BRITISH NAVAL
WEAPONS
OF WORLD WAR TWO

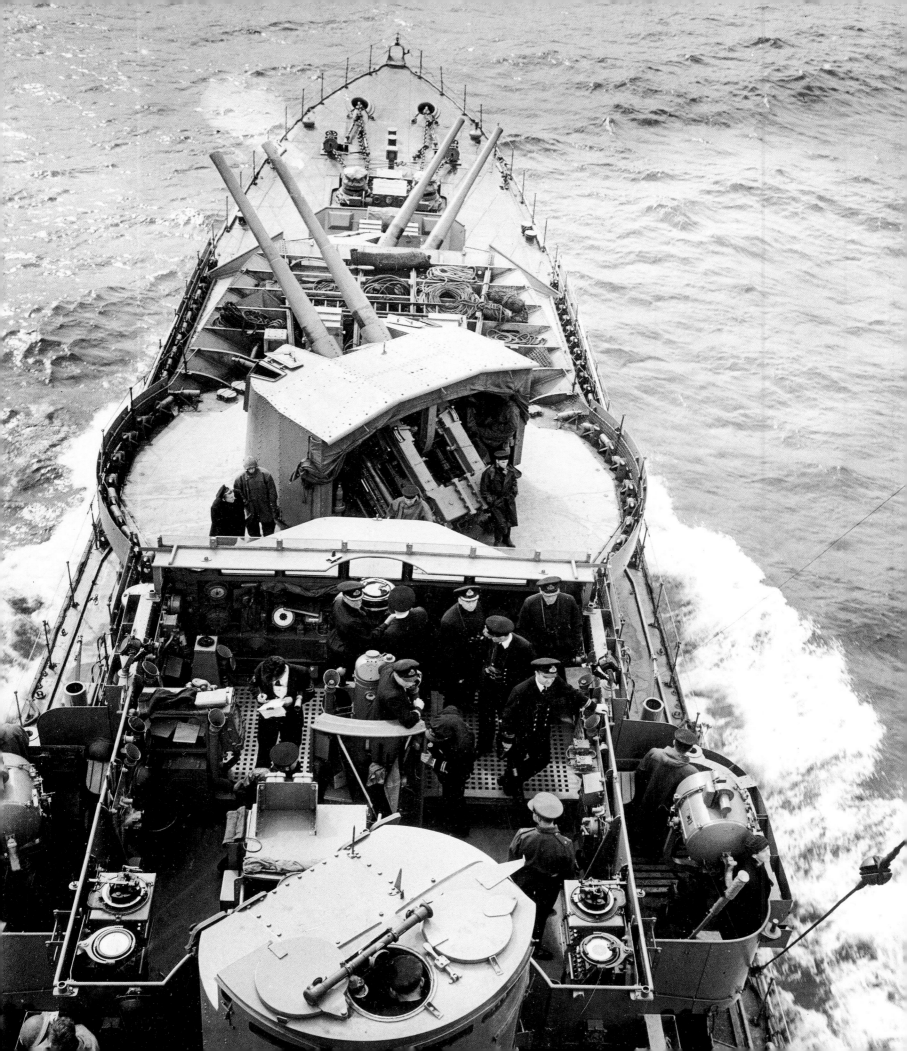

BRITISH NAVAL WEAPONS OF WORLD WAR TWO

THE JOHN LAMBERT COLLECTION

Volume I: Destroyer Weapons

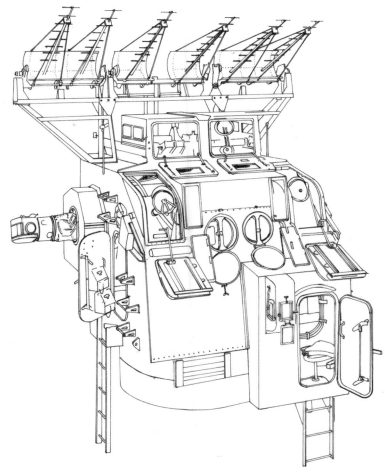

Edited and introduced by

NORMAN FRIEDMAN

Seaforth
PUBLISHING

Frontispiece: An overhead view of a 'J', 'K' or 'N' class destroyer armed with twin 4.7-inch guns in Mk XIX mountings. (John Lambert Collection)

Title page illustration: Mark I Type 'K' HA/LA Director, for 'Z' and 'Ca' class destroyers.

Copyright © Seaforth Publishing 2019
Introduction © Norman Friedman 2019

First published in Great Britain in 2019 by
Seaforth Publishing
An imprint of Pen & Sword Books Ltd
47 Church Street, Barnsley
S Yorkshire S70 2AS

www.seaforthpublishing.com
Email info@seaforthpublishing.com

British Library Cataloguing in Publication Data
A CIP data record for this book is available from the British Library

ISBN 978-1-5267-4767-9 (Hardback)
ISBN 978-1-5267-4769-3 (Kindle)
ISBN 978-1-5267-4768-6 (ePub)

Pen & Sword Books Limited incorporates the imprints of Atlas, Archaeology, Aviation, Discovery, Family History, Fiction, History, Maritime, Military, Military Classics, Politics, Select, Transport, True Crime, Air World, Frontline Publishing, Leo Cooper, Remember When, Seaforth Publishing, The Praetorian Press, Wharncliffe Local History, Wharncliffe Transport, Wharncliffe True Crime and White Owl.

Typeset and designed by Mousemat Design
Printed in China

Contents

Hugh John Lambert

(22 August 1937 – 11 January 2016)

Hugh John Lambert – Hugh to his family, but John to the world at large – was one of a generation of naval writers who were, in the strictest sense, amateurs, but who brought a new level of technical interest, deep personal enthusiasm, and, in John's case, hands-on experience, that radically changed the way warships were described and understood. He was one of a group of like-minded contemporaries that included Antony Preston, Alan Raven and John Roberts, who formed an unofficial club that met in the Draught Room of the National Maritime Museum, presided over by the redoubtable David Lyon. In those days, the Museum's archives only offered full access on weekdays, but David was happy to be at his desk on Saturdays and threw open the Draught Room to anyone he considered a serious researcher. This made it possible for those holding down a full-time job to see original material, especially ships' plans, 'out of hours'. It also became an important forum for discussion and debate, and the mutually beneficial exchange of ideas and information – John regarded joining this select band as a major step forward in his development.

John was trained as a technical draughtsman but showed an early interest in the sea, joining the Royal Naval Volunteer Reserve in order to ensure that his National Service would be in the Royal Navy. Called up in 1956, his engineering background made him a natural candidate for Stoker branch, and he enjoyed naval life so much he signed up for nine years' service, during which time he became familiar with most of the machinery to be found in the warships of that era. Much of his time was spent in aircraft carriers – *Theseus*, *Ocean*, *Albion* and *Bulwark* – which took him around the world and into action at Suez and in the Far East.

He left the Navy as a Petty Officer in 1965 and joined the Metropolitan Police, but in his spare time slowly began a career as a writer on warship topics. Initially, these were short magazine pieces, usually accompanied by one of his own plans, but he soon acquired a following among ship modellers looking for detailed and reliable reference material. As evidence of this demand built up, he began to sell copies of his plans separately and from about 1976 started producing more elaborate drawings specifically for his plans service. By now his Police career was of secondary importance to him, and he regularly turned down promotion in order to have enough freedom to pursue his real interests. Nevertheless, he remained in the force for nearly twenty-five years before taking early retirement.

In the meantime, he continued to write regularly for magazines and periodicals like *Model Boats*, *Airfix Magazine*, *Scale Models*, *Warship*, *Model Shipwright* and *Marine Modelling International*, his output eventually totalling at least 350 articles. His particular obsession was always the smaller types, from destroyers downwards, and especially Coastal Forces, on which he became uniquely expert. Because of his interest in these largely ignored craft, he was forced to become an immensely diligent researcher, seeking out copies of plans, technical manuals, photos and data from obscure archives and any of the wartime builders and suppliers who remained in business at the time. He also tracked down individuals with first-hand knowledge, quizzing them about any and every elusive detail of the ship or weapons system he was working on. A combination of this painstaking research and highly professional draughtsmanship made his plans uniquely valuable.

It was inevitable that his expertise would attract publishing interest, and in 1984 he was commissioned to provide the line illustration for John Campbell's *Naval Weapons of World War Two*. This began a fruitful partnership with Conway Maritime Press, that led to John's first book, *The Fairmile D Motor Torpedo Boat* in the publishers' 'Anatomy of the Ship' series. This was released in 1985, followed in 1986 by another in the same series on *The Submarine Alliance* which he co-wrote with David Hill. He then launched into a broader and more ambitious multi-volume work, *Allied Coastal Forces of World War II*, with the US Navy material being supplied by Al Ross, a long-time American collaborator with shared interests. Volume I: *Fairmile Designs and US Submarine Chasers*, was published in 1990, with Volume II: *Vosper Designs and US ELCOs* following in 1993, but a planned third volume never materialized. The two existing volumes will be reprinted by Seaforth in 2018–2019 and the feasibility of completing the third volume from surviving material is being investigated.

In the new century, John reverted to smaller scale works, publishing *Flower Class Corvettes in World War II* (in the Warship Perspective series) with Alan Raven in 2000, and two 'Specials' in the ShipCraft series (both with Les Brown): *Flower Class Corvettes* in 2008 and *Allied Torpedo Boats* in 2010.

Part of the reason for his apparently low output at this time was that he was working on a large project he clearly expected to become his *magnum opus* – a complete encyclopaedia of British naval weapons used between 1939 and 1945 on destroyer-size and smaller vessels, the rationale being that they were open mountings that would present difficulties to any modeller seeking to portray them in detail. He completed the vast majority of the drawings required, but as his health deteriorated he was not able to write up any of the accompanying text, so the project was a long way from completion when he died in 2016.

Seaforth Publishing acquired all of John's existing drawings, photographs and research materials with a view to fulfilling his ambition, and this book is the first of a series planned to reproduce his weapons drawings in logical, thematic collections. After this one devoted to destroyers, the next volume will cover the weaponry of escorts and minesweepers, which will include much of the deck paraphernalia, electronics and sensors that are not strictly weapons but are nevertheless essential to carrying out their role.

This project will be a posthumous but fitting conclusion to a career of immense significance to all those interested in warships.

Publishers' Note

John Lambert's plans of weapons were drawn on large sheets, usually 32 by 24 inches but a few of 32 by 17 inches. Rather than adopt a specific scale, his style was to make the maximum use of space, so the drawings usually present a very crowded appearance, with details, annotation and the scale bar filling blank areas between the main three-views.

This presents a serious challenge in converting them to book form if material is not to disappear into the gutter between pages. The simplest solutions would be to print them in their entirety on a single page, or else to break them up into a large number of individual parts and scatter them across as many pages as necessary. Each has grave disadvantages. In the first case, it would mean rotating them through 90 degrees; even then, the resulting size would be too small to be useful, and for some annotation too small to read clearly. The second would destroy the relationship between the various parts of the drawings, making it difficult for the reader to see how it all fitted together – and probably making the book much longer and more expensive.

The solution we have adopted is – in effect – to print each drawing across a double-page spread, but digitally separating the two halves, so that nothing of significance is lost in the binding. Because of the way the plans are laid out, in one or two instances this proved impossible, but often it means that there are more part-views on one side of the spread than the other. However, a bit of white space is a small price to pay for having the complete drawings, as large as the page will allow, and all in the same relative positioning as the original.

There is one exception to this. We decided to preface the collection with the most relevant of John Lambert's destroyer drawings to give the reader some examples of where the weapons were fitted. It is impossible to divide a ship across a gutter in any perfect fashion, so we settled for single pages – not ideal, and subject to the disadvantages mentioned above, but as they are something of a bonus to the main coverage of weaponry, we have reluctantly accepted the compromise.

The main portfolio of plans is organised by weapon type – main armament, automatic AA guns, torpedo tubes, etc – and chronologically within those groups from the earliest to the latest and the largest calibre downwards. This project was not quite complete, so not every weapon carried by destroyers is represented, but some of those apparently missing – such as the ubiquitous twin 4in Mk XIX – will be found in the next volume, which is devoted to the weaponry of escorts and minesweepers.

As John Lambert never finished any description to accompany the plans, we are grateful to Norman Friedman for agreeing to sort the material into coherent collections and for providing an introduction that explains the context to the procurement, development and employment of the weapons so exquisitely drawn by John Lambert himself.

A factory view of the Vickers
quad 0.5in LV machine guns
on 'M' Mk III mounting, 1938.
(John Lambert Collection)

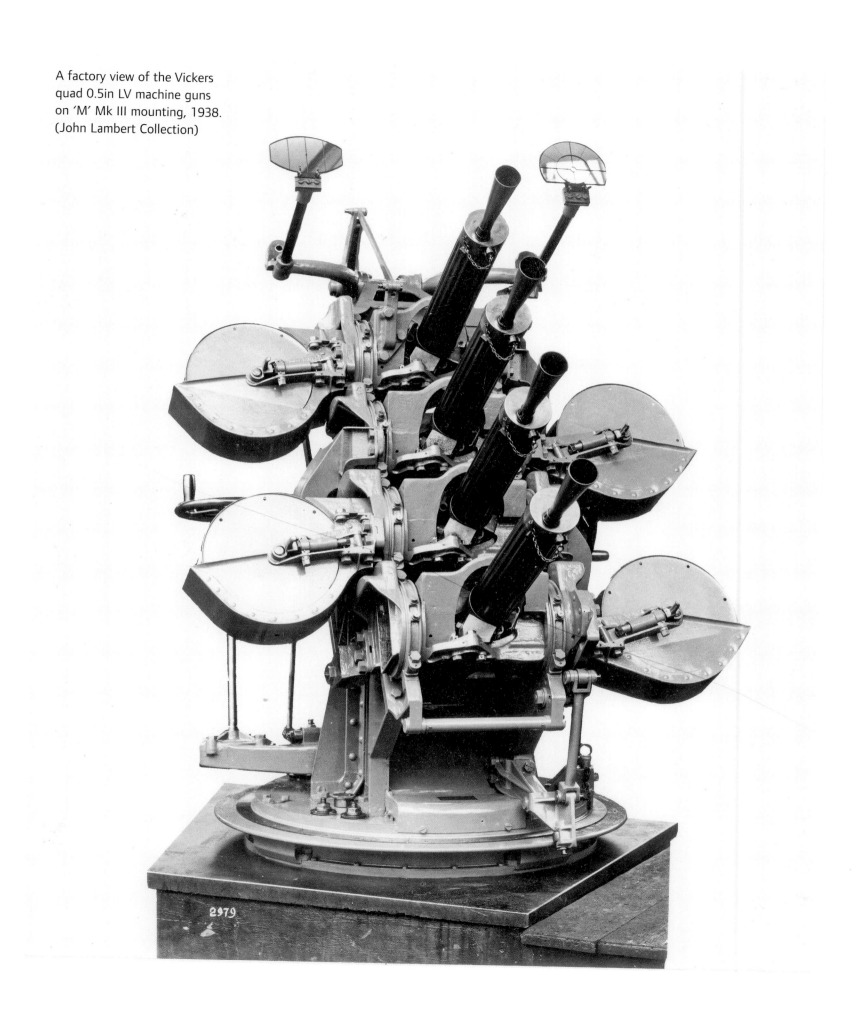

Introduction

Background: World War I

The weapons shown in this book armed British destroyers built between the period before World War I and 1945. The Royal Navy's choice of weapons can be understood in terms of what its destroyers were expected to do. We often think of them as fleet escorts, but for most of this time they were anything but. Initially there was no thought of including destroyers in a British battle fleet. The threat of torpedo attack by *enemy* destroyers was so serious that it was assumed that battleships and cruisers would fire at any destroyer they saw, without taking too much time to be sure of its identity. The idea that destroyers should be integrated with the battle fleet arose in the Royal Navy only after it appeared that the Germans intended to take their own destroyers to sea with their battle fleet. In 1910 the Royal Navy conducted exercises to decide whether and how destroyers should work with the fleet. The answer was that massed destroyer attacks might be effective against an enemy battle line, because as a whole it was so large a target that hits were bound to be made. At the time, however, British destroyers had only two or four torpedo tubes each, partly because British torpedo tubes were relatively heavy. Only in 1913 was a destroyer designed specifically

as a fleet torpedo attacker (with five torpedo tubes and lighter guns), and the outbreak of World War I precluded building it. During the war, it was discovered that a triple tube could be built on about the weight of the previous twin, and eventually it armed the 'V&W' class destroyers and their leaders.

The ships were called 'torpedo boat destroyers' because the first British destroyers were intended to operate in the approaches to French torpedo boat bases, intercepting torpedo boats as they emerged. That particularly applied to the Channel, and to French ideas of raiding British shipping there. Speed was essential if the destroyer was to stay with the torpedo boat long enough to neutralise or sink her. The destroyers had alternative armaments for this role and as what amounted to ocean-going torpedo boats. In

The triple torpedo tube was adopted in the 'V&W' class; in effect, it was the earlier twin mounting with a third tube added above. Some ships had an additional barrel-shaped fitting atop the upper tube. The two post-war prototypes *Amazon* and *Ambuscade* had similar torpedo tubes, but all later British torpedo tubes had their barrels on the same level. (John Lambert Collection)

the latter role they would hunt enemy warships. Nearly up to the outbreak of World War I the Royal Navy retained the ideas of blockading enemy ocean-going torpedo craft and also of hunting enemy heavy ships in packs. British destroyers exercised simulated blockades of the German naval bases. That idea died off as it turned out that a continuous blockade would have required far more destroyers than the Royal Navy wanted to buy or operate. As for hunting, the 1913 manoeuvres showed that, however narrow the North Sea might look on a map, actually finding an enemy fleet or squadron in it would be extremely difficult. Asked for examples of successful hunting, the exercise commanders had to admit that there had been none: the hunting destroyers had found nothing at all at night.

This was the background against which destroyers were incorporated into the Grand Fleet formed in 1914. They were conceived as a torpedo attack force, which at the least could help break up an enemy formation and make it vulnerable to gun attack. It seemed inevitable that a line of closely-packed enemy capital ships would suffer numerous hits from such a 'browning' attack. The phrase came from the army term for firing 'into the brown' of massed enemy troops. If attacks could be mounted during a gun action (an idea the Germans exercised), the enemy might have to evade, and that in turn would ruin his gunnery – contemporary British fire control generally required the shooter to steer a steady course.

The hunting idea lived on in the formation of Force T at Harwich under Commodore Tyrwhitt. It would normally operate independently in the southern part of the North Sea and could be assigned to rendezvous with the Grand Fleet to enlarge its destroyer force. In fact, it proved nearly impossible to arrange the desired rendezvous, and to its great disappointment Force T did not participate in the Battle of Jutland.

The great problem of operating destroyers integral with the fleet was their limited endurance. Fortunately, by 1914 all modern British destroyers burned oil rather than coal. British battleships generally burned oil as well as coal (only the *Queen Elizabeth*s and later ships were all-oil). For a time it was thought that destroyers at shore bases could be ordered to meet the fleet at sea once action was imminent; the Harwich Force of destroyers exemplified this idea. That proved impractical. The Grand Fleet learned that it could extend destroyer endurance by fuelling at sea, typically by towing a destroyer while passing an oil hose over the battleship's stern. For the Royal Navy, then, oil fuel turned destroyers into an integral component of the Grand Fleet. It eliminated the considerable problem of setting a rendezvous, when the timing of the battle was not at all certain. Even at Jutland, when the British knew the Germans were coming out and knew roughly what they were doing, the actual time and position of the collision between the two fleets could not have been predicted. The Germans, who burned coal and could not refuel their destroyers at sea, seem to have accepted that the effective endurance of their fleet was set by the endurance of their destroyers.

Commanding the Grand Fleet, Admiral Sir John Jellicoe saw things somewhat differently. He was aware that his light cruisers were supposed to be his primary anti-destroyer weapon. Compared to destroyers, they were much better gun platforms and also had more powerful batteries. Jellicoe believed that the Germans would emphasise torpedo attack. After all, the creator of their battle fleet, Admiral von Tirpitz, had begun his career as a torpedo specialist. The Germans certainly talked about integrating their destroyers with their capital ships, and in pre-war exercises they often practised a splashy manoeuvre in which destroyers slipped between battleships in line ahead formation, steaming out between the two engaged fleets to attack enemy battleships and disrupt their line. Although the British 1910 exercises showed that any such manoeuvres would be rather dangerous, they had the potential to wreck British gunnery. The British *Iron Duke* and later classes of capital ships were given protected 6in secondary guns specifically to deal with this threat. Previous classes had had unprotected secondary (anti-torpedo boat) batteries because it seemed obvious that destroyer torpedo attacks would come only before or after the gun battle.

Jellicoe was generally pessimistic. He felt that he did not have anything like enough light cruisers, so he wanted his considerable destroyer force to concentrate on defending his battleships against enemy destroyers. He generally considered his fleet's guns his primary weapon. To the extent that torpedoes mattered in a general engagement, they would be the torpedoes fired by his capital ships, from their underwater tubes.

Jellicoe's failure at Jutland brought about re-thinking of British battle tactics. Jellicoe had thought that the Germans would not send their fleet to sea unless they thought it equal to or superior to his own, whose power he tended to underrate. Since the Germans had fewer capital ships, it seemed to him that they must rely on torpedo power, particularly that of their destroyers, to make up the difference. In fact, Jutland was very much a chance encounter. German commander Admiral Scheer considered his force inferior; he spent most of the battle trying to extricate it. The British soon understood that: for them the great question was how to keep a German force which they had intercepted (due to grossly superior British intelligence) from escaping, as Scheer had. It was soon clear, for example, that British shells could not immobilise German battleships, as they had to in order to give the Grand Fleet enough time to win decisively. Enormous effort was concentrated on solving the shell problem, with positive effects by 1918.

Until that had been done, the most effective Grand Fleet weapon was the torpedo, wielded by destroyers, light cruisers, and capital ships. Hence, among other things, the importance of the triple tube which replaced twin tubes in the 'V&W' class, giving them 50 per cent more torpedoes to fire. Longer-range torpedoes were developed, to be fired by destroyers as well as by larger ships. By late in the war, British designers were working on 24.5in weapons, which offered better hydrodynamics than the usual 21in

A 4in/40 QF Mk IV gun, on a P.IX pedestal mounting. Note the characteristic recoil cylinder above the gun, and the unusual curved shield. The Australian *Anzac* seems to have had curved shields, but they were extremely rare. The big wheel allowed the layer to set sights for a set range. That having been done, he elevated and depressed the gun to compensate for the motion of the ship. This gun was adopted after it was reported in August 1910 that it was difficult to work BL guns on board a destroyer; it was a QF equivalent of the earlier BL Mk VIII, using fixed ammunition and a trigger for firing (electrical firing might fail due to spray). It armed *Marksman* and *Grenville* class leaders, the last seven 'K' class destroyers, and all 'L', 'M', 'R', and 'S' class destroyers plus the *Talisman* class. The standard wartime P.IX class mounting could elevate to 15 degrees; it was replaced on board 'Improved S' and 'W' class destroyers by the CP Mk III, which could elevate to 30 degrees (range 12,400 vs 7900yds). The difference between P and CP (central pivot) mountings was that a pedestal was fixed, the rotating mass being the gun and its ancillary equipment and shield, whereas in a central pivot mounting the entire mass turned. (John Lambert Collection)

type. Post-war it proved impossible to fit destroyers with such huge weapons (they appeared only on board the battleships *Nelson* and *Rodney*), but the British did develop quadruple and then quintuple (pentad) torpedo tubes.

Anti-Submarine Warfare

During World War I British destroyers also filled other roles, which required other weapons. Since destroyers were expected to operate with the fleet, they were considered the fleet's natural anti-submarine screen. The Royal Navy concentrated considerable effort on anti-submarine measures before 1914, developing explosive sweeps destroyers could tow. In theory, but unfortunately not in practice, a submarine trying to attack the battleships had to pass through the danger space of these sweeps. The anti-submarine role, rather than the torpedo attack role, seems to explain why Admiral Jellicoe demanded more and more destroyers to work with the Grand Fleet in 1914–1916. During the war many destroyers were provided with explosive paravanes as anti-submarine weapons. A destroyer could tow a paravane at considerable speed, and if it contacted a submarine it could be detonated. This weapon did not prove particularly effective during World War I.

During World War I destroyers served as anti-submarine escorts, although they were much outnumbered by other types of ships. Depth charges and thrown anti-submarine bombs replaced the ineffective sweeps. A depth charge thrower was developed (by Thornycroft) and deployed; it was the standard thrower after World War I. There were also stick bombs, the stick protruding into a gun barrel, so that a charge could fire it. This weapon did not survive World War I.

British destroyers deployed with the fleet and as convoy escorts carried very few depth charges. They had little real chance of detecting a submerged U-boat unless she attacked, because the only submarine detectors available, hydrophones (low-frequency passive sonar), were effective almost only when a ship stopped. Depth charges were introduced in 1916, the initial standard being two depth charges in chutes, one with a manual and one with a hydraulic release (destroyers fitted for minesweeping had only one charge). By mid-June 1917 it was clear that a U-boat could withstand far more depth-charging, and batteries were doubled. Two throwers, each carrying one depth charge (range 40yds) were added beginning in August 1917. A typical destroyer had throwers bearing 50 degrees abaft the beam, and a typical attack was three charges (throwers plus the stern chute). The Royal Navy also experimented with circling torpedoes (about 120 were modified),

which were issued to about thirty destroyers and torpedo boats on escort duty.

Some destroyers were assigned to hunting groups and provided with many more depth charges, typically 30 to 50, sometimes at the expense of guns. For example, in February 1918 the destroyer *Cockatrice* had a 3-charge reload rack alongside each thrower and a 20-charge rail. HMS *Lookout* had 50 charges: 4 throwers (16 charges), 2 chutes (30 charges), and 4 spares on deck. There were also stick bombs. In theory hunting was based on intelligence, either signals intelligence or reports of U-boat sightings and

A massive increase on the World War I standard, HMS *Scimitar* shows her heavy ASW configuration in 1940. She, *Sabre*, and *Skate* were all converted at that time. Their torpedo tubes and midships and after 4in guns were landed, together with their pom-poms. Asdic and eight thowers were installed, as shown here, with two 5-charge rails at the stern; she had 30 charges on deck, 32 at the throwers, and 40 in her after magazine, a total of 112 charges. She could deliver a 14-charge attack, from the throwers (one set doubled up), plus four from the tracks. By mid-1942 *Sardonyx* and *Shikari* also had the heavy battery, and the 14-charge pattern also applied to the *Havant*s (110 charges: 18 in the rails, 32 at the throwers, 26 more on upper deck, and 34 in the torpedo warhead room. Some newer destroyers had these heavy patterns as armament alternatives, 'X' gun being landed, if they joined ASW hunting forces.

attacks. The hunters searched the indicated positions. Unfortunately, in practice using hydrophones it was nearly impossible to find a U-boat near its reported position.

U-boats were not the only threat to shipping. The Germans also had surface warships, and the British could not bottle them up. In November 1917 two fast German cruisers massacred a convoy to Scandinavia, in the process sinking the two destroyers escorting it. The Germans tried to do the same thing using much of their fleet in April 1918. This time German intelligence was so poor that the Germans were unaware that the convoy schedule had changed, but had that not happened another massacre might well have occurred. The lesson for the future, which certainly applied to the Eastern Atlantic in World War II, was that the convoy problem had to include counters to enemy surface ships. During World War II, aircraft were added to the threats.

Mines

Before World War I, the British learned that their Japanese allies had used floating mines effectively at Tsushima, and as Director of Naval Ordnance then-Captain Jellicoe called for development of a British floating mine which destroyers could lay in the path of an enemy fleet. Some of the pre-war destroyers (the 'L' class) were provided with mine rails, but it proved impossible to develop a suitable mine. This experience probably explains why Admiral Jellicoe assumed that German battle tactics would include minelaying, to the point where, in his battle orders, he warned against crossing the wake of the German fleet. Some of the German destroyers and cruisers certainly were fitted to lay mines, but it seems that the Germans had something much more conventional in mind. Certainly, their mines were superior to those of the Royal Navy, and as early as the autumn of 1914 they had succeeded in sinking the new British battleship *Audacious*.

More generally, the Russo-Japanese War convinced many navies, including the Royal Navy, that mines would be an important feature of any future war. The Royal Navy converted some old cruisers to minelayers, and it worked on minesweeping technology. In addition to converted torpedo gunboats, the pre-1914 Admiralty earmarked trawlers, stockpiled equipment, and trained crews. The expectation was that the Germans would mine the approaches to bases, and that local minesweepers could deal with this threat. The mine problem turned out to be far more massive than had been imagined, and among other things the fleet needed its own organic means of neutralising or detecting (for evasion) mines in its path. Since destroyers were expected to accompany the fleet, they took on this role, using towed sweeps (the battleships also had paravanes for self-defence).

It took the British until 1917 to begin producing a truly reliable mine of their own, the Vickers H.2, which borrowed heavily from the designs of captured German mines. By that time the British saw mines as an extremely valuable anti-submarine weapon. To wield it,

they needed a large minelaying force, including fast minelaying destroyers which could penetrate waters nominally controlled by the enemy. Destroyer minelaying would continue to be a staple of the British destroyer force through and after World War II, particular destroyers being fitted for the purpose. There were also larger minelayers and, in World War II, specially designed ones. Beginning in 1916 towed paravanes were issued to ships as shields against mines. Destroyers were issued with them as a means of sweeping ahead of the capital ships. There were special destroyer mine sweeps. Their post-1918 successor was the Two-Speed Destroyer Sweep (TSDS).

The Battle of the Narrow Seas

Probably the greatest surprise for the World War I destroyer force was the battle of the narrow seas, the southern neck of the North Sea and the Channel. Late in the war the Germans based destroyers at Zeebrugge, and they operated against British and Allied shipping. The Harwich Force found itself fighting these destroyers. In this type of war guns mattered far more than torpedoes, although there was considerable interest in snap-shot torpedo attacks on German destroyers which suddenly appeared. The snap-shot problem led to installation of broadside 18in torpedo tubes in

The late-war 'V&W' class destroyers armed with 4in guns had Mk V guns firing separate rather than fixed ammunition on CP Mk II central pivot mountings. HMS *Viscount* is shown in 1943 as a long-range escort, her forward boilers replaced by oil fuel tanks. This photo, intended to aid in recognition, was received by the US Navy in June 1943, but was probably taken earlier. Note the extensive splinter mats and also the fixed splinter shields abreast 'A' and 'B' positions ('A' gun has been replaced by a Hedgehog, which is under canvas). The 'lantern' atop the bridge covers the antenna of a Type 271 surface search radar; at the masthead is the antenna of a Type 291 air warning set. The pole mainmast carries the 'birdcage' HF/DF antenna.

some 'S' class destroyers. They did not long survive the end of World War I.

Almost to the end of the war, British destroyers were armed with 4in quick-firing (QF) guns, meaning that they fired rounds whose powder was in cartridge cases (see drawings **G 1**, **G 2**). In larger ships improved breech mechanisms made it possible to achieve a high rate of fire using bagged powder, the guns being designated BL (breech-loading), but in lively destroyers it was far easier to handle fixed ammunition. The 4in calibre was deemed the largest whose full rounds (shell plus cartridge) could easily be manhandled, the limit being about 63lbs.

When the Germans were reported to be installing more powerful guns (5.9in, in the event), the Royal Navy adopted a more powerful destroyer gun. Then and later the question was how large a gun a destroyer should mount. In the Royal Navy's view, that depended on how large a shell a man standing on a destroyer's rolling, pitching deck could quickly manhandle into a gun. The 5.9in gun fired a shell weighing about 100lbs, which was universally accepted as the limit for a manhandled cruiser weapon. The Royal Navy view was that it was too much for the far livelier destroyers; the limit was something more like 50lbs. The British gun firing this sort of shell was an army 4.7in, and it was adopted. This became the standard British destroyer calibre through World War II. The situation was too urgent to begin making cartridge cases, so the 4.7in Mk I was a BL weapon using bagged powder, which was understood to be somewhat difficult to handle on a destroyer deck. This weapon armed the leaders of the 'V&W' class

Seen from aft in 1942, *Viscount* shows a pair of single 2pdr pom-poms abaft her funnel, and four depth charge throwers, two of them in place of her after torpedo tubes. The shielded gun is a 12pdr, which replaced after tubes in older destroyers.

as well as later 'W' class destroyers (see **G 3**).

Post-war tests showed that the 4.7in gun was powerful enough to do its job: a single hit on the captured German destroyer *V 44* put one of her machinery compartments out of action. In December 1924 Director of Naval Ordnance announced development of a 4.7in QF (cased ammunition) semi-automatic gun for future destroyers: QF (or GFSA) Mk IX, which was formally adopted for future destroyers in 1926. Semi-automatic meant that as it recoiled it automatically ejected its spent cartridge case. British destroyer gun mountings often incorporated netting behind the breech to catch the cartridge before it could hit members of the gun crew. The new gun armed the two prototype destroyers *Amazon* and *Ambuscade*.

One of the wartime surprises was that destroyers were firing at much greater ranges. The 'M' class introduced a simple rangefinder and some simple calculators (a Dumaresq and a Vickers Clock, to estimate enemy range based on estimated enemy speed and bearing). The instruments had to go into a protected Transmitting Station, as in larger ships, in this case in an enlarged charthouse under the bridge. Earlier destroyers were modified similarly, and torpedo controls were installed on the bridge. A director (train only, not elevation) was tried successfully in 1916. In the autumn

'V&W' class leaders and later 'W' class destroyers had 4.7in BL Mk I guns on CP Mk VI* mountings similar to those of the 4in guns. HMS *Whitehall* is shown in April 1943 as a long-range escort, all her torpedo tubes having been landed, and her 'A' gun replaced by a Hedgehog. Note the fixed splinter plating outboard of 'B' gun, and the absence of splinter matting.

of 1918 all destroyer leaders were given full (lightweight) directors, with gyro gear which made it possible to keep tracking a target even if it disappeared intermittently in North Sea mists. It was needed at the much longer ranges now contemplated. This type of control was later extended to the whole 'V&W' class. By the end of World War I destroyers were being adapted for concentration (group) fire, using American-supplied radio-telephones for coordination.

Another development was anti-aircraft weapons. In 1913 destroyers were assigned first Maxim 0.303in machine guns and then 1½pdr pom-poms, 38 of which were soon ordered. Later the 2pdr pom-pom became the standard destroyer anti-aircraft weapon. A general policy adopted in August 1916 called for 6pdr guns or 12pdr 8cwt guns on board earlier destroyers. Those at Dover and the later types would have single 2pdr pom-poms. By

the end of the war, 'V' class destroyers had 3in HA III guns, which were later replaced by 2pdr pom-poms.

The Destroyer Force After 1918

The interwar destroyer force was largely shaped by a radical shift in British naval priorities after 1918. War in the North Sea no longer seemed at all likely nor, for that matter, was war anywhere in European waters. Both of the surviving Continental naval powers, France and Italy, had been World War I allies. They soon returned to their pre-1914 rivalry and enmity, but that seemed unlikely to involve the British Empire. Japan, also a World War I ally, was a very different proposition. During World War I Japan had sheltered subversives from the Asian part of the Empire, and had sometimes espoused a doctrine of 'Asia for the Asians'. When Admiral Jellicoe toured the Empire in 1919 to advise the dominions on naval defence, his topic was generally how they could defend themselves in the event of Japanese expansionism. As this was hardly British official policy at the time, Jellicoe's reports were largely suppressed, at least publicly. However, the British Government let the alliance with Japan lapse in 1921, and by 1923–24 the needs of a Far Eastern war were the basis of British naval planning.

Another important interwar factor was naval arms control. In 1919 there was a widespread understanding that the gruesome experience of World War I would not and could not be repeated. Even if war was unlikely, governments might seek naval superiority in hopes of pressuring each other. The British and other governments sought a way out in the form of naval arms agreements. If, after all, what mattered was relative strengths, why not fix those strengths at lower and lower levels? The first naval arms treaty, signed at Washington in 1921, cut numbers of capital ships, although it did not preclude modernisation. The next step was 'auxiliary' warships, which at the time meant cruisers, destroyers, and submarines. A conference called at Geneva in 1927 failed to produce a treaty, but the 1930 London Naval Conference was much more successful, at least from the point of view of economy. By that time the Great Depression had begun, and the British Government badly needed to reduce defence spending. During the run-up to the 1930 conference planned ships were either not ordered or were cancelled outright as an earnest of British sincerity about arms control.

An annual building program of one flotilla (leader plus eight destroyer) began with the 'A' class in the 1927/28 Estimates. One of the measures the British Government took to show its commitment to arms control was to cut the 1929/30 flotilla from eight to four destroyers ('C' class). However, the 1929/30 leader was built (HMS *Kempenfelt*). The four 'C' class plus the two prototype post-war destroyers were considered three-quarters of a flotilla. However, they were tactically awkward, and eventually all

four 'C' class destroyers were sold to Canada. That other governments did not reciprocate the cuts the British made should perhaps have shown that they were a lot less interested.

Going into the conference, the Admiralty told the Government that it needed all the destroyers it had, because in the event of war older destroyers would be required as convoy escorts and for other anti-submarine roles. It thought the Government agreed that any limit on destroyer tonnage and numbers would be predicated on a successful agreement to limit or even eliminate submarines. Among the Board's charges of bad faith on the Government's part was its embrace of massive cuts in British destroyer tonnage without corresponding cuts in world submarine forces. It did not help that neither France nor Italy agreed to the new Treaty limits on destroyers and cruisers. Since neither seemed likely to be a future enemy, that was dismissed. In 1930 Japan seemed to be the only potential enemy which counted.

HMS *Fury* shows war modifications, probably about 1941, as she lays smoke after a dummy torpedo attack. Her after torpedo tubes have been replaced by a 3in 20cwt gun (the older destroyers got 12cwt guns), and she has single 20mm guns in her bridge wings to supplement the quadruple 0.5in guns further aft. Note the extensive splinter matting around her bridge, and the narrow fixed splinter shields abeam her 4.7in guns. The MF/DF coil forward of the bridge was also a wartime modification. Splinter matting seems to have been removed from 1941 on, so that a December 1942 photograph of *Foxhound* does not show it.

The outcome of the cruiser negotiation in 1930 affected British destroyer development. Going into the conference, the Admiralty told the Government that the British Empire needed at least 70 cruisers, not only for the fleet but also to defend British shipping. World War I seemed to show that convoys, escorted by (among other things) destroyers, could neutralise a submarine offensive. An enemy's cruisers could wipe out relatively weak ships used as convoy escorts, as well as hunting groups. It was also argued that only enemy surface ships could hunt shipping while observing the agreed 'cruiser rules'. German refusal to follow those rules during World War I had brought the United States into the war and, in many eyes, had cost Germany the war. Unfortunately for the Admiralty, the US negotiating position was to demand parity or near-parity as a sop to domestic politics, even though there was no corresponding US shipping protection requirement.

Money was extremely tight due to a combination of the Great Depression and the after-effects of World War I. The British Government view was that some agreement was essential as a way of limiting spending. The earlier Washington Treaty had limited cruisers to 10,000 tons and 8in guns. In 1930 the Admiralty badly wanted to ban future large (ie, expensive) cruisers in the interest of building enough smaller ones. Since small cruisers could not stand up to those with 8in guns, unless some agreement was reached, the Royal Navy would never be able to afford enough viable cruisers. It wanted 8in guns banned, 6 inches (actually 6.1, to meet French requirements) to be the maximum permissible calibre. That happened to be the largest size of gun which could be hand-loaded, hence which could be installed on board converted merchant ships as extemporised wartime cruisers. With the world's largest merchant fleet, such conversions were an important feature of British mobilisation planning. The British managed to ban 8in guns on board future cruisers (with some minor exceptions for the United States), but they accepted what amounted to a 50-cruiser limit. The new treaty would expire at the end of 1936, and it was sometimes pointed out that the Royal Navy would have found it difficult in any case to build up to a higher limit before then.

Unfortunately, the Admiralty had not realised that other navies might not equate smaller guns with smaller ships. Neither the Americans nor the Japanese saw things as the Admiralty did; both ordered big cruisers (*Brooklyn* and *Mogami* classes) armed with 6in guns. The Admiralty found itself forced to buy big 6in cruisers of its own (*Southampton* class). The new treaty limited total cruiser tonnage. The larger the individual ships, the fewer the Royal Navy could have – but it needed numbers for the two cruiser roles, the fleet screen (against enemy destroyers) and trade protection.

To make matters worse, the comfortable assumption that war was unlikely began to unravel. The British Government went into the treaty negotiations under the Ten-Year Rule: the British Empire would not be involved in a major war within a decade. That had made it possible to slash defence, including naval, spending, particularly on consumables such as ammunition. Cuts much

affected emergency plans to convert merchant ships, including fishing trawlers and drifters, into the vast number of warships needed in wartime, as opposed to the peacetime fleet. In peacetime, destroyers and minesweeping sloops were the most numerous British warships, but the numbers which could be maintained in peacetime did not approach what would be needed in a war. The interwar British merchant fleet was by far the largest in the world. It was both what the Royal Navy had to protect in wartime and an important source of wartime strength, both in hulls and in officers and seamen. This resource does not figure in the current book, but it certainly does figure heavily in the planned next volume on escorts and minesweepers. During World War II the merchant fleet also supplied emergency carrier hulls, including some ships which retained their cargo capacity. The US Navy and the Imperial Japanese Navy also made extensive use of merchant ships taken up from trade, but in different ways. The interwar United States retained a large number of merchant ships built in 1918–1921 under programs to overcome the depredations of the U-boats, but they were not suited to most naval roles. The active US merchant fleet was quite small. Wartime US ships with merchant ship hulls were mainly built for the navy by the US Maritime Commission, created in 1936 to revitalise the very weak active US merchant fleet. The Japanese went so far as to design some large merchant ships specifically for wartime use (for example as semi-fleet carriers), and ultimately many small Japanese ships became escorts. At least in the US case, there was no equivalent to the Admiralty's plans for wartime conversions using a mass of stored weapons and ammunition. The British stocks left over from World War I did not take into account the radical new technology of the interwar period in both anti-submarine and anti-air warfare. The Admiralty understood as much, but unfortunately the stocks which the Ten-Year Rule slashed included quartz for Asdic (sonar) transducers for emergency escorts such as trawlers. Mass production of major anti-aircraft weapons did not really begin until after the Ten-Year Rule lapsed.

The Admiralty had never been comfortable with the Rule; through the 1920s British warships had been involved in all sorts of local incidents bordering on war. The Far East was particularly restive, with ongoing major civil conflict in China, a very important place for the British economy. The Admiralty was well aware of Japanese attempts to dominate China during World War I. Nothing had reduced their ambitions, and the ongoing Chinese civil wars were a considerable opportunity for Japanese intervention and, eventually, invasion. How important China was to Britain is reflected in the considerable strength of the China Fleet, which through much of the interwar period included an aircraft carrier. No foreign fleet in the area was nearly as powerful. In 1929 the Admiralty planned a further increase; it wanted to station the three active battlecruisers at Singapore. That would have been quite expensive, and the idea died with the excuse that there was no need to provoke the Japanese. It was impossible to station the entire battle fleet at Singapore in peacetime, because there was so little infrastructure, and because Singapore was considered unsuitable for the families of the fleet's sailors. Malta was far better. In wartime the Mediterranean Fleet would have provided the bulk of the War Fleet which would move its base to Singapore. That strategic calculation translated into a requirement for long destroyer range, meaning more fuel tankage.

From a destroyer design point of view, the two hull requirements were speed and range. Range meant added fuel weight, which made it more difficult to attain high speed in a hull limited by treaty. In theory the interwar scheme of limitation took different navies' range requirements into account by omitting fuel and reserve feed water from displacement. However, even if the fuel itself was not counted, its tankage made for a larger, heavier hull. Armament weight certainly was not omitted from treaty-regulated tonnage, so in effect it had to be traded off against fuel and speed. Even the destroyers conceived between wars for the Far East were short-legged, to the point where during World War II they could not match the endurance of the new frigates, which did not have to be nearly so fast. In many cases destroyers were able to escort trans-Atlantic convoys only because they were adapted to fuel at sea from tankers in the convoys.

When late in 1930 the Admiralty asked the Foreign Office whether the annually-renewed Ten-Year Rule was still valid, the answer must have been shocking. Instead of its usual assurance that nothing could possibly go wrong, this time its Permanent Under Secretary Robert Vansittart wrote that the era of international goodwill was fading; Europe was full of 'pre-war' thinking. As it happened, the shock which ended the Ten-Year Rule and corresponding thinking was Japanese aggression in China, where the

Japanese showed that they wanted to take over Asia and that they would show no mercy to British civilians in areas they conquered. Although China was hardly part of the Empire, British companies in China were too important to Britain for this sort of behaviour to be ignored. In 1932 the League of Nations held a general disarmament conference. By late that year the committee which had been formed to write British proposals for it had become the Defence Requirements Committee, charged with repairing the effects of the Ten-Year Rule. However, the government was still bound by the 1930 treaty it had signed, British finances were still extremely weak, and the British public still imagined that the promises of long-term peace were valid. Any improvement to the naval position had to be made at minimum cost, within the agreed limits.

In the wake of the 1930 treaty, the Government went back to its pre-Treaty policy of building a flotilla each year: the 'D' class in 1930/31, the 'E' class in 1931/32, the 'F' class in 1932/33, the 'G' class in 1933/34, and the 'H' class in 1934/35, each an incremental improvement over the previous year's ships. These were successive versions of the same design. The 'H' class was a repeat 'G', except that HMS *Hereward* was trials ship for the twin 4.7in mounting developed for the 'Tribal' class. This class also introduced the angled bridge face characteristic of later British destroyers through World War II. Initially the 1935/36 destroyers would have been a repeat 'H' class except that they introduced quintuple (pentad) torpedo tubes. They were originally to have had high-angle fire control systems, but in the end that was dropped, and a proposal to adopt heavier (62lb) 4.7in shells was also abandoned.

HMS *Grenade* was a typical interwar destroyer of the 'A' to 'I' classes, with four 4.7in guns and two sets of torpedo tubes. She is shown in 1936.

The 'Tribal' Class: Quasi-Cruisers

In 1933 the Admiralty became aware of the big US and Japanese cruisers to be built despite the London treaty. Now the question was how to maintain a sufficient fleet screening force against enemy destroyers while using up so much of the available cruiser tonnage to build big ships. The solution turned out to be a twin version of the existing 4.7in gun (see **G 7**). Initially it was proposed in 1933 as a solution to providing the existing type of destroyer with sufficient ahead fire, as waves frequently broke over 'A' gun in such small ships. Officers complained that the emphasis on torpedoes pushed the guns to the wet ends of ships whose overall length was severely limited. At the same time, some destroyer officers wanted a more powerful gun; a 5in 62½lb shell was being considered. This weapon had already been proposed in 1929 in view of the Japanese

move to 5in guns in their *Fubuki* class, which were considered flotilla leaders rather than destroyers. At the time, the Naval Staff argued that adopting this gun in mass-production destroyers would be an unnecessary provocation to the Japanese; this advice was in tune with the Foreign Office claim that hostilities with Japan were unlikely for the foreseeable future. Since the French were already using a 5.1in destroyer gun, that calibre was soon chosen for tests. In May 1930 the flotilla leader *Kempenfelt* was chosen for trials, the

A twin 4.7in gun on board the destroyer *Nubian*, with HMS *Packenham* leading. Note the ready-use shells (*not* the cartridges) of two types, stacked vertically around the splinter shield, and open loading tray for the right-hand gun. The objects in the foreground are twin Lewis guns. (John Lambert Collection)

The twin 4.7in mounting Mk XIX in a 'Tribal' was a double version of the Mk XVIII single mounting. Here it is being loaded on board HMS *Zulu*, September 1940. Two men are on each side because they are separately loading the shell and its cartridge. The nets catch the cartridges the gun ejects automatically as it recoils. (John Lambert Collection)

A twin 4.7in mounting (Mk XIX) with a shell in the loading tray, pointed into the horizontal sliding-block breech, seen from the layer's side. Under the loading tray is the rammer cylinder. The vertical handle visible above and to the right of the loading tray is the handle of the breech-operating lever. The objects standing up at the left and right are fuze-setting pedestals; a shell was pushed into one nose down so that its time fuze (for anti-aircraft fire) could be set by the ship's fire control system. Levers atop the structure on each side are to change over between quick-firing and semi-automatic fire. Nets catch ejected cartridge cases. (John Lambert Collection)

gun being mounted in 'B' position. It turned out that the new shell was too heavy for easy handling on board a destroyer.

Since the enemy destroyers were unarmoured, the 4.7in gun had sufficient punch. If it could be mounted in sufficient numbers on board a ship within the agreed destroyer tonnage (1850 tons), these ships could provide some or much of the screen otherwise assigned to small cruisers. In a destroyer, all the guns are lined up lengthwise; length is a more important parameter than displacement. Displacement limited available length, which meant the allowable number of gun mountings. Because the twin mount took up little more length than the single, it was quite conceivable that by using it firepower could be doubled within an acceptable ship length. Moreover, it could be argued that a twin 4.7 in would have more hitting power than the single 6in in existing 'C' and 'D' class cruisers, which had to be replaced. That was the genesis of the 'Tribal' class. In order to maximise their gun power, they would have only a single set of torpedo tubes.

Initially the new ships were to have had five twin 4.7in gun mounts, but during the design process a quadruple (Mk VII) pom-pom replaced one of them.

The twin 4.7in mounting was power-trained and -elevated. Its shield, open at the back, was neither gas- nor splinter-proof, which was a problem. As of 1 March 1935, when the decision had been made to build the big cruiser-substitute, Director of Naval Ordnance (DNO) had to admit that the fully-enclosed mounting he preferred, carrying 62pdr guns, would not be ready in time for these 1935/36 ships. He hoped to have ballistics ready in April 1937. That is why the 'Tribals' had the twin mounting carrying a pair of 50pdr guns. At the time it was hoped that the second series of these ships (1936/37) would have the more powerful gun, but that proved impossible.

This was hardly the kind of destroyer the Admiralty had been building, and for a time alternative designations, including 'V Leader', were proposed. Ultimately the 'Tribals' were classed as destroyers, but as envisaged at the time they would hardly have been the ocean-going torpedo craft of the past.

The Far East War Plan and the Destroyer Force

The 'Tribals' and the more conventional 'A' through 'I' class destroyers were conceived in the context of a dramatic change in British war planning. Existing destroyers and cruisers lacked the range needed in the vast spaces of the Far Eastern war the Admiralty contemplated. It wrote of a new 'oceanic' fleet to replace the earlier North Sea fleet. New longer-legged ones were badly needed, though even the new ones had limited endurance. At 20kts the wartime 'V&W' class, the largest World War I destroyers, had a rated endurance of 1800 nautical miles (nm), but the post-war 'D' class was rated at 4000nm. At 12kts, the 'D' class had more than double the endurance of the 'V&W': 6350nm vs 3120nm. When the British Government first proclaimed the 'Ten-Year Rule' in 1919 the Admiralty saw it not only as an economy measure but

A quadruple torpedo tube on board an unidentified interwar destroyer of the 'B' to 'E' classes (excluding the minelayers), looking aft. This photograph was probably taken in 1942–43 at a Canadian or US yard. Unusual features are the narrow (as opposed to wide) spreaders for radio antennas, and the Oerlikons on deck rather than in tubs on the upper level of the searchlight platform. HMCS *Ottawa* (ex-*Griffin*), and perhaps others, had these features. Note the pipe rack surrounding the Oerlikon to prevent it from firing into the ship as its operator tracked an airplane. The ship's HF/DF mast is visible abaft the searchlight platform. The short cylinder above the tubes, near the breech, is the explosion chamber for the powder which launches the torpedo; there is one per barrel. A device just ahead of it set gyro angle. Torpedoes could also be set to pattern-run (30-degree zig-zag). A wheel further forward (perhaps the shrouded object) set running depth. (John Lambert Collection)

also as an understanding that the Royal Navy had a decade to buy what it needed for the Far East. Given the 1921 Washington Treaty, the navy could not buy new capital ships apart from the two *Nelson*s, but the existing ones had much longer ranges than existing destroyers and cruisers. Up to 1928 successive British Governments did buy new cruisers and destroyers on a reasonably regular basis.

The fleet was slowly modernised. After 1929 the financial situation deteriorated badly. Unfortunately, at about the same time the likely scale of air attack in a future war began to grow, and the anti-submarine problem grew considerably worse.

The Far Eastern war plan the Admiralty envisaged, the one which dominated its efforts through the mid-1930s, was intended ultimately to strangle Japan by blockade. The barrier to any blockade was the Japanese battle fleet. It could crush the relatively small ships which would enforce any blockade. Thus the Admiralty focused on what was needed to destroy the Japanese battle fleet, which generally meant what would be needed in a future fleet action. From time to time it was suggested that the blockade could be enforced by British cruisers in distant waters (for example, off North America and far to the south of Japan), but the war plan generally envisaged a fleet action. Ships were certainly designed with that in mind, and their Staff Requirements (*eg*, for the new *King George V* class battleships) took Far Eastern distances into account. A Japanese fleet free to operate in the Indian Ocean was probably seen as far too dangerous to the Empire as a whole, given the importance of India and Burma.

Far Eastern war plans required that the war fleet steam east, initially to its war base at Singapore. The main threats during that passage would be mines and long-range submarines, against which the destroyers going east had to offer protection. That meant Asdic (sonar) and depth charges on board two of the six fleet destroyer flotillas and also the TSDS mine sweep – not so much to neutralise mines as to provide warning so that the fleet could turn away.

The Japanese had spent heavily to modernise their capital ships, including increasing their gun range beyond that of British capital ships (other than the *Nelson*s and perhaps *Hood*), so the Admiralty emphasised equalisers such as destroyers intended to make massed long-range torpedo attacks. That made the number of British destroyers – actually the number of torpedoes they wielded – very important. Numbers meant minimising the tonnage of individual destroyers, which in turn meant relatively short ships which could not accommodate more than two banks of torpedo tubes. Short length was also prized for handiness. Proposals to replace 'Y' gun with a third set of torpedo tubes generally failed because it would be subject to spray and to blast, and because it was so much larger than a single 4.7in gun. Hence the interest in quadruple and then quintuple tubes to supersede the triple tubes in service at the end of World War I (see **T 1, T 2, T 5**).

The principal British World War I destroyer torpedo was the 21in Mk IV, which weighed 3208lbs and carried a 400lb warhead. Range was 8000yds at 35kts and 13,500yds at 25kts. The first two classes of post-war destroyers had Mk V, introduced in 1918. It typically weighed 3736lbs and carried a 500lb warhead; rated performance was 9500yds at 35kts and 14,500yds at 29kts. It was conceived as a 15,000yd torpedo which could be fired from all existing tubes. It was initially assigned to many larger ships as well as destroyer leaders and 'W' class destroyers. The data are as initially delivered, but it turned out that ships could not generate the desired air pressure, and the torpedo was down-rated to 12,500yds at 29kts. From the 'C' class on, the standard destroyer torpedo was Mk IX, which introduced a burner (fuel-burning) propulsion cycle for much greater performance. It weighed 3732lbs, with a 727lb TNT warhead (from 1944, 815lbs of

Torpex). A version with an improved engine went to sea in the summer of 1939 on board 'J' and 'K' class destroyers. It offered 40kts to 11,000yds with over-run (*ie*, a run at lower and lower speed, but still viable) to 17,000. At 35kts it could reach 15,000yds at full speed, with an over-run to 19,000. The 15,000yd figure was significant because that was also the preferred British gun battle range. Angling gear (60-0-60) was fitted during the war to British destroyer torpedoes, which were redesignated Mk 9** Mod 1, enabling destroyers to fire without the previous large turn before firing. During World War II the advent of radar made it possible to fire torpedoes blind from very long range, requiring longer running range, if possible at higher speeds, so as to minimise the time of flight and therefore the chance of a miss. During the war, as the British became aware of the Japanese 'Long Lance,' they became interested in lengthening the existing Mk 9 by 12 inches (4000lbs all-up weight) with an enlarged warhead, for a total of 930lbs of Torpex. That compared to the 1200lb Japanese warhead; it seemed reasonable to suppose that the Japanese standard of protection of capital ships was 1000lbs. This enlarged torpedo could not be introduced before the end of the war.

The requirement for ahead fire (*ie*, without the large turn) came from the Home Fleet, whose destroyers were frustrated during the Channel Dash by the German *Scharnhorst* and *Gneisenau*, when none of the attacking destroyers managed to hit despite closing the range; *Worcester* was nearly crippled as she turned to fire. The alternative to angling would have been ahead-firing tubes, which could not have been used in the usual line-ahead formation. That was still essential at night. Torpedoes were modified so that they could turn 60 degrees when fired from tubes locked on the beam. The associated centreline pedestal sights were only getting to sea at the end of the war.

According to the official history of wartime British torpedo development, destroyers fired 606 torpedoes in action during World War II, making 86 certain and 12 probable hits, amounting to 16.3 per cent, in 207 attacks. Of these, 91 were considered successful (44 per cent). Destroyer torpedo attacks on *Bismarck* the night before she was sunk seem to have helped keep her personnel awake and thus seriously degrade their performance the next day (the ship's gunnery was extremely poor). During the Battle of the Barents Sea, the deterrent effect of destroyer torpedoes seems to have had a considerable effect. Near the end of the war, a division of British destroyers executed the classic torpedo attack which sank the Japanese cruiser *Haguro*. Destroyer torpedoes contributed to the sinking of the Italian cruisers *Fiume*, *Pola*, and *Zara* at Matapan and *Colleoni* off Cape Bon, and destroyer torpedoes sank the cruisers *Giussano* and *Barbiano* there.

Destroyer Guns

It was generally imagined that a fleet action would be preceded by a 'dog fight' between massed destroyers. The British had to provide their destroyers with powerful enough guns to punch through the

Amazon and *Ambuscade* were the transitional destroyers between the World War I ships and the interwar 'A' to 'I' classes. This is HMS *Amazon*, in a print obtained by the US Navy. She had the same 4.7in guns as World War I destroyers, in the same small shields (CP Mk VI** mountings), and the same triple torpedo tubes, but her bridge structure was that adopted in later destroyers. She had only a rangefinder, without the elaborate director control tower of later classes.

enemy ships, and one lesson of World War I was that those guns needed sophisticated fire control. As during World War I, the most powerful gun which seemed suited to destroyers was the 4.7in. The 1930 London Naval Treaty made 5.1 inches the maximum allowable destroyer calibre. One reason the French refused to sign the treaty was that they were building numerous very large destroyers armed with 5.5in guns as a counter to big Italian destroyers. They did not want these ships classed as cruisers and therefore limited in numbers. The treaty calibre was 5.1 inches because smaller French destroyers were armed with such weapons. The British built an experimental 5.1in gun to see whether it was worth adopting. Trials on board a destroyer showed that its ammunition was unwieldy. The difference between British and French perceptions may have been a difference between the relatively calm waters of the Mediterranean and the rougher waters in which the British expected to operate.

Destroyer Gun Fire Control

Effective gun power depended on fire control. The two prototype destroyers *Amazon* and *Ambuscade* had Barr & Stroud fire control computers instead of the simple Vickers clocks of the wartime 'V&W' class. The 'A' class lacked anything that elaborate, but a fire control and a DCT (director control tower) were introduced in the 'B' class. They also had a Type 31 wireless set, which was used to coordinate the fire of several ships (concentration fire). The 'C' class introduced a Vickers-developed computer (the Admiralty Fire Control Clock, or AFCC) and a new DCT. The combination of DCT and AFCC finally provided a version of the standard Admiralty fire control system, in which the results of spotting were fed back into a computer to adjust input enemy speed and range.

Directors had two separate purposes. One was to cancel out roll and pitch, firing only when guns were level. That was the original director role. A second was fire control – not only gun aiming but supporting prediction of target motion so that guns could hit. Those in the DCT visually tracked the target, periodically finding its range (in some systems the rangefinder was separate from the director). The AFCC in the Transmitting Station developed a fire control solution and then transmitted it back up to the director, where it could be compared with actual target motion. The clock projected ahead target motion so that guns could be laid and aimed, information being transmitted to the dials at the guns (where layers and aimers 'followed the pointers' to aim their weapons). Data from the fire control computer were also transmitted back to the director so that those aloft could check on the accuracy of the fire control solution; for example, when the computed solution drove their binoculars off the target, they could insert corrections. Unlike the large-ship Admiralty Fire Control Table (AFCT), the AFCC was not associated with a plot of consecutive target observations. Omission of a plot was justified by the short range at which a destroyer could be expected to fire.

To accommodate the DCT, the bridge structure in the 'D' class was split, the forward element being the steering and signal house, with the open bridge on top. Atop it were the DCT and the separate rangefinder (see **F 2**). The AFCC proved successful enough that it was installed in modified form (as AFCC II) on board 'A' and 'B' class destroyers. They could not, however, accommodate the DCT, which offered automatic feedback to the AFCC. Instead they had modified 'W' class directors.

In a 'Tribal' class destroyer, the director contained three operators and three officers. The operators were a trainer, a layer (elevation operator), and a cross-level operator. Laying meant adjustment in elevation. The layer dealt with the apparent up and down motion of the target corresponding mainly to the ship's roll. The cross-level operator cancelled out motion at right angles, mainly pitch. Each of the three officers above and behind them had his own large sighting port: a Control Officer flanked by a Spotting Officer and a Rate Officer. The Control Officer designated targets, the Spotting Officer estimated errors in range and the Rate Officer errors in direction (line), which were associated with errors in estimating target course and speed. Rate meant how fast the target was apparently moving, so that the ship's guns could lead it properly. The layer and the cross-level operator tracked the horizon (in two directions at right angles), in effect sensing the ship's pitch and roll so that the system could compensate (in battleships a gyro was usually used for this purpose). The trainer and layer had gyro-stabilised binocular sights and telescopes. Their observations fed target bearing into the AFCC. The associated rangefinder, with its own operator, fed in target range. The AFCC in turn transmitted elevation and train orders to the guns via devices which automatically corrected for parallax and for roll and pitch, based on measurements at the DCT. The guns themselves had follow-the-pointer receivers. The AFCC also transmitted its predicted target bearing back to the director. If it drove his sight line off the target, the Rate Officer made corrections which went back into the Transmitting Station. The Spotting Officer corrected for range errors, based on the range displayed by a counter on the inside of the front of the director shield.

Prior to the 'Tribals', a separate 9ft three-man rangefinder was mounted above and abaft the director control tower. The 'Tribals' had their 12ft rangefinder integrated into a rangefinder director Mk II in the usual director position, abaft and above the DCT (see **F 3**). For surface fire Mk II was a simple rangefinder, its crew following 'follow the pointer' instructions from the Transmitting

Station to stay on the surface target. However, for anti-aircraft fire it functioned as a separate high-angle director in its own right, driven by the FKC. During World War II these directors were fitted with antennas for Type 285 range-only radar.

In the next ('J') class the DCT was modified to provide anti-aircraft capability, a simple three-man rangefinder replacing the rangefinder director of the 'Tribal's (see **F 4**). The rangefinder was manned only by range-taker, trainer, and layer; the director cued it to the appropriate elevation (see **F 5**). This arrangement proved impractical, and was completely revised in 1941. The DCT was limited to surface fire. The rangefinder was modified to function as a rangefinder director. A control officer's seat was added, with angle of presentation (effectively elevation angle measuring) binoculars

The bridge (compass platform) of a destroyer armed with twin 4.7in guns in Mk XIX mountings, the DCT with its short rangefinder turned to port. The tall tube covers the ship's compass; the circular object just abaft the windscreen is the pelorus, for taking bearings of objects seen from the ship. Asdic (sonar) instruments are on the inside of the windbreak, to port. A port in the floor of the bridge allows officers there to see the plot on the deck below. The helm is also on the deck below, in the protruding portion visible above the breech of 'B' mounting. Helm orders are issued via a voice pipe. Note the shallow fixed splinter plating visible at the edges of the 'B' gun platform. (John Lambert Collection)

The high-angle director of the destroyer *Legion*, which was completed with 4in rather than 4.7in guns. The framework above carries the Type 285 range-only radar. The Control Officer at right rear has a speed ring and angle-of-presentation glasses; the angle of presentation was the angle the course of the airplane made to the line across the director. It was an essential input into the high-angle fire control system. In front of him is the barrel of the rangefinder, its operator to the left. In front of them are the director layer and trainer, of which the layer is visible, behind his half of the two-sided director sight. He also has a telescope with a speed ring. This was a posed photograph; note the helmets at right. Most destroyer directors were fully enclosed. (John Lambert Collection)

and means of transmitting data to the Transmitting Station below decks, for the FKC. A windshield was added to protect the operators as they turned the director, and a Type 285 radar mounted on top. The layer had a director firing pistol. These arrangements were repeated in the 'K' and 'N' classes, which were repeat 'J's. This was also the arrangement in the destroyers of the later 'E 'to 'I' classes.

The 'L' and 'M' classes had a new dual-purpose (HA/LA) power-trained Director Mk IV Type TP, which may have been related to the combined DCT/rangefinders which were being installed onboard export destroyers for Brazil and Turkey (see **F 7**). It was turret-shaped rather than cylindrical, with its rangefinder near its after side. The P indicated a P-type gyro-stabilised sight, employing a master gyro to stabilise the layer's, trainer's, and control and rate officer's binocular sights and the rangefinder, but not the associated Radar 285, which was added after the units had been designed. Elevation limits were +65 and -20 degrees. Reportedly it was unsuccessful against aircraft. The anti-aircraft version of the 'L' class had a modified rangefinder director of quite different design. Mk IV (and Mk V, below) was mechanically linked to the Transmitting Station by shafts which in effect replaced the earlier wiring with its synchros. Presumably the shift away from electrical transmission reflected a known shortage of precision electrical manufacturing capacity. The shafts had to be kept relatively short, so the directors in these ships were set low and their Transmitting Stations were immediately below in the superstructure.

'Hunt' class light (escort) destroyers had Mk V or V*, with FKC Mk III and FCB Mk II in the Transmitting Station. The director was manned by two officers (Control Officer and Rate Officer) and three ratings (trainer, layer, and range-taker). For low-angle control, the Control Officer had an alternative position on the Compass Platform outside the director. Instruments on the Compass Platform were receivers for gun range and deflection sent up from the Transmitting Station, so that the Control Officer could see whether the system was properly following the target; and a gun deflection receiver indicating the bearing to which the gun was being set. The officer had a telephone and voice pipe to the Transmitting Station. Mk V** was employed in the first two Emergency destroyer classes, the 'O's and 'P's (see **F 8**). Like the 'Hunt's, they lacked surface directors. The first star indicated a windscreen and the second a radar (Type 285). This version had a specially strengthened rangefinder mounting to overcome the vibration of a ship running at high speed. The Transmitting Station contained an FKC and a sloop-type Fire Control Box (FCB) rather than a Clock. These directors were hand-operated, but during the war they were fitted with power follow-ups stabilising the line of sight as the director trained.

The wartime 'Q' through 'V' class destroyers reverted to the 'Tribal' class system, with a surface DCT (see **F 9**) and a Rangefinder Director Mk II (W) for anti-aircraft fire; the W indicated a windscreen. Data were electrically transmitted, but the director was not power-stabilised. The 'W' class introduced a single dual-purpose HA/LA rangefinder director, Mk III (W) (see **F 6**).

While these ships were being built, an entirely new Mk VI dual-purpose director was being developed. It was not ready for the 'Z' and 'Ca' classes. Instead they had a HA/LA director Mk I Type K, the K referring to a gyro-stabilised surface sight. There was a separate anti-aircraft sight. This director resembled that in the 'L' and 'M' classes, with its self-contained dual-purpose rangefinder and a Type 285 radar on the roof. As in pre-war practice, it had separate ports for level and cross-level (sightings of the horizon). The device was supervised by a Control Officer and a Rate Officer standing side by side at its rear, each with a separate sighting port. The layer had a stabilised high-angle binocular sight and a separate unstabilised low-angle binocular sight, side by side; below was the sight itself. Alongside him were similar optics for the trainer.

Mk VI was an entirely new medium-calibre director intended to

HMS *Sluys* exemplifies the final World War II Royal Navy destroyer, with two power-worked dual-purpose 4.5in guns forward, controlled by the big stabilized Mk VI director visible above her bridge, carrying the two antennas of a Type 275 radar. All of her light anti-aircraft weapons were Bofors – single power mountings on her signal deck, twin STAAGs aft.

Sailors carry the fixed ammunition of a 4in HA gun. This was apparently the maximum unit weight which could be man-handled on board a lively destroyer. Anti-aircraft fire required that the gun be loaded at very high angles and that it be able to recoil without hitting the deck. Hence the platform on which the gun-layer is standing – a feature which was considered unacceptable in a heavier destroyer gun. The ship is a 'J', 'K', or 'N' class destroyer. (John Lambert Collection)

work with a new air defence computer (Flyplane) and a new version of the AFCC (Mk XII). It was fully gyro-stabilised, hence well adapted to tachymetric operation. Unlike previous destroyer directors, Mk VI had a freely-trainable selector sight permitting the control officer to seek further targets while the director tracked a chosen one. At least in its initial form, Mk VI had an integral rangefinder and a pair of nacelles for its Type 275 radar (lightweight post-war versions often dispensed with the rangefinder). Mk VI was designed to control remotely power controlled guns – RP 40 system (see **F 10**). It appeared in later 'C' class destroyers and in some units of the 'Battle' class (others had US-supplied Mk 37s modified with British ballistics).

Anti-Aircraft Heavy Gun Firepower

The need for numbers, hence for minimum destroyer size, affected gun elevation. Ultimately that was set by the height of the trunnions above deck. At maximum elevation, the gun would recoil down towards the deck. Its trunnions, on which it elevated, had to be high enough above the deck to keep the breech from hitting the deck. At zero elevation, with the breech at maximum height, it had to be well within reach of a seaman wielding a heavy shell. Requirements originally written for the 'A' class, the first post-war destroyers, called for an elevation of 40 degrees, with one gun (preferably 'B' gun) elevating to 60, with a special high-angle control system serving it. Even 40 degrees was a problem, and when the ships were built they had four 4.7in guns elevating to 30 degrees, as in earlier destroyers. Problems with the prototype 60-degree mounting slipped it to the 'B' class. Tests on board HMS *Bulldog* (the last of the 'B' class) failed; it seemed that the best that could be done was 40 degrees, and even that was a problem. The 40-degree CP Mk XVII mounting was adopted for the 'E' class (1931/32 Estimates) and for their successors the 'F' and 'G' classes (the earlier 30-degree mounting was CP Mk XVI). Meanwhile the destroyer *Acheron* carried out trials to determine the heaviest shell which could easily be manhandled on board a destroyer, using 50lb, 62lb, and 70lb shells. The last was the estimated weight of a 5.1in shell. Trials on board HMS *Kempenfelt* showed that it was too heavy, but initially the Admiralty was unwilling to abandon it altogether before it was tested in comparison to the 4.7in gun. For a time it seemed that the 4.7in guns would be given 62lb shells, as it seemed that in calm weather a ship could develop about the same rate of fire with them.

As for the 4.7in destroyer mounting, even 40-degree elevation presented problems. In the 'E' class the solution was a shallow (12in deep) well under the gun, covered by portable plates to be used for low-angle fire. Guns used loading trays, which in effect considerably lengthened their breeches. The tray made it possible to use separate ammunition (separate shell and cartridge case). At high angles the two elements of the round could be rammed together (shells had to be rammed to ensure that they seated properly, and did not fall back while the cartridge was being loaded). The tray was swung into place to load, the next round being ready while the last was being fired. In 1933 Director of Naval Ordnance pointed out that without the tray no well would

The CP Mk XVIII mounting shows its loading tray (with shell and cartridge on it) deployed, and also the massive counterweights atop and below the gun, well behind the horizontal sliding breech, which is barely visible. The shield carried platforms for the layer, trainer, sight-setter, and breech worker, but the loaders stood on deck and followed the gun around. The gun was loaded from its left side, the loading tray tilting up to match up with the breech opening. The vertical hand lever was used to close the breech. The gun was hand-rammed using a hand grip on the other side, the rammer being reset by pulling it back to the rear of the loading tray (which is on the other side of the gun). This was a semi-automatic gun, ejecting its cartridge case into the net visible here after it fired. (John Lambert Collection)

The first approach to higher elevation for 4.7in guns was the CP Mk XVII mounting, which employed a pit under the gun to fire at even a modest elevation. It was carried in the 'E' to 'G' classes – this is *Foxhound* in August 1943. In these ships the bridge front at the compass platform level was bulged forward slightly to accommodate an Asdic display. What appears to be a cut in the front of the bridge is actually the sponson supporting the MF/DF coils. Note the absence of splinter mattresses, which were standard early in the war but gone by about 1942. The light anti-aircraft guns visible alongside the bridge structure are single Oerlikons, which were specified as early as the spring of 1941, but were presumably added later, replacing quadruple 0.5in machine guns (twin Oerlikons became available in the fall of 1942). (John Lambert Collection)

have been needed, and that it would not have been difficult to reach 50 degrees elevation. The extra length also made it difficult to adopt longer higher-velocity guns. With the tray, the Royal Navy used a 4.7in/45, but without it a 4.7in/50 could have been adopted. The 50-calibre gun could fire a much heavier (62lb) shell. Ultimately it was adopted in a power mounting in the 'L' and 'M' classes. Plans to produce a single version substantially affected the design of the Emergency destroyer ('O' class). An important factor in the choice of calibres was that the largest complete round which could be rammed 'uphill' without the aid of a loading tray and rammer was the 4in, and even it weighed 63lbs.

Trials showed that a 62pdr shell could be hand-rammed up to an elevation of only 15 degrees. Between 15 and 50 degrees a hand-worked wire rammer might be usable; above 50 degrees power-ramming was necessary. A fully dual-purpose mounting (70-degree elevation) would require power training and ramming, although it

The gun on a CP Mk XVIII mounting being loaded. Shell and cartridge have been placed together in the loading tray, which is about to be tipped up into position just behind the breech. The man on the right has his hand on the breech handle, so that he can close it as soon as the shell has been rammed into place. Note the way the counterweight is shaped to clear the deck at maximum elevation. Note also the difference between the HE shell in the loading tray and the pointed AP shell being brought to the gun. (John Lambert Collection)

could be power-elevated. A single 4.7in/50 mounting would weigh about 10½ tons if it had to elevate only to 40 degrees, but 14½ tons for 70 degrees. That compared to about 8.6 tons for the CP XIV mounting in 'A' to 'D' class destroyers, and to 8.8 tons for the 40-degree CP XVII in the 'E' class. It was also argued that a dual-purpose mounting had too high a silhouette for a destroyer trying to make stealthy torpedo attacks, and that it would be too complex for her small crew to maintain. A 1936 Admiralty memorandum cautioned against any consideration of high-angle fire 'which prejudice low-angle fire until such time as aircraft threaten the successful accomplishment of the destroyer's main object – which is delivery of a torpedo attack.'

The well was needed because at high elevation the breech was so far down, but that in turn was because of the position of the trunnions on which the gun was balanced. If the trunnions could be moved closer to the breech, it would not come so low when the gun elevated to 40 degrees. The solution adopted in the CP Mk XVIII mounting (for 'H' and later classes) was a heavy counterweight (see **G 6.**) That moved the centre of balance of the gun back towards the breech, so that there was no longer any need for a well. The new version of the gun was Mk IX**. This was also the version employed in the 'Tribal' class twin mounting. The counterweight was not quite enough to turn a low-angle gun into a high-angle one; it took quite enough lead to add 10 degrees of elevation, and loading at really high angles was still a problem.

The alternative solution to higher-angle fire, which was adopted by the US Navy, was a loading platform above the ship's deck, bringing the breech into a comfortable position. However, that raised the centre of gravity of the gun. Raising any weight in the ship made her less stable for a given size. If the destroyer were not to grow, she could not accommodate the sort of gun mounting which enabled high-angle fire.

In the face of air attack, moreover, it could be argued that even 40 degrees would enable a destroyer to keep firing at level bombers through most of their approach to the fleet. The ship would no longer be able to engage the aircraft once they came closer, but it was argued that this would be true for so short a time that it could not really matter. This argument set the elevation of the twin 4.7in guns designed for the 'Tribal, class, which was intended to provide fleet anti-aircraft protection.

Anti-Aircraft Fire Control

Unfortunately, the small destroyers lacked the necessary fire control system. Shells had to be set to burst near the approximate position of the air target. It was virtually impossible to put a long-range anti-aircraft shell into an airplane, but it was reasonable to imagine placing it to explode within lethal range. Anti-aircraft fire control was further complicated because that target speed could not be measured directly. For low-angle (surface) fire, the target moved slowly enough that the director could train to follow it, and so could measure its bearing rate. Similarly, range rate could be deduced from a series of rangefinder observations.

It did not help that the Royal Navy rejected stereoscopic rangefinding, which would have provided something close to three-dimensional views of the target. Instead it continued to rely on coincidence rangefinders. It called its anti-air instruments height-finders, which was somewhat misleading. What it meant was that the height-finder was a conventional rangefinder linked to a fire control system. The coincidence device measured the distance between rangefinder and target, but the fire control system calculated the distance between the observer and a point directly below the airplane. The difference gave height. In a British system, up until the end of World War II, the anti-aircraft fire control system fed the height-finder with range to the point below the airplane, and the height-finder calculated height from the difference between that and the actual range. The destroyer anti-air computer was called a Fuze Keeping Clock (FKC), because its output gave the appropriate time setting for shells.

For air targets the Royal Navy chose to rely on its fire control officers to estimate target speed based on their knowledge of aircraft and apparent sizes, using what amounted to a ring sight (an image of a ring projected on a screen). As aircraft speeds increased, such estimation became less and less precise. The control officer tracked the airplane using Angle of Presentation (A/P) binoculars, from which the target's elevation and bearing were transmitted to the FKC. The rate set on the clock was calculated from A/P readings. The control officer could adjust the set rate to put the visible bursts of shell fire in line with the target. A range operator at the clock tuned (set) the clock to the rangefinder range and adjusted the set rate so that the fire control system tracked the target. The FKC could drive the control officer's binoculars so that he could see whether the solution was correct. As feedback the FKC set the rangefinder, so its operator could tell whether the system was generating an accurate range. The system also drove the CO's glasses so that he could see whether the target was being hit. When the range-taker got the range to a target, he hit a pedal to cut lamps

at the receivers in the Transmitting Station; range was transmitted down in 50-yard steps (and the range that was sent was repeated back at the rangefinder so that it could be checked). Tuning range and rate together turned out to require considerable skill.

This system (and other Royal Navy and foreign anti-air systems as well) was designed on the assumption that the target was moving at a constant altitude, which made sense for level and torpedo bombers, but not at all for dive bombers. Unlike a large-ship high-angle computer, the FKC had no plot and was not self-contained, calculating corrections only for anti-aircraft fire. Fuze settings were based entirely on the FKC rate clock (ie, on projecting ahead a deduced target range rate). The FKC was first tested on board the sloop *Fleetwood*. To the surprise of many, it offered results as good as those of the large-ship HACS (high-angle control system) in good weather. Wartime sloops and 'Hunt' class escort destroyers were stabilised largely to insure that they would have effective fire control systems.

British anti-air fire control technology was developed in the 1920s, when British gyro technology was not yet capable of tracking fast air targets precisely enough. Such tracking from shipboard required good stabilisation, another gyro role. By way of contrast, the interwar US Navy had good gyro technology and developed systems which measured speed (in angular terms) directly; they were called tachymetric. The British realised that such systems were inherently better, but they began development only in 1938, too late for the war. As of 1939 it seemed that tachymetric anti-aircraft systems would be in general use by 1942–43, but that could not happen. The Royal Navy did deploy a small tachymetric system to control automatic anti-aircraft guns (equivalent to the US Mk 51), and the late-war Mk 6 director was finally tachymetric.

However, there was an attempt to modify the existing systems with gyro elements: Gyro Rate Units (GRUs) and associated Gyro Rate Unit Boxes (GRUBs) which could measure target angular speed. A GRU aloft transmitted the vertical and horizontal rates it measured to the GRUB in the Transmitting Station. GRU was most accurate at high angular rates, which meant at short ranges. Using GRUB, the rates could be inserted into the calculator. Like much of the rest of the British system, GRUB was designed to deal with targets flying straight and level, projecting ahead their angular positions; but GRU could measure rates for a manoeuvring or diving target. Appropriate GRUB settings would cause the fire control system to generate the appropriate deflections. Adding GRU/GRUB did not turn earlier systems into effective tachymetric ones, because British fire control calculators were not designed to accept rates (or line of sight ranges, for that matter) directly. An entirely new computer was needed: Flyplane. It did not enter service until after the war.

Automatic Weapons

The air threats of the 1920s and early 1930s were low-flying torpedo bombers (later they could drop their weapons from higher

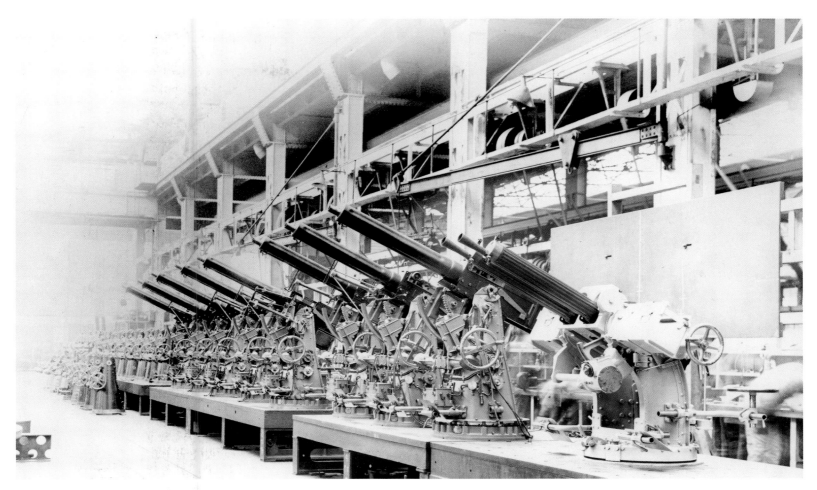

Vickers' delivery line shows the two standard naval automatic weapons of the interwar period: the 2pdr pom-pom and the 0.5in machine gun, both water-cooled. The 2pdr was of 40mm calibre, so between the wars ships credited with 40mm guns had the pom-pom – at least until Bofors started selling its twin naval gun in the late 1930s. In the foreground is a twin 0.5in gun on a naval mounting, a type the Royal Navy did not adopt. As far as the mechanism was concerned, the 2pdr was a scaled-up 0.5in gun. (John Lambert Collection)

altitudes) and higher-altitude level bombers. Both tactics required multiple attackers to be sure of hitting. It seems to have been assumed that a group of level bombers dropping bombs in a set pattern had a good chance of hitting, but only if enough of them attacked together. Similarly, to hit a manoeuvring target, torpedo bombers had to coordinate so that the target could not escape all of their weapons. Both types of attack were certainly threats to major warships, but a destroyer was hardly worth their efforts. During World War I destroyers were fitted with single 3in high-angle guns abaft their funnels, but there was no means of high-angle fire control, and these weapons were more a means of annoying or deterring aircraft than anything else. Post-1918 analysis showed that the main air threat to destroyers would be strafing. To deal with it, the destroyer needed a few automatic weapons.

In the 1920s that typically meant a few single Vickers 2pdr pom-poms, the standard heavy automatic anti-aircraft guns of World War I (see **A 1**) They were in effect much larger versions of the army's heavy water-cooled 0.303in machine gun. They were generally mounted on the searchlight platform between the two banks of torpedo tubes. They were never considered entirely effective. The first post-war version of the standard interwar destroyer ('A' class) had two pom-poms amidships plus Lewis guns. Initially they would have had a 60-degree mounting for one of their four 4.7in guns, but that had to be delayed, as noted, to the 'B' class, and it never materialised. In theory, any large high-angle gun needed a dedicated high-angle control system, although initially it seemed that a high-angle rangefinder might be enough.

The follow-on 'B' class was stiffened to take a 60-degree gun (CP Mk XIII mounting) in 'B' position, and it was tested unsuccessfully on board HMS *Bulldog*, the last in the class (see **G 4**). The 2pdrs were not well liked, so in the 'D' class they were replaced by a 3in high-angle gun (which was retroactively added to the 'C' class, under construction) and by two of the new quadruple 0.5in Vickers machine guns, on the forecastle (see **A 2**). The latter guns were mounted on board the last four 'D's (*Dainty*, *Decoy*, *Duchess*, and *Delight*); the others in the 'D' class were still awaiting them when war broke out, as demand for the 0.5in guns was so great. In 1939 the anti-aircraft destroyers ('Wair's), the 'S' class ASW destroyers, and *Shikari* all had 0.5in guns.

33

The 2pdrs and 0.5in guns were backed by a portable 'tree trunk' mounting for twin 0.303in Lewis light machine guns. These weapons never figured in official armament statements because they were not permanent, but they were very widely deployed. Often the two sets of Lewis guns were alongside the forward superstructure, on the upper deck.

In 1932 the Naval Anti-Aircraft Gunnery Committee recommended abandoning the 3in gun, and increasing the elevation of all four 4.7in guns to 40 degrees. All destroyers should

The quadruple 0.5in Vickers machine gun was a standard close-in destroyer weapon through the early part of World War II. It is shown aboard HMCS *Assiniboine* (ex-HMS *Kempenfelt*) early in the war. Note the shield, which protected the gunner but not the ammunition drums or most of the gun mechanism. (RCN)

have fire control systems adapted to high-angle fire. That was the origin of the CP Mk XVI mounting in the 'E' class.

In the 1930s a replacement light automatic gun, the sextuple

0.661in, was developed (see **A 6**). A prototype was ordered from Vickers in 1935; it was expected to fire 300 rounds per gun per minute. Properly aimed, it would get far more hits than the pom-pom, although the shells would be far lighter (3oz each). Muzzle velocity was 3112ft/sec. It might replace both the quadruple pom-pom and the 0.50-calibre machine gun. In 1936 DNO proposed that the new 'L' class have two such mounts in place of both types of gun. Unfortunately, estimated weight grew too rapidly. At first it was 2.75 tons; for the 'L' class it was to weigh 3.4 tons, but at the mock-up stage in 1938 it was expected to weigh 4 tons, nearly as much as the quadruple pom-pom. Many in the fleet suspected that it lacked hitting power. It was cancelled in 1938. In effect, the 2pdr and the 0.5in machine gun were replaced during World War II by the 20mm Oerlikon.

The quadruple 2pdr was a standard destroyer weapon from the 'Tribal's onwards, until it was superseded by the Hazemeyer Bofors. It was fired by a rating standing between the layer and trainer, initially using a crank and later an electric firing motor drive. This is the original version, with vertical firing handles visible at the rear of the mounting. (John Lambert Collection)

By 1934, there was a new factor: dive bombing. It had been developed mainly by the US Navy; it is not clear to what extent the Admiralty was aware of Japanese interest. The Royal Navy and the other big carrier navies (the US and Japanese) were aware that dive bombers could not be expected to sink capital ships; their bombs did not attain sufficient terminal velocity. That left cruisers, carriers, and destroyers as valid targets. The Royal Navy did not, apparently, understand that it was now perfectly economical for an enemy to attack destroyers from the air. In the context of a fleet action, stripping away destroyers before the battleships came into contact could eliminate an important British equaliser. Furthermore, to the extent that British destroyers were part of the anti-destroyer shield of the battle fleet, wiping them out would have left the way open for enemy destroyers. At this time, the US Navy, which had far more experience with dive bombers, was certainly impressed by the stripping power of its dive bombers in the context of a fleet action. The Admiralty was sufficiently impressed by the new type of attack that it bought a dive bomber, the Blackburn Skua, specifically to gain air superiority in a future Far Eastern war by neutralising Japanese carriers.

A single dive bomber turned out to have an excellent chance of

hitting a single manoeuvring ship, because the pilot could keep adjusting his aim as he dived. Moreover, contemporary forms of anti-aircraft fire were unlikely to deter a dive bomber pilot. Generally, they entailed adjusting the time fuze of a shell so that it would burst at a predicted point in the sky, as predicted by the fire control system. As with other kinds of gunnery, fire control involved an initial estimate, spotting, and corrections. In the case of an aircraft, that was particularly difficult because the target was moving so fast. A dive bomber descended far too quickly for the cycle of firing, spotting, correction, and fuze-setting to follow. The only possible antidote was a powerful automatic weapon which could hose the tube of sky down which the bomber flew. In the 1930s that meant a multiple pom-pom, which was typically a capital ship or cruiser weapon – certainly not the sort of weapon which could fit on board a 1400-ton destroyer.

The 'Tribal's were given a quadruple pom-pom in place of one of the planned five twin 4.7in mountings as a means of self-defence against dive bombers attempting to roll back the fleet's air defence. Larger ships had off-mount directors for their pom-poms, but a destroyer, even a large one, offered no space for one. Unlike its

Gunner's side of the quadruple pom-pom, with two joysticks, the double horizontal handles. They could be used to power-control elevation and train (but note that the training control was not on the same side as the trainer). Normally the layer and pointer trained their cranks in power-assisted mode; the joysticks allowed the mount captain to slew the mount rapidly onto the appropriate bearing. The firing quadrant was on the left side of the right-hand joystick. (John Lambert Collection)

larger eight-barrel brother, the quadruple destroyer pom-pom was controlled from its mounting. Its development had been proposed by the same 1931 Naval Anti-Aircraft Gunnery Committee which had called for 40-degree guns in destroyers. The existing eight-barrel pom-pom was far too massive for destroyers or small cruisers. The quadruple pom-pom was tested on board HMS *Crusader* in 1935–36 (see **A 3**, **A 4**, **A 5**). Although initially it was considered only as an anti-aircraft weapon, by 1937 it was also seen as an effective counter to motor torpedo boats. The Italians had built many of them, and they were a prominent factor of the 1935–36 Mediterranean crisis. Faith in the weapon was enormous; during discussions leading up to construction of the 'Tribal's it was pointed

This is the Mk VII version of the quadruple 2pdr with remote power control (RP), designated RP 50.
(John Lambert Collection)

The rear of the Mk VII RP 50 2pdr. The elaborate pantograph and bar and arcs are sight linkages. The layer's back sight is visible at left behind the speed ring. The dials visible at right are the trainer's receiver for instructions from a director. Each of the boxes shown contained 112 rounds, belt-fed into its gun in 14-round segments. The yoke and cranks on the right trained the gun; similar cranks on the other side elevated it. Under the plate at right was a hydraulic training motor. To move the mounting more rapidly, the layer had a joystick, under the horizontal handle at left. The funnel let in cooling water.
(John Lambert Collection)

out that its value might lie more in the enemy's knowledge of its existence than in its actual ability to shoot down aircraft. It was a quadruple version of the single 2pdr pom-pom which had been a fixture of British anti-aircraft batteries since World War I. This weapon enjoyed considerable export success as well. It was a 40mm/39, and as such is the 40mm gun which features in armament lists of many ships completed before 1936, when the 40mm Bofors gun appeared. Muzzle velocity was low, typically 2040ft/sec (later 2400) vs the 2890 of the later Bofors gun, and it used a lighter projectile (1.6 vs 2lbs). The Mk VII mounting could fire up to 115 rounds per minute. Without any computing director, and with its low velocity, it was unlikely to get many hits beyond 1000yd range (trials on board the battleship *Centurion* suggested 5 per cent hits). As for driving off enemy aircraft, pom-poms were not supplied with tracer ammunition pre-war, on the theory that it would distract gunners. Without seeing tracer coming their way, pilots would not even know that they were under fire. Wartime experience showed that guns were useful far more for their ability to drive off or distract attackers than for their ability to destroy them.

New Problems of the Late 1930s – The Air Threat to Shipping

Until the end of 1936, the Royal Navy destroyer force was limited in both total tonnage and in the tonnage of individual ships, only a few of which could displace 1830 rather than 1500 tons. By the time a new London Naval Conference had been called, the conditions which had justified the 1930 treaty had evaporated. Given the situation in 1930, it had seemed reasonable to sign a treaty with Japan and the United States, even though France and Italy had both backed out. By 1935 the Italians seemed to be on the march. They invaded Ethiopia (Abyssinia), and the League of Nations imposed sanctions, particularly on oil. The British found themselves enforcing the sanctions, and for a time it seemed that the Royal Navy would be fighting in the Mediterranean. Meanwhile, in March 1934 the Japanese announced that they were withdrawing from the limits agreed under the Washington Treaty. They had argued against the 5:5:3 ratio in capital ships imposed in 1921 (and had been granted a larger cruiser ratio in London); now they rejected the entire system. They agreed to attend the 1935 conference, but soon walked out. It was impossible simply to terminate the conference, because the public still believed that arms control was not only possible but desirable. The resulting 1936 London Naval Treaty imposed limits on individual ship size and firepower, but the totals were abandoned altogether. Navies were enjoined to circulate details of ships before they were laid down, in hopes that they could not then spring surprises which would cause bursts of construction by others. Since the treaty was signed only by the United Kingdom, the United States, and France, none of whom was antagonistic to the others, this meant very little.

By the time the London conference met, Adolf Hitler had taken power in Germany, determined to rearm. German naval rearmament presented the British with a terrible dilemma. Even if the Germans did not fight, the British would have to retain a powerful fleet in European waters to counter them. That in turn would reduce the fleet which could steam to the Far East to face an increasingly powerful Imperial Japanese Navy. The British could, however, hope to convince the Germans to limit their naval effort. In 1935 they negotiated a treaty under which the Germans agreed to limit themselves to 35 per cent of British surface warship tonnage. They also agreed to limit submarine construction, but unfortunately the treaty allowed them to build up to 100 per cent of the British figure if they decided that their security demanded it. Perhaps more unfortunately, the British concluded their agreement with the Germans without consulting the French. The only way the British could expect to send a big enough fleet East while facing potentially hostile German and Italian fleets was for the French to secure their position in European waters. After 1936 the Admiralty's main conclusion was that the Empire needed a far larger fleet, including many more destroyers.

It was also necessary to contemplate a war in Europe. British shipping in a Far Eastern war would be far from Japan. The only Japanese threats would be submarines and raiding cruisers, not aircraft. European waters were very different. In 1935, when the British faced war against Italy, the Italians had a large land-based air force. There were no carriers to sink to gain air superiority, and no one believed that any sort of air attack could put land bases out of action permanently.

Although the British did not yet have to fight the Italians, the Italians and the Germans soon demonstrated what aircraft could do to merchant ships. When civil war broke out in Spain, they backed Franco's nationalist rebels, who were the bulk of the Spanish army. The defending Spanish Republic badly needed arms and other supplies, which had to come mainly by sea. Interdiction efforts included not only bombing but also attacks by anonymous submarines. The Royal Navy became involved, one of its roles being to deal with those submarines. The air campaign against merchant ships was impressive. It seemed to foreshadow an entirely possible future of European warfare.

Germany had not yet built a large navy, and it still seemed unlikely that U-boats would repeat the kind of unrestricted submarine campaign they had pursued in 1917–1918. Such a campaign would inevitably involve neutral ships. In 1917, German sinkings had brought the United States into the war, with ruinous consequences for Germany. Too, the convoys introduced in 1917 had largely neutralised the U-boats by clearing the sea of ships: U-boats had found it more and more difficult even to find targets. Aircraft were a very different proposition. They could search rapidly, and they might even be able to discriminate between possible targets. At the least, a future war would require large numbers of escorts with effective anti-aircraft (high-angle) batteries. Thus the need to provide protection for British shipping in the narrow seas around Europe translated into a need for ships with effective long-range high-angle batteries. The only candidate was the new twin 4in high-angle guns with effective fire control. The sloops already being built as anti-submarine escorts were redesigned with powerful 4in batteries. New fast escorts (the 'Hunt' class light destroyers) were designed. Older cruisers and 'V&W' class destroyers were refitted as anti-aircraft ships. Plans were also prepared to convert some fast merchant ships into emergency anti-aircraft escorts. Because the twin 4in guns involved were so prominent in escorts, the drawing of this weapon and its fire control will be found in the next volume of John Lambert's drawings. Note that the twin 4in was definitely not comparable to the 4.7in gun, as it had nothing like the punch needed to deal with a destroyer.

Now the limit on new construction was money, not negotiated limits. New Admiralty policy doubled the annual destroyer building program to two flotillas, the goal being to maintain sixteen modern destroyer flotillas (eight ships each: flotilla leaders were no longer separate). Thus the 1935/36 program paid for both a flotilla of 'Tribal's and the 'I' class, the last of the interwar standard type. Under the 1936/37 program a second flotilla of 'Tribal's and a new 'J' class of large destroyers were built.

In theory, there was still a limit on the tonnage of individual destroyers, but since the total number of cruisers was no longer set, the only limit which mattered was the 8000-ton limit on cruisers. The real limit on the size of individual destroyers was set by their cost. For a time the Admiralty contemplated a 2750-tonner armed with three of the 5.25in dual-purpose turrets adopted for *Dido* class light cruisers, two quadruple torpedo tubes, two quadruple pom-poms, and two of the new 0.661in machine guns. It would supersede both the *Dido*s and the 'Tribal's. It would have the same sort of seakeeping as a small cruiser. The main deterrent to building such ships was that they would raise the general standard of destroyer size, so that it would become ruinously expensive to compete.

The big new 'J' class combined the new twin 4.7in gun with a destroyer-type pair of torpedo tube mountings and the quadruple pom-pom adopted in the 'Tribal's. The 1937/38 program included two more flotillas, the 'K' and 'L' classes. The 'K's were simply repeat 'J's. The 'L' class was conceived as a modified version armed with an enclosed twin 4.7in mounting developed in response to fleet reactions to the 'K' class. It seemed that enclosing the mounting would make it possible to move the 'A' and 'B' mountings closer together, as the crew of 'A' would not be subject to blast from 'B' mounting. The added weight of an enclosed mounting would be made up for by reduction in personnel. Work on the 'L' design was therefore paced by progress with the new mounting.

Unfortunately, the new Mk XX mounting grew far beyond initial estimates (see **G 9**). In February 1937 estimated weight was

Shown at Malta at the end of the war, HMS *Marne* gives an idea of just how massive the 4.7in Mk XX mounting was. The 'fishbone' atop her director is the antenna of a Type 285 radar. Atop her lattice mast is the 'lantern' of a Type 272 radar. The X-shaped antenna at the masthead is for a Type 291 air warning radar; its active elements are the barely visible horizontal ones. Lattice masts were fitted to support increasingly heavy radars. Note the power-operated twin Oerlikons on the signal deck ('A' deck) below her bridge wing and on the platform between her two torpedo tubes. (John Lambert Collection)

38 tons 2cwt and 2qtr, compared to about 29 tons for the 'J' class mounting. In April, however, it was 40.8 tons. Delays in design did not help; in November 1937 the mounting was only at the sketch stage. Maximum elevation, which would determine trunnion height, had not even been fixed (it would be 62in for 40 degrees, 84in for the 50 degrees ultimately chosen). In May 1939, DNO admitted that he could not give final weights until the mount was completed the following year. The Constructor, A P Cole, hoped that it would be within 50 tons (DNO thought 42½). As a weight-saver, guns were hand- rather than power-elevated (as in the 'J' and 'K' classes). In contrast to the twin mounting in the earlier ships, they were on individual trunnions, which required more space.

As a further complication, two pom-poms were wanted, leaving enough space for only one set of torpedo tubes. It was given power drive, on the theory that the single set might have to shift rapidly from beam to beam. Pending supply of enough pom-poms, the ship was given two sets of torpedo tubes. The second pom-pom never appeared. It turned out that a hand-powered pentad weighed about as much as a power-trained quadruple tube, so that was adopted. Ultimately, however, the ships were given quadruple tubes.

In the end, the complicated power mounting could not be produced fast enough, so four of the L class were completed with four twin 4in guns and, despite some proposals, never rearmed.

Given the problems of the 'L' class, it is no surprise that the 1938/39 destroyer program consisted of one repeat 'J' class ('N' class) and one repeat 'L' class ('M' class) flotilla. With the 'N' class, the sixteen desired modern flotillas were complete, so no new destroyers were included in the 1939/40 program – in peacetime.

It seemed unlikely that ships as complex as the 'M' class could be mass-produced in wartime, yet World War I had shown that there were never anything like enough destroyers. In the autumn of

HMS *Jervis,* seen at Malta on 27 December 1945, shows how much smaller the twin Mk XIX 4.7in mounting was than the twin power mounting (Mk XX) of the 'L' and 'M' classes. Note that 'X' gun is now trained aft instead of forward, as it originally did. By this time her after set of torpedo tubes had been reinstated, replacing the 4in anti-aircraft gun. Her lattice mast, which supported a Type 276 surface search radar, was fitted during a May 1945 refit. (John Mortimer collection)

1938, moreover, war seemed quite likely, even though Prime Minister Chamberlain had returned from Munich announcing 'peace in our time'. He must have meant a sufficient breathing space to solve British defence problems, both naval and in the air, as at the time the British radar system was only nearing readiness, and the fighters were not at all adequate. After Munich, the Admiralty began ordering a whole list of ships classed as 'useful only in war', such as 'Flower' class corvettes.

Since no single 62pdr existed (and the power-operated twin was so far behind schedule), the obvious choice to arm any Emergency destroyer was a single 50pdr, backed by a pom-pom and two quadruple torpedo tubes. The standing mobilisation plan called for 'G' class destroyers, but they were obsolete, and a new design was badly wanted. Work was ordered on 28 January 1939, before the decision to make the 'N' class repeat 'J's. To avoid a new machinery design, the new ships would use the existing 'J' class machinery, but a new smaller hull was designed. It would be armed with single 50pdrs, with provision for later replacement by 62pdrs, which meant that they had to be further apart than in previous ships. The planned new DCT and AFCC would not be ready in time, so they would be fitted with 'Hunt' class systems but could later take the better ones. Shipbuilders were asked to produce working drawings on the understanding that they would be paid if war did not break out and the Emergency destroyers were not wanted. As it was, the

three yards involved (Denny, Fairfield, and Hawthorn Leslie) received sketches on 2 September, and war was declared the next day. The first flotilla ('O' class) was ordered on 3 September and a repeat flotilla ('P' class) on 2 October. (However, the wartime Emergency destroyers were built to a different design.) In January 1941 it was decided to rearm eight of the ships with five single 4in anti-aircraft guns and one set of torpedo tubes. The ships so armed were all given 'P' names, some 'O' ships being renamed. Early in 1945 *Petard* was refitted with two twin 4in guns ('B' and 'X' positions), apparently as part of a more general project to rearm the class. *Obdurate*, *Obedient*, *Opportune*, and *Orwell* were all completed as minelayers.

The early War Emergency destroyer *Obdurate* was completed with 4in high-angle guns rather than the planned 4.7in weapons. She is shown as a minelayer in December 1946, with the quadruple 2pdr of early emergency destroyers abaft her funnel, and single 20mm guns between her torpedo tubes, replacing her searchlights.

HMS *Onslaught* was one of the initial War Emergency destroyers. She is shown in July 1942, with a 4in high-angle gun replacing her after torpedo tubes.

ASW Revisited

Once the 1930 conference failed to kill off the submarine, but also promised to kill off the older destroyers, the Royal Navy began building specialised anti-submarine escorts – sloops. The Admiralty was uncomfortably aware that in 1918 over 5000 anti-submarine ships had been mobilised when the Germans had only 148 U-boats, only a third of them at sea at any one time. The question in the interwar period was how the new technology of Asdic could or would change the situation.

Asdic was what would later be called a searchlight sonar, with a beam about 15 degrees wide. It was vastly superior to the World War I hydrophones. It could be used at speed; the Royal Navy developed a dome filled with water which enabled a ship to ping at speeds as high as 24kts. It could detect a submarine whether or not the submarine emitted any noise, and its high-frequency ping avoided much of the usual ocean sound. An operator typically sent out a ping, listened for an echo. If there was none, he turned to search in an adjacent direction. If there was a ping, he worked back and forth in 5 degree steps to find the direction more precisely. That took time. Pre-war exercises suggested that he would probably find a nearby submarine, although there was some evidence that a submarine could slip by as the ship moved and the pattern of beams moved with it. On the other hand, once a submarine was detected, Asdic could usually track it and regain contact after the water had been roiled by a depth charge attack. Maximum sonar range depended on water conditions, but it was typically about 2500yds.

The Asdic beam tilted downwards, so as a ship approached a submarine she would pass out of the beam (the rule of thumb was that depth was a third of the range at which the submarine vanished). The attacker had to pass over the submarine to release depth charges. A canny submarine skipper could tell when the pings ceased (and the hunting ship accelerated), and a violent manoeuvre might well save him. Tiltable Asdics, which could

maintain contact, were not developed until World War II. It was never easy to manoeuvre a ship's stern into position to attack, so depth charge patterns were an attempt to make up for some of the uncertainty in the submarine's position and depth. For example, wartime ten-charge patterns employed a 'sandwich' of two five-charge layers.

The first standard destroyer set was Type 118, first installed in the 'B' class, and optimised for Mediterranean conditions and for a maximum search speed of 18–20kts. These ships introduced a bridge loudspeaker (for echoes) and bridge control of Asdic transducer training. Type 119 introduced an integrated teacher, which could inject signals for training purposes. Type 121 ('D' to 'G' classes) introduced a gyro-stabilised transducer. Type 124 ('C' and 'H' classes) had the first chemical range recorder (to determine the optimum attack time) and an improved amplifier; its dome retracted electrically at 24kts. This set was controlled from a 'silent' cabinet on the lower deck, with secondary control on the bridge. The last pre-war destroyer set was Type 128 (1937, initially for the 'L' class). It had a range recorder and a new amplifier, and it incorporated improvements developed for the trawler sets. It was mechanically trained, controlled from a hut on the bridge. Although generally it had a housing dome, at least initially, as installed in the 'Hunts' it used a fixed dome, which cost about a knot, and permanently rigged wires, which added some further resistance. Type 128A and later versions were gyro-stabilised and electrically trained and formed the basis for the World War II Type 144.

HMS *Intrepid* shows early wartime modifications. She was a minelayer/sweeper (note the sponsoned track leading down, and the paravanes aft), so she did not have fantail space devoted to depth charge throwers. Instead, they were mounted on a platform forward of that for 'X' gun. Note the shield for the quadruple 0.5in machine guns, and the splinter matting limited to the searchlight platform.

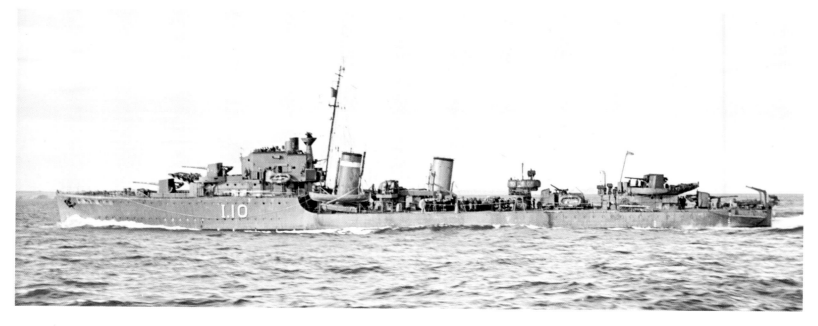

When the Royal Navy began building new destroyers in quantity in 1927, at first it specified that all should be adapted for Asdic installation if desired, though not all would initially be fitted. The final World War I fleet destroyer depth charge battery had been 12 depth charges in a 'V&W' class ship. For the new ones, a five-charge attack was specified, to blanket a submarine approximately under a ship's stern. That amounted to two thrown charges plus three over the stern, from tracks or releases, to form a diamond shape, with one in the centre. However, the new 'A' class (which had no Asdic) was given only six depth charges, the World War I standard, dropped from three chutes (two to starboard).

The 'B' class (1928/29 Estimates) were given Asdic (the first British production set) plus a full five-charge pattern (two throwers, three ready-use charges on a rail) and 15 depth charges, enough for three attacks. Policy was to split the destroyer force into Asdic and TSDS ships, the latter carrying the six-charge World War I battery. In 1929 it seemed that some ships might be 'special submarine killers' for convoy work, with 40 depth charges, a laughable number by World War II standards, but impressive at the time. In September 1931, the Admiralty Board decided that all future destroyers should have Asdic (this did not apply to the 'C' class, which was already well advanced). That was particularly urgent given the Treaty-mandated cuts in the British destroyer force. Although all the new destroyers were adapted for Asdic installation, and although Asdic sets might be stockpiled, installation would take too long in an emergency. The 'E' class was the first affected by this new policy, boiler rooms being shortened to make space for an Asdic trunk. Policy at this time was to fit all new destroyers so that they could be converted quickly to either minelaying or to the TSDS mine sweep. However, *Esk* and *Express* were built as minelayers from the outset.

By 1938, the standard outfit was 30 depth charges, for six five-charge patterns (see **M 2**). Ships typically carried 10 charges in peacetime; in wartime the others would be stowed in the torpedo warhead magazines. A few ships without Asdic had only 10 charges each. Typically, each thrower had three charges. In wartime a depth charge was always carried in the thrower, so the total on leaving port was four. With no stowage below decks, a 'V&W' class destroyer had single five-charge rails. Much heavier loads were ordered once war broke out in 1939.

Asdic would affect both anti-submarine ways of using destroyers in World War I: hunting and convoy. Hunting had failed largely because there was no way of closing in on a submarine betrayed by some form of intelligence. Asdic promised to solve that problem. World War I convoy operations had been mainly a means of preserving shipping, not of killing U-boats. Although convoy was often advertised as a way of bringing U-boats into contact with anti-submarine ships, typically attacks by escorts drove off U-boats but did not kill them. Convoy concentrated the targets and thus made them far more difficult for U-boats to find, and, furthermore, the U-boats found it difficult to attack so many merchant ships in the short time the convoy made them available.

The pre-1939 Royal Navy knew that it would be a long time before it could have very many anti-submarine ships. Its approach to convoy was to provide a few escorts, whose job would be to drive off an attacking submarine. For hunting it would provide a few older destroyers with unusually heavy depth charge batteries, sufficient to attack again and again until a U-boat had been sunk. Hunting was essential a coastal operation, because the open sea was just too wide to enable hunters to get to the hunted quickly enough.

British intelligence seems to have been unaware that the Germans had also thought deeply about the lessons of World War I submarine warfare. They planned to abandon operations near the British coasts in favour of direct attacks on convoys in the open ocean. Convoys would be located using signals intelligence, and attacks would be made by multiple U-boats working together, under control from the shore. The Germans apparently had no idea of what Asdic was, but by 1939 their U-boat commander Admiral Dönitz was telling his captains to attack on the surface at night. Abandoning attacks near the British coasts would make hunting, even with good intelligence, ineffective. Concentrating the U-boats into wolf packs would frustrate the limited number of escorts the Royal Navy could deploy. The impact on the Royal Navy destroyer force was that ships designed for fleet action had to be rearmed as long-range convoy escorts, to make up badly-needed numbers. U-boats did operate near coasts, particularly when that was safe (as they did off the US coast in 1942), but not to anything like the extent they had in 1917–1918. That in turn made many of the coastal ASW craft the Royal Navy pressed into service considerably less useful.

Inherent in the war plan to send a fleet to Singapore was the need to ensure that it would not suffer from possible Japanese minelaying en route. The World War I High Speed Mine Sweep was replaced post-war by the Two-Speed Destroyer Sweep (TSDS), which combined the functions of sweeping for and cutting mine moorings at high and low speeds, respectively (see **M 1**). The sweep consisted of a paravane (depressor) towed right astern, from which were towed two sweep paravanes on either side. They could be set for any depth between 20ft and 60ft. Maximum speed was 25kts, the two paravanes being spread 320yds at low speed and 150yds at high speed. TSDS could be used ahead of a fleet as a search sweep or else as a clearance sweep. At its high-speed setting it was considered effective against simple moored mines at 12kts and above, and against anti-sweep devices at and above 18kts.

War Again

Destroyers had a far more active war in 1939–1945 than they had had in 1914–1918. Contrary to much of its pre-war thinking, the Royal Navy found itself engaged mainly in European rather than Far Eastern waters. It fought a hard, protracted Battle of the Atlantic. As forecast years earlier, older destroyers were modified to work with more specialised escorts, many of them being rebuilt for that role. In the Mediterranean and in the Arctic, convoy support included a large measure of anti-air warfare, as the submarine and surface threats to convoys were backed by substantial enemy air forces, including numerous dive bombers and, in 1943 and afterwards, by bombers launching the first guided anti-ship missiles. Although destroyer torpedoes figured in the war, destroyers functioned far more as fleet or convoy support ships, which included anti-submarine warfare and anti-air warfare. For example, destroyers surrounding heavy ships helped create an umbrella of shellfire above the formation.

Radar and HF/DF

From a technology point of view, the single most significant World War II development was electronic: radar and, not too far behind, shipboard high-frequency direction-finding (HF/DF: 'huff-duff'). Radar had enormous impact on ship air defence, and also on surface and anti-submarine warfare. Radar development began before the war, and at the outbreak of war many British warships had rudimentary HF/DF in the form of diamond-shaped antennas

on their masts. However, for destroyers the story of both advances was very much a wartime one.

The first destroyer radars (called RDF at the time) was Type 286, developed about mid-1940 from Coastal Command's ASV Mk I. Its metric wavelength drastically limited its ability to see surface targets, but it was considered valuable as a warning set. As on the airplane, it used fixed antennas: one in the middle to transmit, two on the sides to receive. The ship had to swing to rotate its beam. Its ability to warn that aircraft were approaching over an 80-degree sector was valuable enough to justify producing

HMCS *Restigouche* (ex-HMS *Comet*) shows the first significant wartime destroyer radar, Type 286, on her foremast. The frame is most visible, the active elements being the double horizontal dipoles visible on the centreline and the sides (the latter angled off to each side). The antenna was fixed, the ship turning to determine direction. The antenna on the mast aft is a 'birdcage' for HF/DF. The circular crossed antennas atop the bridge are for MF/DF. Note the strip of splinter plating abreast 'A' gun. As in other destroyers, the ship's after funnel has been cut down to clear sky arcs. (RCN)

about 200 sets. Type 286M (derived from ASV Mk II) also had a fixed antenna, but it could measure target direction to within 10 degrees. A rotating version (Type 286P), with a 38-degree beam, appeared in February 1941. The final 286PQ offered higher power and better range resolution. It was completely redesigned as Type 290 (which was not successful) and then as Type 291. None of these radars had a narrow enough beam to designate targets to fire

control systems. Eventually the Royal Navy introduced a narrow beam Type 293 radar which 'indicated' targets clearly enough to assign them to directors. Type 291 became the standard wartime Royal Navy destroyer air search (air warning) radar. It could detect an airplane flying at 10,000ft at about 30nm, and a destroyer at 6 to 6.5nm.

German surface attack tactics made it vital to detect surfaced submarines at night. That took much shorter-wave (centimetric) radars, initially Type 271. The magnetron power tube which made it possible was first tested in February 1940. Trials that November and December suggested that such a radar could detect a surfaced or awash submarine. By the time the prototype Type 271X was ready for trials on board the corvette *Orchis* in February 1941, 150 had been ordered. The existing Type 286 could not detect a surfaced U-boat beyond 2000yds, but in March 1941 *Orchis* detected a surfaced submarine at 5000yds and a periscope at 1500yds. The much more powerful 271Q obtained about 40 per cent better range. The antenna was housed inside a protective 'lantern', which became a typical feature of corvettes, frigates, and destroyers. Type 271 did not rotate automatically, and it did not

HMCS *Haida* in June 1949, showing wartime modifications but not yet rebuilt. Thus she shows a Type 293 target indication radar atop her lattice foremast, with an HF/DF 'birdcage' above it, and the antenna of a Type 291 air search radar aft. The ship still has twin 20mm on the platform abreast the bridge, but elsewhere these have been replaced by single 40mm weapons in 'Boffin' mountings. The low-angle director normally forward of her high-angle director is gone. This class had an unusually congested bridge. She also no longer has the usual wartime splinter shields. The shielded object on her after superstructure protects a Hazemeyer. It appears that her after twin 4.7in gun in 'X' position had been landed; the gun aft is a twin 4in high-angle mounting. (Canadian DND)

have a PPI (map-like) display. Type 272 was a destroyer version, differing mainly in that the antenna was separated from the electronics for easier installation. It proved unsatisfactory, and a new set (Type 276) was developed with a much more powerful magnetron (500 kW rather than 100kW) and a new single- rather than double-cheese antenna.

New-generation radars (with PPIs) which appeared in 1943 included Type 293, which became standard onboard destroyers. In effect, it was a high-definition air search set, a modified 276 with its half-cheese antenna tilted up at a 15-degree angle and enlarged to give a narrower beam (4 rather than 6 degrees wide). The narrow beam gave target bearing accurately enough to pass data for fire control. The radar plan approved in April 1943 called for Type 293 to replace Type 272 on board all fleet destroyers. Late in May 1943, once the new heavy radars had been ordered, it was necessary to strengthen destroyer masts: the existing poles were ordered replace by a lattice (not immediately fitted, however) in all fleet destroyers

of 'Tribal' and later classes and in all 'Hunt's, to carry 272P, 276, or 293 radars in the best possible position.

Alongside the search sets were fire control sets, initially operating at about 50cm (rather than the 150cm of Type 286/291)

The War Emergency destroyer *Wessex* is shown at Sydney in 1945 with other units of the British Pacific Fleet. She has twin power-worked 20mm guns, not yet having been refitted with 40mm 'Boffins'; one is visible on her signal deck alongside her bridge. The high-angle director carries the 'fishbones' of a Type 285 radar. Her lattice foremast carries the antenna of a Type 276 surface-search radar (the apparently similar Type 293 was tipped up). An HF/DF 'birdcage' is partly visible at the top of the pole topmast. Barely visible at the near end of the yardarm are the vertical and horizontal dipoles of the Type 87 bridge-to-bridge radio. Note the absence of splinter plating outside 'B' 4.5in mounting, although the strip of splinter plating abreast 'A' mounting is visible. (Alan C Green via State Library of Victoria)

wavelength. By 1940 there was a series of range-only sets using 'fishbone' antennas, including Type 285 for heavy anti-aircraft guns and Type 282 for pom-poms. They needed optical back-up because their beams were so broad. Type 285M/P (1942) had beam-switching, which made it possible for the radar to keep pointed directly at a target. However, the radar could not measure altitude, so blind fire was impossible.

The new 10cm technology which made surface search possible was also applied to fire control, the only important wartime destroyer application being Type 275 on the Mk VI director. It used a pair of antennas (transmission and reception) which could scan their beams conically, in effect using three-dimensional beam-switching to track a target in all three dimensions. It could not track a target automatically. Instead, an operator below decks manually corrected for the beam position error measured by the radar.

HF/DF was introduced at about the same time as air search radar. The anti-convoy tactics developed by the Germans before World War II relied heavily on operational and even tactical control from shore, the theory being that it was too dangerous to rely on any single U-boat to command others. An attack would collapse if it were sunk or disabled. That in turn required reliable long-range radio contact between the shore headquarters and the U-boats. The relatively new technology of high-frequency (HF) radio made such tactics possible, and the Germans convinced themselves that it was impossible for a ship to intercept messages from U-boats. The logic seems to have been that the long-range component of HF signals was directed upwards at an angle, hence could not be detected nearby. However, an HF radio also produced a surface wave which could be detected out to about 30nm. The Germans also thought that even if the signal could be intercepted, it would be too short for direction-finding. They were thinking in terms of pre-war techniques, in which an operator scanned back and forth, looking for maximum and minimum signal strengths. The British used what amounted to radar receiver technology, continuously comparing signal strength in various directions and displaying a pattern on a screen. Short inherent range was actually an asset, since detection indicated a U-boat within about 30nm, and a fast ship could be assigned to run down the line of bearing to deal with the U-boat. The main British set was FH 4. Air search radars competed for masthead space with HF/DF. Late in 1940 the installation of HF/DF in the main wireless office (ie, on the foremast) was suspended to allow installation of Type 286. In November 1941 a pole stub mast for HF/DF was approved at the fore end of the after superstructure for the 'Q' and later classes.

By itself, a radar provided a snap-shot of the current situation (without a PPI, it only provided range and bearing on a few selected targets, which was even less). When radar entered service, the Royal Navy was well aware that tactical decisions should be based on a plot of available information; radar ranges and bearings were added. It was soon clear that all available information had to

be integrated by a new Action Information Organisation (AIO). The space in which that was done was alternatively called an Action Information Centre (AIC), an AIO, or an Operations Room. The AIC was broadly comparable to the US Combat Information Center, but in larger ships there might be several plots rather than the fully centralised one the US Navy preferred. It was natural for ships to devise their own methods for integrating sensor data. Because the plot on one ship had to be able to feed the plot on another operating in company, techniques in any one fleet were standardised. As the war continued, ships were often transferred from fleet to fleet, so the Admiralty developed a standardised AIO doctrine. A committee to define AIO requirements was set up in June 1943. The Royal Navy began to install AIO in destroyers in 1944. At a September 1944 meeting Home Fleet officers approved a layout in which space was made by extending the existing Charthouse/Plotting Office (to starboard abaft the pilothouse, alongside the Asdic office) to starboard to the side of B gun deck. This modification had recently been approved and carried out in *Kempenfelt* (the 'W' Class leader) and was about to be done in *Vigilant*. Some ships were fitted while building. A new scheme promulgated in January 1945 envisaged an Operations Room (including the charthouse extended to starboard), a Target Indicating Room (TIR), a device allowing those on the open bridge (compass platform) to view the PPI and the plot in the Operations Room (OR), and a 'Y' (radio warfare) receiving room (designated QD). The latter superseded the Third Wireless Room of pre-war practice. In leaders, it was a separate space; in destroyers, it was combined with the HF/DF office. From a ship design point of view, the advent of the AIO meant an urgent requirement for more space adjacent to, or more likely immediately under, the compass platform/bridge. Hence the redesigned bridge structure in the *Daring* class, in which space was obtained by in effect pushing out the lower level of the structure. Because the AIO concentrated all available shipboard tactical information, there were some wartime experiments in which a ship was fought from it. However, officers preferred to see the ships and aircraft around them. That was hardly irrational, since even the best radar could not adequately show quick manoeuvres by either.

The 'Battle's, 'Weapon's, Canadian 'Tribal's, and the later 'C' class had the full scheme. Emergency ships completing after June 1944 got the TIU. The 'Ca' class received the full scheme except for *Cambrian*, *Caprice*, and *Cassandra*, completing May through June 1944, which received only Operations Rooms. Of the 10th Emergency Flotilla, only *Zest*, *Zodiac*, *Zambesi*, and *Zealous* received Operations Rooms, to suit their structures. Earlier ships of the 'A' and later classes were fitted as convenient. As of the spring of 1944, a few ships were already being fitted: *Nubian* (full scheme but no TIU), *Kelvin* (full scheme, but no TIU), *Tartar* (OR only), *Obdurate* (full scheme, but no TIU), *Musketeer* (OR only), *Savage* (OR only), *Scourge* (OR plus QD but no 'Y' receiver), *Escapade* (OR only), *Derwent* (OR and QD), *Holderness* (OR and QD), and

Badworth (OR and QD). That this list was so short illustrates just how hard-pressed British shipbuilders were in the spring of 1944, and also why the 'C' class was in such greater demand than earlier destroyer classes immediately after the war, before much could be done in the way of structural modification to existing ships.

Anti-Aircraft Weapons

When war broke out in 1939, the Royal Navy was probably better equipped with anti-aircraft weaponry than any other, but it was not nearly enough. The 1940 campaign off Norway offered a taste of dive bombing, and the fight off Dunkirk showed that German dive bombers were entirely capable of concentrating on individual destroyers. On 17 May 1940 Controller held an emergency meeting to develop solutions. The only available weapons were 3in and 4in guns, and no fire control systems were available. Instructions were issued on 11 June: a 12pdr would replace the after torpedo tubes in the old 'V&W' class (see **G 15**). A 3in 20cwt gun would replace the after torpedo tubes in the 'A' to 'I' classes (see **G 14**). A 4in twin would replace 'X' gun in the 'Tribal's, and the 'J's and 'K's would have a 4in gun instead of their after torpedo tubes (see **G 13**). The single Mk V guns were World War I weapons (which had armed destroyers) on new high-angle mountings. A month later the 4in gun was approved for the 'O' and 'P' classes. Soon the 'N' class was ordered similarly modified to the 'J's and 'K's, and a similar modification was ordered for the 'L' and 'M' classes (except for ships completed with all-4in armament using the same Mk V gun). Similar changes were made to the Emergency destroyers then in the early stages of construction. Without any fire control system, the weapons were justified as a means of driving off approaching aircraft. There was some hope, moreover, that the 'E' to 'I' classes could be fitted with effective fire controls once a three-man rangefinder then under development was ready; they would get FKCs. *Faulknor* and *Foxhound* had new rangefinder directors and FKCs fitted (*Fury* seems to have had an FKC). It is not clear whether any other ships were so fitted (wartime lists of materiel to be landed for escort conversion usually included the director and FKC). The *Havant*s were completed with combined DCTs and, presumably, with FKCs. Some destroyers were not rearmed.

By December 1941 the Admiralty had concluded that the 3in (4in in later ships) was useless, even when controlled by an FKC. It was less effective than an Oerlikon against a dive bomber up to 3000ft, and considerably less effective than a four-barrel pom-pom up to 10,000ft. Torpedo tubes should be restored to 'E' through 'I' class destroyers (more Oerlikons could also be fitted). Director of Plans concluded in April 1942 that except in the Mediterranean, where more effective anti-aircraft weapons might be installed, the second set of tubes should be restored. It is not clear how many ships were refitted this way, because in the official armament list the torpedo battery was either two sets of tubes or one set and a 3in gun, not saying which ship had which.

After the carrier *Illustrious* was knocked out by German dive

This 4in Mk V gun in a high-angle mounting replaced a bank of torpedo tubes early in World War II. On a low-angle mounting, the same gun had armed destroyers during World War I. Note the headphones on the gun's layer, to the right in the photograph, and the muzzles of two of the four guns of a quadruple pom-pom visible behind the searchlight. (John Lambert Collection)

bombers in January 1941, Prime Minister Winston Churchill personally demanded action: he saw a real risk that the navy would be run out of the central Mediterranean. He thought that new weapons, such as the rockets (Unrotated Projectiles, or UPs) might be a solution. An Admiralty meeting concluded that the main requirement was to force enemy aircraft higher so that they could not attack so accurately. The existing pom-pom was the most effective close-range anti-aircraft weapon, 'known to be feared' by the enemy. Projected improvements were high velocity bright tracer ammunition, with remote power control using a tachymetric predictor to come. Other current efforts were the installation of 4in guns on board destroyers and also installation of captured Italian Breda 20mm guns on board selected ships.

Despite the Admiralty's relatively rosy evaluation of the current situation, the Royal Navy suffered badly again in May 1941 when it evacuated British troops from Crete. German dive bombers sank

A typical destroyer 4in high-angle gun and mounting, with the usual low splinter shield surrounding it, but no other protection for the crew. The two cylinders atop the gun are spring recuperators, which returned the gun to position after it recoiled. They identified this mounting as Mk III**, all other versions having hydro-pneumatic recuperators. As usual, layer and trainer stand on either side, presumably looking through their telescopes. The rear platform on the left was for the sight-setter. The lever-operated horizontal sliding breechblock is visible to the right as the loader shoves the round into the open breech. The object below the breech is a spent-cartridge deflector. The ship is the Polish-manned *Piorun*, ex-HMS *Nerissa*, in late 1940.
(John Lambert Collection)

many of the destroyers. Battleship anti-aircraft batteries were not enough; the Royal Navy needed destroyers with real anti-aircraft capability. Since the Norwegian campaign there had been interest in such a ship, although as late as April 1941 opinion did not universally favour it. A sketch design shown to the Admiralty Board in September 1941 showed two twin 4.7in dual-purpose mountings, which did not yet exist. The Board found itself accepting a high-low mix of new destroyers: the new dual-purpose type plus a War Emergency type based on previous practice, armed with low-angle guns.

The only British dual-purpose weapon remotely suited to a destroyer was the twin 4.5in between-decks mounting which had been adopted for carriers and for rebuilt capital ships (see **G 10**). It was too large for existing destroyers, and it used fixed (unit) ammunition impossible to manhandle aboard a destroyer. However, it could be adapted to fire separate shells and cartridges. A new much larger destroyer – which became the 'Battle' class – was designed to accommodate it (see **G 12**). The smaller destroyer *Savage* had one such mounting installed in place of her two forward guns, as a test. The British were interested in the US 5in/38, which they hoped to obtain under Lend-Lease, but US entry into the war in December 1941 made that impossible (the cruiser *Delhi* was rearmed with these weapons). The 1942 war program included two flotillas of the big destroyers (the 'Battle' class) and three of Emergency destroyers. The 1943 program included repeat 'Battles' because the follow-on destroyer weapon, the Mk VI used for the *Daring* class (1944 program) could not be ready in time. It was considerably lighter than the Mk IV used in the 'Battle' class, hence could be mounted in greater numbers on much the same sort of hull.

The 1942 ships had the British Mk VI director; the 1943 group had the US-supplied Mk 37 fire control system, which was considered far in advance of anything the Royal Navy then had (the British had been trying to buy it in quantity since 1941). The supply of Mk 37 systems determined how many 1943 'Battles' there could be. The system had to be modified for British ballistics, each version entailing a considerable effort. The US Navy chose 5.25in and 4.5in. It offered 42 fire control systems, four of which (5.25in ballistics) were assigned to the battleship *Vanguard*. Of the 38 with 4.5in ballistics, 12 were needed for three new *Ark Royal* class carriers. The 26 left over set the maximum number of 1943 'Battle' class destroyers, but there was considerable confusion as to how many would be built to a repeat 1942 design and how many to a new design. Building capacity set the entire 1943 program at 40 destroyers –5 flotillas – as in 1942. Initial plans (October 1942) called for four flotillas of large and one of smaller destroyers, but Mk 37 supplies limited the large destroyers to slightly over three

Vickers' shop test prototype of the twin 4.5in gun Mk 3 which armed the 'Battle' class. Unlike the single open 4.7in and 4.5in mountings, this was a 'between decks' mounting. The later Mk 6 mounting in the *Daring*s was an upper deck mounting; despite its apparently greater bulk, it was considerably lighter. (John Lambert Collection)

The later 'Battles' had US Mk 37 directors, but with British Type 275 radars. This is HMS *Agincourt*. The gun abaft the funnel is a 4.5in Mk V which replaced the 4in guns intended to fire star shell in some of the earlier ships. By the time this photo was taken, the wartime Hazemeyers were gone, together with their successors the STAAGs, in favour of simplified twin utility mountings visible here. (A D Baker III)

HMS *Scourge* was a War Emergency destroyer armed with 55-degree 4.7in guns. Photographed in August 1943, she shows a Hazemeyer Bofors amidships.

flotillas, the remaining two being the smaller Emergency destroyers.

The Emergency Destroyers and Their Main Batteries

The late pre-war 'O' and 'P' class Emergency destroyers were considered too small; the demand that they be restricted to 1500 tons limited their endurance. A design based on the larger 'J' class hull, developed in 1939, became the basis for twelve wartime flotillas: the 'Q' to 'Z' classes and the 'C' series ('Ca', 'Ch', 'Co', and 'Cr' classes), a total of 96 ships. The 1940 ships were the 3rd to the 6th Emergency Flotillas ('Q' through 'T' classes). Later building capacity was given as five flotillas per year. When the big 'Battle' class destroyers were introduced in the 1942 program, the Emergency type was described as 'Intermediate' between them and the small 'Hunt's.

The 50pdr 4.7in gun in a single mount was chosen at the outset, although DNO hoped that later he could provide a non-weatherproof twin 62pdr mounting. It never materialised. Given the simplified armament, fire control was the main bottleneck. As in the 'J' class, the design showed a quadruple 2pdr and the usual 30 depth charges (an increase to 45 had recently been approved for the 'J' and 'K' classes). Groups were conceived in pairs and

progressively improved through the war. At the outset they were considered too large, their 'J' class hulls under-loaded; at the end they were too small to be fitted with what was now considered essential.

By May 1940 it was clear that the 40-degree mounting was inadequate, and that September DNO pointed out that he could increase elevation to 55 degrees relatively easily. To do that he extended the ideas embodied in the 40-degree mountings. The trunnions were pushed as close to the breech as possible. They were raised as high as possible, compatible with ease of loading, and the recoil was shortened. At high angles some form of power ramming was necessary. To provide that, some of the recoil energy went into cocking a spring rammer, which was released as soon as the loading tray came into line with the breech. The mounting weighed 3 tons more than its predecessors, but the big hulls of the Emergency destroyers could easily absorb that. Most of the weight went into strength to withstand the shorter recoil and into a heavier counterweight. The gun shield was made considerably more substantial. This new CP Mk XXII mounting would be ready in time for the 'S' and 'T' classes (5th and 6th Emergency Flotillas – see **G 8**). It could be recognised by its steeply inclined face, previous destroyer shields having nearly vertical faces.

Because construction of the 4th Flotilla ('R' class) had been suspended for a time during the 1940 crisis, these ships were arranged to take the 55-degree gun, with the understanding that they would be completed with 40-degree guns (but they were never rearmed). There were, moreover, reports (which were false) that German destroyer guns could elevate to 80 degrees. Was the 55-degree gun no more than a poor compromise? In October 1940 VCNS ordered that in principle future destroyer guns should be true dual-purpose weapons elevating to 70 or 80 degrees or more, leading directly to the design of the 'Battle' class. This was when the US Navy was approached for 5in/38 guns. Given delays obtaining US weapons, in February 1941 the Sea Lords decided that all 40 ships of the 1941 program (7th to 11th Flotillas: 'U' and later classes) would be armed with 55-degree mountings and two sets of torpedo tubes plus one heavy close-range weapon and four Oerlikons. The 55-degree mounting was considered close enough to full anti-aircraft capacity that the 4in high-angle gun was no longer needed.

The 5th and 6th Emergency Flotillas ('S' and 'T' classes) were ordered early in 1941 as repeat 'R's but with 55-degree mountings, the 40-degree mounting being the fall-back if the new one was not yet ready. Once a 4.5in gun had been selected for the big dual-purpose destroyers ('Battles') it seemed logical to use the same gun in a 55-degree mounting for the smaller destroyers ordered in the same 1942 program. The 4.5in gun fired a heavier shell (55lbs) than the 4.7in and it had better ballistics. The heavy ships used fixed ammunition, but experience in the small cruisers *Scylla* and *Charybdis*, which had upper deck versions of the twin 4.5in, showed that it was difficult to handle. Destroyers would be far livelier, so the decision was taken to develop separate ammunition for them and then to modernise the battleships and carriers to use the same ammunition. For the Emergency destroyers, the 4.5in gun was placed on the existing 55-degree mounting. Alternatives,

such as adopting a US-style loading platform, were rejected. Once the new gun had been chosen for the 1942 ships (12th and 13th Flotillas) it was made retroactive to the 10th and 11th ('Z' and 'Ca' classes). The new mounting was designated 4.5in CP Mk V (see **G 11**), the twin destroyer mounting being Mk IV.

Fire control was also a problem. No dual-purpose DCT light enough for destroyer installation existed in 1940. The 1940 ships received low-angle directors and separate Mk D rangefinders. As of August 1941, it was hoped that the first ships of the 1941 program (8th Flotilla: 'U' class) could have the new Mk III (W) rangefinder director, and there was also some hope that some ships could have US Mk 37s. The rest of the 1941 ships, it was hoped, would have dual-purpose DCTs. To accommodate the new directors, the after ends of bridges were widened and extended, a modification extended to the 'P' and 'Q' classes. Like the big 1942 destroyers ('Battles'), the 1942 Emergency class ('Ch', 'Co', 'Cr' classes) was given the Mk VI DCT, the first fully dual-purpose director in British service. As weight compensation for the director and also the associated remote power control for the 4.5in guns, these ships had one rather than two sets of torpedo tubes.

Photographed in 1947, HMS *Contest* shows the final development of the War Emergency destroyer, with a big Mk VI director atop her bridge. As weight compensation, she had to surrender one of her two sets of torpedo tubes. She shows a single Oerlikon on her signal bridge, and the guns on the two power mountings amidships seem too stubby to be Bofors; they may be single 2pdr pom-poms, an alternative weapon. Note that she lacks the usual splinter protection strips near her 4.5in guns. (Alan C Green via State Library of Victoria)

Automatic Weapons

It also seemed that the pom-pom should be replaced. The Swedish Bofors gun had been adopted by the British army, and in 1941 a few were taken over by the Royal Navy. Its great advantage was its high muzzle velocity. Unlike the pom-pom, the Bofors was entirely self-contained; it could keep firing even if a ship lost power. Other navies had adopted a power-worked twin version. In 1940 the Dutch warship *Willem van der Zaan*, fleeing to the United Kingdom as the Germans invaded, carried a version stabilised in three axes, which promised good shooting even on board a violently rolling, pitching ship. The British decided to put this Hazemeyer mounting into production as Mk IV (see **A 7**). By this time the British were relying heavily on US production, the two navies merging their weapon designations. The Dutch demonstration had convinced the US Navy to adopt a twin Bofors as its Mk I (in preference to the pom-pom, which the US Navy almost put into production), but without stabilisation, using a stabilised Mk 51 director. The US quadruple version became Mk II; a single hand-worked army mounting (which was sometimes mounted on board ships) became Mk III. The first single Bofors (ex-army) were mounted on board some large British warships in 1941.

The Dutch had used an optical rangefinder and a predictor sight. By this time the British had a range-only Type 282 radar which they were using in pom-pom directors. They added it to the Hazemeyer. The Hazemeyer turned out to be rather temperamental, and through the war the Royal Navy sought a better alternative. Its lightweight 'utility' Mk V was biaxially rather than tri-axially stabilised and lacked any onboard director (it used remote power control). It was widely installed. The goal, however, was a better self-contained unit. Development of a twin triaxially-stabilised Buster (Bofors Universal Stabilised Tachymetric Electric Radar) was abandoned late in the war, but the twin biaxially-stabilised STAAG (Stabilised Tachymetric AA Gun) saw considerable post-war service (see **A 9**). Like the Hazemeyer, it developed a bad reputation for unreliability. The original Hazemeyer appeared for the first time on board wartime 'S' class Emergency destroyers.

During the war the navalised Bofors Mk VII superseded the Mk III in British (but not US) service. These mountings replaced Oerlikons at the end of the war (for ships bound for the Pacific) and post-war. Mk VI was a sextuple Bofors intended to replace the octuple pom-poms on board large ships; it was too massive for destroyers.

Initially it seemed that the Hazemeyer would be so effective that the single 4in anti-aircraft gun might no longer be worthwhile: ships could have their full complement of two sets of torpedo tubes. Thus in January 1941 the planned armament of the 5th and 6th Emergency Flotillas ('S' and 'T' classes) was four 55-degree 4.7in guns, one twin Bofors, four Oerlikons, and two sets of quadruple torpedo tubes, with a single 4in gun still carried as an alternative to one set of tubes (the ships were, however, ordered without the 4in

gun). Ships of the 3rd and 4th Flotillas, which had been allocated 4in guns, were completed instead with two sets of torpedo tubes and 40-degree guns (**T 4**). They had quadruple pom-poms and six Oerlikons each (as approved in June 1941). On 21 February the First Sea Lord's meeting on the subject decided that the 7th ('U' Class) and later Flotillas would have two sets of tubes, although it was impossible to guarantee that there would be enough torpedoes to fill them. Builders were told to complete the 7th and later flotillas with two sets of tubes but to retain structural provision for a 4in gun.

The wartime companion to the Bofors (and the pom-pom) was the 20mm Oerlikon, designed in Switzerland but mass-produced in the United States. It needed no power, and a single operator could aim and fire it, using shoulder pads to wield it. The Royal Navy became aware of it before the outbreak of war, initially buying Swiss guns. Because it did not need a source of power, the Oerlikon was easy to install almost anywhere on board a ship. It offered considerable potential against dive bombers. Because it was so light, the Oerlikon offered the possibility of giving a destroyer a real

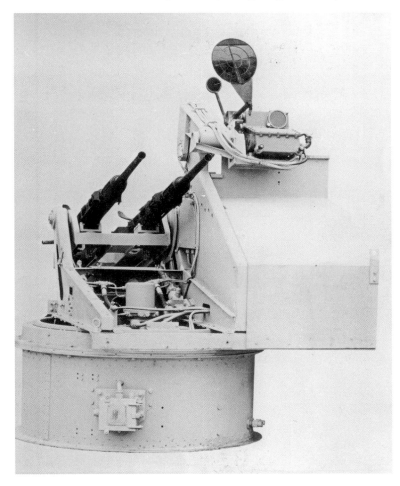

A twin 20mm power mounting (Mk V) equipped with a US-supplied Mk 14 gyro sight (at right, on the front of the operator's cab). This mounting was widely used, and it was the basis of the single power Bofors mounting ('Boffin'). (John Lambert Collection)

The Dutch Hazemeyer 40mm mounting on board the destroyer *Isaac Sweers*, which escaped to England when the Netherlands fell. It retained its on-mount rangefinder even though it was also equipped with a British Type 282 range-only radar, using the antennas above the mounting. This was the mounting the Royal Navy adopted. (John Lambert Collection)

capability to engage several aircraft more or less simultaneously. Until about 1942 it was the main new weapon installed on board British ships. A twin version of the Oerlikon turned out to be little heavier than the single mounting.

In 1942 twin power-worked Oerlikons were introduced to supplement the single hand-worked type (see **A 10**). The policy was initially to provide the maximum number of such guns, on the grounds that the ships involved had too few close-range guns. However, Fleet commanders wanted to limit the number of such weapons for several reasons. One was that the total number of independent weapons (channels of fire) was being reduced. Another was that the twins depended on a ship's electric power,

which could be disabled. A third was that the single was easier to manipulate, hence quicker on a target. Policy was therefore changed to 50 per cent hand-worked, or a minimum of two hand-worked guns if 50 per cent were unworkable, *ie* where such alteration would give unsymmetrical and unbalanced 20mm

Indian sailors clean the 20mm guns of a Mk V mounting on board the sloop HIMS *Narbada*, 1943. The enclosure to the right is the cab for the power control, the operator using the visible ring sight. (John Lambert Collection)

armament. Ultimately, US-type twin hand-worked guns would be used. Thus the approved battery of four twin Mk V in a 1942 'Battle' would be replaced by two twin Mk V and two hand-worked mounts. As of January 1944, the Emergency Flotillas had an approved battery of four Mk V (but the 'Q' and 'R' classes were assigned two twins and two single Mk V); the 'P' class was assigned four twins, the 'O' class two twins and two singles, the 'L' and 'M' class four twins and two singles; the 'J', 'K', and 'N' class was assigned four twin Mk V, the 'Tribal's were assigned four twin Mk V and two singles (except the beamier Canadian 'Tribal's, which had six twins).

The Royal Navy continued to emphasise the Oerlikon well after the US Navy had concluded that it was a secondary weapon, to the point that in 1945 the British Pacific Fleet command had to recommend the elimination of such weapons in favour of Bofors guns because they had proven so ineffective against Kamikazes. When the British Pacific Fleet was formed, it was assumed that one Bofors barrel could be equated to two Oerlikons, but Oerlikon hits were not lethal enough. Before that, in March 1944 the Mediterranean Fleet ordered pairs of Army-type single Bofors guns fitted to 'T' class destroyers. For some time the Mediterranean Fleet had been reporting that the best German pilots were pressing home attacks despite Oerlikon fire, or from beyond Oerlikon range. In effect they were harbingers of what the British Pacific Fleet could expect.

The new power Oerlikon mounting invited replacement of its guns by something more powerful, initially a single 2pdr and later, when the British Pacific Fleet reached Australia, by a single Bofors gun, the result being called a 'Boffin'. Even the 2pdr version was considered worth employing on board carriers in 1945. The initial British reaction to the Kamikazes was to refit destroyers as they steamed East with single Army-type Bofors guns instead of Oerlikons.

On 24 February 1946, HMS *Grenville* ('U' class, flotilla leader) heads home from the Pacific, trailing a paying-off pennant. She shows a Type 293 target indication radar atop her lattice mast, with the antenna of her bridge-to-bridge radio atop her pole topmast. The antenna just abaft the Type 293 is an IFF interrogator associated with her air search radar. Her signal deck and other positions show 40mm 'Boffins' converted from twin power 20mm mountings in Australia. Her after pole mast carries the antenna of a Type 291 air search radar, with a twin 40mm Hazemeyer mounting abaft it. She shows splinter plating around the bases of all her 4.7in guns.
(Alan C Green via State Library of Victoria)

Photographed on 9 February 1946, HMS *Tumult* shows single 40mm 'Boffins' and a twin Hazemeyer Bofors gun between her sets of torpedo tubes. The object on the fore side of her pole mainmast is an IFF transponder; unlike the interrogator on the foremast, it is omni-directional. (Alan C Green via State Library of Victoria)

As for earlier automatic weapons, by October 1940 there were still not enough quadruple 0.5in machine guns, so ships without them were given pairs of 2pdr Mk II pom-poms in sided positions. The surviving World War I 'S' class (except A/S destroyers and *Shikari*) were given a second 2pdr. In the *Scott* and *Shakespeare* classes two 2pdrs replaced No 3 main gun. By this time arrangements were being made to mount two Oerlikons in the 'E' and later classes as they came in hand for refit or repair. Somewhat later in 1940 plans called for fitting two Oerlikons on the signal decks of *Amazon*, *Ambuscade*, and the 'A' through 'I' classes. As of January 1941, plans had been drawn up to install four Oerlikons on the 'A', 'B', 'C', 'E', and 'F' classes. Only two per ship had been authorised, presumably due to shortage of the guns. By this time *Defender* and *Diamond* each had 0.5in machine guns. Close-range guns were rearranged beginning in the spring of 1941 to ensure clear arcs, and Oerlikons began to appear. By the autumn of 1942 twin Oerlikons were available to replace singles. Stability was so limited that some ships could not be fitted with them, including the old 'S' class and the 4.7in 'V&W's and the old leaders. The latter ships traded their 2pdrs for additional Oerlikons, but the 2pdrs were retained by the East Coast ships: *Mackay*, *Campbell*,

Skate in December 1942, showing the need to balance anti-aircraft self-protection against anti-submarine attack. She had a pair of Oerlikons in bandstands and a 12pdr 12cwt heavy anti-aircraft gun. The antenna on her foremast was for a Type 291 air warning radar.

Montrose, *Whitshed*, and *Worcester*. Other ships which could not take twin Oerlikons were the 'Wair's, *Amazon*, and the *Havant* and 'I' classes. None of the older destroyers was ever fitted with Bofors guns, but *Faulknor* received a quadruple 2pdr in place of her long-gone 'Q' 4.7in mounting.

In March 1944 it seemed that the Buster twin Bofors mounting was about to enter production. It could replace a set of torpedo tubes in the 'J', 'K', 'N', or the Emergency classes, and, with extra ballast, it could replace the quadruple pom-pom in the 'Tribal' to 'P' classes (the later Emergency destroyers lacked sufficient space on their gun platforms, and in later ships with Mk VI directors stability precluded installation). As the projected weight of the mounting grew, projected numbers had to be reduced, to two mountings on board the 1943 'Battle's. Buster died at the end of the war, the 'Battle's being fitted with the lighter STAAGs.

The planned shift of the fleet to the Pacific in 1944–45 prompted rearmament, both planned and executed. In the autumn of 1944, for example, the Admiralty considered rearming surviving 'A' through 'I' class destroyers with twin 4in guns plus a single Hedgehog in 'A' or 'B' position. A few ships had enough reserve stability to add a 'Hunt'-style dual-purpose fire control system. The alternative was a full anti-aircraft battery (three twin 4in guns, a twin Bofors, and six Oerlikons) plus a five-charge pattern and perhaps a Hedgehog (which was low on the priority list). Torpedo tubes would have been landed. The result would essentially have been a faster equivalent of a 'Hunt' Type III. None of the refits was

carried out, but HMS *Petard* was rearmed with twin 4in guns in 1945.

The Narrow Seas

The Germans seized the North Sea coast of Europe, as they had in World War I. This time they deployed a considerable force of large motor torpedo boats (S-boats, which the British called E-boats) to attack the mass of coastal shipping. Even after the fall of France, Britain relied heavily on coastal shipping to supply London. Conventional guns were hardly well-adapted to shooting at fast motor craft. British measures to fight the E-boats included deploying British coastal forces and also modifying the armament of destroyers operating on the British East Coast. The E-boat problem may explain why a quadruple pom-pom was mounted on board the anti-aircraft (escort) destroyer *Wallace*. Typically, ships on East Coast convoy duty were given single 2pdr pom-poms as bow chasers. Destroyer examples were HMS *Beagle* and *Bulldog* and the

long-range escort *Watchman*, as well as many 'Hunt's. HMS *Mackay* and some 'W' class destroyers operating on the East Coast were given army-type twin 6pdr rapid-fire gun in place of their 'A' gun (see **A 11**).

A few destroyers were fitted with army-type rapid-firing twin 6pdr guns specifically to engage German torpedo boats ('E-boats') in the southern North Sea. *Vivacious* was the prototype for the twin 6pdr installation. The 1 September 1943 proposal for the production version covered two leaders (*Campbell* and *Montrose*; *Mackay* was later added) and five 'W' class: *Whitshed*, *Worcester*, *Witherington*, *Wivern*, and *Wolverine*. After conversion *Worcester* almost immediately suffered severe mine damage (23 December 1943); she was hulked. Type 272 radar was considered essential in order to fight E-boats, as were two 20in bridge searchlights. It was installed on a lattice mast on the former searchlight position in *Whitshed*, *Wivern*, and *Wolverine*. This 6pdr is in *Mackay*. (John Lambert Collection)

The twin 6pdr showing its vertical breechblocks linked so that one was always closed when the other was open. Ammunition was fixed.
(John Lambert Collection)

The twin 6pdr at full elevation, HMS *Mackay*. (John Lambert Collection)

ASW

The best of the wartime Asdics was Type 144, which introduced a bearing recorder alongside the range recorder of previous types. Its stabilised transducer stepped automatically over an 80-degree arc ahead of a ship; the operator had only to start and stop the scan. Automation freed him to concentrate on listening and on watching the range recorder, the device used to tell when to attack. Whenever he heard an echo the operator pressed a key, marking the paper in the bearing recorder. That made early detection more likely. The bearing recorder made it easier to choose an attack course. There was also a depth-finding sonar (Type 147) using a stabilised tiltable transducer. As U-boats dived deeper, the Q attachment made it possible to maintain contact below the usual beam.

In contrast to pre-war expectation, the wartime Royal Navy found itself operating in submarine-infested waters. All of its destroyers had to have Asdics and substantial depth charge batteries. Indeed, the need for large numbers of depth charges was an important reason that wartime Emergency destroyers were so much larger than their pre-war ancestors. It turned out that Asdic-

directed attacks required large numbers of depth charges, which in turn meant depth charge throwers as well as depth charge tracks at the stern. Wartime experience showed that it was far easier to fire a weapon at a submarine detected ahead of a ship than to try to manoeuvre the ship's stern to place it over an evading U-boat. By 1941 the Royal Navy had an ahead-throwing weapon, the Hedgehog, and in 1943 it also had an ahead-throwing depth charge mortar (Squid). In a destroyer, Hedgehog replaced a gun; it appeared in older destroyers modified as anti-submarine escorts. Fleet destroyers could not accommodate it. However, Squid did not

This interwar destroyer, seen in October 1940, has been modified to deliver the 10-charge pattern (two sandwiched 5-charge patterns) made standard in mid-1940. The new pattern required an extra thrower on each side and a second rail; the standard load was 60 charges (6 attacks). 'Y' gun was surrendered as weight compensation. The 4.7in gun is probably on the original low-angle Mk XIV mounting (it shows no counterweight). The splinter shield around the base of the 4.7in mounting was a war modification. (John Lambert Collection)

'Y' mounting has been removed from this interwar destroyer as weight compensation for a heavy depth charge battery; note the two Thornycroft throwers and the spare arbors, with a loading davit visible and another on the other side. The windbreak on the after deckhouse is for the emergency steering position aft. (John Lambert Collection)

have to be at the fore end of a ship. The big 'Battle's had Squids on their quarterdecks, firing over their superstructure.

By mid-1940 the standard attack doubled to a 10-charge pattern (two diamonds at different depths, to sandwich a submarine). That required a second rail and another set of throwers, with more charges stowed above decks. Typical weight compensation was landing 'Y' gun. The standard load was 60 charges (six attacks), reduced to 50 in 'V&W's (not repeat ships with 4.7in guns). Ships designed for TSDS could carry 60 charges if that gear was landed. 'Wair's and ships without TSDS would carry 50 charges (in fact the 'Wair's carried 45). Leaders would carry 60 (26 below deck, 18 in rails and 16 at throwers). Many ships did not receive the extra charges, hence did not surrender their 'Y' guns. Ships converted for escort work were given 14-charge batteries; the need for heavy depth charge batteries split fleet destroyers from escort destroyers. The 14-charge pattern required four more throwers. Conversely, many ships serving with the fleet did not receive even the 50-charge loadout, retaining all four guns. Late in 1943 the 14-charge pattern was abolished because calculation showed that the chance of success was about the same as with a 10-charge attack. Eliminating four throwers and the carriers of their depth charges made it possible to carry more charges, and would also save personnel. Moreover, trials had shown that there was some mutual interference between charges in a 14-charge attack.

In 1943 a new one-ton Mk X depth charge was introduced. Typically ships carried two of them in a set of torpedo tubes, the two remaining torpedoes being locally controlled. The favoured tactic seems to have been to fire two Mk X to sandwich a submarine, just as the 10- and 14-charge patterns were intended to do. Mk X* could explode deeper. Many escort destroyers carried two Mk X and two Mk X* together in one quadruple torpedo tube.

As of April 1941, the 'A', 'B' (except *Boreas*), 'D', 'F', 'G', 'H', and 'I' classes all had their early-war depth charge outfits (5-charge patterns). An undated (probably December 1941) description of changes to the 'G', 'H', and 'I' classes lists only *Garland* as having landed her TSDS and 'Y' gun for the 10-charge pattern. Much the same was true as late as April 1943, the 'A' and 'B' classes having 10-charge patterns (70 charges each), *Duncan* and the 'D' class heavy patterns (98 charges, 14-charge pattern, in *Duncan*). Of the

'F' class, *Foxhound* and *Fortune* had 70 charges (10-charge pattern), but the others retained their earlier 38-charge loadout. However, by this time some ships were re-rated as escort destroyers: *Beagle*, *Bulldog*, *Escapade*, and *Fame* all converted with only two 4.7in guns (Hedgehog and 70 depth charges). As of December 1943, *Foxhound* and *Boreas* were undergoing similar conversions.

All depth charge attacks were difficult, and well before 1939 there was interest in an ahead-firing weapon which could simply be aimed at a submarine. Given the imprecision of existing Asdics, such a weapon had to fire a pattern of charges. The two alternatives were depth charges, which exploded at a set depth, and contact-fuzed bombs, which exploded only when they hit a submarine. Both were tried at about the same time, but the contact-fuzed Hedgehog (tested in the spring of 1941) was adopted first. It produced a circular 100ft pattern of 24 bombs which entered the water 200yds ahead of a ship. Ships generally carried one salvo in the Hedgehog, two more in ready-use stowage nearby, and four or

HMS *Havant* was a Brazilian destroyer bought on an emergency basis and equipped for ASW rather than for fleet duties; note that she had only a rangefinder, and no director. Her 'Y' gun was eliminated as weight compensation for a heavy depth charge load. The diamond-shaped antenna on her mainmast was a common pre-war HF/DF device, but by about 1941 it had been superseded by the 'birdcage' and a much more sophisticated receiver.

more below deck. Typically, Hedgehog replaced 'A' gun in destroyers converted for escort service, although plans to convert the 'G', 'H', 'I', and *Havant* classes showed it in 'B' position. In these ships the 3in anti-aircraft gun was removed as weight compensation for additional depth charges (as many as 107 on deck in a 'G' class escort destroyer) or 90 in an 'H' or 'I' (with 35 more below decks). Split Hedgehog, which appeared early in 1943, could be mounted to either side of 'A' gun, the deck underneath being strengthened, offering more ahead fire. Typically, installation of split Hedgehog was coupled with replacement of the 24in searchlight amidships; it was replaced by two 20in searchlights sponsoned out from 'B' deck. It was apparently considered impractical to install split Hedgehog in the 'G' class, *Hotspur*, *Hero*, the 'I' class, *Inglefield* and the *Havant*s. In other ships it was a welcome way to add forward-firing firepower to deal with surfaced U-boats.

If the submarine's depth could be determined, big depth charges offered greater killing power. In 1941 a long-range five-barrel depth charge thrower, nick-named the 'Five Wide Virgins,' was tested on board HMS *Whitehall*. The proposed installation was either five barrels in place of 'A' gun or two pairs on either side. Range was 300yds. This device was not adopted, but the idea was embodied in the Squid depth charge mortar tested on board HMS *Ambuscade* in May 1943. It was widely installed on board escorts (see the

HMS *Escapade* shows modifications which would have been extended to the fleet of escort destroyers had the war continued. Having suffered a Hedgehog explosion, she was fitted with the new Squid ASW mortar in 'A' position. The radar atop her bridge was the new Type 277 dish, for surface search, in place of the earlier 'cheeses'. Ships like this were unlikely to encounter air attack, so she had single hand-worked Oerlikons and no supplementary high-angle gun in place of her after torpedo tubes. The torpedo tubes were removed as weight compensation for a heavy depth charge battery. This photograph was taken on 12 February 1945.

forthcoming escort volume), but the only wartime escort destroyer to be fitted was HMS *Escapade*, which had been severely damaged when her split Hedgehog mis-fired in action on 20 September 1943. When repairs were completed on 30 December 1944, she carried double Squid in 'A' position, 4.7in guns in 'B' and 'X' ('B' mount also carried rocket flare rails), and six Oerlikons. She had the new Type 277 dish instead of the usual Type 271 radar lantern, with the usual Type 291 at her foremast, and a stub pole mast aft for HF/DF. Squid armed many destroyers post-war.

The Germans introduced an anti-escort homing torpedo, T-5, which the Royal Navy called GNAT (German Navy Acoustic Torpedo). Some destroyers towed the Foxer noise-making decoy. Its main drawback was that its emissions could interfere with Asdic.

S 1 HMS *Whitehall*, as completed July 1924, a 'Modified W' class fleet destroyer

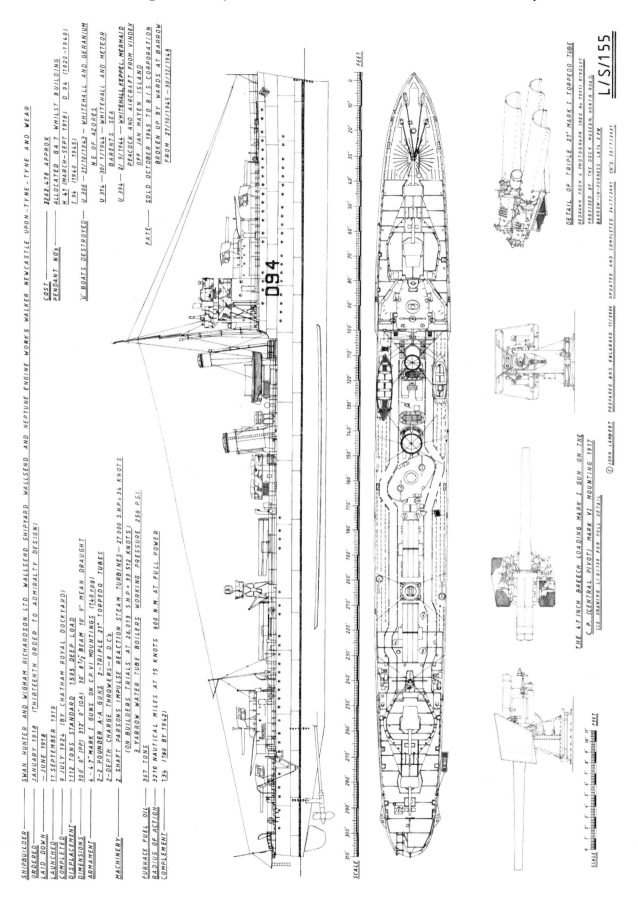

SHIPBUILDER —— SWAN HUNTER AND WIGHAM RICHARDSON LTD WALLSEND SHIPYARD WALLSEND AND NEPTUNE ENGINE WORKS WALKER NEWCASTLE UPON-TYNE-TYNE AND WEAR
ORDERED —— JANUARY 1918 (THIRTEENTH ORDER TO ADMIRALTY DESIGN)
LAID DOWN —— — JUNE 1918
LAUNCHED —— 11 SEPTEMBER 1919
COMPLETED —— 9 JULY 1924 (BY CHATHAM ROYAL DOCKYARD)
DISPLACEMENT —— 1,112 TONS STANDARD 1505 DEEP LOAD
DIMENSIONS —— 300' 0" (PP) 312' 0" (OA) 30' 8½' BEAM 10' 9" MEAN DRAUGHT
ARMAMENT —— 4-4·7" MARK I GUNS ON C.P.VI MOUNTINGS (140 r.p.g)
2-2 POUNDER A-A GUNS 2-TRIPLE 21" TORPEDO TUBES
2-DEPTH CHARGE THROWERS—8 D.C's
MACHINERY —— 2 SHAFT PARSONS IMPULSE REACTION STEAM TURBINES—27,000 S.H.P=34 KNOTS
(ON BUILDERS TRIALS AT 26,013 S.H.P.=33.512 KNOTS)
3 YARROW WATER TUBE BOILERS WORKING PRESSURE 250 P.S.I.
FURNACE FUEL OIL —— 367 TONS
RADIUS OF ACTION —— 3210 NAUTICAL MILES AT 15 KNOTS 600 N.M. AT FULL POWER
COMPLEMENT —— 134 (160 BY 1942)

COST —— £262,678 APPROX
PENDANT NO's —— ALLOCATED GA 7 WHILST BUILDING
H 41 (MARCH-SEPT 1918) D 94 (1920-1940)
1.94 (1940-1945)
'U' BOATS DESTROYED —— U·306 — 31/10/1943 — WHITEHALL AND GERANIUM
N.E OF AZORES
U·314 — 30/1/1944 — WHITEHALL AND METEOR
BARENTS SEA
U·394 — 2/9/1944 — WHITEHALL,KEPPEL, MERMAID
PEACOCK AND AIRCRAFT FROM VINDEX
OFF JAN MAYEN ISLAND
FATE —— SOLD OCTOBER 1945 TO B.I.S CORPORATION
BROKEN UP BY WARDS AT BARROW
FROM 27/10/1945 — 30/12/1948

FEET

L/S/155

DETAIL OF TRIPLE 21" MARK I TORPEDO TUBE
REDRAWN FROM A PHOTOGRAPH (NEG No 7605) KINDLEY
PROVIDED BY THE DOCK MUSEUM, NORTH ROAD,
BARROW-IN-FURNESS LA14 2PW
© JOHN LAMBERT PREPARED AND ENLARGED 11/2000 UPDATED AND COMPLETED 24/7/2001 CHT'D 24/7/2001

THE 4·7 INCH BREECH LOADING MARK I GUN ON THE
C.P (CENTRAL PIVOT) MARK VI MOUNTING 1917
SEE DRAWING L/G/180 FOR FULL DETAIL

SCALE

S 2 HMS *Harvester* (ex-*Handy*, ex-*Jurua*), May 1940

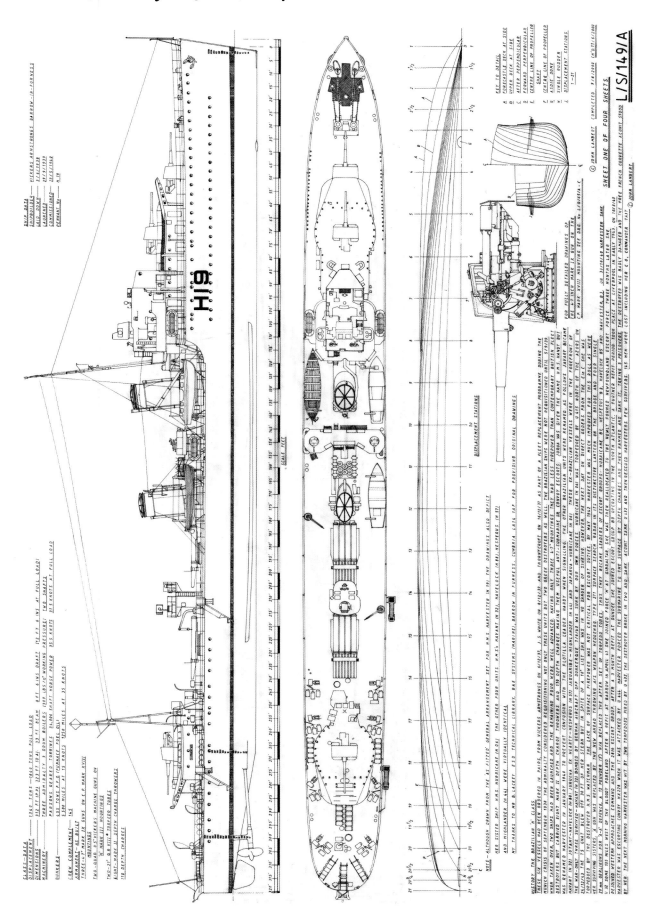

S 2 HMS *Harvester*, enlarged detail as fitted

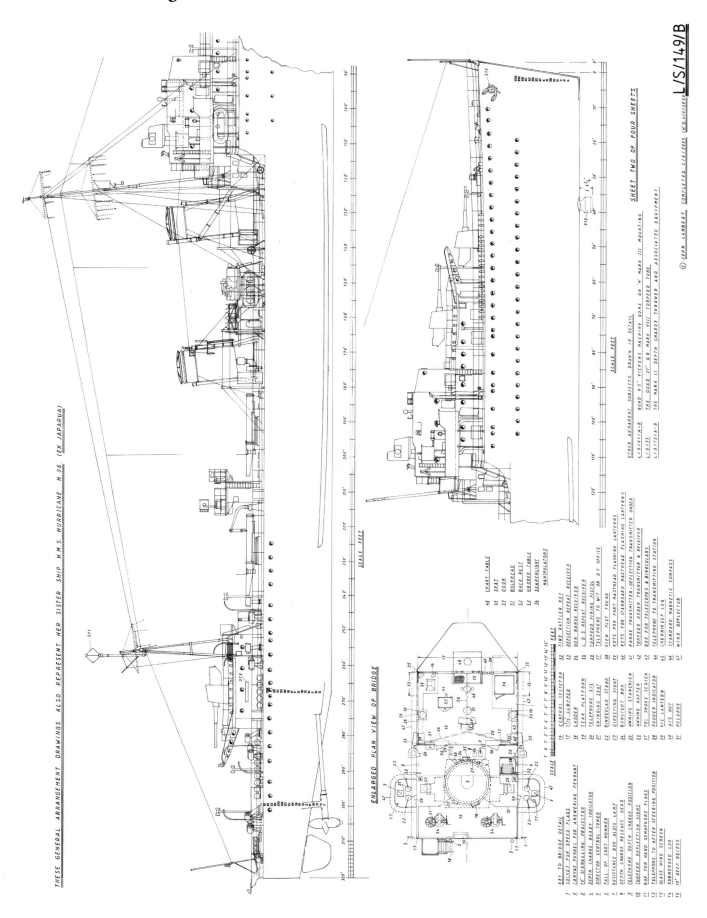

THESE GENERAL ARRANGEMENT DRAWINGS ALSO REPRESENT HER SISTER SHIP H.M.S. HURRICANE H 06 (EX JAPARUA)

L/S/1149/B

SHEET TWO OF FOUR SHEETS

© JOHN LAMBERT COMPLETED 2/6/2000

KEY TO BRIDGE DETAIL

1 SOCKET FOR SPEED FLAGS
2 CANVAS FUNNEL FOR ANSWERING PENDANT
3 10" SIGNALLING PROJECTOR
4 DEPTH CHARGE READY INDICATOR
5 DIRECTOR CONTROL TOWER
6 FALL OF SHOT HUMMER
7 RESISTANCE BOX ALDIS LAMP
8 DEPTH CHARGE RELEASE GEAR
9 TELEPHONE DEPTH CHARGE POSITION
10 TORPEDO DEFLECTION SIGHT
11 BOX FOR HAND SEMAPHORE FLAGS
12 TELEPHONE TO AFTER STEERING POSITION
13 GLASS WIND SCREEN
14 SUBMERGED LOG
15 10" DEEP RECESS

16 CONTROL TELECTOR
17 1/2 SCUPPER
18 LADDER
19 TEAK PLATFORM
20 TELEPHONE S/L
21 SWINGING SEAT
22 BINOCULAR STAND
23 DIRECTING SIGHT
24 BOWLIGHT BOX
25 AWNING STANCHION
26 AWNING RAFTER
27 TEL SMOKE SCREEN
28 RUDDER INDICATOR
29 V/C LANTERN
30 A/S HUT
31 PELORUS

32 FIRE RATTLER KEY
33 DEFLECTION REPEAT RECEIVER
34 GUN RANGE RECEIVER
35 L.O.S REPEAT RECEIVER
36 TORPEDO FIRING PISTOL
37 TELEPHONE TO W/T OR D/F OFFICE
38 VIEW PLOT TRUNK
39 KEYS FOR PORT MASTHEAD FLASHING LANTERNS
40 KEYS FOR STARBOARD MASTHEAD FLASHING LANTERNS
41 RANGE TRANSMITTER–DEFLECTION RECEIVER
42 TORPEDO ORDER TRANSMITTER & RECEIVER
43 BOX FOR TELESCOPES & BINOCULARS
44 TELEPHONE TO TRANSMITTING STATION
45 CHERNIKEEF LOG
46 STANDARD MAGNETIC COMPASS
47 WIND DEFLECTOR

48 CHART TABLE
49 SEAT
50 DOOR
51 BULKHEAD
52 BACK REST
53 HOODED TABLE
54 SEARCHLIGHT
MANIPULATORS

ENLARGED PLAN VIEW OF BRIDGE

SCALE FEET

SCALE FEET

SCALE FEET

OTHER ARMAMENT: SUBJECTS DRAWN IN DETAIL
QUAD 0·5" VICKERS MACHINE GUNS ON 'M' MARK III MOUNTING
L/O/81A–B
L/O/33   THE QUAD 21" Q.R MARK VIII. TORPEDO TUBE
L/S/727A–B   THE MARK II DEPTH CHARGE THROWER AND ASSOCIATED EQUIPMENT

66

S 2 HMS *Harvester*, enlarged detail as fitted

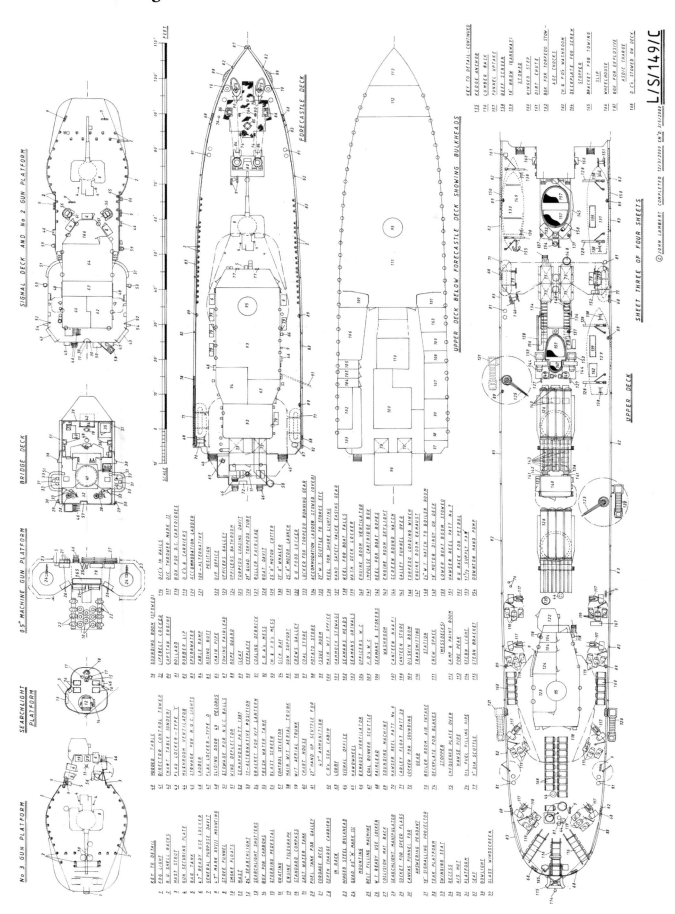

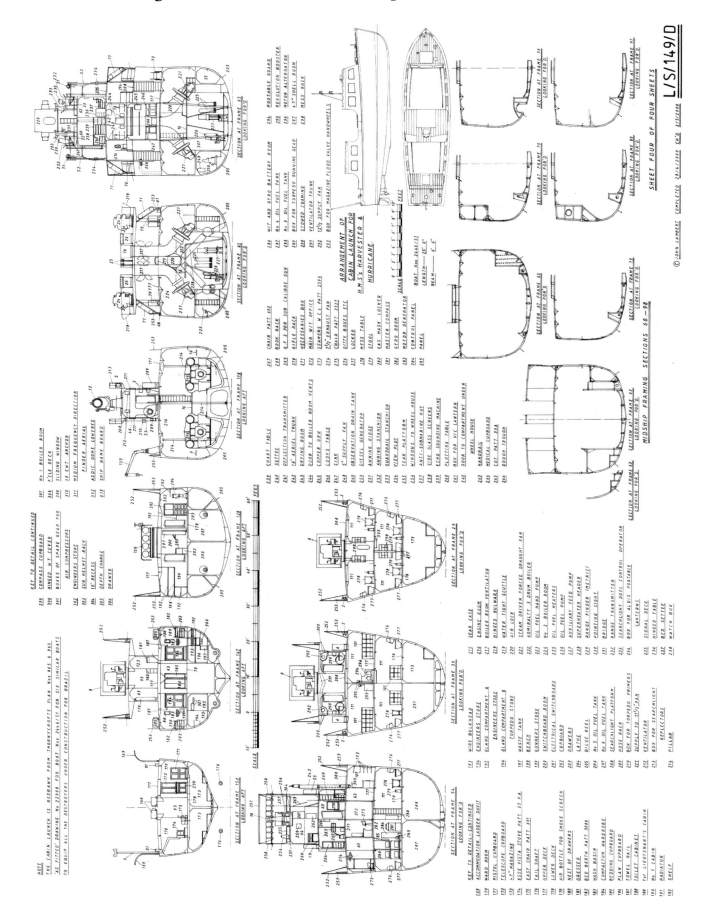

S 3 HMS *Matabele*, 'Tribal' class fleet destroyer, January 1939 [Note that the hull sections for this plan were never completed]

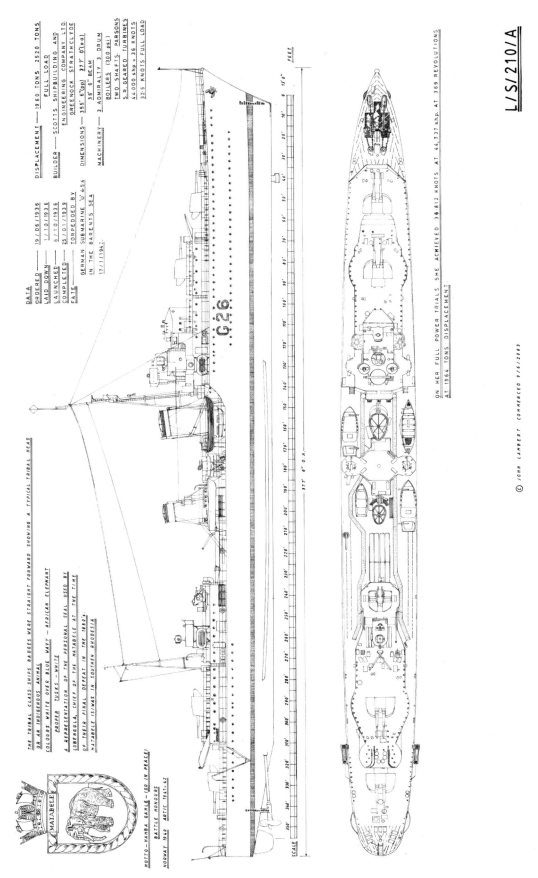

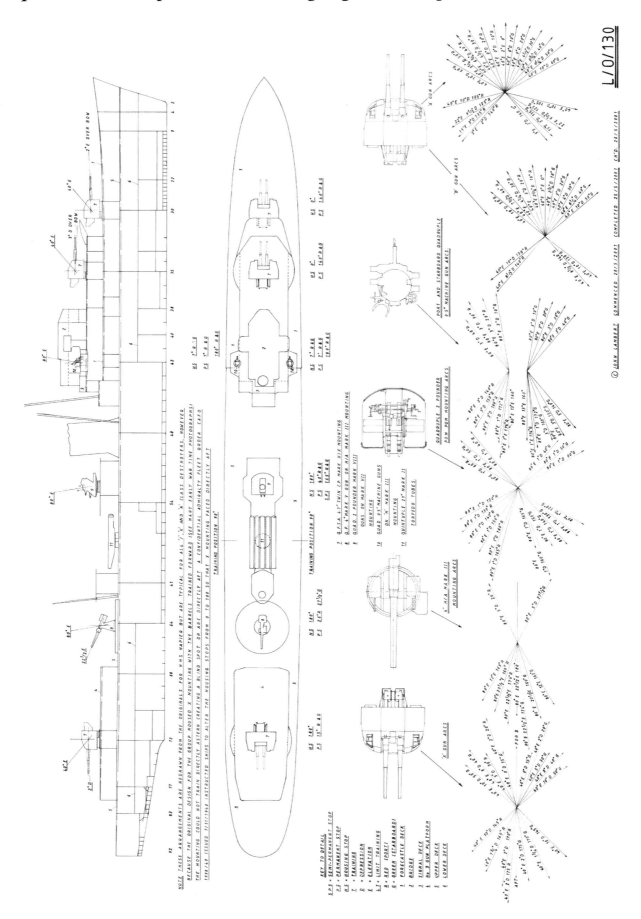

© JOHN LAMBERT

S 5 Sketch design of 1939 for the flotilla leader of the 'Q' class (3rd Emergency Flotilla), HMS *Quilliam*

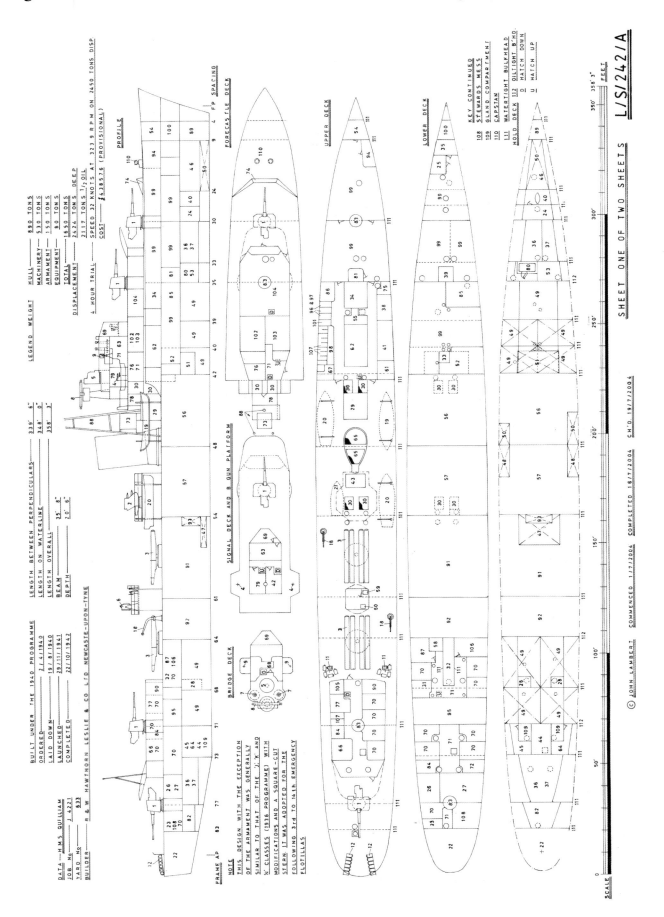

S 5 'Q' class detail – modified stern and alternative armament proposals for improved depth charge stowage

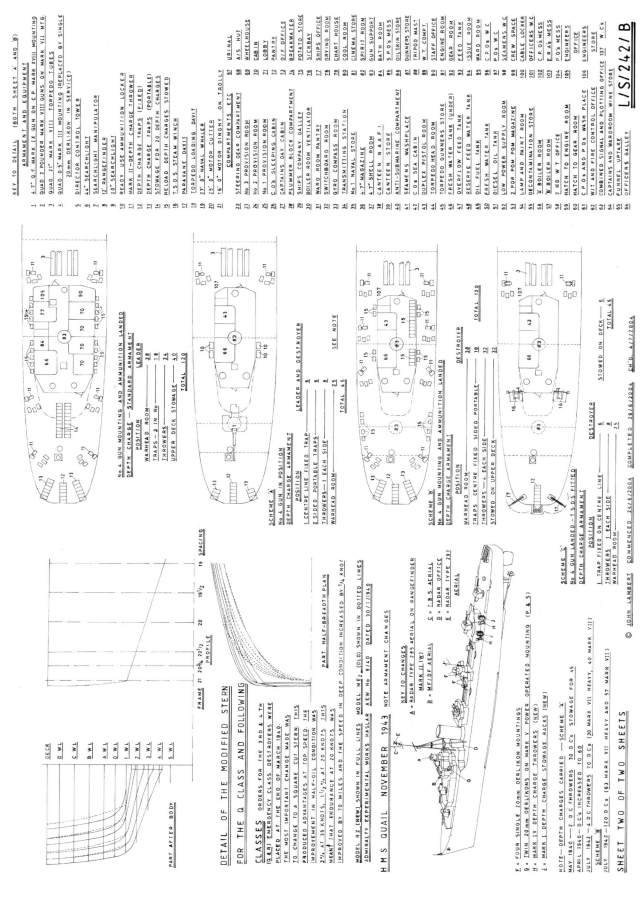

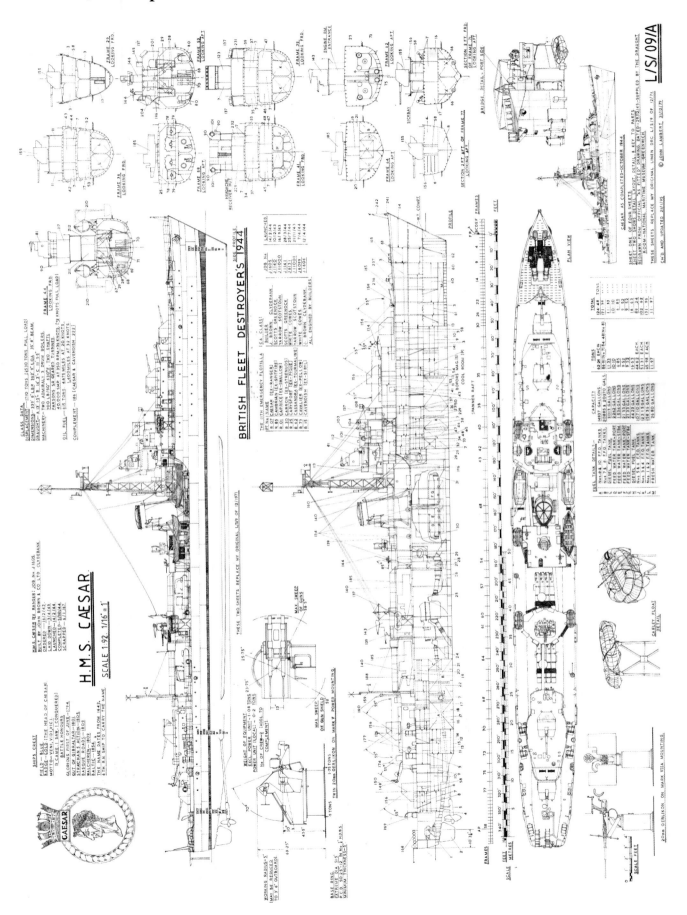

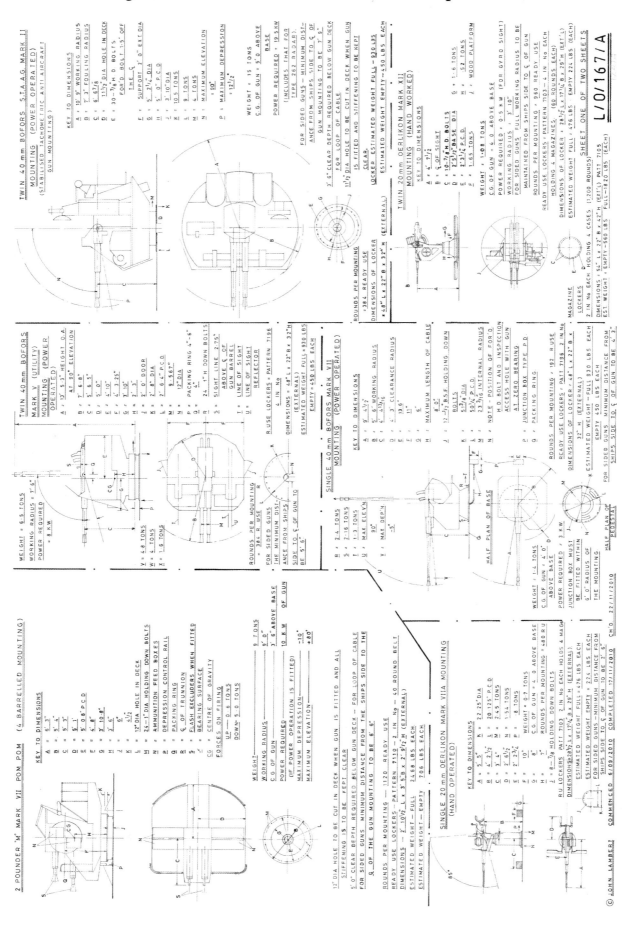

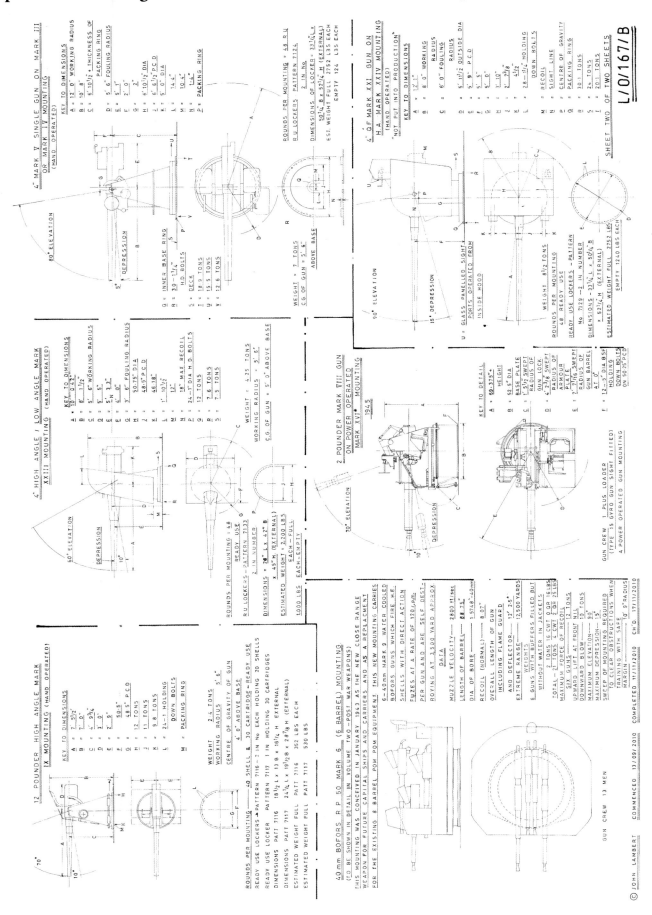

G 1 4in QF Mk IV on P.IX mounting, 1916–1945

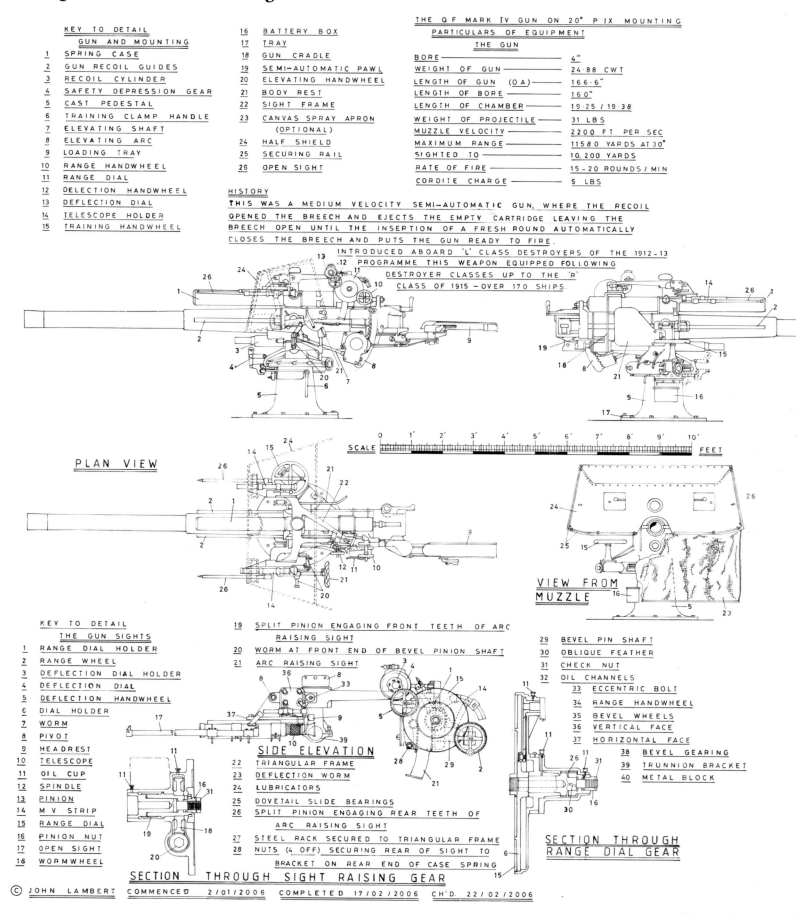

KEY TO DETAIL
GUN AND MOUNTING
1 SPRING CASE
2 GUN RECOIL GUIDES
3 RECOIL CYLINDER
4 SAFETY DEPRESSION GEAR
5 CAST PEDESTAL
6 TRAINING CLAMP HANDLE
7 ELEVATING SHAFT
8 ELEVATING ARC
9 LOADING TRAY
10 RANGE HANDWHEEL
11 RANGE DIAL
12 DEFLECTION HANDWHEEL
13 DEFLECTION DIAL
14 TELESCOPE HOLDER
15 TRAINING HANDWHEEL
16 BATTERY BOX
17 TRAY
18 GUN CRADLE
19 SEMI-AUTOMATIC PAWL
20 ELEVATING HANDWHEEL
21 BODY REST
22 SIGHT FRAME
23 CANVAS SPRAY APRON
   (OPTIONAL)
24 HALF SHIELD
25 SECURING RAIL
26 OPEN SIGHT

THE QF MARK IV GUN ON 20° P IX MOUNTING
PARTICULARS OF EQUIPMENT
THE GUN

BORE	4"
WEIGHT OF GUN	24·88 CWT
LENGTH OF GUN (O.A)	166·6"
LENGTH OF BORE	160"
LENGTH OF CHAMBER	19·25 / 19·38
WEIGHT OF PROJECTILE	31 LBS
MUZZLE VELOCITY	2200 FT PER SEC
MAXIMUM RANGE	11580 YARDS AT 30°
SIGHTED TO	10,200 YARDS
RATE OF FIRE	15-20 ROUNDS/MIN
CORDITE CHARGE	5 LBS

HISTORY

THIS WAS A MEDIUM VELOCITY SEMI-AUTOMATIC GUN, WHERE THE RECOIL OPENED THE BREECH AND EJECTS THE EMPTY CARTRIDGE LEAVING THE BREECH OPEN UNTIL THE INSERTION OF A FRESH ROUND AUTOMATICALLY CLOSES THE BREECH AND PUTS THE GUN READY TO FIRE.
INTRODUCED ABOARD 'L' CLASS DESTROYERS OF THE 1912-13 PROGRAMME THIS WEAPON EQUIPPED FOLLOWING DESTROYER CLASSES UP TO THE 'R' CLASS OF 1915 - OVER 170 SHIPS.

PLAN VIEW

SCALE 0 1' 2' 3' 4' 5' 6' 7' 8' 9' 10' FEET

VIEW FROM MUZZLE

KEY TO DETAIL
THE GUN SIGHTS
1 RANGE DIAL HOLDER
2 RANGE WHEEL
3 DEFLECTION DIAL HOLDER
4 DEFLECTION DIAL
5 DEFLECTION HANDWHEEL
6 DIAL HOLDER
7 WORM
8 PIVOT
9 HEADREST
10 TELESCOPE
11 OIL CUP
12 SPINDLE
13 PINION
14 M V STRIP
15 RANGE DIAL
16 PINION NUT
17 OPEN SIGHT
18 WORMWHEEL

19 SPLIT PINION ENGAGING FRONT TEETH OF ARC
   RAISING SIGHT
20 WORM AT FRONT END OF BEVEL PINION SHAFT
21 ARC RAISING SIGHT
22 TRIANGULAR FRAME
23 DEFLECTION WORM
24 LUBRICATORS
25 DOVETAIL SLIDE BEARINGS
26 SPLIT PINION ENGAGING REAR TEETH OF
   ARC RAISING SIGHT
27 STEEL RACK SECURED TO TRIANGULAR FRAME
28 NUTS (4 OFF) SECURING REAR OF SIGHT TO
   BRACKET ON REAR END OF CASE SPRING

SECTION THROUGH SIGHT RAISING GEAR

SIDE ELEVATION

29 BEVEL PIN SHAFT
30 OBLIQUE FEATHER
31 CHECK NUT
32 OIL CHANNELS
33 ECCENTRIC BOLT
34 RANGE HANDWHEEL
35 BEVEL WHEELS
36 VERTICAL FACE
37 HORIZONTAL FACE
38 BEVEL GEARING
39 TRUNNION BRACKET
40 METAL BLOCK

SECTION THROUGH RANGE DIAL GEAR

© JOHN LAMBERT COMMENCED 2/01/2006 COMPLETED 17/02/2006 CH'D. 22/02/2006

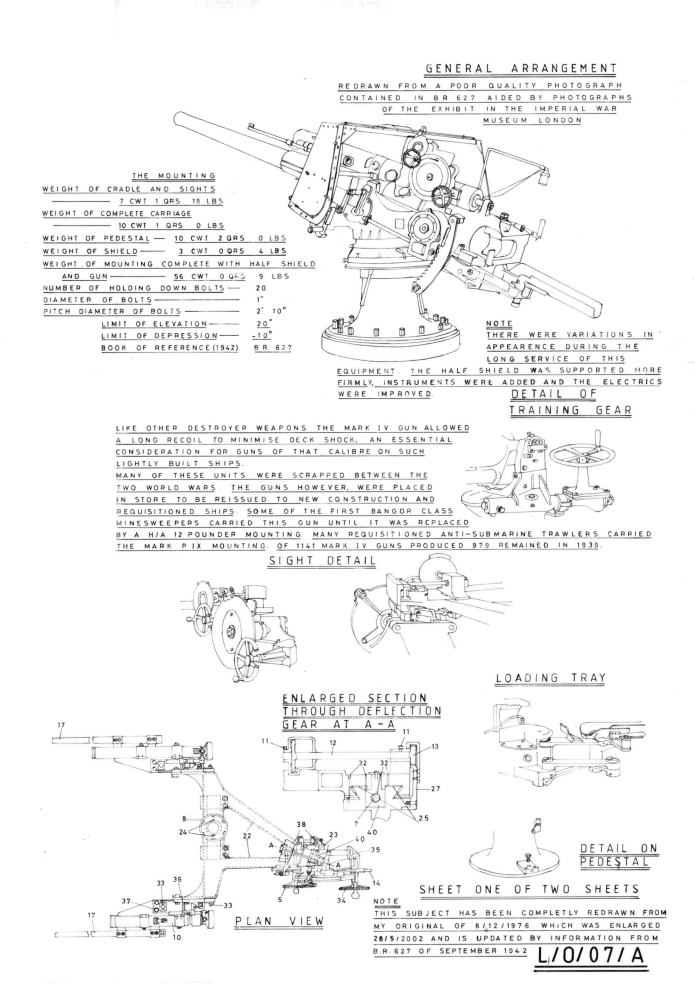

GENERAL ARRANGEMENT

REDRAWN FROM A POOR QUALITY PHOTOGRAPH
CONTAINED IN BR 627 AIDED BY PHOTOGRAPHS
OF THE EXHIBIT IN THE IMPERIAL WAR
MUSEUM LONDON

THE MOUNTING

WEIGHT OF CRADLE AND SIGHTS
— 7 CWT 1 QRS 18 LBS

WEIGHT OF COMPLETE CARRIAGE
— 10 CWT 1 QRS 0 LBS

WEIGHT OF PEDESTAL — 10 CWT 2 QRS 0 LBS

WEIGHT OF SHIELD — 3 CWT 0 QRS 4 LBS

WEIGHT OF MOUNTING COMPLETE WITH HALF SHIELD
AND GUN — 56 CWT 0 QRS 9 LBS

NUMBER OF HOLDING DOWN BOLTS — 20

DIAMETER OF BOLTS — 1"

PITCH DIAMETER OF BOLTS — 2' 10"

LIMIT OF ELEVATION — 20°

LIMIT OF DEPRESSION — -10°

BOOK OF REFERENCE (1942) BR 627

NOTE
THERE WERE VARIATIONS IN
APPEARENCE DURING THE
LONG SERVICE OF THIS
EQUIPMENT. THE HALF SHIELD WAS SUPPORTED MORE
FIRMLY, INSTRUMENTS WERE ADDED AND THE ELECTRICS
WERE IMPROVED.

DETAIL OF TRAINING GEAR

LIKE OTHER DESTROYER WEAPONS THE MARK IV GUN ALLOWED
A LONG RECOIL TO MINIMISE DECK SHOCK, AN ESSENTIAL
CONSIDERATION FOR GUNS OF THAT CALIBRE ON SUCH
LIGHTLY BUILT SHIPS.
MANY OF THESE UNITS WERE SCRAPPED BETWEEN THE
TWO WORLD WARS. THE GUNS HOWEVER, WERE PLACED
IN STORE TO BE REISSUED TO NEW CONSTRUCTION AND
REQUISITIONED SHIPS. SOME OF THE FIRST BANGOR CLASS
MINESWEEPERS CARRIED THIS GUN UNTIL IT WAS REPLACED
BY A H/A 12 POUNDER MOUNTING. MANY REQUISITIONED ANTI-SUBMARINE TRAWLERS CARRIED
THE MARK P IX MOUNTING. OF 1141 MARK IV GUNS PRODUCED 979 REMAINED IN 1939.

SIGHT DETAIL

LOADING TRAY

ENLARGED SECTION THROUGH DEFLECTION GEAR AT A-A

DETAIL ON PEDESTAL

PLAN VIEW

SHEET ONE OF TWO SHEETS

NOTE
THIS SUBJECT HAS BEEN COMPLETLY REDRAWN FROM
MY ORIGINAL OF 8/12/1976 WHICH WAS ENLARGED
28/5/2002 AND IS UPDATED BY INFORMATION FROM
B.R. 627 OF SEPTEMBER 1942

L/O/07/A

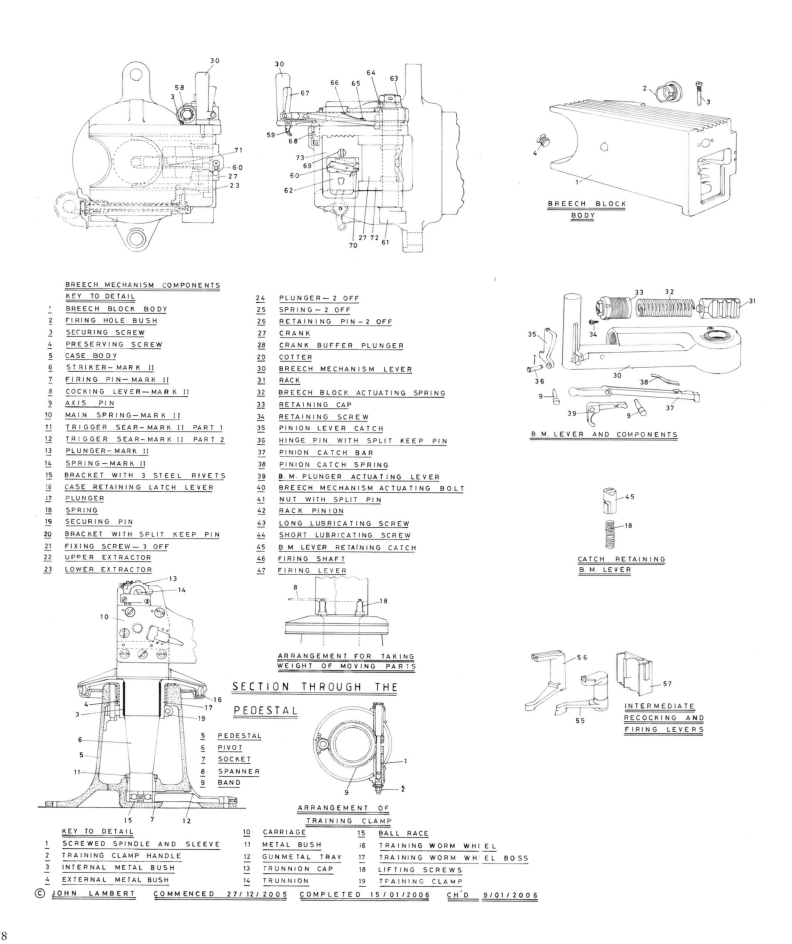

BREECH BLOCK
BODY

BREECH MECHANISM COMPONENTS
KEY TO DETAIL

1	BREECH BLOCK BODY	24	PLUNGER — 2 OFF
2	FIRING HOLE BUSH	25	SPRING — 2 OFF
3	SECURING SCREW	26	RETAINING PIN — 2 OFF
4	PRESERVING SCREW	27	CRANK
5	CASE BODY	28	CRANK BUFFER PLUNGER
6	STRIKER — MARK II	29	COTTER
7	FIRING PIN — MARK II	30	BREECH MECHANISM LEVER
8	COCKING LEVER — MARK II	31	RACK
9	AXIS PIN	32	BREECH BLOCK ACTUATING SPRING
10	MAIN SPRING — MARK II	33	RETAINING CAP
11	TRIGGER SEAR — MARK II PART 1	34	RETAINING SCREW
12	TRIGGER SEAR — MARK II PART 2	35	PINION LEVER CATCH
13	PLUNGER — MARK II	36	HINGE PIN WITH SPLIT KEEP PIN
14	SPRING — MARK II	37	PINION CATCH BAR
15	BRACKET WITH 3 STEEL RIVETS	38	PINION CATCH SPRING
16	CASE RETAINING LATCH LEVER	39	B. M. PLUNGER ACTUATING LEVER
17	PLUNGER	40	BREECH MECHANISM ACTUATING BOLT
18	SPRING	41	NUT WITH SPLIT PIN
19	SECURING PIN	42	RACK PINION
20	BRACKET WITH SPLIT KEEP PIN	43	LONG LUBRICATING SCREW
21	FIXING SCREW — 3 OFF	44	SHORT LUBRICATING SCREW
22	UPPER EXTRACTOR	45	B M LEVER RETAINING CATCH
23	LOWER EXTRACTOR	46	FIRING SHAFT
		47	FIRING LEVER

B.M. LEVER AND COMPONENTS

CATCH RETAINING
B.M. LEVER

INTERMEDIATE
RECOCKING AND
FIRING LEVERS

ARRANGEMENT FOR TAKING
WEIGHT OF MOVING PARTS

SECTION THROUGH THE
PEDESTAL

5 PEDESTAL
6 PIVOT
7 SOCKET
8 SPANNER
9 BAND

ARRANGEMENT OF
TRAINING CLAMP

KEY TO DETAIL

1	SCREWED SPINDLE AND SLEEVE	10	CARRIAGE	15	BALL RACE
2	TRAINING CLAMP HANDLE	11	METAL BUSH	16	TRAINING WORM WHEEL
3	INTERNAL METAL BUSH	12	GUNMETAL TRAY	17	TRAINING WORM WHEEL BOSS
4	EXTERNAL METAL BUSH	13	TRUNNION CAP	18	LIFTING SCREWS
		14	TRUNNION	19	TRAINING CLAMP

© JOHN LAMBERT COMMENCED 27/12/2005 COMPLETED 15/01/2006 CH'D 9/01/2006

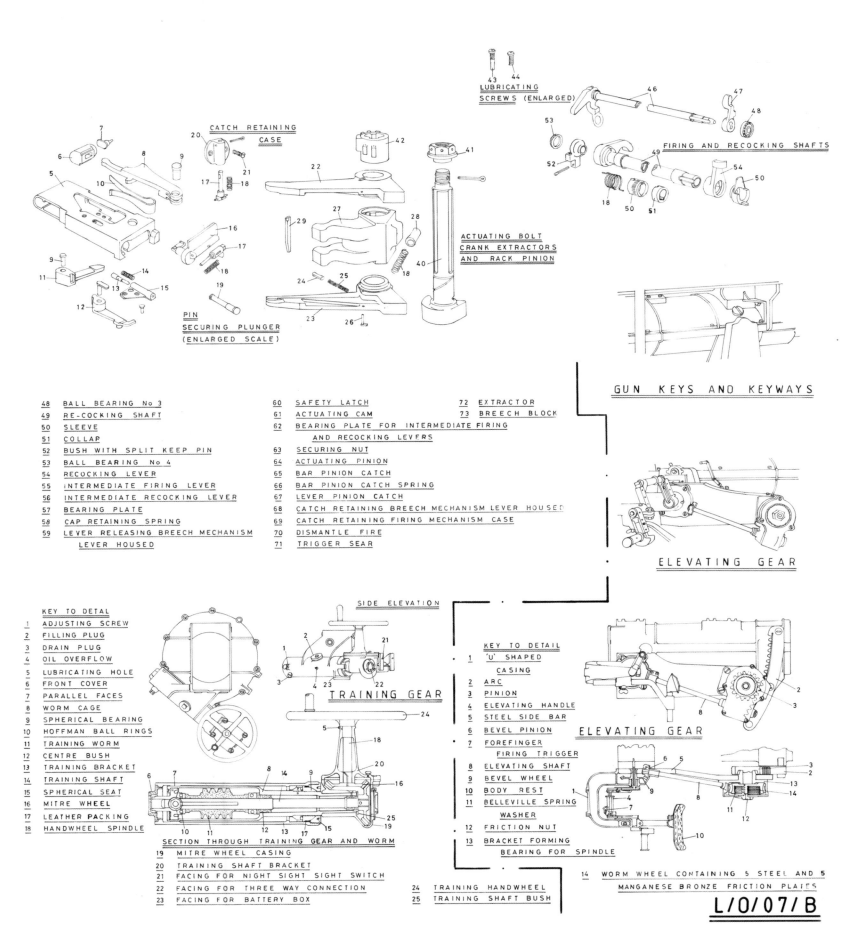

LUBRICATING SCREWS (ENLARGED)

CATCH RETAINING CASE

FIRING AND RECOCKING SHAFTS

ACTUATING BOLT CRANK EXTRACTORS AND RACK PINION

PIN SECURING PLUNGER (ENLARGED SCALE)

GUN KEYS AND KEYWAYS

ELEVATING GEAR

48 BALL BEARING No 3
49 RE-COCKING SHAFT
50 SLEEVE
51 COLLAR
52 BUSH WITH SPLIT KEEP PIN
53 BALL BEARING No 4
54 RECOCKING LEVER
55 INTERMEDIATE FIRING LEVER
56 INTERMEDIATE RECOCKING LEVER
57 BEARING PLATE
58 CAP RETAINING SPRING
59 LEVER RELEASING BREECH MECHANISM
 LEVER HOUSED

60 SAFETY LATCH
61 ACTUATING CAM
62 BEARING PLATE FOR INTERMEDIATE FIRING
 AND RECOCKING LEVERS
63 SECURING NUT
64 ACTUATING PINION
65 BAR PINION CATCH
66 BAR PINION CATCH SPRING
67 LEVER PINION CATCH
68 CATCH RETAINING BREECH MECHANISM LEVER HOUSED
69 CATCH RETAINING FIRING MECHANISM CASE
70 DISMANTLE FIRE
71 TRIGGER SEAR

72 EXTRACTOR
73 BREECH BLOCK

KEY TO DETAIL
1 ADJUSTING SCREW
2 FILLING PLUG
3 DRAIN PLUG
4 OIL OVERFLOW
5 LUBRICATING HOLE
6 FRONT COVER
7 PARALLEL FACES
8 WORM CAGE
9 SPHERICAL BEARING
10 HOFFMAN BALL RINGS
11 TRAINING WORM
12 CENTRE BUSH
13 TRAINING BRACKET
14 TRAINING SHAFT
15 SPHERICAL SEAT
16 MITRE WHEEL
17 LEATHER PACKING
18 HANDWHEEL SPINDLE

SIDE ELEVATION

TRAINING GEAR

SECTION THROUGH TRAINING GEAR AND WORM
19 MITRE WHEEL CASING
20 TRAINING SHAFT BRACKET
21 FACING FOR NIGHT SIGHT SIGHT SWITCH
22 FACING FOR THREE WAY CONNECTION
23 FACING FOR BATTERY BOX
24 TRAINING HANDWHEEL
25 TRAINING SHAFT BUSH

KEY TO DETAIL
1 'U' SHAPED
 CASING
2 ARC
3 PINION
4 ELEVATING HANDLE
5 STEEL SIDE BAR
6 BEVEL PINION
7 FOREFINGER
 FIRING TRIGGER
8 ELEVATING SHAFT
9 BEVEL WHEEL
10 BODY REST
11 BELLEVILLE SPRING
 WASHER
12 FRICTION NUT
13 BRACKET FORMING
 BEARING FOR SPINDLE

ELEVATING GEAR

14 WORM WHEEL CONTAINING 5 STEEL AND 5
 MANGANESE BRONZE FRICTION PLATES

L/0/07/B

G 2 4in BL Mk VIII gun on P (Pedestal) Mk VII mounting, 1911–12 and later destroyers

THIS LOW VELOCITY 4 INCH BREECH
LOADING WEAPON WAS THE MAIN
GUN ARMAMENT FOR THE
ACASTA OR "K" CLASS

LEFT HAND SIDE WITH HALF SHIELD

DESTROYERS OF THE 1911-12 PROGRAMME
AND THE FOLLOWING SPECIALS.
H.M.S's ACASTA, ACHATES, AMBUSCADE,
CHRISTOPHER, COCKATRICE, CONTEST, SHARK,
SPARROWHAWK, SPITFIRE, LYNX, MIDGE & OWL.
SPECIALS — HARDY, PARAGON, PORPOISE, UNITY,
VICTOR, ARDENT, FORTUNE & GARLAND.
(3 GUNS PER SHIP)

SCALE 0 1' 2' 3' 4' 5' 6' 7' 8' 9' 10' FEET

GUN DATA	
LENGTH	= 166·4"
CALIBRE	= 4" / 40
WEIGHT	= 26 CWT
BORE LENGTH	= 159·2"
CALIBRES	= 39·8
LENGTH OF RIFLING	= 140·73"
CALIBRES	= 35·2
CHAMBER LENGTH	= 15·92"
CHAMBER VOLUME	= 208 CUBIC"
RIFLING GROOVES	= 32
TWIST	= 1/30
DEPTH	= 0·04"
WIDTH	= 0·27"
LAND	= 0·1227"

IT WAS ALSO MOUNTED ABOARD THE
'E' CLASS SUBMARINES - E2, E11, E12, E14,
E21, & E22. SOME 'P' CLASS PATROL
BOATS AND FLY CLASS RIVER
GUN BOATS.

PLAN VIEW WITH HALF SHIELD

DETAIL TRAINING HOUSING
AND DEPRESSION STOPS

DETAIL OF MODIFIED
DESIGN OF BREECH
MECHANISM.

SECTION THROUGH BUFFER & SPRING CASE

KEY TO DETAIL

1	36 INCH WORKING RECOIL	4	10° DEPRESSION	8	BUFFER SPRING
2	GUN HORIZONTAL	5	POSITION OF GUN STOPS TO SUIT MOUNTING	9	PADDED BODY REST
3	EDGE OF OIL BATH	6	ELEVATING ARC	10	HAND TRAINING HANDLE
		7	SPRING CASE	11	FIRING TRIGGER

© JOHN LAMBERT   COMMENCED 9/02/2012   COMPLETED 12/03/2012   CH D 16/03/2012

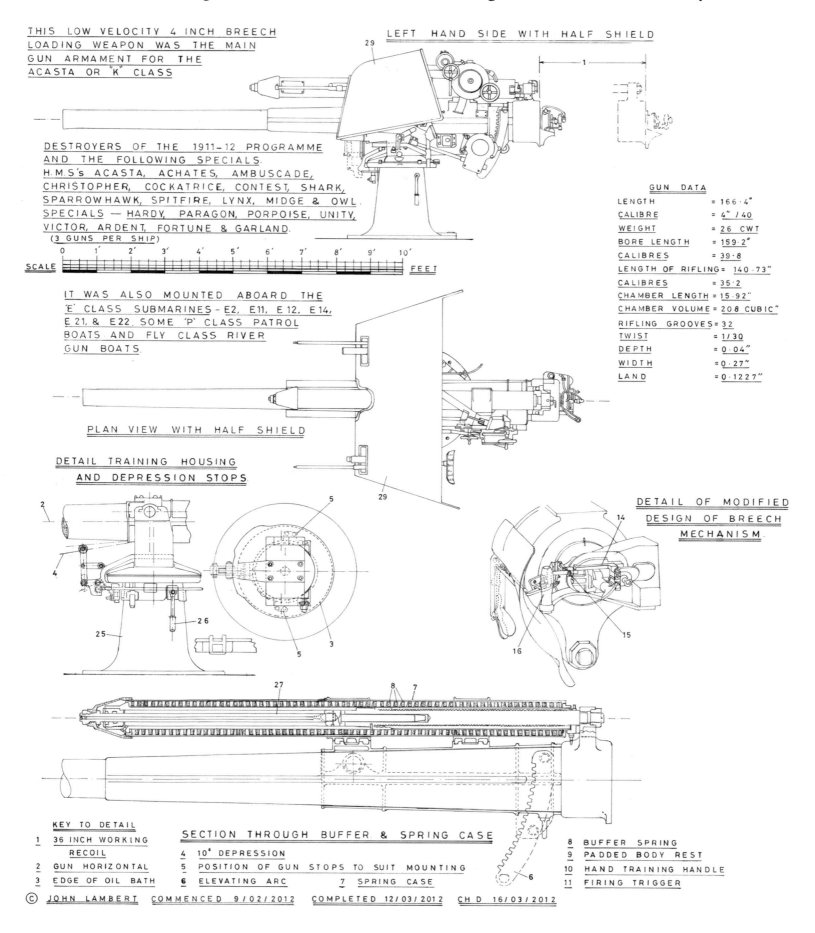

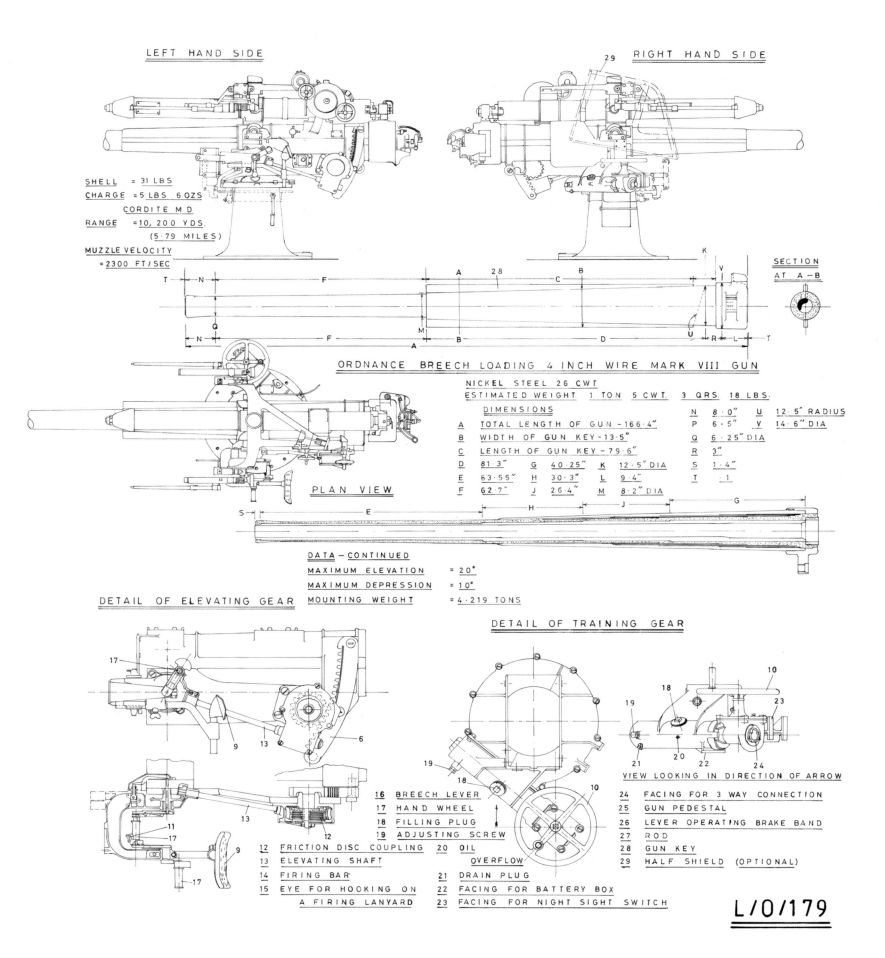

LEFT HAND SIDE

SHELL = 31 LBS
CHARGE = 5 LBS 6 OZS
CORDITE M D
RANGE = 10, 200 YDS.
(5·79 MILES)
MUZZLE VELOCITY
= 2300 FT / SEC

RIGHT HAND SIDE

SECTION
AT A-B

PLAN VIEW

ORDNANCE BREECH LOADING 4 INCH WIRE MARK VIII GUN

NICKEL STEEL 26 CWT
ESTIMATED WEIGHT   1 TON 5 CWT.   3 QRS. 18 LBS.
DIMENSIONS

A	TOTAL LENGTH OF GUN -166·4"		N	8·0"	U	12·5" RADIUS
B	WIDTH OF GUN KEY-13·5"		P	6·5"	V	14·6" DIA
C	LENGTH OF GUN KEY-79·6"		Q	6·25" DIA
D	81·3"	G	40·25"	K	12·5" DIA	R	3"
E	63·55"	H	30·3"	L	9·4"	S	1·4"
F	62·7"	J	26·4"	M	8·2" DIA	T	·1

DATA - CONTINUED
MAXIMUM ELEVATION   = 20°
MAXIMUM DEPRESSION   = 10°
MOUNTING WEIGHT   = 4·219 TONS

DETAIL OF ELEVATING GEAR

DETAIL OF TRAINING GEAR

VIEW LOOKING IN DIRECTION OF ARROW

16 BREECH LEVER
17 HAND WHEEL
18 FILLING PLUG
19 ADJUSTING SCREW
12 FRICTION DISC COUPLING
13 ELEVATING SHAFT
14 FIRING BAR
15 EYE FOR HOOKING ON
     A FIRING LANYARD
20 OIL
     OVERFLOW
21 DRAIN PLUG
22 FACING FOR BATTERY BOX
23 FACING FOR NIGHT SIGHT SWITCH
24 FACING FOR 3 WAY CONNECTION
25 GUN PEDESTAL
26 LEVER OPERATING BRAKE BAND
27 ROD
28 GUN KEY
29 HALF SHIELD (OPTIONAL)

L/O/179

G 3 4.7in BL Mk I gun CP Mk VI mounting, 1917

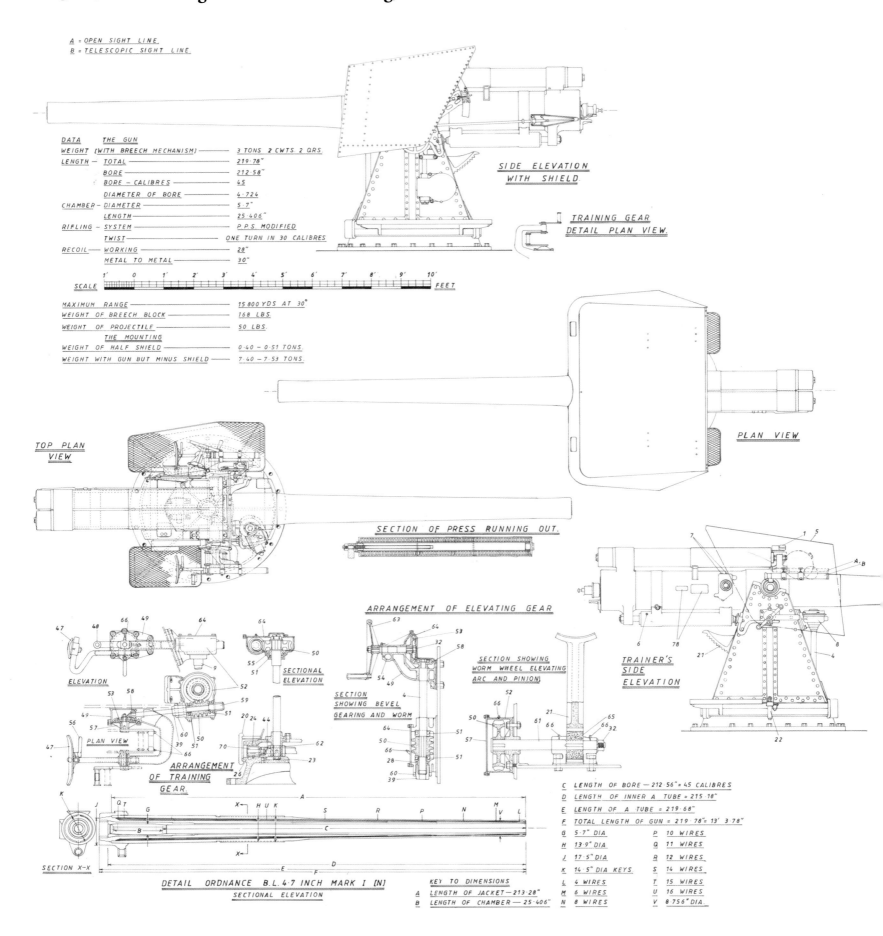

A = OPEN SIGHT LINE
B = TELESCOPIC SIGHT LINE

DATA THE GUN

WEIGHT [WITH BREECH MECHANISM]	—	3 TONS 2 CWTS 2 QRS.
LENGTH — TOTAL	—	219·78″
BORE	—	212·58″
BORE — CALIBRES	—	45
DIAMETER OF BORE	—	4·724
CHAMBER — DIAMETER	—	5·7″
LENGTH	—	25·406″
RIFLING — SYSTEM	—	P.P.S. MODIFIED
TWIST	—	ONE TURN IN 30 CALIBRES
RECOIL — WORKING	—	28″
METAL TO METAL	—	30″

SCALE ... FEET

MAXIMUM RANGE	—	15 800 YDS AT 30°
WEIGHT OF BREECH BLOCK	—	168 LBS.
WEIGHT OF PROJECTILE	—	50 LBS.
THE MOUNTING		
WEIGHT OF HALF SHIELD	—	0·40 — 0·51 TONS.
WEIGHT WITH GUN BUT MINUS SHIELD	—	7·40 — 7·53 TONS.

SIDE ELEVATION
WITH SHIELD

TRAINING GEAR
DETAIL PLAN VIEW.

PLAN VIEW

TOP PLAN
VIEW

SECTION OF PRESS RUNNING OUT.

ARRANGEMENT OF ELEVATING GEAR

SECTION SHOWING
WORM WHEEL ELEVATING
ARC AND PINION)

SECTION
SHOWING BEVEL
GEARING AND WORM

TRAINER'S
SIDE
ELEVATION

ELEVATION

SECTIONAL
ELEVATION

PLAN VIEW

ARRANGEMENT
OF TRAINING
GEAR.

SECTION X—X

DETAIL ORDNANCE B.L. 4·7 INCH MARK I [N]
SECTIONAL ELEVATION

	KEY TO DIMENSIONS	
C	LENGTH OF BORE — 212·56″ = 45 CALIBRES	
D	LENGTH OF INNER A TUBE = 215·18″	
E	LENGTH OF A TUBE = 219·68″	
F	TOTAL LENGTH OF GUN = 219·78″ = 13′ 3·78″	
G	5·7″ DIA	P 10 WIRES
H	13·9″ DIA	Q 11 WIRES
J	17·5″ DIA	R 12 WIRES
K	14·5″ DIA KEYS	S 14 WIRES
L	4 WIRES	T 15 WIRES
M	6 WIRES	U 16 WIRES
N	8 WIRES	V 8·756″ DIA
A	LENGTH OF JACKET — 213·28″	
B	LENGTH OF CHAMBER — 25·406″	

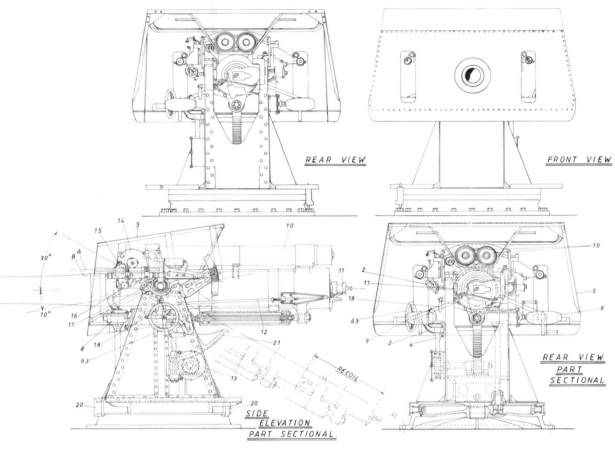

REAR VIEW

FRONT VIEW

SIDE ELEVATION PART SECTIONAL

30°

10°

RECOIL

REAR VIEW PART SECTIONAL

HISTORY

THE 4·7" CALIBRE WAS ADOPTED BY THE ROYAL NAVY FOR FITTING TO DESTROYERS FROM 1917 FOR THE UNITS OF THE SHAKESPEARE AND THE MODIFIED 'W' CLASSES, AS A RESULT OF INTELLIGENCE GATHERED THAT GERMAN DESTROYERS CARRIED A LIGHTER 4·1" GUN AND HAD DESIGNED THEIR S-113 AND V-116 CLASSES WITH FOUR 5·9" CALIBRE GUNS. IN APRIL 1916 WITH THE R.N's 'V' CLASS UNDER CONSIDERATION, JOHN THORNYCROFT AND SON HAD SUBMITTED A DESIGN FOR A DESTROYER LEADER WITH A GUN ARMAMENT OF SIX 4" MOUNTINGS OR FIVE 5" MOUNTINGS. AS A 5" GUN WOULD NEED TO BE DESIGNED AND PROOF FIRED, THE SUGGESTION WAS PUT FORWARD TO MODIFY THE EXISTING ARMY PATTERN 4·7" CALIBRE FIELD GUN TO SAVE VALUABLE TIME. DESPITE THE DRAWBACK OF USING A SEPARATE SHELL AND CARTRIDGE THE SIMPLICITY OF THE WEAPON AND INCREASE IN SHELL WEIGHT FROM THE 32 LBS OF THE 4" GUN TO 45 LBS FULLY JUSTIFIED THE CHANGE. THE NEW CALIBRE WAS ADOPTED FOR ALL THE FOLLOWING DESTROYER CLASSES UP UNTIL 1943 WHEN THE 4·5" SHELL BECAME THE NEW FLEET DESTROYER CALIBRE.

NOTE: THE GUNSHIELD ELEVATES WITH THE GUN.

THIS SUBJECT HAS BEEN REDRAWN FROM TWO OFFICIAL SOURCES THE GUNNERY HANDBOOK OF 1917 WHICH PROVIDED COMPONENT DETAIL, HELD AT THE HAMPSHIRE COUNTY RECORD OFFICE WINCHESTER AND THE ROYAL ORDNANCE FACTORY G/A DRG. No. 57972 G. DATED 18/1/17 HELD AT THE CUMBRIA RECORD OFFICE BARROW-IN-FURNESS. MY THANKS TO BOTH.

ARRANGEMENT OF CRADLE [SHOWING RECOIL AND RUN OUT SYSTEM].

© JOHN LAMBERT 15/1/98. CH'D. 16/1/98.

ARRANGEMENT OF BASE.

L/O/100

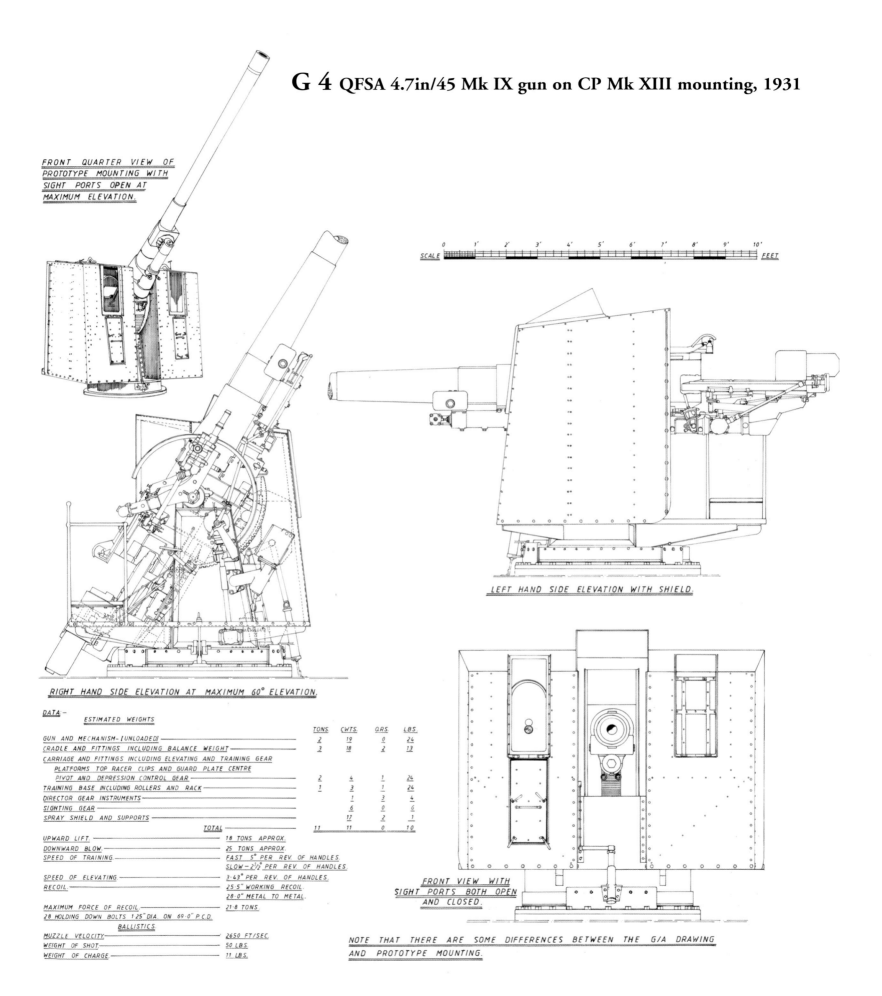

G 4 QFSA 4.7in/45 Mk IX gun on CP Mk XIII mounting, 1931

FRONT QUARTER VIEW OF
PROTOTYPE MOUNTING WITH
SIGHT PORTS OPEN AT
MAXIMUM ELEVATION.

SCALE | 0 1' 2' 3' 4' 5' 6' 7' 8' 9' 10' | FEET

LEFT HAND SIDE ELEVATION WITH SHIELD.

RIGHT HAND SIDE ELEVATION AT MAXIMUM 60° ELEVATION.

DATA:-

ESTIMATED WEIGHTS

	TONS	CWTS.	Q.RS.	LBS.
GUN AND MECHANISM- (UNLOADED)	2	19	0	24
CRADLE AND FITTINGS INCLUDING BALANCE WEIGHT	3	18	2	13
CARRIAGE AND FITTINGS INCLUDING ELEVATING AND TRAINING GEAR PLATFORMS TOP RACER CLIPS AND GUARD PLATE CENTRE PIVOT AND DEPRESSION CONTROL GEAR	2	4	1	24
TRAINING BASE INCLUDING ROLLERS AND RACK	1	3	1	24
DIRECTOR GEAR INSTRUMENTS		1	3	4
SIGHTING GEAR		6	0	6
SPRAY SHIELD AND SUPPORTS		17	2	1
TOTAL	11	11	0	10

UPWARD LIFT.	18 TONS APPROX.
DOWNWARD BLOW.	25 TONS APPROX.
SPEED OF TRAINING.	FAST 5° PER REV. OF HANDLES.
	SLOW - 2½° PER REV. OF HANDLES.
SPEED OF ELEVATING.	3·43° PER REV. OF HANDLES.
RECOIL.	25·5" WORKING RECOIL.
	28·0" METAL TO METAL.
MAXIMUM FORCE OF RECOIL.	21·8 TONS.

28 HOLDING DOWN BOLTS 1·25" DIA. ON 69·0" P.C.D.

BALLISTICS

MUZZLE VELOCITY	2650 FT/SEC.
WEIGHT OF SHOT	50 LBS.
WEIGHT OF CHARGE	11 LBS.

FRONT VIEW WITH
SIGHT PORTS BOTH OPEN
AND CLOSED.

NOTE THAT THERE ARE SOME DIFFERENCES BETWEEN THE G/A DRAWING
AND PROTOTYPE MOUNTING.

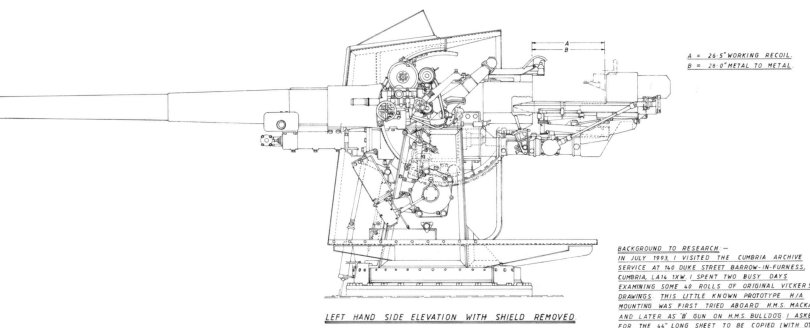

$A = 26.5"$ WORKING RECOIL.
$B = 28.0"$ METAL TO METAL.

LEFT HAND SIDE ELEVATION WITH SHIELD REMOVED.

BACKGROUND TO RESEARCH:—
IN JULY 1993, I VISITED THE CUMBRIA ARCHIVE
SERVICE AT 140 DUKE STREET BARROW-IN-FURNESS,
CUMBRIA, LA14 1XW. I SPENT TWO BUSY DAYS
EXAMINING SOME 40 ROLLS OF ORIGINAL VICKERS
DRAWINGS. THIS LITTLE KNOWN PROTOTYPE H/A
MOUNTING WAS FIRST TRIED ABOARD H.M.S. MACKAY
AND LATER AS 'B' GUN ON H.M.S. BULLDOG. I ASKED
FOR THE 44" LONG SHEET TO BE COPIED (WITH OTHERS)
IN DECEMBER 1993, I VISITED THE RESERVE COLLECTION
AT THE BARROW MUSEUM WHERE I CHECKED THROUGH
A VAST COLLECTION OF OLD VICKERS GLASS PLATE
NEGATIVES. AFTER FURTHER RESEARCH I WAS ABLE TO
IDENTIFY AND HAVE COPIED A NUMBER OF THE
NEGATIVES.
MY THANKS TO DAVID HUGHES AND DAVID TULL,
WITHOUT THEIR ASSISTANCE THIS SUBJECT WOULD NOT
HAVE BEEN POSSIBLE.

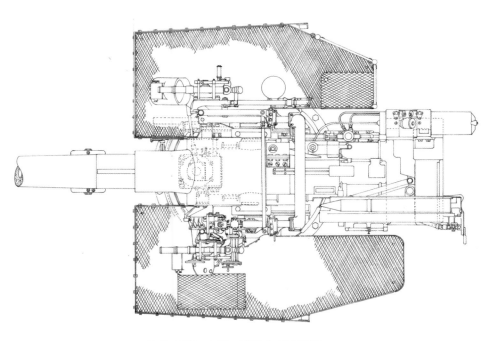

PLAN VIEW WITH SHIELD REMOVED.

HISTORY:—THE C.P. MARK XIII MOUNTING WAS AN ATTEMPT
TO PUT THE 4·7 INCH STANDARD FLEET DESTROYER GUN
IN A HIGH ANGLE 60° MOUNTING FOR ANTI-AIRCRAFT
DEFENCE. THE PROTOTYPE MOUNTING WAS BUILT BY
VICKERS AND UNDERWENT SEA TRIALS ABOARD THE
NEW FLEET DESTROYER H.M.S. BULLDOG BUILT BY SWAN
HUNTER WITH THE NEW MOUNTING CARRIED IN 'B'
POSITION. HER 3 OTHER MOUNTINGS BEING C.P. MARK XIV
WITH 30° ELEVATION. BULLDOG HAD TO BE STRENGTHEND TO
TAKE THE H/A MOUNTING. THE SEA TRIALS PROVED THAT
THE TRUNNION HEIGHT OF 68" WAS QUITE UNACCEPTABLE
FOR LOW ANGLE FIRING WITHOUT A LOADING PLATFORM
AND A DEFINITE HANDICAP TO A HIGH RATE OF FIRE
WITH A LOADING PLATFORM, THUS THIS H/A MOUNTING
WAS NOT PUT INTO PRODUCTION.

CH'D. 31/8/94

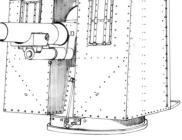

PROTOTYPE MOUNTING AT 0° ELEVATION.
WITH SIGHT PORTS CLOSED.

REDRAWN FROM VICKERS DRG. NO. 94592.
PLUS VICKERS NEGATIVES NO. X2086
AND X2087.
© JOHN LAMBERT 7/7/94

L/0/45

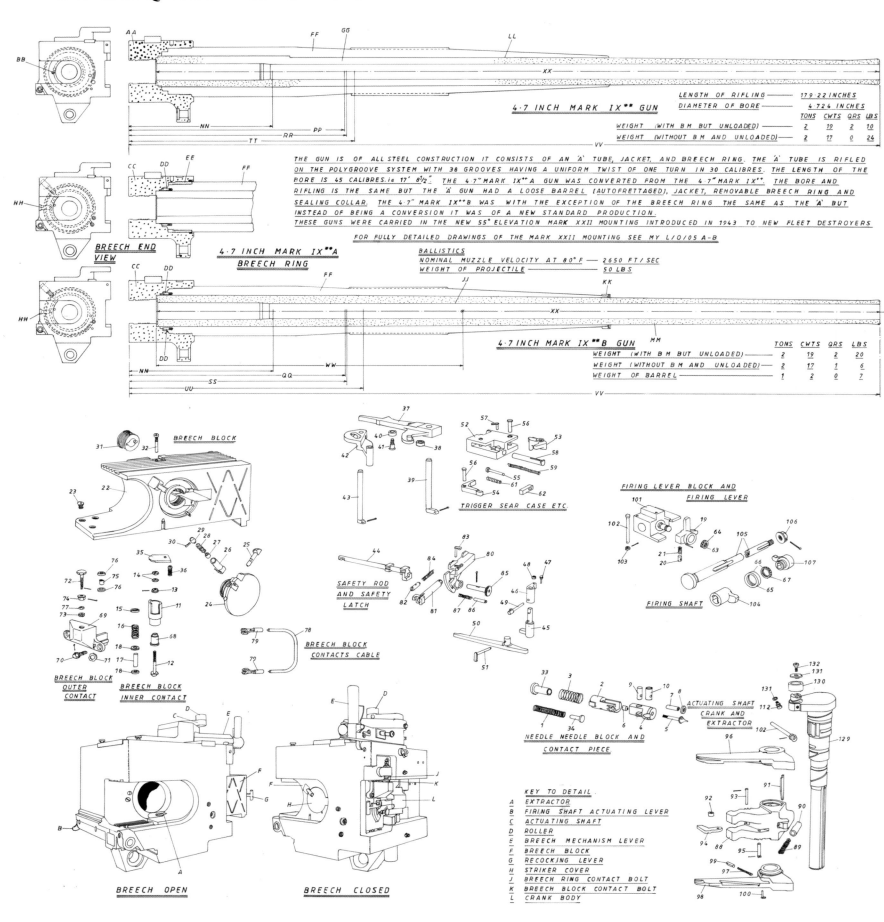

4·7 INCH MARK IX GUN**

	LENGTH OF RIFLING			179·22 INCHES	
	DIAMETER OF BORE			4·724 INCHES	
		TONS	CWTS	QRS	LBS
WEIGHT (WITH B M BUT UNLOADED)		2	19	2	10
WEIGHT (WITHOUT B M AND UNLOADED)		2	17	0	24

THE GUN IS OF ALL STEEL CONSTRUCTION IT CONSISTS OF AN 'A' TUBE, JACKET, AND BREECH RING. THE 'A' TUBE IS RIFLED ON THE POLYGROOVE SYSTEM WITH 38 GROOVES HAVING A UNIFORM TWIST OF ONE TURN IN 30 CALIBRES. THE LENGTH OF THE BORE IS 45 CALIBRES. ie 17' 8½". THE 4·7" MARK IX**A GUN WAS CONVERTED FROM THE 4·7" MARK IX**. THE BORE AND RIFLING IS THE SAME BUT THE 'A' GUN HAD A LOOSE BARREL (AUTOFRETTAGED), JACKET, REMOVABLE BREECH RING AND SEALING COLLAR. THE 4·7" MARK IX**B WAS WITH THE EXCEPTION OF THE BREECH RING THE SAME AS THE 'A' BUT INSTEAD OF BEING A CONVERSION IT WAS OF A NEW STANDARD PRODUCTION.

THESE GUNS WERE CARRIED IN THE NEW 55° ELEVATION MARK XXII MOUNTING INTRODUCED IN 1943 TO NEW FLEET DESTROYERS

FOR FULLY DETAILED DRAWINGS OF THE MARK XXII MOUNTING SEE MY L/O/05 A-B

BREECH END VIEW

4·7 INCH MARK IXA BREECH RING**

BALLISTICS
NOMINAL MUZZLE VELOCITY AT 80° F — 2650 FT / SEC
WEIGHT OF PROJECTILE — 50 LBS

4·7 INCH MARK IXB GUN**

	TONS	CWTS	QRS	LBS
WEIGHT (WITH B M BUT UNLOADED)	2	19	2	20
WEIGHT (WITHOUT B M AND UNLOADED)	2	17	1	6
WEIGHT OF BARREL	1	2	0	7

BREECH BLOCK

TRIGGER SEAR CASE ETC.

FIRING LEVER BLOCK AND FIRING LEVER

SAFETY ROD AND SAFETY LATCH

FIRING SHAFT

BREECH BLOCK CONTACTS CABLE

BREECH BLOCK OUTER CONTACT

BREECH BLOCK INNER CONTACT

NEEDLE NEEDLE BLOCK AND CONTACT PIECE

ACTUATING SHAFT CRANK AND EXTRACTOR

BREECH OPEN

BREECH CLOSED

KEY TO DETAIL
A EXTRACTOR
B FIRING SHAFT ACTUATING LEVER
C ACTUATING SHAFT
D ROLLER
E BREECH MECHANISM LEVER
F BREECH BLOCK
G RECOCKING LEVER
H STRIKER COVER
J BREECH RING CONTACT BOLT
K BREECH BLOCK CONTACT BOLT
L CRANK BODY

KEY TO DETAIL

AA BREECH RING
BB SCREW SECURING BREECH RING
CC REMOVABLE BREECH RING
DD SCREWS SECURING LOOSE BARREL
EE BUSH
FF JACKET
GG 'A' TUBE
HH SCREW STOP BREECH RING
JJ TAPER ·01 PER INCH ON DIAMETER
KK SEALING COLLAR
LL TAPER ·004 PER INCH ON DIAMETER
MM LOOSE BARREL [AUTOFRETTAGED].
NN TO 1" FROM COMMENCEMENT OF RIFLING = 42·4"
PP C OF G [WITH B.M & LOADED] = 63·54 INCHES
QQ C OF G [WITH B.M & LOADED] = 63·64 INCHES
RR C OF G [WITH B.M BUT UNLOADED] = 63·86 INCHES
SS C OF G [WITH B.M BUT UNLOADED] = 63·96 INCHES
TT C OF G [WITHOUT B.M & UNLOADED] BARE GUN = 66·3 INCHES
UU C OF G [WITHOUT B.M & UNLOADED] BAR GUN = 66·4 INCHES
VV TOTAL LENGTH OF GUN = 220·62 INCHES
WW C OF G OF BARREL ONLY = 90·14 INCHES
XX LENGTH OF BORE 212·58 = 45 CALIBRES.

THE BREECH MECHANISM

THE BREECH MECHANISM IS OF THE HORIZONTAL
SLIDING BLOCK TYPE. THE B.M. LEVER IS PIVOTED
ON THE ACTUATING SHAFT ON TOP OF THE BREECH
END AT THE RIGHT HAND SIDE. THE FIRING MECH-
ANISM IS OF THE COMBINED ELECTRIC AND PER-
CUSSION TYPE IN WHICH THE PERCUSSION STRIKER
IS COCKED DURING THE OPENING OF THE BREECH AND
REMAINS COCKED UNLESS PERCUSSION FIRING HAS BEEN
EMPLOYED.

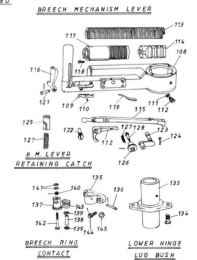

BREECH MECHANISM LEVER

B.M. LEVER
RETAINING CATCH

BREECH RING
CONTACT

LOWER HINGE
LUG BUSH

PART VIEW SHOWING A SHELL IN THE BREECH

THIS SUBJECT HAS BEEN REDRAWN FROM ORIGINAL
MATERIAL CONTAINED IN B.R. 1245 (43).
DATED 12/10/1943

COMPONENT PARTS OF BREECH AND THE FIRING MECHANISM

1	NEEDLE BLOCK SPRING
2	STRIKER
3	STRIKER SPRING
4	NEEDLE BLOCK BODY
5	NEEDLE
6	NUT
7	INSULATING BUSH
8	INSULATING WASHER
9	CONTACT PIECE
10	INSULATING BUSH
11	BREECH BLOCK INNER CONTACT BUSH
12	BOLT
13	NUT WITH KEEP SPLIT PIN
14	TERMINAL NUT — [2 OFF]
15	SHEATH COLLAR
16	SPRING
17	INSULATING BOLT BUSH
18	INSULATING BOLT WASHER
19	FIRING LEVER WITH RIVET
20	PLUNGER
21	SPRING
22	BREECH BLOCK
23	PRESERVING SCREW
24	STRIKER COVER
25	CATCH LEVER HINGE PIN
26	CATCH LEVER
27	CATCH PLUNGER
28	CATCH SPRING
29	CATCH PLUG
30	RETAINING PIN
31	FIRING HOLE BUSH
32	FIXING SCREW
33	STRIKER SPRING BEARING GUIDE
34	NEEDLE BLOCK SPRING GUIDE
35	INNER CONTACT COVER
36	SECURING SCREW
37	COCKING LEVER
38	ROLLER
39	AXIS PIN WITH KEEP SPLIT PIN
40	RETRACTION ROLLER
41	AXIS STUD
42	RECOCKING LEVER
43	AXIS RECOCKING LEVER PIN WITH SPLIT KEEP PIN
44	SAFETY ROD
45	TRIGGER PART I
46	TRIGGER PART II
47	PIN
48	ROLLER
49	RETAINING PIN
50	INTERMEDIATE FIRING LEVER
51	RETAINING PIN
52	TRIGGER SEAR CASE BODY
53	TRIGGER SEAR
54	SAFETY LEVER
55	PLUNGER
56	AXIS PIN
57	RETAINING COCKING LEVER PLUNGER PIN.
58	COCKING LEVER PLUNGER
59	SPRING
60	TRIGGER SEAR AXIS PIN
61	SAFETY LEVER PLUNGER SPRING.
62	PLATE RETAINING TRIGGER SEAR
63	BALL BEARING No 1-[2 OFF]
64	CAGE
65	BALL BEARING No 5-[2 OFF]
66	OUTER BALL RACE [2 OFF]
67	CAGE—[2 OFF]
68	SHEATH
69	BREECH BLOCK INNER CONTACT CASING
70	FIXING SCREW WITH KEEP SPLIT PIN—[2 OFF]
71	LOCKING PLATE—[2 OFF]
72	BOLT WITH SPLIT KEEP PIN
73	SPRING WASHER
74	NUT WITH SPLIT KEEP PIN
75	INSULATING BUSH
76	INSULATING WASHER—[2 OFF]
77	TERMINAL NUT
78	BREECH BLOCK CONTACTS CABLE
79	TAG — [2 OFF]
80	SAFETY LATCH LEVER
81	PLUNGER WITH ROLLER AND ROLLER AXIS RIVET
82	PLUG
83	RETAINING PIN
84	SPRING
85	RETAINING CATCH HANDLE
86	RETAINING CATCH PLUG
87	RETAINING CATCH SPRING
88	CRANK BODY
89	CRANK BUFFER SPRING
90	PLUNGER
91	COTTER
92	CRANK ROLLER
93	AXIS PIN WITH SPLIT KEEP PIN
94	RETRACTING LEVER
95	PIN
96	UPPER EXTRACTOR LEVER
97	PLUNGER SPRING— [2 OFF]
98	LOWER EXTRACTOR LEVER
99	PLUNGER — [2 OFF]
100	RETAINING PIN — [2 OFF]
101	FIRING GEAR BLOCK FIRING LEVER WITH AXIS STUD AND RIVET
102	RETAINING PIN
103	COLLAR WITH SPLIT KEEP PIN
104	LEVER ACTUATING FIRING LEVER
105	FIRING SHAFT
106	NUT WITH SPLIT KEEP RING
107	LEVER ACTUATING FIRING SHAFT
108	BREECH MECHANISM BODY LEVER
109	PLATE LOCKING AXIS PINS.
110	FIXING SCREW
111	No 28 TECALEMIT NIPPLE WASHER
112	TECALEMIT NIPPLE No 28
113	SPRING ACTUATING BREECH BLOCK
114	RACK
115	PINION CATCH LEVER
116	RELEASING LEVER
117	CAP
118	CHECK SCREW
119	PINION CATCH LEVER SPRING
120	RELEASING RETAINING CATCH LEVER
121	AXIS PIN
122	AXIS PIN [2 OFF]
123	PINION RETAINING CATCH LEVER
124	RETAINING SCREW
125	PLUNGER
126	HEAD WITH SPLIT KEEP PIN
127	SPRING
128	PLUNGER
129	ACTUATING SHAFT
130	ROLLER
131	WASHER
132	SECURING SCREW
133	LOWER HINGE LUG BUSH
134	SECURING SCREW-[2 OFF]
135	BREECH RING CONTACT BRACKET
136	PIN
137	BOLT BUSH
138	BOLT INSULATING SLEEVE
139	BOLT INSULATING WASHER
140	RETAINING NUT
141	TERMINAL NUT — [2 OFF]
142	BOLT
143	BOLT BUSH SPRING
144	SCREW FIXING BRACKET-[2 OFF]
145	LOCKING PLATE-[2 OFF]

L/0/113

G 6 QFSA 4.7in/45 Mk IX** gun on CP Mk XVIII mounting, 1934–1942

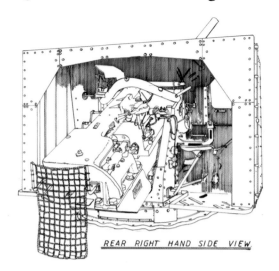

REAR RIGHT HAND SIDE VIEW.

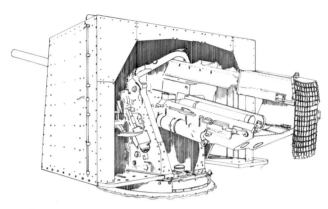

REAR LEFT HAND SIDE VIEW.

FRONT VIEW WITH SHIELD.
SIGHT DOORS SHOWN OPEN AND CLOSED.

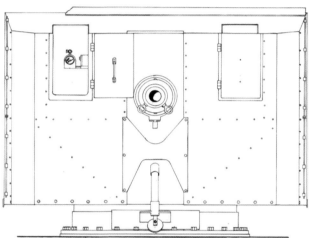

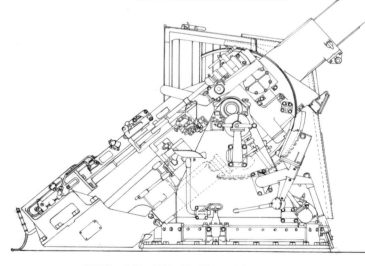

RIGHT HAND SIDE AT FULL ELEVATION.—SHIELD REMOVED.

DATA–C.P. MARK XVIII MOUNTING

WORKING RECOIL	26·5"	SPEED OF ELEVATION	34°/ REVOLUTION OF HANDLE
METAL TO METAL	28"	SPEED OF TRAINING	SLOW 2°/ REV. OF HANDLE
FORCE OF RECOIL	20·5 TONS		FAST 4°/ REV OF HANDLE
DOWNWARD BLOW	19·2 TONS APPROX	GUN CREW	6.
UPWARD LIFT	12·7 TONS APPROX	BOOKS OF REFERENCE	O.U.5489/36 AND B.R. 966/38.
MAXIMUM ELEVATION	40°	RATE OF FIRE	10 R.P.M. APPROX.
MAXIMUM DEPRESSION	–10°		

DATA – THE Q.F.S.A. 4·7 INCH (45 CALIBRES) MARK IX GUN.

BORE	4·724"
MUZZLE VELOCITY	2650 FT/SEC.
WEIGHT INCLUDING BREECH MECHANISM	2·963 / 2·989 TONS.
LENGTH OVERALL	220·62"
LENGTH OF BORE	212·58"
LENGTH OF CHAMBER	30·55"
VOLUME OF CHAMBER	620 CUBIC".
LENGTH OF RIFLING	179·2125"
GROOVES	(38) 0·037" DEEP x 0·27"
LANDS	0·1205"
TWIST	UNIFORM 1 IN 30
APPROX LIFE	1400 E.F.C. WITH NF/S 4200
MAXIMUM RANGE	16970 YARDS AT 40° ELEVATION.
WEIGHT OF PROJECTILE	50 LBS
PROPELLANT CHARGE	11·58 LB SC109 OR 13·13 LBS.
	NF/S 164–048
WORKING PRESSURE	20 TONS / SQ."

DATA – C.P. (HAND OPERATED) MARK XVIII MOUNTING

WEIGHTS	TONS.	CWTS.	QRS.	LBS.
GUN AND MECHANISM UNLOADED	2	19	2	10
CRADLE AND FITTINGS INCLUDING BALANCE WEIGHT	2	14	1	0
CARRIAGE AND FITTINGS INCLUDING ELEVATING AND TRAINING GEAR ARMS SUPPORTING D.F.G INSTRUMENTS TOP RACER. CENTRAL PIVOTS CLIPS GUARD PLATES AND DEPRESSION CONTROL GEAR	2	3	0	0
TRAINING BASE INCLUDING ROLLERS RACK AND HOUSING PAWL BRACKET		19	3	4
DIRECTOR GEAR INCLUDING INSTRUMENTS		3	1	14
SIGHTING GEAR		5	1	0
SPRAY SHIELD PLATFORMS BALANCE WEIGHT AND SUPPORTS	1	5	0	0
TOTAL	10	10	1	0
TOTAL TRAINING MASS	9	10	1	24

(SEE SHEET 'C' FOR OFFICIAL DATA CONTAINED IN GUNNERY MANUALS)

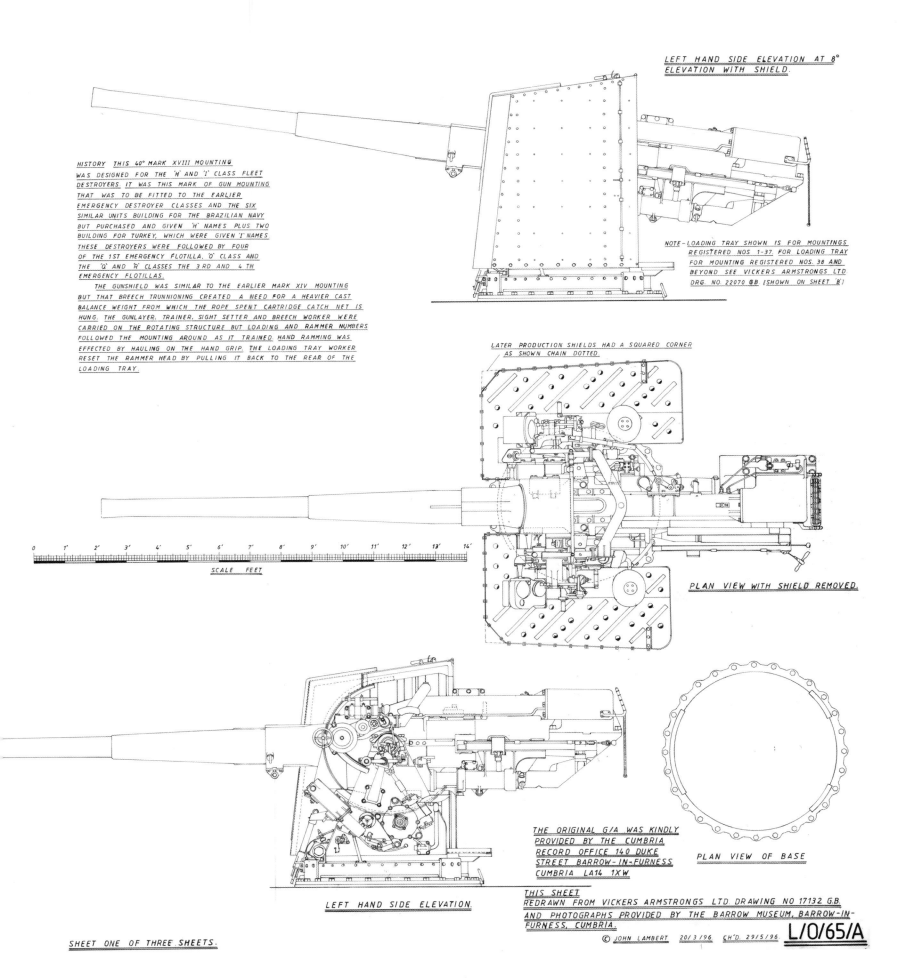

LEFT HAND SIDE ELEVATION AT 8°
ELEVATION WITH SHIELD.

HISTORY THIS 40° MARK XVIII MOUNTING
WAS DESIGNED FOR THE 'H' AND 'I' CLASS FLEET
DESTROYERS. IT WAS THIS MARK OF GUN MOUNTING
THAT WAS TO BE FITTED TO THE EARLIER
EMERGENCY DESTROYER CLASSES AND THE SIX
SIMILAR UNITS BUILDING FOR THE BRAZILIAN NAVY
BUT PURCHASED AND GIVEN 'H' NAMES PLUS TWO
BUILDING FOR TURKEY, WHICH WERE GIVEN 'I' NAMES
THESE DESTROYERS WERE FOLLOWED BY FOUR
OF THE 1ST EMERGENCY FLOTILLA, 'O' CLASS AND
THE 'Q' AND 'R' CLASSES THE 3RD AND 4TH
EMERGENCY FLOTILLAS.
   THE GUNSHIELD WAS SIMILAR TO THE EARLIER MARK XIV MOUNTING
BUT THAT BREECH TRUNNIONING CREATED A NEED FOR A HEAVIER CAST
BALANCE WEIGHT FROM WHICH THE ROPE SPENT CARTRIDGE CATCH NET IS
HUNG. THE GUNLAYER, TRAINER, SIGHT SETTER AND BREECH WORKER WERE
CARRIED ON THE ROTATING STRUCTURE BUT LOADING AND RAMMER NUMBERS
FOLLOWED THE MOUNTING AROUND AS IT TRAINED. HAND RAMMING WAS
EFFECTED BY HAULING ON THE HAND GRIP. THE LOADING TRAY WORKER
RESET THE RAMMER HEAD BY PULLING IT BACK TO THE REAR OF THE
LOADING TRAY.

NOTE-LOADING TRAY SHOWN IS FOR MOUNTINGS
REGISTERED NOS 1-37. FOR LOADING TRAY
FOR MOUNTING REGISTERED NOS. 38 AND
BEYOND SEE VICKERS ARMSTRONGS LTD.
DRG. NO. 22070 GB. (SHOWN ON SHEET 'B')

LATER PRODUCTION SHIELDS HAD A SQUARED CORNER
AS SHOWN CHAIN DOTTED.

0 1' 2' 3' 4' 5' 6' 7' 8' 9' 10' 11' 12' 13' 14'

SCALE FEET

PLAN VIEW WITH SHIELD REMOVED.

THE ORIGINAL G/A WAS KINDLY
PROVIDED BY THE CUMBRIA
RECORD OFFICE 140 DUKE
STREET BARROW-IN-FURNESS
CUMBRIA LA14 1XW

PLAN VIEW OF BASE

THIS SHEET
REDRAWN FROM VICKERS ARMSTRONGS LTD DRAWING NO 17132 G.B.
AND PHOTOGRAPHS PROVIDED BY THE BARROW MUSEUM, BARROW-IN-
FURNESS, CUMBRIA.

LEFT HAND SIDE ELEVATION.

© JOHN LAMBERT 20/3/96 CH'D. 29/5/96   L/0/65/A

SHEET ONE OF THREE SHEETS.

G 6 QFSA 4.7in/45 Mk IX**(N) steel 60cwt gun and Mk XVIII mounting, 1938, detail

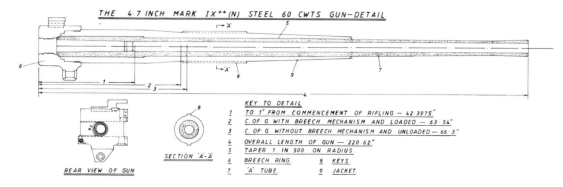

THE 4.7 INCH MARK IX**(N) STEEL 60 CWTS GUN-DETAIL

REAR VIEW OF GUN

SECTION 'A'-'A'

KEY TO DETAIL
1. TO 1" FROM COMMENCEMENT OF RIFLING — 42·3975"
2. C. OF G WITH BREECH MECHANISM AND LOADED — 63·54"
3. C. OF G WITHOUT BREECH MECHANISM AND UNLOADED — 66·3"
4. OVERALL LENGTH OF GUN — 220·62"
5. TAPER 1 IN 500 ON RADIUS
6. BREECH RING.   8. KEYS.
7. 'A' TUBE.   9. JACKET.

NOTE — THE GUN IS RIFLED ON THE POLYGROOVE SYSTEM WITH 38 GROOVES HAVING A UNIFORM TWIST OF ONE TURN IN 30 CALIBRES. THE GUN WAS TO BE INSPECTED AFTER EACH SERIES OF 100 EQUIVALENT FULL CHARGE ROUNDS. THE PROVISIONAL CONDEMING LIMIT WAS 0·226" MAXIMUM WEAR AT 1" FROM THE COMMENCEMENT OF THE RIFLING. THE PROBABLE LIFE OF THE RIFLING WAS 700 E.F.C's

DETAIL—LOADING TRAY MOUNTINGS 1-37.

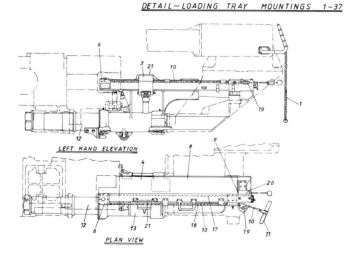

LEFT HAND ELEVATION

PLAN VIEW

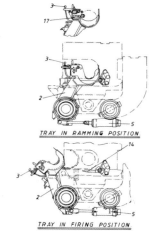

TRAY IN RAMMING POSITION.

TRAY IN FIRING POSITION

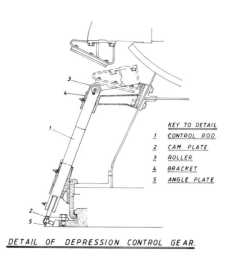

KEY TO DETAIL
1. CONTROL ROD
2. CAM PLATE
3. ROLLER
4. BRACKET
5. ANGLE PLATE

DETAIL OF DEPRESSION CONTROL GEAR.

DETAIL—LOADING TRAY MOUNTINGS 38 AND BEYOND.

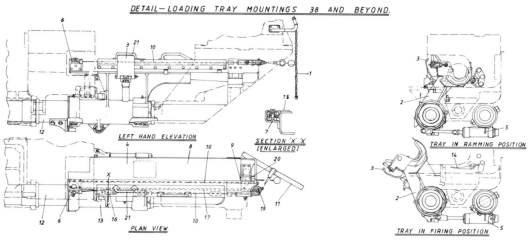

LEFT HAND ELEVATION

SECTION 'X' 'X' (ENLARGED)

PLAN VIEW

TRAY IN RAMMING POSITION

TRAY IN FIRING POSITION

PART SECTION OF BASE PLATE.

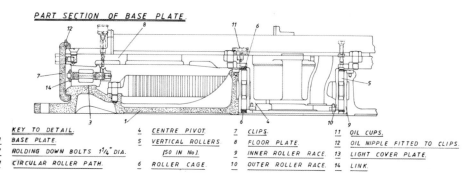

KEY TO DETAIL.
1. BASE PLATE.
2. HOLDING DOWN BOLTS 1¼" DIA.
3. CIRCULAR ROLLER PATH.
4. CENTRE PIVOT.
5. VERTICAL ROLLERS. (50 IN No.)
6. ROLLER CAGE.
7. CLIPS.
8. FLOOR PLATE.
9. INNER ROLLER RACE.
10. OUTER ROLLER RACE.
11. OIL CUPS.
12. OIL NIPPLE FITTED TO CLIPS.
13. LIGHT COVER PLATE.
14. LINK.

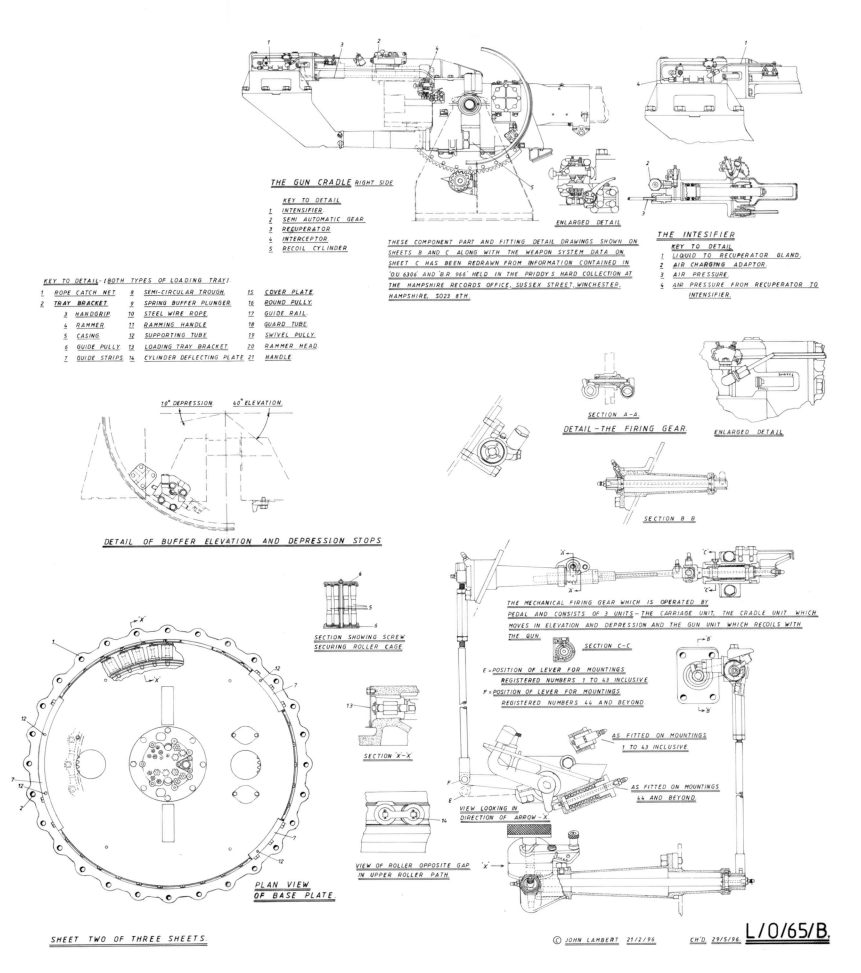

THE GUN CRADLE RIGHT SIDE

KEY TO DETAIL
1 INTENSIFIER.
2 SEMI AUTOMATIC GEAR
3 RECUPERATOR.
4 INTERCEPTOR.
5 RECOIL CYLINDER

ENLARGED DETAIL

THESE COMPONENT PART AND FITTING DETAIL DRAWINGS SHOWN ON SHEETS B AND C ALONG WITH THE WEAPON SYSTEM DATA ON SHEET C HAS BEEN REDRAWN FROM INFORMATION CONTAINED IN 'O.U. 6306' AND 'B.R. 966' HELD IN THE PRIDDY'S HARD COLLECTION AT THE HAMPSHIRE RECORDS OFFICE, SUSSEX STREET, WINCHESTER, HAMPSHIRE, SO23 8TH.

THE INTESIFIER
KEY TO DETAIL
1 LIQUID TO RECUPERATOR GLAND.
2 AIR CHARGING ADAPTOR.
3 AIR PRESSURE.
4 AIR PRESSURE FROM RECUPERATOR TO INTENSIFIER.

KEY TO DETAIL-(BOTH TYPES OF LOADING TRAY).

1	ROPE CATCH NET.	8	SEMI-CIRCULAR TROUGH.	15	COVER PLATE.
2	TRAY BRACKET	9	SPRING BUFFER PLUNGER.	16	ROUND PULLY.
3	HANDGRIP.	10	STEEL WIRE ROPE.	17	GUIDE RAIL.
4	RAMMER.	11	RAMMING HANDLE.	18	GUARD TUBE.
5	CASING.	12	SUPPORTING TUBE.	19	SWIVEL PULLY.
6	GUIDE PULLY.	13	LOADING TRAY BRACKET.	20	RAMMER HEAD.
7	GUIDE STRIPS.	14	CYLINDER DEFLECTING PLATE	21	HANDLE.

10° DEPRESSION.   40° ELEVATION.

DETAIL OF BUFFER ELEVATION AND DEPRESSION STOPS

SECTION A-A

DETAIL-THE FIRING GEAR.   ENLARGED DETAIL

SECTION B B

SECTION SHOWING SCREW SECURING ROLLER CAGE

THE MECHANICAL FIRING GEAR WHICH IS OPERATED BY PEDAL AND CONSISTS OF 3 UNITS – THE CARRIAGE UNIT, THE CRADLE UNIT WHICH MOVES IN ELEVATION AND DEPRESSION AND THE GUN UNIT WHICH RECOILS WITH THE GUN.

SECTION C-C

E = POSITION OF LEVER FOR MOUNTINGS REGISTERED NUMBERS 1 TO 43 INCLUSIVE
F = POSITION OF LEVER FOR MOUNTINGS REGISTERED NUMBERS 44 AND BEYOND.

AS FITTED ON MOUNTINGS 1 TO 43 INCLUSIVE

SECTION 'X'-'X'

AS FITTED ON MOUNTINGS 44 AND BEYOND.

VIEW LOOKING IN DIRECTION OF ARROW-'X'

VIEW OF ROLLER OPPOSITE GAP IN UPPER ROLLER PATH

PLAN VIEW OF BASE PLATE.

SHEET TWO OF THREE SHEETS.

© JOHN LAMBERT 21/2/96   CH'D 29/5/96.   L/0/65/B.

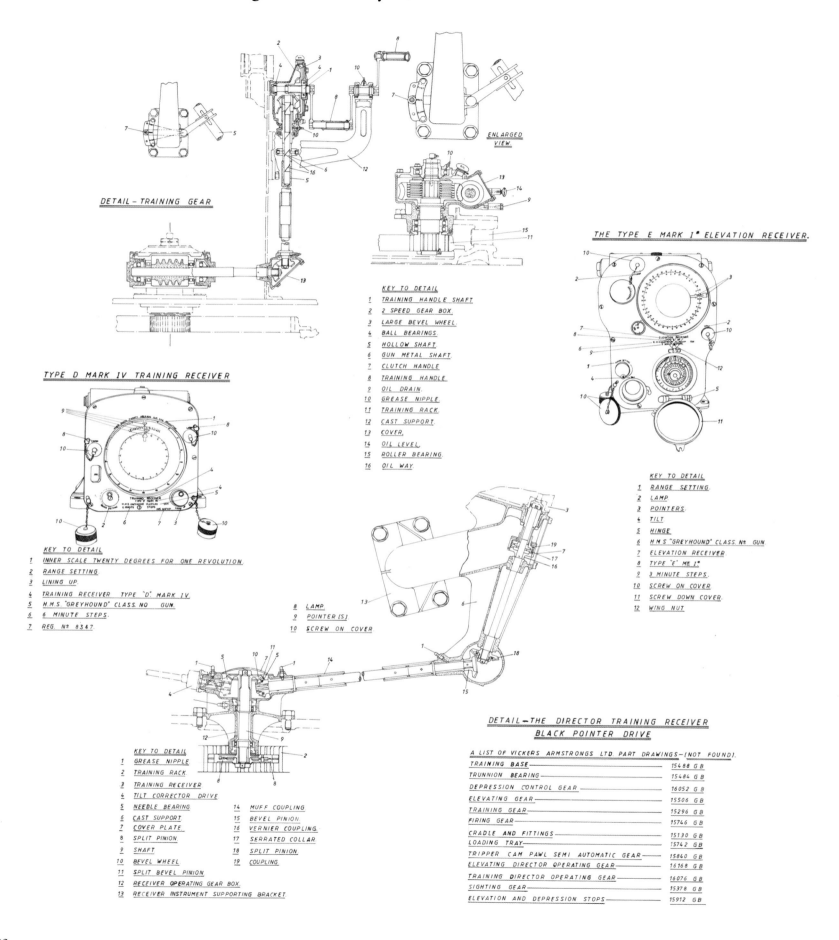

DETAIL - TRAINING GEAR

ENLARGED VIEW.

TYPE D MARK IV TRAINING RECEIVER

THE TYPE E MARK I* ELEVATION RECEIVER.

KEY TO DETAIL

1 TRAINING HANDLE SHAFT
2 2 SPEED GEAR BOX.
3 LARGE BEVEL WHEEL.
4 BALL BEARINGS.
5 HOLLOW SHAFT.
6 GUN METAL SHAFT.
7 CLUTCH HANDLE.
8 TRAINING HANDLE.
9 OIL DRAIN.
10 GREASE NIPPLE.
11 TRAINING RACK.
12 CAST SUPPORT.
13 COVER.
14 OIL LEVEL.
15 ROLLER BEARING.
16 OIL WAY.

KEY TO DETAIL

1 RANGE SETTING.
2 LAMP.
3 POINTERS.
4 TILT.
5 HINGE.
6 H.M.S. "GREYHOUND" CLASS. Nº GUN.
7 ELEVATION RECEIVER.
8 TYPE "E" Mk I*.
9 3 MINUTE STEPS.
10 SCREW ON COVER.
11 SCREW DOWN COVER.
12 WING NUT.

KEY TO DETAIL

1 INNER SCALE TWENTY DEGREES FOR ONE REVOLUTION.
2 RANGE SETTING.
3 LINING UP.
4 TRAINING RECEIVER TYPE "D" MARK IV.
5 H.M.S. "GREYHOUND" CLASS. NO. GUN.
6 6 MINUTE STEPS.
7 REG. Nº 8347.

8 LAMP.
9 POINTER [S].
10 SCREW ON COVER.

DETAIL - THE DIRECTOR TRAINING RECEIVER
BLACK POINTER DRIVE

KEY TO DETAIL

1 GREASE NIPPLE.
2 TRAINING RACK.
3 TRAINING RECEIVER.
4 TILT CORRECTOR DRIVE.
5 NEEDLE BEARING.   14 MUFF COUPLING.
6 CAST SUPPORT.   15 BEVEL PINION.
7 COVER PLATE.   16 VERNIER COUPLING.
8 SPLIT PINION.   17 SERRATED COLLAR.
9 SHAFT.   18 SPLIT PINION.
10 BEVEL WHEEL.   19 COUPLING.
11 SPLIT BEVEL PINION.
12 RECEIVER OPERATING GEAR BOX.
13 RECEIVER INSTRUMENT SUPPORTING BRACKET.

A LIST OF VICKERS ARMSTRONGS LTD. PART DRAWINGS - [NOT FOUND].

TRAINING BASE	15488 G B
TRUNNION BEARING	15484 G B
DEPRESSION CONTROL GEAR	16052 G B
ELEVATING GEAR	15506 G B
TRAINING GEAR	15296 G B
FIRING GEAR	15746 G B
CRADLE AND FITTINGS	15130 G B
LOADING TRAY	15742 G B
TRIPPER CAM PAWL SEMI AUTOMATIC GEAR	15840 G B
ELEVATING DIRECTOR OPERATING GEAR	16168 G B
TRAINING DIRECTOR OPERATING GEAR	16076 G B
SIGHTING GEAR	15378 G B
ELEVATION AND DEPRESSION STOPS	15912 G B

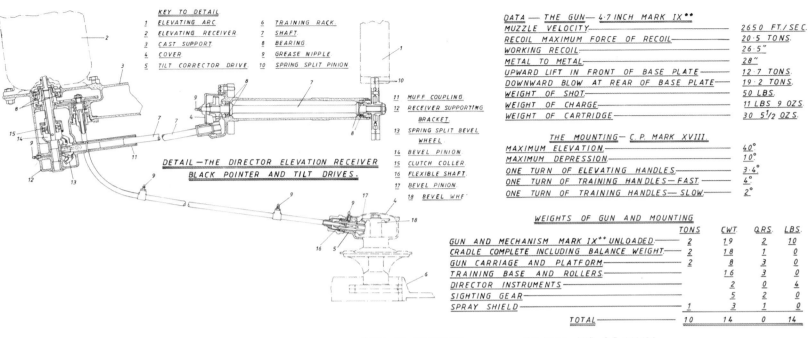

KEY TO DETAIL

1	ELEVATING ARC
2	ELEVATING RECEIVER
3	CAST SUPPORT
4	COVER
5	TILT CORRECTOR DRIVE
6	TRAINING RACK
7	SHAFT
8	BEARING
9	GREASE NIPPLE
10	SPRING SPLIT PINION
11	MUFF COUPLING
12	RECEIVER SUPPORTING BRACKET
13	SPRING SPLIT BEVEL WHEEL
14	BEVEL PINION
15	CLUTCH COLLER
16	FLEXIBLE SHAFT
17	BEVEL PINION
18	BEVEL WHF

DETAIL — THE DIRECTOR ELEVATION RECEIVER BLACK POINTER AND TILT DRIVES.

DATA — THE GUN — 4·7 INCH MARK IX**

MUZZLE VELOCITY	2650 FT./SEC.
RECOIL MAXIMUM FORCE OF RECOIL	20·5 TONS.
WORKING RECOIL	26·5"
METAL TO METAL	28"
UPWARD LIFT IN FRONT OF BASE PLATE	12·7 TONS
DOWNWARD BLOW AT REAR OF BASE PLATE	19·2 TONS.
WEIGHT OF SHOT	50 LBS.
WEIGHT OF CHARGE	11 LBS 9 OZS.
WEIGHT OF CARTRIDGE	30 5½ OZS.

THE MOUNTING — C.P. MARK XVIII

MAXIMUM ELEVATION	40°
MAXIMUM DEPRESSION	10°
ONE TURN OF ELEVATING HANDLES	3·4°
ONE TURN OF TRAINING HANDLES — FAST	4°
ONE TURN OF TRAINING HANDLES — SLOW	2°

WEIGHTS OF GUN AND MOUNTING

	TONS	CWT.	QRS.	LBS.
GUN AND MECHANISM MARK IX** UNLOADED	2	19	2	10
CRADLE COMPLETE INCLUDING BALANCE WEIGHT	2	18	1	0
GUN CARRIAGE AND PLATFORM	2	8	3	0
TRAINING BASE AND ROLLERS		16	3	0
DIRECTOR INSTRUMENTS		2	0	4
SIGHTING GEAR		5	2	0
SPRAY SHIELD	1	3	1	0
TOTAL	10	14	0	14

BOOK OF REFERENCE ———— O.U. 6306 AND B.R. 966/3B.

FLEET DESTROYERS FITTED WITH THE 4.7" MARK IX** GUN ON C.P. MARK XVIII MOUNTING [FOUR MOUNTINGS PER SHIP]

1934 PROGRAMME – 'H' CLASS – HARDY, HERO, HEREWARD, HOSTILE, HOTSPUR, HASTY, HAVOCK, HUNTER & HYPERION.

EX-BRAZILIAN ORDERS – HIGHLANDER, HESPERUS, HAVELOCK, HAVANT, HARVESTER & HURRICANE.

1935 PROGRAMME – I CLASS – INGLEFIELD, INTREPID, IMPULSIVE, ICARUS, ILEX, IMOGEN, IMPERIAL, ISIS & IVANHOE

EX-TURKISH ORDERS – ITHURIEL & INCONSTANT.

1ST EMERGENCY FLOTILLA – ORIBI, OFFA, ONSLAUGHT, ONSLOW [THE REMAINDER WERE FITTED WITH SINGLE 4" MARK V* H.A/LA 80° MOUNTINGS].

3RD EMERGENCY FLOTILLA – QUILLIAM, QUADRANT, QUAIL, QUALITY, QUEENBOROUGH, QUENTIN, QUIBERON & QUICKMATCH.

4TH EMERGENCY FLOTILLA – ROTHERHAM, RELENTLESS, REDOUBT, RACEHORSE, ROCKET, ROEBUCK, RAPID & RAIDER.

[A TOTAL OF 184 MOUNTINGS PLUS SPARES.

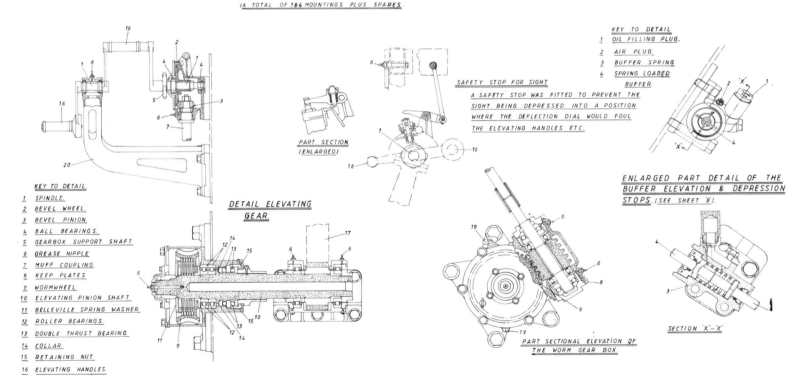

KEY TO DETAIL

1	SPINDLE.
2	BEVEL WHEEL
3	BEVEL PINION
4	BALL BEARINGS.
5	GEARBOX SUPPORT SHAFT
6	GREASE NIPPLE
7	MUFF COUPLING.
8	KEEP PLATES
9	WORMWHEEL
10	ELEVATING PINION SHAFT
11	BELLEVILLE SPRING WASHER.
12	ROLLER BEARINGS.
13	DOUBLE THRUST BEARING
14	COLLAR.
15	RETAINING NUT.
16	ELEVATING HANDLES
17	ELEVATING ARC
18	OIL FILLING CAP
19	OIL DRAIN PLUG
20	CAST SUPPORT

DETAIL ELEVATING GEAR.

SAFETY STOP FOR SIGHT

A SAFETY STOP WAS FITTED TO PREVENT THE SIGHT BEING DEPRESSED INTO A POSITION WHERE THE DEFLECTION DIAL WOULD FOUL THE ELEVATING HANDLES ETC.

PART SECTION [ENLARGED]

KEY TO DETAIL

1	OIL FILLING PLUG.
2	AIR PLUG.
3	BUFFER SPRING
4	SPRING LOADED BUFFER

ENLARGED PART DETAIL OF THE BUFFER ELEVATION & DEPRESSION STOPS. [SEE SHEET 'B'].

SECTION 'X'-'X'

PART SECTIONAL ELEVATION OF THE WORM GEAR BOX

NOTE:—

ALTHOUGH "H.M.S. GREYHOUND" IS NAMED ON THE TRAINING AND ELEVATION RECEIVERS SHOWN, AND THE E, F AND G CLASS DESTROYERS CARRIED THE EARLIER C.P. MARK XVII 40° MOUNTING. — THE SAME INSTRUMENTS FOLLOWED ON, BEING PART OF THE EQUIPMENT THEN STANDARD WITH THE EXISTING GUNNERY DIRECTOR CONTROL TOWER, COMMON TO FLEET DESTROYERS OF THE C, D, E, F, G, H AND I CLASSES.

SHEET THREE OF THREE SHEETS.

CH'D 29/5/96
© JOHN LAMBERT 30/3/96

L/0/65/C

G 7 QFSA 4.7in/45 CP twin mounting Mk XIX. Prototype mounting in HMS *Hereward* dated 13 April 1937

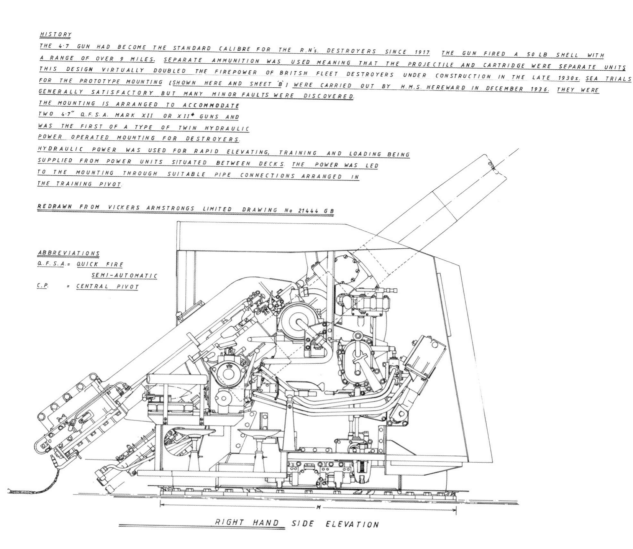

HISTORY

THE 4.7 GUN HAD BECOME THE STANDARD CALIBRE FOR THE R.N's. DESTROYERS SINCE 1917. THE GUN FIRED A 50 LB SHELL WITH A RANGE OF OVER 9 MILES. SEPARATE AMMUNITION WAS USED MEANING THAT THE PROJECTILE AND CARTRIDGE WERE SEPARATE UNITS. THIS DESIGN VIRTUALLY DOUBLED THE FIREPOWER OF BRITSH FLEET DESTROYERS UNDER CONSTRUCTION IN THE LATE 1930s. SEA TRIALS FOR THE PROTOTYPE MOUNTING (SHOWN HERE AND SHEET 'B') WERE CARRIED OUT BY H.M.S. HEREWARD IN DECEMBER 1936. THEY WERE GENERALLY SATISFACTORY BUT MANY MINOR FAULTS WERE DISCOVERED.

THE MOUNTING IS ARRANGED TO ACCOMMODATE TWO 4.7" Q.F.S.A. MARK XII OR XII* GUNS AND WAS THE FIRST OF A TYPE OF TWIN HYDRAULIC POWER OPERATED MOUNTING FOR DESTROYERS.

HYDRAULIC POWER WAS USED FOR RAPID ELEVATING, TRAINING AND LOADING BEING SUPPLIED FROM POWER UNITS SITUATED BETWEEN DECKS. THE POWER WAS LED TO THE MOUNTING THROUGH SUITABLE PIPE CONNECTIONS ARRANGED IN THE TRAINING PIVOT.

REDRAWN FROM VICKERS ARMSTRONGS LIMITED DRAWING No 21444 GB

ABBREVIATIONS
Q.F.S.A.= QUICK FIRE
          SEMI-AUTOMATIC
C.P.   = CENTRAL PIVOT

RIGHT HAND SIDE ELEVATION

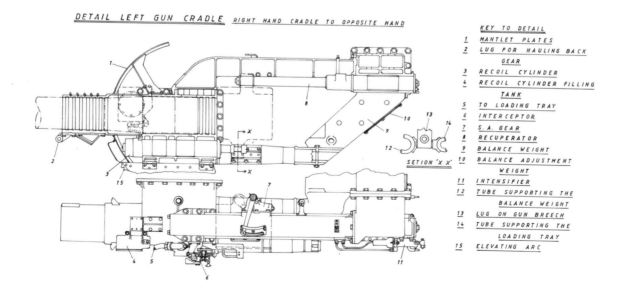

DETAIL LEFT GUN CRADLE RIGHT HAND CRADLE TO OPPOSITE HAND

SETION 'X X'

KEY TO DETAIL
1 MANTLET PLATES
2 LUG FOR HAULING BACK
   GEAR
3 RECOIL CYLINDER
4 RECOIL CYLINDER FILLING
   TANK
5 TO LOADING TRAY
6 INTERCEPTOR
7 S.A. GEAR
8 RECUPERATOR
9 BALANCE WEIGHT
10 BALANCE ADJUSTMENT
   WEIGHT
11 INTENSIFIER
12 TUBE SUPPORTING THE
   BALANCE WEIGHT
13 LUG ON GUN BREECH
14 TUBE SUPPORTING THE
   LOADING TRAY
15 ELEVATING ARC

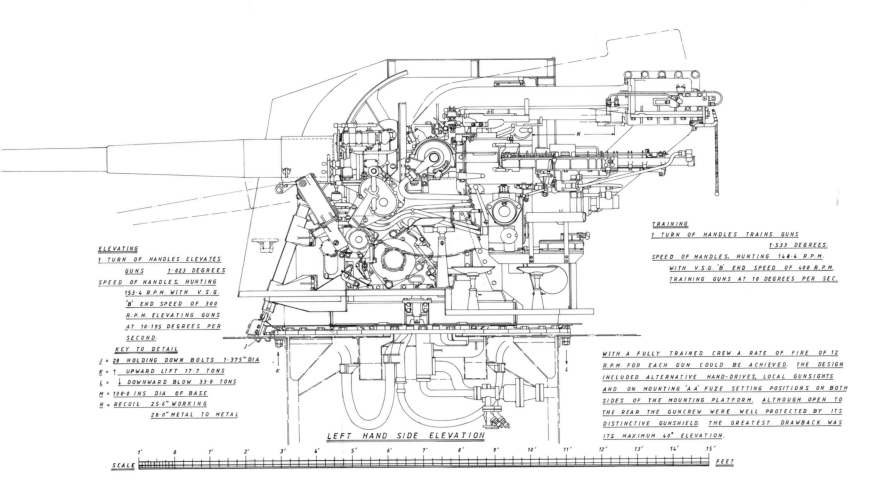

ELEVATING

1 TURN OF HANDLES ELEVATES
GUNS 1·023 DEGREES
SPEED OF HANDLES, HUNTING
153·4 R.P.M. WITH V.S.G.
'B' END SPEED OF 300
R.P.M. ELEVATING GUNS
AT 10·195 DEGREES PER
SECOND.

KEY TO DETAIL

J = 28 HOLDING DOWN BOLTS 1·375"DIA
K = ↑ UPWARD LIFT 17·7 TONS
L = ↓ DOWNWARD BLOW 33·0 TONS
M = 100·0 INS DIA OF BASE
N = RECOIL 25·6" WORKING
28·0" METAL TO METAL

TRAINING

1 TURN OF HANDLES TRAINS GUNS
1·533 DEGREES.
SPEED OF HANDLES, HUNTING 148·4 R.P.M.
WITH V.S.G. 'B' END SPEED OF 400 R.P.M.
TRAINING GUNS AT 10 DEGREES PER SEC.

WITH A FULLY TRAINED CREW A RATE OF FIRE OF 12
R.P.M. FOR EACH GUN COULD BE ACHIEVED. THE DESIGN
INCLUDED ALTERNATIVE HAND-DRIVES, LOCAL GUNSIGHTS
AND ON MOUNTING 'AA' FUZE SETTING POSITIONS ON BOTH
SIDES OF THE MOUNTING PLATFORM. ALTHOUGH OPEN TO
THE REAR THE GUNCREW WERE WELL PROTECTED BY ITS
DISTINCTIVE GUNSHIELD. THE GREATEST DRAWBACK WAS
ITS MAXIMUM 40° ELEVATION.

LEFT HAND SIDE ELEVATION

SCALE 1' 0 1' 2' 3' 4' 5' 6' 7' 8' 9' 10' 11' 12' 13' 14' 15' FEET

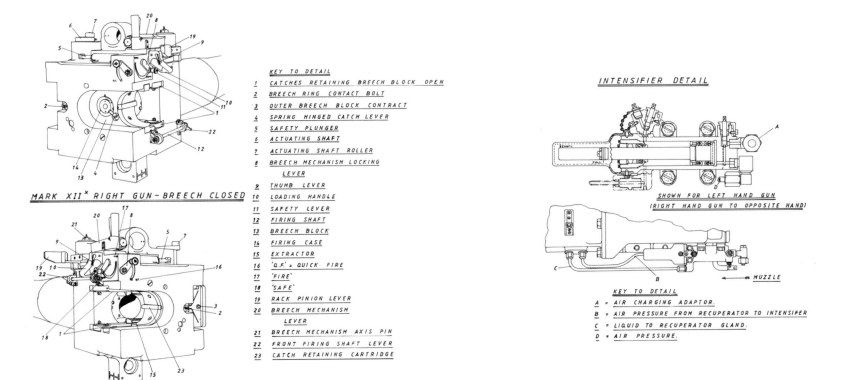

MARK XII* RIGHT GUN – BREECH CLOSED

MARK XII* LEFT GUN – BREECH OPEN

KEY TO DETAIL

1 CATCHES RETAINING BREECH BLOCK OPEN
2 BREECH RING CONTACT BOLT
3 OUTER BREECH BLOCK CONTRACT
4 SPRING HINGED CATCH LEVER
5 SAFETY PLUNGER
6 ACTUATING SHAFT
7 ACTUATING SHAFT ROLLER
8 BREECH MECHANISM LOCKING
   LEVER
9 THUMB LEVER
10 LOADING HANDLE
11 SAFETY LEVER
12 FIRING SHAFT
13 BREECH BLOCK
14 FIRING CASE
15 EXTRACTOR
16 'Q.F.' = QUICK FIRE
17 'FIRE'
18 'SAFE'
19 RACK PINION LEVER
20 BREECH MECHANISM
   LEVER
21 BREECH MECHANISM AXIS PIN
22 FRONT FIRING SHAFT LEVER
23 CATCH RETAINING CARTRIDGE

INTENSIFIER DETAIL

SHOWN FOR LEFT HAND GUN
(RIGHT HAND GUN TO OPPOSITE HAND)

MUZZLE →

KEY TO DETAIL

A = AIR CHARGING ADAPTOR.
B = AIR PRESSURE FROM RECUPERATOR TO INTENSIFIER
C = LIQUID TO RECUPERATOR GLAND.
D = AIR PRESSURE.

L/0/116/A

G 7 QFSA 4.7in/45 CP twin mounting Mk XIX. Construction and detail: plan view of prototype mounting, front view of early production mounting, sighting arrangements and hand ramming gear for production mountings

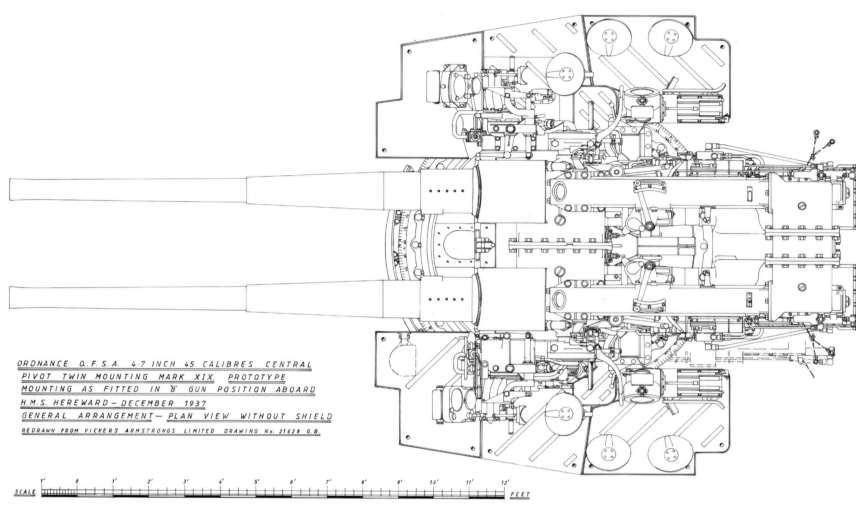

ORDNANCE Q.F.S.A. 4.7 INCH 45 CALIBRES CENTRAL
PIVOT TWIN MOUNTING MARK XIX. PROTOTYPE
MOUNTING AS FITTED IN 'B' GUN POSITION ABOARD
H.M.S. HEREWARD – DECEMBER 1937
GENERAL ARRANGEMENT – PLAN VIEW WITHOUT SHIELD
REDRAWN FROM VICKERS ARMSTRONGS LIMITED DRAWING No. 21628 G.B.

SCALE ... FEET

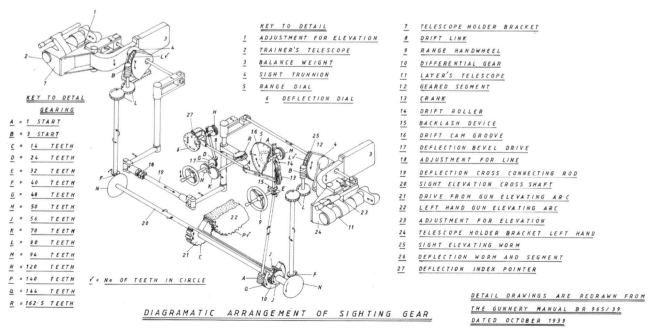

KEY TO DETAIL

1 ADJUSTMENT FOR ELEVATION
2 TRAINER'S TELESCOPE
3 BALANCE WEIGHT
4 SIGHT TRUNNION
5 RANGE DIAL
6 DEFLECTION DIAL
7 TELESCOPE HOLDER BRACKET
8 DRIFT LINK
9 RANGE HANDWHEEL
10 DIFFERENTIAL GEAR
11 LAYER'S TELESCOPE
12 GEARED SEGMENT
13 CRANK
14 DRIFT ROLLER
15 BACKLASH DEVICE
16 DRIFT CAM GROOVE
17 DEFLECTION BEVEL DRIVE
18 ADJUSTMENT FOR LINE
19 DEFLECTION CROSS CONNECTING ROD
20 SIGHT ELEVATION CROSS SHAFT
21 DRIVE FROM GUN ELEVATING ARC
22 LEFT HAND GUN ELEVATING ARC
23 ADJUSTMENT FOR ELEVATION
24 TELESCOPE HOLDER BRACKET LEFT HAND
25 SIGHT ELEVATING WORM
26 DEFLECTION WORM AND SEGMENT
27 DEFLECTION INDEX POINTER

KEY TO DETAIL
GEARING

A = 1 START
B = 3 START
C = 14 TEETH
D = 24 TEETH
E = 32 TEETH
F = 40 TEETH
G = 48 TEETH
H = 50 TEETH
J = 56 TEETH
K = 70 TEETH
L = 90 TEETH
M = 94 TEETH
N = 120 TEETH
P = 140 TEETH
Q = 144 TEETH
R = 162.5 TEETH

⅄ = No OF TEETH IN CIRCLE

DIAGRAMATIC ARRANGEMENT OF SIGHTING GEAR

DETAIL DRAWINGS ARE REDRAWN FROM
THE GUNNERY MANUAL BR 965/39
DATED OCTOBER 1939

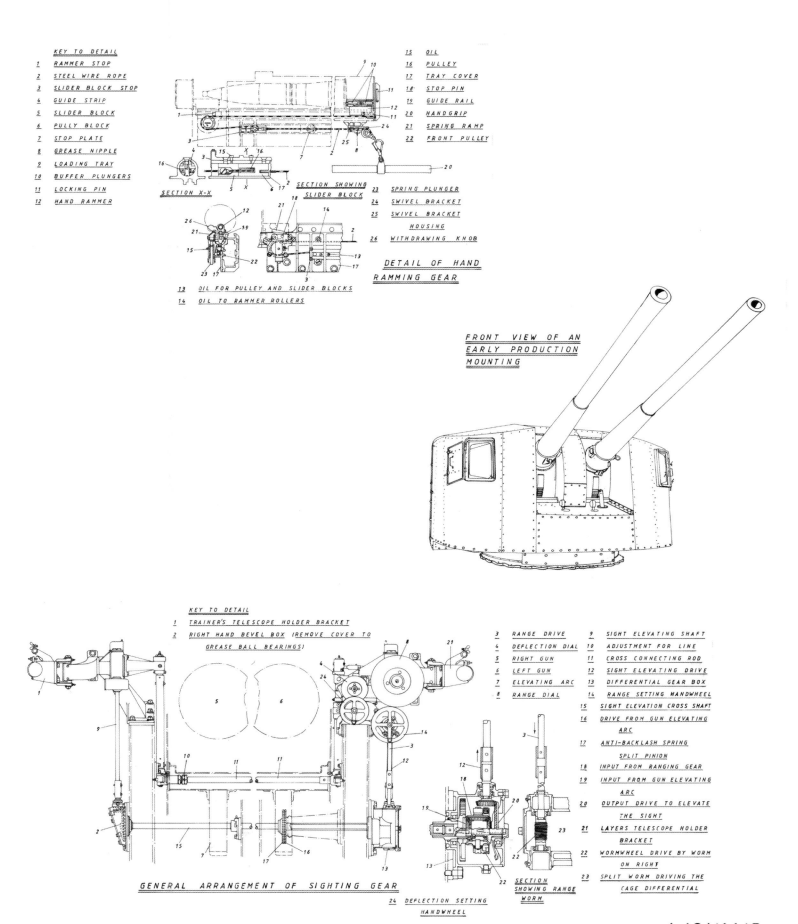

KEY TO DETAIL

1	RAMMER STOP
2	STEEL WIRE ROPE
3	SLIDER BLOCK STOP
4	GUIDE STRIP
5	SLIDER BLOCK
6	PULLY BLOCK
7	STOP PLATE
8	GREASE NIPPLE
9	LOADING TRAY
10	BUFFER PLUNGERS
11	LOCKING PIN
12	HAND RAMMER

15	OIL
16	PULLEY
17	TRAY COVER
18	STOP PIN
19	GUIDE RAIL
20	HANDGRIP
21	SPRING RAMP
22	FRONT PULLEY

SECTION X-X

SECTION SHOWING SLIDER BLOCK

23	SPRING PLUNGER
24	SWIVEL BRACKET
25	SWIVEL BRACKET HOUSING
26	WITHDRAWING KNOB

DETAIL OF HAND RAMMING GEAR

13 OIL FOR PULLEY AND SLIDER BLOCKS
14 OIL TO RAMMER ROLLERS

FRONT VIEW OF AN EARLY PRODUCTION MOUNTING

KEY TO DETAIL

1 TRAINER'S TELESCOPE HOLDER BRACKET
2 RIGHT HAND BEVEL BOX (REMOVE COVER TO GREASE BALL BEARINGS)

3	RANGE DRIVE
4	DEFLECTION DIAL
5	RIGHT GUN
6	LEFT GUN
7	ELEVATING ARC
8	RANGE DIAL

9	SIGHT ELEVATING SHAFT
10	ADJUSTMENT FOR LINE
11	CROSS CONNECTING ROD
12	SIGHT ELEVATING DRIVE
13	DIFFERENTIAL GEAR BOX
14	RANGE SETTING HANDWHEEL
15	SIGHT ELEVATION CROSS SHAFT
16	DRIVE FROM GUN ELEVATING ARC
17	ANTI-BACKLASH SPRING SPLIT PINION
18	INPUT FROM RANGING GEAR
19	INPUT FROM GUN ELEVATING ARC
20	OUTPUT DRIVE TO ELEVATE THE SIGHT
21	LAYERS TELESCOPE HOLDER BRACKET
22	WORMWHEEL DRIVE BY WORM ON RIGHT
23	SPLIT WORM DRIVING THE CAGE DIFFERENTIAL

GENERAL ARRANGEMENT OF SIGHTING GEAR

24 DEFLECTION SETTING HANDWHEEL

SECTION SHOWING RANGE WORM

L/0/116/B

G 7 QFSA 4.7in/45 Mk XXII or XXII* guns on Mk XIX mounting 1938–1945.
As fitted to fleet destroyers of the 'Tribal', 'J', 'K' and 'N' classes

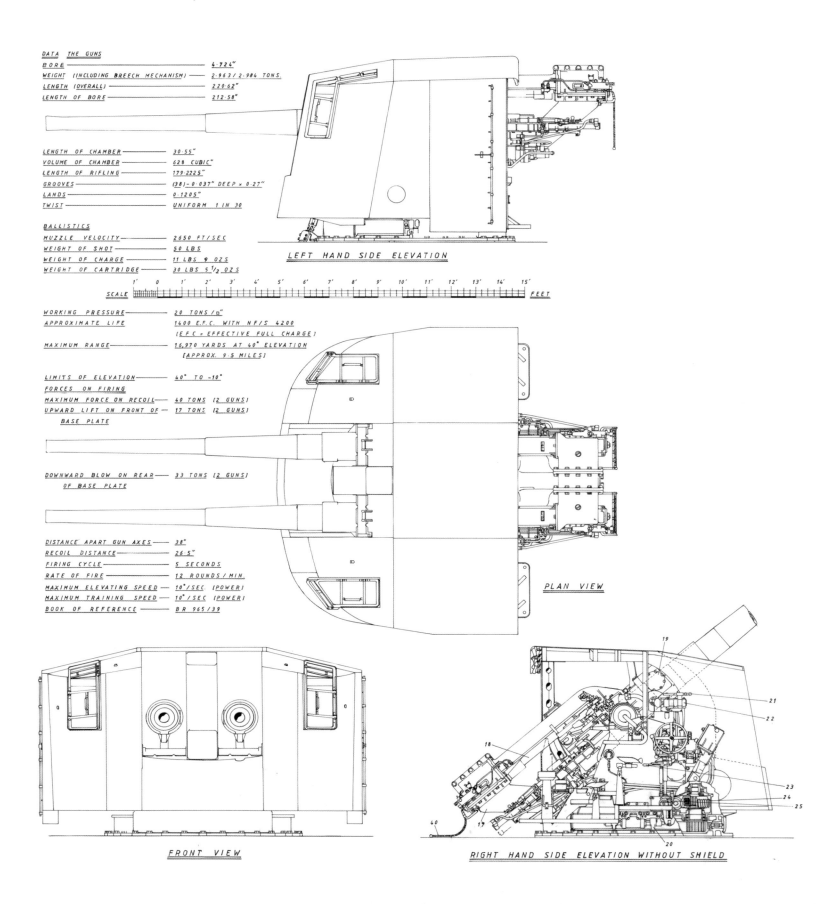

DATA THE GUNS
BORE — 4·724"
WEIGHT (INCLUDING BREECH MECHANISM) — 2·963/2·984 TONS.
LENGTH (OVERALL) — 220·62"
LENGTH OF BORE — 212·58"

LENGTH OF CHAMBER — 30·55"
VOLUME OF CHAMBER — 628 CUBIC"
LENGTH OF RIFLING — 179·2225"
GROOVES — (38)-0·037" DEEP × 0·27"
LANDS — 0·1205"
TWIST — UNIFORM 1 IN 30

BALLISTICS
MUZZLE VELOCITY — 2650 FT/SEC
WEIGHT OF SHOT — 50 LBS
WEIGHT OF CHARGE — 11 LBS 9 OZS
WEIGHT OF CARTRIDGE — 30 LBS 5 1/2 OZS

LEFT HAND SIDE ELEVATION

1' 0 1' 2' 3' 4' 5' 6' 7' 8' 9' 10' 11' 12' 13' 14' 15'
SCALE   FEET

WORKING PRESSURE — 20 TONS/□"
APPROXIMATE LIFE — 1400 E.F.C. WITH NF/S 4200
    (EFC = EFFECTIVE FULL CHARGE)
MAXIMUM RANGE — 16,970 YARDS AT 40° ELEVATION
    (APPROX. 9·5 MILES)

LIMITS OF ELEVATION — 40° TO -10°
FORCES ON FIRING
MAXIMUM FORCE ON RECOIL — 40 TONS (2 GUNS)
UPWARD LIFT ON FRONT OF — 17 TONS (2 GUNS)
    BASE PLATE

DOWNWARD BLOW ON REAR — 33 TONS (2 GUNS)
    OF BASE PLATE

DISTANCE APART GUN AXES — 38"
RECOIL DISTANCE — 26·5"
FIRING CYCLE — 5 SECONDS
RATE OF FIRE — 12 ROUNDS/MIN.
MAXIMUM ELEVATING SPEED — 10°/SEC. (POWER)
MAXIMUM TRAINING SPEED — 10°/SEC (POWER)
BOOK OF REFERENCE — BR 965/39

PLAN VIEW

FRONT VIEW

RIGHT HAND SIDE ELEVATION WITHOUT SHIELD

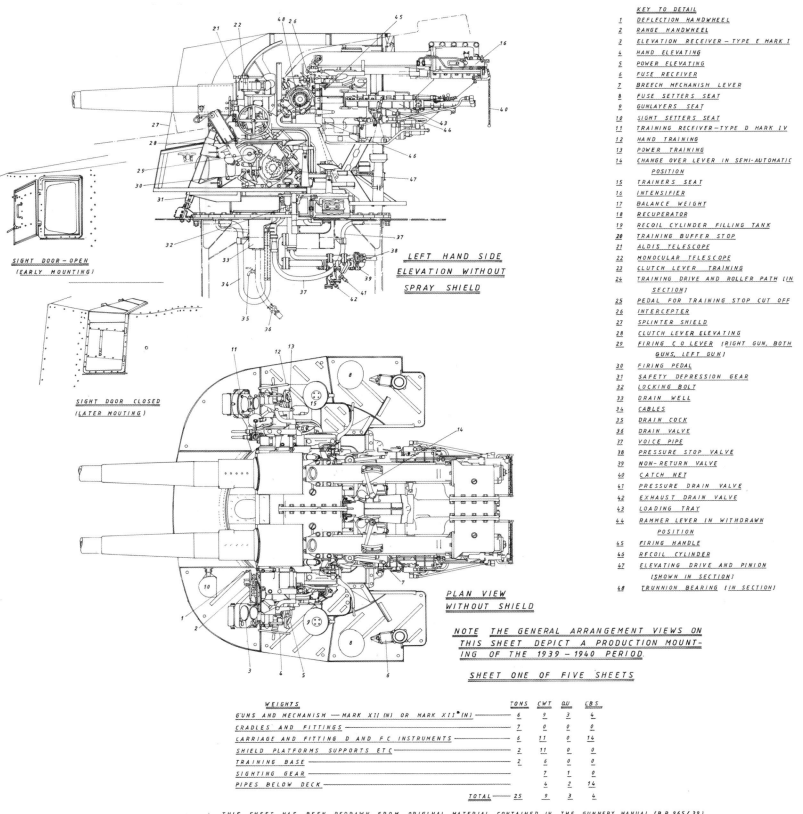

KEY TO DETAIL

1 DEFLECTION HANDWHEEL
2 RANGE HANDWHEEL
3 ELEVATION RECEIVER — TYPE E MARK I
4 HAND ELEVATING
5 POWER ELEVATING
6 FUSE RECEIVER
7 BREECH MECHANISM LEVER
8 FUSE SETTERS SEAT
9 GUNLAYERS SEAT
10 SIGHT SETTERS SEAT
11 TRAINING RECEIVER — TYPE D MARK IV
12 HAND TRAINING
13 POWER TRAINING
14 CHANGE OVER LEVER IN SEMI-AUTOMATIC
     POSITION
15 TRAINERS SEAT
16 INTENSIFIER
17 BALANCE WEIGHT
18 RECUPERATOR
19 RECOIL CYLINDER FILLING TANK
20 TRAINING BUFFER STOP
21 ALDIS TELESCOPE
22 MONOCULAR TELESCOPE
23 CLUTCH LEVER TRAINING
24 TRAINING DRIVE AND ROLLER PATH [IN
     SECTION]
25 PEDAL FOR TRAINING STOP CUT OFF
26 INTERCEPTER
27 SPLINTER SHIELD
28 CLUTCH LEVER ELEVATING
29 FIRING C O LEVER [RIGHT GUN, BOTH
     GUNS, LEFT GUN]
30 FIRING PEDAL
31 SAFETY DEPRESSION GEAR
32 LOCKING BOLT
33 DRAIN WELL
34 CABLES
35 DRAIN COCK
36 DRAIN VALVE
37 VOICE PIPE
38 PRESSURE STOP VALVE
39 NON-RETURN VALVE
40 CATCH NET
41 PRESSURE DRAIN VALVE
42 EXHAUST DRAIN VALVE
43 LOADING TRAY
44 RAMMER LEVER IN WITHDRAWN
     POSITION
45 FIRING HANDLE
46 RECOIL CYLINDER
47 ELEVATING DRIVE AND PINION
     [SHOWN IN SECTION]
48 TRUNNION BEARING [IN SECTION]

SIGHT DOOR – OPEN
(EARLY MOUNTING)

SIGHT DOOR CLOSED
(LATER MOUTING)

LEFT HAND SIDE
ELEVATION WITHOUT
SPRAY SHIELD

PLAN VIEW
WITHOUT SHIELD

NOTE THE GENERAL ARRANGEMENT VIEWS ON
THIS SHEET DEPICT A PRODUCTION MOUNT-
ING OF THE 1939 – 1940 PERIOD.

SHEET ONE OF FIVE SHEETS

WEIGHTS	TONS	CWT	QU	LBS
GUNS AND MECHANISM — MARK XII [N] OR MARK XII*[N]	6	9	3	4
CRADLES AND FITTINGS	7	0	0	0
CARRIAGE AND FITTING D AND FC INSTRUMENTS	6	11	0	14
SHIELD PLATFORMS SUPPORTS ETC	2	11	0	0
TRAINING BASE	2	6	0	0
SIGHTING GEAR		7	1	0
PIPES BELOW DECK		4	2	14
TOTAL	25	9	3	4

THIS SHEET HAS BEEN REDRAWN FROM ORIGINAL MATERIAL CONTAINED IN THE GUNNERY MANUAL [BR 965/39]
AND VICKERS DRG No 22970 GB OF THE SPRAY SHIELD

ⓒ JOHN LAMBERT COMPLETED 16/6/2000 CH'D. 2/7/2000

L/0/116/C

G 7 Mk XIX mounting. Detail and construction of gun shield and gun sighting ports

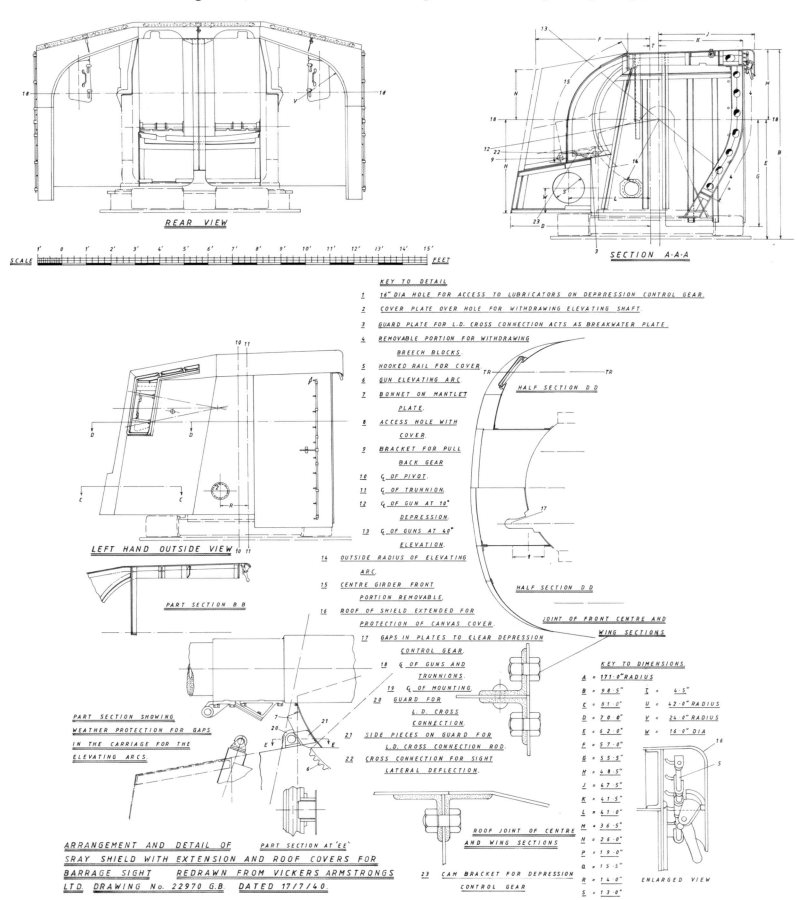

REAR VIEW

SECTION A·A·A

SCALE ⊢⊢⊢⊢⊢⊢ FEET

LEFT HAND OUTSIDE VIEW

PART SECTION B B

PART SECTION SHOWING
WEATHER PROTECTION FOR GAPS
IN THE CARRIAGE FOR THE
ELEVATING ARCS.

ARRANGEMENT AND DETAIL OF
SRAY SHIELD WITH EXTENSION AND ROOF COVERS FOR
BARRAGE SIGHT   REDRAWN FROM VICKERS ARMSTRONGS
LTD. DRAWING No. 22970 G.B.   DATED 17/7/40.

PART SECTION AT 'EE'

HALF SECTION D D

HALF SECTION D D

JOINT OF FRONT CENTRE AND
WING SECTIONS

ROOF JOINT OF CENTRE
AND WING SECTIONS

ENLARGED VIEW

KEY TO DETAIL

1   16" DIA HOLE FOR ACCESS TO LUBRICATORS ON DEPRESSION CONTROL GEAR.
2   COVER PLATE OVER HOLE FOR WITHDRAWING ELEVATING SHAFT.
3   GUARD PLATE FOR L.D. CROSS CONNECTION ACTS AS BREAKWATER PLATE.
4   REMOVABLE PORTION FOR WITHDRAWING
    BREECH BLOCKS.
5   HOOKED RAIL FOR COVER.
6   GUN ELEVATING ARC.
7   BONNET ON MANTLET
    PLATE.
8   ACCESS HOLE WITH
    COVER.
9   BRACKET FOR PULL
    BACK GEAR.
10 ℄ OF PIVOT.
11 ℄ OF TRUNNION.
12 ℄ OF GUN AT 10°
    DEPRESSION.
13 ℄ OF GUNS AT 40°
    ELEVATION.
14 OUTSIDE RADIUS OF ELEVATING
    ARC.
15 CENTRE GIRDER FRONT
    PORTION REMOVABLE.
16 ROOF OF SHIELD EXTENDED FOR
    PROTECTION OF CANVAS COVER.
17 GAPS IN PLATES TO CLEAR DEPRESSION
    CONTROL GEAR.
18 ℄ OF GUNS AND
    TRUNNIONS.
19 ℄ OF MOUNTING.
20 GUARD FOR
    L.D. CROSS
    CONNECTION.
21 SIDE PIECES ON GUARD FOR
    L.D. CROSS CONNECTION ROD.
22 CROSS CONNECTION FOR SIGHT
    LATERAL DEFLECTION.
23 CAM BRACKET FOR DEPRESSION
    CONTROL GEAR

KEY TO DIMENSIONS

A = 171·0"RADIUS		
B = 98·5"	I = 4·5"	
C = 81·0"	U = 42·0" RADIUS	
D = 70·0"	V = 24·0" RADIUS	
E = 62·0"	W = 16·0" DIA	
F = 57·0"		
G = 55·5"		
H = 48·5"		
J = 47·5"		
K = 41·5"		
L = 41·0"		
M = 36·5"		
N = 26·0"		
P = 19·0"		
Q = 15·5"		
R = 14·0"		
S = 13·0"		

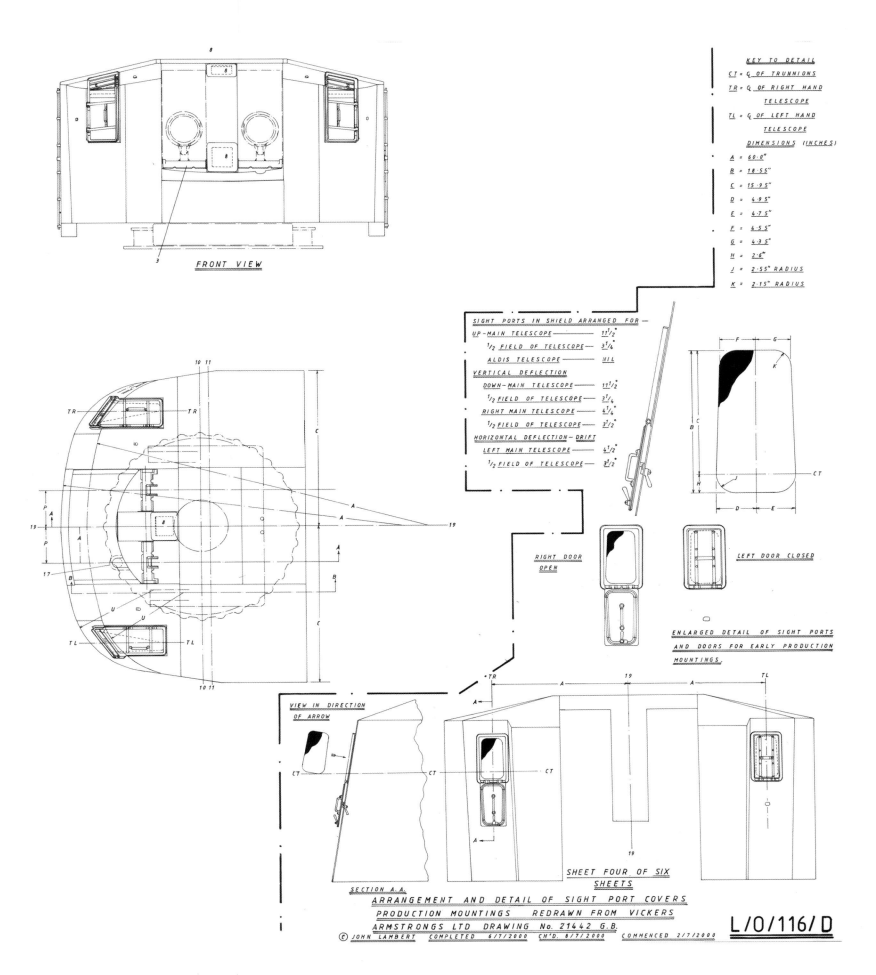

FRONT VIEW

KEY TO DETAIL

CT = ℄ OF TRUNNIONS
TR = ℄ OF RIGHT HAND
        TELESCOPE
TL = ℄ OF LEFT HAND
        TELESCOPE
DIMENSIONS (INCHES)

A = 60·0"
B = 18·55"
C = 15·95"
D = 4·95"
E = 4·75"
F = 4·55"
G = 4·35"
H = 2·6"
J = 2·55" RADIUS
K = 2·15" RADIUS

SIGHT PORTS IN SHIELD ARRANGED FOR —
UP-MAIN TELESCOPE ——— 11½°
  ½ FIELD OF TELESCOPE ——— 3¼°
ALDIS TELESCOPE ——— NIL
VERTICAL DEFLECTION
DOWN-MAIN TELESCOPE ——— 11½°
  ½ FIELD OF TELESCOPE ——— 3¼°
RIGHT MAIN TELESCOPE ——— 4¼°
  ½ FIELD OF TELESCOPE ——— 3½°
HORIZONTAL DEFLECTION—DRIFT
LEFT MAIN TELESCOPE ——— 4½°
  ½ FIELD OF TELESCOPE ——— 3½°

RIGHT DOOR
OPEN

LEFT DOOR CLOSED

ENLARGED DETAIL OF SIGHT PORTS
AND DOORS FOR EARLY PRODUCTION
MOUNTINGS.

VIEW IN DIRECTION
OF ARROW

SECTION A.A.

SHEET FOUR OF SIX
SHEETS

ARRANGEMENT AND DETAIL OF SIGHT PORT COVERS
PRODUCTION MOUNTINGS   REDRAWN FROM VICKERS
ARMSTRONGS LTD   DRAWING No. 21442 G.B.
© JOHN LAMBERT   COMPLETED 6/7/2000   CH'D. 8/7/2000   COMMENCED 2/7/2000

L/O/116/D

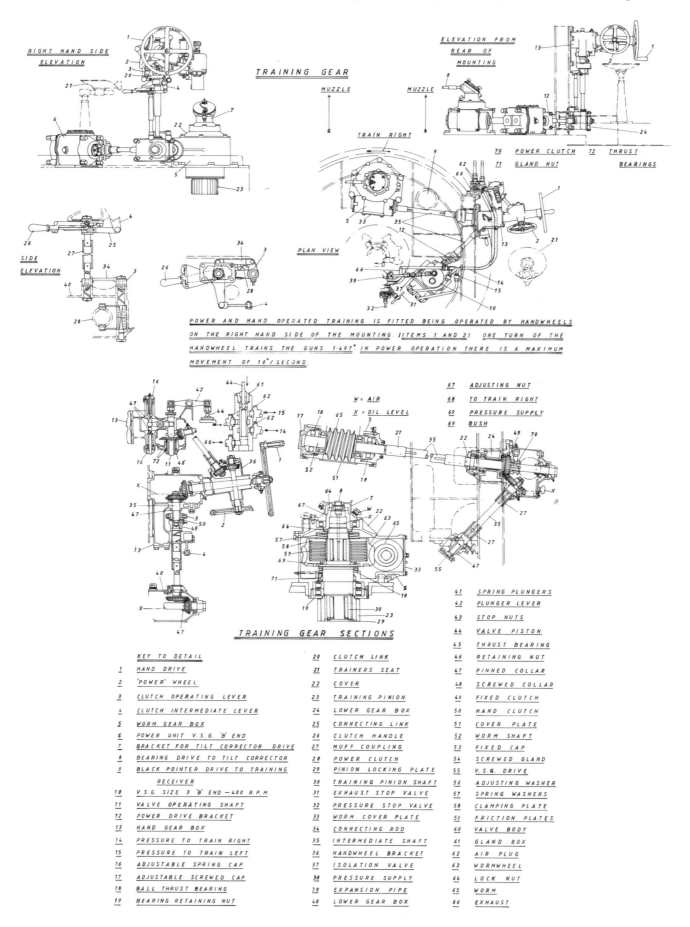

RIGHT HAND SIDE ELEVATION

SIDE ELEVATION

TRAINING GEAR

MUZZLE

ELEVATION FROM REAR OF MOUNTING

MUZZLE

TRAIN RIGHT

PLAN VIEW

70 POWER CLUTCH   72 THRUST
71 GLAND NUT   BEARINGS

POWER AND HAND OPERATED TRAINING IS FITTED BEING OPERATED BY HANDWHEELS
ON THE RIGHT HAND SIDE OF THE MOUNTING. (ITEMS 1 AND 2) ONE TURN OF THE
HANDWHEEL TRAINS THE GUNS 1·497° IN POWER OPERATION THERE IS A MAXIMUM
MOVEMENT OF 10°/SECOND.

W = AIR
X = OIL LEVEL

67   ADJUSTING NUT
68   TO TRAIN RIGHT
69   PRESSURE SUPPLY
69   BUSH

TRAINING GEAR SECTIONS

41   SPRING PLUNGERS
42   PLUNGER LEVER
43   STOP NUTS
44   VALVE PISTON
45   THRUST BEARING

KEY TO DETAIL			
1	HAND DRIVE	20	CLUTCH LINK	46	RETAINING NUT
2	'POWER' WHEEL	21	TRAINERS SEAT	47	PINNED COLLAR
3	CLUTCH OPERATING LEVER	22	COVER	48	SCREWED COLLAR
4	CLUTCH INTERMEDIATE LEVER	23	TRAINING PINION	49	FIXED CLUTCH
5	WORM GEAR BOX	24	LOWER GEAR BOX	50	HAND CLUTCH
6	POWER UNIT V.S.G. 'B' END	25	CONNECTING LINK	51	COVER PLATE
7	BRACKET FOR TILT CORRECTOR DRIVE	26	CLUTCH HANDLE	52	WORM SHAFT
8	BEARING DRIVE TO TILT CORRECTOR	27	MUFF COUPLING	53	FIXED CAP
9	BLACK POINTER DRIVE TO TRAINING RECEIVER	28	POWER CLUTCH	54	SCREWED GLAND
		29	PINION LOCKING PLATE	55	V.S.G. DRIVE
10	V.S.G. SIZE 3 'B' END — 400 R.P.M.	30	TRAINING PINION SHAFT	56	ADJUSTING WASHER
11	VALVE OPERATING SHAFT	31	EXHAUST STOP VALVE	57	SPRING WASHERS
12	POWER DRIVE BRACKET	32	PRESSURE STOP VALVE	58	CLAMPING PLATE
13	HAND GEAR BOX	33	WORM COVER PLATE	59	FRICTION PLATES
14	PRESSURE TO TRAIN RIGHT	34	CONNECTING ROD	60	VALVE BODY
15	PRESSURE TO TRAIN LEFT	35	INTERMEDIATE SHAFT	61	GLAND BOX
16	ADJUSTABLE SPRING CAP	36	HANDWHEEL BRACKET	62	AIR PLUG
17	ADJUSTABLE SCREWED CAP	37	ISOLATION VALVE	63	WORMWHEEL
18	BALL THRUST BEARING	38	PRESSURE SUPPLY	64	LOCK NUT
19	BEARING RETAINING NUT	39	EXPANSION PIPE	65	WORM
		40	LOWER GEAR BOX	66	EXHAUST

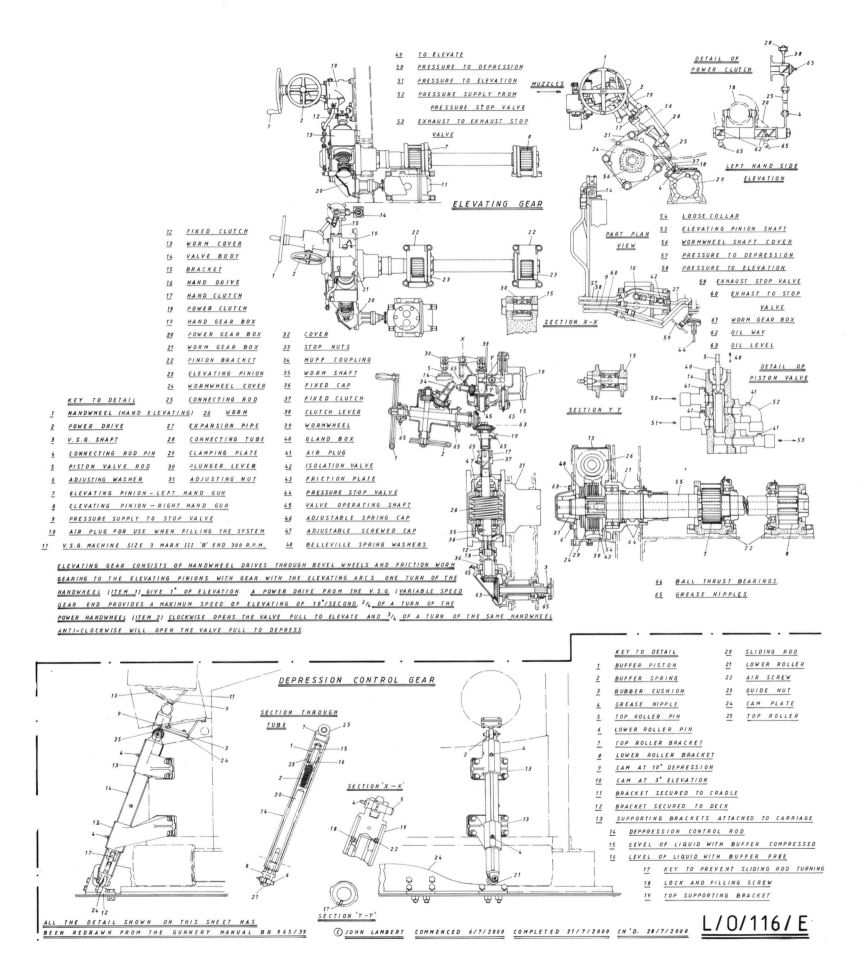

ELEVATING GEAR

49 TO ELEVATE
50 PRESSURE TO DEPRESSION
51 PRESSURE TO ELEVATION
52 PRESSURE SUPPLY FROM PRESSURE STOP VALVE
53 EXHAUST TO EXHAUST STOP VALVE

MUZZLES

DETAIL OF POWER CLUTCH

LEFT HAND SIDE ELEVATION

PART PLAN VIEW

SECTION X-X

SECTION Y Y

DETAIL OF PISTON VALVE

12 FIXED CLUTCH
13 WORM COVER
14 VALVE BODY
15 BRACKET
16 HAND DRIVE
17 HAND CLUTCH
18 POWER CLUTCH
19 HAND GEAR BOX
20 POWER GEAR BOX
21 WORM GEAR BOX
22 PINION BRACKET
23 ELEVATING PINION
24 WORMWHEEL COVER

KEY TO DETAIL
1 HANDWHEEL (HAND ELEVATING)
2 POWER DRIVE
3 V.S.G. SHAFT
4 CONNECTING ROD PIN
5 PISTON VALVE ROD
6 ADJUSTING WASHER
7 ELEVATING PINION – LEFT HAND GUN
8 ELEVATING PINION – RIGHT HAND GUN
9 PRESSURE SUPPLY TO STOP VALVE
10 AIR PLUG FOR USE WHEN FILLING THE SYSTEM
11 V.S.G. MACHINE SIZE 3 MARK III 'B' END 300 R.P.M.

25 CONNECTING ROD
26 WORM
27 EXPANSION PIPE
28 CONNECTING TUBE
29 CLAMPING PLATE
30 PLUNGER LEVER
31 ADJUSTING NUT
32 COVER
33 STOP NUTS
34 MUFF COUPLING
35 WORM SHAFT
36 FIXED CAP
37 FIXED CLUTCH
38 CLUTCH LEVER
39 WORMWHEEL
40 GLAND BOX
41 AIR PLUG
42 ISOLATION VALVE
43 FRICTION PLATE
44 PRESSURE STOP VALVE
45 VALVE OPERATING SHAFT
46 ADJUSTABLE SPRING CAP
47 ADJUSTABLE SCREWED CAP
48 BELLEVILLE SPRING WASHERS

54 LOOSE COLLAR
55 ELEVATING PINION SHAFT
56 WORMWHEEL SHAFT COVER
57 PRESSURE TO DEPRESSION
58 PRESSURE TO ELEVATION
59 EXHAUST STOP VALVE
60 EXHAUST TO STOP VALVE
61 WORM GEAR BOX
62 OIL WAY
63 OIL LEVEL

64 BALL THRUST BEARINGS.
65 GREASE NIPPLES

ELEVATING GEAR CONSISTS OF HANDWHEEL DRIVES THROUGH BEVEL WHEELS AND FRICTION WORM
GEARING TO THE ELEVATING PINIONS WITH GEAR WITH THE ELEVATING ARCS ONE TURN OF THE
HANDWHEEL (ITEM 1) GIVE 1° OF ELEVATION. A POWER DRIVE FROM THE V.S.G (VARIABLE SPEED
GEAR END PROVIDES A MAXIMUM SPEED OF ELEVATING OF 10°/SECOND 3/4 OF A TURN OF THE
POWER HANDWHEEL (ITEM 2) CLOCKWISE OPENS THE VALVE FULL TO ELEVATE AND 3/4 OF A TURN OF THE SAME HANDWHEEL
ANTI-CLOCKWISE WILL OPEN THE VALVE FULL TO DEPRESS.

DEPRESSION CONTROL GEAR

SECTION THROUGH TUBE

SECTION 'X-X'

SECTION 'Y-Y'

KEY TO DETAIL
1 BUFFER PISTON
2 BUFFER SPRING
3 RUBBER CUSHION
4 GREASE NIPPLE
5 TOP ROLLER PIN
6 LOWER ROLLER PIN
7 TOP ROLLER BRACKET
8 LOWER ROLLER BRACKET
9 CAM AT 10° DEPRESSION
10 CAM AT 3° ELEVATION
11 BRACKET SECURED TO CRADLE
12 BRACKET SECURED TO DECK
13 SUPPORTING BRACKETS ATTACHED TO CARRIAGE
14 DEPRESSION CONTROL ROD
15 LEVEL OF LIQUID WITH BUFFER COMPRESSED
16 LEVEL OF LIQUID WITH BUFFER FREE
17 KEY TO PREVENT SLIDING ROD TURNING
18 LOCK AND FILLING SCREW
19 TOP SUPPORTING BRACKET
20 SLIDING ROD
21 LOWER ROLLER
22 AIR SCREW
23 GUIDE NUT
24 CAM PLATE
25 TOP ROLLER

ALL THE DETAIL SHOWN ON THIS SHEET HAS
BEEN REDRAWN FROM THE GUNNERY MANUAL BR 965/39

© JOHN LAMBERT COMMENCED 6/7/2000 COMPLETED 21/7/2000 CH'D. 28/7/2000

L/0/116/E

103

G 8 4.7in Mk IX** on Mk XXII mounting, 1943

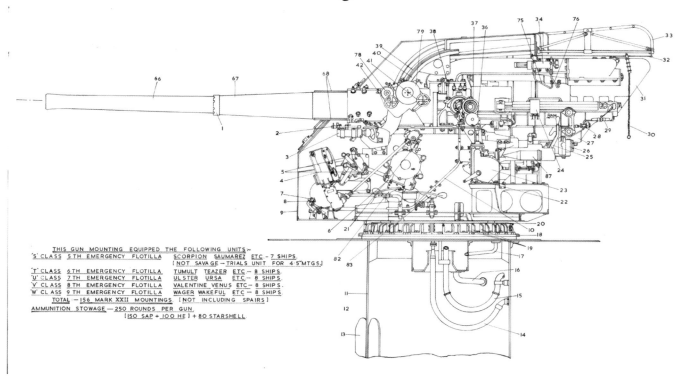

THIS GUN MOUNTING EQUIPPED THE FOLLOWING UNITS:-
'S' CLASS 5TH EMERGENCY FLOTILLA SCORPION SAUMAREZ ETC.- 7 SHIPS.
　　　　　　　　　　　　　　[NOT SAVAGE – TRIALS UNIT FOR 4·5"MTGS.]
'T' CLASS 6TH EMERGENCY FLOTILLA TUMULT TEAZER ETC.- 8 SHIPS.
'U' CLASS 7TH EMERGENCY FLOTILLA ULSTER URSA ETC.- 8 SHIPS.
'V' CLASS 8TH EMERGENCY FLOTILLA VALENTINE VENUS ETC.- 8 SHIPS.
'W' CLASS 9TH EMERGENCY FLOTILLA WAGER WAKEFUL ETC.- 8 SHIPS.
　　　TOTAL – 156 MARK XXII MOUNTINGS. [NOT INCLUDING SPAIRS.]
AMMUNITION STOWAGE – 250 ROUNDS PER GUN.
　　　　　　　[150 SAP + 100 HE] + 80 STARSHELL

A NEW AND MUCH IMPROVED GUN MOUNTING FOR NEW FLEET DESTROYERS FROM 1943.

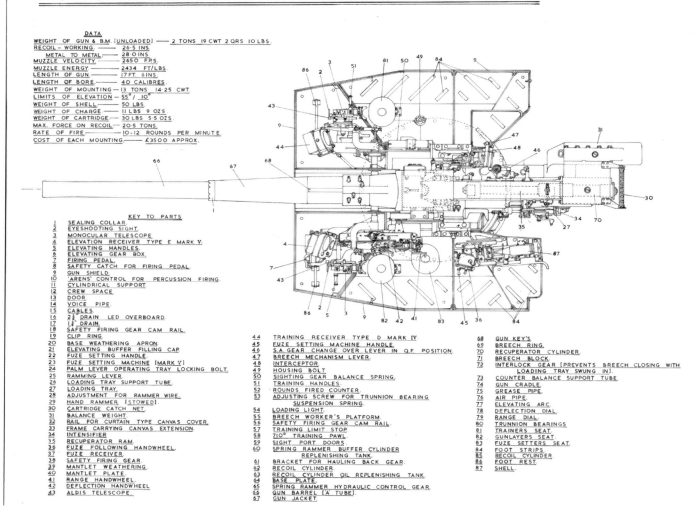

DATA
WEIGHT OF GUN & B.M. [UNLOADED] — 2 TONS 19 CWT 2 QRS 10 LBS.
RECOIL – WORKING. — 26·5 INS.
　　METAL TO METAL. — 28·0 INS.
MUZZLE VELOCITY. — 2650 F.P.S.
MUZZLE ENERGY — 2434 FT/LBS.
LENGTH OF GUN. — 17 FT. 6 INS.
LENGTH OF BORE. — 40 CALIBRES.
WEIGHT OF MOUNTING — 13 TONS 14·25 CWT.
LIMITS OF ELEVATION — 55° / 10°
WEIGHT OF SHELL — 50 LBS.
WEIGHT OF CHARGE — 11 LBS 9 OZS.
WEIGHT OF CARTRIDGE — 30 LBS 5·5 OZS.
MAX. FORCE ON RECOIL — 20·5 TONS.
RATE OF FIRE. — 10-12 ROUNDS PER MINUTE.
COST OF EACH MOUNTING. — £3500 APPROX.

KEY TO PARTS

1	SEALING COLLAR.
2	EYESHOOTING SIGHT.
3	MONOCULAR TELESCOPE.
4	ELEVATION RECEIVER TYPE E MARK V.
5	ELEVATING HANDLES.
6	ELEVATING GEAR BOX.
7	FIRING PEDAL.
8	SAFETY CATCH FOR FIRING PEDAL.
9	GUN SHIELD.
10	'ARENS' CONTROL FOR PERCUSSION FIRING.
11	CYLINDRICAL SUPPORT.
12	CREW SPACE.
13	DOOR.
14	VOICE PIPE.
15	CABLES.
16	2½" DRAIN LED OVERBOARD.
17	1¼" DRAIN.
18	SAFETY FIRING GEAR CAM RAIL.
19	CLIP RING.
20	BASE WEATHERING APRON.
21	ELEVATING BUFFER FILLING CAP.
22	FUZE SETTING HANDLE.
23	FUZE SETTING MACHINE [MARK V]
24	PALM LEVER OPERATING TRAY LOCKING BOLT.
25	RAMMING LEVER.
26	LOADING TRAY SUPPORT TUBE.
27	LOADING TRAY.
28	ADJUSTMENT FOR RAMMER WIRE.
29	HAND RAMMER [STOWED]
30	CARTRIDGE CATCH NET.
31	BALANCE WEIGHT.
32	RAIL FOR CURTAIN TYPE CANVAS COVER.
33	FRAME CARRYING CANVAS EXTENSION.
34	INTENSIFIER.
35	RECUPERATOR RAM.
36	FUZE FOLLOWING HANDWHEEL.
37	FUZE RECEIVER.
38	SAFETY FIRING GEAR.
39	MANTLET WEATHERING.
40	MANTLET PLATE.
41	RANGE HANDWHEEL.
42	DEFLECTION HANDWHEEL.
43	ALDIS TELESCOPE.

44	TRAINING RECEIVER TYPE D MARK IV
45	FUZE SETTING MACHINE HANDLE.
46	S.A GEAR CHANGE OVER LEVER IN Q.F. POSITION.
47	BREECH MECHANISM LEVER.
48	INTERCEPTOR.
49	HOUSING BOLT.
50	SIGHTING GEAR BALANCE SPRING.
51	TRAINING HANDLES.
52	ROUNDS FIRED COUNTER.
53	ADJUSTING SCREW FOR TRUNNION BEARING SUSPENSION SPRING.
54	LOADING LIGHT.
55	BREECH WORKER'S PLATFORM.
56	SAFETY FIRING GEAR CAM RAIL.
57	TRAINING LIMIT STOP
58	710° TRAINING PAWL
59	SIGHT PORT DOORS
60	SPRING RAMMER BUFFER CYLINDER REPLENISHING TANK.
61	BRACKET FOR HAULING BACK GEAR.
62	RECOIL CYLINDER.
63	RECOIL CYLINDER OIL REPLENISHING TANK
64	BASE PLATE.
65	SPRING RAMMER HYDRAULIC CONTROL GEAR.
66	GUN BARREL [A TUBE].
67	GUN JACKET.

68	GUN KEY'S
69	BREECH RING.
70	RECUPERATOR CYLINDER.
71	BREECH BLOCK.
72	INTERLOCK GEAR [PREVENTS BREECH CLOSING WITH LOADING TRAY SWUNG IN].
73	COUNTER BALANCE SUPPORT TUBE.
74	GUN CRADLE.
75	GREASE PIPE.
76	AIR PIPE.
77	ELEVATING ARC.
78	DEFLECTION DIAL.
79	RANGE DIAL.
80	TRUNNION BEARINGS
81	TRAINERS SEAT.
82	GUNLAYERS SEAT.
83	FUZE SETTERS SEAT.
84	FOOT STRIPS
85	RECOIL CYLINDER
86	FOOT REST.
87	SHELL.

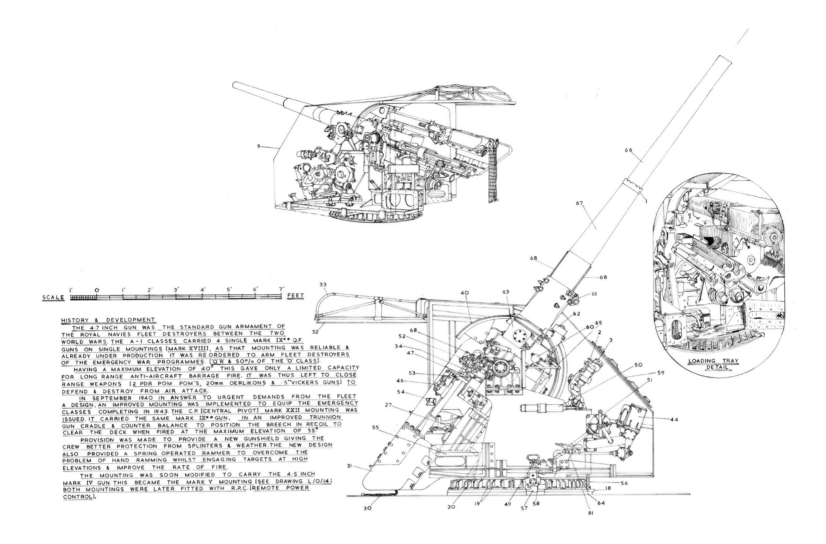

SCALE ⊢ 1' 0 1' 2' 3' 4' 5' 6' 7' FEET

LOADING TRAY DETAIL

HISTORY & DEVELOPMENT

THE 4·7 INCH GUN WAS THE STANDARD GUN ARMAMENT OF THE ROYAL NAVIES FLEET DESTROYERS BETWEEN THE TWO WORLD WARS. THE A-I CLASSES CARRIED 4 SINGLE MARK IX** Q.F. GUNS ON SINGLE MOUNTINGS [MARK XVIII]. AS THAT MOUNTING WAS RELIABLE & ALREADY UNDER PRODUCTION IT WAS RE-ORDERED TO ARM FLEET DESTROYERS OF THE EMERGENCY WAR PROGRAMMES. [Q'R & 50% OF THE 'O' CLASS].

HAVING A MAXIMUM ELEVATION OF 40° THIS GAVE ONLY A LIMITED CAPACITY FOR LONG RANGE ANTI-AIRCRAFT BARRAGE FIRE. IT WAS THUS LEFT TO CLOSE RANGE WEAPONS [2 PDR POM POM'S, 20mm OERLIKONS & ·5"VICKERS GUNS] TO DEFEND & DESTROY FROM AIR ATTACK.

IN SEPTEMBER 1940 IN ANSWER TO URGENT DEMANDS FROM THE FLEET A DESIGN, AN IMPROVED MOUNTING WAS IMPLEMENTED TO EQUIP THE EMERGENCY CLASSES COMPLETING IN 1943. THE C.P. [CENTRAL PIVOT] MARK XXII MOUNTING WAS ISSUED. IT CARRIED THE SAME MARK IX** GUN, IN AN IMPROVED TRUNNION GUN CRADLE & COUNTER BALANCE TO POSITION THE BREECH IN RECOIL TO CLEAR THE DECK WHEN FIRED AT THE MAXIMUM ELEVATION OF 55°.

PROVISION WAS MADE TO PROVIDE A NEW GUNSHIELD GIVING THE CREW BETTER PROTECTION FROM SPLINTERS & WEATHER. THE NEW DESIGN ALSO PROVIDED A SPRING OPERATED RAMMER TO OVERCOME THE PROBLEM OF HAND RAMMING WHILST ENGAGING TARGETS AT HIGH ELEVATIONS & IMPROVE THE RATE OF FIRE.

THE MOUNTING WAS SOON MODIFIED TO CARRY THE 4·5 INCH MARK IV GUN. THIS BECAME THE MARK V MOUNTING [SEE DRAWING L/O/14] BOTH MOUNTINGS WERE LATER FITTED WITH R.P.C. [REMOTE POWER CONTROL].

FOR CONSTRUCTION DETAIL OF THE 4·7" MARK IX** GUN SEE MY L/O/113

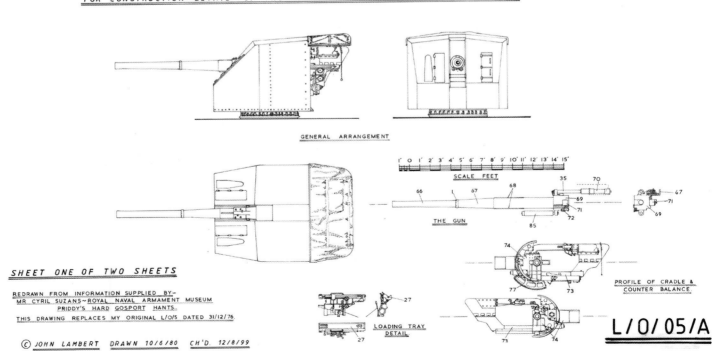

GENERAL ARRANGEMENT

SCALE FEET ⊢ 1' 0 1' 2' 3' 4' 5' 6' 7' 8' 9' 10' 11' 12' 13' 14' 15'

THE GUN

PROFILE OF CRADLE & COUNTER BALANCE

LOADING TRAY DETAIL

SHEET ONE OF TWO SHEETS

REDRAWN FROM INFORMATION SUPPLIED BY-
MR CYRIL SUZANS ~ ROYAL NAVAL ARMAMENT MUSEUM
PRIDDY'S HARD GOSPORT HANTS.
THIS DRAWING REPLACES MY ORIGINAL L/O/5 DATED 31/12/76.

© JOHN LAMBERT DRAWN 10/6/80 CH'D. 12/8/99

L/O/05/A

G 8 4.7in Mk XXII mounting, detail

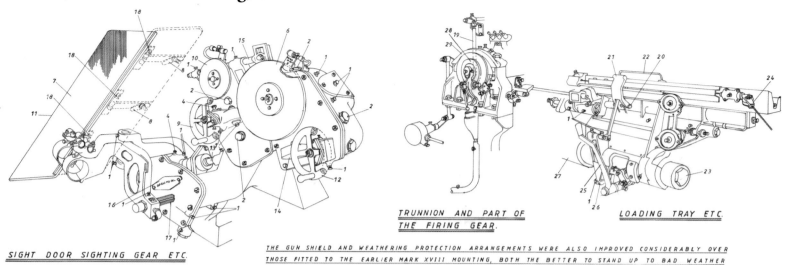

SIGHT DOOR SIGHTING GEAR ETC.

TRUNNION AND PART OF THE FIRING GEAR.

LOADING TRAY ETC.

THE GUN SHIELD AND WEATHERING PROTECTION ARRANGEMENTS WERE ALSO IMPROVED CONSIDERABLY OVER THOSE FITTED TO THE EARLIER MARK XVIII MOUNTING, BOTH THE BETTER TO STAND UP TO BAD WEATHER AND TO GIVE IMPROVED SPLINTER PROTECTION TO THE GUN'S CREW

REDRAWN FROM ORIGINAL MATERIAL CONTAINED IN B.R.1245 (43) DATED 12/11/43.
KINDLEY PROVIDED BY THE HAMPSHIRE RECORD OFFICE
SUSSEX STREET WINCHESTER SO23 8TH. HOLDERS OF THE PRIDDY'S HARD COLLECTION

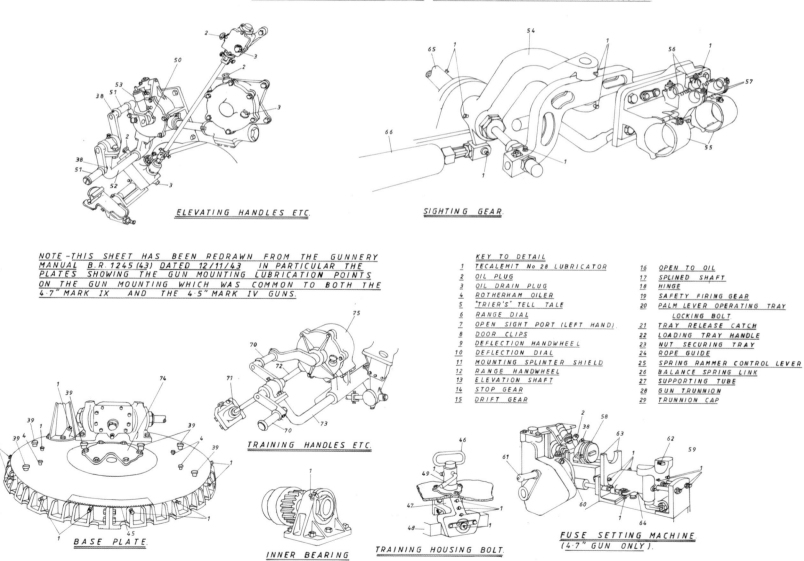

ELEVATING HANDLES ETC.

SIGHTING GEAR.

NOTE - THIS SHEET HAS BEEN REDRAWN FROM THE GUNNERY MANUAL B.R.1245 (43) DATED 12/11/43 IN PARTICULAR THE PLATES SHOWING THE GUN MOUNTING LUBRICATION POINTS ON THE GUN MOUNTING WHICH WAS COMMON TO BOTH THE 4.7" MARK IX AND THE 4.5" MARK IV GUNS.

KEY TO DETAIL

1 TECALEMIT No 28 LUBRICATOR	16 OPEN TO OIL
2 OIL PLUG	17 SPLINED SHAFT
3 OIL DRAIN PLUG	18 HINGE
4 ROTHERHAM OILER	19 SAFETY FIRING GEAR
5 "TRIER'S" TELL TALE	20 PALM LEVER OPERATING TRAY
6 RANGE DIAL	LOCKING BOLT
7 OPEN SIGHT PORT (LEFT HAND).	21 TRAY RELEASE CATCH
8 DOOR CLIPS	22 LOADING TRAY HANDLE
9 DEFLECTION HANDWHEEL	23 NUT SECURING TRAY
10 DEFLECTION DIAL	24 ROPE GUIDE
11 MOUNTING SPLINTER SHIELD	25 SPRING RAMMER CONTROL LEVER
12 RANGE HANDWHEEL	26 BALANCE SPRING LINK
13 ELEVATION SHAFT	27 SUPPORTING TUBE
14 STOP GEAR	28 GUN TRUNNION
15 DRIFT GEAR	29 TRUNNION CAP

TRAINING HANDLES ETC.

BASE PLATE.

INNER BEARING ELEVATING PINION.

TRAINING HOUSING BOLT.

FUSE SETTING MACHINE (4.7" GUN ONLY).

THE 4.7 INCH MARK XXII MOUNTING WAS DESIGNED TO MEET, SO FAR AS POSSIBLE, THE DEMAND FOR INCREASED ELEVATION IN DESTROYER MAIN ARMAMENT GUNS WITHOUT AN UNACCEPTABLE INCREASE OF WEIGHT OVER THE FORMER STANDARD FLEET DESTROYER MOUNTING THE 4.7 INCH C.P. XVIII (SEE DRG L/O/65/A-C) IT MOUNTS THE SAME 4.7 INCH MARK IX** GUN BUT THE ELEVATION HAS BEEN INCREASED TO 55° IN THE MARK XXII COMPARED WITH 40° IN THE EARLIER MARK XVIII MOUNTING. AT THE SAME TIME OTHER IMPROVEMENTS HAD BEEN INCORPORATED PRINCIPALLY WITH THE OBJECT OF IMPROVING THE RATE OF FIRE AND THE ABILITY OF THE MOUNTING TO STAND UP TO DESTROYER CONDITIONS. THE MAJOR ALTERATION WAS THE INTRODUCTION OF A SPRING-OPERATED RAMMER, DESIGNED TO OVERCOME THE DIFFICULTY OF HAND-RAMMING AT HIGHER ELEVATIONS.

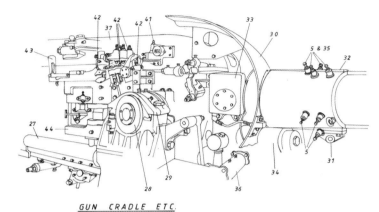

GUN CRADLE ETC.

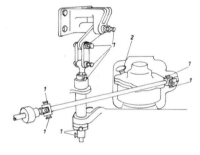

PART OF SAFETY FIRING GEAR AND TILT DRIVE TO THE ELEVATION RECEIVER.

43 BREECH MECHANISM LEVER
44 BREECH RING
45 TRAINING RACK
46 HOUSING HANDLE TO SECURE THE GUN MOUNTING.
47 SUPPORTING BRACKET
48 HOUSING STOP
49 CLAMP
50 FRICTION COVER PLATE
51 ELEVATING HANDLE
52 BRACKET SUPPORTING THE ELEVATING HANDLES.
53 FILLING PLUG
54 SIGHT TRUNNION BRACKET
55 CLAMP FOR TRAINERS MONOCULAR TELESCOPE.
56 CLAMP FOR TRAINERS ALDIS TELESCOPE
57 CLAMP FOR TRAINERS EYE SHOOTING SIGHT ALSO USED AS A BARRAGE SIGHT.
58 SLIDING HEAD
59 FUZE SETTING TRAY
60 INNER AND OUTER CRANK.
61 FUZE SETTING HANDLE
62 SHELL GRIPS
63 HORNS
64 SLIDING BRACKET
65 ELEVATION CROSS CONNECTING TUBE
66 SIGHT BALANCING SPRING CASE
67 SIGHT PINION
68 DIRECTOR ARC
69 SIGHT GEAR BOX
70 TRAINING HANDLES
71 TRAINING PINION
72 WORM SHAFT
73 BRACKET SUPPORTING TRAINING HANDLES
74 CABLE GLAND PLATE COVER
75 WORM GEAR BOX.

30 MANTLET PLATE
31 SLIP GEAR BRACKET
32 GUN KEY
33 RECOIL MAKE UP TANK
34 RECOIL CYLINDER
35 TELL TALE GREASE LUBRICATOR
36 SIGHT CROSS CONNECTION SHAFT
37 SUPPORTING BEAM
38 SPRINGWELL OIL CUP
39 LUBRICATORS ON BASE
40 OIL HOLES
41 TUCKERS OILER No.14
42 TUCKERS OILER No.19

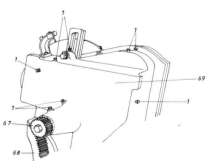

SIGHTING GEAR. [LEFT HAND INSIDE].
© JOHN LAMBERT PART DRAWN 13/8/1999

PARTICULARS OF GUN AND MOUNTING — WEIGHTS

	TONS	CWT	QRS.	LBS
GUN WITH MECHANISM UNLOADED	2	19	2	10
SIGHTING GEAR		4	3	0
GUN SHIELD AND PLATFORMS ETC	2	7	0	24
BASE AND FITTINGS	1	2	1	2
REMAINDER OF MOUNTING	7	0	1	21
WEIGHT OF MOUNTING	13	14	1	1
RECOILING MASS	3	2	3	18
ELEVATING MASS	7	2	0	0
TRAINING MASS	12	12	0	19
TRAINING MASS WITH MEN AND AMMUNITION	13	0	0	0

FORCES ON FIRING (IN TONS)

MAXIMUM FORCE OF RECOIL	20·5
UPWARD LIFT	13·0
DOWNWARD BLOW	22·5

L/O/05/B

COMPLETED 22/12/2000 CH'D. 21/12/00

G 9 Twin 4.7in QFSA Mk XI guns on Mk XX mounting, 1942

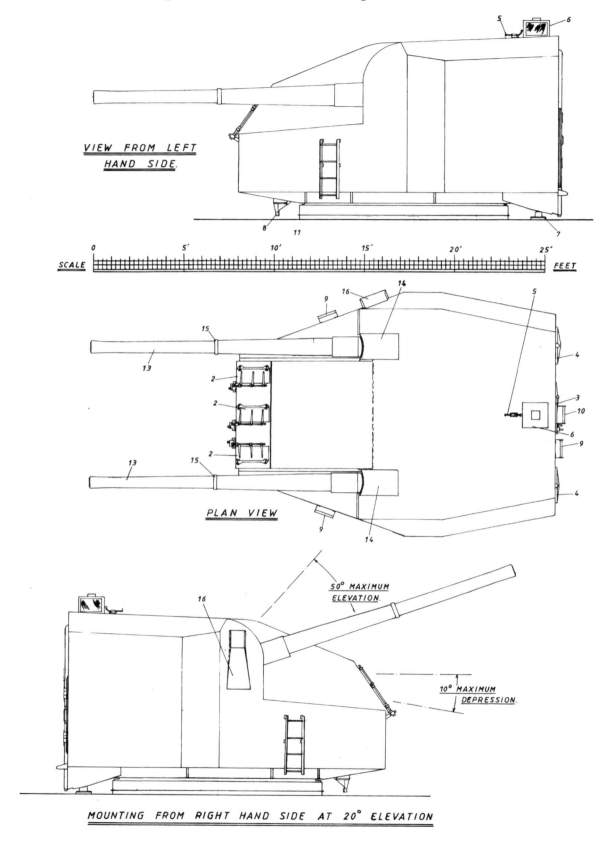

VIEW FROM LEFT HAND SIDE.

SCALE   FEET

PLAN VIEW

50° MAXIMUM ELEVATION.

10° MAXIMUM DEPRESSION.

MOUNTING FROM RIGHT HAND SIDE AT 20° ELEVATION

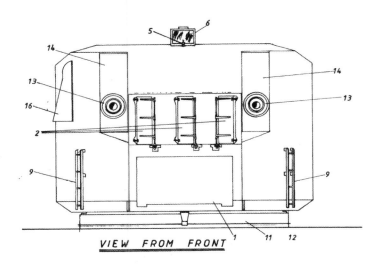

VIEW FROM FRONT

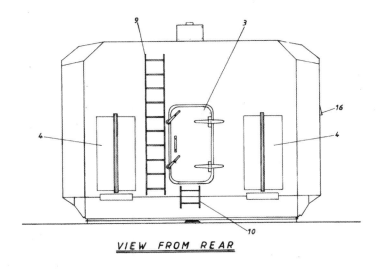

VIEW FROM REAR

ENLARGED PLAN VIEW
OF CLOSED SIGHT
PORTS.

SCALE |0 1' 2' 3'| FEET

KEY TO EXTERNAL DETAIL

1 REMOVABLE ACCESS PANEL.
2 SIGHT PORTS - [CLOSED]
3 ENTRY DOOR TO MOUNTING.
4 DOOR FOR CHUTE FOR
      EJECTED CYLINDERS.
5 SAFETY TRAINERS SIGHT
6 LOOKOUT HOOD.
7 TRAINING HOUSING STOP.
8 TRAINING BUFFER STOP.
9 LADDER
10 STEP
11 PORTABLE PLATES TO
      ROLLER PATH
12 LEATHER APRON.
13 4·7 INCH Q.F. S.A. MARK IX GUN.
14 MANTLET PLATE
15 SEALING COLLAR.
16 7$\frac{1}{2}$" VENTILATION FAN.

ENLARGED SIDE ELEVATION OF TRAINING
BASE ROLLERS. [NO SCALE]

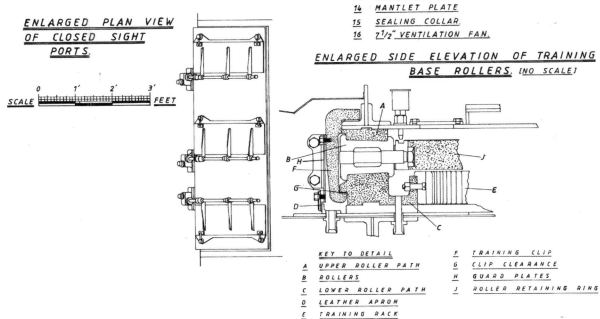

KEY TO DETAIL

A UPPER ROLLER PATH   F TRAINING CLIP
B ROLLERS   G CLIP CLEARANCE
C LOWER ROLLER PATH   H GUARD PLATES
D LEATHER APRON   J ROLLER RETAINING RING
E TRAINING RACK

L/0/87/A

G 9 Twin 4.7in QFSA Mk XI guns on Mk XX mounting, 1942

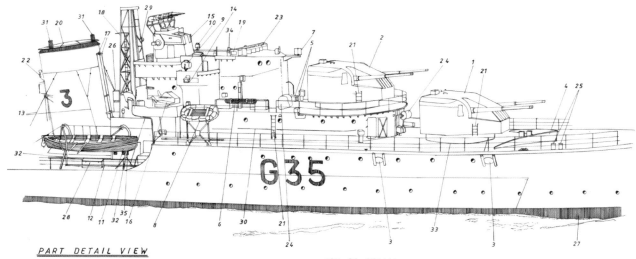

PART DETAIL VIEW
FOR'D. END OF H.M.S. MARNE — DEC. 1945

KEY TO DETAIL:

1	'A' MARK XX MOUNTING.	21	LADDER.
2	'B' MARK XX MOUNTING.	22	STEAM SIREN.
3	ESCAPE HATCH.	23	WIND DEFLECTOR.
4	BREAKWATER.	24	ROPE REEL.
5	VENTILATOR TRUNK.	25	BOLLARDS.
6	CORK LIFEFLOAT.	26	AERIAL TRUNK.
7	M.F.D.F. AERIAL.	27	BOOT TOPPING.
8	CARLEY FLOAT.	28	WASHDECK LOCKER.
9	20" SEARCHLIGHT.	29	LOUDSPEAKER.
10	10" SEARCHLIGHT.	30	HANDRAIL.
11	27' WHALER.	31	GALLEY FUNNEL.
12	BOAT BOOM [STOWED].	32	BOAT DAVIT.
13	FUNNEL GUYS.	33	GUARD RAIL.
14	STARBOARD NAVIGATION LIGHT.	34	COMPASS
15	MARK IV TYPE TP HA/LA. DIRECTOR.		
16	TWIN 20mm MARK V [P.Q] OERLIKON MOUNTING.		
17	BOILER ROOM EXHAUST PIPES FROM THE BOILER		
	'SAFETY VALVES'		
18	LATTICE MAST.	35	BOILER ROOM AIR INTAKE.
19	WINDSCREEN.		
20	FUNNEL SPIDER.		

DESIGN AND DATA —

THE 4.7" MARK XX MOUNTING WAS DESIGNED TO ACCOMMODATE TWO 4.7" Q.F. MARK GUNS WHICH FIRE THE HEAVY (62 LB) SHELL IN A WEATHERPROOF ENCLOSED GUNHOUSE IN WHICH THE AMMUNITION SUPPLY ARRANGEMENTS ARE ALSO CONTAINED. DUE TO THE CENTRAL AMMUNITION HOIST DESIGN, THE AMOUNT OF HANDLING OF AMMUNITION REQUIRED WAS GREATLY REDUCED COMPARED WITH PREVIOUS DESTROYER DESIGNS WHICH ENABLED THE HEAVIER SHELL TO BE MORE EASILY USED. TO PROVIDE MORE EFFECTIVE ANTI-AIRCRAFT FIRE THE MOUNTING HAS A 50° ELEVATION COMPARED WITH THE MORE USUAL 40° AND MECHANICAL FUZE SETTERS WERE PROVIDED. THE LENGTHS OF THE TRUNKS OF THE MOUNTINGS VARIED WITH THE POSITION IN THE SHIP OCCUPIED BY THE MOUNTINGS. THIS NEW MOUNTING WAS THE MAIN GUN ARMAMENT OF THE FOUR FLEET DESTROYERS OF THE 'L' CLASS —[LAFOREY LIGHTNING LOYAL AND LOOKOUT] AND THE EIGHT UNITS OF THE 'M' CLASS. A TOTAL OF 87 GUNS WERE MADE.

THE MARK XX MOUNTING PROVIDED A POWERFUL ANTI-SHIP CAPACITY AND EXCELLENT SUPPORT IN THE 'BOMBARDMENT ROLE [ALTHOUGH MORE BRAWN WAS REQUIRED TO HANDLE THE HEAVY SHELLS]. THE GUNHOUSE SOMEWHAT RESEMBLED THE CONTEMPORARY BATTLESHIP AND DIDO CLASS CRUISERS 5.25" DUEL PURPOSE TWIN TURRET. DESTROYER MEN WERE IMPRESSED BY ITS IMPOSING SIZE, INDIVIDUAL ELEVATION ARRANGEMENTS AND THE CLEVER AMMUNITION SUPPLY SYSTEM BETWEEN THE WIDELY SPACED GUNS. A FIRST CLASS ANTI-SHIP WEAPON IT COULD NOT COPE WITH DIVE BOMBERS ANY MORE THAN THE 40° MOUNTINGS.

BALLISTICS

NOMINAL MUZZLE VELOCITY	2543 FT/SEC
RANGE TABLE MUZZLE VELOCITY FULL CHARGE	{MAX 2575 FT/SEC. MIN 2400 FT/SEC.
RANGE TABLE MUZZLE VELOCITY REDUCED CHARGE	{MAX 1900 FT/SEC MIN 1800 FT/SEC
WEIGHT OF CHARGE	12.81 LBS.
WEIGHT OF CARTRIDGE (CASE AND CHARGE)	32.6 LBS.

DATA — THE GUN

BORE	4.724 INCHES
WEIGHT INCLUDING BREECH MECHANISM	3.351 TONS
LENGTH OVERALL	247.7 INCHES
LENGTH OF BORE	236.2 = 50 CALIBRES
LENGTH OF CHAMBER	28.0 INCHES
LENGTH OF LOOSE BARREL	236.2 INCHES
LENGTH OF JACKET	149.09 INCHES
VOLUME OF CHAMBER	670 CUBIC INCHES
LENGTH OF RIFLING	204.88 INCHES
GROOVES	(38) — 0.0365" DEEP x 0.27"
LANDS	0.1205 INCHES.
TWIST	UNIFORM — 1 IN 30
WEIGHT OF PROJECTILE	62 LBS.
MUZZLE VELOCITY	2538 FT/SEC.
WORKING PRESSURE	20.5 TONS/SQU. INCH
APPROX BARREL LIFE	800 E.F.C. WITH NF/S 3200
MAXIMUM RANGE	21,240 YARDS AT 45° ELEVATION

DATA — THE MOUNTING

DISTANCE APART OF GUN AXES	96 INCHES
RECOIL DISTANCE	26.5 INCHES
FIRING CYCLE	6 SECONDS
SHIELD THICKNESS	0.25 INCHES

WEIGHTS

	TONS	CWTS	QRS	LBS
TWO GUNS AND MECHANISM'S UNLOADED	7	2	0	0
SIGHTING GEAR		12	3	5
GUN SHIELD	6	7	2	18
BASE AND FITTINGS	2	1	3	12
REMAINDER OF MOUNTING	21	8	3	11
WEIGHT OF MOUNTING	37	13	0	19
DECK FITTINGS		8	0	18
HOIST (B MOUNTING)	5	14	1	0
HAND OPERATING GEAR FOR HOIST		10	0	24
HYDRAULIC INSTALLATION COMPLETE WITH OIL COOLER ('B' MOUNTING) ON FIXED STRUCTURE	3	19	1	0
AIR BLAST GEAR ON FIXED STRUCTURE		11	0	7
TOTAL WEIGHT OF EQUIPMENT	48	16	0	12
RECOILING MASS	3	13	2	5
ELEVATING MASS	7	1	0	0
TRAINING MASS	35	11	1	7
TRAINING MASS INCLUDING MEN AND AMMUNITION	37	7	1	0
ROLLER PATH DIAMETER	10 FT. 7 INS.			
BOOK OF REFERENCE	B. 4167 DATED 3/4/42.			
	LATER B.R. 916.			
COOLER				
CAPACITY	1050 GALLONS/HOUR.			

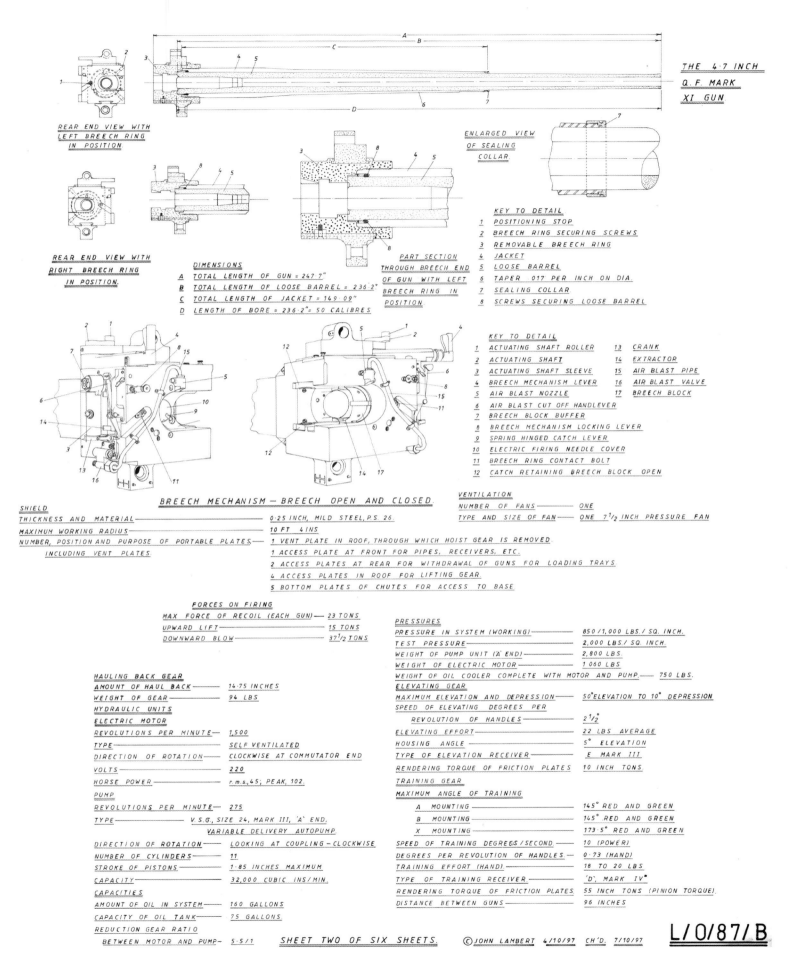

THE 4·7 INCH
Q.F. MARK
XI GUN

**REAR END VIEW WITH
LEFT BREECH RING
IN POSITION.**

**REAR END VIEW WITH
RIGHT BREECH RING
IN POSITION.**

**ENLARGED VIEW
OF SEALING
COLLAR.**

**PART SECTION
THROUGH BREECH END
OF GUN WITH LEFT
BREECH RING IN
POSITION.**

DIMENSIONS
A   TOTAL LENGTH OF GUN = 247·7"
B   TOTAL LENGTH OF LOOSE BARREL = 236·2"
C   TOTAL LENGTH OF JACKET = 149·09"
D   LENGTH OF BORE = 236·2" = 50 CALIBRES

KEY TO DETAIL
1   POSITIONING STOP
2   BREECH RING SECURING SCREWS
3   REMOVABLE BREECH RING
4   JACKET
5   LOOSE BARREL
6   TAPER ·017 PER INCH ON DIA
7   SEALING COLLAR.
8   SCREWS SECURING LOOSE BARREL

KEY TO DETAIL
1   ACTUATING SHAFT ROLLER   13   CRANK
2   ACTUATING SHAFT   14   EXTRACTOR
3   ACTUATING SHAFT SLEEVE   15   AIR BLAST PIPE
4   BREECH MECHANISM LEVER   16   AIR BLAST VALVE
5   AIR BLAST NOZZLE   17   BREECH BLOCK
6   AIR BLAST CUT OFF HANDLEVER
7   BREECH BLOCK BUFFER
8   BREECH MECHANISM LOCKING LEVER
9   SPRING HINGED CATCH LEVER
10 ELECTRIC FIRING NEEDLE COVER
11 BREECH RING CONTACT BOLT
12 CATCH RETAINING BREECH BLOCK OPEN

BREECH MECHANISM — BREECH OPEN AND CLOSED.

SHIELD
THICKNESS AND MATERIAL————————————————— 0·25 INCH, MILD STEEL, P.S. 26.
MAXIMUM WORKING RADIUS————————————————— 10 FT 4 INS
NUMBER, POSITION AND PURPOSE OF PORTABLE PLATES,— 1 VENT PLATE IN ROOF, THROUGH WHICH HOIST GEAR IS REMOVED.
        INCLUDING VENT PLATES.   1 ACCESS PLATE AT FRONT FOR PIPES, RECEIVERS, ETC.
                                                  2 ACCESS PLATES AT REAR FOR WITHDRAWAL OF GUNS FOR LOADING TRAYS
                                                  4 ACCESS PLATES IN ROOF FOR LIFTING GEAR.
                                                  5 BOTTOM PLATES OF CHUTES FOR ACCESS TO BASE

VENTILATION
NUMBER OF FANS———————— ONE
TYPE AND SIZE OF FAN———— ONE 7½ INCH PRESSURE FAN

FORCES ON FIRING
MAX FORCE OF RECOIL (EACH GUN)—— 23 TONS
UPWARD LIFT————————————————— 15 TONS
DOWNWARD BLOW———————————————— 37½ TONS

PRESSURES
PRESSURE IN SYSTEM (WORKING)———————— 850/1,000 LBS./SQ. INCH.
TEST PRESSURE————————————————————— 2,000 LBS./SQ. INCH.
WEIGHT OF PUMP UNIT ('A' END)————————— 2,800 LBS.
WEIGHT OF ELECTRIC MOTOR——————————— 1,060 LBS
WEIGHT OF OIL COOLER COMPLETE WITH MOTOR AND PUMP.—— 750 LBS.

ELEVATING GEAR
MAXIMUM ELEVATION AND DEPRESSION———— 50° ELEVATION TO 10° DEPRESSION
SPEED OF ELEVATING DEGREES PER
        REVOLUTION OF HANDLES———————— 2½°
ELEVATING EFFORT—————————————————— 22 LBS AVERAGE
HOUSING ANGLE————————————————————— 5° ELEVATION
TYPE OF ELEVATION RECEIVER————————— E MARK III
RENDERING TORQUE OF FRICTION PLATES 10 INCH TONS.

HAULING BACK GEAR
AMOUNT OF HAUL BACK——————— 14·75 INCHES
WEIGHT OF GEAR——————————— 94 LBS
HYDRAULIC UNITS
ELECTRIC MOTOR
REVOLUTIONS PER MINUTE——— 1,500
TYPE——————————————————— SELF VENTILATED
DIRECTION OF ROTATION—— CLOCKWISE AT COMMUTATOR END
VOLTS————————————————— 220
HORSE POWER—————————— r.m.s., 45; PEAK, 102.
PUMP
REVOLUTIONS PER MINUTE— 275
TYPE—————————————— V.S.G, SIZE 24, MARK III, 'A' END,
                      VARIABLE DELIVERY AUTOPUMP.
DIRECTION OF ROTATION———— LOOKING AT COUPLING — CLOCKWISE
NUMBER OF CYLINDERS———————— 11
STROKE OF PISTONS—————————— 1·85 INCHES MAXIMUM
CAPACITY————————————————— 32,000 CUBIC INS/MIN.
CAPACITIES
AMOUNT OF OIL IN SYSTEM——— 160 GALLONS
CAPACITY OF OIL TANK————— 75 GALLONS
REDUCTION GEAR RATIO
    BETWEEN MOTOR AND PUMP— 5·5/1

TRAINING GEAR
MAXIMUM ANGLE OF TRAINING
    A MOUNTING————————————— 145° RED AND GREEN
    B MOUNTING————————————— 145° RED AND GREEN
    X MOUNTING————————————— 173·5° RED AND GREEN
SPEED OF TRAINING DEGREES/SECOND.—— 10 (POWER)
DEGREES PER REVOLUTION OF HANDLES — 0·73 (HAND)
TRAINING EFFORT (HAND)————————— 18 TO 20 LBS
TYPE OF TRAINING RECEIVER————— 'D', MARK IV.
RENDERING TORQUE OF FRICTION PLATES 55 INCH TONS (PINION TORQUE).
DISTANCE BETWEEN GUNS————————— 96 INCHES

SHEET TWO OF SIX SHEETS.   ©JOHN LAMBERT 4/10/97   CH'D. 7/10/97

L/0/87/B

111

G 10 Twin QF 4.5in Mk I or III guns on HA Mk II BD mountings, 1938
[Note that this drawing is unfinished]

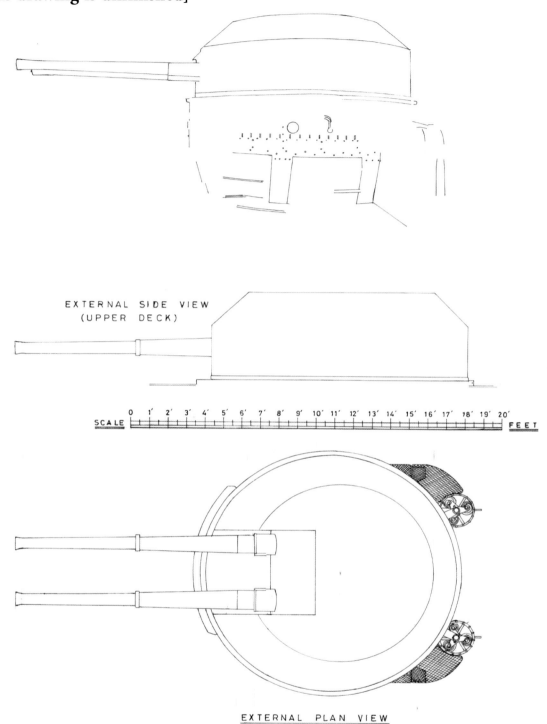

EXTERNAL SIDE VIEW
(UPPER DECK)

SCALE | 0 1' 2' 3' 4' 5' 6' 7' 8' 9' 10' 11' 12' 13' 14' 15' 16' 17' 18' 19' 20' | FEET

EXTERNAL PLAN VIEW

© JOHN LAMBERT COMMENCED 13/11/2012

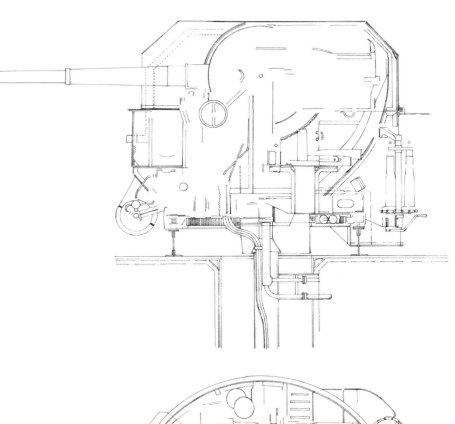

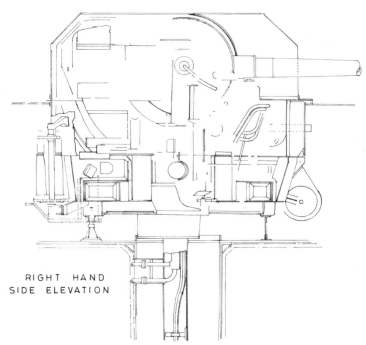

RIGHT HAND
SIDE ELEVATION

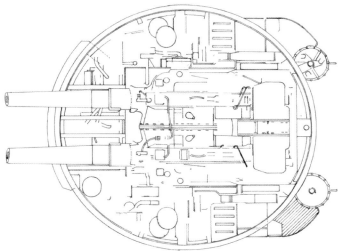

PLAN VIEW WITH THE ROOF REMOVED

DATA 4·5″ Q.F. MARK I III AND V GUN.	
BORE	4·45″
WEIGHT INCLUDING BREECH MECH.	2·814 TONS
LENGTH OVERALL	211·75″
LENGTH OF BORE	200·25″
LENGTH OF CHAMBER	25·06/25·15″
VOLUME OF CHAMBER	600 CUBIC″
LENGH OF RIFLING	170·92″
GROOVES	32 0·037″ DEEP x 0·291″
LANDS	0·1459″
TWISTS	UNIFORM 1 IN 25
WEIGHT OF PROJECTILE	55 LBS.
PROPELLANT CHARGE	
MUZZLE VELOCITY	2449 FT/SEC
WORKING PRESSURE	20·5 TONS/□″
APPROXIMATE LIFE	750 E.F.C.
MAXIMUM RANGE	20,750 YARDS AT 45
CEILING	41,000 AT 80°

MARK II H/A B.D. MOUNTING	
WEIGHT	37·95 TONS
ROLLER PATH DIAMETER	9′ 5″
DISTANCE APART OF GUN AXES	38″
RECOIL	18″
MAX. SPEED OF ELEVATION	10°/SEC
MAX. SPEED OF TRAINING	15°/SEC
FIRING CYCLE	5 SECONDS
TURRET SHIELD	0·5″
RATE OF FIRE	12 ROUNDS/MIN
MAXIMUM ELEVATION	70°
BOOK OF REFERENCE	B.R. 917/40 (H'Bk.)
BOOK OF REFERENCE	B.R. 948 (DRILL)

SHEET ONE OF TWO SHEETS

L/0/184/A

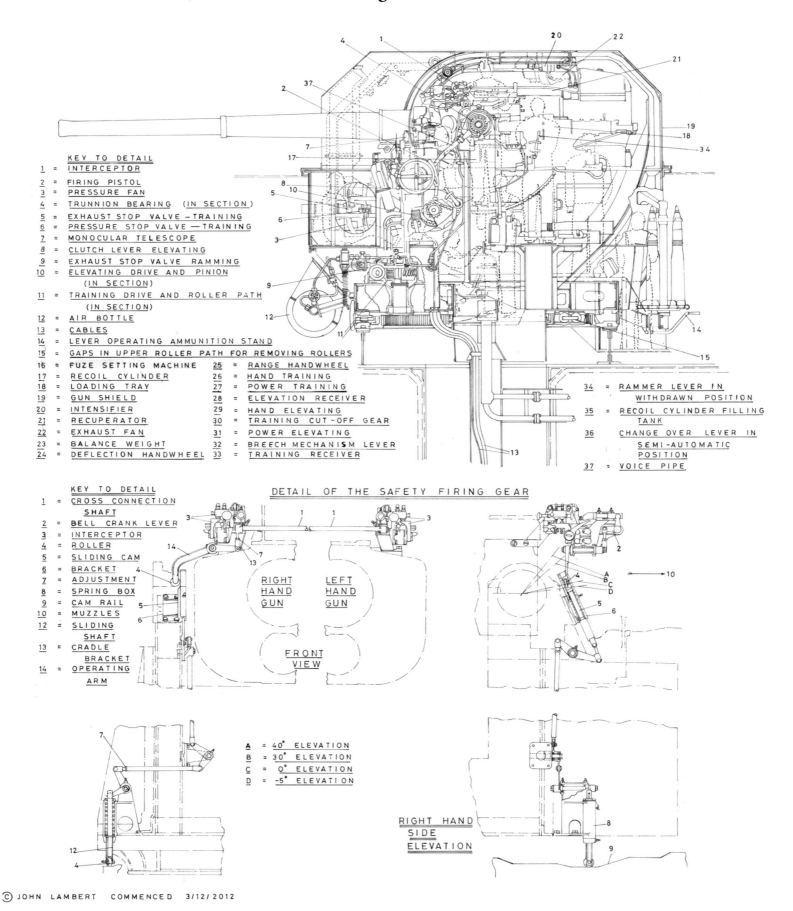

G 10 The Mk II BD (Between Deck) mounting, detail

KEY TO DETAIL

 1 = INTERCEPTOR
 2 = FIRING PISTOL
 3 = PRESSURE FAN
 4 = TRUNNION BEARING (IN SECTION)
 5 = EXHAUST STOP VALVE – TRAINING
 6 = PRESSURE STOP VALVE – TRAINING
 7 = MONOCULAR TELESCOPE
 8 = CLUTCH LEVER ELEVATING
 9 = EXHAUST STOP VALVE RAMMING
10 = ELEVATING DRIVE AND PINION
     (IN SECTION)
11 = TRAINING DRIVE AND ROLLER PATH
     (IN SECTION)
12 = AIR BOTTLE
13 = CABLES
14 = LEVER OPERATING AMMUNITION STAND
15 = GAPS IN UPPER ROLLER PATH FOR REMOVING ROLLERS
16 = FUZE SETTING MACHINE
17 = RECOIL CYLINDER
18 = LOADING TRAY
19 = GUN SHIELD
20 = INTENSIFIER
21 = RECUPERATOR
22 = EXHAUST FAN
23 = BALANCE WEIGHT
24 = DEFLECTION HANDWHEEL

25 = RANGE HANDWHEEL
26 = HAND TRAINING
27 = POWER TRAINING
28 = ELEVATION RECEIVER
29 = HAND ELEVATING
30 = TRAINING CUT-OFF GEAR
31 = POWER ELEVATING
32 = BREECH MECHANISM LEVER
33 = TRAINING RECEIVER

34 = RAMMER LEVER IN
     WITHDRAWN POSITION
35 = RECOIL CYLINDER FILLING
     TANK
36 = CHANGE OVER LEVER IN
     SEMI-AUTOMATIC
     POSITION
37 = VOICE PIPE

KEY TO DETAIL

 1 = CROSS CONNECTION
     SHAFT
 2 = BELL CRANK LEVER
 3 = INTERCEPTOR
 4 = ROLLER
 5 = SLIDING CAM
 6 = BRACKET
 7 = ADJUSTMENT
 8 = SPRING BOX
 9 = CAM RAIL
10 = MUZZLES
12 = SLIDING
     SHAFT
13 = CRADLE
     BRACKET
14 = OPERATING
     ARM

DETAIL OF THE SAFETY FIRING GEAR

RIGHT
HAND
GUN

LEFT
HAND
GUN

FRONT
VIEW

A = 40° ELEVATION
B = 30° ELEVATION
C = 0° ELEVATION
D = -5° ELEVATION

RIGHT HAND
SIDE
ELEVATION

© JOHN LAMBERT COMMENCED 3/12/2012

114

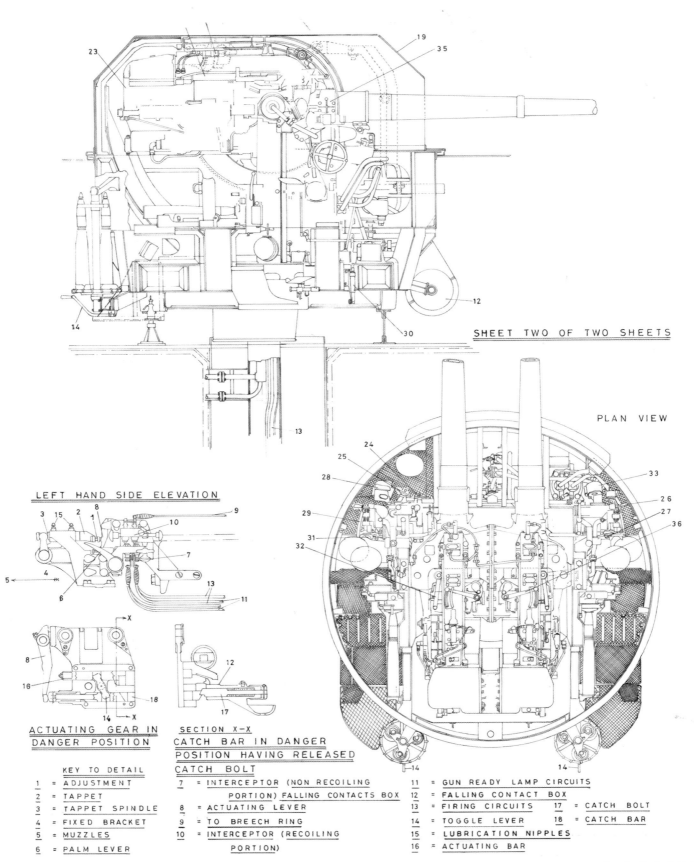

SHEET TWO OF TWO SHEETS

PLAN VIEW

LEFT HAND SIDE ELEVATION

ACTUATING GEAR IN
DANGER POSITION

SECTION X-X
CATCH BAR IN DANGER
POSITION HAVING RELEASED
CATCH BOLT

KEY TO DETAIL

1	= ADJUSTMENT	7	= INTERCEPTOR (NON RECOILING	11	= GUN READY LAMP CIRCUITS	
2	= TAPPET		PORTION) FALLING CONTACTS BOX	12	= FALLING CONTACT BOX	
3	= TAPPET SPINDLE	8	= ACTUATING LEVER	13	= FIRING CIRCUITS	17 = CATCH BOLT
4	= FIXED BRACKET	9	= TO BREECH RING	14	= TOGGLE LEVER	18 = CATCH BAR
5	= MUZZLES	10	= INTERCEPTOR (RECOILING	15	= LUBRICATION NIPPLES	
6	= PALM LEVER		PORTION)	16	= ACTUATING BAR	

L/0/184/B

115

G 11 4.5in Mk IV gun on Mk V Mod 2 mounting, 1945

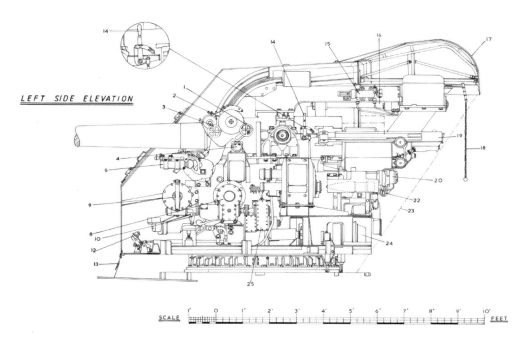

LEFT SIDE ELEVATION

SCALE | 1' 0 1' 2' 3' 4' 5' 6' 7' 8' 9' 10' FEET

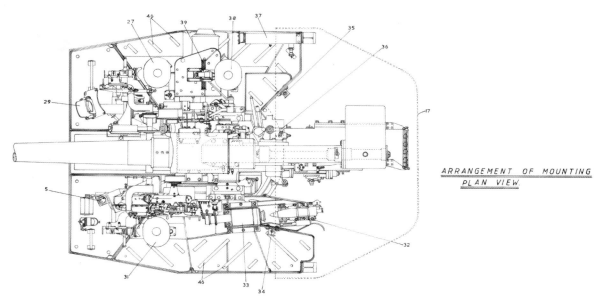

ARRANGEMENT OF MOUNTING
PLAN VIEW.

MOUNTING DETAILS

1	RANGE HANDWHEEL.
2	SIGHT GEARBOX.
3	DEFLECTION HANDWHEEL.
4	GUN POSITION INDICATOR [ELEVATING].
5	GUN POSITION INDICATOR [TRAINING].
6	MONOCULAR & ALDIS TELESCOPES [LAYERS].
7	MONOCULAR & ALDIS TELESCOPES [TRAINERS].
8	ELEVATING ARC & WORM GEARBOX.
9	SPIRAL GEARBOX & ELEVATING HANDLES.
10	HAND POWER CHANGE OVER LEVER [ELEVATING].
11	HAND POWER CHANGE OVER LEVER [TRAINING].
12	PEDAL FIRING GEAR.
13	NYLON SKIRTING.
14	LOADING LEVER.
15	INTENSIFIER.
16	RECUPERATOR.
17	CANOPY.
18	CATCH NET.
19	LOADING TRAY & RAMMER.
20	LOADING TRAY SUPPORT TUBE.
21	LOADING TRAY.
22	TRAY SWINGING GEAR.
23	NYLON COVER.
24	ELEVATING MOTOR.
25	ELEVATING GEARBOX.
26	ELEVATING CONTROLLER.
27	TRAINERS SEAT.
28	TRAINING CONTROLLER.
29	TRAINING RECEIVER.
30	TRAINING MOTOR.

31	LAYERS SEAT.
32	FUZE SETTING TRAY.
33	FUZE SETTING MACHINE.
34	SAFETY FIRING SWITCH [LH] ROCKET FLARE LAUNCHER
35	SAFETY FIRING SWITCH [RH] ROCKET FLARE LAUNCHER
36	S.A. GEAR [LEVER IN Q.F. POSITION].
37	TANK FOR WINDOW WASHING.
38	SEAT FOR JOYSTICK OPERATOR.
39	JOYSTICK.
40	SAFETY SWITCH.
41	RUN OUT CONTACTS.
42	S.A. CAM GEAR.
43	SAFETY FIRING GEAR.
44	BREECH MECHANISM LEVER.
45	BALANCE WEIGHT.
46	FOOT STRIPS.
47	TRAINING STOP.
48	HOUSING BOLT.
49	TRAINING BUFFER.
50	CLIP RING & TRAINING BASE.
51	SPIRAL GEARBOX & TRAINING HANDLES.
52	BARRAGE SIGHT HOOD.
53	SIGHT.
54	WINDOW WIPING GEAR.
55	RECOIL BUFFER REPLENISHING TANK.
56	MANTLET PLATE.
57	RECOIL BUFFER.
58	SIGHT PORT DOORS.
59	BALANCE SPRING FOR SIGHT.
60	LIMIT SWITCH ELEVATION & DEPRESSION.

HISTORY

THE C.P. MARK XXII 4 7 INCH MOUNTING WAS MODIFIED TO CARRY THE 4.5 INCH MARK IV GUN. THE NECESSARY ALTERATIONS WERE MADE TO THE CRADLE AND LOADING TRAY TO ACCOMMODATE NEW BARREL AND AMMUNITION THE NEW MOUNTING BEING THE MARK V.

BOTH THE 4.7" & 4.5" MOUNTINGS WERE LATER EQUIPPED WITH R.P.C. (REMOTE POWER CONTROL). THE 4.5 INCH MTG. SAW SERVICE IN H.M.S. SAVAGE. 'Z' & 'C' (CA, CH & CO) EMERGENCY DESTROYERS THE MOUNTING WAS ALSO FITTED AMIDSHIPS IN LATER UNITS OF THE BATTLE CLASS.

WITH THE INTRODUCTION OF THE TRIBAL CLASS FRIGATES BUILT BETWEEN 1961-1964, TWO OF THESE MOUNTINGS WERE FITTED TO EACH OF THE SEVEN UNITS.

4.5 INCH MARK V* MOD 2 MOUNTING WITH R.P.50 CONTROL

A HAND LOADED MOUNTING AND IS BASICALLY A 4.5" R.P.50 MK.V* MOD 1 MTG. FOR D.C. SHIPS WHICH HAS BEEN MADE SUITABLE FOR CONTROL BY M.R.S 3 IN A.C. SHIPS. REMOTE CONTROL FOR BOTH VERSIONS WAS BY THE R.P. 50 SYSTEM. ALTERNATIVE LOCAL CONTROL THROUGH THE METADYNE SET BY JOYSTICK BEING PROVIDED. HAND ELEVATING AND TRAINING GEAR WAS FITTED FOR USE IN THE EVENT OF POWER FAILURE AND FOR THE PURPOSE OF ASSISTING WITH MAINTENANCE, THE METADYNE EQUIPMENT WAS LOCATED OFF THE MOUNTING.

AMMUNITION WAS LOADED BY HAND ONTO THE GUN LOADING TRAY. RECOIL ENERGY WAS UTILISED TO SWING THE TRAY TO AND FROM THE BREECH AND FOR RAMMING HOME THE ROUND. RAMMING WAS INITIATED AUTOMATICALLY IMMEDIATELY THE TRAY ARRIVED IN LINE WITH THE GUN.

A BARRAGE SIGHT HOOD FOR THE JOYSTICK OPERATOR WAS PROVIDED IN THE ROOF OF THE GUNSHIELD. THE SPLINTER SHIELD BEING SUPPORTED FROM THE PLATFORMS AND CARRIAGE SIDES, AND WAS EXTENDED TO THE REAR BY A CANOPY FROM WHICH NYLON CURTAIN TYPE COVERS WERE SUSPENDED TO ENCLOSE THE REAR OF THE MOUNTING.

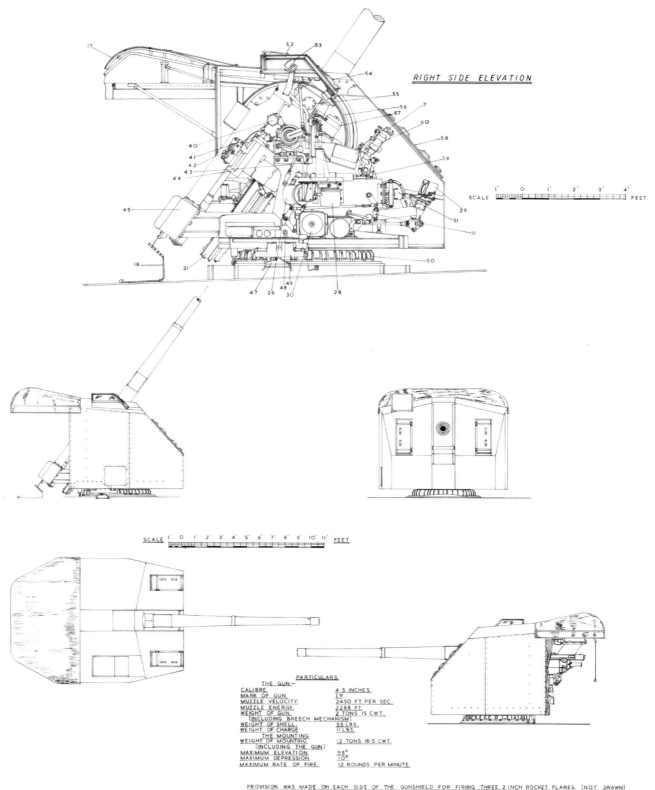

RIGHT SIDE ELEVATION

SCALE 1' 0 1' 2' 3' 4' FEET

SCALE 1' 0 1' 2' 3' 4' 5' 6' 7' 8' 9' 10' 11' FEET

PARTICULARS

THE GUN:-
CALIBRE.	4·5 INCHES.
MARK OF GUN.	IV.
MUZZLE VELOCITY.	2450 FT. PER SEC.
MUZZLE ENERGY.	2288 FT.
WEIGHT OF GUN.	2 TONS 15 CWT.
[INCLUDING BREECH MECHANISM]	
WEIGHT OF SHELL.	55 LBS.
WEIGHT OF CHARGE.	11 LBS.

THE MOUNTING:
WEIGHT OF MOUNTING.	12 TONS 18·5 CWT.
[INCLUDING THE GUN]	
MAXIMUM ELEVATION.	55°
MAXIMUM DEPRESSION.	10°
MAXIMUM RATE OF FIRE.	12 ROUNDS PER MINUTE.

PROVISION WAS MADE ON EACH SIDE OF THE GUNSHIELD FOR FIRING THREE 2 INCH ROCKET FLARES. [NOT DRAWN]
SAFETY FIRING GEAR PREVENTED ROCKET DISCHARGE ON DANGEROUS BEARINGS.

REDRAWN FROM DETAILS SUPPLIED BY VICKERS ARMAMENT DIVISION BARROW IN FURNESS.

SHEET ONE OF TWO SHEETS   © JOHN LAMBERT   COMPLETED 2/12/1978   UPDATED 4/2/2001   CH'D. 6/2/2001   L/0/14/A

G 11 4.5in Mk V mounting, detail

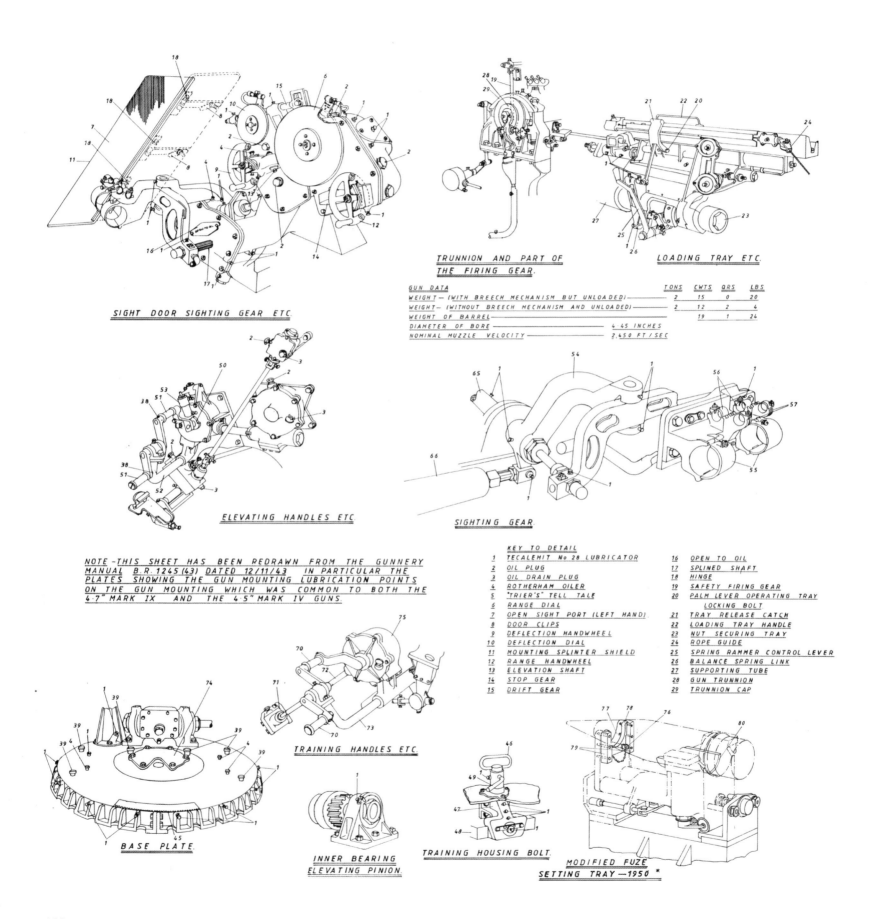

SIGHT DOOR SIGHTING GEAR ETC.

TRUNNION AND PART OF THE FIRING GEAR.

LOADING TRAY ETC.

GUN DATA	TONS	CWTS	QRS	LBS
WEIGHT — (WITH BREECH MECHANISM BUT UNLOADED)	2	15	0	20
WEIGHT — (WITHOUT BREECH MECHANISM AND UNLOADED)	2	12	2	4
WEIGHT OF BARREL		19	1	24
DIAMETER OF BORE		4·45 INCHES		
NOMINAL MUZZLE VELOCITY		2,450 FT / SEC		

ELEVATING HANDLES ETC.

SIGHTING GEAR.

NOTE—THIS SHEET HAS BEEN REDRAWN FROM THE GUNNERY MANUAL B.R.1245(43) DATED 12/11/43 IN PARTICULAR THE PLATES SHOWING THE GUN MOUNTING LUBRICATION POINTS ON THE GUN MOUNTING WHICH WAS COMMON TO BOTH THE 4.7" MARK IX AND THE 4.5" MARK IV GUNS.

KEY TO DETAIL

1	TECALEMIT No 28 LUBRICATOR	16	OPEN TO OIL
2	OIL PLUG	17	SPLINED SHAFT
3	OIL DRAIN PLUG	18	HINGE
4	ROTHERHAM OILER	19	SAFETY FIRING GEAR
5	"TRIER'S" TELL TALE	20	PALM LEVER OPERATING TRAY
6	RANGE DIAL		LOCKING BOLT
7	OPEN SIGHT PORT (LEFT HAND)	21	TRAY RELEASE CATCH
8	DOOR CLIPS	22	LOADING TRAY HANDLE
9	DEFLECTION HANDWHEEL	23	NUT SECURING TRAY
10	DEFLECTION DIAL	24	ROPE GUIDE
11	MOUNTING SPLINTER SHIELD	25	SPRING RAMMER CONTROL LEVER
12	RANGE HANDWHEEL	26	BALANCE SPRING LINK
13	ELEVATION SHAFT	27	SUPPORTING TUBE
14	STOP GEAR	28	GUN TRUNNION
15	DRIFT GEAR	29	TRUNNION CAP

TRAINING HANDLES ETC.

BASE PLATE.

INNER BEARING ELEVATING PINION.

TRAINING HOUSING BOLT.

MODIFIED FUZE SETTING TRAY —1950 *

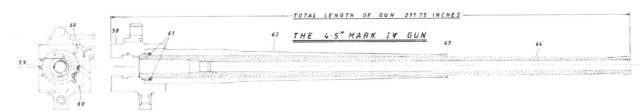

TOTAL LENGTH OF GUN 211.75 INCHES

THE 4.5" MARK IV GUN

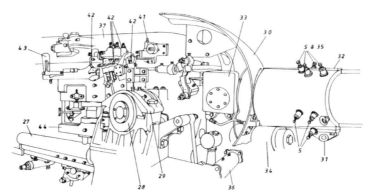

GUN CRADLE ETC.

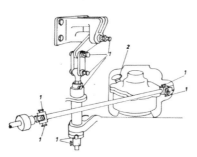

PART OF SAFETY FIRING GEAR
AND TILT DRIVE TO THE
ELEVATION RECEIVER.

30	MANTLET PLATE
31	SLIP GEAR BRACKET
32	GUN KEY
33	RECOIL MAKE UP TANK
34	RECOIL CYLINDER
35	TELL TALE GREASE LUBRICATOR
36	SIGHT CROSS CONNECTION SHAFT
37	SUPPORTING BEAM
38	SPRINGWELL OIL CUP
39	LUBRICATORS ON BASE
40	OIL HOLES
41	TUCKERS OILER No 14
42	TUCKERS OILER No 19

43	BREECH MECHANISM LEVER
44	BREECH RING
45	TRAINING RACK
46	HOUSING HANDLE TO SECURE THE GUN MOUNTING.
47	SUPPORTING BRACKET
48	HOUSING STOP
49	CLAMP
50	FRICTION COVER PLATE
51	ELEVATING HANDLE
52	BRACKET SUPPORTING THE ELEVATING HANDLES.
53	FILLING PLUG
54	SIGHT TRUNNION BRACKET
55	CLAMP FOR TRAINERS MONOCULAR TELESCOPE.
56	CLAMP FOR TRAINERS ALDIS TELESCOPE
57	CLAMP FOR TRAINERS EYE SHOOTING SIGHT ALSO USED AS A BARRAGE SIGHT.
58	REMOVABLE BREECH RING
59	SCREW STOP BREECH RING
60	SCREWS SECURING BREECH RING
61	SCREWS SECURING LOOSE BARREL
62	JACKET
63	SEALING COLLAR
64	LOOSE BARREL (AUTOFRETTAGED)
65	ELEVATION CROSS CONNECTING TUBE
66	SIGHT BALANCING SPRING CASE
67	SIGHT PINION
68	DIRECTOR ARC
69	SIGHT GEAR BOX
70	TRAINING HANDLES
71	TRAINING PINION
72	WORM SHAFT
73	BRACKET SUPPORTING TRAINING HANDLES
74	CABLE GLAND PLATE COVER
75	WORM GEAR BOX

* DETAIL OF THE MODIFIED FUZE SETTING TRAY
TO ACCOMMODATE STAR SHELL, SHORT RANGE
MARK IB AS FITTED TO THE SINGLE MARK V
MOUNTING CARRIED BY THE SECOND GROUP (1943)
BATTLE CLASS DESTROYERS IN THE LATE 1940's

76	DROP NOSE SECURING PIN
77	FORWARD SUPPORT OPENED OUT TO ACCOMMODATE STAR SHELL.
78	LOOSE HORN PLATE TO ACCOMMODATE H.E (HIGH EXPLOSIVE) SHELL.
79	RIGHT AND LEFT GUIDES SECURED TO THE FORWARD SUPPORT
80	PLATE TRAY CUT BACK TO CLEAR THE DRIVING BAND OF THE SHELL

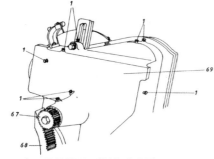

SIGHTING GEAR, (LEFT
HAND INSIDE).

REDRAWN FROM INFORMATION CONTAINED IN THE GUNNERY MANUAL
B.R.1245 (43) DATED 12/11/1943. PART OF THE PRIDDY'S HARD
COLLECTION HELD AT THE HAMPSHIRE ARCHIVE TRUST HAMPSHIRE
RECORD OFFICE SUSSEX STREET WINCHESTER SO23 8TH

SHEET TWO OF TWO SHEETS   © JOHN LAMBERT PART DRAWN 13/8/1999 COMPLETED 4/2/2001 CH'D. 6/2/2001

L/0/14/B

G 12 Twin 4.5in Mk 3(N) QFSA guns on Mk 4 and Mk 4* mounting, 1945. For the 1942 and 1943 'Battle' class destroyers

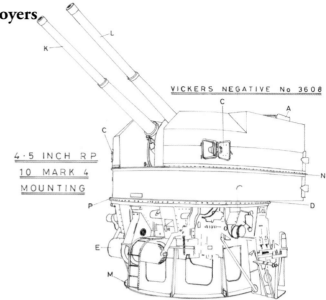

VICKERS NEGATIVE No 3608

4·5 INCH RP
10 MARK 4
MOUNTING

INTRODUCTION

THE 4·5 INCH TWIN MARKS 4 AND 4* MOUNTINGS WERE DEVELOPED FROM
THE 4·5 INCH MARK 2 MOUNTING AS AN EMERGENCY WARTIME MEASURE TO
PROVIDE A TURRET MOUNTING WITH A REVOLVING TRUNK FOR FITTING IN
FLEET DESTROYERS. AS A RESULT CERTAIN COMPROMISES HAD TO BE
ACCEPTED IN THE DESIGN OF THE AMMUNITION SUPPLY WHICH LIMITED
THE SUSTAINED MAXIMUM OUTPUT OF THE TURRET TO 12 rpm PER GUN,
THIS RATE OF FIRE COULD BE MAINTAINED AT ALL ELEVATIONS.
THE MARK 4 MOUNTING WAS FITTED IN THE 1942 BATTLE CLASS DEST-
ROYERS IN CONJUNCTION WITH THE MARK 6 DIRECTOR AND THE ASSOC-
IATED A.F.C.C.MARK 1, WHICH HAS A MAXIMUM RANGE OF 18,000 YARDS
(10·22 MILES). THE MARK 4* MOUNTING WAS FITTED TO THE 1943 BATTLE CLASS
IN CONJUNCTION WITH THE MARK 37 DIRECTOR SYSTEM WHICH HAD A MAX.
SURFACE RANGE OF 17,000 YARDS (9·65 MILES), BUT WITH AN ADDITIONAL
2 200 YARDS FOR ELEVATION SPOTTING. THE MAXIMUM RANGE OF THE MARK
3 GUN IS 21,000 YARDS (11·93 MILES)
THE MOUNTING COULD BE ELEVATED AN TRAINED IN FOUR DIFFERENT WAYS:-

A AUTO -IN WHICH THE MOUNTING AUTOMATICALLY FOLLOWS ELEVATING AND TRAINING TRANSMISSIONS THIS IS THE
       NORMAL STATE.
B POWER - IN WHICH THE MOUNTING IS MOVED BY THE LAYER AND TRAINER OPERATING THEIR
       HANDWHEELS AND FOLLOWING POINTERS. THIS WOULD BE USED IF AUTO FAILED.
C JOYSTICK -IN WHICH THE JOYSTICK OPERATOR MOVES THE MOUNTING IN ELEVATION AND
       TRAINING. THIS WAS USED IN LOCAL CONTROL AGAINST AERIAL TARGETS.
D HAND OPERATION.
EACH GUN WAS PROVIDED WITH A SHELL AND CORDITE HOIST OF THE PUSHER TYPE TO PASS
       THE AMMUNITION INTO THE GUNHOUSE FROM THE DECK BELOW. ON ACCOUNT OF ITS
       UNWIELDY NATURE FIXED AMMUNITION WAS ABANDONED FOR THESE MOUNTINGS AND SEPARATE
       AMMUNITION SUBSTITUTED.
TWO FIXED HOISTS OF THE ENDLESS CHAIN TYPE WERE FITTED IN EACH GUN BAY TO PROVIDE
BOTH SHELL AND CORDITE FROM THE SHELLROOM AND MAGAZINE.

DRAWINGS ARE REDRAWN FROM B.R. (BOOK OF REFERENCE) 1635 (51)
GUN DATA
NOMINAL MUZZLE VELOCITY ——————————— 2429 FT/SEC
WEIGHT OF 2 GUNS & MECHANISMS MARK 3 N UNLOADED — 5 TON 12 CWT 2Q 8LB
MAXIMUM FORCE ON RECOIL (TWO GUNS)——————— 60 TONS
UPWARD LIFT ———————————————— 31 TONS
DOWNWARD BLOW ————————————————— 57 TONS

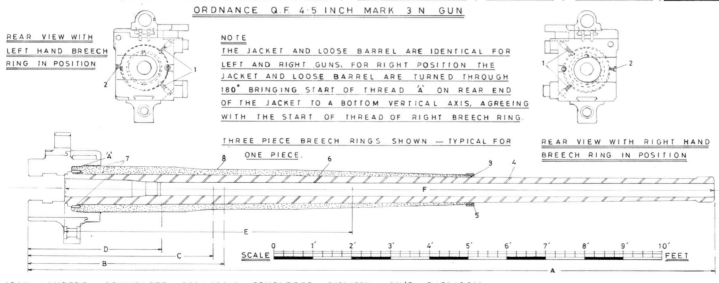

ORDNANCE Q.F. 4·5 INCH MARK 3 N GUN

REAR VIEW WITH
LEFT HAND BREECH
RING IN POSITION

NOTE
THE JACKET AND LOOSE BARREL ARE IDENTICAL FOR
LEFT AND RIGHT GUNS, FOR RIGHT POSITION THE
JACKET AND LOOSE BARREL ARE TURNED THROUGH
180° BRINGING START OF THREAD 'A' ON REAR END
OF THE JACKET TO A BOTTOM VERTICAL AXIS, AGREEING
WITH THE START OF THREAD OF RIGHT BREECH RING.

THREE PIECE BREECH RINGS SHOWN — TYPICAL FOR
ONE PIECE.

REAR VIEW WITH RIGHT HAND
BREECH RING IN POSITION

SCALE 0 1' 2' 3' 4' 5' 6' 7' 8' 9' 10' FEET

© JOHN LAMBERT COMMENCED 30/11/2010 COMPLETED 3/01/2011 CH'D 7/01/2011

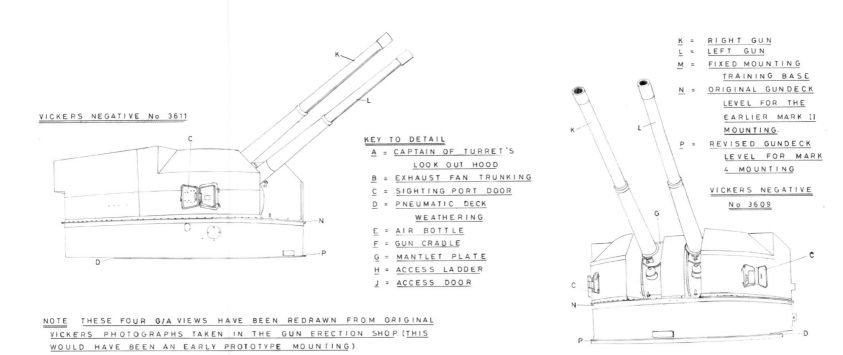

VICKERS NEGATIVE No 3611

K = RIGHT GUN
L = LEFT GUN
M = FIXED MOUNTING
      TRAINING BASE
N = ORIGINAL GUNDECK
      LEVEL FOR THE
      EARLIER MARK II
      MOUNTING.
P = REVISED GUNDECK
      LEVEL FOR MARK
      4 MOUNTING

VICKERS NEGATIVE
No 3609

KEY TO DETAIL
A = CAPTAIN OF TURRET'S
      LOOK OUT HOOD
B = EXHAUST FAN TRUNKING
C = SIGHTING PORT DOOR
D = PNEUMATIC DECK
      WEATHERING
E = AIR BOTTLE
F = GUN CRADLE
G = MANTLET PLATE
H = ACCESS LADDER
J = ACCESS DOOR

NOTE   THESE FOUR G/A VIEWS HAVE BEEN REDRAWN FROM ORIGINAL
VICKERS PHOTOGRAPHS TAKEN IN THE GUN ERECTION SHOP. (THIS
WOULD HAVE BEEN AN EARLY PROTOTYPE MOUNTING).
SEE   DOCK MUSEUM, NORTH ROAD, BARROW-IN-FURNESS, CUMBRIA
      LA14 2PW   TEL 01229 894444 E-MAIL dockmuseum @ barrowbc.gov.uk

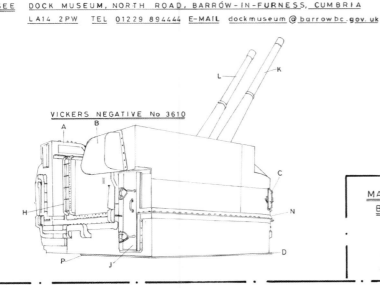

VICKERS NEGATIVE No 3610

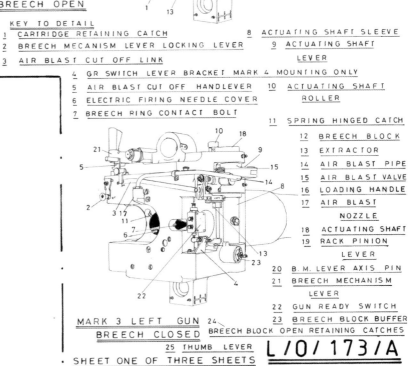

MARK 3 RIGHT GUN
BREECH OPEN

KEY TO DETAIL
1   CARTRIDGE RETAINING CATCH
2   BREECH MECANISM LEVER LOCKING LEVER
3   AIR BLAST CUT OFF LINK
4   GR SWITCH LEVER BRACKET MARK 4 MOUNTING ONLY
5   AIR BLAST CUT OFF HANDLEVER
6   ELECTRIC FIRING NEEDLE COVER
7   BREECH RING CONTACT BOLT

8   ACTUATING SHAFT SLEEVE
9   ACTUATING SHAFT
      LEVER
10 ACTUATING SHAFT
      ROLLER

11 SPRING HINGED CATCH
12 BREECH BLOCK
13 EXTRACTOR
14 AIR BLAST PIPE
15 AIR BLAST VALVE
16 LOADING HANDLE
17 AIR BLAST
      NOZZLE
18 ACTUATING SHAFT
19 RACK PINION
      LEVER
20 B.M. LEVER AXIS PIN
21 BREECH MECHANISM
      LEVER
22 GUN READY SWITCH
23 BREECH BLOCK BUFFER
24 BREECH BLOCK OPEN RETAINING CATCHES
25 THUMB LEVER

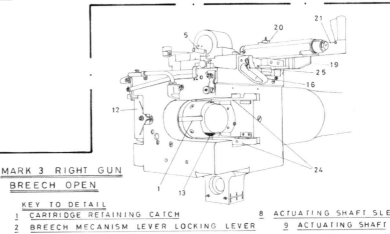

KEY TO DIMENSIONS
A = TOTAL LENGTH OF GUN = 211·75"
B = C OF G (WITHOUT BREECH MECHANISM AND UNLOADED)
      BARE GUN = 60·55"
C = C OF G (WITH BREECH MECHANISM AND LOADED) = 57·13"
D = TO 1" FROM COMMENCENT OF RIFLING = 41·83"
E = C OF G OF BARREL ONLY = 87·63"
F = LENGTH OF BORE = 200·25" = 45 CALIBRES
      KEY TO DETAIL
      1 = SCREWS SECURING BREECH RING
      2 = SCREW STOP BREECH RING
      3 = ASBESTOS PACKING
      4 = LOOSE BARREL (AUTOFRETTAGED)
      5 = SEALING COLLAR
      6 = TAPER ·01 PER INCH ON DIAMETER
      7 = SCREWS SECURING LOOSE BARREL
      8 = JACKET

WEIGHT (WITH BM BUT UNLOADED)
      2 TONS 16 CWT 1 QRS 4 LBS
WEIGHT (WITHOUT BM & UNLOADED) BARE GUN
      2 TONS 12 CWT 3 QRS 1 LB

MARK 3 LEFT GUN
BREECH CLOSED

SHEET ONE OF THREE SHEETS

L/O/173/A

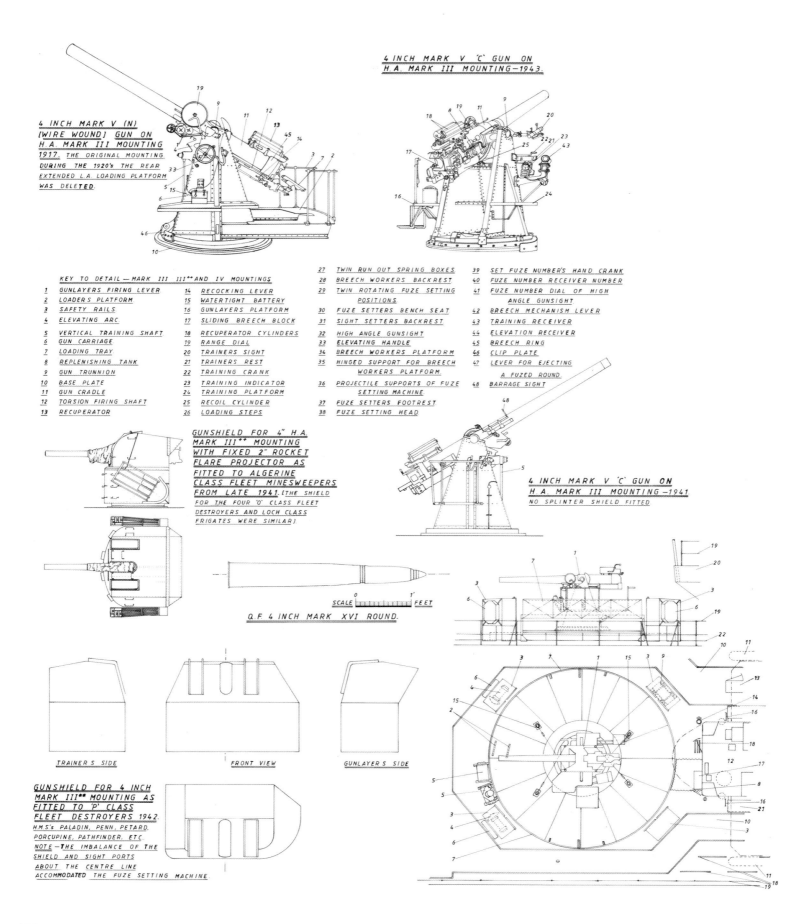

4 INCH MARK V 'C' GUN ON
H.A. MARK III MOUNTING—1943.

4 INCH MARK V (N)
[WIRE WOUND] GUN ON
H.A. MARK III MOUNTING
1917. THE ORIGINAL MOUNTING.
DURING THE 1920's THE REAR
EXTENDED L.A. LOADING PLATFORM
WAS DELETED.

KEY TO DETAIL — MARK III III AND IV MOUNTINGS**

1	GUNLAYERS FIRING LEVER	14	RECOCKING LEVER	27	TWIN RUN OUT SPRING BOXES.
2	LOADERS PLATFORM	15	WATERTIGHT BATTERY	28	BREECH WORKERS BACKREST
3	SAFETY RAILS.	16	GUNLAYERS PLATFORM	29	TWIN ROTATING FUZE SETTING
4	ELEVATING ARC	17	SLIDING BREECH BLOCK		POSITIONS
5	VERTICAL TRAINING SHAFT	18	RECUPERATOR CYLINDERS	30	FUZE SETTERS BENCH SEAT
6	GUN CARRIAGE	19	RANGE DIAL	31	SIGHT SETTERS BACKREST
7	LOADING TRAY	20	TRAINERS SIGHT	32	HIGH ANGLE GUNSIGHT
8	REPLENISHING TANK	21	TRAINERS REST	33	ELEVATING HANDLE
9	GUN TRUNNION	22	TRAINING CRANK	34	BREECH WORKERS PLATFORM
10	BASE PLATE	23	TRAINING INDICATOR	35	HINGED SUPPORT FOR BREECH
11	GUN CRADLE	24	TRAINING PLATFORM		WORKERS PLATFORM.
12	TORSION FIRING SHAFT	25	RECOIL CYLINDER	36	PROJECTILE SUPPORTS OF FUZE
13	RECUPERATOR	26	LOADING STEPS		SETTING MACHINE.
				37	FUZE SETTERS FOOTREST
				38	FUZE SETTING HEAD

39	SET FUZE NUMBER'S HAND CRANK
40	FUZE NUMBER RECEIVER NUMBER
41	FUZE NUMBER DIAL OF HIGH
	ANGLE GUNSIGHT
42	BREECH MECHANISM LEVER
43	TRAINING RECEIVER
44	ELEVATION RECEIVER
45	BREECH RING
46	CLIP PLATE
47	LEVER FOR EJECTING
	A FUZED ROUND.
48	BARRAGE SIGHT

GUNSHIELD FOR 4" H.A.
MARK III** MOUNTING
WITH FIXED 2" ROCKET
FLARE PROJECTOR AS
FITTED TO ALGERINE
CLASS FLEET MINESWEEPERS
FROM LATE 1941. [THE SHIELD
FOR THE FOUR 'O' CLASS FLEET
DESTROYERS AND LOCH CLASS
FRIGATES WERE SIMILAR].

4 INCH MARK V 'C' GUN ON
H.A. MARK III MOUNTING—1941.
NO SPLINTER SHIELD FITTED.

SCALE |||||||||| FEET
0   1'

Q.F. 4 INCH MARK XVI ROUND.

TRAINER'S SIDE   FRONT VIEW   GUNLAYER'S SIDE

GUNSHIELD FOR 4 INCH
MARK III** MOUNTING AS
FITTED TO 'P' CLASS
FLEET DESTROYERS 1942.
H.M.S's PALADIN, PENN, PETARD,
PORCUPINE, PATHFINDER, ETC.
NOTE—THE IMBALANCE OF THE
SHIELD AND SIGHT PORTS
ABOUT THE CENTRE LINE
ACCOMMODATED THE FUZE SETTING MACHINE.

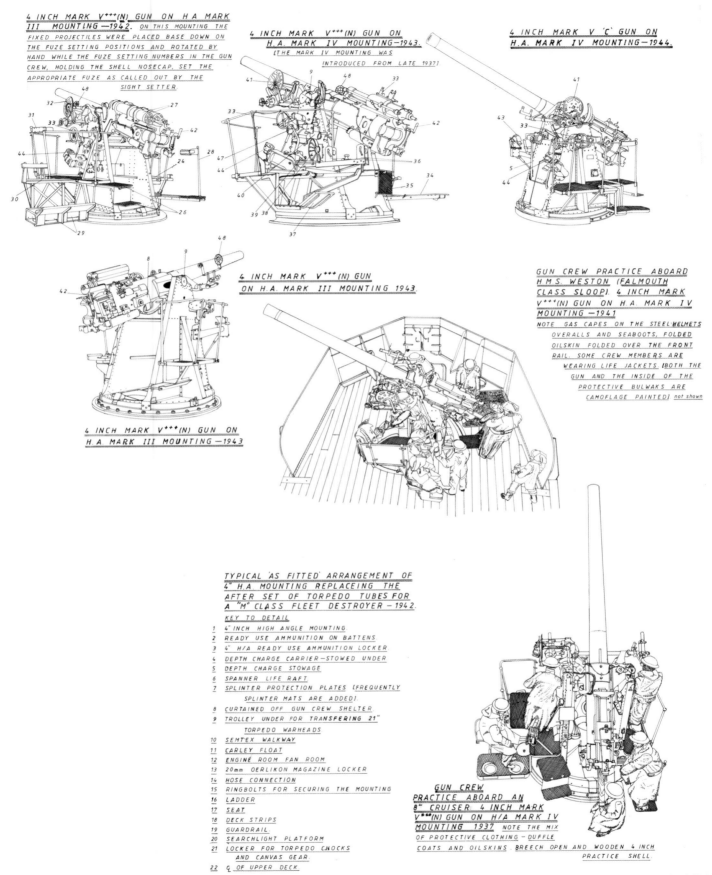

4 INCH MARK V+++(N) GUN ON H.A MARK III MOUNTING —1942. ON THIS MOUNTING THE FIXED PROJECTILES WERE PLACED BASE DOWN ON THE FUZE SETTING POSITIONS AND ROTATED BY HAND WHILE THE FUZE SETTING NUMBERS IN THE GUN CREW, HOLDING THE SHELL NOSECAP, SET THE APPROPRIATE FUZE AS CALLED OUT BY THE SIGHT SETTER.

4 INCH MARK V+++(N) GUN ON H.A. MARK IV MOUNTING —1943. [THE MARK IV MOUNTING WAS INTRODUCED FROM LATE 1937]

4 INCH MARK V 'C' GUN ON H.A. MARK IV MOUNTING —1944.

4 INCH MARK V+++(N) GUN ON H.A. MARK III MOUNTING 1943.

4 INCH MARK V+++(N) GUN ON H.A. MARK III MOUNTING —1943

GUN CREW PRACTICE ABOARD H.M.S. WESTON (FALMOUTH CLASS SLOOP). 4 INCH MARK V+++(N) GUN ON H.A. MARK IV MOUNTING —1941
NOTE GAS CAPES ON THE STEEL HELMETS OVERALLS AND SEABOOTS, FOLDED OILSKIN FOLDED OVER THE FRONT RAIL. SOME CREW MEMBERS ARE WEARING LIFE JACKETS [BOTH THE GUN AND THE INSIDE OF THE PROTECTIVE BULWAKS ARE CAMOFLAGE PAINTED] not shown

TYPICAL 'AS FITTED' ARRANGEMENT OF 4" H.A. MOUNTING REPLACEING THE AFTER SET OF TORPEDO TUBES FOR A "M" CLASS FLEET DESTROYER —1942.

KEY TO DETAIL

1 4" INCH HIGH ANGLE MOUNTING.
2 READY USE AMMUNITION ON BATTENS.
3 4" H/A READY USE AMMUNITION LOCKER.
4 DEPTH CHARGE CARRIER—STOWED UNDER
5 DEPTH CHARGE STOWAGE
6 SPANNER LIFE RAFT.
7 SPLINTER PROTECTION PLATES [FREQUENTLY SPLINTER MATS ARE ADDED].
8 CURTAINED OFF GUN CREW SHELTER
9 TROLLEY UNDER FOR TRANSFERING 21" TORPEDO WARHEADS
10 SEMTEX WALKWAY
11 CARLEY FLOAT
12 ENGINE ROOM FAN ROOM
13 20mm OERLIKON MAGAZINE LOCKER
14 HOSE CONNECTION
15 RINGBOLTS FOR SECURING THE MOUNTING
16 LADDER
17 SEAT
18 DECK STRIPS
19 GUARDRAIL
20 SEARCHLIGHT PLATFORM
21 LOCKER FOR TORPEDO CHOCKS AND CANVAS GEAR.
22 ℄ OF UPPER DECK

GUN CREW PRACTICE ABOARD AN 8" CRUISER. 4 INCH MARK V+++(N) GUN ON H/A MARK IV MOUNTING 1937 NOTE THE MIX OF PROTECTIVE CLOTHING—DUFFLE COATS AND OILSKINS. BREECH OPEN AND WOODEN 4 INCH PRACTICE SHELL.

Ⓒ JOHN LAMBERT COMPLETED 27/5/1997 CH'D. 23/10/1997

L/0/86/A

G 13 High Angle Mk III mountings, fittings detail 1943–1945

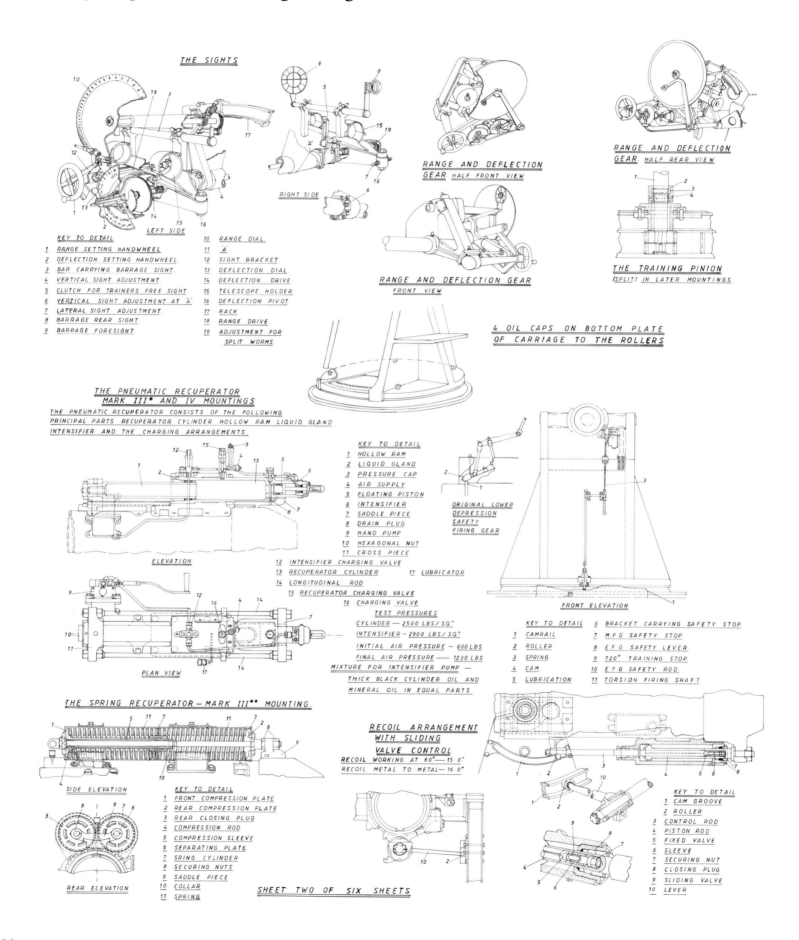

THE SIGHTS

RANGE AND DEFLECTION GEAR. HALF FRONT VIEW

RANGE AND DEFLECTION GEAR. HALF REAR VIEW

RIGHT SIDE

LEFT SIDE

KEY TO DETAIL
1 RANGE SETTING HANDWHEEL
2 DEFLECTION SETTING HANDWHEEL
3 BAR CARRYING BARRAGE SIGHT
4 VERTICAL SIGHT ADJUSTMENT
5 CLUTCH FOR TRAINERS FREE SIGHT
6 VERTICAL SIGHT ADJUSTMENT AT 'A'
7 LATERAL SIGHT ADJUSTMENT
8 BARRAGE REAR SIGHT
9 BARRAGE FORESIGHT
10 RANGE DIAL
11 'A'
12 SIGHT BRACKET
13 DEFLECTION DIAL
14 DEFLECTION DRIVE
15 TELESCOPE HOLDER
16 DEFLECTION PIVOT
17 RACK
18 RANGE DRIVE
19 ADJUSTMENT FOR SPLIT WORMS

RANGE AND DEFLECTION GEAR
FRONT VIEW

THE TRAINING PINION
(SPLIT) IN LATER MOUNTINGS

4 OIL CAPS ON BOTTOM PLATE OF CARRIAGE TO THE ROLLERS

THE PNEUMATIC RECUPERATOR MARK III* AND IV MOUNTINGS

THE PNEUMATIC RECUPERATOR CONSISTS OF THE FOLLOWING PRINCIPAL PARTS RECUPERATOR CYLINDER HOLLOW RAM LIQUID GLAND INTENSIFIER AND THE CHARGING ARRANGEMENTS

KEY TO DETAIL
1 HOLLOW RAM
2 LIQUID GLAND
3 PRESSURE CAP
4 AIR SUPPLY
5 FLOATING PISTON
6 INTENSIFIER
7 SADDLE PIECE
8 DRAIN PLUG
9 HAND PUMP
10 HEXAGONAL NUT
11 CROSS PIECE
12 INTENSIFIER CHARGING VALVE
13 RECUPERATOR CYLINDER
14 LONGITUDINAL ROD
15 RECUPERATOR CHARGING VALVE
16 CHARGING VALVE
17 LUBRICATOR

ELEVATION

PLAN VIEW

ORIGINAL LOWER DEPRESSION SAFETY FIRING GEAR

TEST PRESSURES
CYLINDER — 2500 LBS/SQ"
INTENSIFIER — 2900 LBS/SQ"
INITIAL AIR PRESSURE — 600 LBS
FINAL AIR PRESSURE — 1230 LBS
MIXTURE FOR INTENSIFIER PUMP —
THICK BLACK CYLINDER OIL AND
MINERAL OIL IN EQUAL PARTS

FRONT ELEVATION

KEY TO DETAIL
1 CAMRAIL
2 ROLLER
3 SPRING
4 CAM
5 LUBRICATION
6 BRACKET CARRYING SAFETY STOP
7 M.F.G SAFETY STOP
8 E.F.G SAFETY LEVER
9 720° TRAINING STOP
10 E.F.G SAFETY ROD
11 TORSION FIRING SHAFT

THE SPRING RECUPERATOR – MARK III** MOUNTING.

SIDE ELEVATION

REAR ELEVATION

KEY TO DETAIL
1 FRONT COMPRESSION PLATE
2 REAR COMPRESSION PLATE
3 REAR CLOSING PLUG
4 COMPRESSION ROD
5 COMPRESSION SLEEVE
6 SEPARATING PLATE
7 SRING CYLINDER
8 SECURING NUTS
9 SADDLE PIECE
10 COLLAR
11 SPRING

RECOIL ARRANGEMENT WITH SLIDING VALVE CONTROL

RECOIL WORKING AT 80° — 15 0"
RECOIL METAL TO METAL — 16 0"

KEY TO DETAIL
1 CAM GROOVE
2 ROLLER
3 CONTROL ROD
4 PISTON ROD
5 FIXED VALVE
6 SLEEVE
7 SECURING NUT
8 CLOSING PLUG
9 SLIDING VALVE
10 LEVER

SHEET TWO OF SIX SHEETS

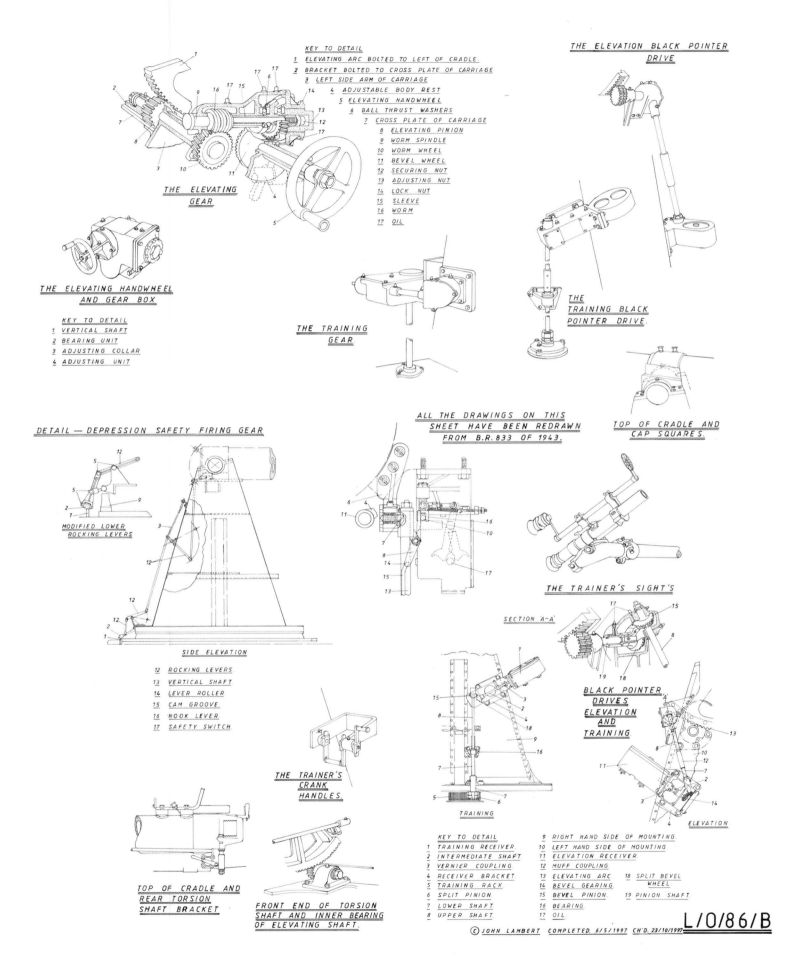

KEY TO DETAIL

1 ELEVATING ARC BOLTED TO LEFT OF CRADLE.
2 BRACKET BOLTED TO CROSS PLATE OF CARRIAGE
3 LEFT SIDE ARM OF CARRIAGE
4 ADJUSTABLE BODY REST
5 ELEVATING HANDWHEEL
6 BALL THRUST WASHERS
7 CROSS PLATE OF CARRIAGE
8 ELEVATING PINION
9 WORM SPINDLE
10 WORM WHEEL
11 BEVEL WHEEL
12 SECURING NUT
13 ADJUSTING NUT
14 LOCK NUT
15 SLEEVE
16 WORM
17 OIL

THE ELEVATING GEAR

THE ELEVATION BLACK POINTER DRIVE

THE ELEVATING HANDWHEEL AND GEAR BOX

KEY TO DETAIL
1 VERTICAL SHAFT
2 BEARING UNIT
3 ADJUSTING COLLAR
4 ADJUSTING UNIT

THE TRAINING GEAR.

THE TRAINING BLACK POINTER DRIVE.

DETAIL — DEPRESSION SAFETY FIRING GEAR

MODIFIED LOWER ROCKING LEVERS

SIDE ELEVATION

12 ROCKING LEVERS
13 VERTICAL SHAFT
14 LEVER ROLLER
15 CAM GROOVE.
16 HOOK LEVER
17 SAFETY SWITCH.

ALL THE DRAWINGS ON THIS SHEET HAVE BEEN REDRAWN FROM B.R.833 OF 1943.

TOP OF CRADLE AND CAP SQUARES.

THE TRAINER'S SIGHT'S

SECTION 'A-A'

BLACK POINTER DRIVES ELEVATION AND TRAINING.

THE TRAINER'S CRANK HANDLES.

TOP OF CRADLE AND REAR TORSION SHAFT BRACKET

FRONT END OF TORSION SHAFT AND INNER BEARING OF ELEVATING SHAFT.

TRAINING

ELEVATION

KEY TO DETAIL
1 TRAINING RECEIVER
2 INTERMEDIATE SHAFT
3 VERNIER COUPLING
4 RECEIVER BRACKET
5 TRAINING RACK
6 SPLIT PINION
7 LOWER SHAFT
8 UPPER SHAFT
9 RIGHT HAND SIDE OF MOUNTING
10 LEFT HAND SIDE OF MOUNTING
11 ELEVATION RECEIVER
12 MUFF COUPLING
13 ELEVATING ARC
14 BEVEL GEARING
15 BEVEL PINION.
16 BEARING
17 OIL
18 SPLIT BEVEL WHEEL
19 PINION SHAFT

© JOHN LAMBERT COMPLETED. 6/5/1997 CH'D. 23/10/1997

L/0/86/B

G 13 The 4in High Angle Mk III mounting of 1917 and Mk V*(N), V***(N) and V (C) guns of 1943

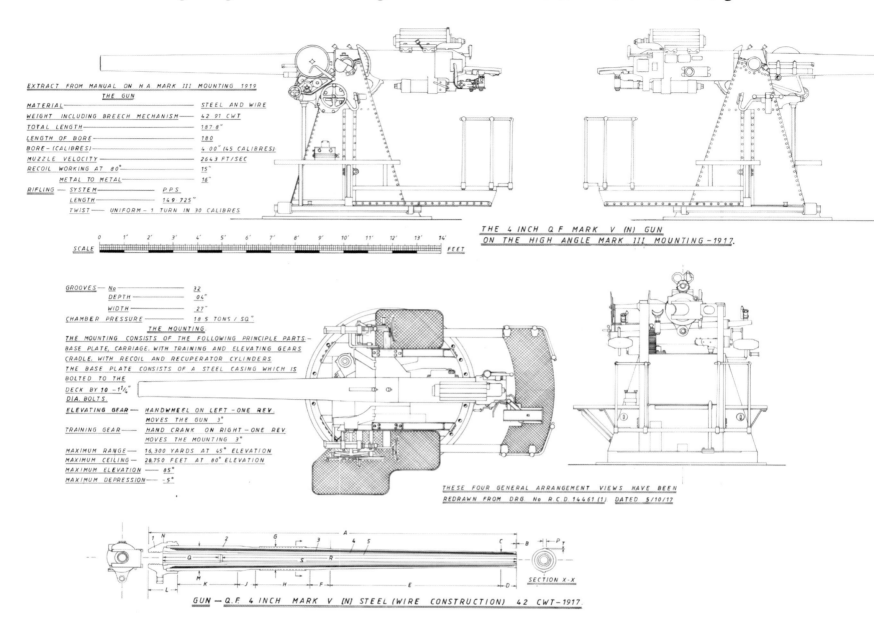

EXTRACT FROM MANUAL ON H.A MARK III MOUNTING 1919
THE GUN

MATERIAL	STEEL AND WIRE
WEIGHT INCLUDING BREECH MECHANISM	42.91 CWT
TOTAL LENGTH	187.8"
LENGTH OF BORE	180
BORE - (CALIBRES)	4.00" (45 CALIBRES)
MUZZLE VELOCITY	2643 FT/SEC
RECOIL WORKING AT 80°	15"
METAL TO METAL	16"
RIFLING - SYSTEM	P.P.S
LENGTH	149.725"
TWIST - UNIFORM - 1 TURN IN 30 CALIBRES	

SCALE — 0 1' 2' 3' 4' 5' 6' 7' 8' 9' 10' 11' 12' 13' 14' — FEET

THE 4 INCH Q.F MARK V (N) GUN
ON THE HIGH ANGLE MARK III MOUNTING - 1917.

GROOVES — No	32
DEPTH	.04"
WIDTH	.27"
CHAMBER PRESSURE	18.5 TONS / SQ"

THE MOUNTING

THE MOUNTING CONSISTS OF THE FOLLOWING PRINCIPLE PARTS-
BASE PLATE, CARRIAGE, WITH TRAINING AND ELEVATING GEARS
CRADLE, WITH RECOIL AND RECUPERATOR CYLINDERS
THE BASE PLATE CONSISTS OF A STEEL CASING WHICH IS
BOLTED TO THE
DECK BY 10 - 1¼"
DIA. BOLTS.

ELEVATING GEAR —	HANDWHEEL ON LEFT - ONE REV. MOVES THE GUN 3°
TRAINING GEAR —	HAND CRANK ON RIGHT - ONE REV. MOVES THE MOUNTING 3°
MAXIMUM RANGE —	16,300 YARDS AT 45° ELEVATION
MAXIMUM CEILING —	28,750 FEET AT 80° ELEVATION
MAXIMUM ELEVATION —	85°
MAXIMUM DEPRESSION —	-5°

THESE FOUR GENERAL ARRANGEMENT VIEWS HAVE BEEN
REDRAWN FROM DRG. No R.C.D. 14461 (1) DATED 5/10/17

SECTION X-X

GUN — Q.F. 4 INCH MARK V (N) STEEL (WIRE CONSTRUCTION) 42 CWT - 1917.

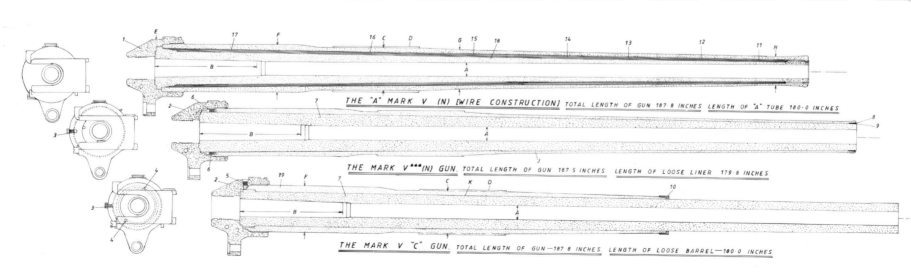

THE "A" MARK V (N) [WIRE CONSTRUCTION] TOTAL LENGTH OF GUN 187.8 INCHES LENGTH OF "A" TUBE 180.0 INCHES

THE MARK V***(N) GUN. TOTAL LENGTH OF GUN 187.5 INCHES. LENGTH OF LOOSE LINER 179.8 INCHES

THE MARK V "C" GUN. TOTAL LENGTH OF GUN — 187.8 INCHES. LENGTH OF LOOSE BARREL — 180.0 INCHES

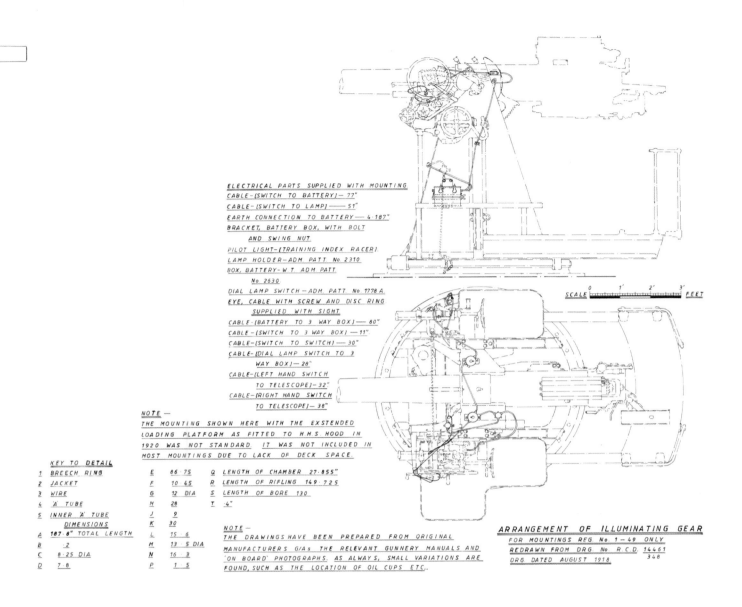

ELECTRICAL PARTS SUPPLIED WITH MOUNTING
CABLE-(SWITCH TO BATTERY)— 77"
CABLE-(SWITCH TO LAMP)——— 51"
EARTH CONNECTION TO BATTERY— 4·187"
BRACKET, BATTERY BOX, WITH BOLT
   AND SWING NUT.
PILOT LIGHT-(TRAINING INDEX RACER).
LAMP HOLDER-ADM. PATT. No. 2310
BOX, BATTERY-W.T. ADM. PATT.
   No. 2630.
DIAL LAMP SWITCH—ADM. PATT. No. 1778 A.
EYE, CABLE WITH SCREW AND DISC RING
   SUPPLIED WITH SIGHT
CABLE-(BATTERY TO 3 WAY BOX)— 80"
CABLE-(SWITCH TO 3 WAY BOX)— 11"
CABLE-(SWITCH TO SWITCH)— 30"
CABLE-(DIAL LAMP SWITCH TO 3
   WAY BOX)— 28"
CABLE-(LEFT HAND SWITCH
   TO TELESCOPE)— 32"
CABLE-(RIGHT HAND SWITCH
   TO TELESCOPE)— 38"

NOTE—
THE MOUNTING SHOWN HERE WITH THE EXSTENDED
LOADING PLATFORM AS FITTED TO H.M.S. HOOD IN
1920 WAS NOT STANDARD. IT WAS NOT INCLUDED IN
MOST MOUNTINGS DUE TO LACK OF DECK SPACE.

KEY TO DETAIL
1 BREECH RING
2 JACKET
3 WIRE
4 'A' TUBE
5 INNER 'A' TUBE
      DIMENSIONS
A 187·8" TOTAL LENGTH
B ·2
C 8·25 DIA
D 7·8
E 86·75
F 10·45
G 12 DIA
H 28
J 9
K 30
L 15·6
M 13·5 DIA
N 16·3
P 1·5
Q LENGTH OF CHAMBER 27·855"
R LENGTH OF RIFLING 149·725
S LENGTH OF BORE 130
T ·4"

NOTE—
THE DRAWINGS HAVE BEEN PREPARED FROM ORIGINAL
MANUFACTURERS G/As THE RELEVANT GUNNERY MANUALS AND
'ON BOARD' PHOTOGRAPHS. AS ALWAYS, SMALL VARIATIONS ARE
FOUND, SUCH AS THE LOCATION OF OIL CUPS ETC..

SCALE 0 1' 2' 3' FEET

ARRANGEMENT OF ILLUMINATING GEAR
FOR MOUNTINGS REG. No. 1— 49 ONLY
REDRAWN FROM DRG. No. R.C.D. 14461
                                    348
DRG DATED AUGUST 1918

KEY TO DETAIL THE GUNS
1 BREECH RING
2 REMOVABLE BREECH RING
3 SCREW SECURING BREECH RING
4 SCREWS SECURING LOOSE BARREL
5 SCREW STOP BREECH RING
6 SCREWS SECURING LOOSE LINER
7 LOOSE BARREL (AUTOFRETTAGED).
8 SEALING RING
9 PACKING
10 SEALING COLLAR
11 6 WIRES
12 8 WIRES
13 10 WIRES
14 12 WIRES
15 14 WIRES
16 16 WIRES
17 17 WIRES
18 'A' TUBE
19 JACKET

DIMENSIONS
A 4·0" DIA OF BORE.
B LENGTH OF CHAMBER — 28·015"
C 12·0" DIA.
D 24" KEY.
E 16·3" DIA.
F 13·5" DIA.
G 10·85" DIA.
H 8·25" DIA
J TAPER- ·0228 PER INCH ON DIA.
K TAPER- ·004 PER INCH ON DIA.

ALL THE DRAWINGS ON THIS SHEET HAVE BEEN
REDRAWN FROM ORIGINAL MATERIAL KINDLY
PROVIDED BY THE HAMPSHIRE RECORD OFFICE
SUSSEX STREET, WINCHESTER, SO23 8TH.

SHEET THREE OF SIX SHEETS.

© JOHN LAMBERT 26/10/1997 CH'D 26/10/1997

L/O/86/C

G 13 The 4in QF V gun on HA Mk III mountings, 1919

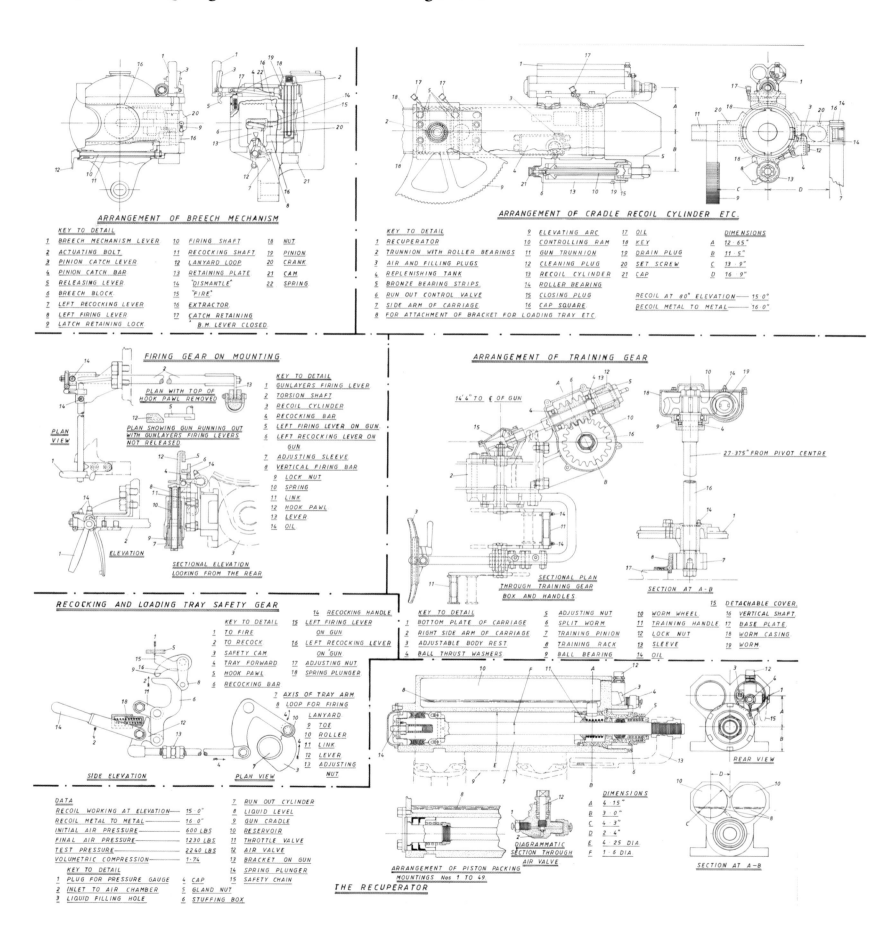

ARRANGEMENT OF BREECH MECHANISM

KEY TO DETAIL

1	BREECH MECHANISM LEVER	10	FIRING SHAFT	18	NUT
2	ACTUATING BOLT	11	RECOCKING SHAFT	19	PINION
3	PINION CATCH LEVER	12	LANYARD LOOP	20	CRANK
4	PINION CATCH BAR	13	RETAINING PLATE	21	CAM
5	RELEASING LEVER	14	"DISMANTLE"	22	SPRING
6	BREECH BLOCK.	15	"FIRE"		
7	LEFT RECOCKING LEVER	16	EXTRACTOR.		
8	LEFT FIRING LEVER	17	CATCH RETAINING		
9	LATCH RETAINING LOCK		B.M. LEVER CLOSED.		

ARRANGEMENT OF CRADLE RECOIL CYLINDER ETC.

KEY TO DETAIL

1	RECUPERATOR	9	ELEVATING ARC	17	OIL	DIMENSIONS
2	TRUNNION WITH ROLLER BEARINGS	10	CONTROLLING RAM	18	KEY	A 12·65"
3	AIR AND FILLING PLUGS	11	GUN TRUNNION	19	DRAIN PLUG	B 11·5"
4	REPLENISHING TANK	12	CLEANING PLUG	20	SET SCREW	C 13·9"
5	BRONZE BEARING STRIPS	13	RECOIL CYLINDER	21	CAP	D 16·9"
6	RUN OUT CONTROL VALVE	14	ROLLER BEARING			
7	SIDE ARM OF CARRIAGE	15	CLOSING PLUG			RECOIL AT 80° ELEVATION — 15·0"
8	FOR ATTACHMENT OF BRACKET FOR LOADING TRAY ETC.	16	CAP SQUARE			RECOIL METAL TO METAL — 16·0"

FIRING GEAR ON MOUNTING.

PLAN WITH TOP OF
HOOK PAWL REMOVED

PLAN SHOWING GUN RUNNING OUT
WITH GUNLAYERS FIRING LEVERS
NOT RELEASED

PLAN VIEW

ELEVATION

SECTIONAL ELEVATION
LOOKING FROM THE REAR

KEY TO DETAIL

1 GUNLAYERS FIRING LEVER
2 TORSION SHAFT
3 RECOIL CYLINDER
4 RECOCKING BAR
5 LEFT FIRING LEVER ON GUN.
6 LEFT RECOCKING LEVER ON
  GUN
7 ADJUSTING SLEEVE
8 VERTICAL FIRING BAR
9 LOCK NUT
10 SPRING
11 LINK
12 HOOK PAWL
13 LEVER
14 OIL

ARRANGEMENT OF TRAINING GEAR

14'4" TO ₵ OF GUN

27·375" FROM PIVOT CENTRE

SECTIONAL PLAN
THROUGH TRAINING GEAR
BOX AND HANDLES

SECTION AT A-B

KEY TO DETAIL

1	BOTTOM PLATE OF CARRIAGE	5	ADJUSTING NUT	10	WORM WHEEL	15	DETACHABLE COVER.
2	RIGHT SIDE ARM OF CARRIAGE	6	SPLIT WORM	11	TRAINING HANDLE	16	VERTICAL SHAFT.
3	ADJUSTABLE BODY REST	7	TRAINING PINION	12	LOCK NUT	17	BASE PLATE.
4	BALL THRUST WASHERS	8	TRAINING RACK	13	SLEEVE	18	WORM CASING.
		9	BALL BEARING	14	OIL	19	WORM.

RECOCKING AND LOADING TRAY SAFETY GEAR

SIDE ELEVATION

PLAN VIEW

KEY TO DETAIL

1 TO FIRE
2 TO RECOCK
3 SAFETY CAM
4 TRAY FORWARD
5 HOOK PAWL
6 RECOCKING BAR
7 AXIS OF TRAY ARM
8 LOOP FOR FIRING
  LANYARD
9 TOE
10 ROLLER
11 LINK
12 LEVER
13 ADJUSTING
  NUT
14 RECOCKING HANDLE
15 LEFT FIRING LEVER
  ON GUN
16 LEFT RECOCKING LEVER
  ON GUN
17 ADJUSTING NUT
18 SPRING PLUNGER

DATA

RECOIL WORKING AT ELEVATION	15·0"
RECOIL METAL TO METAL	16·0"
INITIAL AIR PRESSURE	600 LBS
FINAL AIR PRESSURE	1230 LBS
TEST PRESSURE	2240 LBS
VOLUMETRIC COMPRESSION	1·74

KEY TO DETAIL

1	PLUG FOR PRESSURE GAUGE	4	CAP	7	RUN OUT CYLINDER
2	INLET TO AIR CHAMBER	5	GLAND NUT	8	LIQUID LEVEL
3	LIQUID FILLING HOLE	6	STUFFING BOX	9	GUN CRADLE
				10	RESERVOIR
				11	THROTTLE VALVE
				12	AIR VALVE
				13	BRACKET ON GUN
				14	SPRING PLUNGER
				15	SAFETY CHAIN

DIAGRAMMATIC
SECTION THROUGH
AIR VALVE

ARRANGEMENT OF PISTON PACKING
MOUNTINGS Nos 1 TO 49.

THE RECUPERATOR

DIMENSIONS

A	4·15"
B	3·0"
C	4·3"
D	2·4"
E	4·25 DIA
F	1·6 DIA

REAR VIEW

SECTION AT A-B

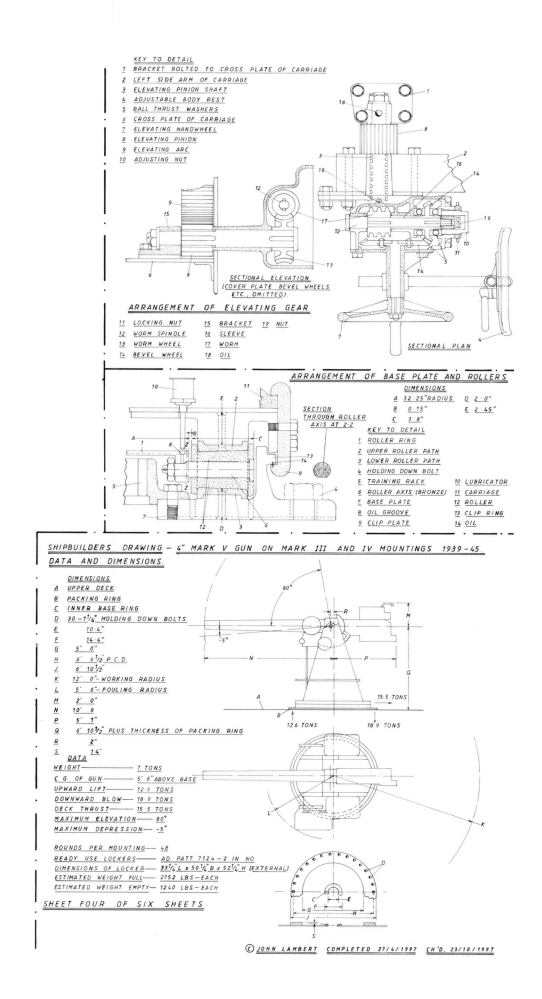

KEY TO DETAIL

1 BRACKET BOLTED TO CROSS PLATE OF CARRIAGE
2 LEFT SIDE ARM OF CARRIAGE
3 ELEVATING PINION SHAFT
4 ADJUSTABLE BODY REST
5 BALL THRUST WASHERS
6 CROSS PLATE OF CARRIAGE
7 ELEVATING HANDWHEEL
8 ELEVATING PINION
9 ELEVATING ARC
10 ADJUSTING NUT

SECTIONAL ELEVATION
(COVER PLATE BEVEL WHEELS
ETC., OMITTED).

ARRANGEMENT OF ELEVATING GEAR

SECTIONAL PLAN

11	LOCKING NUT	15	BRACKET	19	NUT
12	WORM SPINDLE	16	SLEEVE		
13	WORM WHEEL	17	WORM		
14	BEVEL WHEEL	18	OIL		

ARRANGEMENT OF BASE PLATE AND ROLLERS

DIMENSIONS

A 32·25"RADIUS   D 2·0"
B 0·15"   E 2·45"
C 3·8"

SECTION
THROUGH ROLLER
AXIS AT Z-Z

KEY TO DETAIL

1 ROLLER RING
2 UPPER ROLLER PATH
3 LOWER ROLLER PATH
4 HOLDING DOWN BOLT
5 TRAINING RACK   10 LUBRICATOR
6 ROLLER AXIS (BRONZE) 11 CARRIAGE
7 BASE PLATE   12 ROLLER
8 OIL GROOVE   13 CLIP RING
9 CLIP PLATE   14 OIL

SHIPBUILDERS DRAWING – 4" MARK V GUN ON MARK III AND IV MOUNTINGS 1939–45.

DATA AND DIMENSIONS.

DIMENSIONS

A UPPER DECK.
B PACKING RING
C INNER BASE RING
D 30 –1¼" HOLDING DOWN BOLTS
E   10·4"
F   14·4"
G   5' 0"
H   6' 6½" P.C.D.
J   6' 10½"
K 12' 0"–WORKING RADIUS
L   5' 6"–FOULING RADIUS
M   2' 0"
N 10' 8
P   5' 1"
Q   6' 10½" PLUS THICKNESS OF PACKING RING
R   2"
S   14"

DATA

WEIGHT——————— 7 TONS
C G OF GUN———— 5' 6"ABOVE BASE
UPWARD LIFT———— 12·6 TONS
DOWNWARD BLOW—— 18·9 TONS
DECK THRUST——— 15·5 TONS
MAXIMUM ELEVATION— 80°
MAXIMUM DEPRESSION— -5°

ROUNDS PER MOUNTING— 48
READY USE LOCKERS——— AD PATT 7124–2 IN NO.
DIMENSIONS OF LOCKER— 33¼" L x 50¼" B x 52¼" H (EXTERNAL).
ESTIMATED WEIGHT FULL— 2752 LBS–EACH
ESTIMATED WEIGHT EMPTY— 1240 LBS–EACH

SHEET FOUR OF SIX SHEETS

80°
-5°
15·5 TONS
12·6 TONS   18·9 TONS

© JOHN LAMBERT COMPLETED 27/4/1997 CH'D. 23/10/1997

L/0/86/D

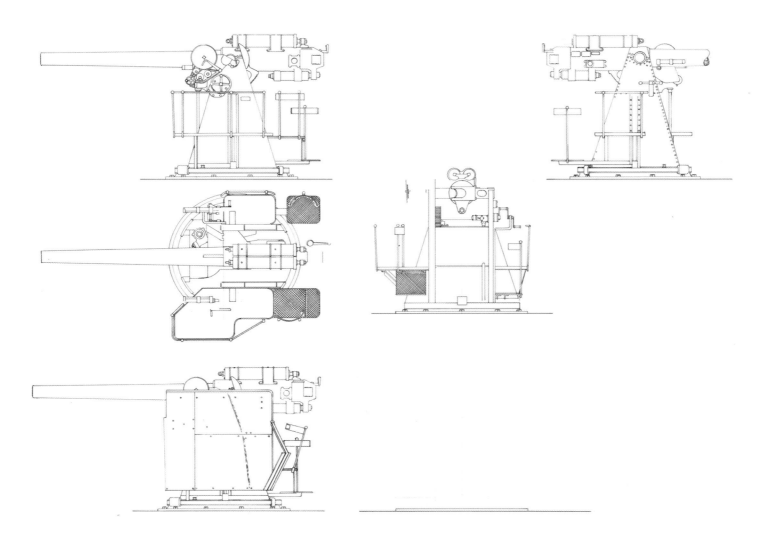

THE 4" Q.F. MARK V V* V** V*** AND V 'C' GUNS ON				
MARK III III III AND IV MOUNTINGS—1943				
DATA				
MUZZLE VELOCITY	2,625 FT./SEC.			
WEIGHT OF PROJECTILE	31 LBS.			
WEIGHT OF MOUNTINGS	MK. III	MK. III*	MK. III**	MK. IV
GUN AND GUN MECHANISM	43 CWT.	43 CWT.	43 CWT.	43 CWT.
CRADLE AND SIGHTS	22½	22½	29	25¼
CARRIAGE—(WITHOUT CRADLE				
AND SIGHTS)	69½	69½	69	6¹
TOTAL	135	135	141	135¼
SHIELD—(FOR MOUNTINGS WITH DUEL FUZE SETTERS				
POSITION ON GUNLAYERS SIDE)	40 CWT.			
SHIELD—(FOR MOUNTINGS WITH FUZE SETTER				
POSITION ON EACH SIDE)	32¾ CWT.			
RECOIL—WORKING	15"			
METAL TO METAL	16"			

FORCES ON FIRING	MARK's III III & IV	MARK III.
MAXIMUM FORCE ON RECOIL	15 TONS	15 TONS
UPWARD LIFT	14½ TONS	13 TONS
DOWNWARD BLOW	20¾ TONS	13 TONS
LIMITS OF ELEVATION	80° TO −5°	
BOOK OF REFERENCE	B.R. 833	

HISTORY AND DEVELOPMENT

THE 4 INCH MARK V GUN DATED FROM 1916 WITH ITS CONSTRUCTION UPDATED AS TIME PASSED. THE ORIGINAL 'A' MARK V GUN CONSISTED OF INNER 'A' AND OUTER 'A' TUBES, JACKET, BREECH RING AND LAYERS OF STEEL WIRE. THE INNER 'A' TUBE WAS PRESSED INTO THE OUTER 'A' TUBE AND WAS PREVENTED FROM MOVING FORWARD BY THE SHOULDERS. LAYERS OF STEEL WIRE WAS WOUND OVER THE 'A' TUBE AND THE JACKET WAS SHRUNK ON OVER THE WIRE. THE BREECH RING BEING SHRUNK ON OVER THE REAR OF THE 'A' TUBE AND SCREWED TO THE JACKET, THUS KEEPING ALL PARTS OF THE GUN TOGETHER. IT WAS FITTED TO RECEIVE THE BREECH BLOCK AND BREECH MECHANISM, HAVING PROJECTIONS ON THE UPPER SIDE FOR ATTACHMENT OF THE RUN-OUT PISTON ROD OR SPRING TIE RODS AND ON THE UNDER SIDE FOR THE RECOIL PISTON ROD. A CLINOMETER PLANE WAS FORMED ON THE LEFT UPPER SIDE. KEYS WERE FORMED ON THE UPPER AND LOWER SIDES OF THE JACKET SERVING AS GUIDES FOR THE GUN IN ITS CRADLE, THUS PREVENTING IT FROM ROTATING UNDER THE REACTION OF THE RIFLING. THE CHAMBER WAS SLIGHTLY CONED THROUGHOUT ITS LENGTH TO FACILITATE THE INSERTION AND EXTRACTION OF THE CARTRIDGE CASE.

THE 'A' MARK V[*?] GUN WAS SIMILAR, EXCEPT THAT THE INNER 'A' AND 'A' TUBES WERE MADE IN ONE PIECE. THE MARK V** AND V*** GUNS WERE FITTED WITH LOOSE LINERS AND THE V 'C' WITH A LOOSE BARREL. THE LOOSE LINERS OF THE MARK V** WERE NOT TO BE FITTED ON BOARD DUE TO THE RISK OF SCORING. THE LOOSE LINERS OF THE MARK V*** AND THE LOOSE BARREL OF THE V 'C' COULD BE EXCHANGED ON BOARD.

THE BREECH BLOCK WAS OF THE HORIZONTAL SLIDING TYPE MOVING ACROSS THE BREECH OPENING IN A SERIES OF GROOVES OF 'BUTTRESS THREAD' SECTION.

554 OF THE EARLIER MARKS WERE BUILT AND 283 MARK V 'C' GUNS FOR THE R.N. SOME 107 WERE PRODUCED FOR THE ARMY BETWEEN 1917 AND 1920; OF THESE 83 WERE LATER TRANSFERRED TO THE NAVY.

THE HIGH ANGLE MOUNTING, A REQUIREMENT BROUGHT ABOUT BY IMPROVING AIRCRAFT PERFORMANCE AS W.W.I DREW TO A CLOSE, BECAME THE MARK III AND BY IMPROVEMENT THE MARK III*, III** AND BY 1938 THE MARK IV, ALL BEING GENERALLY SIMILAR. THE MAIN DIFFERENCES WERE IN THE DESIGN OF THE RECOIL AND RUN OUT CYLINDERS AND THE POSITION OF THE FUZE SETTING PLATFORMS. THE MARK III HAD A POOR HYDROPNEUMATIC CYLINDER AND TWO SMALL PLATFORMS ON EACH SIDE OF THE TRUNNION SUPPORTS. THE MARK III* WAS SIMILAR BUT WITH DRY PNEUMATIC RUN-OUT ARRANGEMENTS. THE MARK III** HAD A PAIR OF LARGE RUN OUT SPRINGS IN PROMINENT TWIN CYLINDERS ABOVE THE GUN CRADLE WITH A DOUBLE HAND FUZE SETTING PLATFORM ON THE LEFT HAND SIDE. THE FINAL, MARK IV VERSION (MOSTLY REMOVED FROM THE 8" COUNTY CLASS CRUISERS AND REPLACED BY TWIN 4" MARK XIX MOUNTINGS) HAD AN IMPROVED PNEUMATIC RUN-OUT CYLINDER OTHERWISE KNOWN AS THE 'RECUPERATOR' WITH A MECHANICAL FUZE SETTING MACHINE ON THE LEFT HAND SIDE. THE GUN WAS NATURALLY BALANCED. IT UTILISED FIXED AMMUNITION, BEING A TYPICAL ANTI-AIRCRAFT GUN OF THE PERIOD WITH A HIGH TRUNNION AXIS. IT WAS PROVIDED WITH A LOADER'S PLATFORM TO EASE THE PROBLEM OF LOADING AT LOW ANGLES OF ELEVATION, THE ANGLED TRUNNION CAPS BEING DESIGNED TO TAKE THE DOWNTHRUST AT HIGH ELEVATION. DURING THE 1920's THEY HAD A RATHER COMPLEX H/A GEARED GUNSIGHT. IT WAS NOT SUCCESSFUL BEING REMOVED WITH THE ADVENT OF THE H/A CONTROL SYSTEM. LATER A SIMPLIFIED SIGHT FOR LOCAL SURFACE CONTROL WAS STANDARD, ALTHOUGH AIMING AT HIGH LEVEL BOMBERS AND SURFACE TARGETS WAS USUALLY BY 'FOLLOW-THE-POINTER', IN DIRECTOR CONTROL. WHEN FIRING AGAINST DIVE BOMBERS THE MOUNTING WENT INTO LOCAL BARRAGE FIRE FOR WHICH A SIMPLE 'CARTWHEEL' SIGHT WAS FITTED.

THE EARLIER H/A MARK I MOUNTINGS GAVE 60° ELEVATION, THE MARK III, 80° AND IT WAS THE STANDARD A-A WEAPON UNTIL REPLACED BY THE NEW TWIN MOUNTING FROM THE LATE 1930's. IT WAS STILL CARRIED ABOARD H.M.S.s REPULSE, EAGLE, HERMES, CANBERRA, YORK AND SYDNEY AT THE TIME OF THEIR LOSS. THEY WERE FITTED ON THE A-A CRUISERS COVENTRY AND CURLEW, FOUR 'O' CLASS AND ALL THE 'P' CLASS DESTROYERS, LOCH CLASS FRIGATES, ALGERINE CLASS FLEET MINESWEEPERS AND SOME 5.25" DIDO CLASS CRUISERS AS STAR SHELL MOUNTINGS. OF THE NUMEROUS SMALL SLOOPS (BRIDGEWATER, HASTINGS, SHOREHAM, GRIMSBY, HALCYON, KINGFISHER AND GUILLEMOT CLASSES) WHICH HAD THEIR LOW ANGLE 4" MAIN ARMAMENT REPLACED BY H/A MOUNTINGS AS THEY REFITTED AND THE H/A MARK III AND IV MOUNTINGS BECAME AVAILABLE.

WITH THIS COMMON EQUIPMENT IN SERVICE FOR MORE THAN 20 YEARS THERE ARE MANY VARIATIONS. THE ORIGINAL MARK III GENERAL ARRANGEMENT VIEW WITH THE EXTENDED REAR PLATFORM WAS REDRAWN FROM ORIGINAL G/AS OF MOUNTINGS FITTED TO H.M.S. HOOD ON HER COMPLETION IN MAY 1920. THERE WERE MANY MODIFICATIONS, ELECTRIC WIRING, IMPROVED SIGHTS AND INSTRUMENTATION. SOME HAD SHIELDS, OTHERS HALF SHIELDS AND MANY WERE UNSHIELDED OR ONLY HAD SPLINTER MATS SECURED TO GUARDRAILS FOR PROTECTION.

OTHER DRAWINGS AND VIEWS ARE REDRAWN FROM B.R. 833/43 AND PHOTOGRAPHS.

L/0/86/E

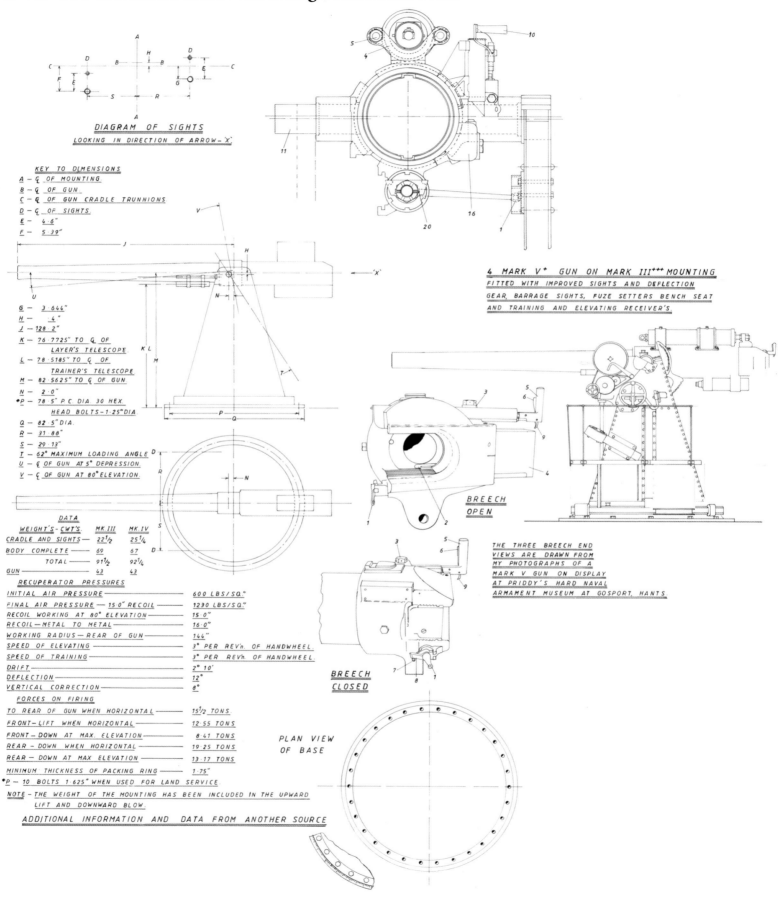

DIAGRAM OF SIGHTS
LOOKING IN DIRECTION OF ARROW 'X'

KEY TO DIMENSIONS
A – ℄ OF MOUNTING.
B – ℄ OF GUN.
C – ℄ OF GUN CRADLE TRUNNIONS.
D – ℄ OF SIGHTS.
E – 4·6"
F – 5·39"

G – 3·644"
H – ·4"
J – 128·2"
K – 76·7725" TO ℄ OF
     LAYER'S TELESCOPE.
L – 78·5185" TO ℄ OF
     TRAINER'S TELESCOPE.
M – 82·5625" TO ℄ OF GUN.
N – 2·0"
*P – 78·5" P.C. DIA 30 HEX.
     HEAD BOLTS – 1·25" DIA.
Q – 82·5" DIA.
R – 31·88"
S – 29·13"
T – 62° MAXIMUM LOADING ANGLE
U – ℄ OF GUN AT 5° DEPRESSION.
V – ℄ OF GUN AT 80° ELEVATION.

4 MARK V* GUN ON MARK III*** MOUNTING
FITTED WITH IMPROVED SIGHTS AND DEFLECTION
GEAR, BARRAGE SIGHTS, FUZE SETTERS BENCH SEAT
AND TRAINING AND ELEVATING RECEIVER'S.

BREECH
OPEN

THE THREE BREECH END
VIEWS ARE DRAWN FROM
MY PHOTOGRAPHS OF A
MARK V GUN ON DISPLAY
AT PRIDDY'S HARD NAVAL
ARMAMENT MUSEUM AT GOSPORT, HANTS.

BREECH
CLOSED

DATA

WEIGHT'S – CWT'S.	MK.III	MK.IV
CRADLE AND SIGHTS –	22½	25¼
BODY COMPLETE –	69	67
TOTAL –	91½	92¼
GUN –	43	43

RECUPERATOR PRESSURES
INITIAL AIR PRESSURE ———————— 600 LBS/SQ."
FINAL AIR PRESSURE – 15·0" RECOIL ——— 1230 LBS/SQ."
RECOIL WORKING AT 80° ELEVATION ——— 15·0"
RECOIL – METAL TO METAL ——————— 16·0"
WORKING RADIUS – REAR OF GUN ———— 144"
SPEED OF ELEVATING ——————— 3° PER REV'n. OF HANDWHEEL.
SPEED OF TRAINING ——————— 3° PER REV'n. OF HANDWHEEL.
DRIFT ————————————————— 2° 10'
DEFLECTION —————————————— 12°
VERTICAL CORRECTION ————————— 8°

FORCES ON FIRING
TO REAR OF GUN WHEN HORIZONTAL ——— 15½ TONS.
FRONT – LIFT WHEN HORIZONTAL ———— 12·55 TONS
FRONT – DOWN AT MAX. ELEVATION ——— 8·41 TONS
REAR – DOWN WHEN HORIZONTAL ———— 19·25 TONS
REAR – DOWN AT MAX ELEVATION ———— 13·17 TONS
MINIMUM THICKNESS OF PACKING RING —— 1·75"
*P – 10 BOLTS 1·625" WHEN USED FOR LAND SERVICE

NOTE – THE WEIGHT OF THE MOUNTING HAS BEEN INCLUDED IN THE UPWARD
LIFT AND DOWNWARD BLOW.

ADDITIONAL INFORMATION AND DATA FROM ANOTHER SOURCE

PLAN VIEW
OF BASE

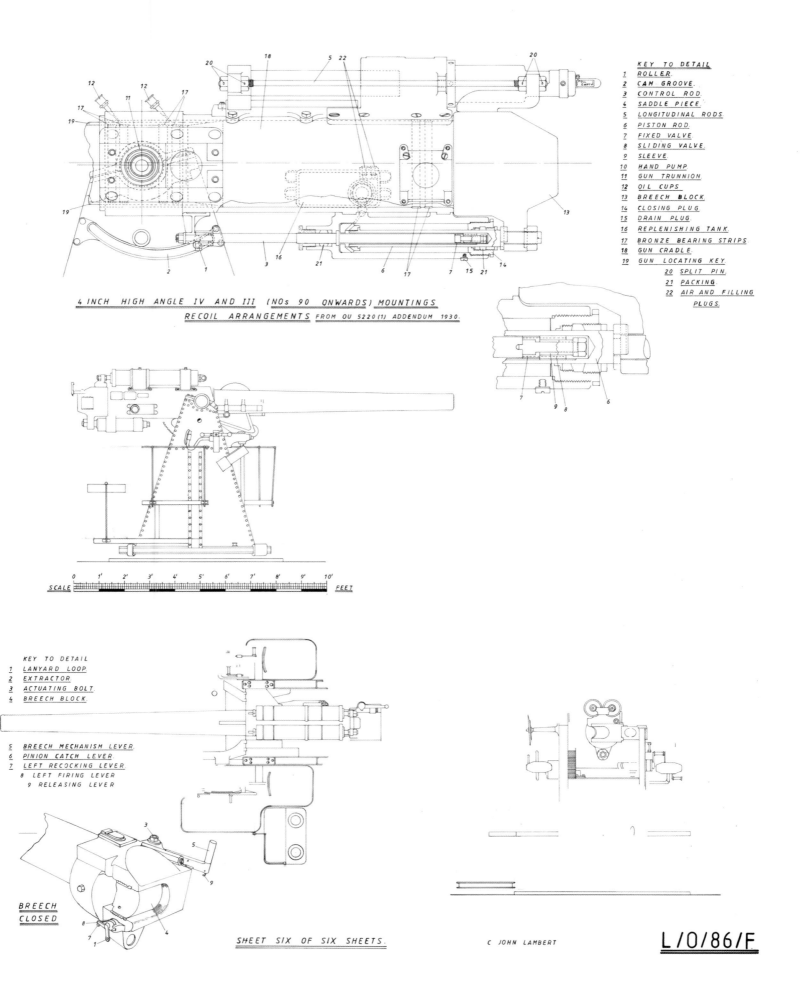

KEY TO DETAIL
1 ROLLER.
2 CAM GROOVE.
3 CONTROL ROD.
4 SADDLE PIECE
5 LONGITUDINAL RODS.
6 PISTON ROD.
7 FIXED VALVE
8 SLIDING VALVE.
9 SLEEVE.
10 HAND PUMP
11 GUN TRUNNION.
12 OIL CUPS
13 BREECH BLOCK.
14 CLOSING PLUG.
15 DRAIN PLUG.
16 REPLENISHING TANK.
17 BRONZE BEARING STRIPS.
18 GUN CRADLE.
19 GUN LOCATING KEY.
20 SPLIT PIN.
21 PACKING.
22 AIR AND FILLING
    PLUGS.

4 INCH HIGH ANGLE IV AND III (NOs 90 ONWARDS) MOUNTINGS
RECOIL ARRANGEMENTS FROM OU 5220(1) ADDENDUM 1930.

SCALE |0 1' 2' 3' 4' 5' 6' 7' 8' 9' 10'| FEET

KEY TO DETAIL
1 LANYARD LOOP.
2 EXTRACTOR
3 ACTUATING BOLT.
4 BREECH BLOCK.

5 BREECH MECHANISM LEVER.
6 PINION CATCH LEVER.
7 LEFT RECOCKING LEVER.
  8 LEFT FIRING LEVER
  9 RELEASING LEVER

BREECH
CLOSED

SHEET SIX OF SIX SHEETS.

C JOHN LAMBERT

L/0/86/F

G 14 3in 20cwt Mk I gun on Mk IVA mounting

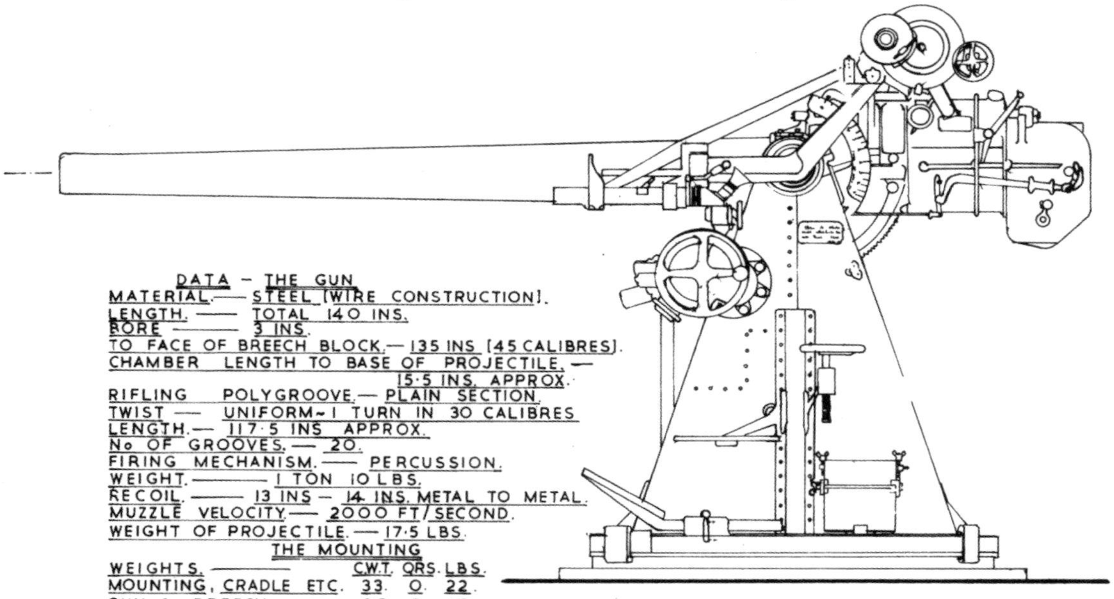

DATA — THE GUN
MATERIAL. — STEEL [WIRE CONSTRUCTION].
LENGTH. — TOTAL 140 INS.
BORE. — 3 INS.
TO FACE OF BREECH BLOCK. — 135 INS [45 CALIBRES].
CHAMBER LENGTH TO BASE OF PROJECTILE. —
        15·5 INS. APPROX.
RIFLING POLYGROOVE. — PLAIN SECTION.
TWIST — UNIFORM~ I TURN IN 30 CALIBRES
LENGTH. — 117·5 INS APPROX.
No OF GROOVES. — 20.
FIRING MECHANISM. — PERCUSSION.
WEIGHT. — 1 TON 10 LBS.
RECOIL. — 13 INS — 14 INS. METAL TO METAL.
MUZZLE VELOCITY — 2000 FT/SECOND.
WEIGHT OF PROJECTILE. — 17·5 LBS.

THE MOUNTING

WEIGHTS.	CWT.	QRS.	LBS.
MOUNTING, CRADLE ETC.	33	O	22
GUN & BREECH.	20	O	10
SIGHTING GEAR.	3	1	16
TOTAL	36	3	6

ELEVATION. — -10°/ 90°
ONE REVOLUTION OF HANDWHEEL = 5° ELEVATON.
71·6 REVOLUTIONS CF HANDWHEEL = ONE REVOLUTION OF MOUNTING.
FORCES ON FIRING. 9 TONS DOWNWARD THRUST.
        6·2 TONS UPWARD THRUST.
RATE OF FIRE ——— 20 –25 R /MIN.

LEFT SIDE ELEVATION

0 1' 2' 3' 4' 5' 6' 7' 8' 9' 10'

SCALE FEET

HISTORY

DEVELOPED UNDER ROYAL NAVY SPONSORSHIP BEFORE WWI IT WAS PLACED IN PRODUCTION FROM 1914 AS A COMMON ANTI-AIRCRAFT GUN FOR BOTH THE NAVY AND ARMY. DUE TO ITS AVAILABILITY IT WAS USED IN THE PROTECTION OF OUR CITY'S. WITH THE LACK OF HARD HITTING A-A WEAPONS FOR WARSHIPS. THE MOUTING WAS FITTED TO A NUMBER OF FLEET & ESCORT DESTROYERS. IN 1942 THIS MOUNTING, WITH THE ADDITION OF A SPLINTER SHIELD, WAS ISSUED TO A NUMBER OF STEAM GUN BOATS. (SEE DRG. L/S/I).

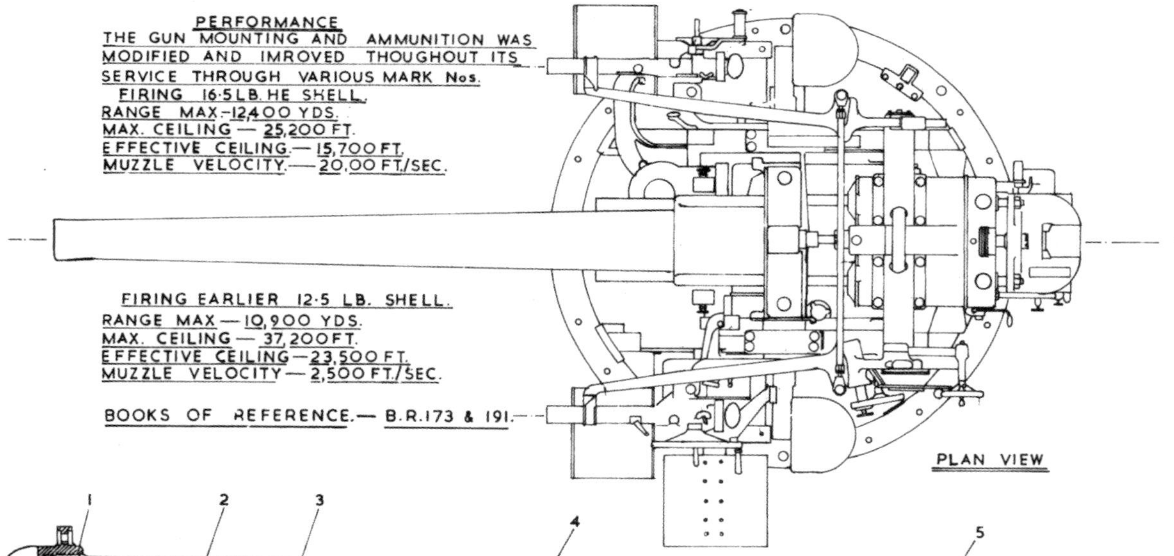

PERFORMANCE

THE GUN MOUNTING AND AMMUNITION WAS MODIFIED AND IMROVED THOUGHOUT ITS SERVICE THROUGH VARIOUS MARK Nos.
        FIRING 16·5 LB. HE SHELL.
RANGE MAX – 12400 YDS.
MAX. CEILING — 25,200 FT.
EFFECTIVE CEILING. — 15,700 FT.
MUZZLE VELOCITY. — 20,00 FT/SEC.

FIRING EARLIER 12·5 LB. SHELL.
RANGE MAX — 10,900 YDS.
MAX. CEILING — 37,200 FT.
EFFECTIVE CEILING – 23,500 FT.
MUZZLE VELOCITY — 2,500 FT./SEC.

BOOKS OF REFERENCE. — B.R.173 & 191.

PLAN VIEW

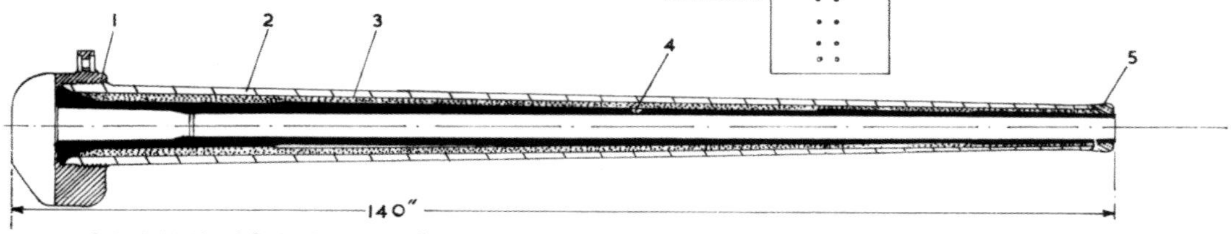

140"

QF 3-INCH 20 CWT MARK I.

1 BREECH RING.
2 JACKET.
3 WIRE.
4 'A' TUBE.
5 STOP RING.

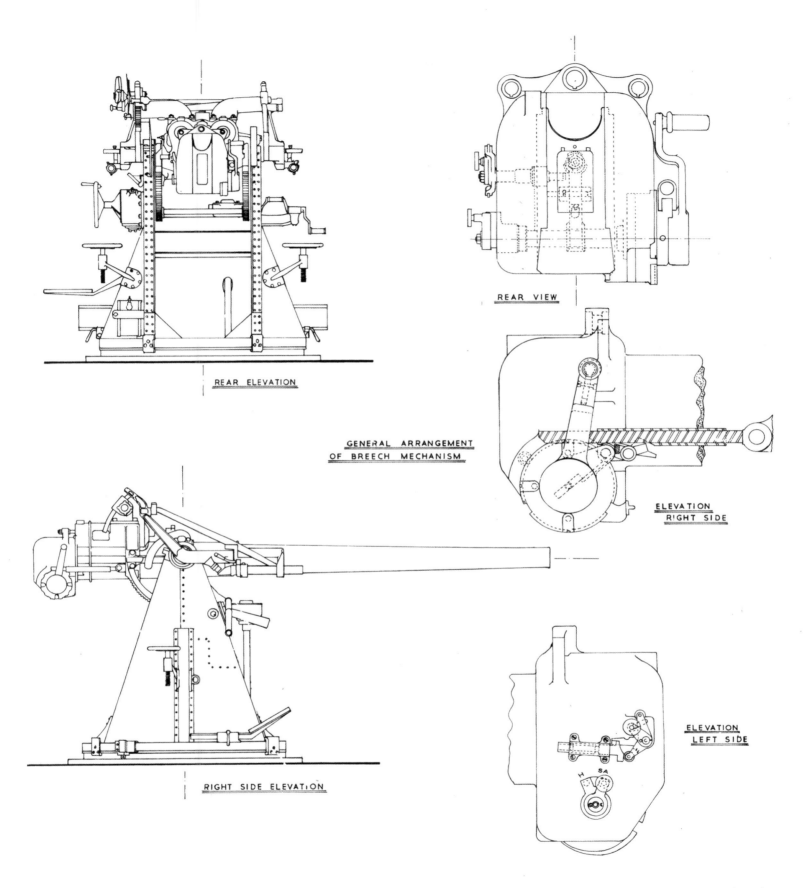

REAR ELEVATION

REAR VIEW

GENERAL ARRANGEMENT
OF BREECH MECHANISM

ELEVATION
RIGHT SIDE

RIGHT SIDE ELEVATION

ELEVATION
LEFT SIDE

L/O/17

(PHOTOGRAPHICALLY ENLARGED 14/11/2000) UPDATED 28/6/94. © JOHN LAMBERT 5/4/79.

135

G 15 12pdr 12cwt gun on HA/LA Mk IX mounting

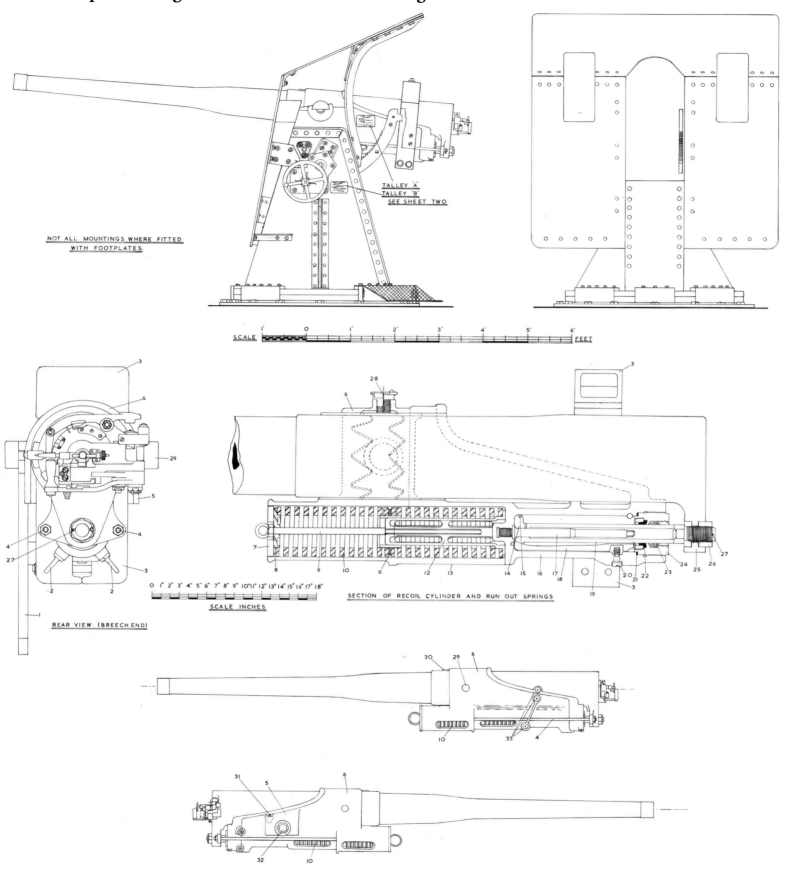

NOT ALL MOUNTINGS WHERE FITTED
WITH FOOTPLATES.

TALLEY 'A'
TALLEY 'B'
SEE SHEET TWO

SCALE   FEET

REAR VIEW (BREECH END)

SCALE INCHES

SECTION OF RECOIL CYLINDER AND RUN OUT SPRINGS

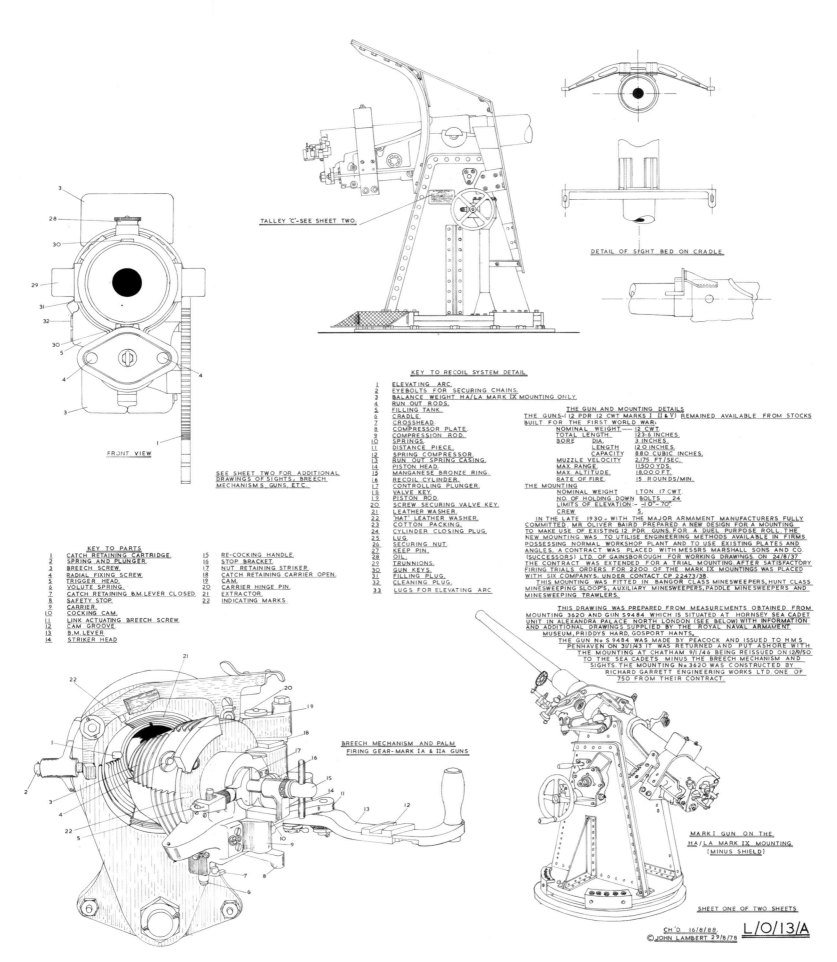

FRONT VIEW

TALLEY 'C'-SEE SHEET TWO.

DETAIL OF SIGHT BED ON CRADLE

SEE SHEET TWO FOR ADDITIONAL
DRAWINGS OF SIGHTS, BREECH
MECHANISMS, GUNS, ETC.

KEY TO RECOIL SYSTEM DETAIL.

1. ELEVATING ARC.
2. EYEBOLTS FOR SECURING CHAINS.
3. BALANCE WEIGHT HA/LA MARK IX MOUNTING ONLY.
4. RUN OUT RODS.
5. FILLING TANK.
6. CRADLE.
7. CROSSHEAD.
8. COMPRESSOR PLATE.
9. COMPRESSION ROD.
10. SPRINGS.
11. DISTANCE PIECE.
12. SPRING COMPRESSOR.
13. RUN OUT SPRING CASING.
14. PISTON HEAD.
15. MANGANESE BRONZE RING.
16. RECOIL CYLINDER.
17. CONTROLLING PLUNGER.
18. VALVE KEY.
19. PISTON ROD.
20. SCREW SECURING VALVE KEY.
21. LEATHER WASHER.
22. 'HAT' LEATHER WASHER.
23. COTTON PACKING.
24. CYLINDER CLOSING PLUG.
25. LUG.
26. SECURING NUT.
27. KEEP PIN.
28. OIL.
29. TRUNNIONS.
30. FILLING PLUG.
31. FILLING PLUG.
32. CLEANING PLUG.
33. LUGS FOR ELEVATING ARC

THE GUN AND MOUNTING DETAILS

THE GUNS-(12 PDR 12 CWT MARKS I II & V) REMAINED AVAILABLE FROM STOCKS
BUILT FOR THE FIRST WORLD WAR.

NOMINAL WEIGHT.	12 CWT.
TOTAL LENGTH.	123·6 INCHES.
BORE DIA.	3 INCHES.
LENGTH	120 INCHES.
CAPACITY	880 CUBIC INCHES.
MUZZLE VELOCITY	2,175 FT/SEC.
MAX. RANGE.	11,500 YDS.
MAX. ALTITUDE.	18,000 FT.
RATE OF FIRE.	15 ROUNDS/MIN.

THE MOUNTING
NOMINAL WEIGHT   1 TON 17 CWT.
NO. OF HOLDING DOWN BOLTS. 24
LIMITS OF ELEVATION:- -10°-70°.
CREW   5.

IN THE LATE 1930s WITH THE MAJOR ARMAMENT MANUFACTURERS FULLY
COMMITTED, MR OLIVER BAIRD PREPARED A NEW DESIGN FOR A MOUNTING
TO MAKE USE OF EXISTING 12 PDR GUNS FOR A DUEL PURPOSE ROLL. THE
NEW MOUNTING WAS TO UTILISE ENGINEERING METHODS AVAILABLE IN FIRMS
POSSESSING NORMAL WORKSHOP PLANT AND TO USE EXISTING PLATES AND
ANGLES. A CONTRACT WAS PLACED WITH MESSRS MARSHALL SONS AND CO.
(SUCCESSORS) LTD. OF GAINSBOROUGH FOR WORKING DRAWINGS ON 24/8/37
THE CONTRACT WAS EXTENDED FOR A TRIAL MOUNTING. AFTER SATISFACTORY
FIRING TRIALS ORDERS FOR 2200 OF THE MARK IX MOUNTINGS WAS PLACED
WITH SIX COMPANYS. UNDER CONTACT CP 22473/38.
THIS MOUNTING WAS FITTED IN BANGOR CLASS MINESWEEPERS, HUNT CLASS
MINESWEEPING SLOOP'S, AUXILIARY MINESWEEPERS, PADDLE MINESWEEPERS AND
MINESWEEPING TRAWLERS.

THIS DRAWING WAS PREPARED FROM MEASUREMENTS OBTAINED FROM
MOUNTING 3620 AND GUN S9484 WHICH IS SITUATED AT HORNSEY SEA CADET
UNIT IN ALEXANDRA PALACE NORTH LONDON (SEE BELOW) WITH INFORMATION
AND ADDITIONAL DRAWINGS SUPPLIED BY THE ROYAL NAVAL ARMAMENT
MUSEUM, PRIDDYS HARD, GOSPORT HANTS.
THE GUN No S9484 WAS MADE BY PEACOCK AND ISSUED TO H.M.S.
PENHAVEN ON 31/1/43 IT WAS RETURNED AND PUT ASHORE WITH
THE MOUNTING AT CHATHAM 9/1/46 BEING REISSUED ON 12/9/50
TO THE SEA CADETS MINUS THE BREECH MECHANISM AND
SIGHTS. THE MOUNTING No 3620 WAS CONSTRUCTED BY
RICHARD GARRETT ENGINEERING WORKS LTD. ONE OF
750 FROM THEIR CONTRACT.

KEY TO PARTS

1. CATCH RETAINING CARTRIDGE.
2. SPRING AND PLUNGER
3. BREECH SCREW.
4. RADIAL FIXING SCREW
5. TRIGGER HEAD.
6. VOLUTE SPRING.
7. CATCH RETAINING B.M. LEVER CLOSED.
8. SAFETY STOP.
9. CARRIER.
10. COCKING CAM.
11. LINK ACTUATING BREECH SCREW.
12. CAM GROOVE.
13. B.M. LEVER
14. STRIKER HEAD.
15. RE-COCKING HANDLE.
16. STOP BRACKET.
17. NUT RETAINING STRIKER.
18. CATCH RETAINING CARRIER OPEN.
19. CAM.
20. CARRIER HINGE PIN.
21. EXTRACTOR.
22. INDICATING MARKS.

BREECH MECHANISM AND PALM
FIRING GEAR-MARK IA & IIA GUNS

MARK I GUN ON THE
HA/LA MARK IX MOUNTING
[MINUS SHIELD]

SHEET ONE OF TWO SHEETS

CH'D. 16/8/88.
© JOHN LAMBERT 29/8/78

L/O/13/A

G 15 12pdr 12cwt gun on HA/LA Mk IX mounting, details

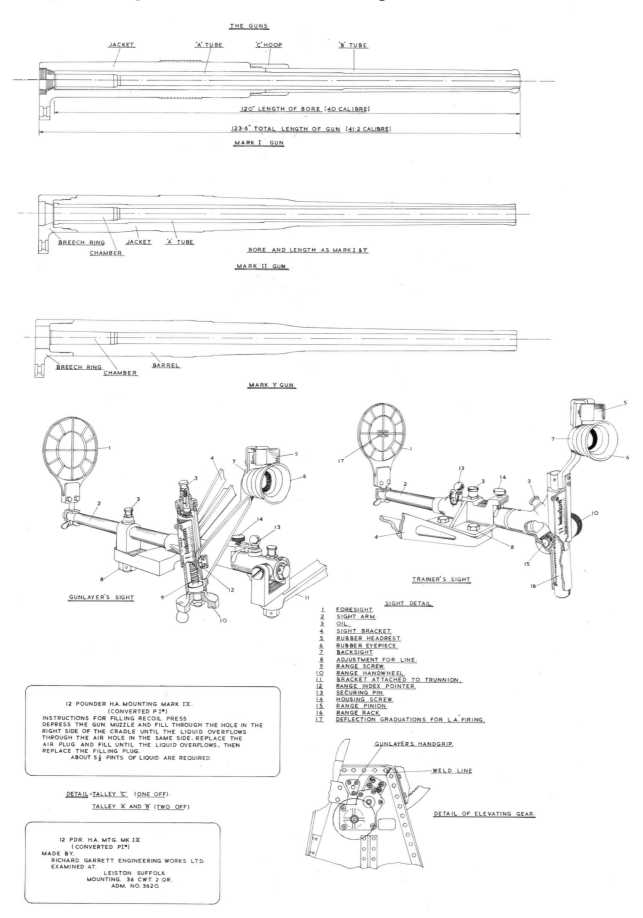

THE GUNS

JACKET   'A' TUBE   'C' HOOP   'B' TUBE

120" LENGTH OF BORE [40 CALIBRE]

123·6" TOTAL LENGTH OF GUN [41·2 CALIBRE]

MARK I GUN

BREECH RING   JACKET   'A' TUBE

CHAMBER

BORE AND LENGTH AS MARK I & V

MARK II GUN

BREECH RING   BARREL

CHAMBER

MARK V GUN

GUNLAYER'S SIGHT

TRAINER'S SIGHT

SIGHT DETAIL

1 FORESIGHT.
2 SIGHT ARM.
3 OIL.
4 SIGHT BRACKET.
5 RUBBER HEADREST.
6 RUBBER EYEPIECE.
7 BACKSIGHT.
8 ADJUSTMENT FOR LINE.
9 RANGE SCREW.
10 RANGE HANDWHEEL.
11 BRACKET ATTACHED TO TRUNNION.
12 RANGE INDEX POINTER.
13 SECURING PIN.
14 HOUSING SCREW.
15 RANGE PINION.
16 RANGE RACK.
17 DEFLECTION GRADUATIONS FOR L.A. FIRING.

12 POUNDER H.A. MOUNTING MARK IX.
(CONVERTED P I*)
INSTRUCTIONS FOR FILLING RECOIL PRESS
DEPRESS THE GUN MUZZLE AND FILL THROUGH THE HOLE IN THE
RIGHT SIDE OF THE CRADLE UNTIL THE LIQUID OVERFLOWS
THROUGH THE AIR HOLE IN THE SAME SIDE. REPLACE THE
AIR PLUG AND FILL UNTIL THE LIQUID OVERFLOWS, THEN
REPLACE THE FILLING PLUG.
ABOUT 5½ PINTS OF LIQUID ARE REQUIRED.

DETAIL - TALLEY 'C' (ONE OFF).

TALLEY 'A' AND 'B' (TWO OFF)

12 PDR. H.A. MTG. MK IX
(CONVERTED PI*)
MADE BY.
RICHARD GARRETT ENGINEERING WORKS LTD.
EXAMINED AT.
LEISTON SUFFOLK
MOUNTING. 36 CWT. 2 QR.
ADM. NO. 3620.

GUNLAYERS HANDGRIP

WELD LINE

DETAIL OF ELEVATING GEAR.

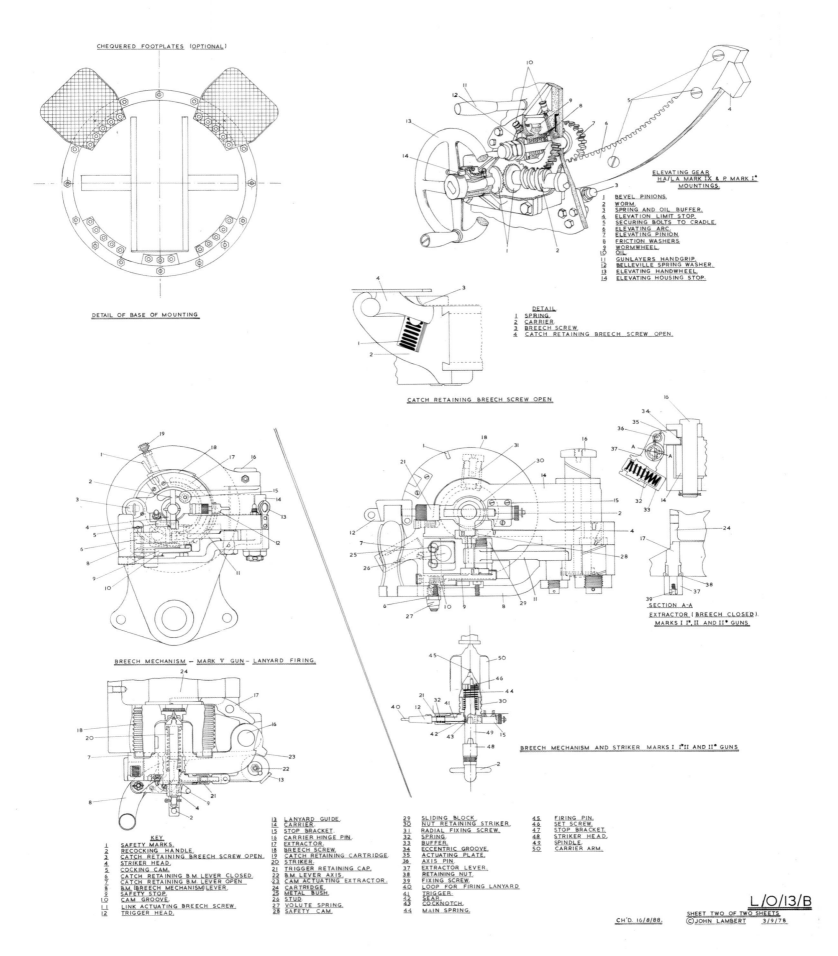

CHEQUERED FOOTPLATES (OPTIONAL)

DETAIL OF BASE OF MOUNTING

ELEVATING GEAR
HA/LA MARK IX & P. MARK I*
MOUNTINGS.

1 BEVEL PINIONS.
2 WORM.
3 SPRING AND OIL BUFFER.
4 ELEVATION LIMIT STOP.
5 SECURING BOLTS TO CRADLE.
6 ELEVATING ARC.
7 ELEVATING PINION.
8 FRICTION WASHERS.
9 WORMWHEEL.
10 OIL.
11 GUNLAYERS HANDGRIP.
12 BELLEVILLE SPRING WASHER.
13 ELEVATING HANDWHEEL.
14 ELEVATING HOUSING STOP.

DETAIL
1 SPRING.
2 CARRIER.
3 BREECH SCREW.
4 CATCH RETAINING BREECH SCREW OPEN.

CATCH RETAINING BREECH SCREW OPEN

BREECH MECHANISM – MARK V GUN – LANYARD FIRING.

SECTION A-A
EXTRACTOR (BREECH CLOSED).
MARKS I I*, II AND II* GUNS

BREECH MECHANISM AND STRIKER MARKS I I*II AND II* GUNS

KEY
1 SAFETY MARKS.
2 RECOCKING HANDLE.
3 CATCH RETAINING BREECH SCREW OPEN.
4 STRIKER HEAD.
5 COCKING CAM.
6 CATCH RETAINING B.M. LEVER CLOSED.
7 CATCH RETAINING B.M. LEVER OPEN.
8 B.M. (BREECH MECHANISM) LEVER.
9 SAFETY STOP.
10 CAM GROOVE.
11 LINK ACTUATING BREECH SCREW.
12 TRIGGER HEAD.

13 LANYARD GUIDE.
14 CARRIER.
15 STOP BRACKET.
16 CARRIER HINGE PIN.
17 EXTRACTOR.
18 BREECH SCREW.
19 CATCH RETAINING CARTRIDGE.
20 STRIKER.
21 TRIGGER RETAINING CAP.
22 B.M. LEVER AXIS.
23 CAM ACTUATING EXTRACTOR.
24 CARTRIDGE.
25 METAL BUSH.
26 STUD.
27 VOLUTE SPRING.
28 SAFETY CAM.

29 SLIDING BLOCK.
30 NUT RETAINING STRIKER.
31 RADIAL FIXING SCREW.
32 SPRING.
33 BUFFER.
34 ECCENTRIC GROOVE.
35 ACTUATING PLATE.
36 AXIS PIN.
37 EXTRACTOR LEVER.
38 RETAINING NUT.
39 FIXING SCREW.
40 LOOP FOR FIRING LANYARD.
41 TRIGGER.
42 SEAR.
43 COCKNOTCH.
44 MAIN SPRING.

45 FIRING PIN.
46 SET SCREW.
47 STOP BRACKET.
48 STRIKER HEAD.
49 SPINDLE.
50 CARRIER ARM.

CH'D. 16/8/88.   © JOHN LAMBERT   3/9/78

L/O/13/B
SHEET TWO OF TWO SHEETS

A 1 Vickers 40mm 2pdr on HA Mk II mounting, 1929

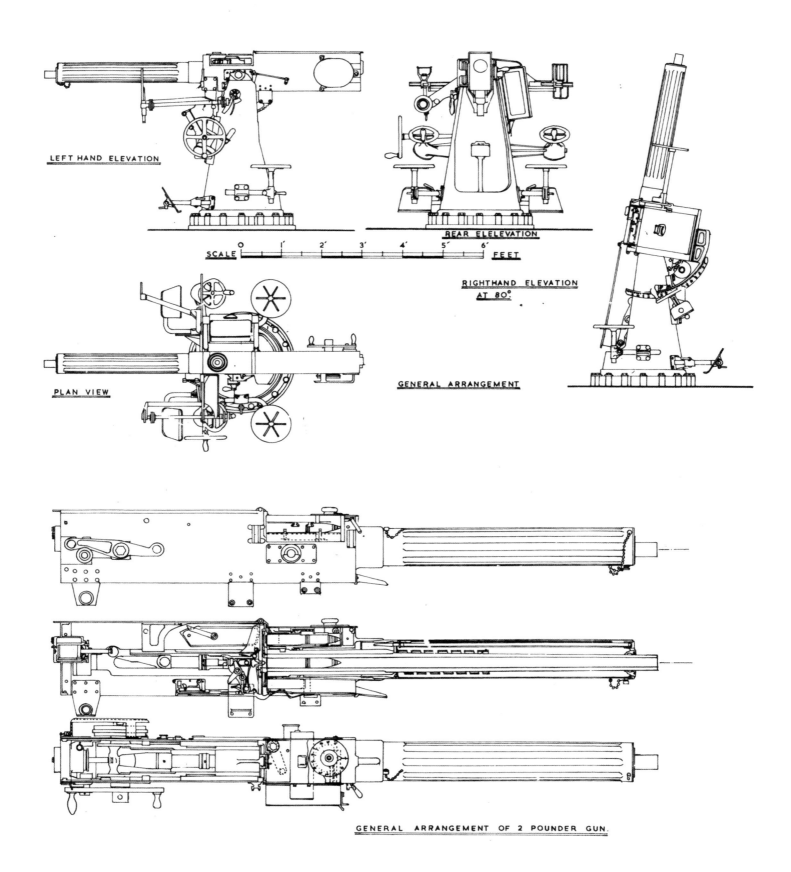

LEFT HAND ELEVATION

REAR ELELEVATION

SCALE 0 1' 2' 3' 4' 5' 6' FEET

RIGHTHAND ELEVATION AT 80°

PLAN VIEW

GENERAL ARRANGEMENT

GENERAL ARRANGEMENT OF 2 POUNDER GUN.

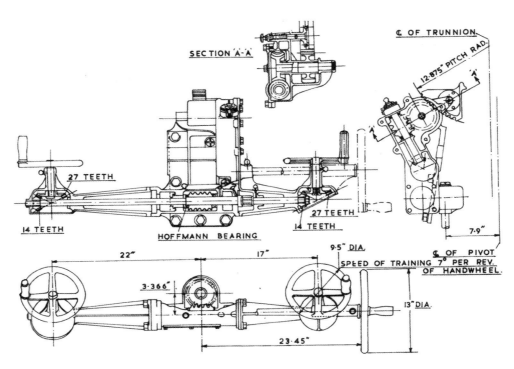

SECTION 'A-A'

℄ OF TRUNNION

12·875" PITCH RAD.

℄ OF PIVOT
SPEED OF TRAINING 7° PER REV.
OF HANDWHEEL.

27 TEETH

14 TEETH

HOFFMANN BEARING

27 TEETH

14 TEETH

7·9"

22"   17"   9·5" DIA.

3·366"

13" DIA.

23·45"

DETAIL :- ELEVATING & TRAINING GEAR.

HISTORY :- A DEVELOPMENT OF THE POM POM CARRIED BY SHIPS OF THE R.N. DURING THE GREAT WAR. THE HIGH ANGLE MARK II MOUNTING WAS INTRODUCED FROM 1929 AND FITTED TO THE DESTROYER CLASSES BUILDING OR COMPLETING, UNTIL THE PRODUCTION OF THE QUAD. ·5 INCH MACHINE GUN FOR ANTI~AIRCRAFT DEFENCE. IN WAR SERVICE BOTH OF THESE WEAPONS SYSTEMS LACKED THE FIREPOWER REQUIRED TO DESTROY MODERN AXIS AIRCRAFT AND FROM 1941-42 THEY WERE GRADUALLY REPLACED BY THE MORE EFFICIENT 20 mm OERLIKON GUN. [ALSO FITTED TO SOME MINESWEEPING SLOOP CLASSES OF 1930's]

DATA - THE GUN

CALIBRE. --------- 1·575 INCHES.
MUZZLE VELOCITY. ------ 2000 FT / SEC.
PRESSURE. -------- 17 TONS / SQ. INCH.
MUZZLE ENERGY. ------ 55·5 FT. TONS.
LENGTH OF BARREL. ---- 39·37 CALIBRES. [62 INCHES.]
LENGTH OF RIFLING. ---- 54·84 INCHES.
TWIST IN RIFLING. ----- 1 TURN IN 30 CALIBRES.
No OF GROOVES. ------- 12.
DEPTH OF GROOVES. ---- ·0156 INCHES.
WIDTH OF GROOVES. ---- ·322 TO ·311 INS.
LENGTH OF RECOIL. ---- 3 INS [METAL TO METAL].
MAX. PULL ON TRUNNIONS. -- 2·1 TONS.
TOTAL LENGTH OF GUN. ---- 95·65 INS.
CAPACITY OF WATER JACKET. -24 PINTS.
RATE OF FIRE. --------- 200 ROUNDS PER MINUTE.
MAX RANGE. --------- 7830 YDS.
HEIGHT ATTAINED BY PROJECTILE AT MAX. ELEVATION. -- 14,515 FT.
TOTAL RANGE AT MAX. ELEVATION. ----- 2400 YDS.
WEIGHT OF GUN COMP WITH AMMUNITION BOX & BRACKET. ---- 584 LBS.
WEIGHT OF 25 ROUNDS IN BELT. ---- 75·5 LBS.
WEIGHT OF AMMUNITION BOX. ------ 17·5 LBS.
WEIGHT OF WATER IN JACKET. ----- 32 LBS.
WEIGHT OF AMMUNITION BOX BRACKET. -- 28 LBS.
    THE MOUNTING
MAX ELEVATION. ------ 80°
MAX DEPRESSION. ----- 6°
UPWARD LIFT. ------- 3 TONS.
DOWNWARD BLOW. ----- 3·5 TONS.
SPEED OF ELEVATION. --- 7° PER 1 REVOLUTION OF HANDWHEEL.
SPEED OF TRAINING. ---- 7° PER 1 REVOLUTION OF HANDWHEEL.
ESTIMATED WEIGHTS.
GUN -------- 4 CWTS 2 QRS 23 LBS.
MOUNTING ----- 9 CWTS 1 QRS 5 LBS.
TOTAL ------ 14 CWTS 0 QRS 0 LBS.

REDRAWN FROM INFORMATION SUPPLIED BY MR INGHAM CURATOR :-
ROYAL NAVY ARMAMENT MUSEUM, PRIDDY'S HARD, GOSPORT HANTS..

FOR FURTHER INFORMATION ON THE GUN SEE DRG. L/0/10.
SHEET ONE OF TWO SHEETS

L/0/29/A

© JOHN LAMBERT 18/12/79

A 1 2pdr HA Mk II mounting, detail

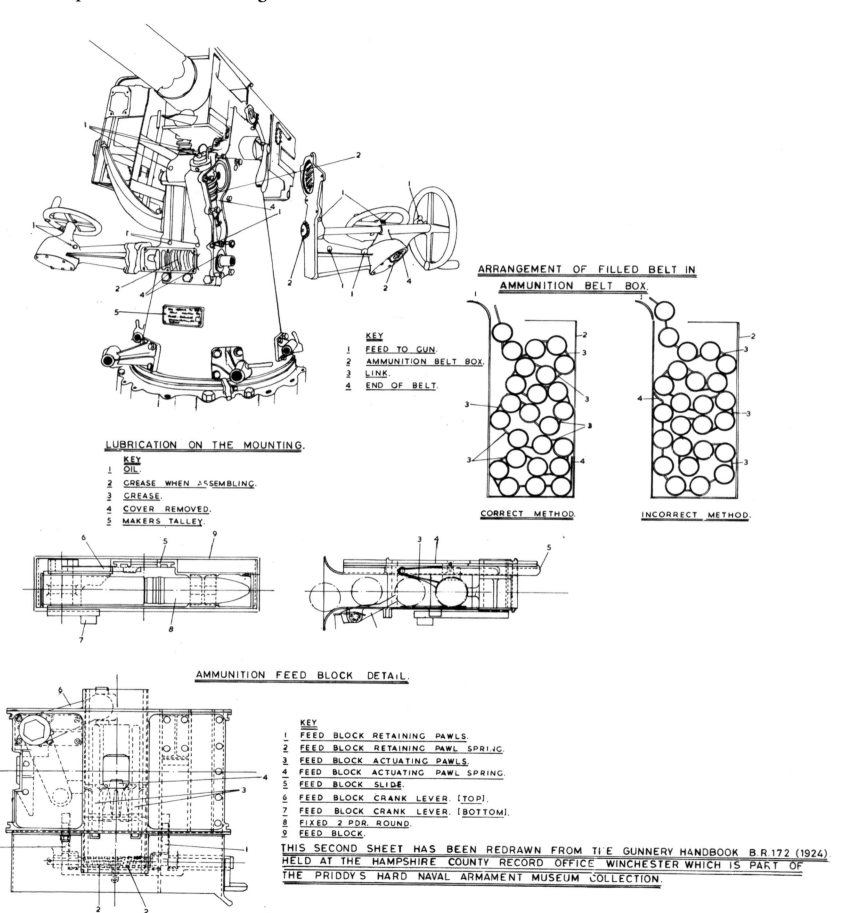

ARRANGEMENT OF FILLED BELT IN AMMUNITION BELT BOX.

KEY
1 FEED TO GUN.
2 AMMUNITION BELT BOX.
3 LINK.
4 END OF BELT.

CORRECT METHOD.

INCORRECT METHOD.

LUBRICATION ON THE MOUNTING.

KEY
1 OIL.
2 GREASE WHEN ASSEMBLING.
3 GREASE.
4 COVER REMOVED.
5 MAKERS TALLEY.

AMMUNITION FEED BLOCK DETAIL.

KEY
1 FEED BLOCK RETAINING PAWLS.
2 FEED BLOCK RETAINING PAWL SPRING.
3 FEED BLOCK ACTUATING PAWLS.
4 FEED BLOCK ACTUATING PAWL SPRING.
5 FEED BLOCK SLIDE.
6 FEED BLOCK CRANK LEVER. [TOP].
7 FEED BLOCK CRANK LEVER. [BOTTOM].
8 FIXED 2 PDR. ROUND.
9 FEED BLOCK.

THIS SECOND SHEET HAS BEEN REDRAWN FROM THE GUNNERY HANDBOOK B.R.172 (1924) HELD AT THE HAMPSHIRE COUNTY RECORD OFFICE WINCHESTER WHICH IS PART OF THE PRIDDY'S HARD NAVAL ARMAMENT MUSEUM COLLECTION.

ARRANGEMENT OF SEATS AND FOOTRESTS

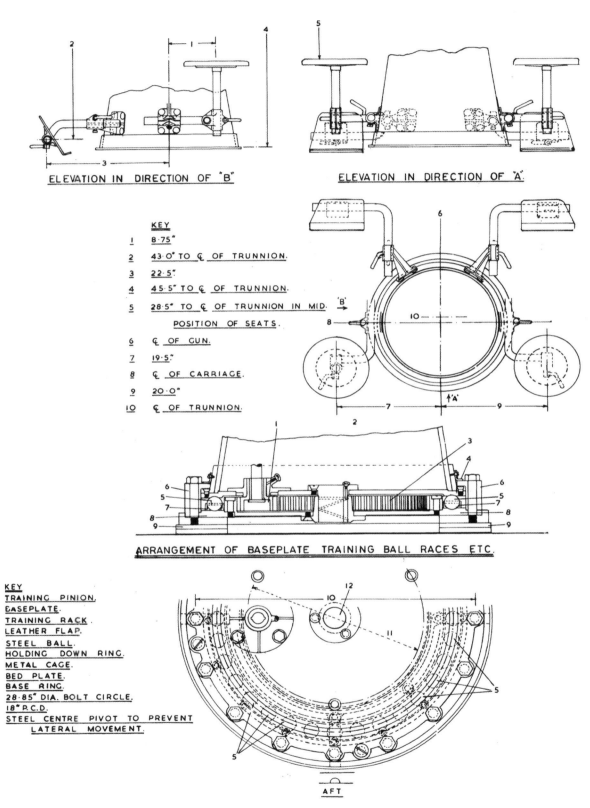

ELEVATION IN DIRECTION OF "B"

ELEVATION IN DIRECTION OF "A"

KEY

1. 8·75"
2. 43·0" TO ₵ OF TRUNNION.
3. 22·5"
4. 45·5" TO ₵ OF TRUNNION.
5. 28·5" TO ₵ OF TRUNNION IN MID. POSITION OF SEATS.
6. ₵ OF GUN.
7. 19·5"
8. ₵ OF CARRIAGE.
9. 20·0"
10. ₵ OF TRUNNION.

ARRANGEMENT OF BASEPLATE TRAINING BALL RACES ETC.

KEY

1. TRAINING PINION.
2. BASEPLATE.
3. TRAINING RACK.
4. LEATHER FLAP.
5. STEEL BALL.
6. HOLDING DOWN RING.
7. METAL CAGE.
8. BED PLATE.
9. BASE RING.
10. 28·85" DIA. BOLT CIRCLE.
11. 18" P.C.D.
12. STEEL CENTRE PIVOT TO PREVENT LATERAL MOVEMENT.

AFT

SHEET TWO OF TWO SHEETS.

© JOHN LAMBERT 30/10/94

L/0/29/B

A 2 Quad Vickers 0.50in machine guns on 'M' Mk III mounting, 1938

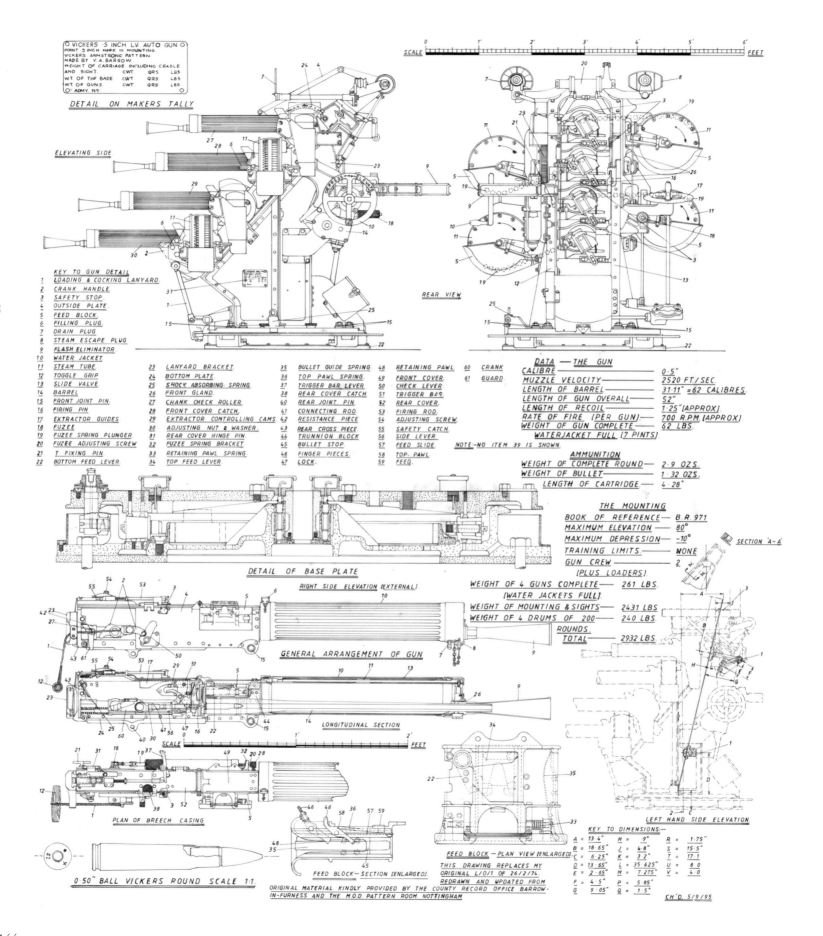

DETAIL ON MAKERS TALLY

ELEVATING SIDE

REAR VIEW

KEY TO GUN DETAIL

1	LOADING & COCKING LANYARD.
2	CRANK HANDLE.
3	SAFETY STOP.
4	OUTSIDE PLATE.
5	FEED BLOCK.
6	FILLING PLUG.
7	DRAIN PLUG.
8	STEAM ESCAPE PLUG.
9	FLASH ELIMINATOR.
10	WATER JACKET.
11	STEAM TUBE.
12	TOGGLE GRIP.
13	SLIDE VALVE.
14	BARREL.
15	FRONT JOINT PIN.
16	FIRING PIN.
17	EXTRACTOR GUIDES.
18	FUZEE.
19	FUZEE SPRING PLUNGER.
20	FUZEE ADJUSTING SCREW.
21	T FIXING PIN.
22	BOTTOM FEED LEVER.

23	LANYARD BRACKET.
24	BOTTOM PLATE.
25	SHOCK ABSORBING SPRING.
26	FRONT GLAND.
27	CRANK CHECK ROLLER.
28	FRONT COVER CATCH.
29	EXTRACTOR CONTROLLING CAMS.
30	ADJUSTING NUT & WASHER.
31	REAR COVER HINGE PIN.
32	FUZEE SPRING BRACKET.
33	RETAINING PAWL SPRING.
34	TOP FEED LEVER.

35	BULLET GUIDE SPRING.
36	TOP PAWL SPRING.
37	TRIGGER BAR LEVER.
38	REAR COVER CATCH.
40	REAR JOINT PIN.
41	CONNECTING ROD.
42	RESISTANCE PIECE.
43	REAR CROSS PIECE.
44	TRUNNION BLOCK.
45	BULLET STOP.
46	FINGER PIECES.
47	LOCK.

48	RETAINING PAWL.
49	FRONT COVER.
50	CHECK LEVER.
51	TRIGGER BAR.
52	REAR COVER.
53	FIRING ROD.
54	ADJUSTING SCREW.
55	SAFETY CATCH.
56	SIDE LEVER.
57	FEED SLIDE.
58	TOP PAWL.
59	FEED.

60	CRANK
61	GUARD.

NOTE - NO ITEM 39 IS SHOWN

DATA — THE GUN

CALIBRE	0.5"
MUZZLE VELOCITY	2520 FT/SEC.
LENGTH OF BARREL	31.11" = 62 CALIBRES.
LENGTH OF GUN OVERALL	52"
LENGTH OF RECOIL	1.25" [APPROX]
RATE OF FIRE [PER GUN]	700 R.P.M. [APPROX]
WEIGHT OF GUN COMPLETE	62 LBS.
WATERJACKET FULL [7 PINTS].	

AMMUNITION

WEIGHT OF COMPLETE ROUND	2.9 OZS.
WEIGHT OF BULLET	1.32 OZS.
LENGTH OF CARTRIDGE	4.28"

THE MOUNTING

BOOK OF REFERENCE	B.R. 971
MAXIMUM ELEVATION	80°
MAXIMUM DEPRESSION	-10°
TRAINING LIMITS	NONE
GUN CREW	2
[PLUS LOADERS].	
WEIGHT OF 4 GUNS COMPLETE	261 LBS.
[WATER JACKETS FULL].	
WEIGHT OF MOUNTING & SIGHTS	2431 LBS.
WEIGHT OF 4 DRUMS OF 200	240 LBS.
ROUNDS	
TOTAL	2932 LBS.

DETAIL OF BASE PLATE

RIGHT SIDE ELEVATION [EXTERNAL].

GENERAL ARRANGEMENT OF GUN

LONGITUDINAL SECTION

SECTION 'A-A'

LEFT HAND SIDE ELEVATION

PLAN OF BREECH CASING

FEED BLOCK — PLAN VIEW [ENLARGED].

THIS DRAWING REPLACES MY
ORIGINAL L/O/1 OF 26/2/74.
REDRAWN AND UPDATED FROM
ORIGINAL MATERIAL KINDLY PROVIDED BY THE COUNTY RECORD OFFICE BARROW-
IN-FURNESS AND THE M.O.D. PATTERN ROOM NOTTINGHAM

FEED BLOCK — SECTION [ENLARGED].

0.50" BALL VICKERS ROUND SCALE 1:1.

KEY TO DIMENSIONS:

A = 13.4"	H = .9"	R = 1.75"
B = 18.65"	J = 4.8"	S = 15.5"
C = 6.25"	K = 3.2"	T = 17.1
D = 13.65"	L = 35.625"	U = 8.0
E = 2.65"	M = 7.275"	V = 4.0
F = 4.5"	P = 5.85"	
G = 9.05"	Q = 1.5"	

CH'D. 5/9/95

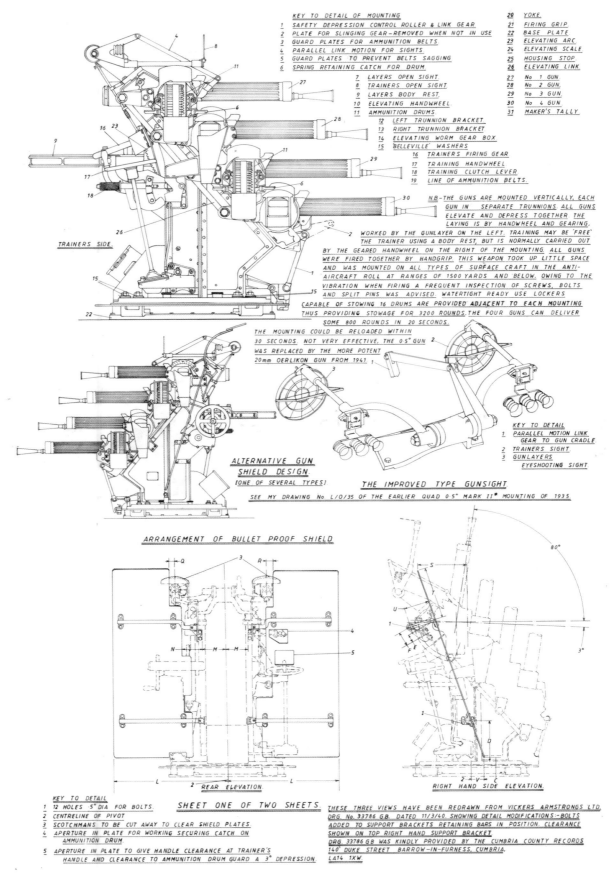

KEY TO DETAIL OF MOUNTING

1	SAFETY DEPRESSION CONTROL ROLLER & LINK GEAR.
2	PLATE FOR SLINGING GEAR - REMOVED WHEN NOT IN USE
3	GUARD PLATES FOR AMMUNITION BELTS.
4	PARALLEL LINK MOTION FOR SIGHTS.
5	GUARD PLATES TO PREVENT BELTS SAGGING
6	SPRING RETAINING CATCH FOR DRUM
7	LAYERS OPEN SIGHT.
8	TRAINERS OPEN SIGHT.
9	LAYERS BODY REST.
10	ELEVATING HANDWHEEL.
11	AMMUNITION DRUMS.
12	LEFT TRUNNION BRACKET.
13	RIGHT TRUNNION BRACKET
14	ELEVATING WORM GEAR BOX
15	'BELLEVILLE' WASHERS
16	TRAINERS FIRING GEAR
17	TRAINING HANDWHEEL
18	TRAINING CLUTCH LEVER.
19	LINE OF AMMUNITION BELTS.

20	YOKE.
21	FIRING GRIP.
22	BASE PLATE
23	ELEVATING ARC
24	ELEVATING SCALE
25	HOUSING STOP.
26	ELEVATING LINK
27	No 1 GUN.
28	No 2 GUN.
29	No 3 GUN.
30	No 4 GUN.
31	MAKER'S TALLY

NB - THE GUNS ARE MOUNTED VERTICALLY, EACH GUN IN SEPARATE TRUNNIONS ALL GUNS ELEVATE AND DEPRESS TOGETHER. THE LAYING IS BY HANDWHEEL AND GEARING, WORKED BY THE GUNLAYER ON THE LEFT. TRAINING MAY BE 'FREE' THE TRAINER USING A BODY REST, BUT IS NORMALLY CARRIED OUT BY THE GEARED HANDWHEEL ON THE RIGHT OF THE MOUNTING. ALL GUNS WERE FIRED TOGETHER BY HANDGRIP. THIS WEAPON TOOK UP LITTLE SPACE AND WAS MOUNTED ON ALL TYPES OF SURFACE CRAFT IN THE ANTI-AIRCRAFT ROLL AT RANGES OF 1500 YARDS AND BELOW. OWING TO THE VIBRATION WHEN FIRING A FREQUENT INSPECTION OF SCREWS, BOLTS AND SPLIT PINS WAS ADVISED. WATERTIGHT READY USE LOCKERS CAPABLE OF STOWING 16 DRUMS ARE PROVIDED ADJACENT TO EACH MOUNTING THUS PROVIDING STOWAGE FOR 3200 ROUNDS. THE FOUR GUNS CAN DELIVER SOME 800 ROUNDS IN 20 SECONDS.

THE MOUNTING COULD BE RELOADED WITHIN 30 SECONDS. NOT VERY EFFECTIVE, THE 0.5" GUN WAS REPLACED BY THE MORE POTENT 20mm OERLIKON GUN FROM 1941.

TRAINERS SIDE.

KEY TO DETAIL

1 PARALLEL MOTION LINK GEAR TO GUN CRADLE.
2 TRAINERS SIGHT
3 GUNLAYERS EYESHOOTING SIGHT

THE IMPROVED TYPE GUNSIGHT

SEE MY DRAWING No L/0/35 OF THE EARLIER QUAD 0.5" MARK II* MOUNTING OF 1935

ALTERNATIVE GUN SHIELD DESIGN.
[ONE OF SEVERAL TYPES]

ARRANGEMENT OF BULLET PROOF SHIELD

REAR ELEVATION.

RIGHT HAND SIDE ELEVATION.

SHEET ONE OF TWO SHEETS.

KEY TO DETAIL

1 12 HOLES .5" DIA FOR BOLTS.
2 CENTRELINE OF PIVOT.
3 SCOTCHMANS TO BE CUT AWAY TO CLEAR SHIELD PLATES.
4 APERTURE IN PLATE FOR WORKING SECURING CATCH ON AMMUNITION DRUM.
5 APERTURE IN PLATE TO GIVE HANDLE CLEARANCE AT TRAINER'S HANDLE AND CLEARANCE TO AMMUNITION DRUM GUARD A 3° DEPRESSION.

THESE THREE VIEWS HAVE BEEN REDRAWN FROM VICKERS ARMSTRONGS LTD. DRG. No. 33786 G.B. DATED 11/3/40 SHOWING DETAIL MODIFICATIONS:- BOLTS ADDED TO SUPPORT BRACKETS RETAINING BARS IN POSITION. CLEARANCE SHOWN ON TOP RIGHT HAND SUPPORT BRACKET
DRG. 33786 GB WAS KINDLY PROVIDED BY THE CUMBRIA COUNTY RECORDS 140 DUKE STREET BARROW-IN-FURNESS, CUMBRIA.
LA14 1XW.

© JOHN LAMBERT 17/7/95.

L/0/01/A

A 2 Quad Vickers 0.50in machine guns on 'M' Mk III mounting, 1938, detail

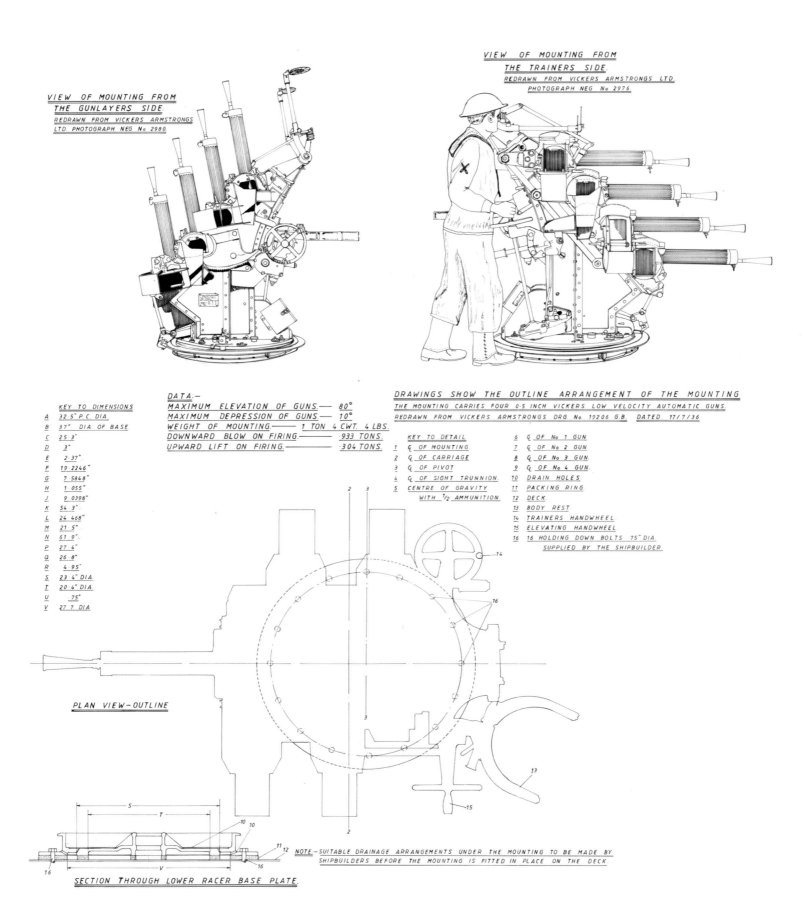

VIEW OF MOUNTING FROM THE GUNLAYERS SIDE.
REDRAWN FROM VICKERS ARMSTRONGS LTD. PHOTOGRAPH NEG No 2980

VIEW OF MOUNTING FROM THE TRAINERS SIDE.
REDRAWN FROM VICKERS ARMSTRONGS LTD PHOTOGRAPH NEG No 2976

KEY TO DIMENSIONS	
A	32·5" P.C. DIA.
B	37" DIA. OF BASE
C	25·3"
D	3"
E	2·37"
F	19·2246"
G	7·5848"
H	1·055"
J	9·0398"
K	54·3"
L	24·468"
M	21·5"
N	61·9"
P	27·4"
Q	26·8"
R	4·95"
S	23·4" DIA
T	20·4" DIA
U	·75"
V	27·7 DIA

DATA:-
MAXIMUM ELEVATION OF GUNS.——— 80°
MAXIMUM DEPRESSION OF GUNS.——— 10°
WEIGHT OF MOUNTING.——— 1 TON 4 CWT. 4 LBS.
DOWNWARD BLOW ON FIRING.——— ·933 TONS.
UPWARD LIFT ON FIRING.——— ·304 TONS.

KEY TO DETAIL	
1	₵ OF MOUNTING
2	₵ OF CARRIAGE
3	₵ OF PIVOT
4	₵ OF SIGHT TRUNNION.
5	CENTRE OF GRAVITY WITH ½ AMMUNITION
6	₵ OF No 1 GUN
7	₵ OF No 2 GUN
8	₵ OF No 3 GUN.
9	₵ OF No 4 GUN.
10	DRAIN HOLES.
11	PACKING RING
12	DECK
13	BODY REST
14	TRAINERS HANDWHEEL
15	ELEVATING HANDWHEEL
16	16 HOLDING DOWN BOLTS ·75" DIA SUPPLIED BY THE SHIPBUILDER

DRAWINGS SHOW THE OUTLINE ARRANGEMENT OF THE MOUNTING
THE MOUNTING CARRIES FOUR 0·5 INCH VICKERS LOW VELOCITY AUTOMATIC GUNS.
REDRAWN FROM VICKERS ARMSTRONGS DRG No 19206 G.B. DATED 17/7/36

PLAN VIEW—OUTLINE

NOTE:- SUITABLE DRAINAGE ARRANGEMENTS UNDER THE MOUNTING TO BE MADE BY SHIPBUILDERS BEFORE THE MOUNTING IS FITTED IN PLACE ON THE DECK

SECTION THROUGH LOWER RACER BASE PLATE.

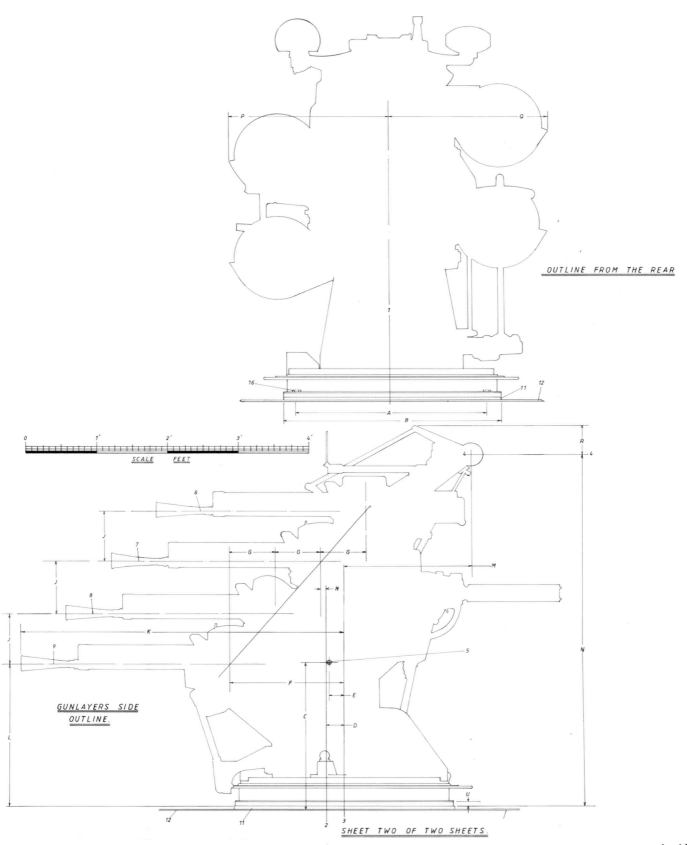

OUTLINE FROM THE REAR

SCALE   FEET

GUNLAYERS SIDE
OUTLINE.

SHEET TWO OF TWO SHEETS.

© JOHN LAMBERT 5/1/97

L/0/01/B

A 3 2pdr Mk VIII LV (low velocity) and Mk VIII* HV (high velocity) guns

NOTE—THE CONNECTING BLOCK [119] DIFFERS IN THE UPPER AND LOWER GUNS. THE UPPER GUN BLOCK IS ABOUT 13" LONGER ON ACCOUNT OF THE SPACE REQUIRED FOR THE CARTRIDGE GANGWAY. WHEN THESE GUNS ARE USED IN THE OUTER POSITION ON OTHER MOUNTINGS [MARK V AND VI] THE EJECTOR TUBE IS LONGER THAN THAT IN A LOWER GUN BUT IS OTHERWISE SIMILAR. THE STEAM TUBE OF A LOWER GUN IS APPROX 9½" LONGER THAN THAT OF THE UPPER GUN. THE FREE LENGTH OF THE BARREL SPRING WHEN UNCOMPRESSED IS BETWEEN 30.5" AND 31". FEED BOXES AND BOTTOM FEED LEVERS ARE MARKED LEFT AND RIGHT AND WERE NOT INTERCHANGEABLE. THE PITCH OF THE BELTED AMMUNITION WAS APPROX 2.4". THE ARTICULATED LINKS ARE SPRING STEEL HARDENED AND TEMPERED. H.E. NOSE FUSED OR INCENDIARY AMMUNITION WAS NOT TO BE FIRED THROUGH THE MUZZLE COVERS. THE BELTS WAS LOADED SO THAT THE FIRST TWO ROUNDS FIRED WERE PRACTICE OR PRACTICE TRACER.

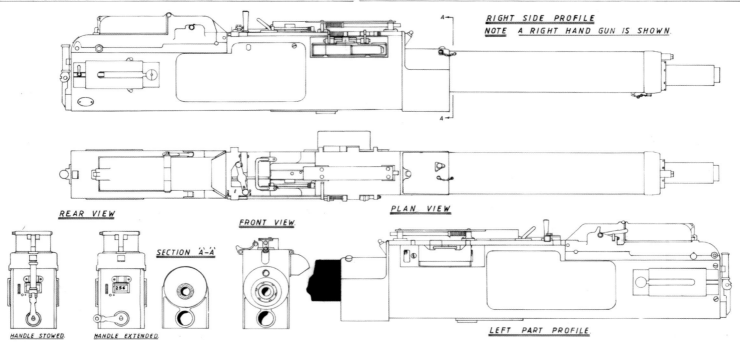

RIGHT SIDE PROFILE
NOTE A RIGHT HAND GUN IS SHOWN.

REAR VIEW

PLAN VIEW

FRONT VIEW

SECTION 'A'-'A'

HANDLE STOWED.

HANDLE EXTENDED.

LEFT PART PROFILE

AS IS USUAL I HAVE NOT FOUND ANY EXTERNAL G/A DRAWINGS. THESE HAVE BEEN PREPARED WITH THE AID OF MY PHOTOGRAPH COLLECTION. OFFICIAL DRAWINGS [REDRAWN ON THESE FOUR SHEETS] AND MEASUREMENTS TAKEN FROM GUN No. S 10835 WHICH IS ON DISPLAY AT THE ROYAL NAVAL ARMAMENT MUSEUM, PRIDDY'S HARD, GOSPORT, HANTS.

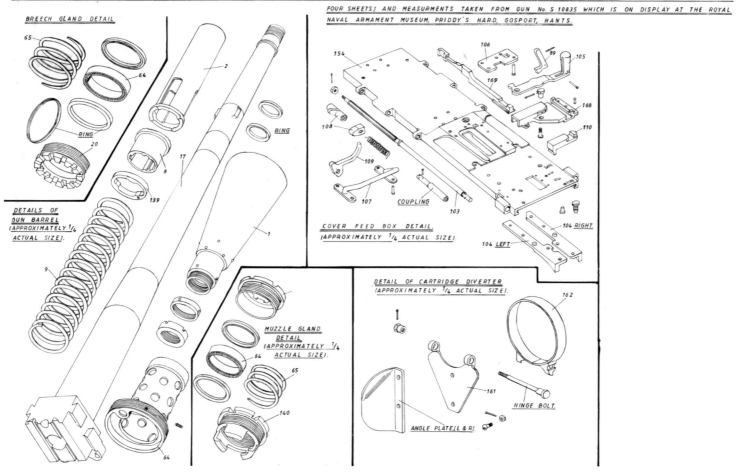

BREECH GLAND DETAIL

RING

RING

DETAILS OF GUN BARREL (APPROXIMATELY ¼ ACTUAL SIZE).

MUZZLE GLAND DETAIL (APPROXIMATELY ¼ ACTUAL SIZE).

COVER FEED BOX DETAIL. (APPROXIMATELY ¼ ACTUAL SIZE).

COUPLING

104 RIGHT

104 LEFT

DETAIL OF CARTRIDGE DIVERTER (APPROXIMATELY ¼ ACTUAL SIZE).

HINGE BOLT.

ANGLE PLATE (L & R).

PART VIEW - GENERAL ARRANGEMENT OF UPPER GUN. [SEE SHEET 'B' FOR LARGER
AND COMPLETE G/A WITH KEY'S TO DETAIL ON SHEETS 'B' & 'C'].

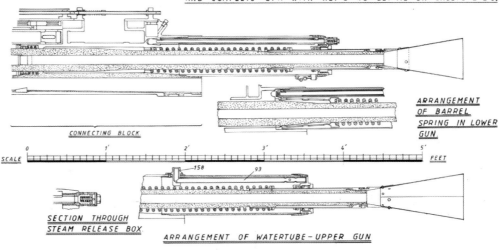

CONNECTING BLOCK

ARRANGEMENT
OF BARREL
SPRING IN LOWER
GUN.

SCALE 0 1' 2' 3' 4' 5' FEET

158   93

SECTION THROUGH
STEAM RELEASE BOX.

ARRANGEMENT OF WATERTUBE - UPPER GUN

STEAM RELEASE
BOX.
WATER TUBE
SUPPORTING
PLUG.

END VIEW OF
WATERJACKET.

70   70   SPINDLE.
PIN.
53

CATCH
84
163
NUT
34
112
85
SLEEVE
CUSHION
111
CRANK STOP BOLT.
159

COVER MECHANISM DETAIL
(APPROXIMATELY 1/4 ACTUAL SIZE).

FEED BOX DETAIL FOR
LEFT GUNS MARK's
VII AND VIIP MOUNTINGS
OF 1944.
(APPROXIMATELY
1/4 ACTUAL
SIZE).
TOP
81
BOTTOM

L.H.

HISTORY –
THIS 40mm, RECOIL OPERATED, WATER COOLED, BELT FED GUN, RATHER LIKE A LARGE
MACHINE GUN, WAS A REDESIGN OF THE EARLIER MARK II GUN TO SUIT 8 BARREL MOUNTING
A PROTOTYPE, 6 BARREL MARK II MOUNTING HAD BEEN TRIED OUT IN 1921-22, FOLLOWED BY
DESIGN WORK CARRIED OUT ON EXPERIMENTAL MULTIPLE GUN MOUNTINGS BOTH BY
ARMSTRONG AND VICKERS. THE VICKERS MOUNTING EVENTUALLY BEING SELECTED FOR PRODUCTION.
A MOCK UP BEING EXAMINED IN JULY 1923, BUT BECAUSE OF TREASURY RESTRICTIONS IT WAS
NOT UNTIL 1927 THAT FIRING TRIALS WERE CARRIED OUT, FOLLOWED BY SEA TRIALS ABOARD
H.M.S. TIGER IN 1928. THE ISSUE OF THE FIRST 8 BARREL SERVICE MOUNTING BEING TO H.M.S.
VALIANT IN LATE 1930. THE HEAVY AND COMPLEX 8 BARREL "M" MOUNTING BEING GRADUALLY
INTRODUCED ABOARD CAPITAL SHIPS FROM 1931 IT WAS IN TURN SUCCEDED BY THE GENERALLY
SIMILAR MARK VI MOUNTING. BOTH HAD CONTROLLED FIRE GUNS' BUT IN 1939 AUTOMATIC FIRE
WAS INTRODUCED. THE MOUNTINGS BECOMING THE MARK VA AND VIA.
A SERIOUS DEFECT OF THE ORIGINAL MARK VIII GUN WAS THE LOW MUZZLE VELOCITY. [2040 FT
/ SEC]. IT WAS FOUND POSSIBLE TO INCREASE THE MUZZLE VELOCITY TO 2400 FT/SEC. MOUNTINGS
WITH THESE GUNS - SHOWN HERE - WERE DISTINGUISHED BY A STAR [*] ADDED TO THE MARK NO
I HAVE REDRAWN THE 2 POUNDER POM POM MARK VIII H.V. GUN FROM OFFICIAL GUNNERY
MANUALS AIDED BY PHOTOGRAPHS. THIS CLOSE RANGE WEAPON WAS IN SERVICE THROUGHOUT
THE WAR, BEING FITTED TO 8, 4 AND SINGLE BARRELLED MOUNTINGS. EARLY MOUNTINGS DID NOT
HAVE A FLAME GUARD FITTED BUT AS WARTIME PRODUCTION INCREASED THE GUN WAS
IMPROVED AS A RESULT OF OPERATIONAL EXPERIENCE. THE GUN HAD A MAXIMUM RANGE
OF 1700 YARDS. THE COMPLEX INTERNAL WORKING MECHANISM REQUIRED CONSIDERABLE
SKILLED MAINTENANCE BY THE SHIPS O.A's. (ORDINANCE ARTIFICERS)

DATA – Q.F. 2 PDR MARK VIII HIGH VELOCITY GUN

MUZZLE VELOCITY	2300 FT./SEC.
LENGTH OF GUN BARREL	62 INS.
DIAMETER OF BORE	1·575 INS. [40mm]
LENGTH OF RIFLING	54·84 INS
TWIST OF RIFLING	1 IN 30 RIGHT HANDED
No. OF GROOVES	12
LENGTH OF RECOIL	
AVERAGE WORKING	7·5 INS.
MAXIMUM [METAL TO METAL]	8·0 INS.
MINIMUM TO ENSURE CORRECT FUNCTIONING OF MECHANISM	7·3 INS.
OVERALL LENGTH OF GUN EXCLUDING FLAME GUARD	8 FT 4·6 INS
OVERALL LENGTH OF GUN INCLUDING FLAME GUARD	9 FT 7·6 INS
CAPACITY OF WATERJACKET	21 PINTS
RATE OF FIRE [AUTOMATIC]	115 ROUNDS/MIN. [APPROX].
CAPACITY OF BUFFER SYSTEM	1 QUART
TOTAL WEIGHT, WATERJACKET AND BUFFER SYSTEM FILLED	7 CWTS.
RANGE TABLES LOW ANGLE	No. 430
RANGE TABLES HIGH ANGLE	No. 431
TRAJECTORY CHART	No. O C 76
BOOKS OF REFERENCE	B.R. 778, B.R. 847/44 & B.R. 258/41.

THIS SUBJECT HAS BEEN REDRAWN MAINLY FROM INFORMATION
PROVIDED BY MY VISIT TO THE HAMPSHIRE RECORD OFFICE
SUSSEX STREET WINCHESTER IN JULY 1993. THE COMPONENT PARTS
BEING FOUND IN BR. 847/44, THE HANDBOOK FOR THE 2 PDR Q.F.
MARK VIII GUN ON MARKS VII AND VII P [QUAD]. MOUNTING 1944
AND SCHEDUAL OF COMPONENT PARTS AND TOOLS. THE DETAILED
COMPONENT PARTS OF THIS GUN, OVER 300 ITEMS, SHOWN ON
THESE THREE SHEETS ARE THE WORK OF UNKNOWN WARTIME
ILLUSTRATORS. THE SERFEIT IS DUE TO THEM.

SHEET ONE OF FOUR SHEETS.

© JOHN LAMBERT 27/7/96 CH'D. 12/8/96 L/0/38/A

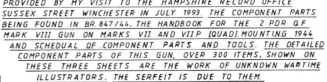

A 3 2pdr Mk VIII* HV gun, 1943

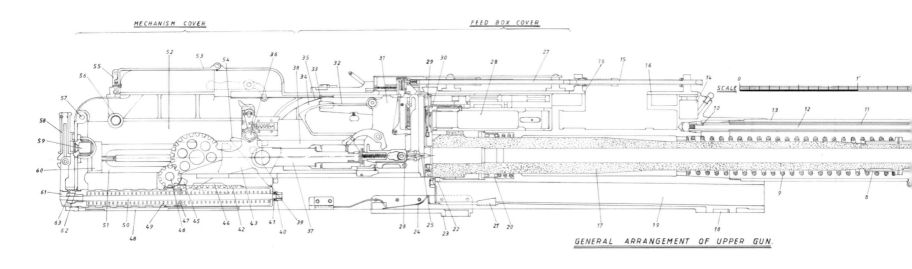

MECHANISM COVER

FEED BOX COVER

SCALE

GENERAL ARRANGEMENT OF UPPER GUN.

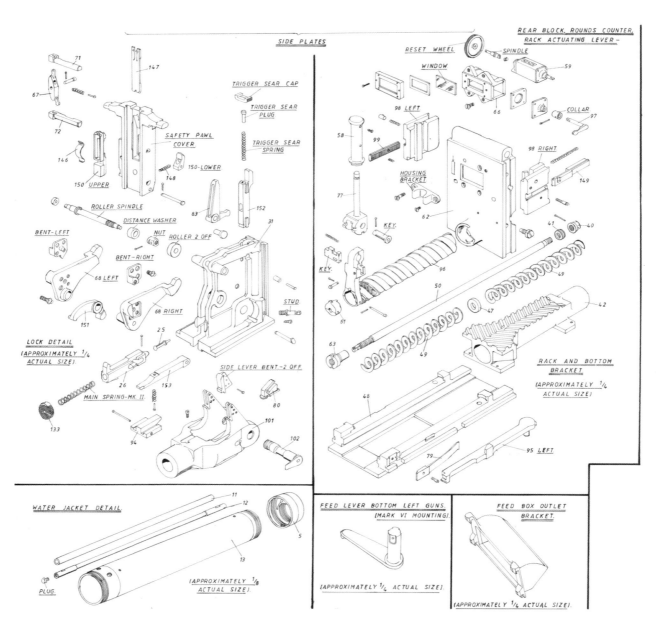

SIDE PLATES

REAR BLOCK, ROUNDS COUNTER,
RACK ACTUATING LEVER —

RESET WHEEL

SPINDLE

WINDOW

TRIGGER SEAR CAP

TRIGGER SEAR
PLUG

COLLAR

SAFETY PAWL
COVER

TRIGGER SEAR
SPRING

150 UPPER

150-LOWER

HOUSING
BRACKET

ROLLER SPINDLE

DISTANCE WASHER

KEY.

BENT-LEFT

NUT

ROLLER 2 OFF

BENT-RIGHT

KEY.

68 LEFT

68 RIGHT

STUD.

151

LOCK DETAIL
(APPROXIMATELY ¼
ACTUAL SIZE).

SIDE LEVER BENT-2 OFF

25

MAIN SPRING-MK.II.

133

94

RACK AND BOTTOM
BRACKET
(APPROXIMATELY ¼
ACTUAL SIZE).

95 LEFT

WATER JACKET DETAIL

FEED LEVER BOTTOM LEFT GUNS.
(MARK VI MOUNTING).

FEED BOX OUTLET
BRACKET

PLUG.

(APPROXIMATELY ¼
ACTUAL SIZE).

(APPROXIMATELY ¼ ACTUAL SIZE).

(APPROXIMATELY ¼ ACTUAL SIZE).

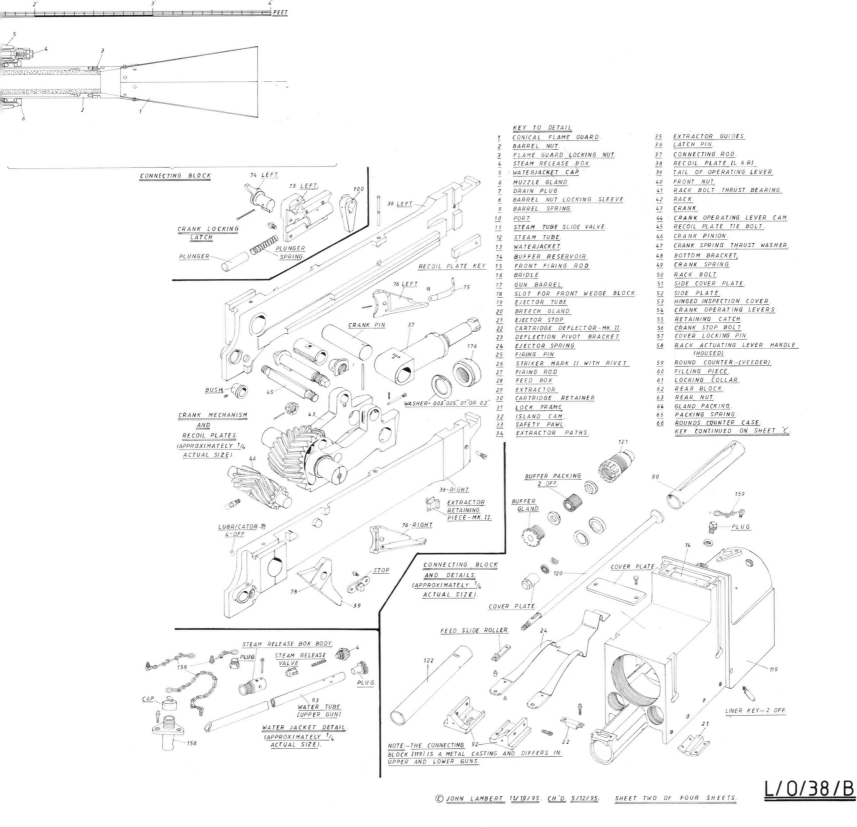

GENERAL DESCRIPTION OF THE MARK VIII DEPICTED HERE IS SIMILAR TO THE RIGHT INNER GUN OF THE EIGHT GUN MARK VI MOUNTING AND WAS USED ON THE SINGLE MARK VIII MOUNTING AND THE MARK XVI POWER OPERATED MOUNTING. IT IS FULLY AUTOMATIC WITH RATE OF FIRE UNCONTROLLED UNLIKE GUNS ON THE MARK VII MOUNTING (FOUR GUN EQUIPMENT) WHICH WERE ADAPTED FOR CONTROLLED FIRE ONLY, AND CERTAIN GUNS ON MARK V (EARLY MOUNTING) AND MARK VI MOUNTINGS WHICH HAD NOT YET BEEN CONVERTED FOR AUTOMATIC FIRE (1943).

NOTE – A PLATE INSCRIBED A.H.V. (AUTOMATIC HIGH VELOCITY) WAS ATTACHED TO THE REAR BLOCK THIS HAD TO BE REPLACED BY ONE MARKED A.L.V. IF AT ANY TIME THE GUN SHOULD BE CONVERTED TO USE LOW VELOCITY AMMUNITION BY SUBSTITUTING THE MARK I BUFFER LINER FOR THE MARK III WHICH WAS NORMALLY FITTED.

FEET

CONNECTING BLOCK

CRANK LOCKING LATCH

PLUNGER

PLUNGER SPRING

RECOIL PLATE KEY

CRANK PIN

BUSH

CRANK MECHANISM AND RECOIL PLATES (APPROXIMATELY 1/4 ACTUAL SIZE)

LUBRICATOR 4-OFF

STOP

EXTRACTOR RETAINING PIECE-MK. II.

BUFFER PACKING 2 OFF

BUFFER GLAND

PLUG

CONNECTING BLOCK AND DETAILS (APPROXIMATELY 1/4 ACTUAL SIZE)

COVER PLATE

FEED SLIDE ROLLER

COVER PLATE

LINER KEY– 2 OFF

STEAM RELEASE BOX BODY

PLUG

STEAM RELEASE VALVE

PLUG

CAP

WATER TUBE (UPPER GUN)

WATER JACKET DETAIL (APPROXIMATELY 1/4 ACTUAL SIZE)

NOTE–THE CONNECTING BLOCK (119) IS A METAL CASTING AND DIFFERS IN UPPER AND LOWER GUNS

KEY TO DETAIL

1	CONICAL FLAME GUARD.
2	BARREL NUT.
3	FLAME GUARD LOCKING NUT.
4	STEAM RELEASE BOX.
5	WATERJACKET CAP.
6	MUZZLE GLAND.
7	DRAIN PLUG.
8	BARREL NUT LOCKING SLEEVE.
9	BARREL SPRING.
10	PORT.
11	STEAM TUBE SLIDE VALVE.
12	STEAM TUBE.
13	WATERJACKET.
14	BUFFER RESERVOIR.
15	FRONT FIRING ROD.
16	BRIDLE.
17	GUN BARREL.
18	SLOT FOR FRONT WEDGE BLOCK.
19	EJECTOR TUBE.
20	BREECH GLAND.
21	EJECTOR STOP.
22	CARTRIDGE DEFLECTOR - MK. II.
23	DEFLECTION PIVOT BRACKET.
24	EJECTOR SPRING.
25	FIRING PIN.
26	STRIKER MARK II WITH RIVET.
27	FIRING ROD.
28	FEED BOX.
29	EXTRACTOR.
30	CARTRIDGE RETAINER.
31	LOCK FRAME.
32	ISLAND CAM.
33	SAFETY PAWL.
34	EXTRACTOR PATHS.
35	EXTRACTOR GUIDES.
36	LATCH PIN.
37	CONNECTING ROD.
38	RECOIL PLATE (L & R).
39	TAIL OF OPERATING LEVER.
40	FRONT NUT.
41	RACK BOLT THRUST BEARING.
42	RACK.
43	CRANK.
44	CRANK OPERATING LEVER CAM.
45	RECOIL PLATE TIE BOLT.
46	CRANK PINION.
47	CRANK SPRING THRUST WASHER.
48	BOTTOM BRACKET.
49	CRANK SPRING.
50	RACK BOLT.
51	SIDE COVER PLATE.
52	SIDE PLATE.
53	HINGED INSPECTION COVER.
54	CRANK OPERATING LEVERS.
55	RETAINING CATCH.
56	CRANK STOP BOLT.
57	COVER LOCKING PIN.
58	RACK ACTUATING LEVER HANDLE (HOUSED).
59	ROUND COUNTER:-(VEEDER).
60	FILLING PIECE.
61	LOCKING COLLAR.
62	REAR BLOCK.
63	REAR NUT.
64	GLAND PACKING.
65	PACKING SPRING.
66	ROUNDS COUNTER CASE.
	KEY CONTINUED ON SHEET 'C'.

© JOHN LAMBERT 11/19/95. CH'D. 5/12/95.   SHEET TWO OF FOUR SHEETS.

L/0/38/B

A 3 2pdr Mk VIII* HV gun and ammunition, detail

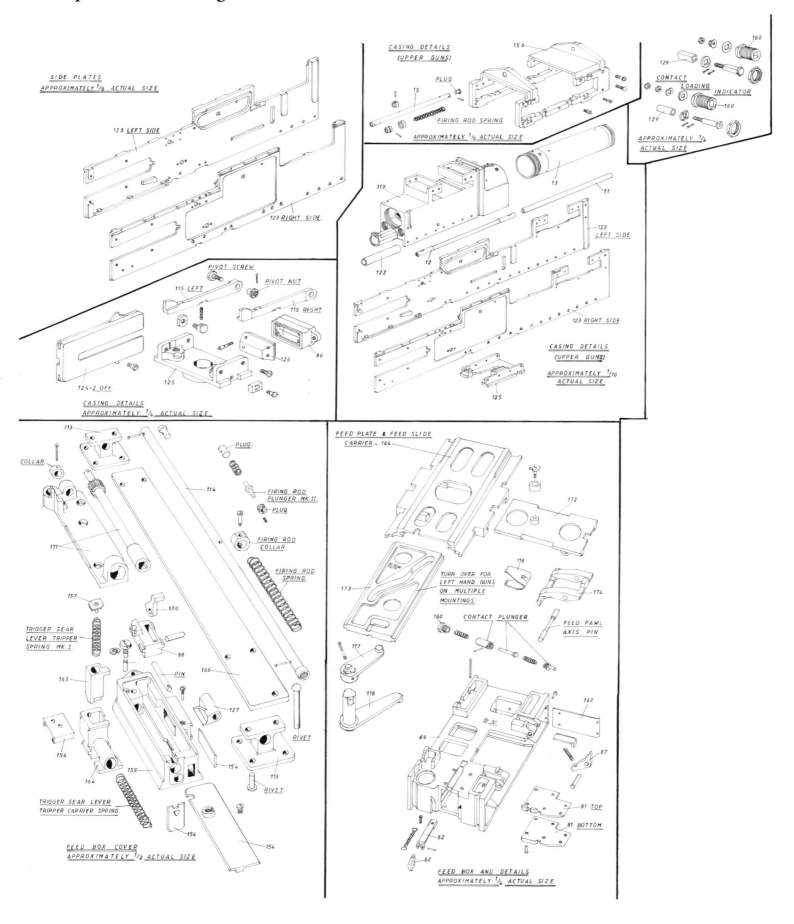

SIDE PLATES
APPROXIMATELY 1/8 ACTUAL SIZE

123 LEFT SIDE

123 RIGHT SIDE.

CASING DETAILS
(UPPER GUNS)

156

PLUG

15

FIRING ROD SPRING

APPROXIMATELY 1/4 ACTUAL SIZE

129

CONTACT
LOADING INDICATOR

160

160

129

APPROXIMATELY 1/4
ACTUAL SIZE

119

13

11

122

12

123
LEFT SIDE

123 RIGHT SIDE

CASING DETAILS
(UPPER GUNS)

APPROXIMATELY 1/10
ACTUAL SIZE

125

PIVOT SCREW

115 LEFT

PIVOT NUT

115 RIGHT

126

86

124-2 OFF.

125

CASING DETAILS
APPROXIMATELY 1/4 ACTUAL SIZE.

113

COLLAR

PLUG.

114

FIRING ROD
PLUNGER MK.II.

PLUG

FIRING ROD
COLLAR

FIRING ROD
SPRING.

171

157

170

TRIGGER SEAR
LEVER TRIPPER
SPRING MK.I.

88

165

PIN.

166

127

154

155

113

164

RIVET

154

RIVET.

TRIGGER SEAR LEVER
TRIPPER CARRIER SPRING.

154

154

FEED BOX COVER
APPROXIMATELY 1/2 ACTUAL SIZE

FEED PLATE & FEED SLIDE
CARRIER.- 164

172

173

TURN OVER FOR
LEFT HAND GUNS
ON MULTIPLE
MOUNTINGS

116

174

160

CONTACT PLUNGER

FEED PAWL
AXIS PIN

117

118

167

69

87

82

81 TOP

81 BOTTOM

82

FEED BOX AND DETAILS
APPROXIMATELY 1/4 ACTUAL SIZE

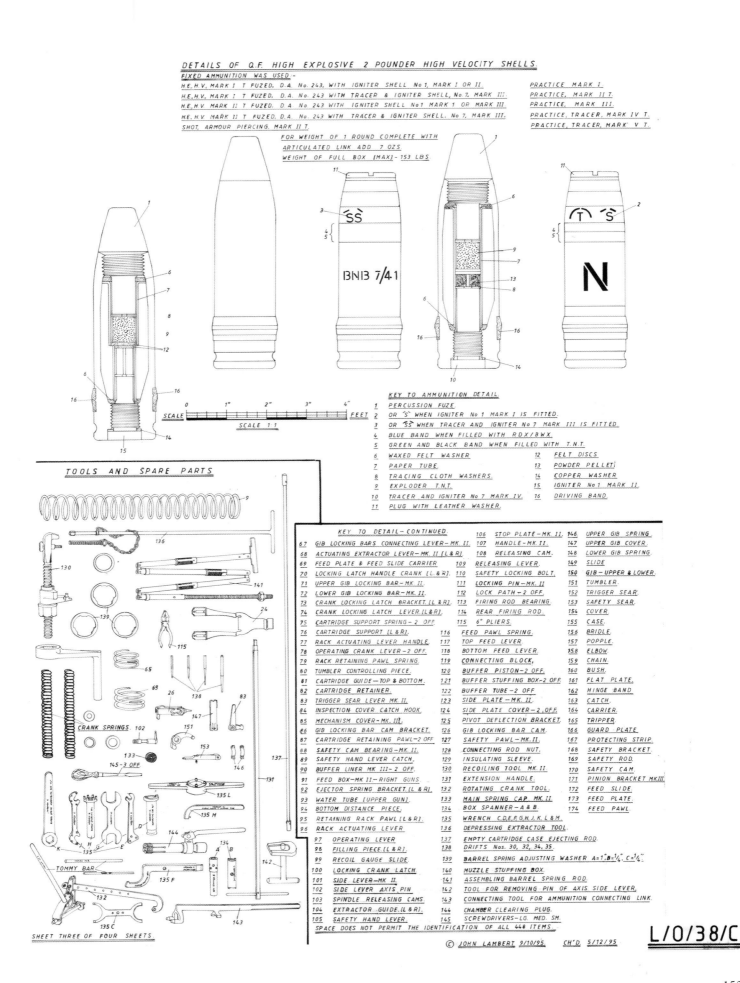

DETAILS OF Q.F. HIGH EXPLOSIVE 2 POUNDER HIGH VELOCITY SHELLS.

FIXED AMMUNITION WAS USED:-

H.E,H.V, MARK I T FUZED, D.A. No.243, WITH IGNITER SHELL No1, MARK I OR II.

H.E,H.V, MARK I T FUZED, D.A. No.243 WITH TRACER & IGNITER SHELL, No.7, MARK III.

H.E.H.V MARK II T FUZED. D.A. No.243 WITH IGNITER SHELL No1 MARK 1 OR MARK III

H.E,H.V MARK II T FUZED, D.A. No.243 WITH TRACER & IGNITER SHELL. No.7, MARK III.

SHOT, ARMOUR PIERCING, MARK II T.

PRACTICE MARK I

PRACTICE, MARK II T.

PRACTICE, MARK III.

PRACTICE, TRACER, MARK IV T.

PRACTICE, TRACER, MARK V T.

FOR WEIGHT OF 1 ROUND COMPLETE WITH
ARTICULATED LINK ADD 7 OZS
WEIGHT OF FULL BOX [MAX]- 153 LBS

BNB 7/41

SCALE |0 | 1" | 2" | 3" | 4"| FEET

SCALE 1:1

KEY TO AMMUNITION DETAIL

1 PERCUSSION FUZE
2 OR 'S' WHEN IGNITER No1 MARK I IS FITTED.
3 OR 'SS' WHEN TRACER AND IGNITER No7 MARK III IS FITTED
4 BLUE BAND WHEN FILLED WITH RDX/BWX.
5 GREEN AND BLACK BAND WHEN FILLED WITH T.N.T.
6 WAXED FELT WASHER
7 PAPER TUBE
8 TRACING CLOTH WASHERS.
9 EXPLODER T.N.T.
10 TRACER AND IGNITER No7 MARK IV.
11 PLUG WITH LEATHER WASHER.
12 FELT DISCS
13 POWDER PELLET
14 COPPER WASHER
15 IGNITER No1 MARK II.
16 DRIVING BAND.

TOOLS AND SPARE PARTS

CRANK SPRINGS. 102

145-3 OFF

TOMMY BAR

SHEET THREE OF FOUR SHEETS

KEY TO DETAIL - CONTINUED.

No.	Description	No.	Description	No.	Description
67	GIB LOCKING BARS CONNECTING LEVER-MK.II	106	STOP PLATE-MK.II	146	UPPER GIB SPRING
68	ACTUATING EXTRACTOR LEVER-MK.II [L&R]	107	HANDLE-MK.II	147	UPPER GIB COVER.
69	FEED PLATE & FEED SLIDE CARRIER	108	RELEASING CAM.	148	LOWER GIB SPRING.
70	LOCKING LATCH HANDLE CRANK [L&R]	109	RELEASING LEVER.	149	SLIDE
71	UPPER GIB LOCKING BAR-MK.II.	110	SAFETY LOCKING BOLT.	150	GIB-UPPER & LOWER.
72	LOWER GIB LOCKING BAR-MK.II.	111	LOCKING PIN-MK.II	151	TUMBLER.
73	CRANK LOCKING LATCH BRACKET.[L&R].	112	LOCK PATH-2 OFF.	152	TRIGGER SEAR.
74	CRANK LOCKING LATCH LEVER.[L&R].	113	FIRING ROD BEARING.	153	SAFETY SEAR.
75	CARTRIDGE SUPPORT SPRING-2 OFF.	114	REAR FIRING ROD.	154	COVER.
76	CARTRIDGE SUPPORT [L&R].	115	6" PLIERS.	155	CASE.
77	RACK ACTUATING LEVER HANDLE.	116	FEED PAWL SPRING.	156	BRIDLE.
78	OPERATING CRANK LEVER-2 OFF.	117	TOP FEED LEVER.	157	POPPLE.
79	RACK RETAINING PAWL SPRING.	118	BOTTOM FEED LEVER.	158	ELBOW.
80	TUMBLER CONTROLLING PIECE.	119	CONNECTING BLOCK,	159	CHAIN.
81	CARTRIDGE GUIDE-TOP & BOTTOM.	120	BUFFER PISTON-2 OFF.	160	BUSH.
82	CARTRIDGE RETAINER.	121	BUFFER STUFFING BOX-2 OFF.	161	FLAT PLATE.
83	TRIGGER SEAR LEVER MK.II.	122	BUFFER TUBE-2 OFF	162	HINGE BAND.
84	INSPECTION COVER CATCH HOOK.	123	SIDE PLATE-MK.II.	163	CATCH.
85	MECHANISM COVER-MK.III.	124	SIDE PLATE COVER-2.OFF.	164	CARRIER.
86	GIB LOCKING BAR CAM BRACKET.	125	PIVOT DEFLECTION BRACKET.	165	TRIPPER.
87	CARTRIDGE RETAINING PAWL-2 OFF	126	GIB LOCKING BAR CAM.	166	GUARD PLATE.
88	SAFETY CAM BEARING-MK.II.	127	SAFETY PAWL-MK.II.	167	PROTECTING STRIP.
89	SAFETY HAND LEVER CATCH.	128	CONNECTING ROD NUT.	168	SAFETY BRACKET.
90	BUFFER LINER MK III-2 OFF.	129	INSULATING SLEEVE.	169	SAFETY ROD.
91	FEED BOX-MK.II-RIGHT GUNS.	130	RECOILING TOOL MK.II.	170	SAFETY CAM.
92	EJECTOR SPRING BRACKET.[L&R].	131	EXTENSION HANDLE.	171	PINION BRACKET MK.III
93	WATER TUBE [UPPER GUN].	132	ROTATING CRANK TOOL.	172	FEED SLIDE.
94	BOTTOM DISTANCE PIECE.	133	MAIN SPRING CAP. MK.II	173	FEED PLATE.
95	RETAINING RACK PAWL [L&R].	134	BOX SPANNER-A & B	174	FEED PAWL.
96	RACK ACTUATING LEVER	135	WRENCH C,D,E,F,G,H,J,K,L & M		
97	OPERATING LEVER	136	DEPRESSING EXTRACTOR TOOL.		
98	FILLING PIECE.[L&R].	137	EMPTY CARTRIDGE CASE EJECTING ROD.		
99	RECOIL GAUGE SLIDE	138	DRIFTS Nos. 30, 32, 34, 35.		
100	LOCKING CRANK LATCH	139	BARREL SPRING ADJUSTING WASHER A=1",B=1/4", C=1/4"		
101	SIDE LEVER-MK.II.	140	MUZZLE STUFFING BOX.		
102	SIDE LEVER AXIS PIN	141	ASSEMBLING BARREL SPRING ROD.		
103	SPINDLE RELEASING CAMS.	142	TOOL FOR REMOVING PIN OF AXIS SIDE LEVER.		
104	EXTRACTOR GUIDE.[L&R].	143	CONNECTING TOOL FOR AMMUNITION CONNECTING LINK.		
105	SAFETY HAND LEVER.	144	CHAMBER CLEARING PLUG.		
		145	SCREWDRIVERS-LG. MED. SM.		

SPACE DOES NOT PERMIT THE IDENTIFICATION OF ALL 448 ITEMS.

© JOHN LAMBERT 9/10/95   CH'D 5/12/95

L/0/38/C

A 3 2pdr Mk VIII gun, working mechanism and detail

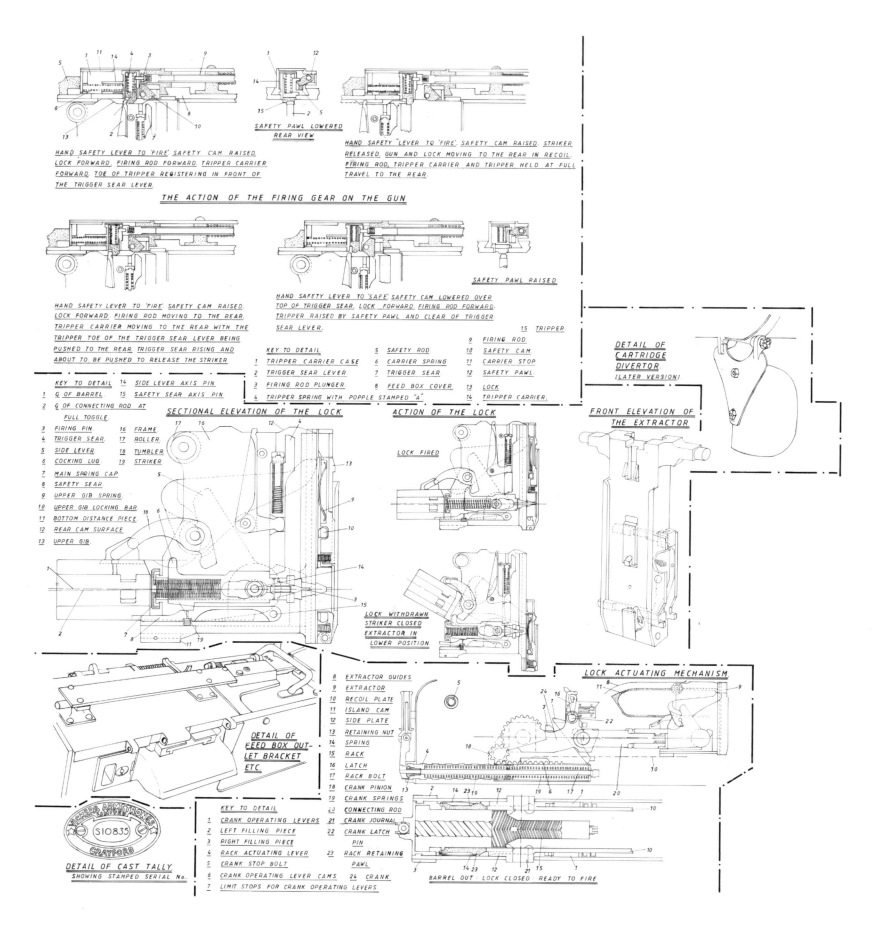

SAFETY PAWL LOWERED
REAR VIEW

HAND SAFETY LEVER TO 'FIRE'. SAFETY CAM RAISED.
LOCK FORWARD. FIRING ROD FORWARD. TRIPPER CARRIER
FORWARD. TOE OF TRIPPER REGISTERING IN FRONT OF
THE TRIGGER SEAR LEVER.

HAND SAFETY 'LEVER TO 'FIRE'. SAFETY CAM RAISED. STRIKER
RELEASED. GUN AND LOCK MOVING TO THE REAR IN RECOIL.
FIRING ROD, TRIPPER CARRIER AND TRIPPER HELD AT FULL
TRAVEL TO THE REAR.

THE ACTION OF THE FIRING GEAR ON THE GUN

SAFETY PAWL RAISED.

HAND SAFETY LEVER TO 'FIRE'. SAFETY CAM RAISED.
LOCK FORWARD. FIRING ROD MOVING TO THE REAR.
TRIPPER CARRIER MOVING TO THE REAR WITH THE
TRIPPER TOE OF THE TRIGGER SEAR LEVER BEING
PUSHED TO THE REAR. TRIGGER SEAR RISING AND
ABOUT TO BE PUSHED TO RELEASE THE STRIKER

HAND SAFETY LEVER TO 'SAFE' SAFETY CAM LOWERED OVER
TOP OF TRIGGER SEAR. LOCK FORWARD. FIRING ROD FORWARD.
TRIPPER RAISED BY SAFETY PAWL AND CLEAR OF TRIGGER
SEAR LEVER.

KEY TO DETAIL
1 TRIPPER CARRIER CASE
2 TRIGGER SEAR LEVER
3 FIRING ROD PLUNGER.
4 TRIPPER SPRING WITH POPPLE STAMPED "A"

5 SAFETY ROD
6 CARRIER SPRING
7 TRIGGER SEAR.
8 FEED BOX COVER.

9 FIRING ROD.
10 SAFETY CAM.
11 CARRIER STOP
12 SAFETY PAWL.
13 LOCK
14 TRIPPER CARRIER.
15 TRIPPER.

DETAIL OF
CARTRIDGE
DIVERTOR.
[LATER VERSION]

KEY TO DETAIL
1 G OF BARREL.
2 G OF CONNECTING ROD AT
   FULL TOGGLE.
3 FIRING PIN.
4 TRIGGER SEAR.
5 SIDE LEVER.
6 COCKING LUG.
7 MAIN SPRING CAP.
8 SAFETY SEAR.
9 UPPER GIB SPRING.
10 UPPER GIB LOCKING BAR.
11 BOTTOM DISTANCE PIECE.
12 REAR CAM SURFACE
13 UPPER GIB.

14 SIDE LEVER AXIS PIN
15 SAFETY SEAR AXIS PIN
16 FRAME.
17 ROLLER.
18 TUMBLER.
19 STRIKER

SECTIONAL ELEVATION OF THE LOCK

ACTION OF THE LOCK

LOCK FIRED

LOCK WITHDRAWN
STRIKER CLOSED
EXTRACTOR IN
LOWER POSITION.

FRONT ELEVATION OF
THE EXTRACTOR

DETAIL OF FEED BOX OUT-
LET BRACKET
ETC.

KEY TO DETAIL
8 EXTRACTOR GUIDES
9 EXTRACTOR
10 RECOIL PLATE
11 ISLAND CAM
12 SIDE PLATE
13 RETAINING NUT
14 SPRING
15 RACK
16 LATCH
17 RACK BOLT
18 CRANK PINION
19 CRANK SPRINGS
20 CONNECTING ROD
21 CRANK JOURNAL
22 CRANK LATCH
   PIN
23 RACK RETAINING
   PAWL
24 CRANK

LOCK ACTUATING MECHANISM

VICKERS ARMSTRONG
S10835
GRAYFORD

DETAIL OF CAST TALLY
SHOWING STAMPED SERIAL No.

KEY TO DETAIL
1 CRANK OPERATING LEVERS
2 LEFT FILLING PIECE
3 RIGHT FILLING PIECE
4 RACK ACTUATING LEVER
5 CRANK STOP BOLT
6 CRANK OPERATING LEVER CAMS
7 LIMIT STOPS FOR CRANK OPERATING LEVERS

BARREL OUT. LOCK CLOSED. READY TO FIRE

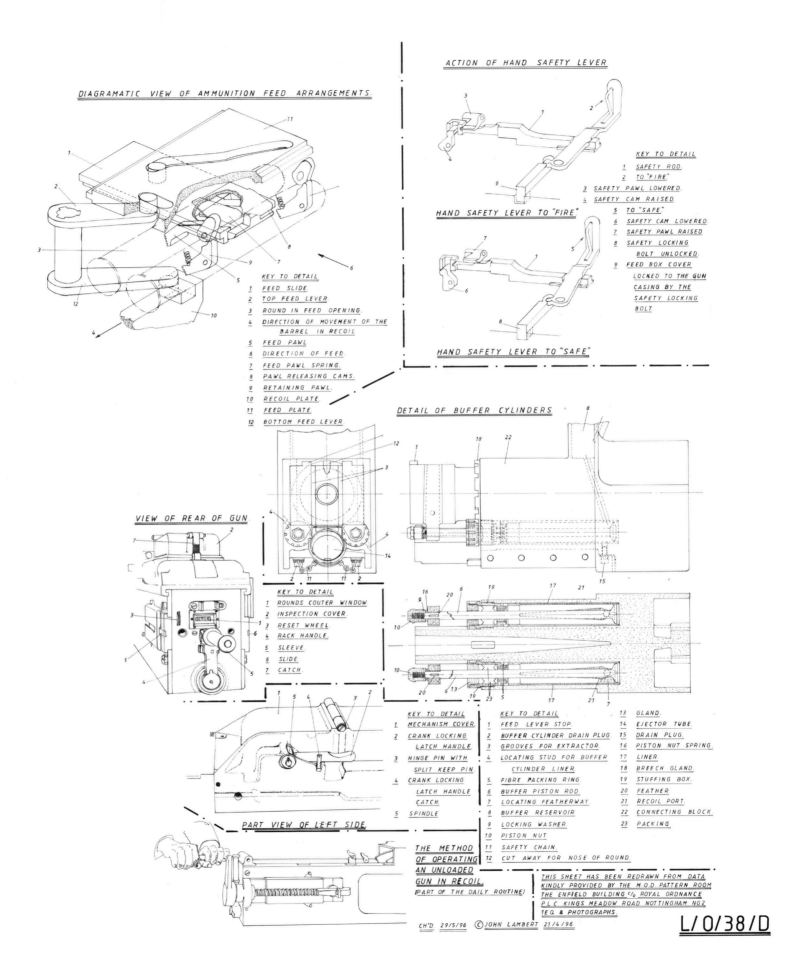

DIAGRAMATIC VIEW OF AMMUNITION FEED ARRANGEMENTS.

ACTION OF HAND SAFETY LEVER

HAND SAFETY LEVER TO "FIRE"

HAND SAFETY LEVER TO "SAFE"

KEY TO DETAIL
1 SAFETY ROD.
2 TO "FIRE"
3 SAFETY PAWL LOWERED.
4 SAFETY CAM RAISED.
5 TO "SAFE"
6 SAFETY CAM LOWERED.
7 SAFETY PAWL RAISED
8 SAFETY LOCKING
   BOLT UNLOCKED.
9 FEED BOX COVER
   LOCKED TO THE GUN
   CASING BY THE
   SAFETY LOCKING
   BOLT

KEY TO DETAIL
1 FEED SLIDE
2 TOP FEED LEVER.
3 ROUND IN FEED OPENING.
4 DIRECTION OF MOVEMENT OF THE
   BARREL IN RECOIL
5 FEED PAWL
6 DIRECTION OF FEED.
7 FEED PAWL SPRING.
8 PAWL RELEASING CAMS.
9 RETAINING PAWL.
10 RECOIL PLATE.
11 FEED PLATE
12 BOTTOM FEED LEVER.

DETAIL OF BUFFER CYLINDERS

VIEW OF REAR OF GUN.

KEY TO DETAIL
1 ROUNDS COUTER WINDOW.
2 INSPECTION COVER.
3 RESET WHEEL
4 RACK HANDLE.
5 SLEEVE
6 SLIDE
7 CATCH.

KEY TO DETAIL
1 MECHANISM COVER.
2 CRANK LOCKING
   LATCH HANDLE
3 HINGE PIN WITH
   SPLIT KEEP PIN
4 CRANK LOCKING
   LATCH HANDLE
   CATCH.
5 SPINDLE

KEY TO DETAIL
1 FEED LEVER STOP
2 BUFFER CYLINDER DRAIN PLUG.
3 GROOVES FOR EXTRACTOR.
4 LOCATING STUD FOR BUFFER
   CYLINDER LINER.
5 FIBRE PACKING RING
6 BUFFER PISTON ROD.
7 LOCATING FEATHERWAY
8 BUFFER RESERVOIR
9 LOCKING WASHER.
10 PISTON NUT.
11 SAFETY CHAIN.
12 CUT AWAY FOR NOSE OF ROUND

13 GLAND.
14 EJECTOR TUBE.
15 DRAIN PLUG.
16 PISTON NUT SPRING
17 LINER
18 BREECH GLAND.
19 STUFFING BOX.
20 FEATHER
21 RECOIL PORT.
22 CONNECTING BLOCK
23 PACKING.

PART VIEW OF LEFT SIDE

THE METHOD
OF OPERATING
AN UNLOADED
GUN IN RECOIL
(PART OF THE DAILY ROUTINE)

THIS SHEET HAS BEEN REDRAWN FROM DATA
KINDLY PROVIDED BY THE M.O.D. PATTERN ROOM
THE ENFIELD BUILDING c/o ROYAL ORDNANCE
PLC KINGS MEADOW ROAD NOTTINGHAM NG2
1EQ & PHOTOGRAPHS.

CH'D. 29/5/96 (C) JOHN LAMBERT 21/4/96

L/0/38/D

A 4 Quad 2pdr mounting 'M' Mk VII

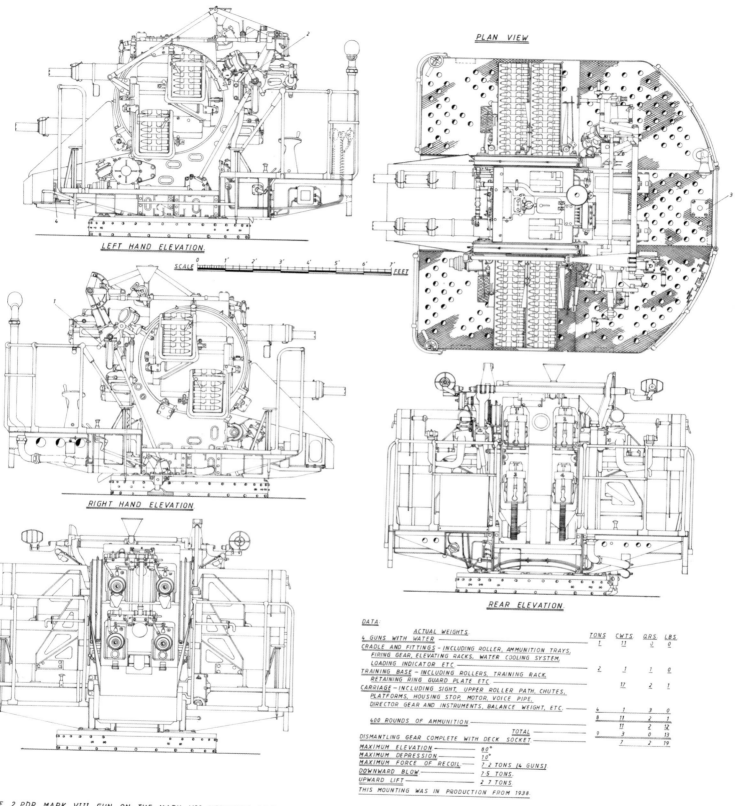

PLAN VIEW

LEFT HAND ELEVATION.

SCALE 0 1' 2' 3' 4' 5' 6' 7' FEET

RIGHT HAND ELEVATION.

REAR ELEVATION.

DATA:

		ACTUAL WEIGHTS.	TONS	CWTS	QRS	LBS
4 GUNS WITH WATER			1	11	0	0
CRADLE AND FITTINGS - INCLUDING ROLLER, AMMUNITION TRAYS, FIRING GEAR, ELEVATING RACKS, WATER COOLING SYSTEM, LOADING INDICATOR ETC			2	1	1	0
TRAINING BASE - INCLUDING ROLLERS, TRAINING RACK, RETAINING RING GUARD PLATE ETC				17	2	1
CARRIAGE - INCLUDING SIGHT, UPPER ROLLER PATH, CHUTES, PLATFORMS, HOUSING STOP, MOTOR, VOICE PIPE, DIRECTOR GEAR AND INSTRUMENTS, BALANCE WEIGHT, ETC.			4	1	3	0
400 ROUNDS OF AMMUNITION			8	11	2	1
				11	2	12
		TOTAL	9	3	0	13
DISMANTLING GEAR COMPLETE WITH DECK SOCKET				7	2	19

MAXIMUM ELEVATION	80°
MAXIMUM DEPRESSION	10°
MAXIMUM FORCE OF RECOIL	7·2 TONS (4 GUNS)
DOWNWARD BLOW	7·5 TONS.
UPWARD LIFT	2·7 TONS.

THIS MOUNTING WAS IN PRODUCTION FROM 1938.

THE 2 PDR MARK VIII GUN ON THE MARK VII MOUNTING WAS FOUND ON CRUISERS DESTROYERS AND SOME SLOOPS. THE MOUNTING WAS FITTED WITH OR WITHOUT A POM POM DIRECTOR AND IN THE FORMER CASE LAYING AND TRAINING WAS BY REMOTE POWER CONTROL (R.P.C) AS A GENERAL RULE POM POM DIRECTORS WERE FITTED IN CRUISERS AND NOT DESTROYERS. THE CREW CONSISTED OF EIGHT MEN. THE CAPTAIN OF THE GUN BEING IN CHARGE AND OPERATING THE FIRING CLUTCH LEVER. THE REMAINDER OF THE CREW WERE GUNLAYER, TRAINER, AMMUNITION FEED NUMBERS AND LOADERS FOR RIGHT AND LEFT GUNS. AMMUNITION WAS SUPPLIED IN BELTS; EIGHT BELTS PER GUN, EACH BELT CONSISTING OF 14 ROUNDS AND LOADED ON TO THE FEED RAILS. THE FIRST AND LAST ROUND OF EACH BELT RESTING ON THE RAILS AND CONNECTED TO THE PREVIOUS BELT BY CONNECTING LINKS. THE REMAINDER OF THE BELT HUNG IN A BIGHT.
ALL DRAWINGS ON THIS SHEET REDRAWN FROM VICKERS ORIGINALS KINDLY PROVIDED BY THE CUMBRIA COUNTY RECORDS OFFICE
140, DUKE STREET, BARROW IN FURNESS CUMBRIA LA14 1XW.

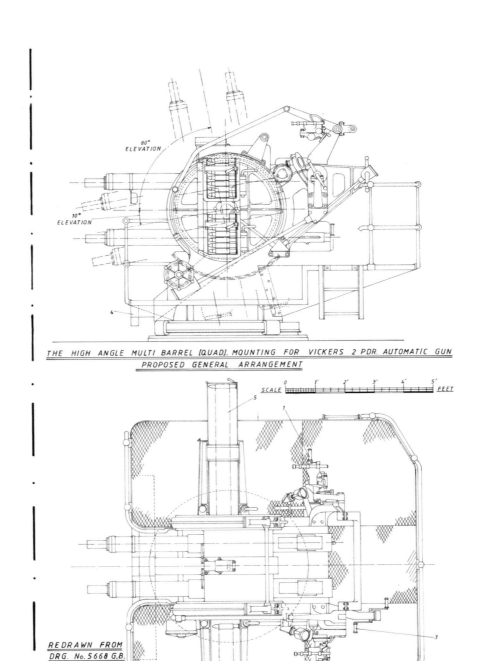

THE HIGH ANGLE MULTI BARREL [QUAD]. MOUNTING FOR VICKERS 2 PDR. AUTOMATIC GUN
PROPOSED GENERAL ARRANGEMENT

SCALE 0 1' 2' 3' 4' 5' FEET

REDRAWN FROM
DRG. No. 5668 G.B.

OTHER 2 POUNDER MOUNTINGS
    DRAWN —

L/O/04	SINGLE MARK VIII MANUAL MOUNTING - 1940
L/O/06 A-B	SINGLE MARK XVI POWER MOUNTING - 1942
L/O/29 A-B	VICKERS 40mm H/A MARK II MOUNTING - 1929
L/O/38 A-D	THE 2 PDR MARK VIII AND VIII* GUN.
L/O/66	THE 8 BARRELLED 'M' MARK V MOUNTING - 1938
L/O/84 A-D	THE 8 BARRELLED MARK VI R.P. 10 MOUNTING - 1945
L/O/138 A-C	THE QUAD MARK VII P MOUNTING - 1944

KEY
1 TRAINING HANDLES.
        1 TURN [FAST] = 7°
        1 TURN [SLOW] = 4°
2 ELEVATING HANDLES.
        1 TURN [FAST] = 7°
        1 TURN [SLOW] = 4°
3 FIRING HANDLES.
4 BALANCE WEIGHT.
5 BOX FOR 150 LINKED ROUNDS.

DATA:-

ESTIMATED WEIGHTS	TONS	CWTS	QRS	LBS
4 GUNS COMPLETE	1	8	3	0
MOUNTING INCLUDING EMPTY AMMUNITION BOXES AND BALACE WEIGHT	5	15	3	0
TOTAL	7	4	2	0

UPWARD LIFT ——————————— 3·4 TONS
DOWNWARD, BLOW ——————————— 6·1 TONS
MAXIMUM FORCE OF RECOIL [4 GUNS] - 6·5 TONS
BALLISTICS
MUZZLE VELOCITY ——————————— 2000 FT/SEC.

FRONT ELEVATION.
GENERAL ARRANGEMENT OF MOUNTING.
FOR MOUNTINGS REGISTERED No 2 & UPWARDS.
REDRAWN FROM DRG. DATED 14/6/39.

KEY
1 TRAINING GEAR — 1 TURN OF HANDLES = 4° ON GUNS.
2 ELEVATING GEAR — 1 TURN OF HANDLES = 4° ON GUNS.
3 COVER PLATE 7·5" x 7·5" OVER 6" DIA. HOLE IN PLATFORM
        FOR DISMANTLING POST WHICH PASSES THROUGH A
        SOCKET SECURED TO THE DECK
4 ELECTRIC MOTOR 220 VOLTS. D.C. 940 RPM

SHEET ONE OF FOUR SHEETS
ⓒ JOHN LAMBERT 18/10/93. CH'D. 15/11/93

L/O/52/A

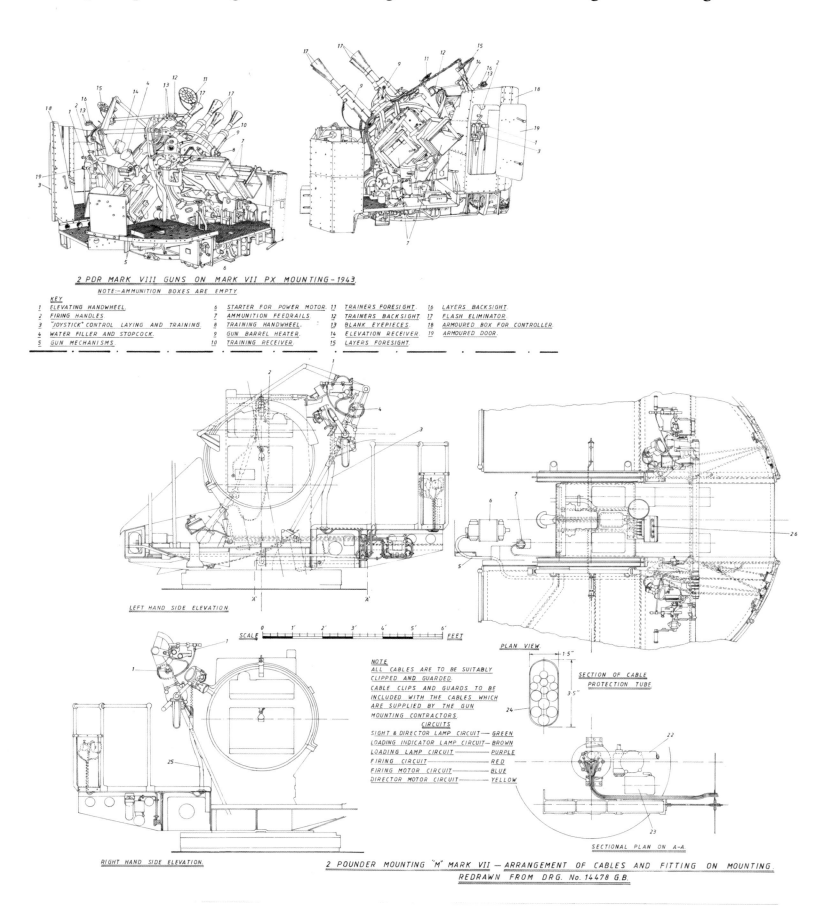

2 PDR MARK VIII GUNS ON MARK VII PX MOUNTING-1943.

NOTE:—AMMUNITION BOXES ARE EMPTY

KEY

1	ELEVATING HANDWHEEL.	6	STARTER FOR POWER MOTOR.	11	TRAINERS FORESIGHT.	16	LAYERS BACKSIGHT.
2	FIRING HANDLES.	7	AMMUNITION FEEDRAILS.	12	TRAINERS BACKSIGHT.	17	FLASH ELIMINATOR.
3	"JOYSTICK" CONTROL LAYING AND TRAINING.	8	TRAINING HANDWHEEL.	13	BLANK EYEPIECES.	18	ARMOURED BOX FOR CONTROLLER.
4	WATER FILLER AND STOPCOCK.	9	GUN BARREL HEATER.	14	ELEVATION RECEIVER.	19	ARMOURED DOOR.
5	GUN MECHANISMS.	10	TRAINING RECEIVER.	15	LAYERS FORESIGHT.		

LEFT HAND SIDE ELEVATION.

SCALE 0 1' 2' 3' 4' 5' 6' FEET

PLAN VIEW

SECTION OF CABLE
PROTECTION TUBE.

NOTE
ALL CABLES ARE TO BE SUITABLY
CLIPPED AND GUARDED.
CABLE CLIPS AND GUARDS TO BE
INCLUDED WITH THE CABLES WHICH
ARE SUPPLIED BY THE GUN
MOUNTING CONTRACTORS.

CIRCUITS

SIGHT & DIRECTOR LAMP CIRCUIT — GREEN
LOADING INDICATOR LAMP CIRCUIT—BROWN
LOADING LAMP CIRCUIT ———— PURPLE
FIRING CIRCUIT ———————— RED
FIRING MOTOR CIRCUIT———— BLUE
DIRECTOR MOTOR CIRCUIT———— YELLOW

RIGHT HAND SIDE ELEVATION.

SECTIONAL PLAN ON A-A.

2 POUNDER MOUNTING "M" MARK VII — ARRANGEMENT OF CABLES AND FITTING ON MOUNTING
REDRAWN FROM DRG. No. 14478 G.B.

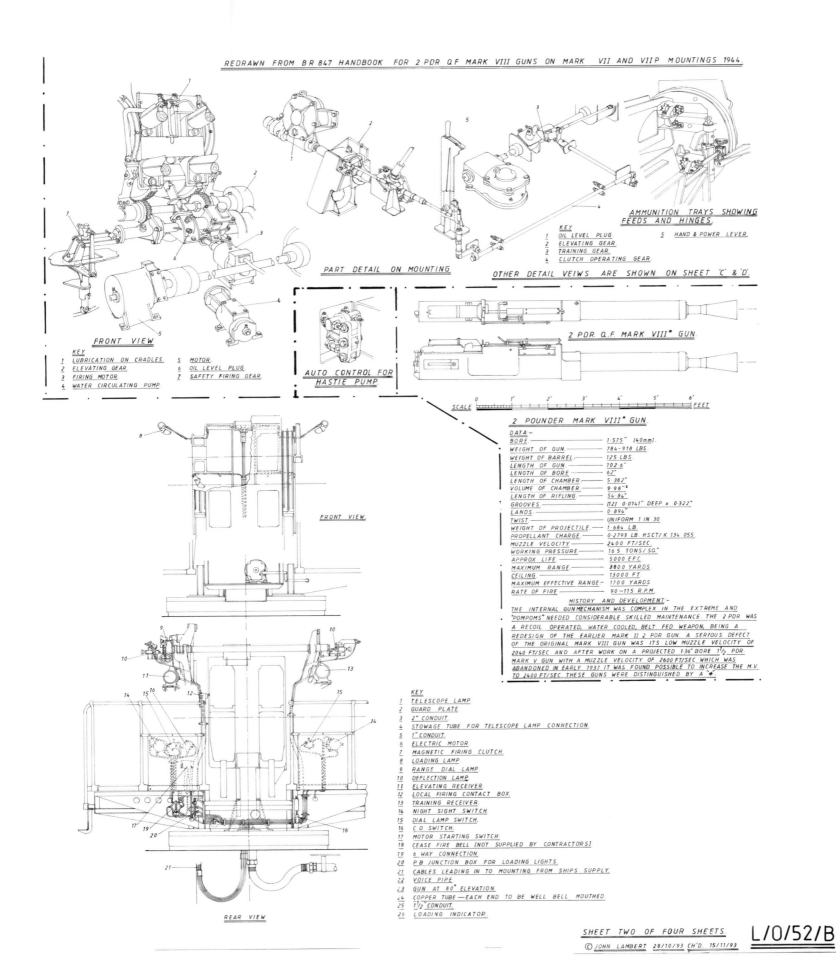

AMMUNITION TRAYS SHOWING FEEDS AND HINGES.

KEY
1 OIL LEVEL PLUG   5 HAND & POWER LEVER.
2 ELEVATING GEAR.
3 TRAINING GEAR.
4 CLUTCH OPERATING GEAR.

PART DETAIL ON MOUNTING

OTHER DETAIL VEIWS ARE SHOWN ON SHEET 'C' & 'D'.

FRONT VIEW

KEY
1 LUBRICATION ON CRADLES.   5 MOTOR.
2 ELEVATING GEAR.   6 OIL LEVEL PLUG.
3 FIRING MOTOR.   7 SAFETY FIRING GEAR.
4 WATER CIRCULATING PUMP.

AUTO CONTROL FOR HASTIE PUMP

2 PDR. Q.F. MARK VIII* GUN.

SCALE |0| |1'| |2'| |3'| |4'| |5'| |6'| FEET

2 POUNDER MARK VIII* GUN.

DATA-
BORE	—	1·575" [40mm].
WEIGHT OF GUN.	—	784-918 LBS.
WEIGHT OF BARREL.	—	125 LBS.
LENGTH OF GUN.	—	102·6"
LENGTH OF BORE.	—	62"
LENGTH OF CHAMBER.	—	5·382"
VOLUME OF CHAMBER.	—	9·98³
LENGTH OF RIFLING.	—	54·84"
GROOVES	—	[12] 0·0141" DEEP x 0·322"
LANDS.	—	0·894"
TWIST.	—	UNIFORM 1 IN 30
WEIGHT OF PROJECTILE.	—	1·684 LB.
PROPELLANT CHARGE.	—	0·2793 LB. HSCT/ K 134 055
MUZZLE VELOCITY	—	2400 FT/SEC.
WORKING PRESSURE	—	16·5 TONS/SQ."
APPROX LIFE.	—	5000 EFC
MAXIMUM RANGE.	—	3800 YARDS
CEILING	—	13000 FT.
MAXIMUM EFFECTIVE RANGE.	—	1700 YARDS
RATE OF FIRE	—	90-115 R.P.M.

HISTORY AND DEVELOPMENT:-
THE INTERNAL GUN MECHANISM WAS COMPLEX IN THE EXTREME AND "POMPOMS" NEEDED CONSIDERABLE SKILLED MAINTENANCE. THE 2 PDR WAS A RECOIL OPERATED, WATER COOLED, BELT FED WEAPON, BEING A REDESIGN OF THE EARLIER MARK II 2 PDR GUN. A SERIOUS DEFECT OF THE ORIGINAL MARK VIII GUN WAS ITS LOW MUZZLE VELOCITY OF 2040 FT/SEC AND AFTER WORK ON A PROJECTED 1·36" BORE 1½ PDR. MARK V GUN WITH A MUZZLE VELOCITY OF 2600 FT/SEC. WHICH WAS ABANDONED IN EARLY 1937 IT WAS FOUND POSSIBLE TO INCREASE THE M.V. TO 2400 FT/SEC. THESE GUNS WERE DISTINGUISHED BY A "*".

FRONT VIEW.

REAR VIEW.

KEY
1 TELESCOPE LAMP
2 GUARD PLATE
3 2" CONDUIT.
4 STOWAGE TUBE FOR TELESCOPE LAMP CONNECTION.
5 1" CONDUIT.
6 ELECTRIC MOTOR.
7 MAGNETIC FIRING CLUTCH.
8 LOADING LAMP.
9 RANGE DIAL LAMP.
10 DEFLECTION LAMP.
11 ELEVATING RECEIVER.
12 LOCAL FIRING CONTACT BOX.
13 TRAINING RECEIVER.
14 NIGHT SIGHT SWITCH.
15 DIAL LAMP SWITCH.
16 C.O. SWITCH.
17 MOTOR STARTING SWITCH.
18 CEASE FIRE BELL [NOT SUPPLIED BY CONTRACTORS]
19 6 WAY CONNECTION.
20 P.B JUNCTION BOX FOR LOADING LIGHTS.
21 CABLES LEADING IN TO MOUNTING FROM SHIPS SUPPLY.
22 VOICE PIPE.
23 GUN AT 80° ELEVATION.
24 COPPER TUBE —EACH END TO BE WELL BELL MOUTHED.
25 1½" CONDUIT.
26 LOADING INDICATOR.

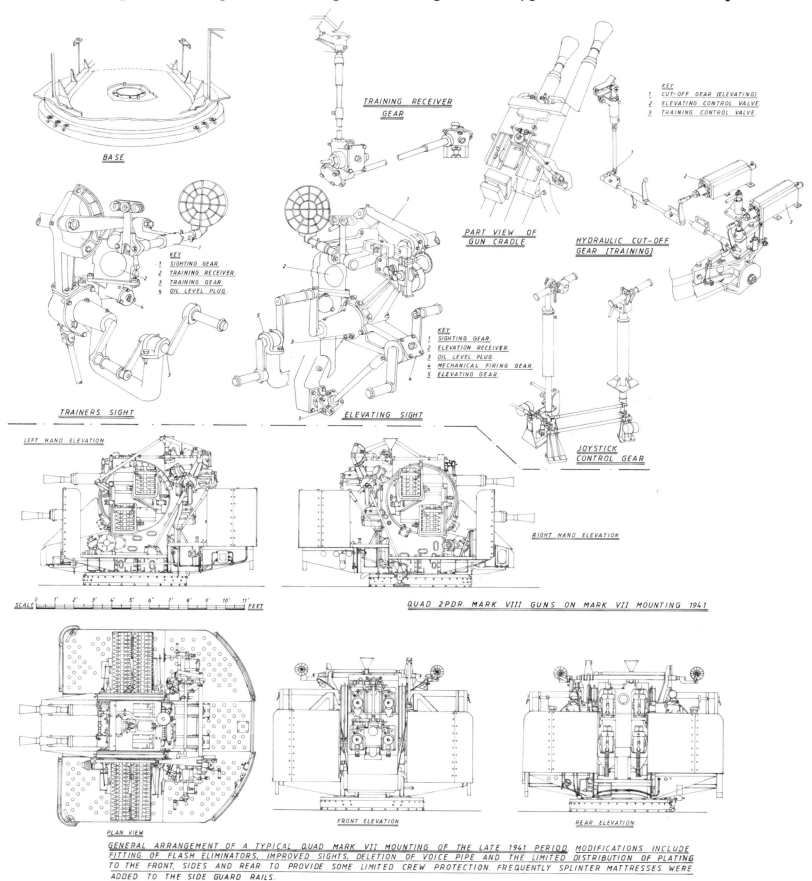

BASE

TRAINING RECEIVER GEAR

PART VIEW OF GUN CRADLE

KEY
1 CUT-OFF GEAR (ELEVATING).
2 ELEVATING CONTROL VALVE.
3 TRAINING CONTROL VALVE.

HYDRAULIC CUT-OFF GEAR (TRAINING).

KEY
1 SIGHTING GEAR.
2 TRAINING RECEIVER.
3 TRAINING GEAR.
4 OIL LEVEL PLUG.

TRAINERS SIGHT

KEY
1 SIGHTING GEAR.
2 ELEVATION RECEIVER.
3 OIL LEVEL PLUG.
4 MECHANICAL FIRING GEAR.
5 ELEVATING GEAR.

ELEVATING SIGHT

JOYSTICK CONTROL GEAR

LEFT HAND ELEVATION

RIGHT HAND ELEVATION

SCALE 0 1' 2' 3' 4' 5' 6' 7' 8' 9' 10' 11' FEET

QUAD 2PDR. MARK VIII GUNS ON MARK VII MOUNTING 1941

PLAN VIEW

FRONT ELEVATION.

REAR ELEVATION.

GENERAL ARRANGEMENT OF A TYPICAL QUAD MARK VII MOUNTING OF THE LATE 1941 PERIOD. MODIFICATIONS INCLUDE FITTING OF FLASH ELIMINATORS, IMPROVED SIGHTS, DELETION OF VOICE PIPE AND THE LIMITED DISTRIBUTION OF PLATING TO THE FRONT, SIDES AND REAR TO PROVIDE SOME LIMITED CREW PROTECTION. FREQUENTLY SPLINTER MATTRESSES WERE ADDED TO THE SIDE GUARD RAILS.

SHEET THREE OF FOUR SHEETS.

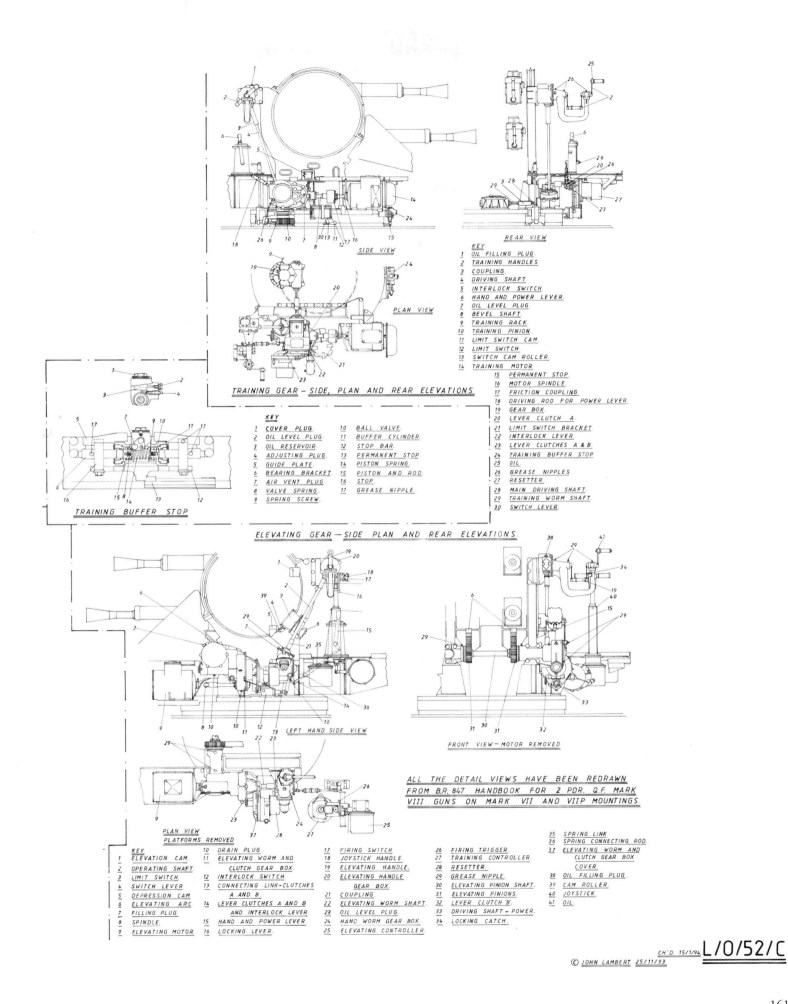

SIDE VIEW

REAR VIEW

PLAN VIEW

KEY.
1 OIL FILLING PLUG.
2 TRAINING HANDLES.
3 COUPLING.
4 DRIVING SHAFT.
5 INTERLOCK SWITCH.
6 HAND AND POWER LEVER.
7 OIL LEVEL PLUG.
8 BEVEL SHAFT.
9 TRAINING RACK.
10 TRAINING PINION.
11 LIMIT SWITCH CAM.
12 LIMIT SWITCH.
13 SWITCH CAM ROLLER.
14 TRAINING MOTOR.
15 PERMANENT STOP.
16 MOTOR SPINDLE.
17 FRICTION COUPLING.
18 DRIVING ROD FOR POWER LEVER.
19 GEAR BOX.
20 LEVER CLUTCH A.
21 LIMIT SWITCH BRACKET.
22 INTERLOCK LEVER.
23 LEVER CLUTCHES A & B.
24 TRAINING BUFFER STOP.
25 OIL.
26 GREASE NIPPLES.
27 RESETTER.
28 MAIN DRIVING SHAFT.
29 TRAINING WORM SHAFT.
30 SWITCH LEVER.

TRAINING GEAR — SIDE, PLAN AND REAR ELEVATIONS

KEY
1 COVER PLUG.   10 BALL VALVE.
2 OIL LEVEL PLUG.   11 BUFFER CYLINDER.
3 OIL RESERVOIR.   12 STOP BAR.
4 ADJUSTING PLUG.   13 PERMANENT STOP.
5 GUIDE PLATE.   14 PISTON SPRING.
6 BEARING BRACKET.   15 PISTON AND ROD.
7 AIR VENT PLUG.   16 STOP.
8 VALVE SPRING.   17 GREASE NIPPLE.
9 SPRING SCREW.

TRAINING BUFFER STOP

ELEVATING GEAR — SIDE PLAN AND REAR ELEVATIONS.

LEFT HAND SIDE VIEW

FRONT VIEW — MOTOR REMOVED

PLAN VIEW
PLATFORMS REMOVED

ALL THE DETAIL VIEWS HAVE BEEN REDRAWN
FROM B.R. 847 HANDBOOK FOR 2 PDR. Q.F. MARK
VIII GUNS ON MARK VII AND VIIP MOUNTINGS.

KEY
1 ELEVATION CAM.   10 DRAIN PLUG.   17 FIRING SWITCH.   26 FIRING TRIGGER.   35 SPRING LINK.
2 OPERATING SHAFT.   11 ELEVATING WORM AND   18 JOYSTICK HANDLE.   27 TRAINING CONTROLLER.   36 SPRING CONNECTING ROD.
3 LIMIT SWITCH.   CLUTCH GEAR BOX.   19 ELEVATING HANDLE.   28 RESETTER.   37 ELEVATING WORM AND
4 SWITCH LEVER.   12 INTERLOCK SWITCH.   20 ELEVATING HANDLE   29 GREASE NIPPLE.   CLUTCH GEAR BOX
5 DEPRESSION CAM.   13 CONNECTING LINK-CLUTCHES   GEAR BOX.   30 ELEVATING PINION SHAFT.   COVER.
6 ELEVATING ARC.   A AND B.   21 COUPLING.   31 ELEVATING PINIONS.   38 OIL FILLING PLUG.
7 FILLING PLUG.   14 LEVER CLUTCHES A AND B 22 ELEVATING WORM SHAFT.   32 LEVER CLUTCH 'B'.   39 CAM ROLLER.
8 SPINDLE.   AND INTERLOCK LEVER.   23 OIL LEVEL PLUG.   33 DRIVING SHAFT - POWER.   40 JOYSTICK.
9 ELEVATING MOTOR.   15 HAND AND POWER LEVER.   24 HAND WORM GEAR BOX.   34 LOCKING CATCH.   41 OIL.
                           16 LOCKING LEVER.   25 ELEVATING CONTROLLER.

CH'D. 15/1/94

© JOHN LAMBERT 25/11/93

L/0/52/C

A 4 2pdr QF Mk VIII gun on Mk VII and VII* P mountings, 1944

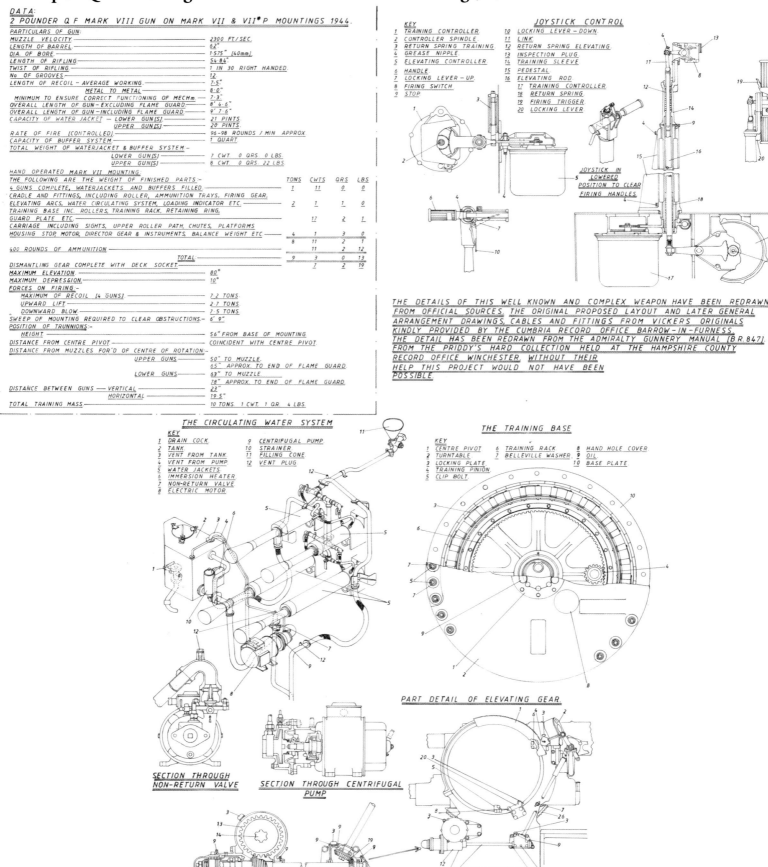

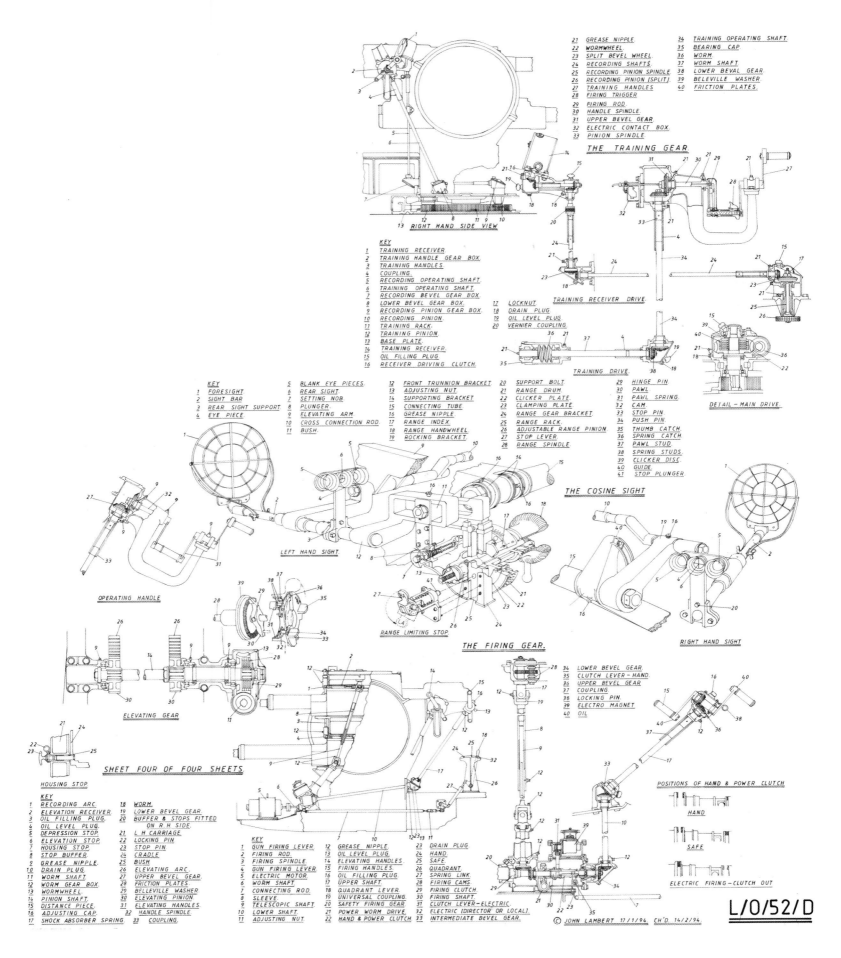

THE TRAINING GEAR

21	GREASE NIPPLE.	34	TRAINING OPERATING SHAFT.
22	WORMWHEEL.	35	BEARING CAP.
23	SPLIT BEVEL WHEEL.	36	WORM.
24	RECORDING SHAFTS.	37	WORM SHAFT.
25	RECORDING PINION SPINDLE.	38	LOWER BEVEL GEAR.
26	RECORDING PINION [SPLIT].	39	BELEVILLE WASHER.
27	TRAINING HANDLES.	40	FRICTION PLATES.
28	FIRING TRIGGER.		
29	FIRING ROD.		
30	HANDLE SPINDLE.		
31	UPPER BEVEL GEAR.		
32	ELECTRIC CONTACT BOX.		
33	PINION SPINDLE.		

RIGHT HAND SIDE VIEW

KEY

1	TRAINING RECEIVER.
2	TRAINING HANDLE GEAR BOX.
3	TRAINING HANDLES.
4	COUPLING.
5	RECORDING OPERATING SHAFT.
6	TRAINING OPERATING SHAFT.
7	RECORDING BEVEL GEAR BOX.
8	LOWER BEVEL GEAR BOX.
9	RECORDING PINION GEAR BOX.
10	RECORDING PINION.
11	TRAINING RACK.
12	TRAINING PINION.
13	BASE PLATE.
14	TRAINING RECEIVER.
15	OIL FILLING PLUG.
16	RECEIVER DRIVING CLUTCH.
17	LOCKNUT.
18	DRAIN PLUG.
19	OIL LEVEL PLUG.
20	VERNIER COUPLING.

TRAINING RECEIVER DRIVE.

TRAINING DRIVE.

DETAIL - MAIN DRIVE.

THE COSINE SIGHT

KEY

1	FORESIGHT.	5	BLANK EYE PIECES.	12	FRONT TRUNNION BRACKET.	20	SUPPORT BOLT.	29	HINGE PIN.
2	SIGHT BAR.	6	REAR SIGHT.	13	ADJUSTING NUT.	21	RANGE DRUM.	30	PAWL.
3	REAR SIGHT SUPPORT.	7	SETTING NOB.	14	SUPPORTING BRACKET.	22	CLICKER PLATE.	31	PAWL SPRING.
4	EYE PIECE.	8	PLUNGER.	15	CONNECTING TUBE.	23	CLAMPING PLATE.	32	CAM.
		9	ELEVATING ARM.	16	GREASE NIPPLE.	24	RANGE GEAR BRACKET.	33	STOP PIN.
		10	CROSS CONNECTION ROD.	17	RANGE INDEX.	25	RANGE RACK.	34	PUSH PIN.
		11	BUSH.	18	RANGE HANDWHEEL.	26	ADJUSTABLE RANGE PINION.	35	THUMB CATCH.
				19	ROCKING BRACKET.	27	STOP LEVER.	36	SPRING CATCH.
						28	RANGE SPINDLE.	37	PAWL STUD.
								38	SPRING STUDS.
								39	CLICKER DISC.
								40	GUIDE.
								41	STOP PLUNGER.

LEFT HAND SIGHT.

RIGHT HAND SIGHT.

OPERATING HANDLE

RANGE LIMITING STOP.

ELEVATING GEAR.

SHEET FOUR OF FOUR SHEETS.

THE FIRING GEAR.

34	LOWER BEVEL GEAR.
35	CLUTCH LEVER - HAND.
36	UPPER BEVEL GEAR.
37	COUPLING.
38	LOCKING PIN.
39	ELECTRO MAGNET.
40	OIL.

POSITIONS OF HAND & POWER CLUTCH

HAND

SAFE

ELECTRIC FIRING - CLUTCH OUT

HOUSING STOP

KEY

1	RECORDING ARC.	18	WORM.
2	ELEVATION RECEIVER.	19	LOWER BEVEL GEAR.
3	OIL FILLING PLUG.	20	BUFFER & STOPS FITTED
4	OIL LEVEL PLUG.		ON R.H. SIDE.
5	DEPRESSION STOP.	21	L H CARRIAGE.
6	ELEVATION STOP.	22	LOCKING PIN.
7	HOUSING STOP.	23	STOP PIN.
8	STOP BUFFER.	24	CRADLE.
9	GREASE NIPPLE.	25	BUSH.
10	DRAIN PLUG.	26	ELEVATING ARC.
11	WORM SHAFT.	27	UPPER BEVEL GEAR.
12	WORM GEAR BOX.	28	FRICTION PLATES.
13	WORMWHEEL.	29	BELLEVILLE WASHER.
14	PINION SHAFT.	30	ELEVATING PINION.
15	DISTANCE PIECE.	31	ELEVATING HANDLES.
16	ADJUSTING CAP.	32	HANDLE SPINDLE.
17	SHOCK ABSORBER SPRING.	33	COUPLING.

KEY

1	GUN FIRING LEVER.	12	GREASE NIPPLE.	23	DRAIN PLUG.
2	FIRING ROD.	13	OIL LEVEL PLUG.	24	HAND.
3	FIRING SPINDLE.	14	ELEVATING HANDLES.	25	SAFE.
4	GUN FIRING LEVER.	15	FIRING HANDLES.	26	QUADRANT.
5	ELECTRIC MOTOR.	16	OIL FILLING PLUG.	27	SPRING LINK.
6	WORM SHAFT.	17	UPPER SHAFT.	28	FIRING CAMS.
7	CONNECTING ROD.	18	QUADRANT LEVER.	29	FIRING SHAFT.
8	SLEEVE.	19	UNIVERSAL COUPLING.	30	FIRING CLUTCH.
9	TELESCOPIC SHAFT.	20	SAFETY FIRING GEAR.	31	CLUTCH LEVER-ELECTRIC.
10	LOWER SHAFT.	21	POWER WORM DRIVE.	32	ELECTRIC [DIRECTOR OR LOCAL].
11	ADJUSTING NUT.	22	HAND & POWER CLUTCH.	33	INTERMEDIATE BEVEL GEAR.

© JOHN LAMBERT 17/1/94 CH'D. 14/2/94

L/0/52/D

A 5 Quad 2pdr Mk VII* P mounting of 1944, with joystick control, power operation and protective plating

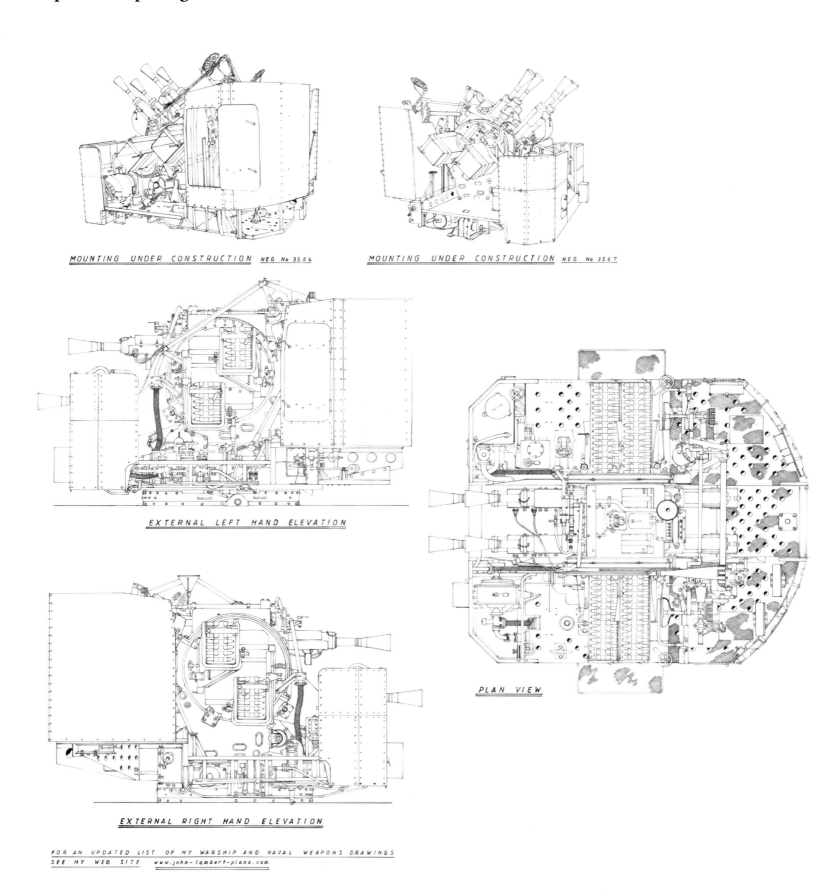

MOUNTING UNDER CONSTRUCTION NEG No 3564

MOUNTING UNDER CONSTRUCTION NEG No 3567

EXTERNAL LEFT HAND ELEVATION

PLAN VIEW

EXTERNAL RIGHT HAND ELEVATION

FOR AN UPDATED LIST OF MY WARSHIP AND NAVAL WEAPONS DRAWINGS
SEE MY WEB SITE www.john-lambert-plans.com

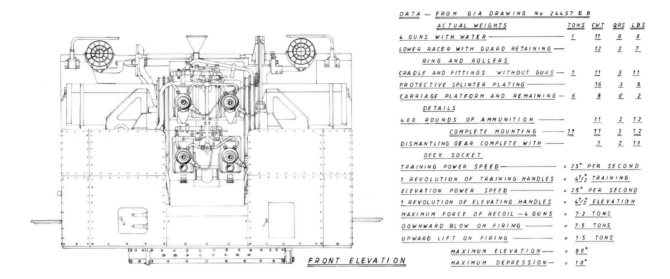

FRONT ELEVATION

DATA — FROM G/A DRAWING No 24457 G B

ACTUAL WEIGHTS	TONS	CWT	QRS	LBS
4 GUNS WITH WATER	1	11	0	0
LOWER RACER WITH GUARD RETAINING RING AND ROLLERS		12	2	7
CRADLE AND FITTINGS WITHOUT GUNS	1	11	3	11
PROTECTIVE SPLINTER PLATING		16	3	8
CARRIAGE PLATFORM AND REMAINING DETAILS	6	8	0	2
400 ROUNDS OF AMMUNITION		11	2	12
COMPLETE MOUNTING	11	11	3	12
DISMANTLING GEAR COMPLETE WITH DECK SOCKET		7	2	19

TRAINING POWER SPEED — = 25° PER SECOND
1 REVOLUTION OF TRAINING HANDLES = 4½° TRAINING
ELEVATION POWER SPEED — = 25° PER SECOND
1 REVOLUTION OF ELEVATING HANDLES = 4½° ELEVATION
MAXIMUM FORCE OF RECOIL — 4 GUNS = 7·2 TONS
DOWNWARD BLOW ON FIRING — = 7·5 TONS
UPWARD LIFT ON FIRING — = 1·5 TONS
MAXIMUM ELEVATION — = 80°
MAXIMUM DEPRESSION — = 10°

SCALE   0 1' 2' 3' 4' 5' 6' 7' 8' 9' 10' 11' 12' 13' 14' 15' 16' 17'   FEET

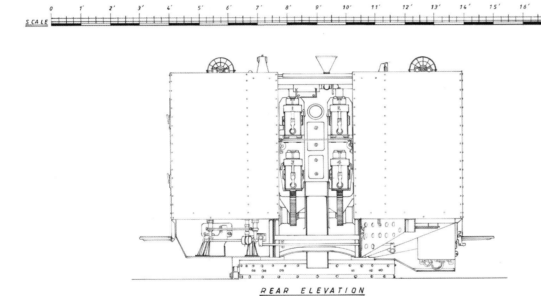

REAR ELEVATION

INTRODUCTION CONTAINED IN PRELIMINARY PAMPHLET — LATER PUBLISHED IN HANDBOOK - B R 847
THIS POWER OPERATED MOUNTING IS BASICALLY THE MARK VII HAND WORKED MOUNTING WITH POWER ADDITION. THE CIRCULATING WATER SYSTEM HAS ALSO BEEN ADDED TO ENSURE MORE EFFICIENT COOLING OF THE GUN BARRELS BUT WAS NOT FITTED INITIALLY TO THE EARLIER MOUNTINGS
WHEN UNDER POWER OPERATION THE MOUNTING WAS CONTROLLED BY EITHER OF TWO INTERCONNECTED JOYSTICKS (SEE SHEET 'C')
THE SOURCE OF POWER FOR THE ELEVATING AND TRAINING GEARS IS AN ELECTRIC MOTOR WHICH DRIVES A HELE-SHAW PUMP. THE HIGH PRESSURE OIL FROM THE PUMP DRIVES THE ELEVATING AND TRAINING HELE SHAW-MOTORS UNDER THE CONTROL OF THE
JOYSTICKS. THE HYDRAULIC SYSTEM WAS NORMALLY FILLED WITH OIL TO SPECIFICATION D.T.D. 44D. EXCEPT IN HOT CLIMATES WHEN IT WAY HAVE BEEN NECESSARY TO REVERT TO ADMIRALTY SPECIAL MINERAL OIL.
THE POWER DRIVE COULD BE CONNECTED OR DISCONNECTED AT WILL BY MEANS OF A SYSTEM OF CLUTCHES. (SEE SHEET 'C')
THE ELECTRIC MOTOR, THE HELE-SHAW PUMP AND THE WATER CIRCULATING PUMP ARE SUPPORTED ON PLATFORMS AT THE FRONT OF THE MOUNTING.
THE TRAINING BASE, CRADLE AND FITTINGS FIRING GEAR SIGHTING GEAR AND THE ELEVATING AND TRAINING RECEIVER DRIVES REMAIN UNALTERED. THE POSITION OF THE EVERSHED O.F·1 HAS BEEN MOVED FROM THE SIGHT ARM BRACKET TO A POSITION IN FRONT OF THE JOYSTICK OPERATORS. FOR SHIPS FITTED WITH MAGSLIP T.B.1 ARRANGEMENTS, AN ADDITIONAL CIM. MARK IV TRAINING RECEIVER, OPERATED BY A FLEXIBLE DRIVE IS BEING FITTED IN FRONT OF THE JOYSTICK OPERATORS. EARLIER MOUNTINGS WERE NOT FITTED WITH THIS GEAR IN THE FIRST INSTANCE.
FOR FULLY DETAILED DRAWINGS OF THE 2 POUNDER MARK VIII LOW VELOCITY AND THE LATER MARK VIII HIGH VELOCITY GUN USED IN THIS MOUNTING SEE L/O/38/A-C FOR FULLY DETAILED DRAWINGS OF THE EARLIER QUAD 2 PDR MARK VII MOUNTING PRIOR TO POWER OPERATION ETC SEE L/O/52/A-D. NOTE MANY OF THESE EARLY MOUNTING WERE REBUILT AND MODIFIED TO MARK VII* P STANDARD.

SHEET ONE OF THREE SHEETS

L/O/138/A

© JOHN LAMBERT   COMMENCED 13/11/2001   COMPLETED 10/2/2002   CH'D 15/2/2002

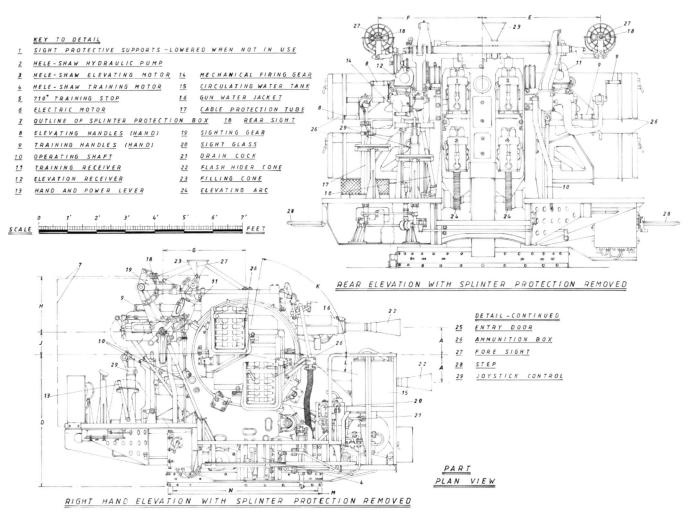

KEY TO DETAIL

1 SIGHT PROTECTIVE SUPPORTS -LOWERED WHEN NOT IN USE
2 HELE-SHAW HYDRAULIC PUMP
3 HELE-SHAW ELEVATING MOTOR   14 MECHANICAL FIRING GEAR
4 HELE-SHAW TRAINING MOTOR   15 CIRCULATING WATER TANK
5 710° TRAINING STOP   16 GUN WATER JACKET
6 ELECTRIC MOTOR   17 CABLE PROTECTION TUBE
7 OUTLINE OF SPLINTER PROTECTION BOX 18 REAR SIGHT
8 ELEVATING HANDLES (HAND)   19 SIGHTING GEAR
9 TRAINING HANDLES (HAND)   20 SIGHT GLASS
10 OPERATING SHAFT   21 DRAIN COCK
11 TRAINING RECEIVER   22 FLASH HIDER CONE
12 ELEVATION RECEIVER   23 FILLING CONE
13 HAND AND POWER LEVER   24 ELEVATING ARC

SCALE 0 1' 2' 3' 4' 5' 6' 7' FEET

REAR ELEVATION WITH SPLINTER PROTECTION REMOVED

DETAIL-CONTINUED
25 ENTRY DOOR
26 AMMUNITION BOX
27 FORE SIGHT
28 STEP
29 JOYSTICK CONTROL

PART PLAN VIEW

RIGHT HAND ELEVATION WITH SPLINTER PROTECTION REMOVED

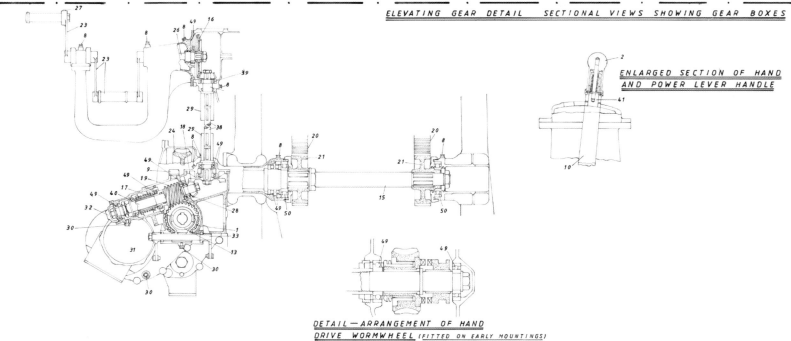

ELEVATING GEAR DETAIL   SECTIONAL VIEWS SHOWING GEAR BOXES

ENLARGED SECTION OF HAND AND POWER LEVER HANDLE

DETAIL—ARRANGEMENT OF HAND DRIVE WORMWHEEL (FITTED ON EARLY MOUNTINGS)

THIS GENERAL ARRANGEMENT REDRAWN FROM
DRAWING No 24457 GB DATED 23/1/1944
ORIGINALLY DRAWN BY G LEATT AT 1/8 SCALE

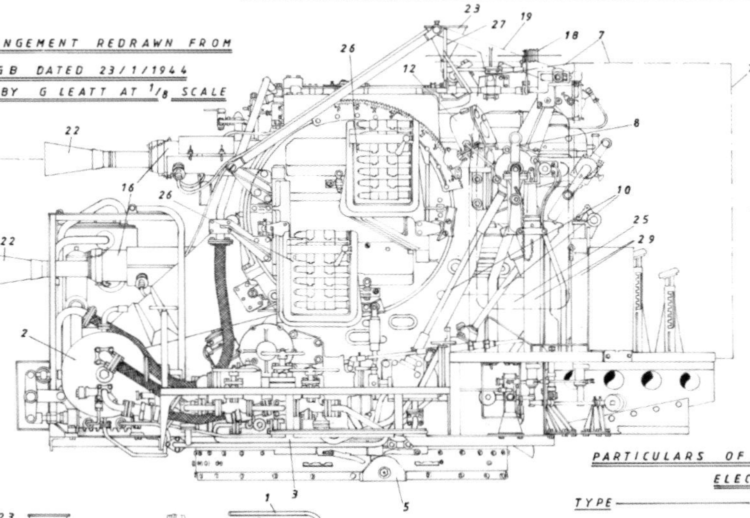

DIMENSIONS

A = 11·5 MEAN CENTRES
B = 9·75 MEAN CENTRES
C = 74·35
D = 56·0
E = 45·0
F = 39·5
G = 34·0
H = 23·812
I = 9·5
K = 80° MAX ELEVATION
L = 10° MAX DEPRESSION
M = 64" DIA OF BASE
N = 60·8" P.C.D. DIA 24
    1" DIA HOLDING
    DOWN BOLTS

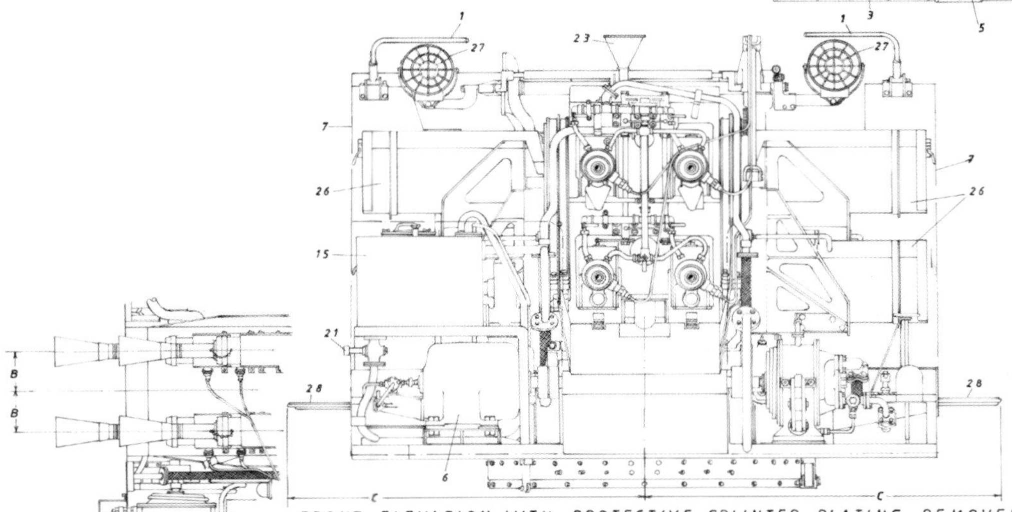

PARTICULARS OF THE MOUNTING
ELECTRIC MOTOR
TYPE —————— 100 AND 220 VOLTS
HORSE POWER —— 3 - 18
SPEED ————— 950 R.P.M.
HYDRAULIC PUMP
TYPE —— HELE-SHAW ROTARY PLUNGER TYPE
No. OF CYLINDERS —— 7
ELEVATING MOTOR
TYPE —— HELE SHAW ROTARY PLUNGER TYPE
No. OF CYLINDERS —— 6
HORSE POWER ———— 3·5
TRAINING MOTOR
TYPE —— HELE-SHAW ROTARY PLUNGER TYPE
No OF CYLINDERS —— 6
HORSE POWER ———— 6
GEAR RATIOS
HAND OPERATION
ELEVATING — 1 REVOLUTION OF HANDLES = 4 1/2° ON CRADLE
TRAINING — 1 REVOLUTION OF HANDLES = 4 1/2° ON MOUNTING
POWER OPERATION
ELEVATING — 360° ON CRADLE   144 REVOLUTIONS OF MOTOR
TRAINING — 360° ON MOUNTING   120 REVOLUTIONS OF MOTOR

FRONT ELEVATION WITH PROTECTIVE SPLINTER PLATING REMOVED

KEY TO DETAIL
1 HAND DRIVE WORMWHEEL (NON REVERSING)
2 HAND AND POWER LEVER HANDLE
3 SPUR GEAR RESETTER DRIVE
4 SPRING CONNECTING ROD
5 DRIVING SHAFT - POWER
6 DRIVING SHAFT - HAND
7 DRIVING PINION - POWER
8 GREASE NIPPLE
9 OIL FILLING PLUG
10 HAND AND POWER LEVER
11 HAND DRIVE WORMWHEEL
12 CLUTCH B - POWER DRIVE
13 CLUTCH A - HAND DRIVE
14 ELEVATING WORM SHAFT
15 ELEVATING PINION SHAFT
16 UPPER BEVEL GEAR
17 COUPLING SHOCK ABSORBER
18 LOWER BEVEL GEAR
19 HAND DRIVE WORM
20 ELEVATING ARCS
21 ELEVATING PINIONS
22 OIL LEVEL PLUG
23 ELEVATING HANDLES
24 ELEVATING WORMWHEEL
25 ELEVATING MOTOR
26 HANDLE SPINDLE
27 OIL
28 SHIM
29 COUPLING
30 DRAIN PLUG
31 RESETTER
32 BEARING CAP
33 CLUTCH SPINDLE
34 FRICTION CLUTCH
35 CLUTCH SLEEVE
36 DISTANCE PIECE
37 CONNECTING LINK
38 OPERATING SHAFT
39 PINION SPINDLE
40 WORM SPINDLE
41 SPRING PLUNGER
42 ELEVATING WORM
43 DRIVING DISC
44 MOTOR SPINDLE
45 INTERLOCK SWITCH
46 BELLEVILLE WASHERS
47 DRIVING WHEEL — POWER
48 FRICTION PLATE
49 BALL BEARING
50 ROLLER THUST BEARING

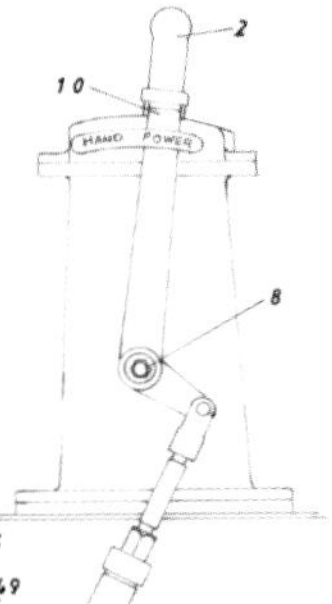

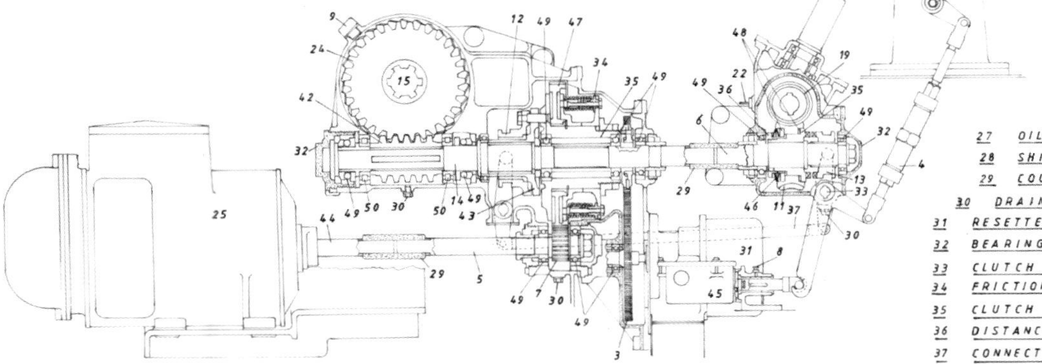

SHEET TWO OF THREE SHEETS

© JOHN LAMBERT COMMENCED 4/01/2002 COMPLETED 2/2/2001 CH'D. 5/2/2002

L/0/138/B

A 5 Quad 2pdr Mk VII* P mounting, detail

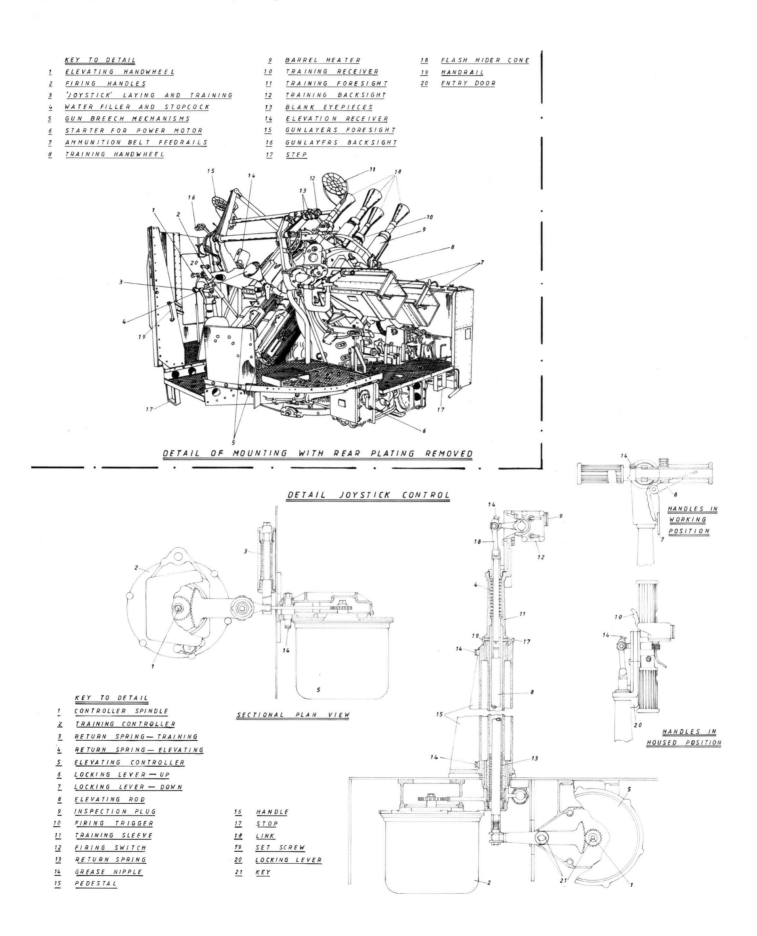

KEY TO DETAIL

1 ELEVATING HANDWHEEL
2 FIRING HANDLES
3 'JOYSTICK' LAYING AND TRAINING
4 WATER FILLER AND STOPCOCK
5 GUN BREECH MECHANISMS
6 STARTER FOR POWER MOTOR
7 AMMUNITION BELT FEEDRAILS
8 TRAINING HANDWHEEL

9   BARREL HEATER
10 TRAINING RECEIVER
11 TRAINING FORESIGHT
12 TRAINING BACKSIGHT
13 BLANK EYEPIECES
14 ELEVATION RECEIVER
15 GUNLAYERS FORESIGHT
16 GUNLAYERS BACKSIGHT
17 STEP

18 FLASH HIDER CONE
19 HANDRAIL
20 ENTRY DOOR

DETAIL OF MOUNTING WITH REAR PLATING REMOVED

DETAIL JOYSTICK CONTROL

SECTIONAL PLAN VIEW

KEY TO DETAIL

1   CONTROLLER SPINDLE
2   TRAINING CONTROLLER
3   RETURN SPRING— TRAINING
4   RETURN SPRING— ELEVATING
5   ELEVATING CONTROLLER
6   LOCKING LEVER — UP
7   LOCKING LEVER — DOWN
8   ELEVATING ROD
9   INSPECTION PLUG
10 FIRING TRIGGER
11 TRAINING SLEEVE
12 FIRING SWITCH
13 RETURN SPRING
14 GREASE NIPPLE
15 PEDESTAL

16 HANDLE
17 STOP
18 LINK
19 SET SCREW
20 LOCKING LEVER
21 KEY

HANDLES IN WORKING POSITION

HANDLES IN HOUSED POSITION

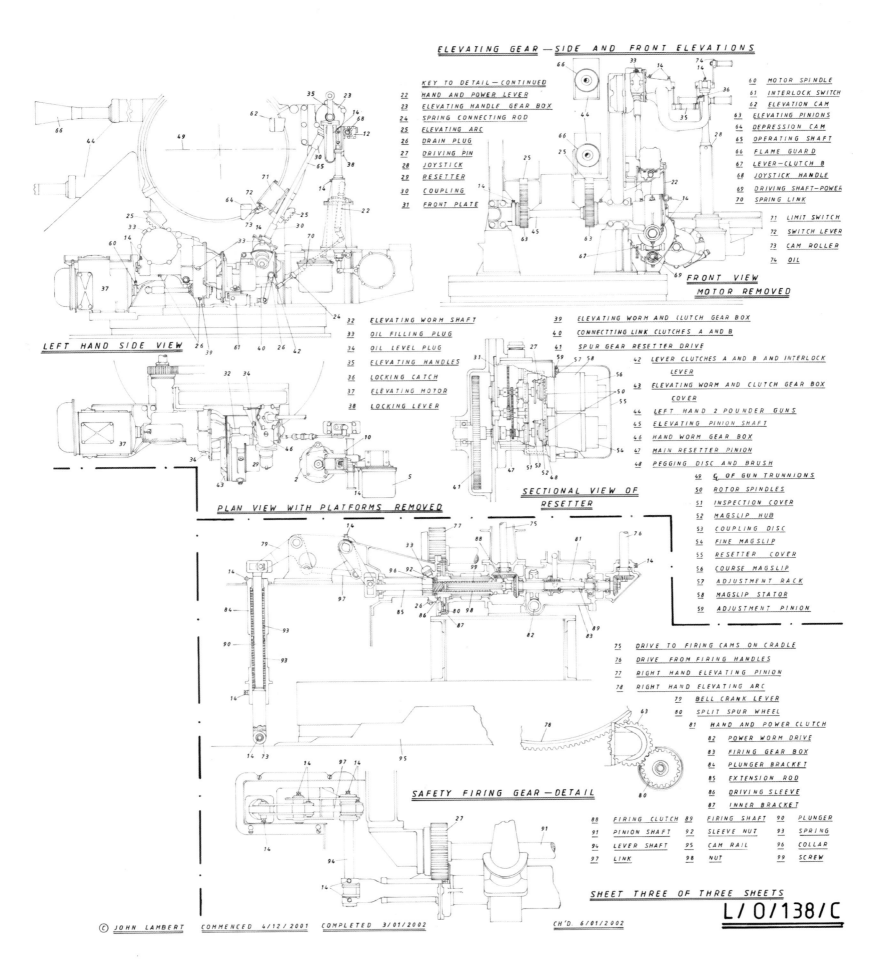

ELEVATING GEAR — SIDE AND FRONT ELEVATIONS

KEY TO DETAIL — CONTINUED

22 HAND AND POWER LEVER
23 ELEVATING HANDLE GEAR BOX
24 SPRING CONNECTING ROD
25 ELEVATING ARC
26 DRAIN PLUG
27 DRIVING PIN
28 JOYSTICK
29 RESETTER
30 COUPLING
31 FRONT PLATE

60 MOTOR SPINDLE
61 INTERLOCK SWITCH
62 ELEVATION CAM
63 ELEVATING PINIONS
64 DEPRESSION CAM
65 OPERATING SHAFT
66 FLAME GUARD
67 LEVER — CLUTCH B
68 JOYSTICK HANDLE
69 DRIVING SHAFT — POWER
70 SPRING LINK

71 LIMIT SWITCH
72 SWITCH LEVER
73 CAM ROLLER
74 OIL

FRONT VIEW
MOTOR REMOVED

LEFT HAND SIDE VIEW

32 ELEVATING WORM SHAFT
33 OIL FILLING PLUG
34 OIL LEVEL PLUG
35 ELEVATING HANDLES
36 LOCKING CATCH
37 ELEVATING MOTOR
38 LOCKING LEVER

39 ELEVATING WORM AND CLUTCH GEAR BOX
40 CONNECTTING LINK CLUTCHES A AND B
41 SPUR GEAR RESETTER DRIVE
42 LEVER CLUTCHES A AND B AND INTERLOCK
   LEVER
43 ELEVATING WORM AND CLUTCH GEAR BOX
   COVER
44 LEFT HAND 2 POUNDER GUNS
45 ELEVATING PINION SHAFT
46 HAND WORM GEAR BOX
47 MAIN RESETTER PINION
48 PEGGING DISC AND BRUSH

49 ₵ OF GUN TRUNNIONS
50 ROTOR SPINDLES
51 INSPECTION COVER
52 MAGSLIP HUB
53 COUPLING DISC
54 FINE MAGSLIP
55 RESETTER COVER
56 COURSE MAGSLIP
57 ADJUSTMENT RACK
58 MAGSLIP STATOR
59 ADJUSTMENT PINION

PLAN VIEW WITH PLATFORMS REMOVED

SECTIONAL VIEW OF
RESETTER

75 DRIVE TO FIRING CAMS ON CRADLE
76 DRIVE FROM FIRING HANDLES
77 RIGHT HAND ELEVATING PINION
78 RIGHT HAND ELEVATING ARC
79 BELL CRANK LEVER
80 SPLIT SPUR WHEEL
81 HAND AND POWER CLUTCH
82 POWER WORM DRIVE
83 FIRING GEAR BOX
84 PLUNGER BRACKET
85 EXTENSION ROD
86 DRIVING SLEEVE
87 INNER BRACKET

SAFETY FIRING GEAR — DETAIL

88 FIRING CLUTCH	89 FIRING SHAFT	90 PLUNGER
91 PINION SHAFT	92 SLEEVE NUT	93 SPRING
94 LEVER SHAFT	95 CAM RAIL	96 COLLAR
97 LINK	98 NUT	99 SCREW

SHEET THREE OF THREE SHEETS

L / 0 / 138 / C

© JOHN LAMBERT   COMMENCED 4/12/2001   COMPLETED 3/01/2002   CH'D 6/01/2002

169

A 6 Projected 0.661in close range automatic gun mounting 'M' (multiple) 6-barrelled Mk I mounting, 1935 (cancelled 1938)

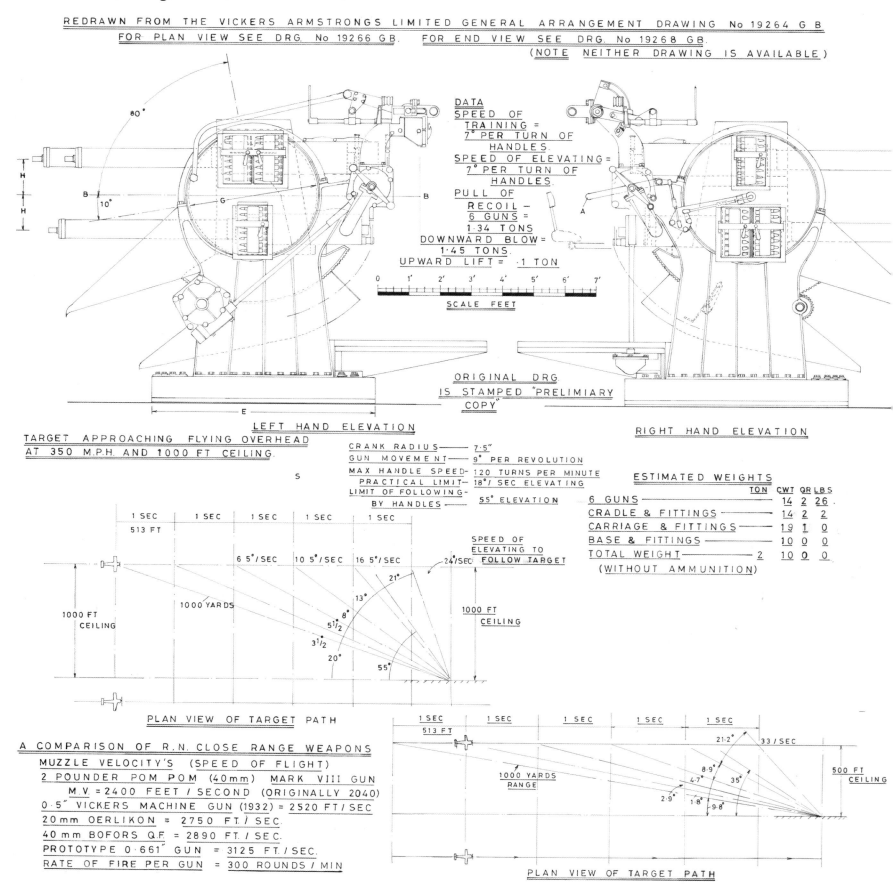

REDRAWN FROM THE VICKERS ARMSTRONGS LIMITED GENERAL ARRANGEMENT DRAWING No 19264 G B

FOR PLAN VIEW SEE DRG. No 19266 G B.   FOR END VIEW SEE DRG. No 19268 G B.

(NOTE NEITHER DRAWING IS AVAILABLE)

DATA
SPEED OF TRAINING = 7° PER TURN OF HANDLES.
SPEED OF ELEVATING = 7° PER TURN OF HANDLES.
PULL OF RECOIL — 6 GUNS = 1·34 TONS
DOWNWARD BLOW = 1·45 TONS.
UPWARD LIFT = ·1 TON

SCALE FEET

ORIGINAL DRG IS STAMPED "PRELIMIARY COPY"

LEFT HAND ELEVATION

RIGHT HAND ELEVATION

TARGET APPROACHING FLYING OVERHEAD AT 350 M.P.H. AND 1000 FT CEILING.

CRANK RADIUS — 7·5"
GUN MOVEMENT — 9° PER REVOLUTION
MAX HANDLE SPEED- PRACTICAL LIMIT — 120 TURNS PER MINUTE 18°/ SEC ELEVATING
LIMIT OF FOLLOWING- BY HANDLES — 55° ELEVATION

ESTIMATED WEIGHTS

	TON	CWT	QR	LBS
6 GUNS		14	2	26
CRADLE & FITTINGS		14	2	2
CARRIAGE & FITTINGS		19	1	0
BASE & FITTINGS		10	0	0
TOTAL WEIGHT	2	10	0	0

(WITHOUT AMMUNITION)

SPEED OF ELEVATING TO FOLLOW TARGET

1 SEC 513 FT
1000 YARDS
1000 FT CEILING

6 5°/SEC   10 5°/SEC   16 5°/SEC   24°/SEC
21°
13°
8°
5 1/2°
3 1/2°
20°
55°

PLAN VIEW OF TARGET PATH

A COMPARISON OF R.N. CLOSE RANGE WEAPONS

MUZZLE VELOCITY'S (SPEED OF FLIGHT)

2 POUNDER POM POM (40mm) MARK VIII GUN M.V. = 2400 FEET / SECOND (ORIGINALLY 2040)

0·5" VICKERS MACHINE GUN (1932) = 2520 FT/SEC

20mm OERLIKON = 2750 FT./ SEC.

40 mm BOFORS Q.F. = 2890 FT./ SEC.

PROTOTYPE 0·661" GUN = 3125 FT./ SEC.

RATE OF FIRE PER GUN = 300 ROUNDS / MIN

1 SEC 513 FT
1000 YARDS RANGE
21·2°   33°/SEC
8·9°
4·7°   35°
2·9°   1·8°
9·8°
500 FT CEILING

PLAN VIEW OF TARGET PATH

THE FULL SIZE 0·661" AMMUNITION TO FIRE
A 3 OZ (85 GM) BULLET AT 3125 FEET / SEC
AT 300 ROUNDS / MINUTE.

ALTERNATIVE CREW POSITIONS AS SHOWN

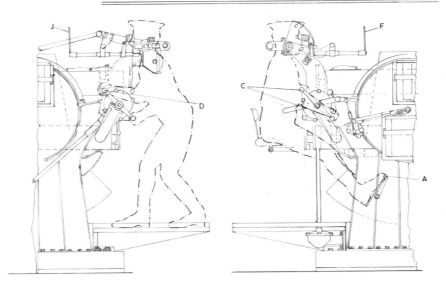

TARGET PASSING AT CEILING OF 500 FEET
AT 350 M P H

J = GUNLAYERS OPEN SIGHT

F = TRAINERS OPEN SIGHT
G = DIA 31·0"
H = 9"

KEY TO DETAIL
A = TRAINERS FIRING GEAR
B = ₵ OF TRUNNIONS
C = TRAINING HANDLES
D = ELEVATING HANDLES
E = DIA OF BASE = 54"

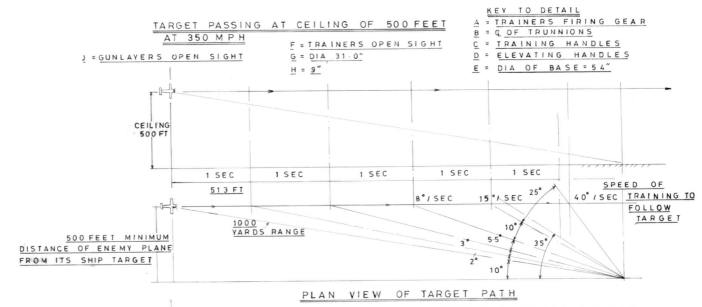

PLAN VIEW OF TARGET PATH

SPEED OF ELEVATING
TO FOLLOW TARGET

ELEVATING BY DOUBLE HANDLES
CRANK RADIUS ———————— 7·5"
GUN MOVEMENT ———————— 9° / TURN
MAXIMUM HANDLE SPEED —— 120 TURNS / MIN
(PRACTICAL LIMIT) ———— 18° / SEC TRAINING

THREE DIAGRAMATIC TRAJECTORY DRAWINGS FOR
AIRBORNE TARGETS REDRAWN FROM DRG No 28120 GB

TRAINING BY DOUBLE HANDLES
CRANK RADIUS ———————— 7·5"
GUN MOVEMENT ———————— 9° / TURN
MAX HANDLE SPEED —— 120 TURNS / MIN
(PRACTICAL LIMIT) —— 18° / SEC TRAINING

SHEET ONE OF TWO SHEETS
NOTE
AS CAN BE SHOWN IF THE
MULTIPLE 0·661" MACHINE GUN
HAD BEEN FULLY DEVELOPED
IT COULD HAVE BEEN VERY
POTENT WEAPON

L / O / 187 / A

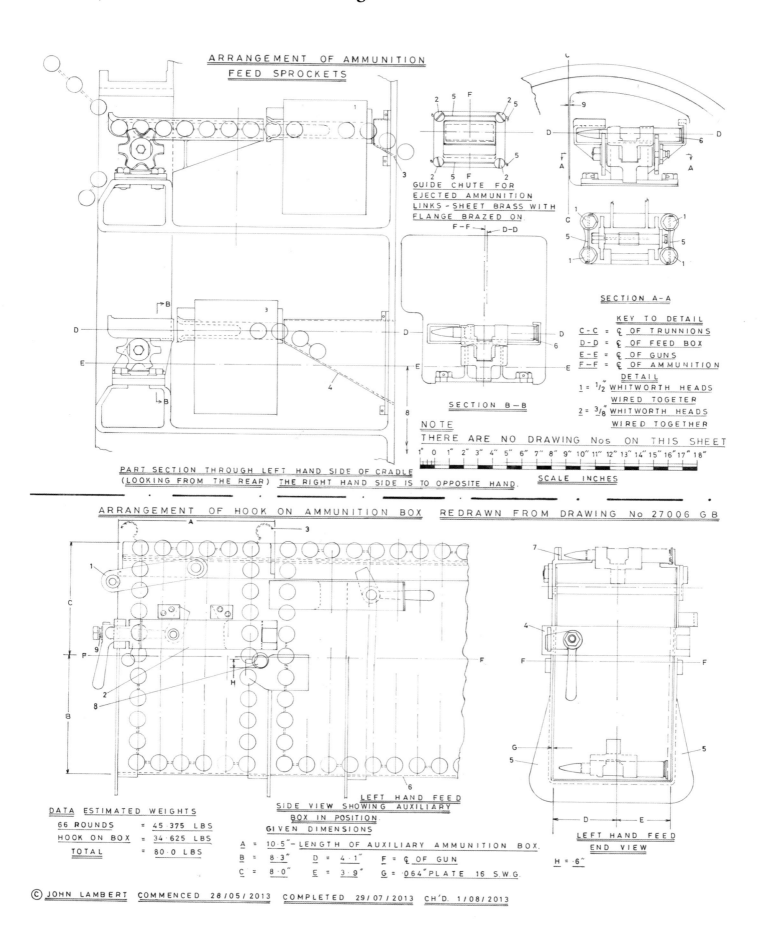

ARRANGEMENT OF AMMUNITION FEED SPROCKETS

GUIDE CHUTE FOR EJECTED AMMUNITION LINKS - SHEET BRASS WITH FLANGE BRAZED ON

SECTION A-A

KEY TO DETAIL

C-C = ₵ OF TRUNNIONS
D-D = ₵ OF FEED BOX
E-E = ₵ OF GUNS
F-F = ₵ OF AMMUNITION

DETAIL
1 = ¹/₂" WHITWORTH HEADS WIRED TOGETER
2 = ³/₈" WHITWORTH HEADS WIRED TOGETHER

NOTE
THERE ARE NO DRAWING Nos ON THIS SHEET

SECTION B-B

SCALE INCHES

PART SECTION THROUGH LEFT HAND SIDE OF CRADLE (LOOKING FROM THE REAR) THE RIGHT HAND SIDE IS TO OPPOSITE HAND.

ARRANGEMENT OF HOOK ON AMMUNITION BOX   REDRAWN FROM DRAWING No 27006 GB

SIDE VIEW SHOWING AUXILIARY BOX IN POSITION

LEFT HAND FEED

LEFT HAND FEED END VIEW

DATA ESTIMATED WEIGHTS

66 ROUNDS   = 45·375 LBS
HOOK ON BOX   = 34·625 LBS
TOTAL   = 80·0 LBS

GIVEN DIMENSIONS

A = 10·5" - LENGTH OF AUXILIARY AMMUNITION BOX.
B = 8·3"   D = 4·1"   F = ₵ OF GUN
C = 8·0"   E = 3·9"   G = ·064" PLATE 16 S.W.G.
H = ·6"

© JOHN LAMBERT COMMENCED 28/05/2013 COMPLETED 29/07/2013 CH'D. 1/08/2013

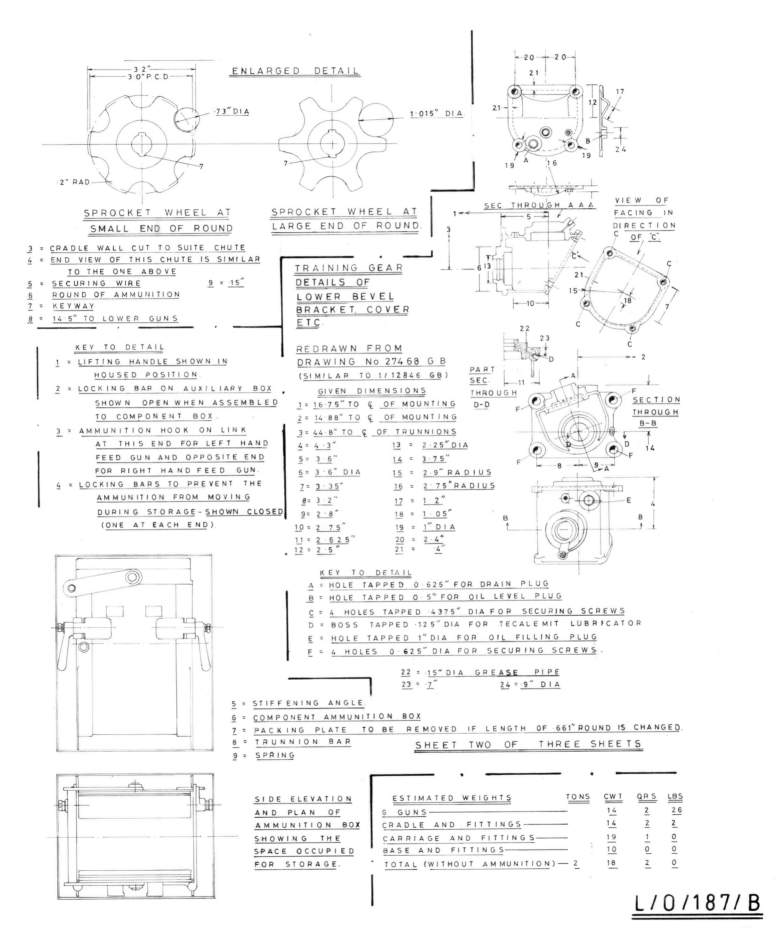

ENLARGED DETAIL

3.2"
3.0" P.C.D
.73" DIA
.2" RAD
7

SPROCKET WHEEL AT
SMALL END OF ROUND

1.015" DIA
7

SPROCKET WHEEL AT
LARGE END OF ROUND.

3 = CRADLE WALL CUT TO SUITE CHUTE
4 = END VIEW OF THIS CHUTE IS SIMILAR
    TO THE ONE ABOVE
5 = SECURING WIRE   9 = .15"
6 = ROUND OF AMMUNITION
7 = KEYWAY
8 = 14.5" TO LOWER GUNS

KEY TO DETAIL
1 = LIFTING HANDLE SHOWN IN
    HOUSED POSITION.
2 = LOCKING BAR ON AUXILIARY BOX
    SHOWN OPEN WHEN ASSEMBLED
    TO COMPONENT BOX.
3 = AMMUNITION HOOK ON LINK
    AT THIS END FOR LEFT HAND
    FEED GUN AND OPPOSITE END
    FOR RIGHT HAND FEED GUN.
4 = LOCKING BARS TO PREVENT THE
    AMMUNITION FROM MOVING
    DURING STORAGE-SHOWN CLOSED
    (ONE AT EACH END).

TRAINING GEAR
DETAILS OF
LOWER BEVEL
BRACKET, COVER
ETC.

REDRAWN FROM
DRAWING No 27468 G B
(SIMILAR TO 1/12846 GB)
GIVEN DIMENSIONS
1 = 16.75" TO ₵ OF MOUNTING
2 = 14.88" TO ₵ OF MOUNTING
3 = 44.8" TO ₵ OF TRUNNIONS
4 = 4.3"   13 = 2.25" DIA
5 = 3.6"   14 = 3.75"
6 = 3.6" DIA   15 = 2.9" RADIUS
7 = 3.35"   16 = 2.75" RADIUS
8 = 3.2"   17 = 1.2"
9 = 2.8"   18 = 1.05"
10 = 2.75"   19 = 1" DIA
11 = 2.625"   20 = 2.4"
12 = 2.5"   21 = .4"

KEY TO DETAIL
A = HOLE TAPPED 0.625" FOR DRAIN PLUG
B = HOLE TAPPED 0.5" FOR OIL LEVEL PLUG
C = 4 HOLES TAPPED .4375" DIA FOR SECURING SCREWS
D = BOSS TAPPED .125" DIA FOR TECALEMIT LUBRICATOR
E = HOLE TAPPED 1" DIA FOR OIL FILLING PLUG
F = 4 HOLES 0.625" DIA FOR SECURING SCREWS.

22 = .15" DIA GREASE PIPE
23 = .7"   24 = .9" DIA

5 = STIFFENING ANGLE.
6 = COMPONENT AMMUNITION BOX
7 = PACKING PLATE TO BE REMOVED IF LENGTH OF .661" ROUND IS CHANGED.
8 = TRUNNION BAR
9 = SPRING

SEC THROUGH A A A

VIEW OF
FACING IN
DIRECTION
OF 'C'

PART
SEC.
THROUGH
D-D

SECTION
THROUGH
B-B

SHEET TWO OF THREE SHEETS

SIDE ELEVATION
AND PLAN OF
AMMUNITION BOX
SHOWING THE
SPACE OCCUPIED
FOR STORAGE.

ESTIMATED WEIGHTS	TONS	CWT	QRS	LBS
6 GUNS		14	2	26
CRADLE AND FITTINGS		14	2	2
CARRIAGE AND FITTINGS		19	1	0
BASE AND FITTINGS		10	0	0
TOTAL (WITHOUT AMMUNITION)	2	18	2	0

L / 0 / 187 / B

A 6 Projected 0.661in multiple machine gun mounting, further design detail

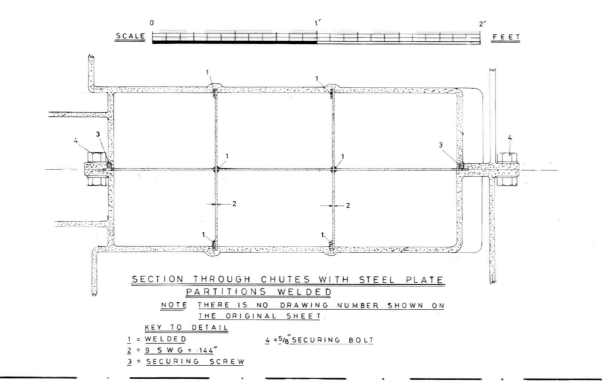

SCALE |0   1'   2'| FEET

SECTION THROUGH CHUTES WITH STEEL PLATE
PARTITIONS WELDED

NOTE THERE IS NO DRAWING NUMBER SHOWN ON
THE ORIGINAL SHEET.

KEY TO DETAIL

1 = WELDED   4 = 5/8" SECURING BOLT

2 = 9 S W G = ·144"

3 = SECURING SCREW

HISTORY AND BACKGROUND

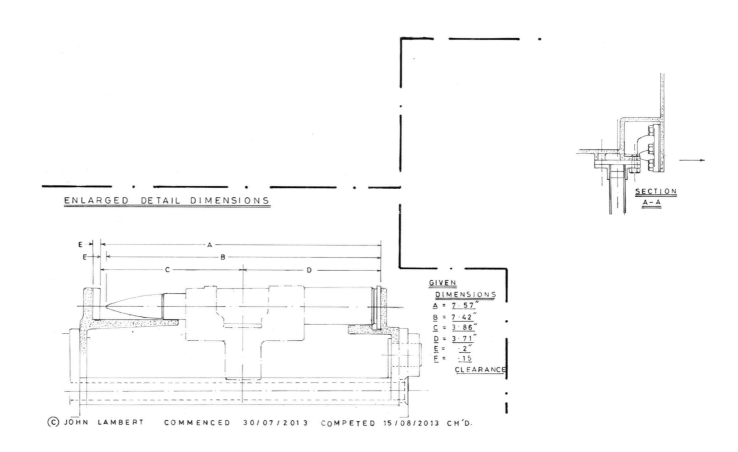

ENLARGED DETAIL DIMENSIONS

GIVEN
DIMENSIONS

A = 7·57"

B = 7·42"

C = 3·86"

D = 3·71"

E = ·2"

F = ·15

CLEARANCE

SECTION
A-A

© JOHN LAMBERT   COMMENCED 30/07/2013   COMPETED 15/08/2013 CH'D.

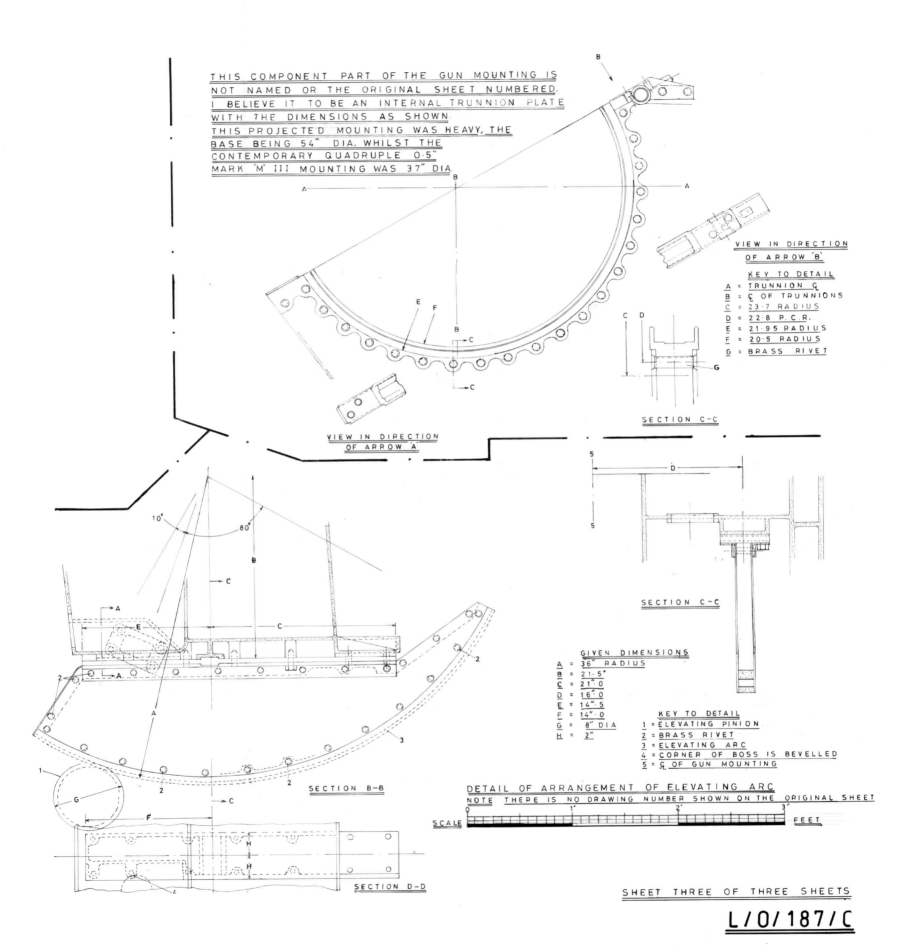

THIS COMPONENT PART OF THE GUN MOUNTING IS
NOT NAMED OR THE ORIGINAL SHEET NUMBERED.
I BELIEVE IT TO BE AN INTERNAL TRUNNION PLATE
WITH THE DIMENSIONS AS SHOWN.
THIS PROJECTED MOUNTING WAS HEAVY, THE
BASE BEING 54" DIA. WHILST THE
CONTEMPORARY QUADRUPLE 0·5"
MARK 'M' III MOUNTING WAS 37" DIA.

VIEW IN DIRECTION
OF ARROW 'B'

KEY TO DETAIL
A = TRUNNION ℄
B = ℄ OF TRUNNIONS
C = 23·7 RADIUS
D = 22·8 P.C.R.
E = 21·95 RADIUS
F = 20·5 RADIUS
G = BRASS RIVET

SECTION C-C

VIEW IN DIRECTION
OF ARROW 'A'

SECTION C-C

10°   80°

GIVEN DIMENSIONS
A = 36" RADIUS
B = 21·5"
C = 21" 0
D = 16" 0
E = 14" 5
F = 14" 0
G = 8" DIA
H = 2"

KEY TO DETAIL
1 = ELEVATING PINION
2 = BRASS RIVET
3 = ELEVATING ARC
4 = CORNER OF BOSS IS BEVELLED
5 = ℄ OF GUN MOUNTING

SECTION B-B

DETAIL OF ARRANGEMENT OF ELEVATING ARC
NOTE THERE IS NO DRAWING NUMBER SHOWN ON THE ORIGINAL SHEET
SCALE   0   1'   2'   3'   FEET

SECTION D-D

SHEET THREE OF THREE SHEETS

L/0/187/C

175

A 7 Twin 40mm Bofors Mk IV* (Hazemeyer) mounting, 1944

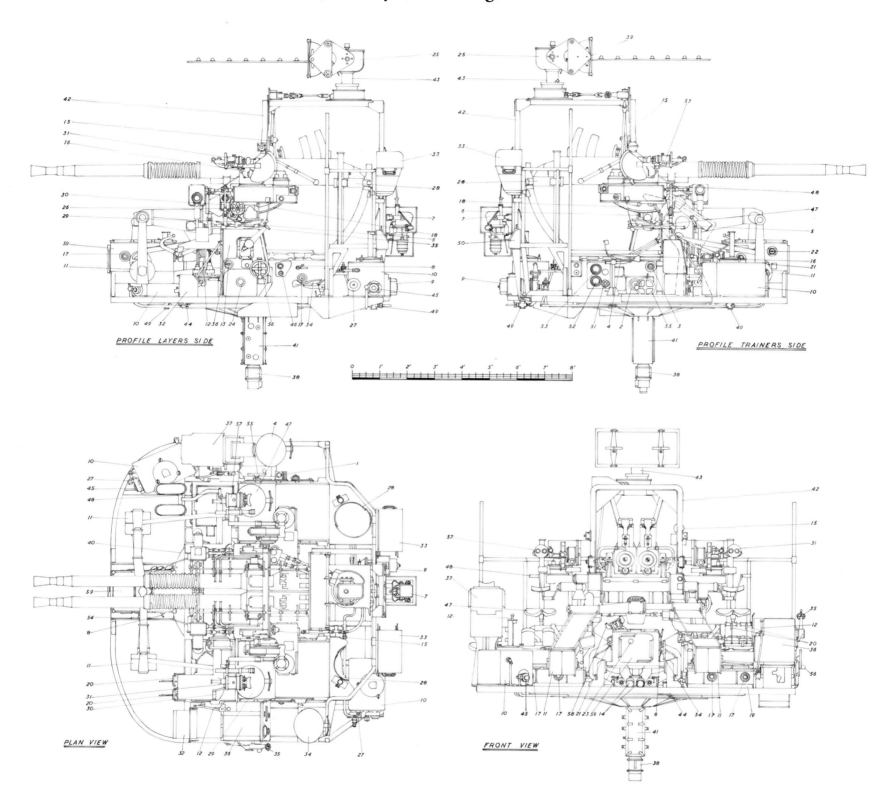

PROFILE LAYERS SIDE

PROFILE TRAINERS SIDE

PLAN VIEW

FRONT VIEW

HISTORY:
THIS EXCELLENT NAVAL ANTI-AIRCRAFT WEAPON CAME TO GREAT BRITAIN AFTER THE FALL OF HOLLAND IN 1940. IT WAS NOTED ABOARD THE MINELAYING DESTROYER 'WILLEM VAN DER ZAAN' WHICH CARRIED TWO MOUNTINGS. HER 40mm MOUNTINGS WERE INSPECTED BY D.N.O. (DIRECTOR OF NAVAL ORDANANCE) & A REPRESENTATIVE FROM D.T.S.D. (DIRECTOR OF TACTICAL SHIP REQUIREMENTS) THE DUTCH MOUNTING INCORPERATED HAZEMEYER FIRE CONTROL INSTRUMENTS ON THE MOUNTING, BEING STABILISED BY GYRO CONTROL OF A THREE AXIS MOUNTING CONTROL OF FIRE BEING TACHYMETRIC. THE OFFICERS THAT WITNESSED THE DEMONSTRATION WERE DULY IMPRESSED & AS A RESULT FIRST ONE, THEN BOTH MOUNTINGS WERE LIFTED FROM THE SHIP TO UNDERGO FURTHER TESTS ASHORE ON A SPECIALLY CONSTRUCTED ROLLING GUN PLATFORM, IN ORDER THAT MANUFACTURING DRAWINGS COULD BE MADE. THE SIZE & WEIGHT OF THE MARK IV (HAZEMEYER) MOUNTING WAS ABOUT THE SAME AS THAT OF THE FOUR BARRELLED MARK VII 2 POUNDER POM POM BUT WITH A HIGHER MUZZLE VELOCITY, LOWER AMMUNITION EXPENDITURE, & GREATER ACCURACY, THE TWIN BOFORS WAS POTENTIALLY MUCH MORE DEADLY. BY DECEMBER 1940, 50 OF THE MARK IV MOUNTING WERE ON ORDER, DELIVERY WAS ANTICIPATED AT 5 SETS A MONTH, WITH UNITS BEING AVAILABLE FROM MID 1942. THE DUTCH NAVY IN EXILE ALSO REQUIRED 2 SETS A MONTH WITH UP TO 48 SETS ON ORDER. THE COST PER SET INCLUDING HAZEMEYER CONTROL INSTRUMENTS & ARRAY FOR TYPE 282P(2) RADAR WAS ESTIMATED AT £10,000, ABOUT THE SAME AS FOR THE 4 GUNNED POM POM & ITS DIRECTOR.

KEY TO FITTINGS & EQUIPMENT

1. AZIMUTH DEFLECTION RATE DRUM.
2. AZIMUTH DEFLECTION DIAL.
3. AZIMUTH SPOTTING RECEIVER.
4. AUXILIARY TRAINERS SEAT.
5. AUXILIARY TRAINERS CLUTCH.
6. AUXILIARY TRAINING HANDWHEEL.
7. BEAM SWITCHING UNIT.
8. BRAKE LEVER.
9. CIRCULATING PUMP.
10. COOLING WATER TANK.
11. CROSS LEVEL BALANCE WEIGHT.
12. CHANGE SPEED LEVER.
13. CONSTANT SPEED MOTOR SWITCH.
14. CARTRIDGE CASE CHUTES.
15. CHECK FIRE BELL.
16. DIMMING SWITCH.
17. DRIERS.
18. ELEVATING ARC.
19. ELEVATING CONTROL UNIT.
20. FIRING PEDALS.
21. GYRO SWITCH.
22. GYRO LOCKING SWITCH.
23. GYRO WINDOW.
24. GYRO INSPECTION WINDOW.
25. GEAR BOX FOR RADAR AERIALS.
26. HOUSING STOP [ELEVATION].
27. IMMERSION HEATER.
28. LOADING NUMBERS BODY SUPPORT.
29. LAYERS SEAT.
30. LAYERS HAND CRANK.
31. LAYERS SIGHT.
32. PORTABLE SPOTTING TRANSMITTER UNIT STOWAGE BOX.
33. READY USE AMMUNITION LOCKER.
34. RANGE OPERATORS SEAT.
35. RANGE HANDWHEEL.
36. RANGE UNIT.
37. REMOTE TRAINING TUBE UNIT.
38. ROTATING CONNECTOR.
39. TYPE 282 P RADAR AERIAL ARRAY.
40. SAFETY FIRING CAM PLATE [TRAINING].
41. SLIP RING CASING.
42. SUPPORTING GANTRY.
43. SUPPORTING PILLAR.
44. SAFETY TRAINING FIRING GEAR
45. STRAINER.
46. SPOTTING RECEIVER DRIVE.
47. TRAINERS SEAT.
48. TRAINING HANDLES.
49. TANK DRAIN COCK.
50. TELEPHONE STOWAGE BOX.
51. WIND SPEED SETTING HANDLE.
52. WIND SPEED DIAL.
53. WIND DIRECTION DIAL.
54. ZERO SETTING [CROSS LEVEL]
55. ZERO SETTING [TRAINING].
56. ZERO SETTING [ELEVATION].
57. TRAINING SIGHT.
58. CROSS LEVEL LOCKING BOLT SWITCH & HANDWHEEL.
59. CROSS LEVEL UNIT.

DATA   THE MOUNTING

SIGHTING BINOCULARS	ROSS 3½ x PATT G372.
EST. DECK BLOWS ON FIRING: DOWNWARD	5 TONS.
UPWARD LIFT	2 TONS.
GUN ELEVATION	-10° TO 90°
TRAINING	ALL ROUND [CONTINUOUS].
CROSS LEVEL CORRECTION	14° RIGHT & LEFT ON MOUNTING.
SIGHT ELEVATION	-10° TO 90°
SIGHT DEFLECTION	25° RIGHT & LEFT.
ARC OF ELEVATING & TRAINING PER TURN OF HANDLES FOR OPERATING BY HAND	5° FAST ½° SLOW.
RADAR EQUIPMENT	TYPE 282 P [2] DUPLEX AERIAL.
WATER COOLING PUMP CAPACITY	10 GALLONS PER MINUTE.
WATER TANK CAPACITY	TWO 20 GALLON TANKS.
FIRING GEAR	MECHANICAL BY RIGHT & LEFT FOOT PEDALS THAT ARE OPERATED BY THE LAYER. [GUNS CAN BE FIRED TOGETHER OR INDEPENDENTLY].
WORKING RADIUS	9 FT 8 INS.
RATE OF FIRE	120 ROUNDS PER BARREL PER MIN.
WEIGHT OF MOUNTING	7 TONS 22 LBS. [COMPLETE MOUNTING WITHOUT WATER AMMUNITION & CREW].

THE GUN

CALIBRE	40 mm OR 1·5748 INCHES.
MUZZLE VELOCITY	2,800 FT PER SECOND.
MAXIMUM EFFECTIVE RANGE	2,500 YARDS.
EXTREME RANGE	12,500 YARDS.
MAXIMUM ALTITUDE	18,000 FEET.

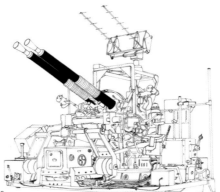

THE MARK IV MOUNTING WAS FIRST CARRIED ABOARD THE DESTROYERS OF THE 5TH EMERGENCY FLOTILLA OR 'S' CLASS WHICH COMPLETED IN THE LATTER HALF OF 1943. THEY WERE CARRIED ON THE CENTRELINE & WERE FITTED TO THE LATER FLEET DESTROYER CLASSES. THE WEAPON SYSTEM WAS ALSO AUTHORISED FOR OTHER ESCORT TYPES. SLOOPS OF THE BLACK SWAN & LATER MODIFIED BLACK SWAN CLASSES. WHICH CARRIED TWO MARK IV MOUNTINGS SIDE BY SIDE

GENERAL ARRANGEMENT

REDRAWN FROM THE OFFICIAL GUNNERY MANUAL FROM THE NATIONAL MARITIME MUSEUM GREENWICH

SHEET ONE OF TWO SHEETS

THIS SHEET REPLACES THE ORIGINAL OF 22.1.72.

© JOHN LAMBERT 1.8.86

L/0/09/A

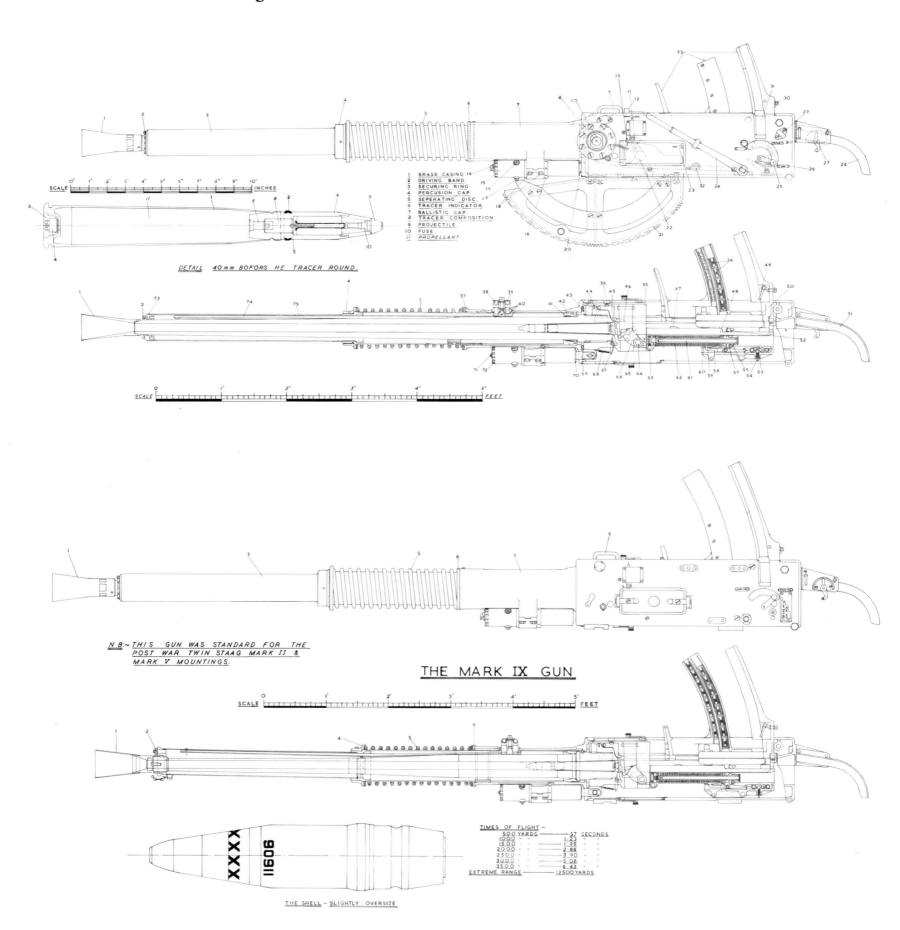

SCALE |0" 1" 2" 3" 4" 5" 6" 7" 8" 9" 10"| INCHES

1 BRASS CASING
2 DRIVING BAND
3 SECURING RING
4 PERCUSION CAP
5 SEPERATING DISC
6 TRACER INDICATOR
7 BALLISTIC CAP
8 TRACER COMPOSITION
9 PROJECTILE
10 FUSE
11 PROPELLANT

DETAIL 40mm BOFORS HE TRACER ROUND.

SCALE |0 1' 2' 3' 4' 5'| FEET

N B:~ THIS GUN WAS STANDARD FOR THE
POST WAR TWIN STAAG MARK II &
MARK V MOUNTINGS.

THE MARK IX GUN

SCALE |0 1' 2' 3' 4' 5'| FEET

TIMES OF FLIGHT ~

500	YARDS	·57	SECONDS
1000	"	1·23	"
1500	"	1·99	"
2000	"	2·88	"
2500	"	3·90	"
3000	"	5·08	"
3500	"	6·43	"
EXTREME RANGE		12500 YARDS	

THE SHELL - SLIGHTLY OVERSIZE

178

DETAILS

1. FLAME GUARD.
2. FORWARD GLAND RING.
3. BARREL WATER JACKET.
4. FORWARD SPRING COLLAR.
5. BARREL SPRING.
6. REAR SPRING COLLAR.
7. BREECH CASING.
8. FIRING PLUNGER.
9. TOP COVER HANDLE.
10. TRUNNION.
11. BREECH INDICATOR.
12. TOP COVER CATCH.
13. BELL CRANK.
14. RUN OUT ADJUSTING VALVE LOCKING PLATE.
15. BUFFER.
16. BUFFER FILLING PLUG.
17. BUFFER DRAIN PLUG.
18. BOLTS SECURING BUFFER.
19. BUFFER SECURING COLLAR.
20. APERTURE COVER.
21. ELEVATING ARC.
22. CRANK.
23. OPERATING COVER AND CATCH.
24. HAND OPERATING LEVER (IN FORWARD POSITION).
25. SAFETY LEVER.
26. REAR COVER.
27. RECOIL INDICATOR.
28. DEFLECTOR.
29. REAR CATCH (FOR HAND OPERATING LEVER).
30. THUMB LEVER ACTUATING FEED CONTROL.
31. CHARGER CHUTE.
32. LOADING STOP.
33. GUIDES.
34. FEED PAWLS.
35. BREECH RING.
36. SCREW AND LOCKIN PLATE RETAINING BARREL CATCH.
37. REAR COLLAR.
38. WATER CONNECTION RETURN.
39. WATER CONNECTION FLOW.
40. WASHERS.
41. PACKING.
42. GLAND RING.
43. RUBBER BUFFER RING.
44. INTERRUPTED THREADS BARREL AND BREECH RING.
45. BARREL CATCH.
46. BREECH BLOCK.
47. LOADING TRAY PAWLS.
48. LOADING TRAY.
49. FEED CONTROL LEVER.
50. FEED CYLINDERS.
51. EMPTY CASE DEFLECTOR.
52. RAMMER LEVERS.
53. CHECK LEVERS.
54. RAMMER CATCH LEVER PLUNGER.
55. RAMMER SHOE.
57. BENT ON RAMMER SHOE.
58. RAMMER RELEASING LEVER.
59. PROJECTION OPERATING RAMMER RELEASE LEVER.
60. CYLINDER CATCH SPINDLE.
61. RAMMER ROD.
62. RAMMER SPRING.
63. LOADING TRAY SECURING BOLT.
64. CRANK SHAFT.
65. BOTTOM COVER CATCH.
66. LEFT INNER CRANK.
67. EXTRACTORS.
68. EXTRACTOR LEVER SPRING.
69. BUFFER PISTON.
70. BUFFER PISTON BUSH.
71. RUN OUT ADJUSTING VALVE.
72. FORWARD BUFFER GLAND.
73. GLAND RING.
74. CIRCULATING TUBE.
75. WATER JACKET.
76. SPRING LOADED PLUNGERS.
77. RAMMER LEVER CLAWS.
78. FEED CHECK LEVER.
79. CENTRE CHECK LEVER.
80. LH CHECK LEVER OPERATED BY FIRING GEAR.
81. CYLINDER CATCH PAWLS.
82. TORSION SPRINGS.
83. FEED CYLINDER CATCHES.
84. CYLINDER CATCH HEAD SPINDLE.

40mm BOFORS GUN (BRITISH AND AMERICAN MANUFACTURE) 1944

THIS GUN WAS SIMILAR TO THAT USED ON LAND SERVICE BUT WITH THE ADDITION OF A WATER JACKET FOR COOLING THE BARREL, CIRCULATION BEING SUPPLIED BY A PUMP ON THE GUN MOUNTING TO OBVIATE THE NECESSITY FOR BARREL CHANGING. OTHER ALTERATIONS BEING MADE TO PERMIT THE GUN TO BE FITTED ON MULTIPLE MOUNTINGS.

THE GUN IS FULLY AUTOMATIC, SIMPLE IN ACTION AND OF ROBUST CONSTRUCTION. THE RECOIL AND RUN OUT BEING UTILISED TO OPEN THE BREECH, EJECT THE EMPTY CASE, FEED DOWN A FRESH ROUND AND PASS IT TO THE CHAMBER, WHEN THE BREECH IS CLOSED BY ITS SPRING AND AFTER IT HAS CLOSED FIRE THE ROUND.

THE RATE OF FIRE IS 120 ROUNDS PER MINUTE AT 60° ELEVATION WHICH GAVE APPROX 140 ROUNDS PER MINUTE WITH THE GUN HORIZONTAL.

CALIBRE —— 40mm OR 1·574B INCHES
MUZZLE VELOCITY —— 2800 FT./SEC.

THIS SHEET UPDATED 2/8/86

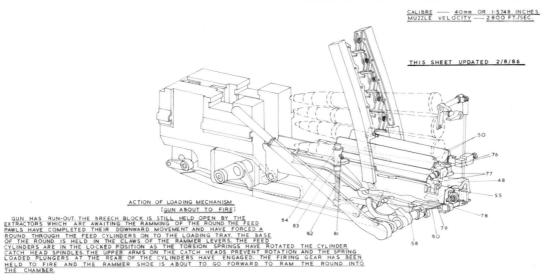

ACTION OF LOADING MECHANISM
(GUN ABOUT TO FIRE)

GUN HAS RUN-OUT. THE BREECH BLOCK IS STILL HELD OPEN BY THE EXTRACTORS WHICH ARE AWAITING THE RAMMING OF THE ROUND. THE FEED PAWLS HAVE COMPLETED THEIR DOWNWARD MOVEMENT AND HAVE FORCED A ROUND THROUGH THE FEED CYLINDERS ON TO THE LOADING TRAY. THE BASE OF THE ROUND IS HELD IN THE CLAWS OF THE RAMMER LEVERS. THE FEED CYLINDERS ARE IN THE LOCKED POSITION AS THE TORSION SPRINGS HAVE ROTATED THE CYLINDER CATCH HEAD SPINDLES. THE UPPER ARMS ON THE CATCH HEADS PREVENT ROTATION AND THE SPRING LOADED PLUNGERS AT THE REAR OF THE CYLINDERS HAVE ENGAGED. THE FIRING GEAR HAS BEEN HELD TO FIRE AND THE RAMMER SHOE IS ABOUT TO GO FORWARD TO RAM THE ROUND INTO THE CHAMBER.

SHEET OF TWO SHEETS

L/O/09/B

© JOHN LAMBERT   28/9/78

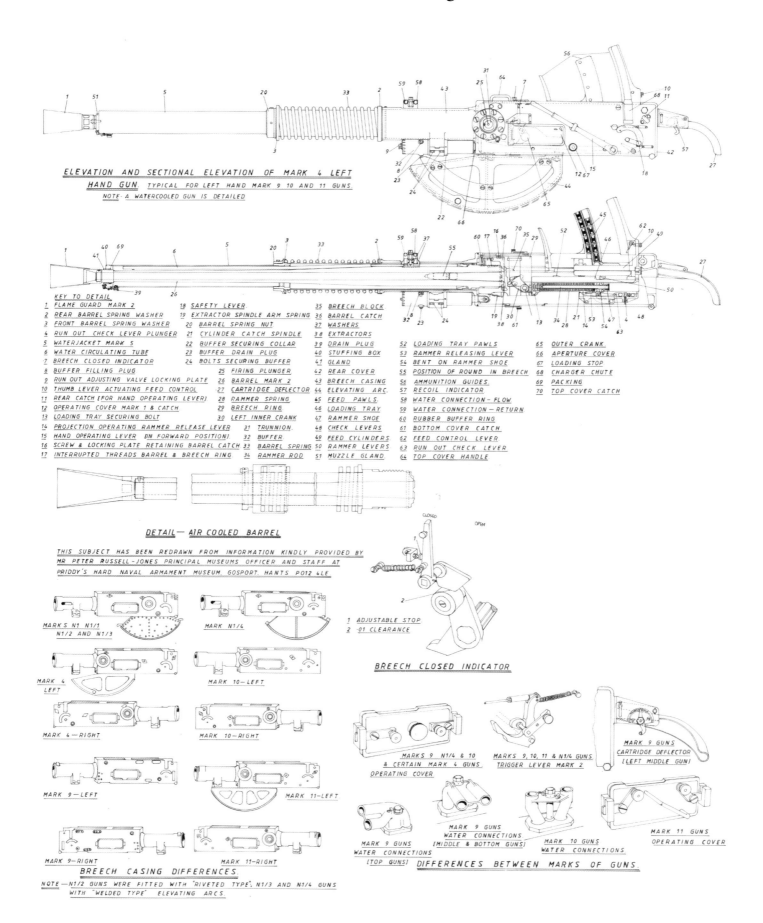

ELEVATION AND SECTIONAL ELEVATION OF MARK 4 LEFT
HAND GUN. TYPICAL FOR LEFT HAND MARK 9 10 AND 11 GUNS.
NOTE. A WATERCOOLED GUN IS DETAILED

KEY TO DETAIL

1 FLAME GUARD MARK 2
2 REAR BARREL SPRING WASHER
3 FRONT BARREL SPRING WASHER
4 RUN OUT CHECK LEVER PLUNGER
5 WATERJACKET MARK 5
6 WATER CIRCULATING TUBE
7 BREECH CLOSED INDICATOR
8 BUFFER FILLING PLUG
9 RUN OUT ADJUSTING VALVE LOCKING PLATE
10 THUMB LEVER ACTUATING FEED CONTROL
11 REAR CATCH (FOR HAND OPERATING LEVER)
12 OPERATING COVER MARK 1 & CATCH
13 LOADING TRAY SECURING BOLT
14 PROJECTION OPERATING RAMMER RELEASE LEVER
15 HAND OPERATING LEVER (IN FORWARD POSITION)
16 SCREW & LOCKING PLATE RETAINING BARREL CATCH
17 INTERRUPTED THREADS BARREL & BREECH RING

18 SAFETY LEVER
19 EXTRACTOR SPINDLE ARM SPRING
20 BARREL SPRING NUT
21 CYLINDER CATCH SPINDLE
22 BUFFER SECURING COLLAR
23 BUFFER DRAIN PLUG
24 BOLTS SECURING BUFFER
25 FIRING PLUNGER
26 BARREL MARK 2
27 CARTRIDGE DEFLECTOR
28 RAMMER SPRING
29 BREECH RING
30 LEFT INNER CRANK
31 TRUNNION.
32 BUFFER
33 BARREL SPRING
34 RAMMER ROD

35 BREECH BLOCK
36 BARREL CATCH
37 WASHERS
38 EXTRACTORS
39 DRAIN PLUG
40 STUFFING BOX
41 GLAND
42 REAR COVER
43 BREECH CASING
44 ELEVATING ARC.
45 FEED PAWLS.
46 LOADING TRAY
47 RAMMER SHOE
48 CHECK LEVERS
49 FEED CYLINDERS.
50 RAMMER LEVERS
51 MUZZLE GLAND.

52 LOADING TRAY PAWLS
53 RAMMER RELEASING LEVER
54 BENT ON RAMMER SHOE
55 POSITION OF ROUND IN BREECH
56 AMMUNITION GUIDES.
57 RECOIL INDICATOR
58 WATER CONNECTION—FLOW
59 WATER CONNECTION—RETURN.
60 RUBBER BUFFER RING
61 BOTTOM COVER CATCH
62 FEED CONTROL LEVER
63 RUN OUT CHECK LEVER
64 TOP COVER HANDLE

65 OUTER CRANK
66 APERTURE COVER
67 LOADING STOP
68 CHARGER CHUTE
69 PACKING
70 TOP COVER CATCH

DETAIL—AIR COOLED BARREL

THIS SUBJECT HAS BEEN REDRAWN FROM INFORMATION KINDLY PROVIDED BY
MR PETER RUSSELL-JONES PRINCIPAL MUSEUMS OFFICER AND STAFF AT
PRIDDY'S HARD NAVAL ARMAMENT MUSEUM, GOSPORT, HANTS PO12 4LE

BREECH CLOSED INDICATOR

1 ADJUSTABLE STOP
2 ·01 CLEARANCE

MARKS N1 N1/1
N1/2 AND N1/3

MARK N1/4

MARK 4
LEFT

MARK 10—LEFT

MARK 4—RIGHT

MARK 10—RIGHT

MARK 9—LEFT

MARK 11—LEFT

MARK 9—RIGHT

MARK 11—RIGHT

BREECH CASING DIFFERENCES.

NOTE—N1/2 GUNS WERE FITTED WITH "RIVETED TYPE". N1/3 AND N1/4 GUNS
WITH "WELDED TYPE" ELEVATING ARCS.

MARKS 9 N1/4 & 10
& CERTAIN MARK 4 GUNS
OPERATING COVER

MARKS 9, 10, 11 & N1/4 GUNS
TRIGGER LEVER MARK 2

MARK 9 GUNS
CARTRIDGE DEFLECTOR
[LEFT MIDDLE GUN]

MARK 9 GUNS
WATER CONNECTIONS
[TOP GUNS]

MARK 9 GUNS
WATER CONNECTIONS
[MIDDLE & BOTTOM GUNS]

MARK 10 GUNS
WATER CONNECTIONS

MARK 11 GUNS
OPERATING COVER

DIFFERENCES BETWEEN MARKS OF GUNS.

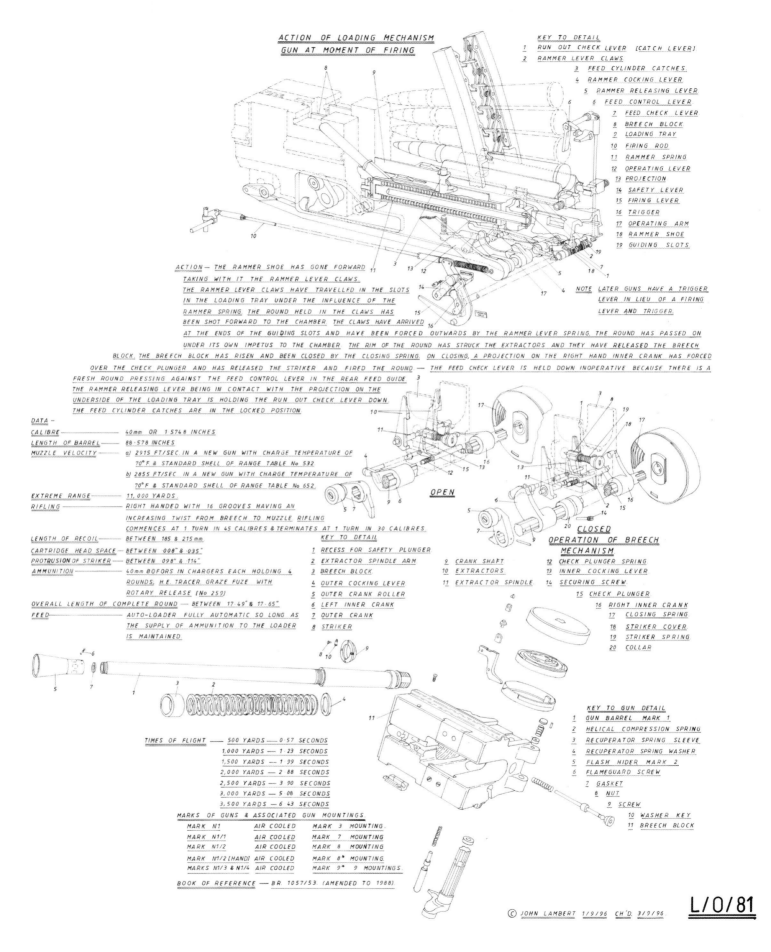

ACTION OF LOADING MECHANISM
GUN AT MOMENT OF FIRING

KEY TO DETAIL
1 RUN OUT CHECK LEVER [CATCH LEVER]
2 RAMMER LEVER CLAWS.
3 FEED CYLINDER CATCHES.
4 RAMMER COCKING LEVER
5 RAMMER RELEASING LEVER
6 FEED CONTROL LEVER
7 FEED CHECK LEVER
8 BREECH BLOCK
9 LOADING TRAY
10 FIRING ROD
11 RAMMER SPRING
12 OPERATING LEVER
13 PROJECTION
14 SAFETY LEVER
15 FIRING LEVER
16 TRIGGER
17 OPERATING ARM
18 RAMMER SHOE
19 GUIDING SLOTS

NOTE LATER GUNS HAVE A TRIGGER
LEVER IN LIEU OF A FIRING
LEVER AND TRIGGER.

ACTION — THE RAMMER SHOE HAS GONE FORWARD
TAKING WITH IT THE RAMMER LEVER CLAWS.
THE RAMMER LEVER CLAWS HAVE TRAVELLED IN THE SLOTS
IN THE LOADING TRAY UNDER THE INFLUENCE OF THE
RAMMER SPRING. THE ROUND HELD IN THE CLAWS HAS
BEEN SHOT FORWARD TO THE CHAMBER. THE CLAWS HAVE ARRIVED
AT THE ENDS OF THE GUIDING SLOTS AND HAVE BEEN FORCED OUTWARDS BY THE RAMMER LEVER SPRING. THE ROUND HAS PASSED ON
UNDER ITS OWN IMPETUS TO THE CHAMBER. THE RIM OF THE ROUND HAS STRUCK THE EXTRACTORS AND THEY HAVE RELEASED THE BREECH
BLOCK. THE BREECH BLOCK HAS RISEN AND BEEN CLOSED BY THE CLOSING SPRING. ON CLOSING, A PROJECTION ON THE RIGHT HAND INNER CRANK HAS FORCED
OVER THE CHECK PLUNGER AND HAS RELEASED THE STRIKER AND FIRED THE ROUND — THE FEED CHECK LEVER IS HELD DOWN INOPERATIVE BECAUSE THERE IS A
FRESH ROUND PRESSING AGAINST THE FEED CONTROL LEVER IN THE REAR FEED GUIDE
THE RAMMER RELEASING LEVER BEING IN CONTACT WITH THE PROJECTION ON THE
UNDERSIDE OF THE LOADING TRAY IS HOLDING THE RUN OUT CHECK LEVER DOWN.
THE FEED CYLINDER CATCHES ARE IN THE LOCKED POSITION.

DATA —
CALIBRE — 40mm OR 1.5748 INCHES
LENGTH OF BARREL — 88.578 INCHES
MUZZLE VELOCITY — a) 2915 FT/SEC. IN A NEW GUN WITH CHARGE TEMPERATURE OF
70°F. & STANDARD SHELL OF RANGE TABLE No 532
b) 2855 FT/SEC. IN A NEW GUN WITH CHARGE TEMPERATURE OF
70°F & STANDARD SHELL OF RANGE TABLE No 652.
EXTREME RANGE — 11,000 YARDS.
RIFLING — RIGHT HANDED WITH 16 GROOVES HAVING AN
INCREASING TWIST FROM BREECH TO MUZZLE. RIFLING
COMMENCES AT 1 TURN IN 45 CALIBRES & TERMINATES AT 1 TURN IN 30 CALIBRES.
LENGTH OF RECOIL — BETWEEN 185 & 215mm.
CARTRIDGE HEAD SPACE — BETWEEN .008" & .035"
PROTRUSION OF STRIKER — BETWEEN .098" & .114"
AMMUNITION — 40mm BOFORS IN CHARGERS EACH HOLDING 4
ROUNDS, H.E. TRACER GRAZE FUZE WITH
ROTARY RELEASE [No 259]
OVERALL LENGTH OF COMPLETE ROUND — BETWEEN 17.49" & 17.65"
FEED — AUTO-LOADER FULLY AUTOMATIC SO LONG AS
THE SUPPLY OF AMMUNITION TO THE LOADER
IS MAINTAINED.

KEY TO DETAIL
1 RECESS FOR SAFETY PLUNGER
2 EXTRACTOR SPINDLE ARM
3 BREECH BLOCK
4 OUTER COCKING LEVER
5 OUTER CRANK ROLLER
6 LEFT INNER CRANK
7 OUTER CRANK
8 STRIKER
9 CRANK SHAFT
10 EXTRACTORS
11 EXTRACTOR SPINDLE

OPEN

CLOSED
OPERATION OF BREECH
MECHANISM
12 CHECK PLUNGER SPRING
13 INNER COCKING LEVER
14 SECURING SCREW.
15 CHECK PLUNGER
16 RIGHT INNER CRANK
17 CLOSING SPRING
18 STRIKER COVER.
19 STRIKER SPRING
20 COLLAR

TIMES OF FLIGHT — 500 YARDS — 0.57 SECONDS
1,000 YARDS — 1.23 SECONDS
1,500 YARDS — 1.99 SECONDS
2,000 YARDS — 2.88 SECONDS
2,500 YARDS — 3.90 SECONDS
3,000 YARDS — 5.08 SECONDS
3,500 YARDS — 6.43 SECONDS

KEY TO GUN DETAIL
1 GUN BARREL MARK 1
2 HELICAL COMPRESSION SPRING
3 RECUPERATOR SPRING SLEEVE
4 RECUPERATOR SPRING WASHER
5 FLASH HIDER MARK 2
6 FLAMEGUARD SCREW
7 GASKET
8 NUT
9 SCREW.
10 WASHER KEY
11 BREECH BLOCK

MARKS OF GUNS & ASSOCIATED GUN MOUNTINGS

MARK N1	AIR COOLED	MARK 3 MOUNTING.
MARK N1/1	AIR COOLED	MARK 7 MOUNTING
MARK N1/2	AIR COOLED	MARK 8 MOUNTING
MARK N1/2 [HAND]	AIR COOLED	MARK 8* MOUNTING.
MARKS N1/3 & N1/4	AIR COOLED	MARK 9* 9 MOUNTINGS.

BOOK OF REFERENCE — BR 1057/53 (AMENDED TO 1988).

© JOHN LAMBERT 1/9/96 CH'D 3/9/96

L/O/81

A 8 Single 40mm Bofors Mk III* naval mounting, 1946

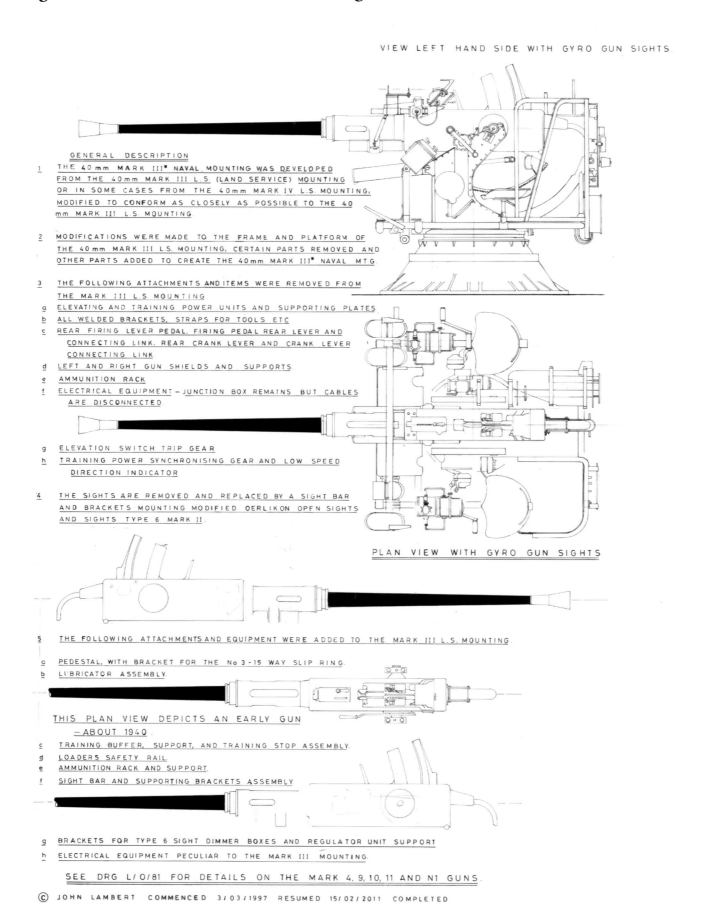

VIEW LEFT HAND SIDE WITH GYRO GUN SIGHTS.

GENERAL DESCRIPTION

1 THE 40mm MARK III* NAVAL MOUNTING WAS DEVELOPED
FROM THE 40mm MARK III L.S. (LAND SERVICE) MOUNTING
OR IN SOME CASES FROM THE 40mm MARK IV L.S. MOUNTING,
MODIFIED TO CONFORM AS CLOSELY AS POSSIBLE TO THE 40
mm MARK III L.S. MOUNTING.

2 MODIFICATIONS WERE MADE TO THE FRAME AND PLATFORM OF
THE 40mm MARK III L.S. MOUNTING, CERTAIN PARTS REMOVED AND
OTHER PARTS ADDED TO CREATE THE 40mm MARK III* NAVAL MTG.

3 THE FOLLOWING ATTACHMENTS AND ITEMS WERE REMOVED FROM
THE MARK III L.S. MOUNTING

a ELEVATING AND TRAINING POWER UNITS AND SUPPORTING PLATES
b ALL WELDED BRACKETS, STRAPS FOR TOOLS ETC
c REAR FIRING LEVER PEDAL, FIRING PEDAL REAR LEVER AND
   CONNECTING LINK, REAR CRANK LEVER AND CRANK LEVER
   CONNECTING LINK
d LEFT AND RIGHT GUN SHIELDS AND SUPPORTS
e AMMUNITION RACK
f ELECTRICAL EQUIPMENT – JUNCTION BOX REMAINS BUT CABLES
   ARE DISCONNECTED.

g ELEVATION SWITCH TRIP GEAR
h TRAINING POWER SYNCHRONISING GEAR AND LOW SPEED
   DIRECTION INDICATOR

4 THE SIGHTS ARE REMOVED AND REPLACED BY A SIGHT BAR
AND BRACKETS MOUNTING MODIFIED OERLIKON OPEN SIGHTS
AND SIGHTS TYPE 6 MARK II.

PLAN VIEW WITH GYRO GUN SIGHTS

5 THE FOLLOWING ATTACHMENTS AND EQUIPMENT WERE ADDED TO THE MARK III L.S. MOUNTING.

a PEDESTAL, WITH BRACKET FOR THE No 3 - 15 WAY SLIP RING.
b LUBRICATOR ASSEMBLY.

THIS PLAN VIEW DEPICTS AN EARLY GUN
   – ABOUT 1940.

c TRAINING BUFFER, SUPPORT, AND TRAINING STOP ASSEMBLY.
d LOADERS SAFETY RAIL.
e AMMUNITION RACK AND SUPPORT.
f SIGHT BAR AND SUPPORTING BRACKETS ASSEMBLY.

g BRACKETS FOR TYPE 6 SIGHT DIMMER BOXES AND REGULATOR UNIT SUPPORT
h ELECTRICAL EQUIPMENT PECULIAR TO THE MARK III MOUNTING.

SEE DRG L/0/81 FOR DETAILS ON THE MARK 4, 9, 10, 11 AND N1 GUNS.

© JOHN LAMBERT COMMENCED 31/03/1997 RESUMED 15/02/2011 COMPLETED

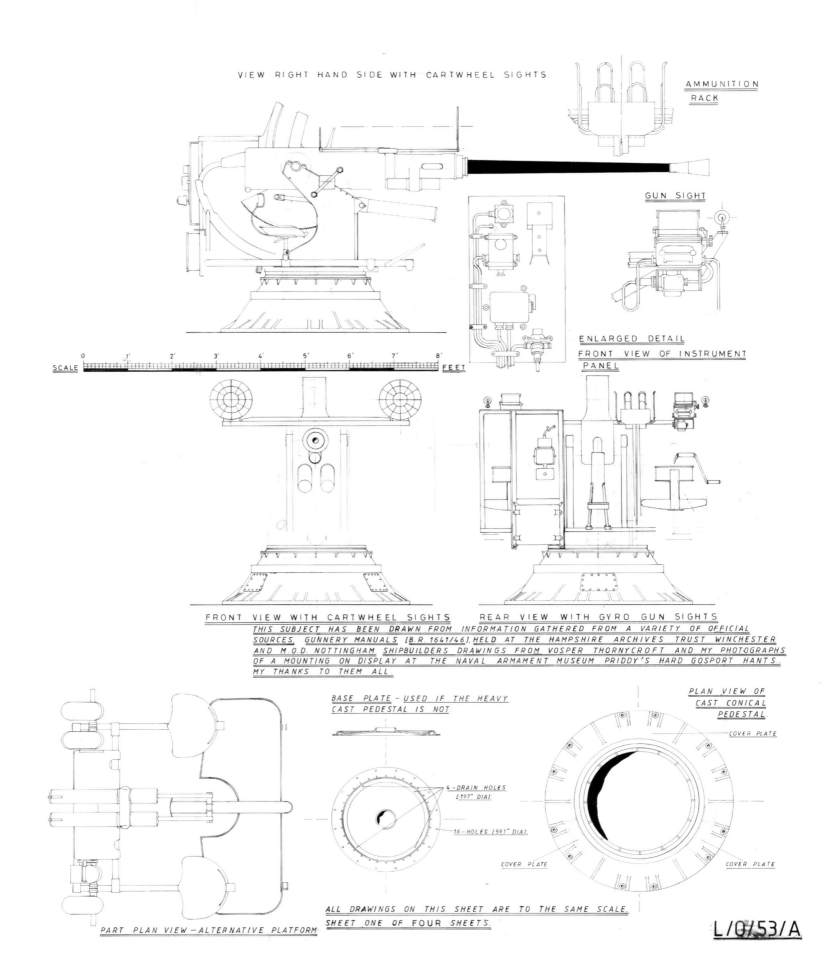

VIEW RIGHT HAND SIDE WITH CARTWHEEL SIGHTS.

AMMUNITION RACK

GUN SIGHT

ENLARGED DETAIL
FRONT VIEW OF INSTRUMENT PANEL

SCALE | 0 1' 2' 3' 4' 5' 6' 7' 8' | FEET

FRONT VIEW WITH CARTWHEEL SIGHTS

REAR VIEW WITH GYRO GUN SIGHTS

THIS SUBJECT HAS BEEN DRAWN FROM INFORMATION GATHERED FROM A VARIETY OF OFFICIAL SOURCES. GUNNERY MANUALS [B.R. 1641/46], HELD AT THE HAMPSHIRE ARCHIVES TRUST WINCHESTER AND M.O.D. NOTTINGHAM. SHIPBUILDERS DRAWINGS FROM VOSPER THORNYCROFT AND MY PHOTOGRAPHS OF A MOUNTING ON DISPLAY AT THE NAVAL ARMAMENT MUSEUM PRIDDY'S HARD GOSPORT HANTS. MY THANKS TO THEM ALL.

BASE PLATE - USED IF THE HEAVY CAST PEDESTAL IS NOT.

PLAN VIEW OF CAST CONICAL PEDESTAL.

COVER PLATE

4-DRAIN HOLES [.197" DIA]

16-HOLES [.591" DIA]

COVER PLATE

COVER PLATE

PART PLAN VIEW — ALTERNATIVE PLATFORM

ALL DRAWINGS ON THIS SHEET ARE TO THE SAME SCALE.
SHEET ONE OF FOUR SHEETS.

L/0/53/A

A 8 Single 40mm Bofors Mk III* naval mounting, detail

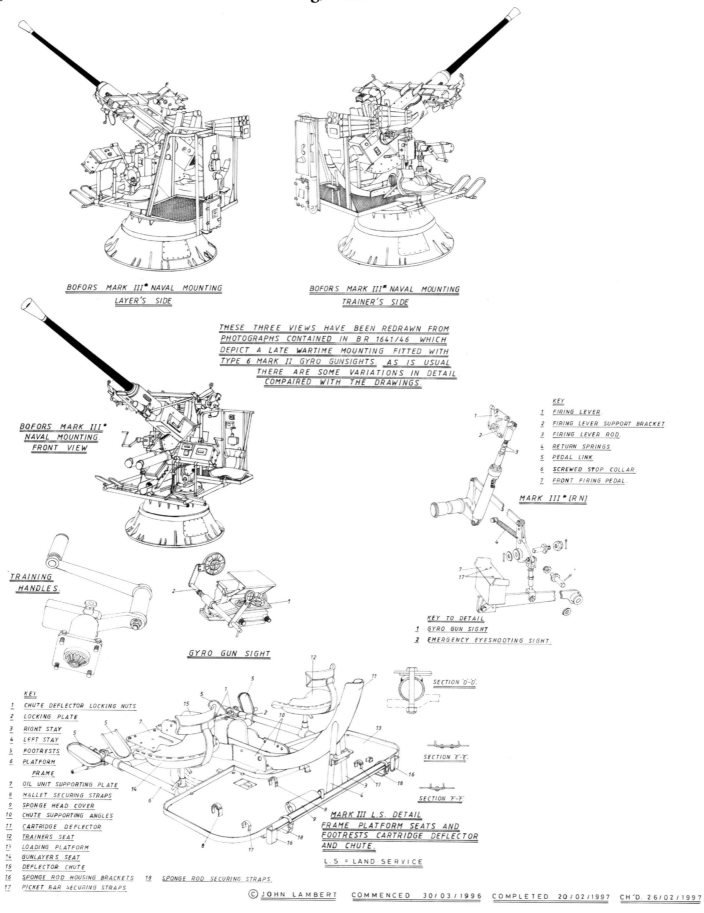

BOFORS MARK III* NAVAL MOUNTING
LAYER'S SIDE

BOFORS MARK III* NAVAL MOUNTING
TRAINER'S SIDE

THESE THREE VIEWS HAVE BEEN REDRAWN FROM
PHOTOGRAPHS CONTAINED IN BR 1641/46 WHICH
DEPICT A LATE WARTIME MOUNTING FITTED WITH
TYPE 6 MARK II GYRO GUNSIGHTS. AS IS USUAL
THERE ARE SOME VARIATIONS IN DETAIL
COMPAIRED WITH THE DRAWINGS.

BOFORS MARK III*
NAVAL MOUNTING.
FRONT VIEW

KEY
1 FIRING LEVER
2 FIRING LEVER SUPPORT BRACKET
3 FIRING LEVER ROD.
4 RETURN SPRINGS
5 PEDAL LINK.
6 SCREWED STOP COLLAR.
7 FRONT FIRING PEDAL.

MARK III* [R N]

KEY TO DETAIL
1 GYRO GUN SIGHT
2 EMERGENCY EYESHOOTING SIGHT.

TRAINING
HANDLES.

GYRO GUN SIGHT

KEY
1 CHUTE DEFLECTOR LOCKING NUTS
2 LOCKING PLATE
3 RIGHT STAY
4 LEFT STAY
5 FOOTRESTS
6 PLATFORM
   FRAME
7 OIL UNIT SUPPORTING PLATE
8 MALLET SECURING STRAPS
9 SPONGE HEAD COVER
10 CHUTE SUPPORTING ANGLES
11 CARTRIDGE DEFLECTOR
12 TRAINERS SEAT
13 LOADING PLATFORM
14 GUNLAYERS SEAT
15 DEFLECTOR CHUTE
16 SPONGE ROD HOUSING BRACKETS
17 PICKET BAR SECURING STRAPS
18 SPONGE ROD SECURING STRAPS.

SECTION 'D'-'D'.

SECTION 'E'-'E'.

SECTION 'F'-'F'.

MARK III L.S. DETAIL
FRAME PLATFORM SEATS AND
FOOTRESTS CARTRIDGE DEFLECTOR
AND CHUTE.

L.S = LAND SERVICE

© JOHN LAMBERT   COMMENCED 30/03/1996 COMPLETED 20/02/1997 CH'D. 26/02/1997.

184

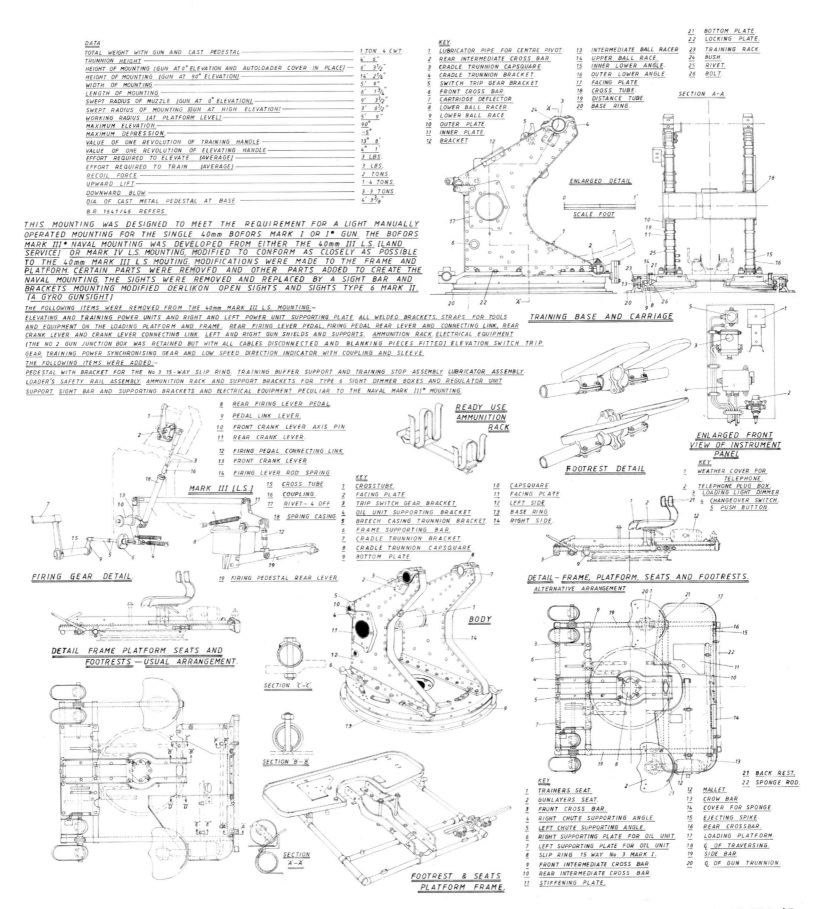

DATA

TOTAL WEIGHT WITH GUN AND CAST PEDESTAL — 1 TON 4 CWT
TRUNNION HEIGHT — 4' 6"
HEIGHT OF MOUNTING [GUN AT 0° ELEVATION AND AUTOLOADER COVER IN PLACE] — 6' 3½"
HEIGHT OF MOUNTING [GUN AT 90° ELEVATION] — 14' 2¼"
WIDTH OF MOUNTING — 5' 9"
LENGTH OF MOUNTING — 6' 1¾"
SWEPT RADIUS OF MUZZLE [GUN AT 0° ELEVATION] — 9' 3½"
SWEPT RADIUS OF MOUNTING [GUN AT HIGH ELEVATION] — 3' 6½"
WORKING RADIUS [AT PLATFORM LEVEL] — 5' 9"
MAXIMUM ELEVATION — 90°
MAXIMUM DEPRESSION — -5°
VALUE OF ONE REVOLUTION OF TRAINING HANDLE — 13° 8'
VALUE OF ONE REVOLUTION OF ELEVATING HANDLE — 4° 1'
EFFORT REQUIRED TO ELEVATE [AVERAGE] — 3 LBS.
EFFORT REQUIRED TO TRAIN [AVERAGE] — 3 LBS.
RECOIL FORCE — 2 TONS
UPWARD LIFT — 1.4 TONS
DOWNWARD BLOW — 3.3 TONS
DIA. OF CAST METAL PEDESTAL AT BASE — 4' 3⅜"
B.R. 1641/46 REFERS

THIS MOUNTING WAS DESIGNED TO MEET THE REQUIREMENT FOR A LIGHT MANUALLY OPERATED MOUNTING FOR THE SINGLE 40mm BOFORS MARK I OR I* GUN. THE BOFORS MARK III* NAVAL MOUNTING WAS DEVELOPED FROM EITHER THE 40mm III L.S. [LAND SERVICE] OR MARK IV L.S. MOUNTING, MODIFIED TO CONFORM AS CLOSELY AS POSSIBLE TO THE 40mm MARK III L.S. MOUTING. MODIFICATIONS WERE MADE TO THE FRAME AND PLATFORM. CERTAIN PARTS WERE REMOVED AND OTHER PARTS ADDED TO CREATE THE NAVAL MOUNTING. THE SIGHTS WERE REMOVED AND REPLACED BY A SIGHT BAR AND BRACKETS MOUNTING MODIFIED OERLIKON OPEN SIGHTS AND SIGHTS TYPE 6 MARK II. [A GYRO GUNSIGHT]

THE FOLLOWING ITEMS WERE REMOVED FROM THE 40mm MARK III L.S. MOUNTING:-
ELEVATING AND TRAINING POWER UNITS AND RIGHT AND LEFT POWER UNIT SUPPORTING PLATE. ALL WELDED BRACKETS, STRAPS FOR TOOLS AND EQUIPMENT ON THE LOADING PLATFORM AND FRAME. REAR FIRING LEVER PEDAL, FIRING PEDAL REAR LEVER AND CONNECTING LINK, REAR CRANK LEVER AND CRANK LEVER CONNECTING LINK. LEFT AND RIGHT GUN SHIELDS AND SUPPORTS. AMMUNITION RACK. ELECTRICAL EQUIPMENT [THE NO 2 GUN JUNCTION BOX WAS RETAINED BUT WITH ALL CABLES DISCONNECTED AND BLANKING PIECES FITTED] ELEVATION SWITCH TRIP GEAR, TRAINING POWER SYNCHRONISING GEAR AND LOW SPEED DIRECTION INDICATOR WITH COUPLING AND SLEEVE.
THE FOLLOWING ITEMS WERE ADDED:-
PEDESTAL WITH BRACKET FOR THE No 3 15-WAY SLIP RING. TRAINING BUFFER SUPPORT AND TRAINING STOP ASSEMBLY. LUBRICATOR ASSEMBLY. LOADER'S SAFETY RAIL ASSEMBLY. AMMUNITION RACK AND SUPPORT BRACKETS FOR TYPE 6 SIGHT DIMMER BOXES AND REGULATOR UNIT SUPPORT. SIGHT BAR AND SUPPORTING BRACKETS AND ELECTRICAL EQUIPMENT PECULIAR TO THE NAVAL MARK III* MOUNTING.

KEY
1 LUBRICATOR PIPE FOR CENTRE PIVOT.
2 REAR INTERMEDIATE CROSS BAR.
3 CRADLE TRUNNION CAPSQUARE.
4 CRADLE TRUNNION BRACKET.
5 SWITCH TRIP GEAR BRACKET.
6 FRONT CROSS BAR.
7 CARTRIDGE DEFLECTOR.
8 LOWER BALL RACER.
9 LOWER BALL RACE.
10 OUTER PLATE.
11 INNER PLATE.
12 BRACKET.
13 INTERMEDIATE BALL RACER.
14 UPPER BALL RACE.
15 INNER LOWER ANGLE.
16 OUTER LOWER ANGLE.
17 FACING PLATE.
18 CROSS TUBE.
19 DISTANCE TUBE.
20 BASE RING.
21 BOTTOM PLATE.
22 LOCKING PLATE.
23 TRAINING RACK.
24 BUSH.
25 RIVET.
26 BOLT.

SECTION A-A

ENLARGED DETAIL

SCALE FOOT

TRAINING BASE AND CARRIAGE

8 REAR FIRING LEVER PEDAL
9 PEDAL LINK LEVER.
10 FRONT CRANK LEVER AXIS PIN
11 REAR CRANK LEVER.
12 FIRING PEDAL CONNECTING LINK
13 FRONT CRANK LEVER.
14 FIRING LEVER ROD SPRING
15 CROSS TUBE.
16 COUPLING.
17 RIVET - 4 OFF
18 SPRING CASING

MARK III [L.S.]

FIRING GEAR DETAIL.

19 FIRING PEDESTAL REAR LEVER.

READY USE AMMUNITION RACK

FOOTREST DETAIL

ENLARGED FRONT VIEW OF INSTRUMENT PANEL
KEY
1 WEATHER COVER FOR TELEPHONE.
2 TELEPHONE PLUG BOX.
3 LOADING LIGHT DIMMER.
4 CHANGEOVER SWITCH.
5 PUSH BUTTON

KEY
1 CROSSTUBE.
2 FACING PLATE.
3 TRIP SWITCH GEAR BRACKET.
4 OIL UNIT SUPPORTING BRACKET.
5 BREECH CASING TRUNNION BRACKET.
6 FRAME SUPPORTING BAR.
7 CRADLE TRUNNION BRACKET.
8 CRADLE TRUNNION CAPSQUARE.
9 BOTTOM PLATE.
10 CAPSQUARE.
11 FACING PLATE.
12 LEFT SIDE.
13 BASE RING.
14 RIGHT SIDE.

BODY

SECTION 'C-C'

SECTION 'B-B'

SECTION 'A-A'

DETAIL FRAME PLATFORM SEATS AND FOOTRESTS - USUAL ARRANGEMENT.

FOOTREST & SEATS PLATFORM FRAME.

DETAIL - FRAME, PLATFORM, SEATS AND FOOTRESTS.
ALTERNATIVE ARRANGEMENT

KEY
1 TRAINERS SEAT.
2 GUNLAYERS SEAT.
3 FRONT CROSS BAR.
4 RIGHT CHUTE SUPPORTING ANGLE.
5 LEFT CHUTE SUPPORTING ANGLE.
6 RIGHT SUPPORTING PLATE FOR OIL UNIT
7 LEFT SUPPORTING PLATE FOR OIL UNIT
8 SLIP RING 15 WAY No 3 MARK I.
9 FRONT INTERMEDIATE CROSS BAR.
10 REAR INTERMEDIATE CROSS BAR.
11 STIFFENING PLATE.
12 MALLET.
13 CROW BAR.
14 COVER FOR SPONGE.
15 EJECTING SPIKE.
16 REAR CROSSBAR.
17 LOADING PLATFORM.
18 ℄ OF TRAVERSING.
19 SIDE BAR.
20 ℄ OF GUN TRUNNION.
21 BACK REST.
22 SPONGE ROD.

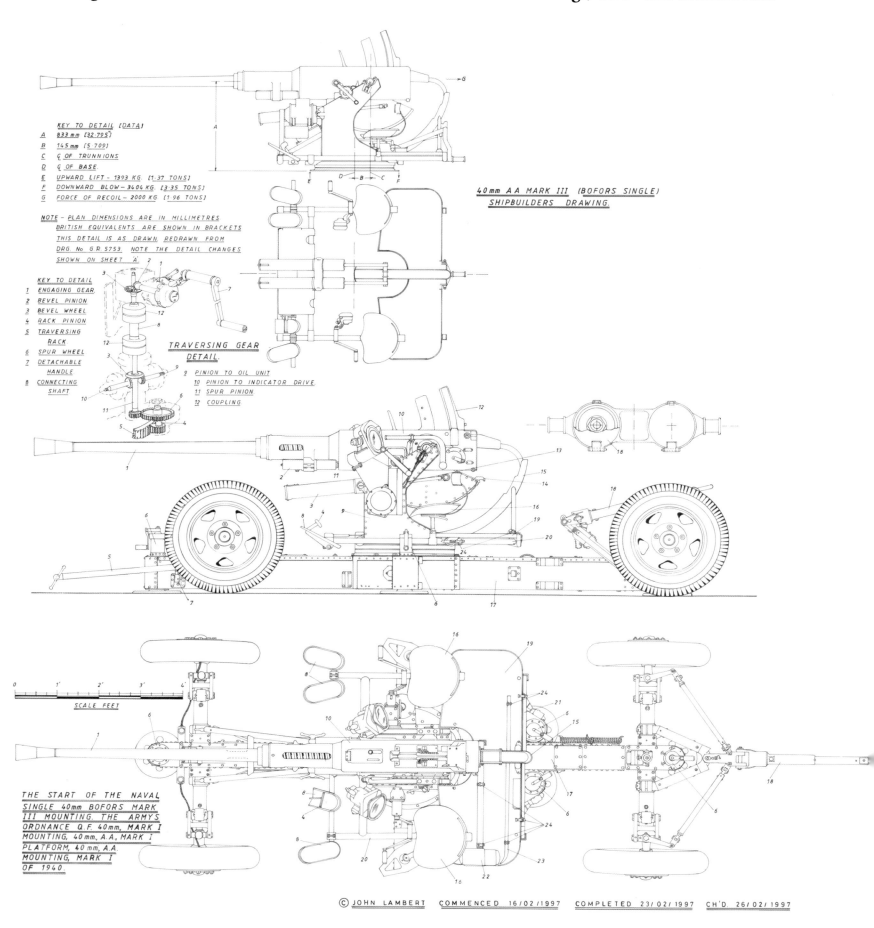

KEY TO DETAIL (DATA)

A 833 mm (32·795")
B 145 mm (5·709")
C ℄ OF TRUNNIONS
D ℄ OF BASE.
E UPWARD LIFT - 1393 KG. (1·37 TONS)
F DOWNWARD BLOW - 3404 KG. (3·35 TONS)
G FORCE OF RECOIL - 2000 KG. (1·96 TONS)

NOTE - PLAN DIMENSIONS ARE IN MILLIMETRES.
BRITISH EQUIVALENTS ARE SHOWN IN BRACKETS
THIS DETAIL IS AS DRAWN. REDRAWN FROM
DRG. No G.R.5753. NOTE THE DETAIL CHANGES
SHOWN ON SHEET 'A'.

KEY TO DETAIL
1 ENGAGING GEAR.
2 BEVEL PINION.
3 BEVEL WHEEL
4 RACK PINION
5 TRAVERSING
   RACK
6 SPUR WHEEL
7 DETACHABLE
   HANDLE
8 CONNECTING
   SHAFT

9   PINION TO OIL UNIT
10 PINION TO INDICATOR DRIVE.
11 SPUR PINION
12 COUPLING.

TRAVERSING GEAR DETAIL.

40mm A A MARK III (BOFORS SINGLE)
SHIPBUILDERS DRAWING.

SCALE FEET

THE START OF THE NAVAL
SINGLE 40mm BOFORS MARK
III MOUNTING. THE ARMYS
ORDNANCE Q.F. 40mm, MARK I
MOUNTING, 40 mm, A.A. MARK I
PLATFORM, 40 mm, A.A.
MOUNTING, MARK I
OF 1940.

© JOHN LAMBERT   COMMENCED 16/02/1997   COMPLETED 23/02/1997   CH'D 26/02/1997

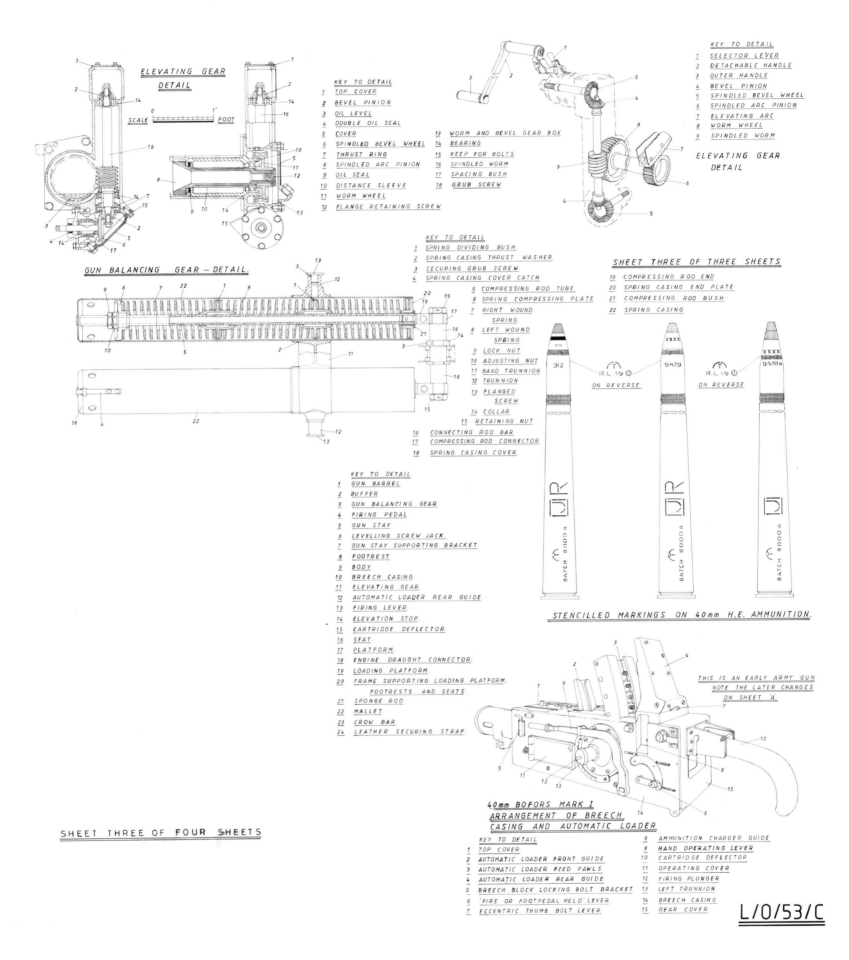

ELEVATING GEAR DETAIL

SCALE 0 — 1' FOOT

KEY TO DETAIL
1 TOP COVER
2 BEVEL PINION
3 OIL LEVEL
4 DOUBLE OIL SEAL
5 COVER
6 SPINDLED BEVEL WHEEL
7 THRUST RING
8 SPINDLED ARC PINION
9 OIL SEAL
10 DISTANCE SLEEVE
11 WORM WHEEL
12 FLANGE RETAINING SCREW
13 WORM AND BEVEL GEAR BOX
14 BEARING
15 KEEP FOR BOLTS
16 SPINDLED WORM
17 SPACING BUSH
18 GRUB SCREW

KEY TO DETAIL
1 SELECTOR LEVER
2 DETACHABLE HANDLE
3 OUTER HANDLE
4 BEVEL PINION
5 SPINDLED BEVEL WHEEL
6 SPINDLED ARC PINION
7 ELEVATING ARC
8 WORM WHEEL
9 SPINDLED WORM

ELEVATING GEAR DETAIL

GUN BALANCING GEAR - DETAIL.

KEY TO DETAIL
1 SPRING DIVIDING BUSH.
2 SPRING CASING THRUST WASHER
3 SECURING GRUB SCREW.
4 SPRING CASING COVER CATCH
5 COMPRESSING ROD TUBE
6 SPRING COMPRESSING PLATE
7 RIGHT WOUND SPRING
8 LEFT WOUND SPRING
9 LOCK NUT
10 ADJUSTING NUT
11 BAND TRUNNION
12 TRUNNION
13 FLANGED SCREW
14 COLLAR
15 RETAINING NUT
16 CONNECTING ROD BAR
17 COMPRESSING ROD CONNECTOR
18 SPRING CASING COVER.

SHEET THREE OF THREE SHEETS
19 COMPRESSING ROD END
20 SPRING CASING END PLATE
21 COMPRESSING ROD BUSH
22 SPRING CASING

KEY TO DETAIL
1 GUN BARREL
2 BUFFER
3 GUN BALANCING GEAR
4 FIRING PEDAL
5 GUN STAY
6 LEVELLING SCREW JACK.
7 GUN STAY SUPPORTING BRACKET
8 FOOTREST
9 BODY
10 BREECH CASING
11 ELEVATING GEAR
12 AUTOMATIC LOADER REAR GUIDE
13 FIRING LEVER
14 ELEVATION STOP.
15 CARTRIDGE DEFLECTOR
16 SEAT
17 PLATFORM.
18 ENGINE DRAUGHT CONNECTOR.
19 LOADING PLATFORM.
20 FRAME SUPPORTING LOADING PLATFORM, FOOTRESTS AND SEATS.
21 SPONGE ROD.
22 MALLET.
23 CROW BAR.
24 LEATHER SECURING STRAP.

312   R.L. V9   ON REVERSE   XXXX   9479   R.L. V9   ON REVERSE   XXXX   9.578A

BATCH 8000A   BATCH 8000A

STENCILLED MARKINGS ON 40mm H.E. AMMUNITION.

THIS IS AN EARLY ARMY GUN NOTE THE LATER CHANGES ON SHEET 'A'

SHEET THREE OF FOUR SHEETS

40mm BOFORS MARK I ARRANGEMENT OF BREECH CASING AND AUTOMATIC LOADER

KEY TO DETAIL
1 TOP COVER
2 AUTOMATIC LOADER FRONT GUIDE
3 AUTOMATIC LOADER FEED PAWLS
4 AUTOMATIC LOADER REAR GUIDE
5 BREECH BLOCK LOCKING BOLT BRACKET
6 "FIRE OR FOOTPEDAL HELD" LEVER
7 ECCENTRIC THUMB BOLT LEVER
8 AMMUNITION CHARGER GUIDE
9 HAND OPERATING LEVER
10 CARTRIDGE DEFLECTOR
11 OPERATING COVER
12 FIRING PLUNGER
13 LEFT TRUNNION
14 BREECH CASING
15 REAR COVER

L/0/53/C

A 8 Single 40mm Bofors Mk III naval mounting, general arrangement as modified with gyro gun sights, 1945

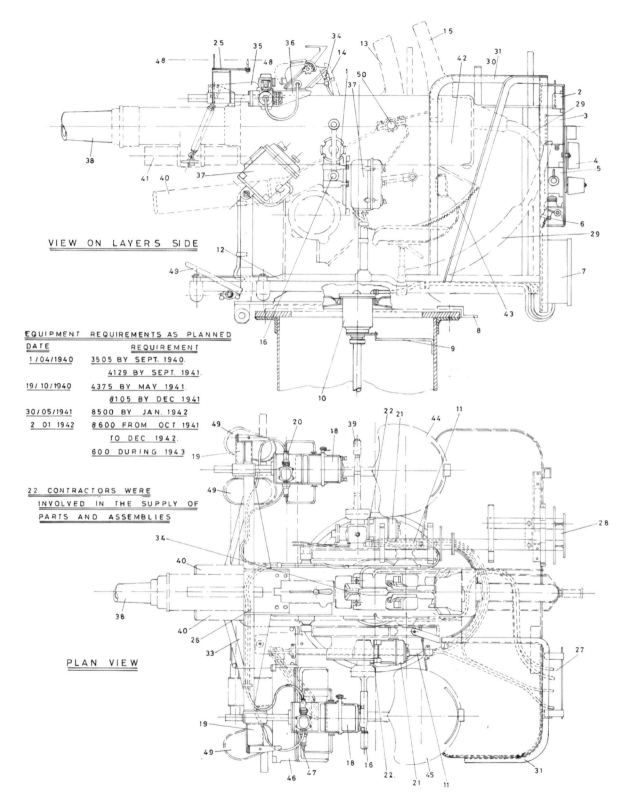

VIEW ON LAYERS SIDE

EQUIPMENT REQUIREMENTS AS PLANNED

DATE	REQUIREMENT
1/04/1940	3505 BY SEPT. 1940.
	4129 BY SEPT. 1941.
19/10/1940	4375 BY MAY 1941.
	8105 BY DEC 1941
30/05/1941	8500 BY JAN. 1942
2 01 1942	8600 FROM OCT 1941
	TO DEC 1942.
	600 DURING 1943

22 CONTRACTORS WERE INVOLVED IN THE SUPPLY OF PARTS AND ASSEMBLIES

PLAN VIEW

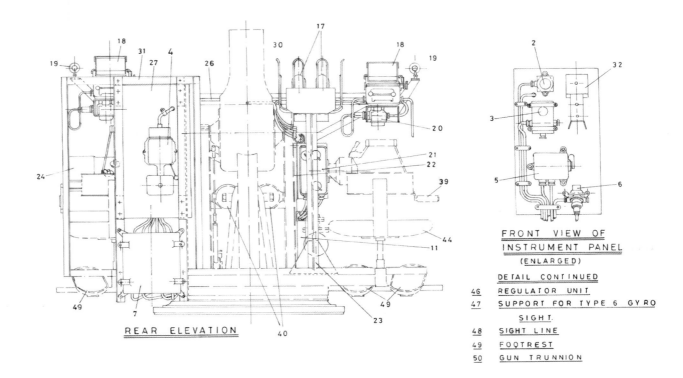

REAR ELEVATION

FRONT VIEW OF
INSTRUMENT PANEL
(ENLARGED)

DETAIL CONTINUED

46	REGULATOR UNIT
47	SUPPORT FOR TYPE 6 GYRO SIGHT.
48	SIGHT LINE
49	FOOTREST
50	GUN TRUNNION

NOTE THESE THREE DRAWING ARE NOT TO THE SAME SCALE BUT REPRESENTATIVE ONLY.
THIS SHEET HAS BEEN REDRAWN FROM THREE PLATES CONTAINED IN THE MANUAL — DRG. GR 7093 ETC.

KEY TO DETAIL

1	BRACKET SUPPORTING DIMMER BOX	17	AMMUNITION RACK (READY USE).	33	SUPPORT FOR REGULATOR UNIT
2	PUSH BUTTON	18	GYRO GUN SIGHT - TYPE 6.	34	LOADING LIGHT
3	LOADING LIGHT DIMMER	19	OPEN GUN SIGHT.	35	BRACKET SUPPORTING SIGHTS
4	CHECK FIRE BELL	20	JUNCTION UNIT.	36	PLATFORM CARRYING GYRO SIGHT AND JUNCTION BOX.
5	CHANGE OVER SWITCH	21	DIMMER UNIT.		
6	TELEPHONE PLUG BOX	22	BRACKET.		
7	JUNCTION BOX	23	AMMUNITION RACK SUPPORT		
8	TRAINING STOP	24	REGULATOR UNIT	37	DIMMER BOX FOR GYRO GUN SIGHT
9	FORK HOLDING SLIP RING UNIT	25	SIGHT SUPPORT		
10	SLIP RING UNIT	26	SIGHT BAR.	38	GUN BARREL
11	1¼" SCREWED CONDUIT — ALL ELBOW JOINTS SHOULD HAVE INSPECTION COVERS.	27	LOADERS SAFETY RAIL AND INSTRUMENT PANEL	39	HAND TRAINING GEAR
		28	AMMUNITION RACK AND SUPPORT	40	GUN BALANCING GEAR
12	END OF CONDUIT FLATTENED			41	BUFFER CYLINDER
13	AUTOMATIC LOADER FEED PAWLS	29	CARTRIDGE DEFECTOR.	42	BREECH CASING
14	AUTOMATIC LOADER FRONT GUIDE	30	BREECH REAR COVER.	43	ELEVATING ARC
15	AUTOMATIC LOADER REAR GUIDE	31	RAIL AROUND LOADER	44	SEAT FOR TRAINING
16	HAND ELEVATING GEAR	32	WEATHER COVER FOR TELEPHONE	45	SEAT FOR ELEVATING

DEVELOPMENT HISTORY

IT WAS AN URGENT REQUIREMENT TO PROVIDE A WEAPON TO COUNTER LOW FLYING AIRCRAFT WHICH LED TO THE ADOPTION OF THIS WEAPON FOR OUR ARMED FORCES. INITIALLY RESEARCH WAS DIRECTED AT PROVIDING A SUITABLE WEAPON OF THE 2 POUNDER POM POM TYPE AS OPPOSED TO ·303" AND 0·5" MACHINE GUNS, BUT THESE LACKED ANY 'PUNCH' VICKERS ARMSTRONG PRODUCED A 40mm 2 POUNDER (POM POM) WHICH WAS CONSIDERED UNSATISFACTORY AT TRIALS IN THE SPRING OF 1937. HOWEVER PRODUCTION INCREASED AS NOTHING ELSE WAS AVAILABLE AND AMMUNITION WAS PLENTIFUL. IT WAS DECIDED TO PROCEED WITH THE 40mm BOFORS DESIGNED AND PRODUCED BY A.B. BOFORS IN SWEDEN AND DESIGNES WERE AVAILABLE FOR A MOBILE TOWED MOUNTING (SEE SHEET 'C'). ORDERS WERE PLACED AND A LICENCE TO MANUFACTURE OBTAINED. ORIGINAL PLANS COVERED MANUFACTURE BY R.C.F NOTTINGHAM, AND THE NUFFIELD ORGANISATION. WARTIME EXPANSION LED TO THE PROVISION OF THE MAJOR ASSEMBLIES ON AN INDEPENDENT BASIS. A MARKED REDUCTION IN WORKING HOURS WAS ACHIEVED DURING THE EARLY YEARS BY TECHNICAL ADVANCES. E.G. LOADING TRAY ORIGINALLY FORGED IN STAINLESS STEEL TO WITHSTAND EROSION IT WAS CHANGED TO NICKEL STEEL PERMITTING FASTER MACHINING TIMES. THE FEED PAWLS WERE REPLACED BY ALUMINIUM BRONZE DIE CASTINGS. FLAME GUARDS —DROP FORGINGS WERE REPLACED BY MALLEABLE IRON CASTINGS OR WELDED FABRICATIONS. BREECH CASING—THE DROP FORGINGS WERE NOW OF WELDED FABRICATION WHILST THE ELEVATING ARC WAS REPLACED BY TWO ALTERNATIVES OF WELDED AND STEEL CASTING. THE MARK III GUN EMBODIED MANY DESIGN ALTERATIONS. THE MAJOR MODIFICATION ENTAILING CONSIDERABLE SIMPLIFICATION TO THE AUTOMATIC LOADER. NEW FACTORIES WERE BUILT AND BROUGHT ONLINE. ANTICIPATED DELIVERY IN JANUARY 1941 RISING TO 100/MONTH BY JUNE.

SHEET FOUR OF FOUR SHEETS L/0/53/0

A 9 Twin 40mm Bofors STAAG Mk 3 mounting

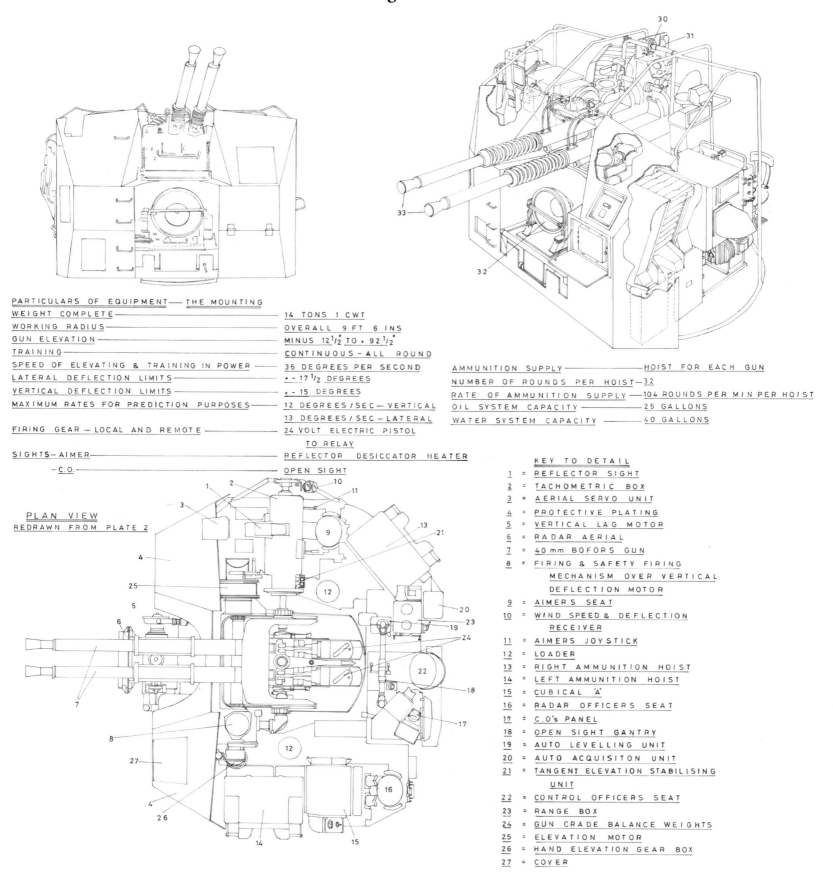

PARTICULARS OF EQUIPMENT — THE MOUNTING

WEIGHT COMPLETE ———————— 14 TONS 1 CWT
WORKING RADIUS ———————— OVERALL 9 FT 6 INS
GUN ELEVATION ———————— MINUS 12½° TO + 92½°
TRAINING ———————— CONTINUOUS — ALL ROUND
SPEED OF ELEVATING & TRAINING IN POWER — 36 DEGREES PER SECOND
LATERAL DEFLECTION LIMITS ———————— + - 17½ DEGREES
VERTICAL DEFLECTION LIMITS ———————— + - 15 DEGREES
MAXIMUM RATES FOR PREDICTION PURPOSES — 12 DEGREES / SEC — VERTICAL
                                        13 DEGREES / SEC — LATERAL
FIRING GEAR — LOCAL AND REMOTE ———————— 24 VOLT ELECTRIC PISTOL
                                        TO RELAY
SIGHTS — AIMER ———————— REFLECTOR DESICCATOR HEATER
       — C.O. ———————— OPEN SIGHT

AMMUNITION SUPPLY ———————— HOIST FOR EACH GUN
NUMBER OF ROUNDS PER HOIST — 32
RATE OF AMMUNITION SUPPLY — 104 ROUNDS PER MIN PER HOIST
OIL SYSTEM CAPACITY ———————— 25 GALLONS
WATER SYSTEM CAPACITY ———————— 40 GALLONS

PLAN VIEW
REDRAWN FROM PLATE 2

KEY TO DETAIL

1 = REFLECTOR SIGHT
2 = TACHOMETRIC BOX
3 = AERIAL SERVO UNIT
4 = PROTECTIVE PLATING
5 = VERTICAL LAG MOTOR
6 = RADAR AERIAL
7 = 40 mm BOFORS GUN
8 = FIRING & SAFETY FIRING
    MECHANISM OVER VERTICAL
    DEFLECTION MOTOR
9 = AIMERS SEAT
10 = WIND SPEED & DEFLECTION
     RECEIVER
11 = AIMERS JOYSTICK
12 = LOADER
13 = RIGHT AMMUNITION HOIST
14 = LEFT AMMUNITION HOIST
15 = CUBICAL 'A'
16 = RADAR OFFICERS SEAT
17 = C.O's PANEL
18 = OPEN SIGHT GANTRY
19 = AUTO LEVELLING UNIT
20 = AUTO ACQUISITON UNIT
21 = TANGENT ELEVATION STABILISING
     UNIT
22 = CONTROL OFFICERS SEAT
23 = RANGE BOX
24 = GUN CRADE BALANCE WEIGHTS
25 = ELEVATION MOTOR
26 = HAND ELEVATION GEAR BOX
27 = COVER

© JOHN LAMBERT   COMMENCED 21/08/2012   COMPLETED 5/09/2012   CH'D. 8/09/2012

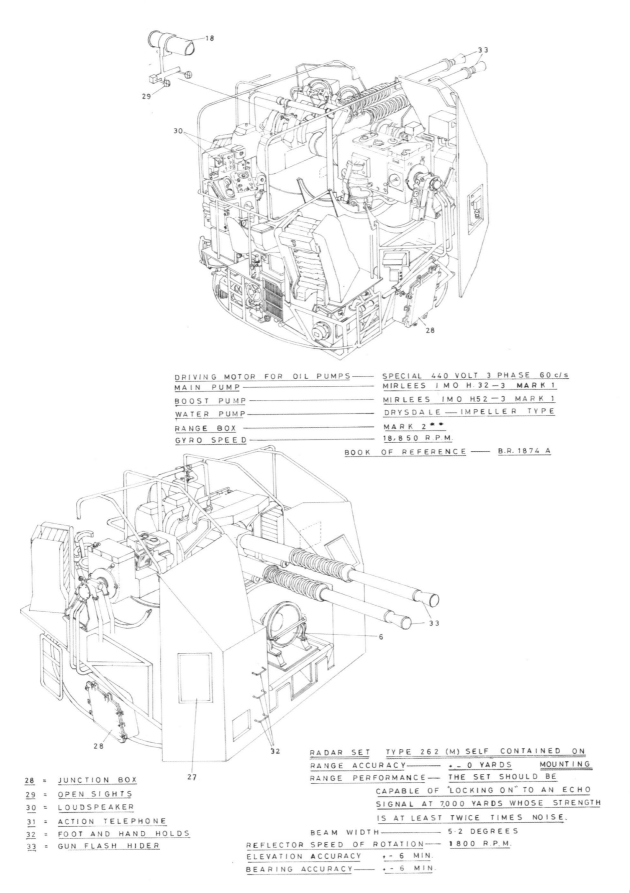

DRIVING MOTOR FOR OIL PUMPS —————— SPECIAL 440 VOLT 3 PHASE 60 c/s
MAIN PUMP ————————————————— MIRLEES I M O H.32—3 MARK 1
BOOST PUMP ————————————————— MIRLEES I M O H52—3 MARK 1
WATER PUMP ————————————————— DRYSDALE —— IMPELLER TYPE
RANGE BOX ————————————————— MARK 2 **
GYRO SPEED ————————————————— 18,850 R.P.M.

BOOK OF REFERENCE —————— B.R.1874 A

28 = JUNCTION BOX
29 = OPEN SIGHTS
30 = LOUDSPEAKER
31 = ACTION TELEPHONE
32 = FOOT AND HAND HOLDS
33 = GUN FLASH HIDER

RADAR SET   TYPE 262 (M) SELF CONTAINED ON
RANGE ACCURACY ——————— +.- 0 YARDS   MOUNTING
RANGE PERFORMANCE —— THE SET SHOULD BE
CAPABLE OF "LOCKING ON" TO AN ECHO
SIGNAL AT 7,000 YARDS WHOSE STRENGTH
IS AT LEAST TWICE TIMES NOISE.
BEAM WIDTH ——————— 5.2 DEGREES
REFLECTOR SPEED OF ROTATION —— 1800 R.P.M.
ELEVATION ACCURACY   +.- 6 MIN.
BEARING ACCURACY ——————— +.- 6 MIN.

L / 0 / 181 / C

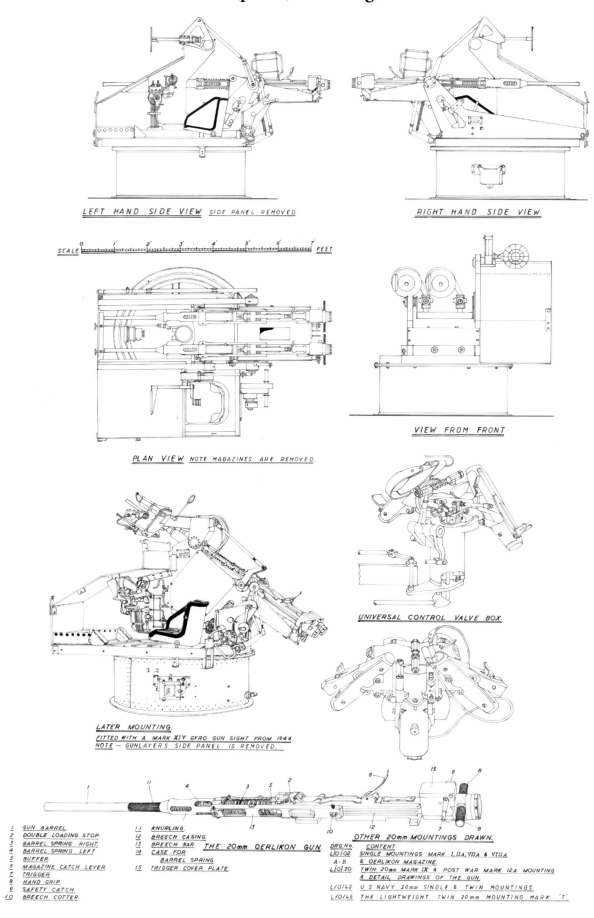

LEFT HAND SIDE VIEW *SIDE PANEL REMOVED*

RIGHT HAND SIDE VIEW.

SCALE 0 1 2 3 4 5 6 7 FEET

VIEW FROM FRONT

PLAN VIEW *NOTE MAGAZINES ARE REMOVED.*

UNIVERSAL CONTROL VALVE BOX.

LATER MOUNTING.
FITTED WITH A MARK XIV GYRO GUN SIGHT FROM 1944.
NOTE — GUNLAYERS SIDE PANEL IS REMOVED.

THE 20mm OERLIKON GUN.

1 GUN BARREL.
2 DOUBLE LOADING STOP.
3 BARREL SPRING RIGHT.
4 BARREL SPRING LEFT
5 BUFFER.
6 MAGAZINE CATCH LEVER
7 TRIGGER.
8 HAND GRIP.
9 SAFETY CATCH.
10 BREECH COTTER.
11 KNURLING.
12 BREECH CASING.
13 BREECH BAR
14 CASE FOR
     BARREL SPRING.
15 TRIGGER COVER PLATE.

OTHER 20mm MOUNTINGS DRAWN.

DRG.No.	CONTENT
L10102.	SINGLE MOUNTINGS MARK I, IIA, VIIA & VIIIA
A-B	& OERLIKON MAGAZINE.
L10130.	TWIN 20mm MARK IX & POST WAR MARK 12A MOUNTING
	& DETAIL DRAWINGS OF THE GUN.
L10140	U S NAVY 20mm SINGLE & TWIN MOUNTINGS
L10146	THE LIGHTWEIGHT TWIN 20mm MOUNTING MARK 'T'

DATA

THE 20mm OERLIKON GUN.
CALIBRE——20mm or ·8 INS APPROX.
MUZZLE VELOCITY.—2725 FT/SEC
RIFLING.——9 RIGHT HAND GROOVES.
LENGTH OVERALL.—8 FT.
WEIGHT—WITH SPLINED BARREL—141 LBS.(NOT SHOWN).
WEIGHT—WITHOUT SPLINED BARREL—150 LBS
RATE OF FIRE.——465—480 ROUNDS PER MIN.
MAX RANGE AT 45° ELEVATION—6250 YARDS.
THE MARK V (POWER) MOUNTING.
WEIGHT OF TURRET (COMPLETE WITH GUNS &
    AMMUNITION).—2247 LBS.
WEIGHT OF CRADLE (FITTED WITH GUN MOUNTING
    BLOCKS).——200 LBS.
ARC OF TRAINING—0°—360°
POWER——HYDRAULIC.
FIRING MECHANISM-HYDRAULIC.
WORKING PRESSURE.—300 LB/SQ"
OIL USED IN SYSTEM—D.T.D. 44D.
HORIZONTAL ROLLERS—19.
VERTICAL ROLLERS.——20.
HOLDING DOWN BOLTS.—12—·5"DIA—50·25"P.C.D.
BASE RING.——51·5" EXTREME DIA.
POSITION OF C.G.-6" BELOW C.L. TRUNNIONS.
WEIGHT OF EQUIPMENT—1·08 TONS.
POWER UNIT.(LOCAL)——0·2 TONS.
No OF CREW——2
EFFECTIVE RANGE—1000—1200 YARDS.
AMMUNITION——2400 ROUNDS PER GUN.
    (C.A.F.O. 1229/45.)
DISTANCE BETWEEN GUNS—13"

HISTORY:-

THE PURPOSE OF THIS EQUIPMENT WAS TO PROVIDE
POWER OPERATION TO A TURRET CONTAINING TWO MARK II
OR MARK IV GUNS WITH ACCURACY & SENSITIVITY OF
CONTROL & WITH THE LEAST POSSIBLE FATIGUE TO
THE GUN LAYER.
INTRODUCED INTO SERVICE IN 1942. THE HYDRAULIC
POWER WAS PROVIDED FROM A PUMP USUALLY DRIVEN
FROM THE MAIN OR AUXILIARY ENGINES IN COASTAL
FORCES. IN LARGER UNITS LOCAL DRIVE UNITS WERE
DRIVEN BY ELECTRIC MOTORS.
BY 1943 PRODUCTION HAD INCREASED & THE MOUNTING
EQUIPPED SHIPS OF ALL TYPES E.G. FLEET DESTROYERS
(4) CRUISERS (8-10) BATTLESHIPS (5-13) BUT BY 1945 THIS
MOUNTING WAS GRADUALLY REPLACED BY THE MORE POTANT
40mm BOFORS MARK III & VII MOUNTINGS.

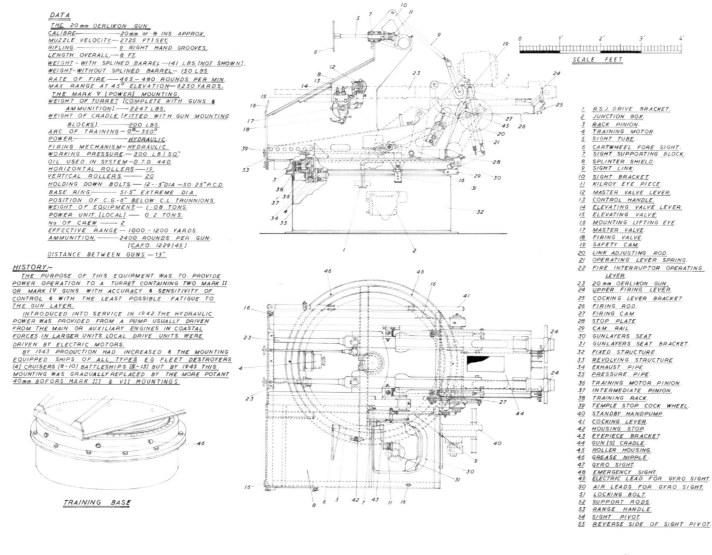

TRAINING BASE

SCALE FEET

1 R.S.J. DRIVE BRACKET.
2 JUNCTION BOX.
3 RACK PINION.
4 TRAINING MOTOR.
5 SIGHT TUBE.
6 CARTWHEEL FORE SIGHT.
7 SIGHT SUPPORTING BLOCK.
8 SPLINTER SHIELD.
9 SIGHT LINK.
10 SIGHT BRACKET.
11 KILROY EYE PIECE.
12 MASTER VALVE LEVER.
13 CONTROL HANDLE.
14 ELEVATING VALVE LEVER.
15 ELEVATING VALVE.
16 MOUNTING LIFTING EYE.
17 MASTER VALVE.
18 FIRING VALVE.
19 SAFETY CAM.
20 LINK ADJUSTING ROD.
21 OPERATING LEVER SPRING.
22 FIRE INTERRUPTOR OPERATING
     LEVER.
23 20mm OERLIKON GUN.
24 UPPER FIRING LEVER.
25 COCKING LEVER BRACKET.
26 FIRING ROD.
27 FIRING CAM.
28 STOP PLATE.
29 CAM RAIL.
30 GUNLAYERS SEAT.
31 GUNLAYERS SEAT BRACKET.
32 FIXED STRUCTURE.
33 REVOLVING STRUCTURE.
34 EXHAUST PIPE.
35 PRESSURE PIPE.
36 TRAINING MOTOR PINION.
37 INTERMEDIATE PINION.
38 TRAINING RACK.
39 TEMPLE STOP COCK WHEEL.
40 STANDBY HANDPUMP.
41 COCKING LEVER.
42 HOUSING STOP.
43 EYEPIECE BRACKET.
44 GUN (S) CRADLE.
45 ROLLER HOUSING.
46 GREASE NIPPLE.
47 GYRO SIGHT.
48 EMERGENCY SIGHT.
49 ELECTRIC LEAD FOR GYRO SIGHT.
50 AIR LEADS FOR GYRO SIGHT.
51 LOCKING BOLT.
52 SUPPORT RODS.
53 RANGE HANDLE.
54 SIGHT PIVOT.
55 REVERSE SIDE OF SIGHT PIVOT.

DRAWN FROM INFORMATION PROVIDED BY THE ROYAL NAVAL ORDNANCE MUSEUM PRIDDY'S HARD GOSPORT HANTS.
FOR DETAIL OF THE 20mm GUN & COMPONENT PARTS SEE - L/0/82.

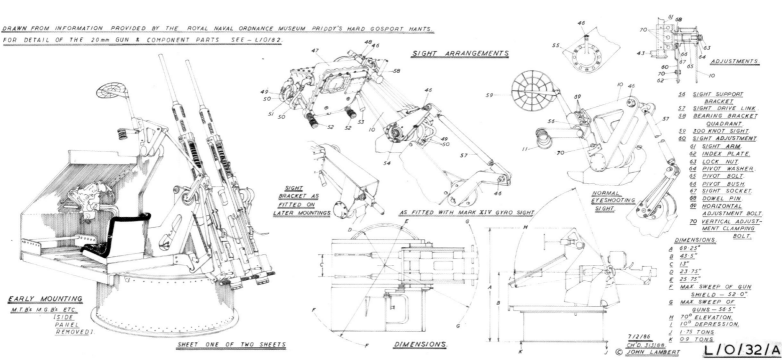

SIGHT ARRANGEMENTS

ADJUSTMENTS

EARLY MOUNTING
M.T.B's M.G.B's ETC.
(SIDE PANEL REMOVED).

SIGHT
BRACKET AS
FITTED ON
LATER MOUNTINGS.

AS FITTED WITH MARK XIV GYRO SIGHT.

NORMAL
EYESHOOTING
SIGHT.

56 SIGHT SUPPORT
     BRACKET
57 SIGHT DRIVE LINK.
58 BEARING BRACKET
     QUADRANT.
59 300 KNOT SIGHT.
60 SIGHT ADJUSTMENT.
61 SIGHT ARM.
62 INDEX PLATE.
63 LOCK NUT.
64 PIVOT WASHER.
65 PIVOT BOLT.
66 PIVOT BUSH.
67 SIGHT SOCKET.
68 DOWEL PIN.
69 HORIZONTAL
     ADJUSTMENT BOLT.
70 VERTICAL ADJUST-
     MENT CLAMPING
     BOLT.

DIMENSIONS.
A 69·25"
B 43·5"
C 13"
D 23·75"
E 25·75"
F MAX SWEEP OF GUN
     SHIELD - 52·0"
G MAX. SWEEP OF
     GUNS - 56·5"
H 70° ELEVATION.
I 10° DEPRESSION.
J 1·75 TONS.
K 0·9 TONS.

DIMENSIONS.

SHEET ONE OF TWO SHEETS

7/2/86
CH'D. 3/3/86.
© JOHN LAMBERT

L/0/32/A

A 10 Twin 20mm Oerlikon on Mk V (power) mounting, details 1942 – 1944

N.B.— THE ARMOURED BLAST PROTECTION BOX WAS DESIGNED TO FIT ON THOSE TWIN 20mm OERLIKON MARK V POWER OPERATED MOUNTINGS WHERE THE CREW WERE SUBJECT TO THE EFFECT OF BLAST FROM LARGER CALIBRE WEAPONS SUCH AS THE TWIN 4" MARK XIX. THIS ADDITION BEING FITTED TO THOSE MOUNTINGS LOCATED ON THE QUARTERDECK OF SOME SLOOPS. E.G. H.M.S's STARLING PEACOCK MERMAID HIND ETC. THIS MODIFICATION WAS PUT IN HAND FROM DECEMBER 1942

SIDE ELEVATION – MARK II OERLIKON WITH MAGAZINE.

SCALE FEET

MAGAZINE FROM FRONT

SIDE VIEW.

DETAIL OF MOUNTING WITH ARMOURED BLAST PROTECTION BOX.
REDRAWN FROM DRG. G. 1739
NOTE – NO HAND EMERGENCY PRESSURE PUMP IS FITTED AND VISION FOR THE GUNLAYER IS MUCH REDUCED BY THE BLAST BOX AND ARMOURED WINDOW.

PLAN VIEW.

MOUNTING MODIFICATION DETAIL
NOT TO SAME SCALE

KEY TO DETAIL – (NOTE DIFFERING SCALE)

1 FOR MODIFICATION TO SIGHT (SEE DRAWING G. 1734) (NEW SIGHT BAR AND BEAD SIGHT TO BE SUPPLIED BY THE CONTRACTOR).
2 EXISTING ARMOUR SHIELD (BEHIND).
3 EXISTING FOOT REST SUPPORT BRACKETS TO BE MODIFIED BY SLOTTING HOLES AND REPOSITIONING BRACKETS AS FOUND NECESSARY.
4 EXISTING PLATFORM PLATE.
5 LATERAL STRUCTURE SUPPORT ANGLE.
6 TRAVERSE STRUCTURE SUPPORT ANGLE.
7 TRUNNION SIDE SUPPORT PLATE.
8 SWEPT CIRCLE (SPLINTER SHIELD) – 4' 4" RADIUS.
9 SWEPT CIRCLE (GUN) – 4' 8 1/8" RADIUS.

1 MODIFY EXISTING FOOT REST SUPPORT BRACKETS AS INDICATED.
2 REMOVE SIGHT FOR MODIFYING TO DRAWING 'G' 1734.
3 POSITION BLAST BOX ON MOUNTING SO THAT.
   (a) PLATE 'F' BEDS AGAINST TRUNNION SIDE SUPPORT PLATE.
   (b) ROOF SEATING FRAME 'G' BEDS AGAINST ARMOUR SHIELD WITH UPPER EDGE FLUSH WITH TOP OF ARMOUR SHIELD.
   (c) BACK PLATE 'H' BEDS AGAINST TRASVERSE STRUCTURE.
   (d) PLATE 'J' ABUTS EDGE OF ARMOUR SHIELD.
4 DRILL ARMOUR SHIELD (3/8" DIA CLEAR) TO SUIT FRAME 'G' BOLT IN POSITION USING BOLTS 'K'.
5 DRILL AND TAP TRUNNION SIDE SUPPORT PLATE 3/8" DIA WHITWORTH AND BOLT PLATE 'F' IN POSITION USING BOLTS 'L'.
6 DRILL TRANSVERSE STRUCTURE SUPPORT ANGLE 3/8" DIA CLEAR TO SUIT PLATE 'H' BOLT IN POSITION USING BOLTS 'M' IN THIS OPERATION INCLUDE DOOR STOP 'N' WHEN BOLTING.
7 POSITION ANGLE A PARRALLEL WITH EDGE OF ARMOUR SHIELD TO FORM DOOR AND FILLING PLATE SEATINGS. DRILL ARMOUR SHIELD (3/8" DIA CLEAR) AND BOLT ANGLE 'A' IN POSITION USING BOLTS 'B'.
8 BOLT SIDE FILLING PLATE 'C' TO ANGLE 'A' USING BOLTS 'D'.
9 DRILL LATERAL STRUCTURE SUPPORT ANGLE (3/16" DIA CLEAR) TO SUIT PLATE 'C' AND BOLT IN POSITION USING BOLTS 'E'.
10 REPLACE MODIFIED SIGHT.

SIGHTING GEAR TRUNNIONS FIRE INTERRUPTER GEAR AND REAR FIRING LEVERS.

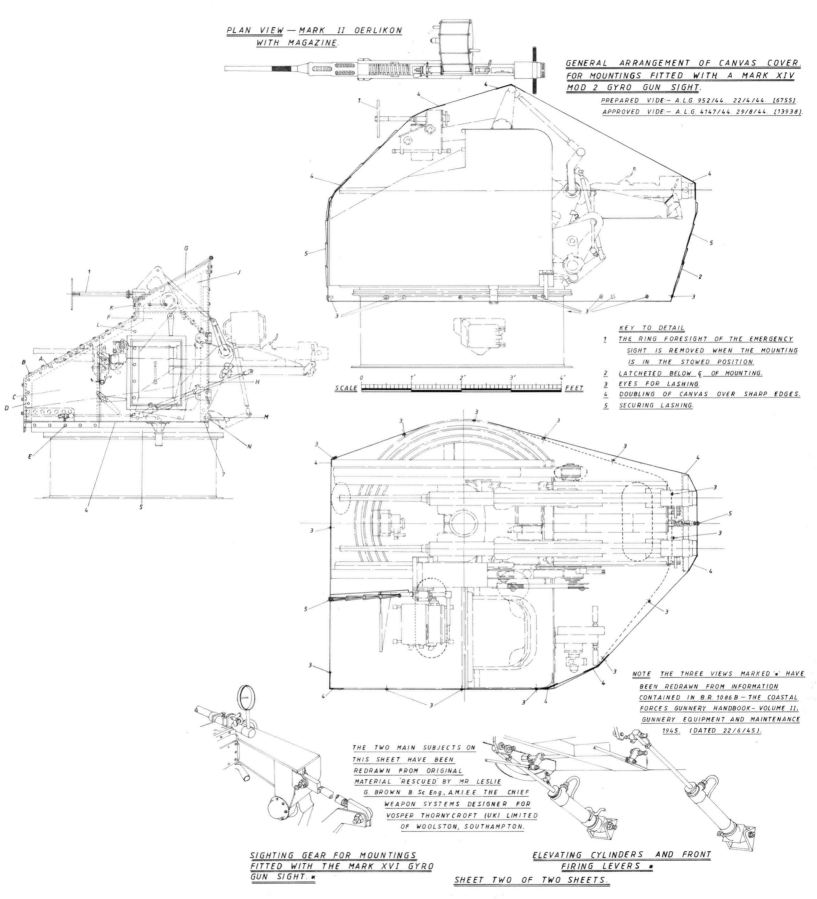

PLAN VIEW — MARK II OERLIKON
WITH MAGAZINE.

GENERAL ARRANGEMENT OF CANVAS COVER.
FOR MOUNTINGS FITTED WITH A MARK XIV
MOD 2 GYRO GUN SIGHT.
PREPARED VIDE:- A.L.G. 952/44. 22/4/44. [6755].
APPROVED VIDE:- A.L.G. 4147/44. 29/8/44. [13938].

KEY TO DETAIL
1 THE RING FORESIGHT OF THE EMERGENCY
   SIGHT IS REMOVED WHEN THE MOUNTING
   IS IN THE STOWED POSITION.
2 LATCHETED BELOW ℄ OF MOUNTING.
3 EYES FOR LASHING.
4 DOUBLING OF CANVAS OVER SHARP EDGES.
5 SECURING LASHING.

SCALE 0 1' 2' 3' 4' FEET

NOTE THE THREE VIEWS MARKED '■' HAVE
BEEN REDRAWN FROM INFORMATION
CONTAINED IN B.R. 1086 B — THE COASTAL
FORCES GUNNERY HANDBOOK— VOLUME II.
GUNNERY EQUIPMENT AND MAINTENANCE
1945. [DATED 22/6/45].

THE TWO MAIN SUBJECTS ON
THIS SHEET HAVE BEEN
REDRAWN FROM ORIGINAL
MATERIAL 'RESCUED' BY MR LESLIE
G. BROWN B.Sc.Eng., A.M.I.E.E. THE CHIEF
WEAPON SYSTEMS DESIGNER FOR
VOSPER THORNYCROFT (UK) LIMITED
OF WOOLSTON, SOUTHAMPTON.

SIGHTING GEAR FOR MOUNTINGS
FITTED WITH THE MARK XVI GYRO
GUN SIGHT. ■

ELEVATING CYLINDERS AND FRONT
FIRING LEVERS ■

SHEET TWO OF TWO SHEETS.

L/0/32/B

A 11 6pdr 10cwt Mk I gun on twin Mk I mounting, 1944

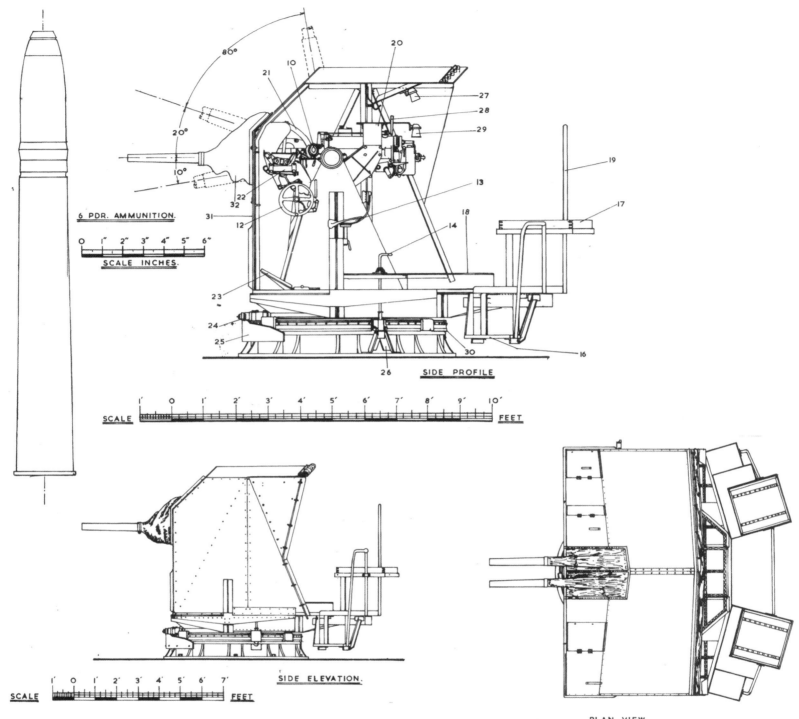

6 PDR. AMMUNITION.

SCALE INCHES.

SIDE PROFILE

SCALE — FEET

SIDE ELEVATION.

SCALE — FEET

PLAN VIEW

HISTORY:~ THE TWIN 6 PDR. DESIGN WAS PUT FOREWARD IN 1925 AS A RAPID FIRING LIGHT WEAPONS SYSTEM AS CLOSE DEFENCE OF HARBOUR ENTRANCES ETC. THE FIRST TWO GUNS WERE PROVED DURING 1928 AND MANUFACTURE STARTED ABOUT 1933. THE FIRST MOUNTINGS BEING FORMALLY APPROVED ON 28/2/34, THEY REMAINED IN SERVICE UNTIL 1956.
22 GUNS WERE ALLOCATED FOR R.N. SERVICE IN 1944, BEING MOUNTED IN "A" GUN POSITON IN PLACE OF THE 4.7" GUN & CARRIED ON ESCORT VESSELS LIKELY TO ENCOUNTER 'E' BOATS ETC. THE DESIGN BEING MODIFIED TO SUIT RN REQUIREMENTS. THE GUN CREW CONSISTING OF 8 RATINGS & A CONTROL OFFICER. THE MOUNTING BEING ASSOCIATED TO UNITS SO FITTED 271 OR 272 RADAR TO ASSIST CONTROL IN VISUAL OR BLIND FIRE PROVIDING TARGET RANGE & BEARING.

TO SUIT RN REQUIREMENTS. THE FOLLOWING ALTERATIONS & ADDITIONS WERE MADE CENTRE PIVOT & VERTICAL ROLLERS FITTED. LUBRICATION IMPROVED & WEATHER PROTECTION FITTED. THE ELEVATION INCREASED TO 20° [80° IN MACKAY] THE SIGHTING WAS CHANGED TO NAVAL SERVICE TELESCOPES. THE GUN SHIELD & PLATFORM WERE REDUCED IN SIZE TO DECREASE THE MOUNTINGS WORKING RADIUS. NAVAL PATTERN SEATS, A CATCH NET FITTED, THE BLAST BAGS REMODELLED & THE FIXED AMMUNITION TRAYS WERE MOVED CLOSER TO THE BREECH WORKERS. SAFETY FIRING GEAR WAS FITTED.

© JOHN LAMBERT COMPLETED 15/09/1979 CH'D. 16/08/1988 UPDATED 24/07/1988 ENLARGED 20/08/2005

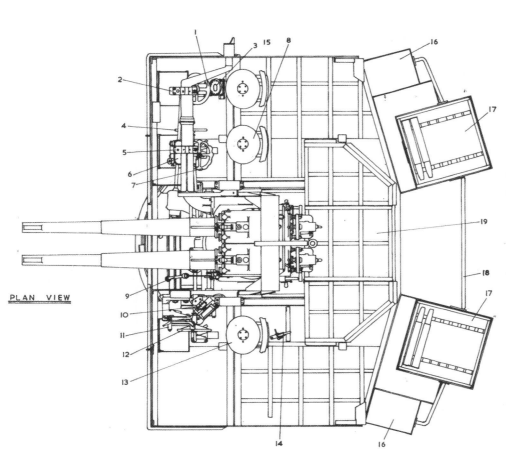

PLAN VIEW

DATA ~ BASED UPON THE ARMY'S TWIN 6 PDR. COAST GUN.
WEIGHT OF GUN & B/MECH. —1060 LBS.
TOTAL LENGTH.—109.72 INS.
LENGTH. OF BORE—105.47 INS.[47 CAL]
RIFLING.— 24 GROOVES UNIFORM R/H.
ELEVATION.— −10°—+7½°
TRAVERSE.—— 360°
WEIGHT IN ACTION.—22132 LBS.
RATE OF FIRE.——120 R.P.M.
MUZZLE VELOCITY.— 2360 FT./SEC.
MAXIMUM RANGE.— 5150 YDS.
ADDITIONAL DATA ON THE R.N.
MOUNTINGS SEE BELOW.

WEIGHT OF R N MOUNTING —— 10 CWT.

BOOK OF REFERENCE —— B R 995

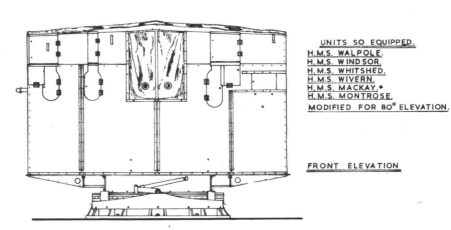

UNITS SO EQUIPPED.
H.M.S. WALPOLE.
H.M.S. WINDSOR.
H.M.S. WHITSHED.
H.M.S. WIVERN.
H.M.S. MACKAY.✱
H.M.S. MONTROSE.
MODIFIED FOR 80° ELEVATION.

FRONT ELEVATION

THESE THREE VIEWS DEPICT H.M.S. MACKAY'S MOUNTING.

REDRAWN FROM INFORMATION SUPPLIED BY THE R.N. ARMAMENT MUSEUM PRIDDY'S HARD, GOSPORT, HANTS.

COMPARISON OF PERFORMANCE	4.7"B.L. MK I	TWIN 6 PDR.
RATE OF FIRE.	6 R.P.M.	72 R.P.M.[NORMAL] 80 R.P.M.[MAX]
LBS. OUTPUT PER MINUTE.	300 LBS/MIN.	432 LBS/MIN.
MAXIMUM RANGE.	16,000 YDS.	5150 YDS.

L / O / 28

F 1 9ft FQ 2 rangefinder on MQ 1 and MQ 12 mountings, 1918–1921
[Note that this was a coincidence rangefinder, not stereoscopic as described in the annotation]

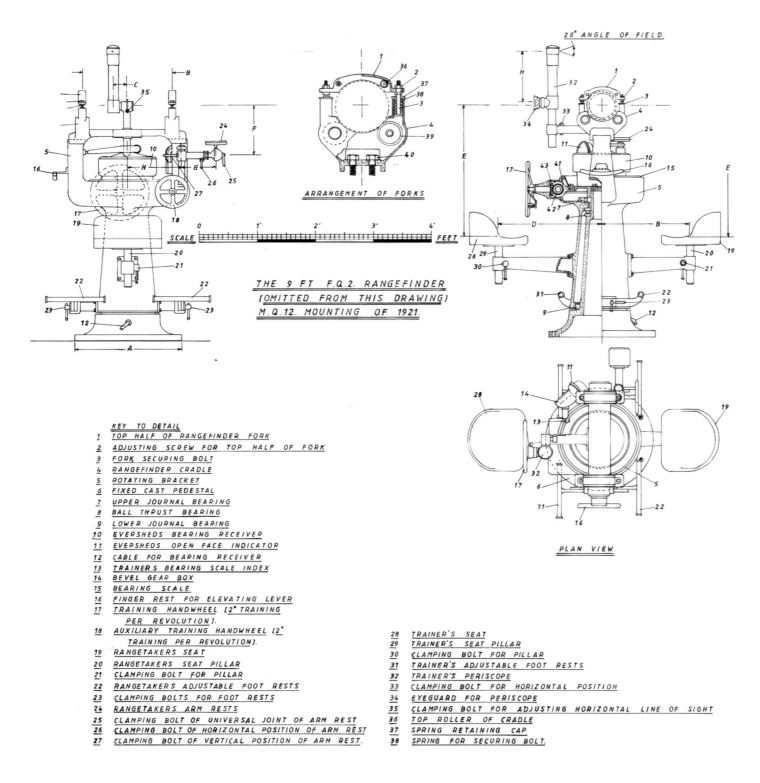

20° ANGLE OF FIELD.

ARRANGEMENT OF FORKS

THE 9 FT. F.Q.2. RANGEFINDER
(OMITTED FROM THIS DRAWING)
M.Q.12. MOUNTING OF 1921.

SCALE   FEET

PLAN VIEW

KEY TO DETAIL

1 TOP HALF OF RANGEFINDER FORK
2 ADJUSTING SCREW FOR TOP HALF OF FORK
3 FORK SECURING BOLT
4 RANGEFINDER CRADLE
5 ROTATING BRACKET
6 FIXED CAST PEDESTAL
7 UPPER JOURNAL BEARING
8 BALL THRUST BEARING
9 LOWER JOURNAL BEARING
10 EVERSHEDS BEARING RECEIVER
11 EVERSHEDS OPEN FACE INDICATOR
12 CABLE FOR BEARING RECEIVER
13 TRAINERS BEARING SCALE INDEX
14 BEVEL GEAR BOX
15 BEARING SCALE
16 FINGER REST FOR ELEVATING LEVER
17 TRAINING HANDWHEEL [2° TRAINING
      PER REVOLUTION].
18 AUXILIARY TRAINING HANDWHEEL [2°
      TRAINING PER REVOLUTION].
19 RANGETAKERS SEAT
20 RANGETAKERS SEAT PILLAR
21 CLAMPING BOLT FOR PILLAR
22 RANGETAKERS ADJUSTABLE FOOT RESTS
23 CLAMPING BOLTS FOR FOOT RESTS
24 RANGETAKERS ARM RESTS
25 CLAMPING BOLT OF UNIVERSAL JOINT OF ARM REST
26 CLAMPING BOLT OF HORIZONTAL POSITION OF ARM REST
27 CLAMPING BOLT OF VERTICAL POSITION OF ARM REST.

28 TRAINER'S SEAT
29 TRAINER'S SEAT PILLAR
30 CLAMPING BOLT FOR PILLAR
31 TRAINER'S ADJUSTABLE FOOT RESTS
32 TRAINER'S PERISCOPE
33 CLAMPING BOLT FOR HORIZONTAL POSITION
34 EYEGUARD FOR PERISCOPE
35 CLAMPING BOLT FOR ADJUSTING HORIZONTAL LINE OF SIGHT
36 TOP ROLLER OF CRADLE
37 SPRING RETAINING CAP
38 SPRING FOR SECURING BOLT.

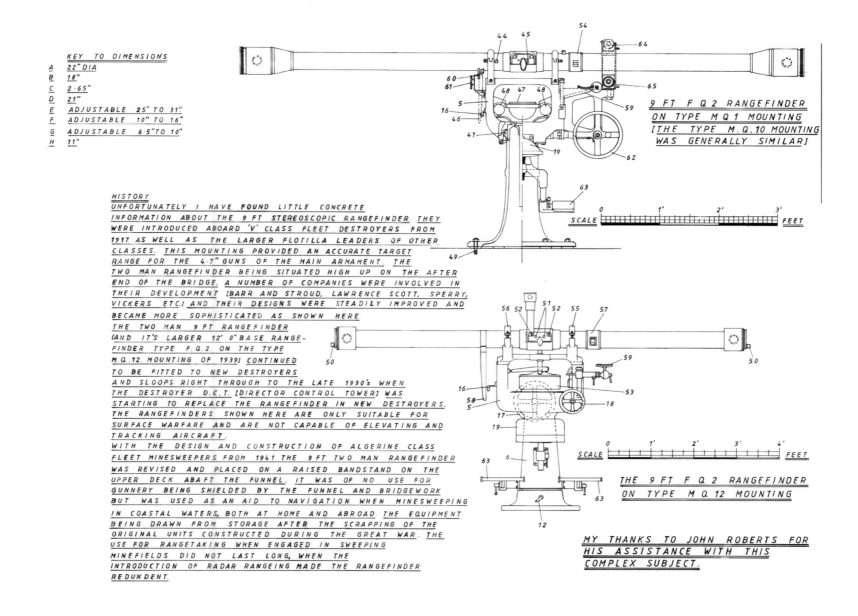

KEY TO DIMENSIONS

A 22" DIA
B 18"
C 2·65"
D 21"
E ADJUSTABLE 25" TO 31"
F ADJUSTABLE 10" TO 16"
G ADJUSTABLE 6·5" TO 10"
H 11"

9 FT F Q 2 RANGEFINDER
ON TYPE M Q 1 MOUNTING
[THE TYPE M.Q.10 MOUNTING
WAS GENERALLY SIMILAR]

SCALE 0 1' 2' 3' FEET

HISTORY

UNFORTUNATELY I HAVE FOUND LITTLE CONCRETE
INFORMATION ABOUT THE 9 FT STEREOSCOPIC RANGEFINDER. THEY
WERE INTRODUCED ABOARD 'V' CLASS FLEET DESTROYERS FROM
1917 AS WELL AS THE LARGER FLOTILLA LEADERS OF OTHER
CLASSES. THIS MOUNTING PROVIDED AN ACCURATE TARGET
RANGE FOR THE 4·7" GUNS OF THE MAIN ARMAMENT. THE
TWO MAN RANGEFINDER BEING SITUATED HIGH UP ON THE AFTER
END OF THE BRIDGE. A NUMBER OF COMPANIES WERE INVOLVED IN
THEIR DEVELOPMENT [BARR AND STROUD, LAWRENCE SCOTT, SPERRY,
VICKERS ETC.] AND THEIR DESIGNS WERE STEADILY IMPROVED AND
BECAME MORE SOPHISTICATED AS SHOWN HERE.
THE TWO MAN 9 FT RANGEFINDER
(AND IT'S LARGER 12' 0" BASE RANGE-
FINDER TYPE F.Q.2. ON THE TYPE
M.Q.12. MOUNTING OF 1939) CONTINUED
TO BE FITTED TO NEW DESTROYERS
AND SLOOPS RIGHT THROUGH TO THE LATE 1930's WHEN
THE DESTROYER D.C.T. [DIRECTOR CONTROL TOWER] WAS
STARTING TO REPLACE THE RANGEFINDER IN NEW DESTROYERS.
THE RANGEFINDERS SHOWN HERE ARE ONLY SUITABLE FOR
SURFACE WARFARE AND ARE NOT CAPABLE OF ELEVATING AND
TRACKING AIRCRAFT.
WITH THE DESIGN AND CONSTRUCTION OF ALGERINE CLASS
FLEET MINESWEEPERS FROM 1941 THE 9 FT TWO MAN RANGEFINDER
WAS REVISED AND PLACED ON A RAISED BANDSTAND ON THE
UPPER DECK ABAFT THE FUNNEL. IT WAS OF NO USE FOR
GUNNERY BEING SHIELDED BY THE FUNNEL AND BRIDGEWORK
BUT WAS USED AS AN AID TO NAVIGATION WHEN MINESWEEPING
IN COASTAL WATERS, BOTH AT HOME AND ABROAD. THE EQUIPMENT
BEING DRAWN FROM STORAGE AFTER THE SCRAPPING OF THE
ORIGINAL UNITS CONSTRUCTED DURING THE GREAT WAR. THE
USE FOR RANGETAKING WHEN ENGAGED IN SWEEPING
MINEFIELDS DID NOT LAST LONG, WHEN THE
INTRODUCTION OF RADAR RANGEING MADE THE RANGEFINDER
REDUNDENT.

SCALE 0 1' 2' 3' 4' FEET

THE 9 FT F Q 2 RANGEFINDER
ON TYPE M Q 12 MOUNTING

MY THANKS TO JOHN ROBERTS FOR
HIS ASSISTANCE WITH THIS
COMPLEX SUBJECT.

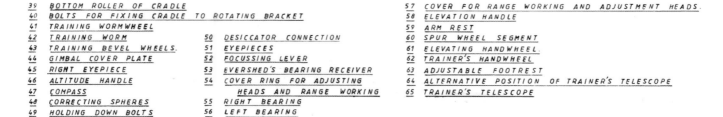

39 BOTTOM ROLLER OF CRADLE
40 BOLTS FOR FIXING CRADLE TO ROTATING BRACKET
41 TRAINING WORMWHEEL
42 TRAINING WORM
43 TRAINING BEVEL WHEELS.
44 GIMBAL COVER PLATE
45 RIGHT EYEPIECE
46 ALTITUDE HANDLE
47 COMPASS
48 CORRECTING SPHERES
49 HOLDING DOWN BOLTS
50 DESICCATOR CONNECTION
51 EYEPIECES
52 FOCUSSING LEVER
53 EVERSHED'S BEARING RECEIVER
54 COVER RING FOR ADJUSTING
    HEADS AND RANGE WORKING
55 RIGHT BEARING
56 LEFT BEARING
57 COVER FOR RANGE WORKING AND ADJUSTMENT HEADS.
58 ELEVATION HANDLE
59 ARM REST
60 SPUR WHEEL SEGMENT
61 ELEVATING HANDWHEEL.
62 TRAINER'S HANDWHEEL
63 ADJUSTABLE FOOTREST
64 ALTERNATIVE POSITION OF TRAINER'S TELESCOPE
65 TRAINER'S TELESCOPE

L/0/105

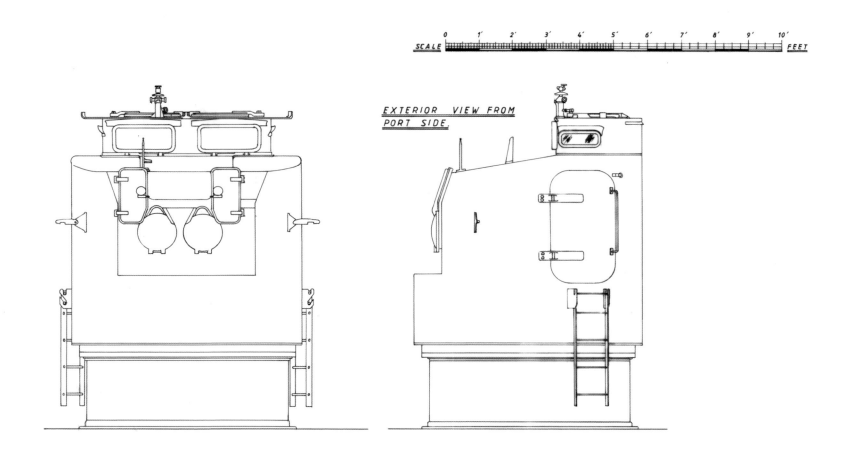

SCALE ‖‖‖‖‖‖‖‖‖ FEET

EXTERIOR VIEW FROM PORT SIDE.

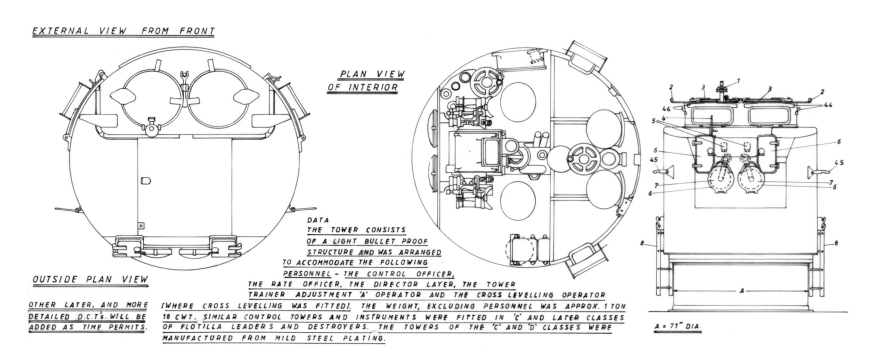

EXTERNAL VIEW FROM FRONT

PLAN VIEW OF INTERIOR

OUTSIDE PLAN VIEW

DATA
THE TOWER CONSISTS OF A LIGHT BULLET PROOF STRUCTURE AND WAS ARRANGED TO ACCOMMODATE THE FOLLOWING PERSONNEL – THE CONTROL OFFICER, THE RATE OFFICER, THE DIRECTOR LAYER, THE TOWER TRAINER ADJUSTMENT 'A' OPERATOR AND THE CROSS LEVELLING OPERATOR [WHERE CROSS LEVELLING WAS FITTED]. THE WEIGHT, EXCLUDING PERSONNEL WAS APPROX. 1 TON 18 CWT. SIMILAR CONTROL TOWERS AND INSTRUMENTS WERE FITTED IN 'C' AND LATER CLASSES OF FLOTILLA LEADERS AND DESTROYERS. THE TOWERS OF THE 'C' AND 'D' CLASSES WERE MANUFACTURED FROM MILD STEEL PLATING.

OTHER LATER, AND MORE DETAILED D.C.T's. WILL BE ADDED AS TIME PERMITS.

A = 71" DIA.

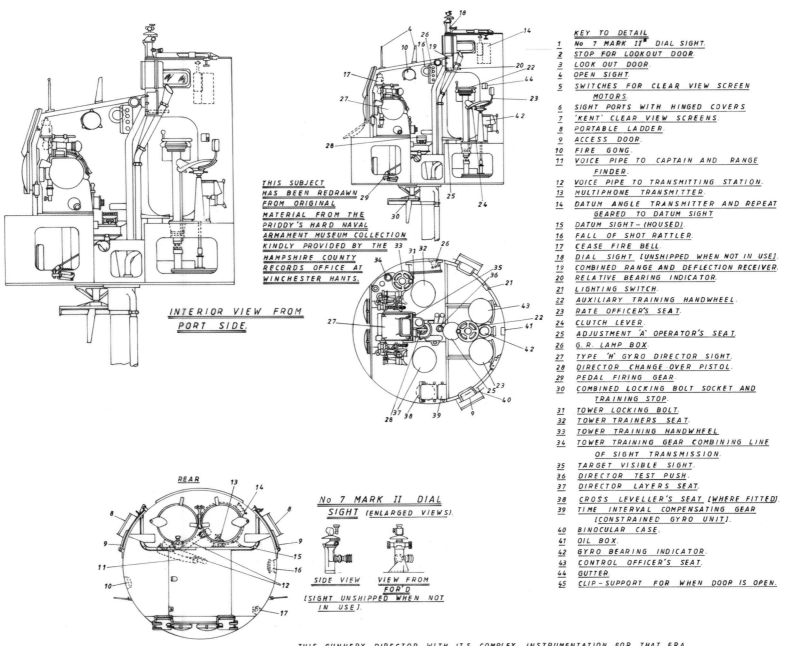

INTERIOR VIEW FROM
PORT SIDE.

THIS SUBJECT
HAS BEEN REDRAWN
FROM ORIGINAL
MATERIAL FROM THE
PRIDDY'S HARD NAVAL
ARMAMENT MUSEUM COLLECTION
KINDLY PROVIDED BY THE
HAMPSHIRE COUNTY
RECORDS OFFICE AT
WINCHESTER HANTS.

REAR

FRONT

No 7 MARK II DIAL
SIGHT (ENLARGED VIEWS).

SIDE VIEW

VIEW FROM
FOR'D

[SIGHT UNSHIPPED WHEN NOT
IN USE].

KEY TO DETAIL

1   No 7 MARK II* DIAL SIGHT.
2   STOP FOR LOOKOUT DOOR.
3   LOOK OUT DOOR.
4   OPEN SIGHT.
5   SWITCHES FOR CLEAR VIEW SCREEN
    MOTORS.
6   SIGHT PORTS WITH HINGED COVERS.
7   'KENT' CLEAR VIEW SCREENS.
8   PORTABLE LADDER.
9   ACCESS DOOR.
10 FIRE GONG.
11 VOICE PIPE TO CAPTAIN AND RANGE
    FINDER.
12 VOICE PIPE TO TRANSMITTING STATION.
13 MULTIPHONE TRANSMITTER.
14 DATUM ANGLE TRANSMITTER AND REPEAT
    GEARED TO DATUM SIGHT
15 DATUM SIGHT - (HOUSED).
16 FALL OF SHOT RATTLER.
17 CEASE FIRE BELL.
18 DIAL SIGHT [UNSHIPPED WHEN NOT IN USE].
19 COMBINED RANGE AND DEFLECTION RECEIVER.
20 RELATIVE BEARING INDICATOR.
21 LIGHTING SWITCH.
22 AUXILIARY TRAINING HANDWHEEL.
23 RATE OFFICER'S SEAT.
24 CLUTCH LEVER.
25 ADJUSTMENT 'A' OPERATOR'S SEAT.
26 G.R. LAMP BOX.
27 TYPE 'H' GYRO DIRECTOR SIGHT.
28 DIRECTOR CHANGE-OVER PISTOL.
29 PEDAL FIRING GEAR.
30 COMBINED LOCKING BOLT SOCKET AND
    TRAINING STOP.
31 TOWER LOCKING BOLT.
32 TOWER TRAINERS SEAT.
33 TOWER TRAINING HANDWHEEL.
34 TOWER TRAINING GEAR COMBINING LINE
    OF SIGHT TRANSMISSION.
35 TARGET VISIBLE SIGHT.
36 DIRECTOR TEST PUSH.
37 DIRECTOR LAYERS SEAT.
38 CROSS LEVELLER'S SEAT [WHERE FITTED].
39 TIME INTERVAL COMPENSATING GEAR
    [CONSTRAINED GYRO UNIT].
40 BINOCULAR CASE.
41 OIL BOX.
42 GYRO BEARING INDICATOR.
43 CONTROL OFFICER'S SEAT.
44 GUTTER.
45 CLIP - SUPPORT FOR WHEN DOOR IS OPEN.

THIS GUNNERY DIRECTOR WITH ITS COMPLEX INSTRUMENTATION FOR THAT ERA
WAS FITTED TO THE FLEET DESTROYERS OF THE 1931 CONSTRUCTION PROGRAMME. IT DOES
NOT HAVE A RANGEFINDER WHICH WAS A SEPARATE ITEM FITTED TO THE REAR OF THE D.C.T.
THE 9 'E' CLASS UNITS WERE ORDERED 1/11/32 AND ALL COMPLETED BY LATE 1934. - ECLIPSE 29/11/34, ECHO 22/10/34,
ENCOUNTER 2/11/34, ELECTRA 13/9/34, ESCORT 30/10/34, ESCAPADE 30/8/34, EXPRESS 2/11/34, ESK 28/9/38, AND THE FLOTTILA
LEADER EXMOUTH 9/11/34. A SIMILAR D.C.T. WAS FITTED TO THE FOLLOWING 'F','G' AND 'H' DESTROYER
CLASSES, WHICH DIFFERED IN MINOR DETAIL ONLY. BOOK OF REFERENCE C.B. 1925 (12) AND B.R. 912 (12).
© JOHN LAMBERT 1/3/99 CH'D. 6/3/99

L/0/108

F 3 Combined rangefinder director Mk I, 1937

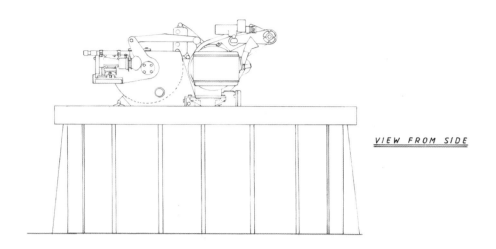

VIEW FROM SIDE

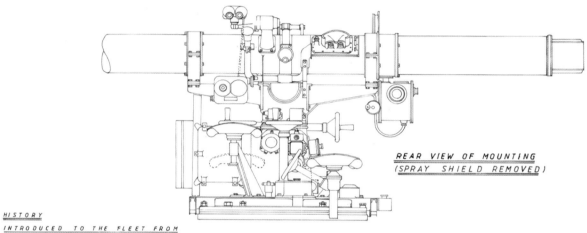

REAR VIEW OF MOUNTING
(SPRAY SHIELD REMOVED)

HISTORY

INTRODUCED TO THE FLEET FROM
1937 THIS EQUIPMENT IS ALSO SHOWN AS "THE FOUR MAN RANGE
FINDER DIRECTOR" BEING FITTED TO THE NEW TRIBAL CLASS
FLEET DESTROYERS. IN MARCH 1935, WHILST STILL AT THE DESIGN
STAGE THAT THE RANGE FINDER AND DIRECTOR CONTROL TOWER WOULD
BE BE KEPT SEPARATE. LATER IN THE WAR THE TWO TWO FUNCTIONS WOULD
BE COMBINED INTO A SINGLE UNIT

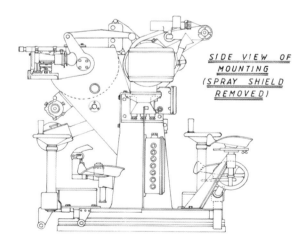

SIDE VIEW OF
MOUNTING
(SPRAY SHIELD
REMOVED)

KEY TO DETAIL

1 PEDESTAL
2 RANGEFINDER
3 LOCKING BOLT
4 LOOKOUT OFFICER'S SEAT BRACKET
5 AUXILIARY TRAINING GEAR BOX SPEED 2°/ REV.
6 TRAINING GEAR BOX FAST SPEED 5°/REV. SLOW SPEED 1°/REV
7 ELEVATOR'S AND TRAINER'S SEAT BRACKET
8 RANGETAKERS SEAT BRACKET
9 ELEVATING GEAR BOX FAST SPEED 3°/REV SLOW SPEED $^1/_2$ / REV
10 ELEVATING GEAR
11 AUXILIARY ELEVATING GEAR SPEED 2°/ REV
12 CONTROL OFFICERS SIGHT BRACKET AND LINK ARMS
13 LEFT RANGEFINDER BEARING
14 RIGHT RANGEFINDER BEARING
15 "WIPE OUT" GEAR
16 FOOTRESTS ON PLATFORM
17 RANGE RATE UNIT IN ACCORDANCE WITH BARR AND
      STROUD LIMITED DRAWING No 11669
18 TRAINERS BINOCULAR AND ALDIS SIGHT DIMMING SWITCH
      ADMIRALTY PATTERN No 5959

✦ IN ACCORDANCE WITH BARR AND STROUD LTD. DRAWING No 11·213·C.

REDRAWN FROM BARR AND STROUD DRAWING No 11746

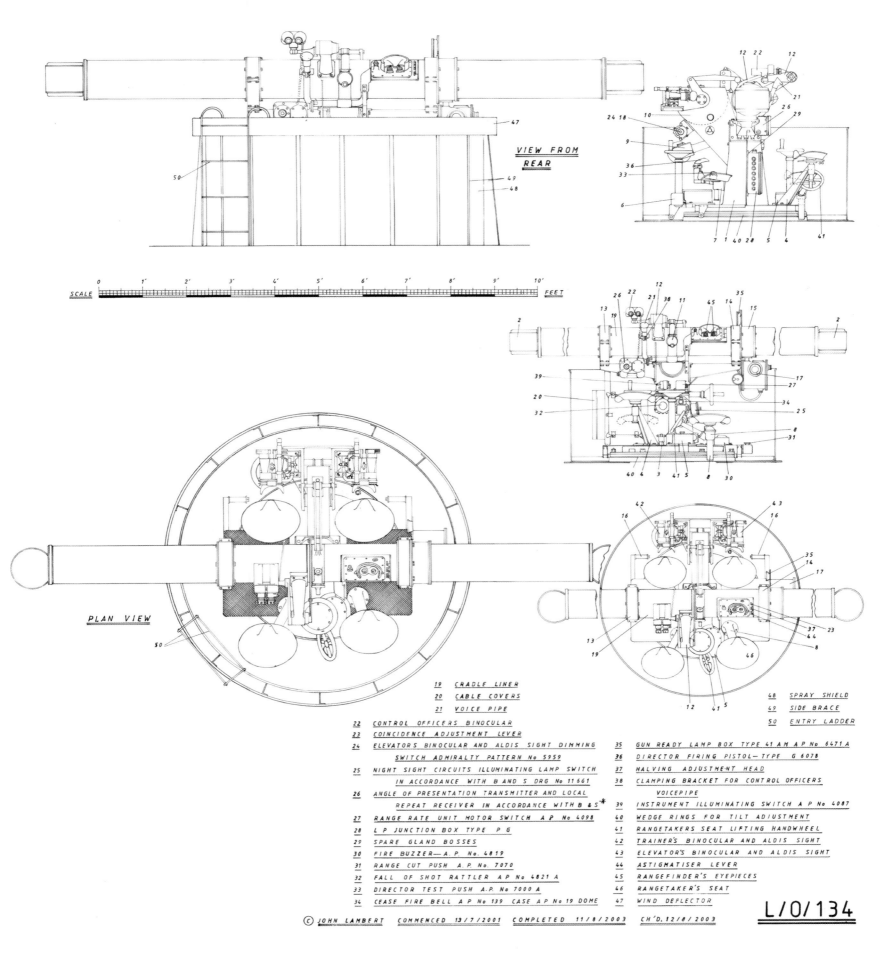

VIEW FROM
REAR

SCALE |0 1' 2' 3' 4' 5' 6' 7' 8' 9' 10'| FEET

PLAN VIEW

19 CRADLE LINER
20 CABLE COVERS
21 VOICE PIPE
22 CONTROL OFFICERS BINOCULAR
23 COINCIDENCE ADJUSTMENT LEVER
24 ELEVATORS BINOCULAR AND ALDIS SIGHT DIMMING
    SWITCH ADMIRALTY PATTERN No 5959
25 NIGHT SIGHT CIRCUITS ILLUMINATING LAMP SWITCH
    IN ACCORDANCE WITH B AND S DRG No 11661
26 ANGLE OF PRESENTATION TRANSMITTER AND LOCAL
    REPEAT RECEIVER IN ACCORDANCE WITH B & S *
27 RANGE RATE UNIT MOTOR SWITCH A P No 4098
28 L P JUNCTION BOX TYPE P G
29 SPARE GLAND BOSSES
30 FIRE BUZZER—A.P. No. 4819
31 RANGE CUT PUSH A.P. No. 7070
32 FALL OF SHOT RATTLER AP No 4821 A
33 DIRECTOR TEST PUSH A.P. No 7000 A
34 CEASE FIRE BELL A P No 139 CASE A P No 19 DOME

35 GUN READY LAMP BOX TYPE 41 AM A P No 6471 A
36 DIRECTOR FIRING PISTOL— TYPE G 6078
37 HALVING ADJUSTMENT HEAD
38 CLAMPING BRACKET FOR CONTROL OFFICERS
    VOICEPIPE
39 INSTRUMENT ILLUMINATING SWITCH A P No 4087
40 WEDGE RINGS FOR TILT ADJUSTMENT
41 RANGETAKERS SEAT LIFTING HANDWHEEL
42 TRAINER'S BINOCULAR AND ALDIS SIGHT
43 ELEVATOR'S BINOCULAR AND ALDIS SIGHT
44 ASTIGMATISER LEVER
45 RANGEFINDER'S EYEPIECES
46 RANGETAKER'S SEAT
47 WIND DEFLECTOR

48 SPRAY SHIELD
49 SIDE BRACE
50 ENTRY LADDER

© JOHN LAMBERT   COMMENCED 13/7/2001   COMPLETED 11/8/2003   CH'D. 12/8/2003

L/0/134

F 4 Director control towers for 1936 Programme destroyers ('J' class), 1939

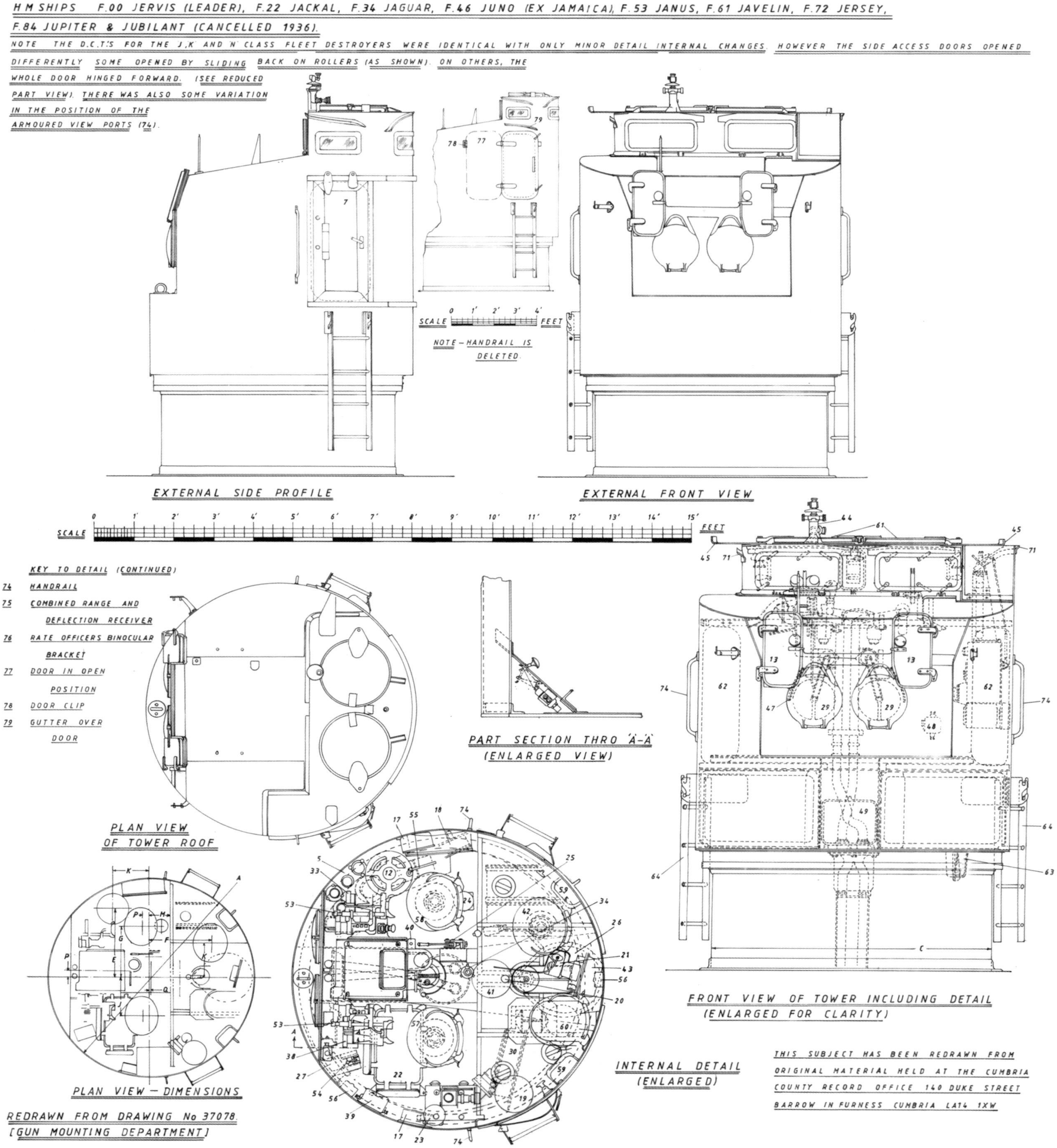

H M SHIPS   F.00 JERVIS (LEADER), F.22 JACKAL, F.34 JAGUAR, F.46 JUNO (EX JAMAICA), F.53 JANUS, F.61 JAVELIN, F.72 JERSEY, F.84 JUPITER & JUBILANT (CANCELLED 1936).

NOTE   THE D.C.T.'S FOR THE J,K AND N CLASS FLEET DESTROYERS WERE IDENTICAL WITH ONLY MINOR DETAIL INTERNAL CHANGES. HOWEVER THE SIDE ACCESS DOORS OPENED DIFFERENTLY. SOME OPENED BY SLIDING BACK ON ROLLERS (AS SHOWN). ON OTHERS, THE WHOLE DOOR HINGED FORWARD. (SEE REDUCED PART VIEW). THERE WAS ALSO SOME VARIATION IN THE POSITION OF THE ARMOURED VIEW PORTS (74).

SCALE 0 1' 2' 3' 4' FEET

NOTE — HANDRAIL IS DELETED.

EXTERNAL SIDE PROFILE

EXTERNAL FRONT VIEW

SCALE 0 1' 2' 3' 4' 5' 6' 7' 8' 9' 10' 11' 12' 13' 14' 15' FEET

KEY TO DETAIL (CONTINUED)

74 HANDRAIL
75 COMBINED RANGE AND
    DEFLECTION RECEIVER
76 RATE OFFICERS BINOCULAR
    BRACKET
77 DOOR IN OPEN
    POSITION
78 DOOR CLIP
79 GUTTER OVER
    DOOR

PLAN VIEW
OF TOWER ROOF

PART SECTION THRO 'A-A'
(ENLARGED VIEW)

FRONT VIEW OF TOWER INCLUDING DETAIL
(ENLARGED FOR CLARITY)

PLAN VIEW — DIMENSIONS

REDRAWN FROM DRAWING No 37078.
[GUN MOUNTING DEPARTMENT]

INTERNAL DETAIL
(ENLARGED)

THIS SUBJECT HAS BEEN REDRAWN FROM
ORIGINAL MATERIAL HELD AT THE CUMBRIA
COUNTY RECORD OFFICE 140 DUKE STREET
BARROW IN FURNESS CUMBRIA LA14 1XW

204

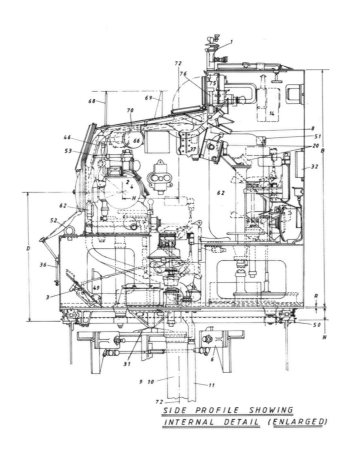

SIDE PROFILE SHOWING
INTERNAL DETAIL (ENLARGED)

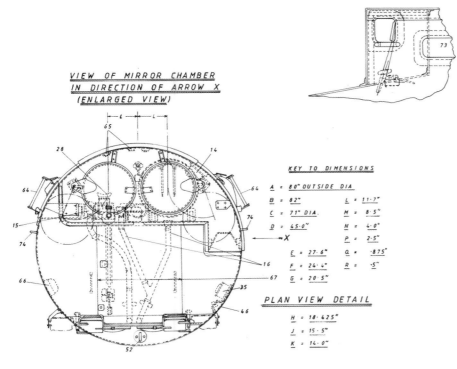

VIEW OF MIRROR CHAMBER
IN DIRECTION OF ARROW X
(ENLARGED VIEW)

KEY TO DIMENSIONS

A = 80" OUTSIDE DIA
B = 82"
C = 71" DIA.
D = 45·0"

L = 11·7"
M = 8·5"
N = 4·0"
P = 2·5"

E = 27·6"
F = 24·4"
G = 20·5"

Q = ·875"
R = ·5"

PLAN VIEW DETAIL

H = 18·425"
J = 15·5"
K = 14·0"

KEY TO DETAIL

1 THIS SIGHT TO BE UNSHIPPED WHEN NOT IN USE
2 H.M.S. JERVIS IS FITTED WITH A TYPE HM MARK II** GYRO
  SIGHT IN PLACE OF A MARK II**
3 PEDAL GEAR FOR DIRECTOR CHANGE OVER FIRING PISTOL
4 TYPE 'H' MARK II** DOUBLE STABILIZED GYRO DIRECTOR SIGHT
5 TOWER TRAINING GEAR COMBINING LINE OF SIGHT
    TRANSMISSION
6 STOP GEAR LIMITING TRAINING TO 440°
7 SLIDING DOOR ON ROLLERS AND GUIDE RAILS
8 RELATIVE BEARING INDICATOR
9 1-2 CORE CABLE A P 4509 FOR HEATING AND LIGHTING
10 4-30 CORE CABLES A P 4515 ALL INSIDE TUBE
11 2 FLEXIBLE VOICE PIPES 2" DIA
12 TOWER TRAINING HANDWHEEL VALVES — 30' AND 3°
13 SIGHT PORTS WITH HINGED DOORS
14 TRANSMITTER AND REPEAT FOR DATUM SIGHT
15 VOICE PIPE TO CAPTAIN AND RANGEFINDER
16 VOICE PIPES TO THE TRANSMITTING STATION
17 STOWAGE BOX FOR TELEPHONES
18 JUNCTION BOX TYPE P J No 3
19 SEAT FOR CROSS-LEVELLING OPERATOR
20 OFFICERS TRAINING HANDLE VALUE 3°
21 DRIVE TO RELATIVE BEARING INDICATOR
22 TIME INTERVAL COMPENSATING GEAR
23 OIL RESERVOIR FOR TRAINERS SEAT
24 OIL RESERVOIR FOR LAYERS SEAT
25 HAND PUMP FOR TRAINERS SEAT
26 AUXILIARY HAND TRAINING GEAR
27 JUNCTION BOX TYPE P B No 10
28 CONTROL OFFICERS BINOCULARS
29 KENTS CLEAR VIEW SCREENS
30 JUNCTION BOX No 2 TYPE P.H.
31 LOCKING BOLT SOCKET
32 5 WAY DISTRIBUTION BOX
33 UNSTABILIZED BINOCULARS
    G. 352
34 DIRECTOR TEST PUSH
35 FALL OF SHOT RATTLER
36 BRACKET SECURING COVERS
37 GUN READY LAMP BOX
38 UNSTABILIZED BINOCULARS
    G 352
39 RELAY FOR GYRO FIRING
40 TARGET VISIBLE SWITCH
41 SIGHT ADJUSTERS SEAT
42 CONTROL OFFICERS SEAT
43 EVERSHED BEARING RECEIVER
44 No 7 MARK II DIAL SIGHT
45 STOP FOR LOOK OUT DOOR
46 CEASE FIRE BELL
47 SPRAY SHIELD
48 SWITCH FOR GYRO
49 RADIATOR
50 LEATHER APRON
51 LIGHTING SWITCH
52 LIFTING RING
53 ALDIS SIGHT G 344
54 HAND PUMP
55 TOWER LOCKING BOLT
56 OIL BOX
57 LAYERS SEAT
58 TRAINERS SEAT
59 BINOCULAR CASE
60 RATE OFFICERS SEAT
61 LOOK-OUT DOORS
62 ENTRY DOOR
63 BUFFER SPRING
64 PORTABLE LADDER
65 TELEPHONE PLUGS
66 FIRE GONG
67 33" PORTABLE PLATE
68 OPEN SIGHT
69 REAR SIGHT
70 HAND GRIP
71 GUTTERING
72 ₵ OF TOWER
73 ARMOURED GLASS
    VIEWING PORT
74 HANDRAIL

[ORIGINAL DRAWN BY W A TOWNSON]
ORDER No 227 D.F.G. 8 SETS. VICKERS ARMSTRONGS LIMITED

© JOHN LAMBERT COMMENCED 1/9/2000 COMPLETED 17/6/2001 CH'D 19/6/2001

L/0/122

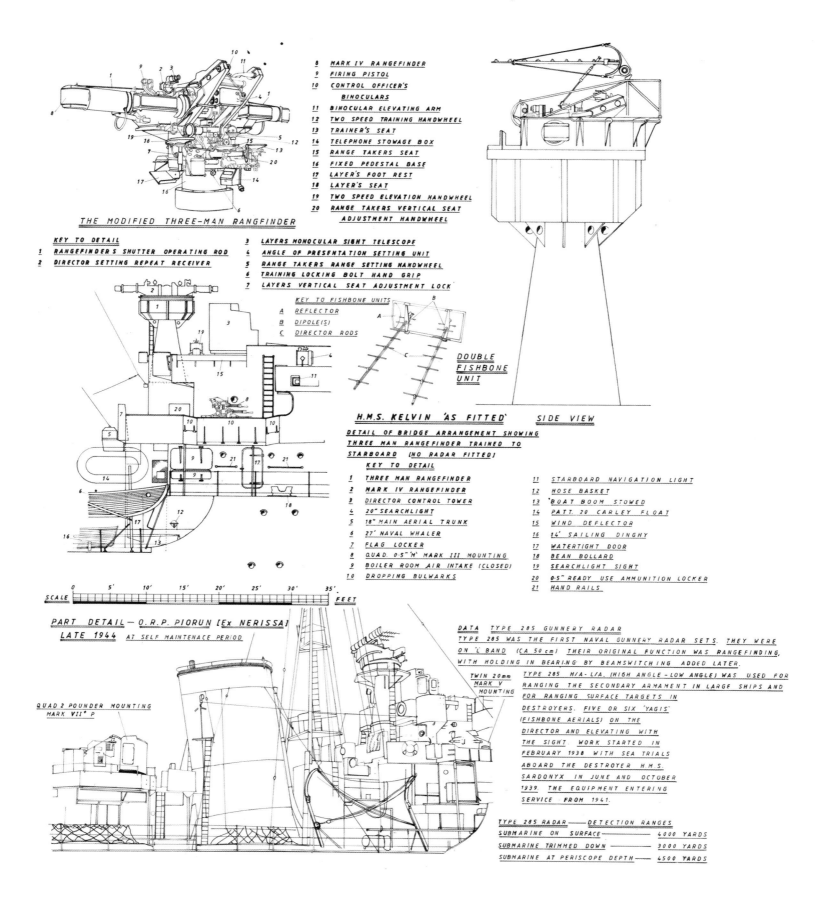

THE MODIFIED THREE-MAN RANGFINDER

8 MARK IV RANGEFINDER
9 FIRING PISTOL
10 CONTROL OFFICER'S BINOCULARS
11 BINOCULAR ELEVATING ARM
12 TWO SPEED TRAINING HANDWHEEL
13 TRAINER'S SEAT
14 TELEPHONE STOWAGE BOX
15 RANGE TAKERS SEAT
16 FIXED PEDESTAL BASE
17 LAYER'S FOOT REST
18 LAYER'S SEAT
19 TWO SPEED ELEVATION HANDWHEEL
20 RANGE TAKERS VERTICAL SEAT ADJUSTMENT HANDWHEEL

KEY TO DETAIL
1 RANGEFINDER'S SHUTTER OPERATING ROD
2 DIRECTOR SETTING REPEAT RECEIVER
3 LAYERS MONOCULAR SIGHT TELESCOPE
4 ANGLE OF PRESENTATION SETTING UNIT
5 RANGE TAKERS RANGE SETTING HANDWHEEL
6 TRAINING LOCKING BOLT HAND GRIP
7 LAYERS VERTICAL SEAT ADJUSTMENT LOCK

KEY TO FISHBONE UNITS
A REFLECTOR
B DIPOLE(S)
C DIRECTOR RODS

DOUBLE FISHBONE UNIT

H.M.S. KELVIN 'AS FITTED'   SIDE VIEW

DETAIL OF BRIDGE ARRANGEMENT SHOWING
THREE MAN RANGEFINDER TRAINED TO
STARBOARD (NO RADAR FITTED)

KEY TO DETAIL
1 THREE MAN RANGEFINDER
2 MARK IV RANGEFINDER
3 DIRECTOR CONTROL TOWER
4 20" SEARCHLIGHT
5 18" MAIN AERIAL TRUNK
6 27' NAVAL WHALER
7 FLAG LOCKER
8 QUAD. 0.5" 'H' MARK III MOUNTING
9 BOILER ROOM AIR INTAKE (CLOSED)
10 DROPPING BULWARKS
11 STARBOARD NAVIGATION LIGHT
12 HOSE BASKET
13 BOAT BOOM STOWED
14 PATT. 20 CARLEY FLOAT
15 WIND DEFLECTOR
16 14' SAILING DINGHY
17 WATERTIGHT DOOR
18 BEAN BOLLARD
19 SEARCHLIGHT SIGHT
20 0.5" READY USE AMMUNITION LOCKER
21 HAND RAILS

SCALE 0 5' 10' 15' 20' 25' 30' 35' FEET

PART DETAIL — O.R.P. PIORUN [Ex NERISSA]
LATE 1944 AT SELF MAINTENACE PERIOD.

QUAD 2 POUNDER MOUNTING MARK VII° P

TWIN 20mm MARK V MOUNTING

DATA TYPE 285 GUNNERY RADAR
TYPE 285 WAS THE FIRST NAVAL GUNNERY RADAR SETS. THEY WERE
ON 'L BAND (CA 50 cm) THEIR ORIGINAL FUNCTION WAS RANGEFINDING,
WITH HOLDING IN BEARING BY BEAMSWITCHING ADDED LATER.

TYPE 285 H/A-L/A (HIGH ANGLE-LOW ANGLE) WAS USED FOR
RANGING THE SECONDARY ARMAMENT IN LARGE SHIPS AND
FOR RANGING SURFACE TARGETS IN
DESTROYERS. FIVE OR SIX 'YAGIS'
(FISHBONE AERIALS) ON THE
DIRECTOR AND ELEVATING WITH
THE SIGHT. WORK STARTED IN
FEBRUARY 1938 WITH SEA TRIALS
ABOARD THE DESTROYER H.M.S.
SARDONYX IN JUNE AND OCTOBER
1939. THE EQUIPMENT ENTERING
SERVICE FROM 1941.

TYPE 285 RADAR	DETECTION RANGES
SUBMARINE ON SURFACE	4000 YARDS
SUBMARINE TRIMMED DOWN	3000 YARDS
SUBMARINE AT PERISCOPE DEPTH	4500 YARDS

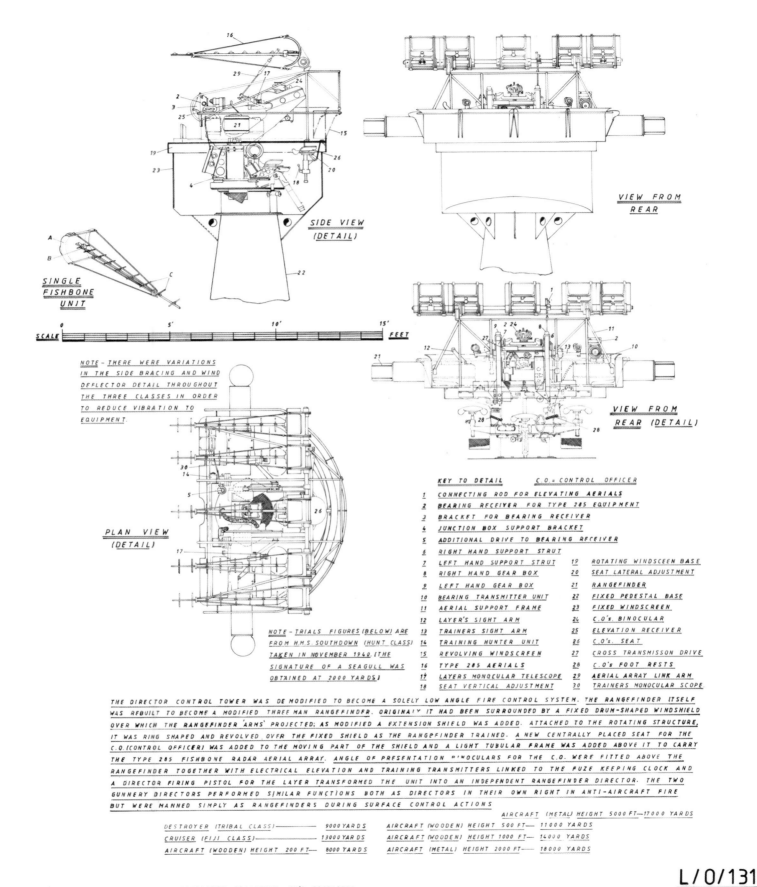

SIDE VIEW
(DETAIL)

VIEW FROM
REAR

SINGLE
FISHBONE
UNIT

VIEW FROM
REAR (DETAIL)

SCALE 0   5'   10'   15' FEET

NOTE - THERE WERE VARIATIONS
IN THE SIDE BRACING AND WIND
DEFLECTOR DETAIL THROUGHOUT
THE THREE CLASSES IN ORDER
TO REDUCE VIBRATION TO
EQUIPMENT.

PLAN VIEW
(DETAIL)

NOTE - TRIALS FIGURES (BELOW) ARE
FROM H.M.S. SOUTHDOWN (HUNT CLASS)
TAKEN IN NOVEMBER 1940. (THE
SIGNATURE OF A SEAGULL WAS
OBTAINED AT 2000 YARDS)

KEY TO DETAIL   C.O. = CONTROL OFFICER
1   CONNECTING ROD FOR ELEVATING AERIALS
2   BEARING RECEIVER FOR TYPE 285 EQUIPMENT
3   BRACKET FOR BEARING RECEIVER
4   JUNCTION BOX SUPPORT BRACKET
5   ADDITIONAL DRIVE TO BEARING RECEIVER
6   RIGHT HAND SUPPORT STRUT
7   LEFT HAND SUPPORT STRUT   19 ROTATING WINDSCEEN BASE
8   RIGHT HAND GEAR BOX   20 SEAT LATERAL ADJUSTMENT
9   LEFT HAND GEAR BOX   21 RANGEFINDER
10 BEARING TRANSMITTER UNIT   22 FIXED PEDESTAL BASE
11 AERIAL SUPPORT FRAME   23 FIXED WINDSCREEN
12 LAYER'S SIGHT ARM   24 C.O's. BINOCULAR
13 TRAINERS SIGHT ARM   25 ELEVATION RECEIVER
14 TRAINING HUNTER UNIT   26 C.O's. SEAT
15 REVOLVING WINDSCREEN   27 CROSS TRANSMISSON DRIVE
16 TYPE 285 AERIALS   28 C.O's FOOT RESTS
17 LAYERS MONOCULAR TELESCOPE   29 AERIAL ARRAY LINK ARM
18 SEAT VERTICAL ADJUSTMENT   30 TRAINERS MONOCULAR SCOPE

THE DIRECTOR CONTROL TOWER WAS DE MODIFIED TO BECOME A SOLELY LOW ANGLE FIRE CONTROL SYSTEM. THE RANGEFINDER ITSELF
WAS REBUILT TO BECOME A MODIFIED THREE MAN RANGEFINDER. ORIGINALLY IT HAD BEEN SURROUNDED BY A FIXED DRUM-SHAPED WINDSHIELD
OVER WHICH THE RANGEFINDER 'ARMS' PROJECTED; AS MODIFIED A EXTENSION SHIELD WAS ADDED. ATTACHED TO THE ROTATING STRUCTURE,
IT WAS RING SHAPED AND REVOLVED OVER THE FIXED SHIELD AS THE RANGEFINDER TRAINED. A NEW CENTRALLY PLACED SEAT FOR THE
C.O.(CONTROL OFFICER) WAS ADDED TO THE MOVING PART OF THE SHIELD AND A LIGHT TUBULAR FRAME WAS ADDED ABOVE IT TO CARRY
THE TYPE 285 FISHBONE RADAR AERIAL ARRAY. ANGLE OF PRESENTATION BINOCULARS FOR THE C.O. WERE FITTED ABOVE THE
RANGEFINDER TOGETHER WITH ELECTRICAL ELEVATION AND TRAINING TRANSMITTERS LINKED TO THE FUZE KEEPING CLOCK AND
A DIRECTOR FIRING PISTOL FOR THE LAYER TRANSFORMED THE UNIT INTO AN INDEPENDENT RANGEFINDER DIRECTOR. THE TWO
GUNNERY DIRECTORS PERFORMED SIMILAR FUNCTIONS BOTH AS DIRECTORS IN THEIR OWN RIGHT IN ANTI-AIRCRAFT FIRE
BUT WERE MANNED SIMPLY AS RANGEFINDERS DURING SURFACE CONTROL ACTIONS

	AIRCRAFT (METAL) HEIGHT 5000 FT—17000 YARDS	
DESTROYER (TRIBAL CLASS)————— 9000 YARDS	AIRCRAFT (WOODEN) HEIGHT 500 FT— 11000 YARDS	
CRUISER (FIJI CLASS)————— 13000 YARDS	AIRCRAFT (WOODEN) HEIGHT 1000 FT— 14000 YARDS	
AIRCRAFT (WOODEN) HEIGHT 200 FT— 8000 YARDS	AIRCRAFT (METAL) HEIGHT 2000 FT— 18000 YARDS	

L/0/131

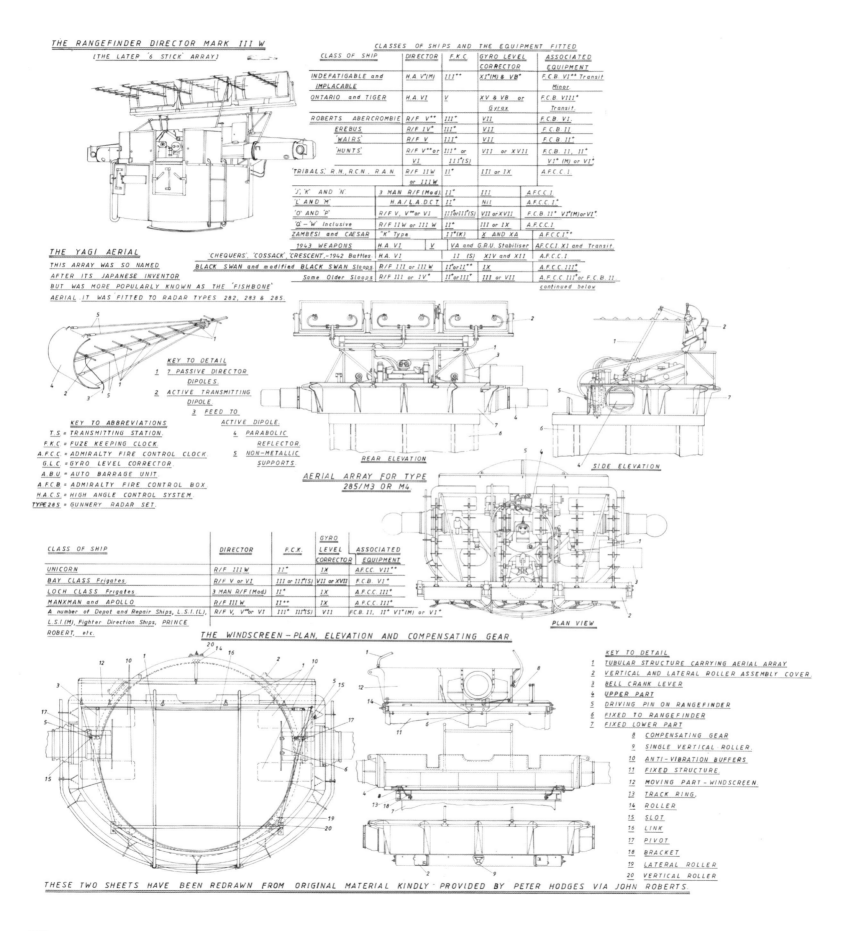

THE RANGEFINDER DIRECTOR MARK III W
[THE LATER '6 STICK' ARRAY]

CLASSES OF SHIPS AND THE EQUIPMENT FITTED

CLASS OF SHIP	DIRECTOR	F.K.C	GYRO LEVEL CORRECTOR	ASSOCIATED EQUIPMENT
INDEFATIGABLE and IMPLACABLE	H.A.V*(M)	III**	XI*(M) & VB*	F.C.B. VI** Transit Minor.
ONTARIO and TIGER	H.A.VI	V	XV & VB or Gyrax	F.C.B. VIII* Transit.
ROBERTS ABERCROMBIE	R/F V**	III*	VII	F.C.B. VI.
EREBUS	R/F IV*	III*	VII	F.C.B.II
'WAIRS'	R/F V	III*	VII	F.C.B II*
'HUNTS'	R/F V** or VI	III* or III*(S)	VII or XVII	F.C.B. II, II* VI* (M) or VI*
'TRIBALS', R.N., R.C.N., R.A.N	R/F II W or III W	II*	III or IX	A.F.C.C.I
'J', 'K' AND 'N'	3 MAN R/F (Mod)	II*	III	A.F.C.C.I
'L' AND 'M'	H.A/L.A.D.C.T	II*	Nil	A.F.C.C.I*
'O' AND 'P'	R/F V, V** or VI	III* or III*(S)	VII or XVII	F.C.B. II* VI*(M) or VI*.
'Q' – 'W' Inclusive	R/F II W or III W	II*	III or IX	A.F.C.C.I
ZAMBESI and CAESAR	"K" Type.	II*(K)	X AND XA	A.F.C.C.I**
1943 WEAPONS	H.A. VI	V	VA and G.R.U. Stabiliser	A.F.C.C.I. XI and Transit
'CHEQUERS', 'COSSACK', 'CRESCENT', -1942 Battles.	H.A. VI		II (S)	XIV and XII	A.F.C.C.I
BLACK SWAN and modified BLACK SWAN Sloops	R/F III or III W	II* or II**	IX	A.F.C.C.III*
Some Older Sloops	R/F III or IV*	II* or III*	III or VII	A.F.C.C III* or F.C.B. II.
				continued below

THE YAGI AERIAL

THIS ARRAY WAS SO NAMED
AFTER ITS JAPANESE INVENTOR
BUT WAS MORE POPULARLY KNOWN AS THE 'FISHBONE'
AERIAL. IT WAS FITTED TO RADAR TYPES 282, 283 & 285.

KEY TO DETAIL
1 7 PASSIVE DIRECTOR
   DIPOLES.
2 ACTIVE TRANSMITTING
   DIPOLE
3 FEED TO
   ACTIVE DIPOLE.
4 PARABOLIC
   REFLECTOR.
5 NON-METALLIC
   SUPPORTS.

KEY TO ABBREVIATIONS
T.S. = TRANSMITTING STATION.
F.K.C. = FUZE KEEPING CLOCK.
A.F.C.C. = ADMIRALTY FIRE CONTROL CLOCK.
G.L.C. = GYRO LEVEL CORRECTOR.
A.B.U. = AUTO BARRAGE UNIT.
A.F.C.B = ADMIRALTY FIRE CONTROL BOX.
H.A.C.S. = HIGH ANGLE CONTROL SYSTEM.
TYPE 285 = GUNNERY RADAR SET.

REAR ELEVATION

SIDE ELEVATION

AERIAL ARRAY FOR TYPE
285/M3 OR M4.

CLASS OF SHIP	DIRECTOR	F.C.K.	GYRO LEVEL CORRECTOR	ASSOCIATED EQUIPMENT
UNICORN	R/F III W	II*	IX	A.F.C.C. VII**
BAY CLASS Frigates.	R/F V or VI	III or III*(S)	VII or XVII	F.C.B. VI*
LOCH CLASS Frigates.	3 MAN R/F (Mod)	II*	IX	A.F.C.C.III*
MANXMAN and APOLLO	R/F III W	II**	IX	A.F.C.C.III*
A number of Depot and Repair Ships, L.S.I.(L), L.S.I.(M), Fighter Direction Ships, PRINCE ROBERT, etc.	R/F V, V**or VI	III* III*(S)	VII	F.C.B. II. II* VI*(M) or VI*

PLAN VIEW

THE WINDSCREEN – PLAN, ELEVATION AND COMPENSATING GEAR.

KEY TO DETAIL
1 TUBULAR STRUCTURE CARRYING AERIAL ARRAY
2 VERTICAL AND LATERAL ROLLER ASSEMBLY COVER
3 BELL CRANK LEVER
4 UPPER PART
5 DRIVING PIN ON RANGEFINDER
6 FIXED TO RANGEFINDER
7 FIXED LOWER PART
8 COMPENSATING GEAR
9 SINGLE VERTICAL ROLLER.
10 ANTI-VIBRATION BUFFERS
11 FIXED STRUCTURE
12 MOVING PART - WINDSCREEN
13 TRACK RING.
14 ROLLER
15 SLOT
16 LINK
17 PIVOT
18 BRACKET
19 LATERAL ROLLER
20 VERTICAL ROLLER

THESE TWO SHEETS HAVE BEEN REDRAWN FROM ORIGINAL MATERIAL KINDLY PROVIDED BY PETER HODGES VIA JOHN ROBERTS.

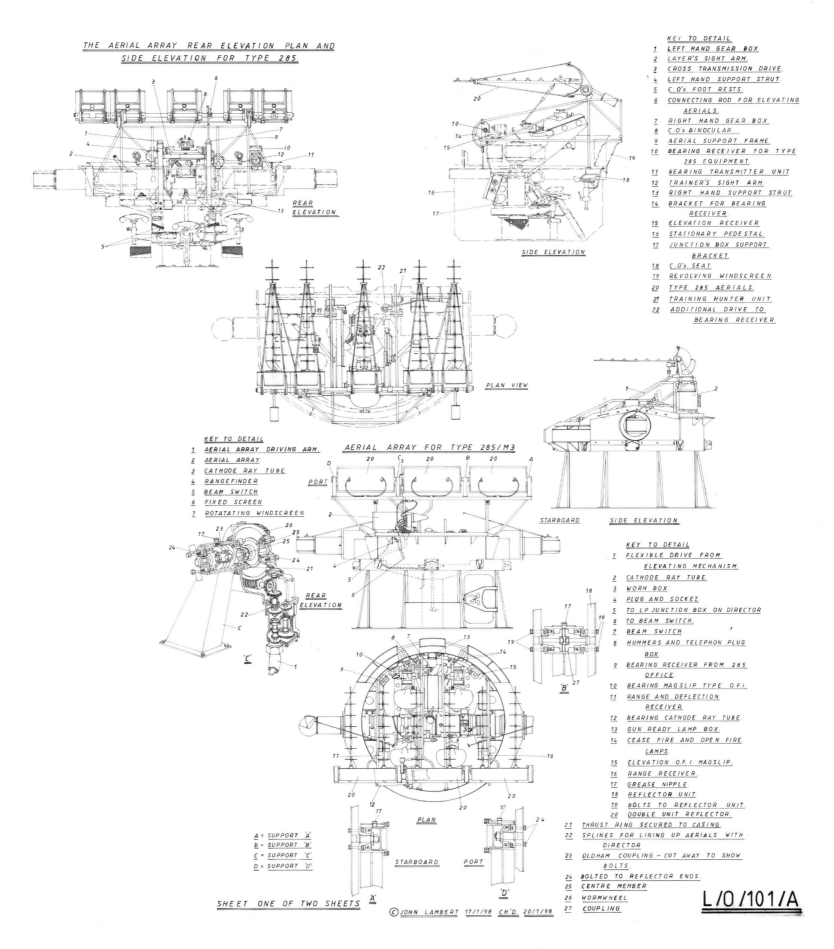

THE AERIAL ARRAY REAR ELEVATION PLAN AND
SIDE ELEVATION FOR TYPE 285.

REAR
ELEVATION

SIDE ELEVATION

PLAN VIEW

AERIAL ARRAY FOR TYPE 285/M3

PORT

REAR
ELEVATION

'C'

STARBOARD   SIDE ELEVATION

KEY TO DETAIL
1 LEFT HAND GEAR BOX.
2 LAYER'S SIGHT ARM.
3 CROSS TRANSMISSION DRIVE.
4 LEFT HAND SUPPORT STRUT.
5 C.O's FOOT RESTS.
6 CONNECTING ROD FOR ELEVATING
   AERIALS.
7 RIGHT HAND GEAR BOX
8 C.O's BINOCULAR.
9 AERIAL SUPPORT FRAME
10 BEARING RECEIVER FOR TYPE
   285 EQUIPMENT
11 BEARING TRANSMITTER UNIT
12 TRAINER'S SIGHT ARM.
13 RIGHT HAND SUPPORT STRUT.
14 BRACKET FOR BEARING
   RECEIVER.
15 ELEVATION RECEIVER
16 STATIONARY PEDESTAL
17 JUNCTION BOX SUPPORT
   BRACKET.
18 C.O's. SEAT.
19 REVOLVING WINDSCREEN
20 TYPE 285 AERIALS.
21 TRAINING HUNTER UNIT.
22 ADDITIONAL DRIVE TO
   BEARING RECEIVER

KEY TO DETAIL
1 AERIAL ARRAY DRIVING ARM.
2 AERIAL ARRAY.
3 CATHODE RAY TUBE
4 RANGEFINDER
5 BEAM SWITCH
6 FIXED SCREEN
7 ROTATATING WINDSCREEN

KEY TO DETAIL
1 FLEXIBLE DRIVE FROM
   ELEVATING MECHANISM.
2 CATHODE RAY TUBE
3 WORM BOX.
4 PLUG AND SOCKET
5 TO LP JUNCTION BOX ON DIRECTOR
6 TO BEAM SWITCH.
7 BEAM SWITCH
8 HUMMERS AND TELEPHON PLUG
   BOX.
9 BEARING RECEIVER FROM 285
   OFFICE.
10 BEARING MAGSLIP TYPE O.F.I.
11 RANGE AND DEFLECTION
   RECEIVER.
12 BEARING CATHODE RAY TUBE
13 GUN READY LAMP BOX.
14 CEASE FIRE AND OPEN FIRE
   LAMPS.
15 ELEVATION O.F.I. MAGSLIP.
16 RANGE RECEIVER
17 GREASE NIPPLE
18 REFLECTOR UNIT
19 BOLTS TO REFLECTOR UNIT.
20 DOUBLE UNIT REFLECTOR.
21 THRUST RING SECURED TO CASING
22 SPLINES FOR LINING UP AERIALS WITH
   DIRECTOR
23 OLDHAM COUPLING – CUT AWAY TO SHOW
   BOLTS.
24 BOLTED TO REFLECTOR ENDS.
25 CENTRE MEMBER
26 WORMWHEEL
27 COUPLING

A = SUPPORT 'A'
B = SUPPORT 'B'
C = SUPPORT 'C'
D = SUPPORT 'D'

'B'

PLAN

STARBOARD   PORT

'A'   'D'

SHEET ONE OF TWO SHEETS

© JOHN LAMBERT 17/1/98 CH'D 20/1/98

L/O/101/A

F 7 Rangefinder director Mk IV in detail, Mk IV HA/LA, Mk I Type K, Mk VI, HACS Mk IV, HA/LA Mk V and V*(M) HA/LA directors, 1942–1945

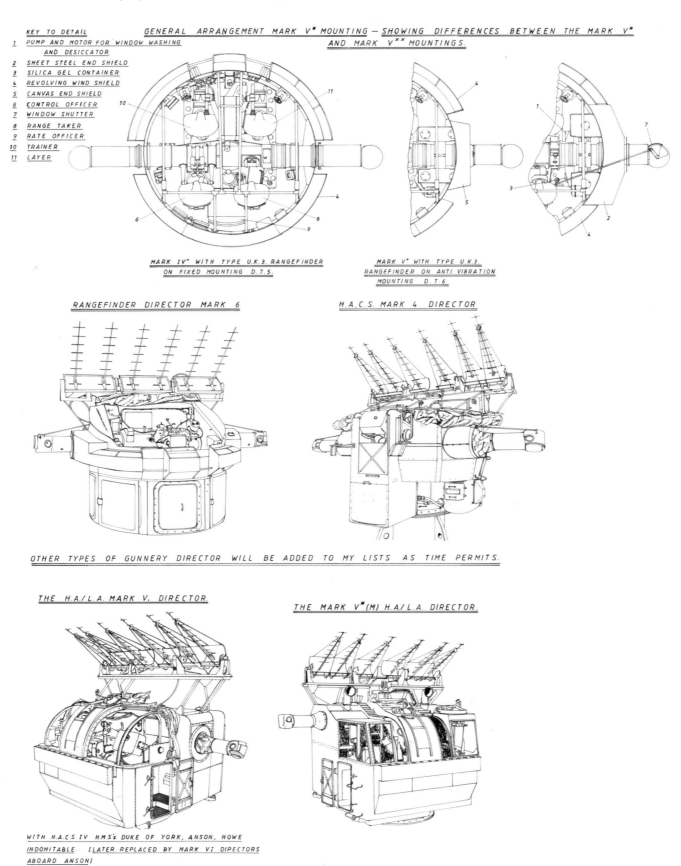

KEY TO DETAIL
1 PUMP AND MOTOR FOR WINDOW WASHING AND DESICCATOR.
2 SHEET STEEL END SHIELD
3 SILICA GEL CONTAINER
4 REVOLVING WIND SHIELD
5 CANVAS END SHIELD
6 CONTROL OFFICER
7 WINDOW SHUTTER
8 RANGE TAKER
9 RATE OFFICER
10 TRAINER
11 LAYER

GENERAL ARRANGEMENT MARK V* MOUNTING – SHOWING DIFFERENCES BETWEEN THE MARK V* AND MARK V** MOUNTINGS.

MARK IV* WITH TYPE U.K.3. RANGEFINDER ON FIXED MOUNTING D.T.S.

MARK V* WITH TYPE U.K.3. RANGEFINDER ON ANTI VIBRATION MOUNTING D.T.6.

RANGEFINDER DIRECTOR MARK 6

H.A.C.S. MARK 4 DIRECTOR

OTHER TYPES OF GUNNERY DIRECTOR WILL BE ADDED TO MY LISTS AS TIME PERMITS.

THE H.A./L.A. MARK V. DIRECTOR.

THE MARK V*(M) H.A./L.A. DIRECTOR.

WITH H.A.C.S. IV H.M.S's DUKE OF YORK, ANSON, HOWE INDOMITABLE. [LATER REPLACED BY MARK VI DIRECTORS ABOARD ANSON]

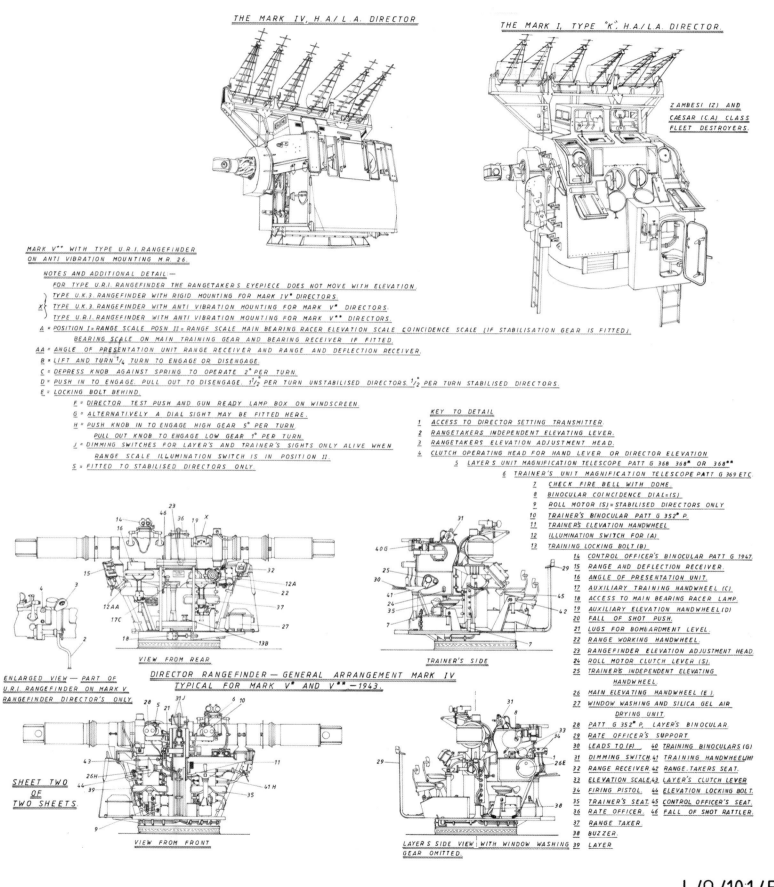

THE MARK IV, H.A./L.A. DIRECTOR

THE MARK I, TYPE "K" H.A./L.A. DIRECTOR.

ZAMBESI (Z) AND CAESAR (CA) CLASS FLEET DESTROYERS.

MARK V** WITH TYPE U.R.I. RANGEFINDER ON ANTI VIBRATION MOUNTING M.R. 26.

NOTES AND ADDITIONAL DETAIL:—

FOR TYPE U.R.I. RANGEFINDER THE RANGETAKERS EYEPIECE DOES NOT MOVE WITH ELEVATION.

X {
TYPE U.K.3. RANGEFINDER WITH RIGID MOUNTING FOR MARK IV* DIRECTORS.
TYPE U.K.3. RANGEFINDER WITH ANTI VIBRATION MOUNTING FOR MARK V* DIRECTORS.
TYPE U.R.I. RANGEFINDER WITH ANTI VIBRATION MOUNTING FOR MARK V** DIRECTORS.

A = POSITION I = RANGE SCALE POSN II = RANGE SCALE MAIN BEARING RACER ELEVATION SCALE COINCIDENCE SCALE (IF STABILISATION GEAR IS FITTED)
    BEARING SCALE ON MAIN TRAINING GEAR AND BEARING RECEIVER IF FITTED.
AA = ANGLE OF PRESENTATION UNIT RANGE RECEIVER AND RANGE AND DEFLECTION RECEIVER.
B = LIFT AND TURN 1/4 TURN TO ENGAGE OR DISENGAGE.
C = DEPRESS KNOB AGAINST SPRING TO OPERATE 2° PER TURN.
D = PUSH IN TO ENGAGE. PULL OUT TO DISENGAGE. 1 1/2° PER TURN UNSTABILISED DIRECTORS. 1/2° PER TURN STABILISED DIRECTORS.
E = LOCKING BOLT BEHIND.
F = DIRECTOR TEST PUSH AND GUN READY LAMP BOX ON WINDSCREEN.
G = ALTERNATIVELY A DIAL SIGHT MAY BE FITTED HERE.
H = PUSH KNOB IN TO ENGAGE HIGH GEAR 5° PER TURN.
    PULL OUT KNOB TO ENGAGE LOW GEAR 1° PER TURN.
J = DIMMING SWITCHES FOR LAYER'S AND TRAINER'S SIGHTS ONLY ALIVE WHEN
    RANGE SCALE ILLUMINATION SWITCH IS IN POSITION II.
S = FITTED TO STABILISED DIRECTORS ONLY.

KEY TO DETAIL

1 ACCESS TO DIRECTOR SETTING TRANSMITTER.
2 RANGETAKERS INDEPENDENT ELEVATING LEVER.
3 RANGETAKERS ELEVATION ADJUSTMENT HEAD.
4 CLUTCH OPERATING HEAD FOR HAND LEVER OR DIRECTOR ELEVATION
5 LAYER'S UNIT MAGNIFICATION TELESCOPE PATT G 368 368* OR 368**
6 TRAINER'S UNIT MAGNIFICATION TELESCOPE PATT G 369 ETC.
7 CHECK FIRE BELL WITH DOME.
8 BINOCULAR COINCIDENCE DIAL=(S)
9 ROLL MOTOR (S) = STABILISED DIRECTORS ONLY
10 TRAINER'S BINOCULAR PATT G 352* P.
11 TRAINER'S ELEVATION HANDWHEEL
12 ILLUMINATION SWITCH FOR (A)
13 TRAINING LOCKING BOLT (B)
14 CONTROL OFFICER'S BINOCULAR PATT G 1947.
15 RANGE AND DEFLECTION RECEIVER
16 ANGLE OF PRESENTATION UNIT.
17 AUXILIARY TRAINING HANDWHEEL (C)
18 ACCESS TO MAIN BEARING RACER LAMP.
19 AUXILIARY ELEVATION HANDWHEEL (D)
20 FALL OF SHOT PUSH.
21 LUGS FOR BOMBARDMENT LEVEL.
22 RANGE WORKING HANDWHEEL.
23 RANGEFINDER ELEVATION ADJUSTMENT HEAD.
24 ROLL MOTOR CLUTCH LEVER (S).
25 TRAINER'S INDEPENDENT ELEVATING HANDWHEEL
26 MAIN ELEVATING HANDWHEEL (E).
27 WINDOW WASHING AND SILICA GEL AIR DRYING UNIT.
28 PATT G 352* P, LAYER'S BINOCULAR.
29 RATE OFFICER'S SUPPORT.
30 LEADS TO (F)
31 DIMMING SWITCH.
32 RANGE RECEIVER.
33 ELEVATION SCALE.
34 FIRING PISTOL.
35 TRAINER'S SEAT.
36 RATE OFFICER.
37 RANGE TAKER.
38 BUZZER.
39 LAYER.
40 TRAINING BINOCULARS (G)
41 TRAINING HANDWHEEL (H)
42 RANGE TAKERS SEAT.
43 LAYER'S CLUTCH LEVER.
44 ELEVATION LOCKING BOLT.
45 CONTROL OFFICER'S SEAT.
46 FALL OF SHOT RATTLER.

VIEW FROM REAR

TRAINER'S SIDE

ENLARGED VIEW — PART OF U.R.I. RANGEFINDER ON MARK V RANGEFINDER DIRECTOR'S ONLY.

DIRECTOR RANGEFINDER — GENERAL ARRANGEMENT MARK IV TYPICAL FOR MARK V* AND V** — 1943.

SHEET TWO OF TWO SHEETS.

VIEW FROM FRONT

LAYER'S SIDE VIEW WITH WINDOW WASHING GEAR OMITTED.

© JOHN LAMBERT 17/1/98 CH'D 20/1/98

L/O/101/B

211

F 8 Destroyer rangefinder director Mk V**, 1943

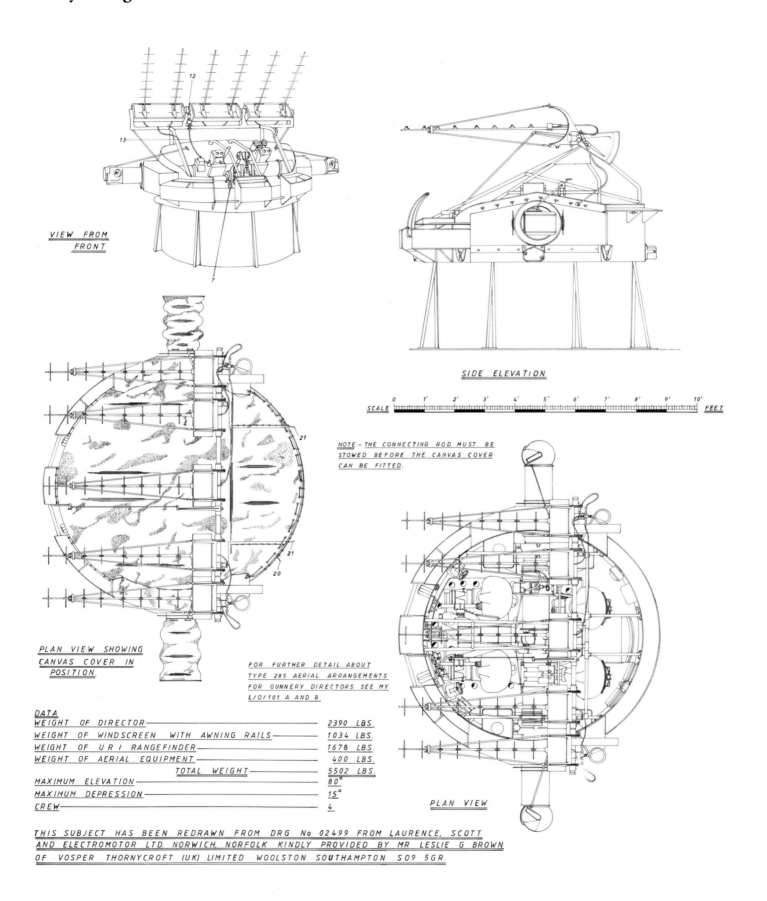

VIEW FROM
FRONT

SIDE ELEVATION

SCALE |0 1' 2' 3' 4' 5' 6' 7' 8' 9' 10'| FEET

NOTE – THE CONNECTING ROD MUST BE
STOWED BEFORE THE CANVAS COVER
CAN BE FITTED.

PLAN VIEW SHOWING
CANVAS COVER IN
POSITION

FOR FURTHER DETAIL ABOUT
TYPE 285 AERIAL ARRANGEMENTS
FOR GUNNERY DIRECTORS SEE MY
L/0/101 A AND B.

DATA
WEIGHT OF DIRECTOR——————————————— 2390 LBS.
WEIGHT OF WINDSCREEN WITH AWNING RAILS—— 1034 LBS.
WEIGHT OF U R I RANGEFINDER—————————— 1678 LBS.
WEIGHT OF AERIAL EQUIPMENT——————————— 400 LBS.
          TOTAL WEIGHT——————— 5502 LBS.
MAXIMUM ELEVATION——————————————————— 80°
MAXIMUM DEPRESSION—————————————————— 15°
CREW————————————————————————————————— 4

PLAN VIEW

THIS SUBJECT HAS BEEN REDRAWN FROM DRG No 02499 FROM LAURENCE, SCOTT
AND ELECTROMOTOR LTD. NORWICH, NORFOLK KINDLY PROVIDED BY MR LESLIE G BROWN
OF VOSPER THORNYCROFT (UK) LIMITED WOOLSTON SOUTHAMPTON SO9 5GR.

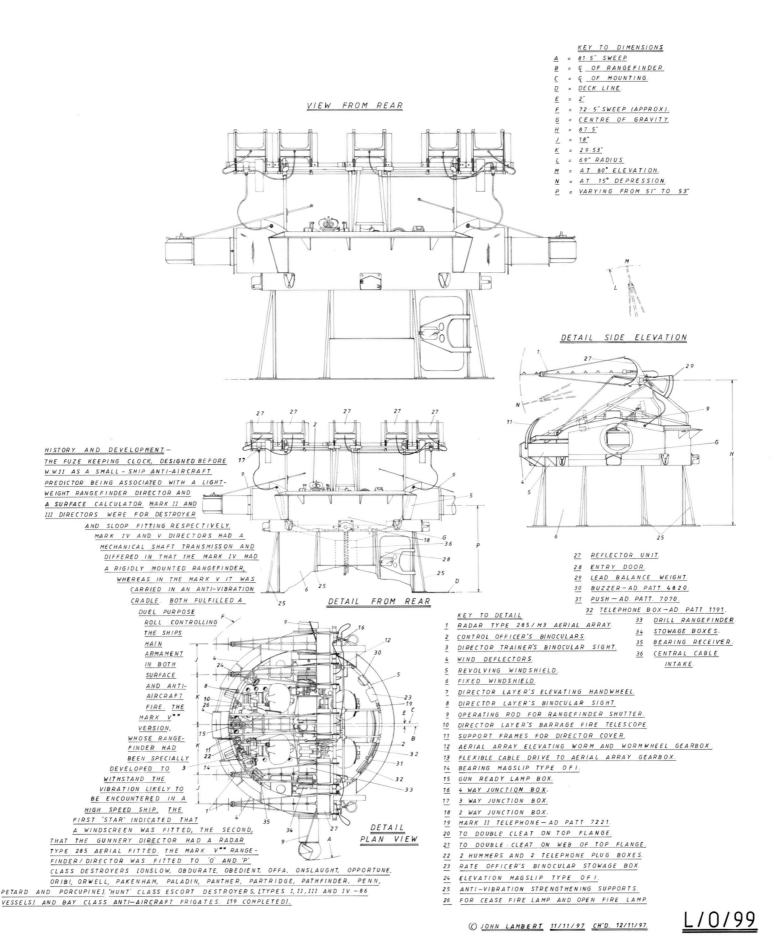

VIEW FROM REAR

DETAIL SIDE ELEVATION

DETAIL FROM REAR

HISTORY AND DEVELOPMENT—
THE FUZE KEEPING CLOCK, DESIGNED BEFORE
W.W.II AS A SMALL-SHIP ANTI-AIRCRAFT
PREDICTOR BEING ASSOCIATED WITH A LIGHT-
WEIGHT RANGEFINDER DIRECTOR AND
A SURFACE CALCULATOR. MARK II AND
III DIRECTORS WERE FOR DESTROYER
AND SLOOP FITTING RESPECTIVELY.
MARK IV AND V DIRECTORS HAD A
MECHANICAL SHAFT TRANSMISSON AND
DIFFERED IN THAT THE MARK IV HAD
A RIGIDLY MOUNTED RANGEFINDER,
WHEREAS IN THE MARK V IT WAS
CARRIED IN AN ANTI-VIBRATION
CRADLE. BOTH FULFILLED A
DUEL PURPOSE
ROLL CONTROLLING
THE SHIPS
MAIN
ARMAMENT
IN BOTH
SURFACE
AND ANTI-
AIRCRAFT
FIRE. THE
MARK V**
VERSION,
WHOSE RANGE-
FINDER HAD
BEEN SPECIALLY
DEVELOPED TO
WITHSTAND THE
VIBRATION LIKELY TO
BE ENCOUNTERED IN A
HIGH SPEED SHIP. THE
FIRST 'STAR' INDICATED THAT
A WINDSCREEN WAS FITTED, THE SECOND,
THAT THE GUNNERY DIRECTOR HAD A RADAR
TYPE 285 AERIAL FITTED. THE MARK V** RANGE-
FINDER/DIRECTOR WAS FITTED TO 'O' AND 'P'
CLASS DESTROYERS (ONSLOW, OBDURATE, OBEDIENT, OFFA, ONSLAUGHT, OPPORTUNE,
ORIBI, ORWELL, PAKENHAM, PALADIN, PANTHER, PARTRIDGE, PATHFINDER, PENN,
PETARD AND PORCUPINE). 'HUNT' CLASS ESCORT DESTROYERS, (TYPES I, II, III AND IV —86
VESSELS) AND BAY CLASS ANTI-AIRCRAFT FRIGATES. (19 COMPLETED).

DETAIL PLAN VIEW

KEY TO DETAIL
1 RADAR TYPE 285/M3 AERIAL ARRAY
2 CONTROL OFFICER'S BINOCULARS.
3 DIRECTOR TRAINER'S BINOCULAR SIGHT.
4 WIND DEFLECTORS.
5 REVOLVING WINDSHIELD.
6 FIXED WINDSHIELD.
7 DIRECTOR LAYER'S ELEVATING HANDWHEEL.
8 DIRECTOR LAYER'S BINOCULAR SIGHT.
9 OPERATING ROD FOR RANGEFINDER SHUTTER.
10 DIRECTOR LAYER'S BARRAGE FIRE TELESCOPE
11 SUPPORT FRAMES FOR DIRECTOR COVER.
12 AERIAL ARRAY ELEVATING WORM AND WORMWHEEL GEARBOX.
13 FLEXIBLE CABLE DRIVE TO AERIAL ARRAY GEARBOX.
14 BEARING MAGSLIP TYPE OF I.
15 GUN READY LAMP BOX.
16 4 WAY JUNCTION BOX.
17 3 WAY JUNCTION BOX.
18 2 WAY JUNCTION BOX.
19 MARK II TELEPHONE—AD PATT 7221.
20 TO DOUBLE CLEAT ON TOP FLANGE.
21 TO DOUBLE CLEAT ON WEB OF TOP FLANGE.
22 2 HUMMERS AND 2 TELEPHONE PLUG BOXES.
23 RATE OFFICER'S BINOCULAR STOWAGE BOX.
24 ELEVATION MAGSLIP TYPE OF I.
25 ANTI-VIBRATION STRENGTHENING SUPPORTS.
26 FOR CEASE FIRE LAMP AND OPEN FIRE LAMP.

27 REFLECTOR UNIT.
28 ENTRY DOOR.
29 LEAD BALANCE WEIGHT.
30 BUZZER—AD. PATT. 4820
31 PUSH—AD. PATT. 7070
32 TELEPHONE BOX—AD PATT 1191.
33 DRILL RANGEFINDER.
34 STOWAGE BOXES.
35 BEARING RECEIVER.
36 CENTRAL CABLE INTAKE.

© JOHN LAMBERT 11/11/97 CH'D. 12/11/97   L/0/99

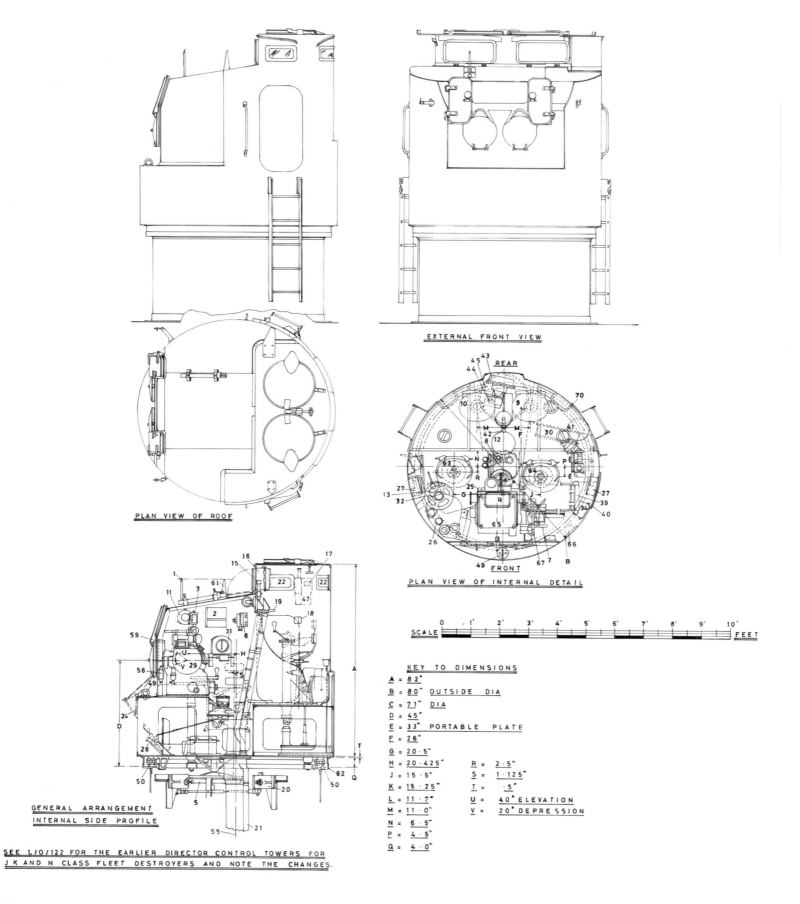

EXTERNAL FRONT VIEW

PLAN VIEW OF ROOF

PLAN VIEW OF INTERNAL DETAIL

GENERAL ARRANGEMENT
INTERNAL SIDE PROFILE

SEE L/O/122 FOR THE EARLIER DIRECTOR CONTROL TOWERS FOR
J K AND N CLASS FLEET DESTROYERS AND NOTE THE CHANGES.

SCALE 0 1' 2' 3' 4' 5' 6' 7' 8' 9' 10' FEET

KEY TO DIMENSIONS

A = 82"
B = 80" OUTSIDE DIA
C = 71" DIA
D = 45"
E = 33" PORTABLE PLATE
F = 26"
G = 20.5"
H = 20.425"   R = 2.5"
J = 15.5"   S = 1.125"
K = 15.25"   T = .5"
L = 11.7"   U = 40° ELEVATION
M = 11.0"   V = 20° DEPRESSION
N = 6.5"
P = 4.5"
Q = 4.0"

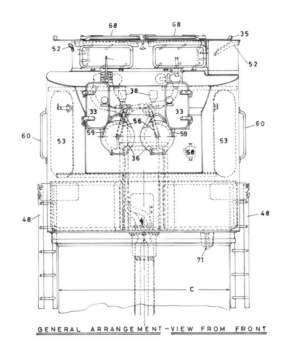

GENERAL ARRANGEMENT-VIEW FROM FRONT

VIEW OF MIRROR CHAMBER
IN DIRECTION OF ARROW "X"

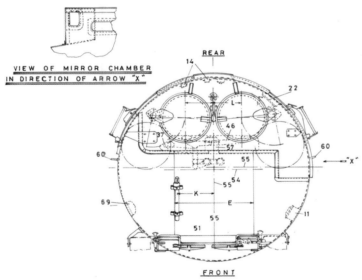

FRONT
PLAN VIEW OF ROOF - GENERAL ARRANGEMENT

NOTE
VARIATION OF TRAINING RACKS (OVERSIZE BY THE FOLLOWING AMOUNTS)

H M SHIPS			H M SHIPS		
QUENTIN	+·032″		QUEENBOROUGH	+·005″
QUIBERON	+·034″		RACEHORSE	+·003″
ROTHERHAM	+·028″		RELENTLESS	+·008″
QUILLIAM	+·022″		QUADRANT	+·0035″
REDOUBT	+·022″		RAPID	+·0035″
QUIQKMATCH	+·022″		QUAIL	+·0015″
RAIDER	+·036″		ROCKET	+·0165″
QUALITY	+·022″		ROEBUCK	+·011″
SPARE — V CLASS	+·0045″		SPARE — V CLASS	+·0045″

KEY TO DETAIL

1	COLLAPSIBLE OPEN SIGHT		58	SWITCH FOR GYRO
2	TELEPHONE STOWAGE BOX		59	SPRAY SHIELD
3	CHECK FIRE BELL		60	HANDRAIL
4	RADIATOR		61	REAR SIGHT
5	LOCKING BOLT SOCKET		62	LEATHER APRON
6	GUN READY LAMP BOX		63	TRAINERS SEAT
7	UNSTABILIZED TELESCOPE		64	LAYERS SEAT
8	DIRECTOR TEST PUSH		65	℄ OF SIGHT
9	RATE OFFICERS SEAT		66	OIL BOX
10	CONTROL OFFICERS SEAT		67	ALDIS TUBE
11	FALL OF SHOT RATTLER		68	LOOK-OUT DOORS
12	SIGHT ADJUSTER SEAT		69	FIRE GONG
13	TOWER LOCKING BOLT		70	BINOCULAR CASE
14	TELEPHONE PLUGS		71	BUFFER SPRING

15   RATE OFFICERS BINOCULAR BRACKET
16   COMBINED RANGE AND DEFLECTION RECEIVER
17   SWITCH FOR INSTRUMENT ILLUMINATION
18   LIGHTING SWITCH - ADMIRALTY PATTERN 4089
19   RELATIVE BEARING INDICATOR
20   STOP GEAR LIMITING TRAINING TO 440°
21   2 FLEXIBLE VOICE PIPES - 2″ DIA
22   ARMOURED PLATE GLASS VIEWING PORT
24   BRACKET SECURING COVERS
25   TARGET VISIBLE SWITCH
26   TOWER TRAINING GEAR COMBINING LINE OF
     SIGHT TRANSMISSION
27   STOWAGE BOX FOR TELEPHONES
28   PEDAL GEAR FOR DIRECTOR CHANGE OVER
     PISTOL
29   TYPE H M MARK V* DOUBLE STABILIZED
     GYRO DIRECTOR SIGHT
30   JUNCTION BOX TYPE PJ
31   BEARING RECEIVER MAG SLIP TYPE C M
     MARK IV
32   TOWER TRAINING HANDWHEEL VALVES 30′
     AND 3°
33   SIGHT PORTS WITH HINGED DOORS
34   RELAY FOR GYRO FIRING
35   STOP FOR LOOK-OUT DOOR
36   KENTS CLEAR VIEW SCREENS
37   VOICE PIPES TO CAPTAIN AND RANGEFINDER
38   SWITCHES FOR CLEAR VIEW SCREEN MOTORS
39   TIME INTERVAL COMPENSATING GEAR
40   INSPECTION PLATE FOR ADJUSTMENT OF
     T I C GEAR
41   SEAT FOR CROSS-LEVELLING OPERATOR
42   OFFICERS TRAINING HANDLE - VALUE 3°
43   EVERSHED BEARING RECEIVER
44   DRIVE TO RELATIVE BEARING INDICATOR
45   AUXILIARY HAND TRAINING GEAR
46   VOICE PIPES TO TRANSMITTING STATION
     OF TOWER
47   TRANSMITTER AND REPEAT FOR DATUM
     SIGHT
48   PORTABLE LADDER
49   LIFTING BOLT - PORTABLE
50   ROLLER BEARING
51   HINGED OPENING
52   EXTERNAL GUTTERING
53   SIDE ENTRY DOORS
54   ℄ OF CIRCULAR PLATING
55   ℄ OF TOWER
56   DRIVE BELTS FOR KENTS CLEAR VIEW SCREENS
57   RANGE AND DEFLECTION RECEIVER

REDRAWN FROM GENERAL ARRANGEMENT DRAWING No 3781
HELD AT THE CUMBRIA COUNTY RECORD OFFICE 140 DUKE STREET BARROW IN FURNESS CUMBRIA LA14 1XW
© JOHN LAMBERT COMMENCED 16/6/2004 COMMENCED 25/6/2004 CH'D. 29/6/2004

L/O/155

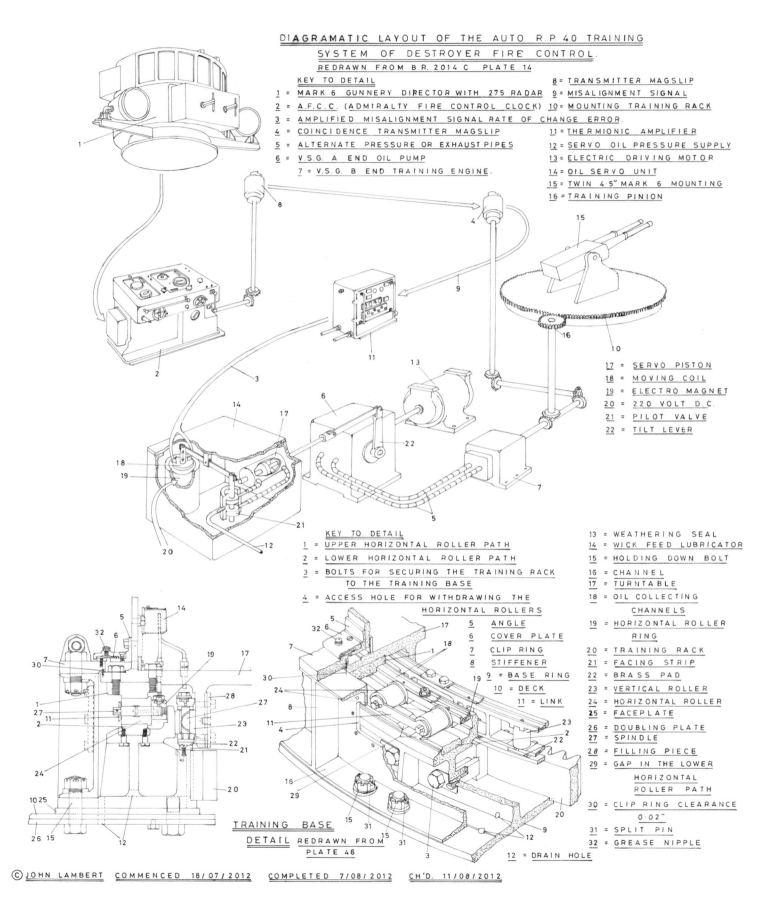

DIAGRAMATIC LAYOUT OF THE AUTO R.P 40 TRAINING
SYSTEM OF DESTROYER FIRE CONTROL.
REDRAWN FROM B.R. 2014 C PLATE 14

KEY TO DETAIL
1 = MARK 6 GUNNERY DIRECTOR WITH 275 RADAR
2 = A.F.C.C. (ADMIRALTY FIRE CONTROL CLOCK)
3 = AMPLIFIED MISALIGNMENT SIGNAL RATE OF CHANGE ERROR.
4 = COINCIDENCE TRANSMITTER MAGSLIP
5 = ALTERNATE PRESSURE OR EXHAUST PIPES
6 = V.S.G. A END OIL PUMP
7 = V.S.G. B END TRAINING ENGINE.

8 = TRANSMITTER MAGSLIP
9 = MISALIGNMENT SIGNAL
10 = MOUNTING TRAINING RACK

11 = THERMIONIC AMPLIFIER
12 = SERVO OIL PRESSURE SUPPLY
13 = ELECTRIC DRIVING MOTOR
14 = OIL SERVO UNIT
15 = TWIN 4·5" MARK 6 MOUNTING
16 = TRAINING PINION

17 = SERVO PISTON
18 = MOVING COIL
19 = ELECTRO MAGNET
20 = 220 VOLT D.C.
21 = PILOT VALVE
22 = TILT LEVER

KEY TO DETAIL
1 = UPPER HORIZONTAL ROLLER PATH
2 = LOWER HORIZONTAL ROLLER PATH
3 = BOLTS FOR SECURING THE TRAINING RACK
    TO THE TRAINING BASE
4 = ACCESS HOLE FOR WITHDRAWING THE
    HORIZONTAL ROLLERS
5 = ANGLE
6 = COVER PLATE
7 = CLIP RING
8 = STIFFENER
9 = BASE RING
10 = DECK
11 = LINK

13 = WEATHERING SEAL
14 = WICK FEED LUBRICATOR
15 = HOLDING DOWN BOLT
16 = CHANNEL
17 = TURNTABLE
18 = OIL COLLECTING
    CHANNELS
19 = HORIZONTAL ROLLER
    RING
20 = TRAINING RACK
21 = FACING STRIP
22 = BRASS PAD
23 = VERTICAL ROLLER
24 = HORIZONTAL ROLLER
25 = FACEPLATE
26 = DOUBLING PLATE
27 = SPINDLE
28 = FILLING PIECE
29 = GAP IN THE LOWER
    HORIZONTAL
    ROLLER PATH
30 = CLIP RING CLEARANCE
    0·02"
31 = SPLIT PIN
32 = GREASE NIPPLE

TRAINING BASE
DETAIL REDRAWN FROM
PLATE 46

12 = DRAIN HOLE

DATA —THE MOUNTING

TYPE OF ELEVATION GEAR	=	HYDRAULIC RAM
MAXIMUM ELEVATION	=	80°
MAXIMUM DEPRESSION	=	-15°
ARC OF TRAINING	=	800° (400° RIGHT 400° LEFT)
GEAR RATIO	=	ENGINE TO RACK 120 TO 1
TRAINING RACK	=	240 TEETH ON 120′ PC DIA

FORCES ON FIRING

WITH GUNS HORIZONTAL	=	18·9 TONS
WITH GUNS AT 80° ELEVATION	=	23 TONS
MAX. UPWARD LIFT AT FRONT OF BASE PLATE	=	18·9 TONS
MAX. DOWNWARD BLOW AT REAR OF BASE PLATE	=	52·7 TONS (INCLUDING 23 TONS)
DISTANCE BETWEEN GUNS		32·5″
RATE OF FIRE		12 –14 ROUNDS / MIN.
GUN RANGE		20,750 YARDS (11·78 MILES)
MAXIMUM HEIGHT		41,000 FEET = (7·76 MILES)
BOOKS OF REFERENCE	=	B.R. 2014 B & C B.R. 1958, B.R. 292, B.R. 1945,
		B.R.1638, B.R. 1644.

GUN SHIELD

THICKNESS	=	0·375″
MATERIAL	=	U X W

GUN RECOIL

WORKING (NOMINAL)	=	20″
METAL TO METAL	=	22″

WEIGHTS TONS		MARK 6 & 6*	MARK 6*MOD 1
1 GUN WITH B.M. BUT UNLOADED	=	3·315	3·315
COMPLETE CRADLE WITH GUNS ETC	=	12·2	12·2
CENTRAL TRUNK	=	1·55	1·55
TRAINING MASS INC. GUNS AND CABLES	=	46 APPROX	43·25 APPROX

TRAINING BASE

HOLDING DOWN BOLTS	=	64	64
DIA	=	1″	1″
PITCH CIRCLE DIA	=	141″	126″

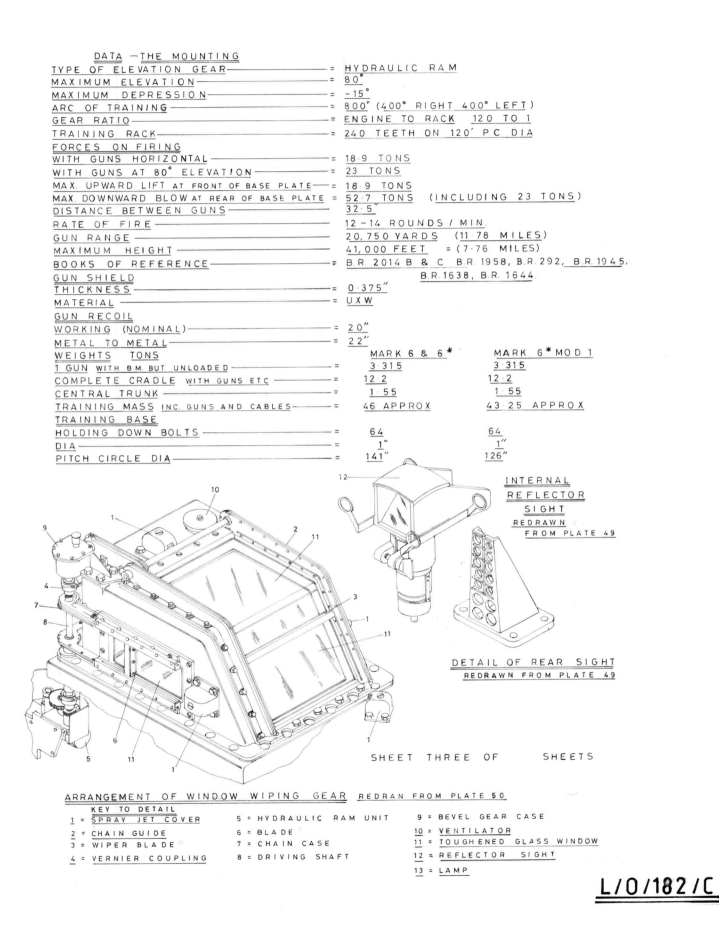

INTERNAL
REFLECTOR
SIGHT
REDRAWN
FROM PLATE 49

DETAIL OF REAR SIGHT
REDRAWN FROM PLATE 49

SHEET THREE OF   SHEETS

ARRANGEMENT OF WINDOW WIPING GEAR REDRAN FROM PLATE 50

KEY TO DETAIL

1 = SPRAY JET COVER	5 = HYDRAULIC RAM UNIT	9 = BEVEL GEAR CASE
2 = CHAIN GUIDE	6 = BLADE	10 = VENTILATOR
3 = WIPER BLADE	7 = CHAIN CASE	11 = TOUGHENED GLASS WINDOW
4 = VERNIER COUPLING	8 = DRIVING SHAFT	12 = REFLECTOR SIGHT
		13 = LAMP

L/O/182/C

T 1 Quadruple 21in torpedo tubes QRE Mk I, 1929

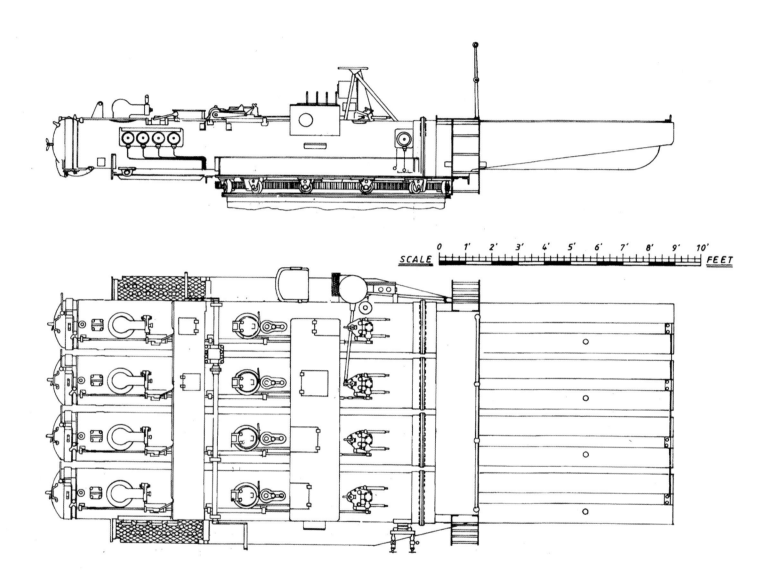

SCALE 0 1' 2' 3' 4' 5' 6' 7' 8' 9' 10' FEET

<u>HISTORY</u>

THE QUADRUPLE REVOLVING [Q.R.] AND PENTAD [P.R] SERIES OF TORPEDO TUBE MOUNTINGS WERE PRE. W.W.II DEVELOPMENTS AND STEMMED, IN THE FIRST INSTANCE FROM THIS Q.R. MARK I MOUNTING, DESIGNED FOR THE CRUISERS H.M.S. EMERALD AND H.M.S. ENTERPRISE OF 1926. THE TWO SHIPS WERE COMPLETED BEFORE THE TORPEDO TUBES AND SO TEMPORARILY SHIPPED TRIPLE REVOLVING [T.R] MARK I's UNTIL THE EIGHT Q.R.[E]. MARK I's WERE COMPLETED AND WERE FITTED DURING THE TWO SHIPS 1928-29 REFITS. THE TWO 'E' CLASS WERE THE LAST OF THE BRITISH WWI PROGRAMMES. THE FOUR MOUNTINGS AND THE RESULTING SIXTEEN TUBES GAVE THEM THE LARGEST TORPEDO ARMAMENT EVER MOUNTED IN A BRITISH SHIP. THE FOLLOWING 8" GUNNED 'KENT' CLASS UNITS REVERTED TO ONLY TWO Q.R. MARK II TUBES.

© JOHN LAMBERT   COMPLETED 6/10/1997   CH D 7/10/1997   ENLARGED 19/08/2005

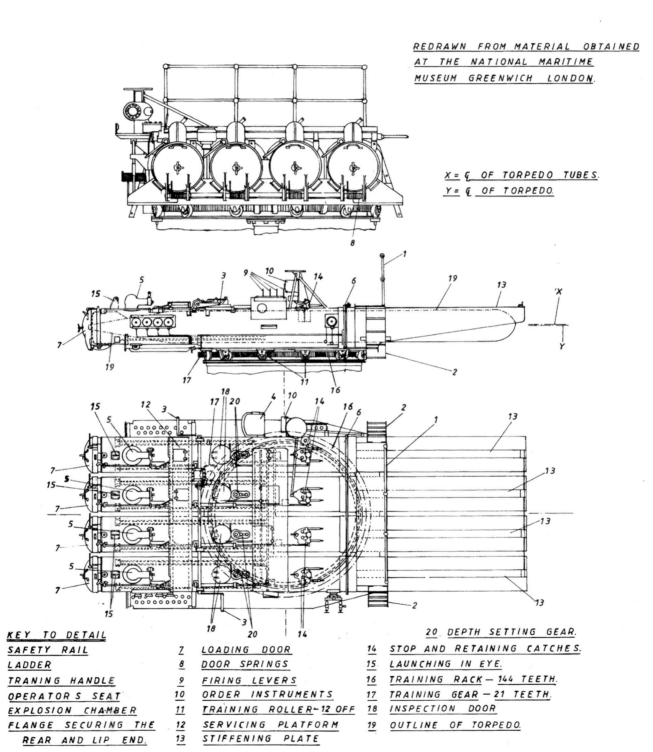

OTHER TORPEDO TUBES DRAWN—

L/0/33 — THE QUADRUPLE 21" Q.R. MARK VIII TORPEDO TUBE.—1943.

L/0/36/A-C- COASTAL FORCES 21" AND 18" TORPEDO TUBES.— 1939—45.

L/0/93/A-B- QUINTUPLE 21" P.R. MARK III TORPEDO TUBES.— 1944.

REDRAWN FROM MATERIAL OBTAINED
AT THE NATIONAL MARITIME
MUSEUM GREENWICH LONDON.

X = ₵ OF TORPEDO TUBES.
Y = ₵ OF TORPEDO.

KEY TO DETAIL

1	SAFETY RAIL	7	LOADING DOOR	14	STOP AND RETAINING CATCHES.
2	LADDER	8	DOOR SPRINGS	15	LAUNCHING IN EYE.
3	TRANING HANDLE	9	FIRING LEVERS	16	TRAINING RACK — 144 TEETH.
4	OPERATOR S SEAT	10	ORDER INSTRUMENTS	17	TRAINING GEAR — 21 TEETH.
5	EXPLOSION CHAMBER	11	TRAINING ROLLER— 12 OFF	18	INSPECTION DOOR
6	FLANGE SECURING THE REAR AND LIP END.	12	SERVICING PLATFORM	19	OUTLINE OF TORPEDO.
		13	STIFFENING PLATE		

20 DEPTH SETTING GEAR.

L/0/95

T 2 Pentad 21in torpedo tubes PR Mk II, 1937, as in 'K' class fleet destroyers

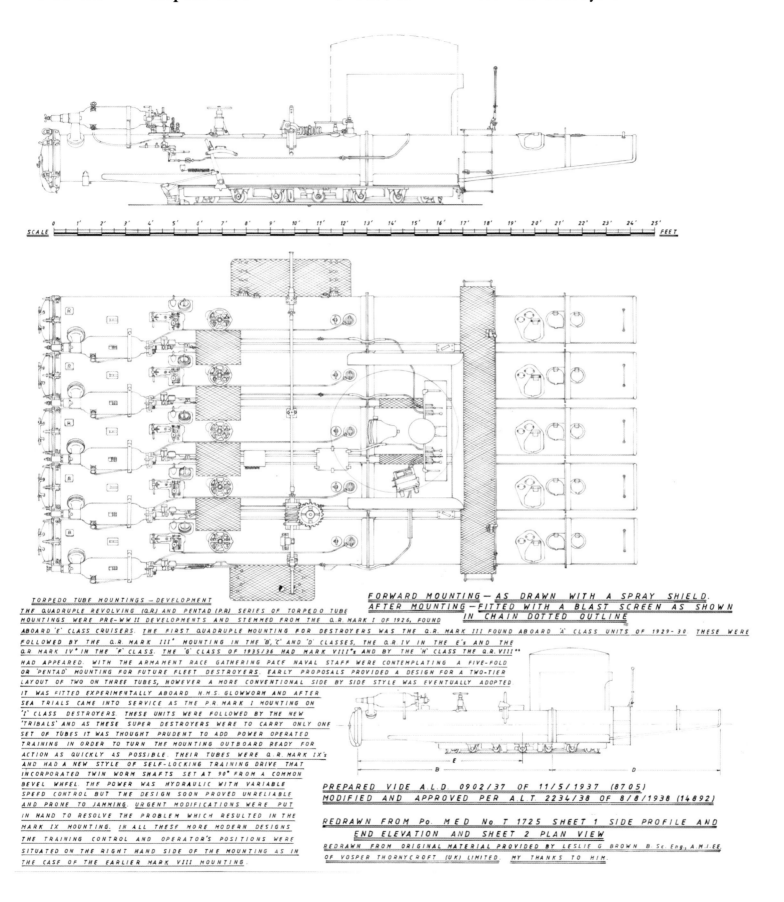

SCALE | 0 1' 2' 3' 4' 5' 6' 7' 8' 9' 10' 11' 12' 13' 14' 15' 16' 17' 18' 19' 20' 21' 22' 23' 24' 25' | FEET

TORPEDO TUBE MOUNTINGS – DEVELOPMENT

THE QUADRUPLE REVOLVING (Q.R.) AND PENTAD (P.R.) SERIES OF TORPEDO TUBE MOUNTINGS WERE PRE-WW II DEVELOPMENTS AND STEMMED FROM THE Q.R. MARK I OF 1926, FOUND ABOARD 'E' CLASS CRUISERS. THE FIRST QUADRUPLE MOUNTING FOR DESTROYERS WAS THE Q.R. MARK III FOUND ABOARD 'A' CLASS UNITS OF 1929-30. THESE WERE FOLLOWED BY THE Q.R. MARK III* MOUNTING IN THE 'B', 'C' AND 'D' CLASSES, THE Q.R. IV IN THE E's AND THE Q.R. MARK IV* IN THE 'F' CLASS. THE 'G' CLASS OF 1935/36 HAD MARK VIII's AND BY THE 'H' CLASS THE Q.R. VIII** HAD APPEARED. WITH THE ARMAMENT RACE GATHERING PACE NAVAL STAFF WERE CONTEMPLATING A FIVE-FOLD OR 'PENTAD' MOUNTING FOR FUTURE FLEET DESTROYERS. EARLY PROPOSALS PROVIDED A DESIGN FOR A TWO-TIER LAYOUT OF TWO ON THREE TUBES, HOWEVER A MORE CONVENTIONAL SIDE BY SIDE STYLE WAS EVENTUALLY ADOPTED. IT WAS FITTED EXPERIMENTALLY ABOARD H.M.S. GLOWWORM AND AFTER SEA TRIALS CAME INTO SERVICE AS THE P.R. MARK I MOUNTING ON 'I' CLASS DESTROYERS. THESE UNITS WERE FOLLOWED BY THE NEW 'TRIBALS' AND AS THESE SUPER DESTROYERS WERE TO CARRY ONLY ONE SET OF TUBES IT WAS THOUGHT PRUDENT TO ADD POWER OPERATED TRAINING IN ORDER TO TURN THE MOUNTING OUTBOARD READY FOR ACTION AS QUICKLY AS POSSIBLE. THEIR TUBES WERE Q.R. MARK IX's AND HAD A NEW STYLE OF SELF-LOCKING TRAINING DRIVE THAT INCORPORATED TWIN WORM SHAFTS SET AT 90° FROM A COMMON BEVEL WHEEL. THE POWER WAS HYDRAULIC WITH VARIABLE SPEED CONTROL BUT THE DESIGN SOON PROVED UNRELIABLE AND PRONE TO JAMMING. URGENT MODIFICATIONS WERE PUT IN HAND TO RESOLVE THE PROBLEM WHICH RESULTED IN THE MARK IX MOUNTING. IN ALL THESE MORE MODERN DESIGNS THE TRAINING CONTROL AND OPERATOR'S POSITIONS WERE SITUATED ON THE RIGHT HAND SIDE OF THE MOUNTING AS IN THE CASE OF THE EARLIER MARK VIII MOUNTING.

FORWARD MOUNTING – AS DRAWN WITH A SPRAY SHIELD.
AFTER MOUNTING – FITTED WITH A BLAST SCREEN AS SHOWN IN CHAIN DOTTED OUTLINE

PREPARED VIDE A.L.D. 0902/37 OF 11/5/1937 (8705)
MODIFIED AND APPROVED PER A.L.T. 2234/38 OF 8/8/1938 (14892)

REDRAWN FROM Po. MED No. T 1725 SHEET 1 SIDE PROFILE AND END ELEVATION AND SHEET 2 PLAN VIEW
REDRAWN FROM ORIGINAL MATERIAL PROVIDED BY LESLIE G BROWN B. Sc. Eng, A.M.I.EE OF VOSPER THORNYCROFT (UK) LIMITED. MY THANKS TO HIM.

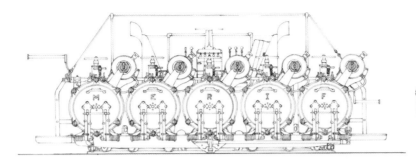

NOTE
THE LETTERING ON THE TORPEDO
TUBE LOADING DOORS IDENTIFIES
THOSE FOR THE FOR'D. TUBES
FITTED WITH THE SPRAY SHIELD.

TORPEDO TUBE MOUNTINGS DEVELOPMENT
- CONTINUED

BY 1938 A SPRAYSHIELD HAD
BEEN FITTED TO ONE MOUNTING
ABOARD THE LIGHT CRUISER
H.M.S. AURORA AS AN EXPERIMENT.
THIS PROVED TO BE SUCH A
SUCCESS THAT THE IDEA WAS
ADOPTED FOR FUTURE DESIGNS.
AT THE SAME PERIOD THE OUT-
BOARD SITING OF THE OPERATING
POSITIONS IN THE MARK VIII AND
VIII*s WAS FOUND TO SUFFER FROM
EXCESSIVE VIBRATION. AS A
RESULT FROM THE 'J' CLASS ONWARDS IT WAS DECIDED TO LOCATE THE OPERATORS POSITION CENTRALLY, ABOVE AND BETWEEN
THE TORPEDO TUBES. A SPRAYSHIELD WAS PROVIDED FOR THE FOR'D. MOUNTING AND AN ENCLOSED BLAST SCREEN (OR CUPOLA)
ON THE AFTER MOUNTING. THIS DID NOT ALTER THE MARK No (DESIGNATED P.R MARK III WHILST IT STILL EMPLOYED THE SAME
HAND WORKED RACK-AND-PINION TRAINING GEAR AS HAD FEATURED IN THE EARLIER MARK VIIIs. THE 'N' CLASS FOLLOWED ON
FROM THE 'J' AND 'K' CLASSES WITH ONLY MINOR MODIFICATIONS TO THEIR TORPEDO TUBES AND DESIGNATED P R MARK II*s.

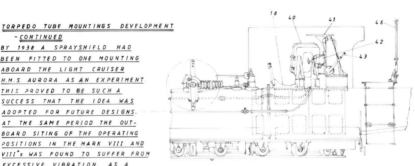

KEY TO PRINCIPAL DIMENSIONS

A	14' 5" RADIUS
B	13' 0"
C	12' 10 1/8" RADIUS
D	11' 2"
E	11' 0" TO ₵ OF PIVOT
F	2' 4 1/2"
G	1' 11 1/2"

DETAIL SHOWING CONTROLS

NOTE
THE ORIGINAL BLUE LINEN SHEET - STILL SMELLING OF
GUN OIL - HAS A HAND WRITTEN NOTE ON THE TOP
EDGE - "RECEIVED WITH LETTER FROM ENGINEERING DEPT.
PORTSMOUTH DOCKYARD - DATED 15/9/1937 (LETTER IN
'J' 'K' FILE No 2241)" IT IS THEREFORE CONCEIVABLE
THAT THIS ORIGINAL DRAWING WAS USED IN THE
CONSTRUCTION OF H.M.S. KIMBERLEY.

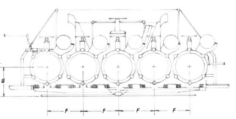

PRINCIPAL DIMENSIONS

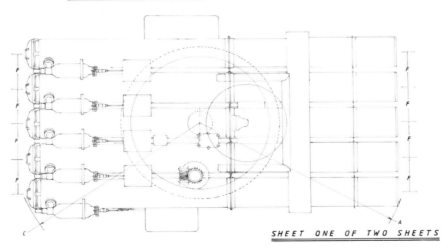

SHEET ONE OF TWO SHEETS

© JOHN LAMBERT COMMENCED 24/7/2001 COMPLETED 5/8/2001 CH'D. 10/8/2001

L/O/132/A

T 3 Quintuple 21in PR Mk III torpedo tubes, 1944, as fitted to the 1943 group of 'Battle' class destroyers

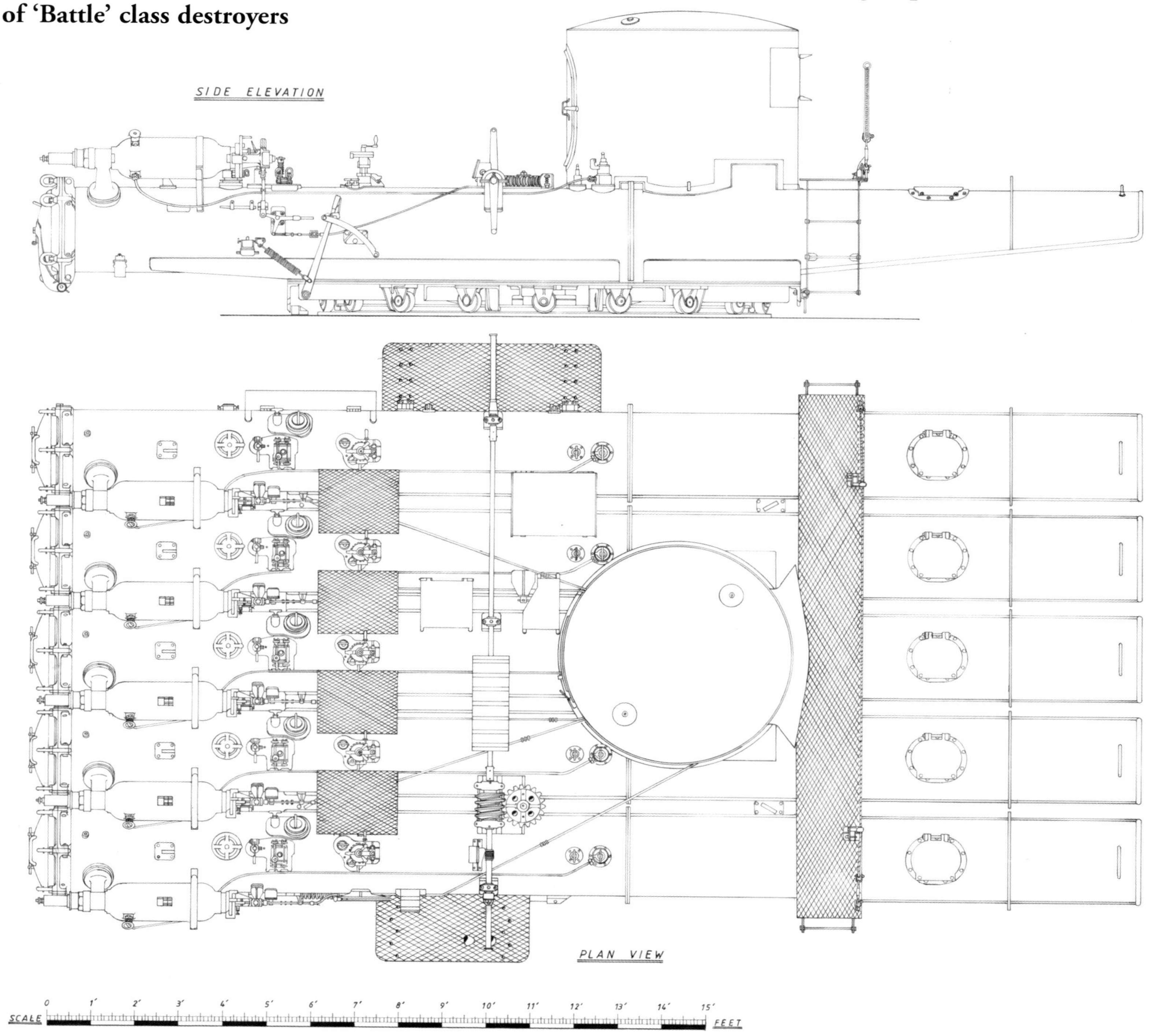

SIDE ELEVATION

PLAN VIEW

SCALE |0 1' 2' 3' 4' 5' 6' 7' 8' 9' 10' 11' 12' 13' 14' 15'| FEET

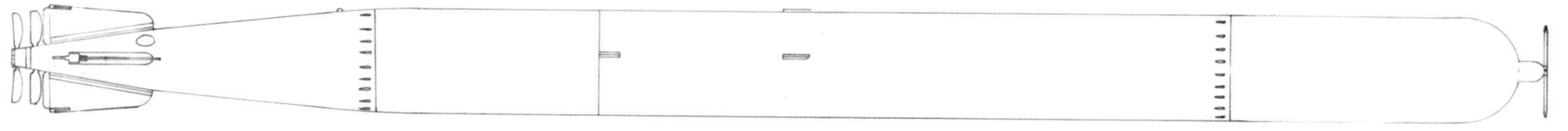

21 INCH MARK IX TORPEDO [TO SAME SCALE] (SEE MY DRG L/O/33 FOR DETAILED TORPEDO DIMENSIONS)

LONGER AND HEAVIER THAN THE PRECEEDING MARK VIII, THE MARK IX WAS DESIGNED AS A GENERAL SERVICE TORPEDO FOR ISSUE TO SURFACE CRAFT. IT WAS DRIVEN BY A SEMI DIESEL INTERNAL COMBUSTION ENGINE ON THE DRY HEATER CYCLE. WHEN ISSUED TO DESTROYERS IT WAS A SINGLE SPEED TORPEDO CAPABLE OF RUNNING 10,500 YARDS (6·94 MILES) AT 35 KNOTS OR 14 000 YARDS (7·9 MILES) AT 29·9 KNOTS. THE DEPTH KEEPING GEAR WAS DESIGNED TO PROVIDE A RECOVERY RANGE OF NOT MORE THAN 400 YARDS. PROVISION WAS MADE TO ADJUST THE OPERATING DEPTH FROM 6 TO 44 FT. HORIZONTAL RUDDER CONTROLLING GEAR WAS FITTED. THE WARHEAD CONTAINED 750 LBS OF T.N.T. THE TORPEDO WEIGHED 3731 LBS. 109 MARK IX's WERE FIRED DURING WORLD WAR II.

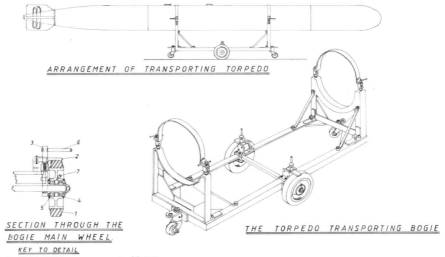

ARRANGEMENT OF TRANSPORTING TORPEDO

SECTION THROUGH THE
BOGIE MAIN WHEEL.

KEY TO DETAIL

1 SOLID TYRE.
2 BRAKE.
3 SCREW DOWN CLAMP
4 BALL BEARING.
5 ROLLER BEARING.

6 'T' BAR.
7 GREASE NIPPLE.

THE TORPEDO TRANSPORTING BOGIE

VIEW FROM FRONT

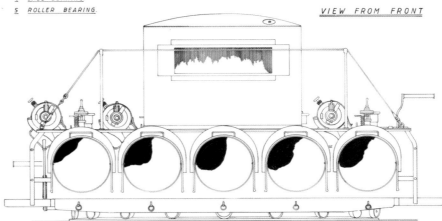

HISTORY —

THESE LATE WAR DESIGNED, HAND WORKED, PENTAD REVOLVING (P.R.) SERIES OF TORPEDO TUBE MOUNTINGS
WERE CARRIED BY THE LATER GROUP OF BATTLES— H.M.S's DUNKIRK, BARROSA, AISNE, JUTLAND,
CORUNNA, AGINCOURT, MATAPAN AND ALAMEIN. (16 VESSELS OF THIS PROGRAMME WERE CANCELLED
OF WHICH 9 HAD BEEN LAUNCHED AND FOR THE FOLLOWING 1944 PROGRAMME, 'G' CLASS—GAEL
GALLANT, GAUNTLET, GIFT
GLOWWORM, GRAFTON.

GREYHOUND AND GUERNSEY—ALL
OF WHICH WERE CANCELLED —12/12/45).
THE TUBES WERE SIMILAR TO THOSE OF THE EARLIER
Q.R. MARK VIII*** MOUNTING AS CARRIED BY THE '1942 BATTLE CLASS.
IMMEDIATELY BEFORE FIRING RUNNING DEPTH, GYRO ANGLING, SPEED
AND IF REQUIRED PATTERN RUNNING (ZIG ZAG) PROVIDED
BY THE 'W' GEAR IN THE GYRO CONTROL. THE TUBE
READY SWITCH WAS CLOSED AND THE TORPEDO(S) FIRED.
THIS REDUCED THE MAXIMUM RANGE OF THE TORPEDO BUT COULD
BE TACTICALLY ADVANTAGEOUS.

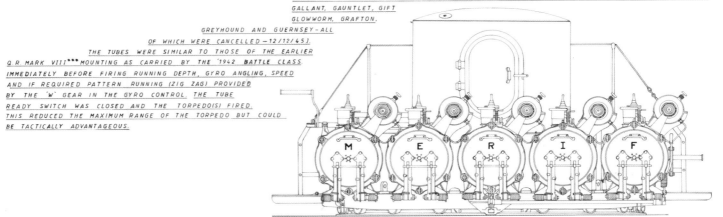

FRONT VIEW—FOR'D MOUNTING

L/0/93/A.

© JOHN LAMBERT 16/11/97   CH'D. 16/11/97.

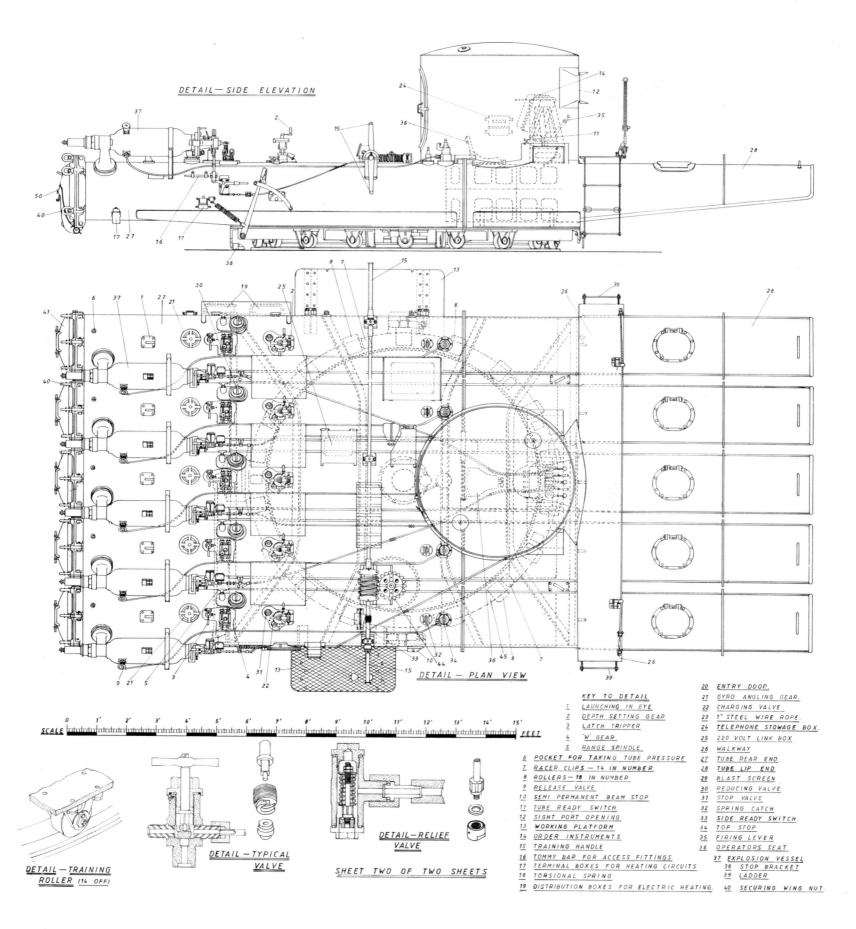

T 3 Quintuple 21in PR Mk III torpedo tubes, 1944, detail

DETAIL—SIDE ELEVATION

DETAIL—PLAN VIEW

SCALE

0 1' 2' 3' 4' 5' 6' 7' 8' 9' 10' 11' 12' 13' 14' 15' FEET

DETAIL—TRAINING ROLLER (14 OFF)

DETAIL—TYPICAL VALVE

DETAIL—RELIEF VALVE

SHEET TWO OF TWO SHEETS

KEY TO DETAIL
1 LAUNCHING IN EYE
2 DEPTH SETTING GEAR
3 LATCH TRIPPER
4 'W' GEAR
5 RANGE SPINDLE
6 POCKET FOR TAKING TUBE PRESSURE
7 RACER CLIPS — 14 IN NUMBER
8 ROLLERS — 18 IN NUMBER
9 RELEASE VALVE
10 SEMI PERMANENT BEAM STOP
11 TUBE READY SWITCH
12 SIGHT PORT OPENING
13 WORKING PLATFORM
14 ORDER INSTRUMENTS
15 TRAINING HANDLE
16 TOMMY BAR FOR ACCESS FITTINGS
17 TERMINAL BOXES FOR HEATING CIRCUITS
18 TORSIONAL SPRING
19 DISTRIBUTION BOXES FOR ELECTRIC HEATING.

20 ENTRY DOOR.
21 GYRO ANGLING GEAR.
22 CHARGING VALVE
23 1" STEEL WIRE ROPE.
24 TELEPHONE STOWAGE BOX.
25 220 VOLT LINK BOX
26 WALKWAY
27 TUBE REAR END.
28 TUBE LIP END
29 BLAST SCREEN
30 REDUCING VALVE
31 STOP VALVE
32 SPRING CATCH
33 SIDE READY SWITCH
34 TOP STOP
35 FIRING LEVER
36 OPERATORS SEAT
37 EXPLOSION VESSEL
38 STOP BRACKET
39 LADDER
40 SECURING WING NUT

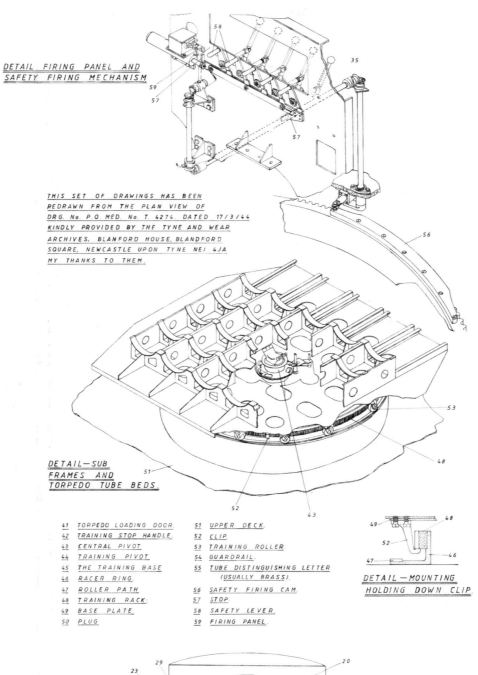

<u>DETAIL FIRING PANEL AND</u>
<u>SAFETY FIRING MECHANISM</u>

THIS SET OF DRAWINGS HAS BEEN
REDRAWN FROM THE PLAN VIEW OF
DRG. No. P.O. MED. No. T. 4274. DATED 17/3/44
KINDLY PROVIDED BY THE TYNE AND WEAR
ARCHIVES, BLANFORD HOUSE, BLANDFORD
SQUARE, NEWCASTLE UPON TYNE NEI 4JA
MY THANKS TO THEM.

<u>DETAIL—SUB</u>
<u>FRAMES AND</u>
<u>TORPEDO TUBE BEDS</u>

41	TORPEDO LOADING DOOR.		51	UPPER DECK.
42	TRAINING STOP HANDLE.		52	CLIP
43	CENTRAL PIVOT		53	TRAINING ROLLER
44	TRAINING PIVOT		54	GUARDRAIL.
45	THE TRAINING BASE		55	TUBE DISTINGUISHING LETTER
46	RACER RING.			(USUALLY BRASS).
47	ROLLER PATH		56	SAFETY FIRING CAM.
48	TRAINING RACK.		57	STOP.
49	BASE PLATE		58	SAFETY LEVER.
50	PLUG		59	FIRING PANEL.

<u>DETAIL—MOUNTING</u>
<u>HOLDING DOWN CLIP.</u>

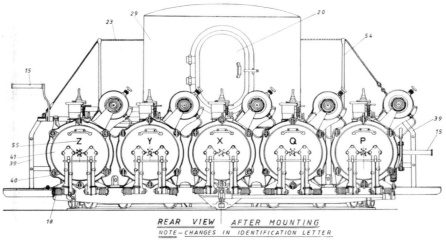

<u>REAR VIEW AFTER MOUNTING</u>
NOTE—CHANGES IN IDENTIFICATION LETTER

© <u>JOHN LAMBERT</u> 2/11/97 CH'D 16/11/97.

<u>L/0/93/B.</u>

T 4 Quadruple 21in QR Mk VIII torpedo tubes and Mk IX torpedo, as carried by Emergency fleet destroyers, 1943

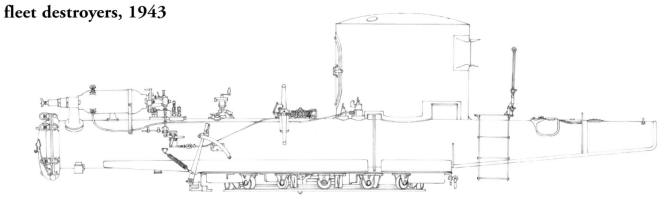

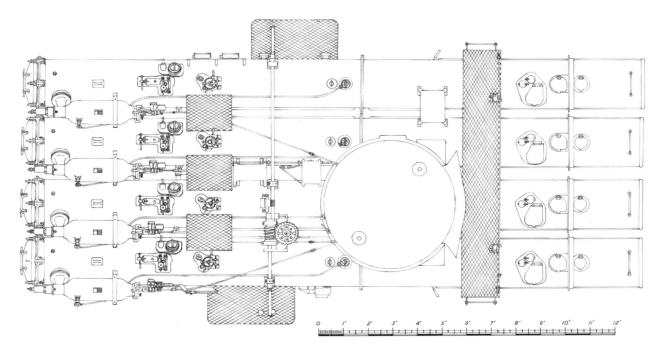

QUADRUPLE 21 INCH Q R MARK VIII TORPEDO TUBES & MARK IX TORPEDO
AS CARRIED BY EMERGENCY FLEET DESTROYERS~1943.

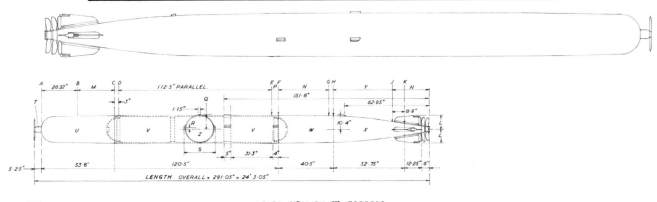

KEY			
A	4·625" DIA.	L	10·501"	W	BALANCE CHAMBER.
B	20·95" DIA.	M	27·48" CONICAL.	X	AFTERBODY.
C	20·98" DIA.	N	STRAIGHT CONE.	Y	25 FT. CURVE.
D	21·0" DIA.	P	5·0"	Z	SECTION SHOWING
E	21·0" DIA.	Q	11·125"		SIDE & TOP LUGS.
F	20·926" DIA.	R	1·75"		
G	20·438" DIA.	S	21·956"		
H	20·356" DIA.	T	FIRING PISTOL.		
J	12·3" DIA.	U	WARHEAD.		
K	9·22" DIA.	V	AIR VESSEL.		

DATA 21" MARK IX TORPEDO.

DESIGNED AS A GENERAL TORPEDO FOR ISSUE TO SURFACE CRAFT IT WAS DRIVEN BY A SEMI DIESEL INTERNAL COMBUSTION ENGINE ON THE DRY HEATER CYCLE. WHEN ISSUED TO DESTROYERS OR LEADERS, IT WAS A SINGLE SPEED TORPEDO CAPABLE OF RUNNING 10500 YARDS (6·94 MILES) AT 35 KNOTS.

WHEN ISSUED TO CRUISERS IT WAS A TWO SPEED TORPEDO CAPABLE OF RUNNING 10500 YARDS AT 35 KNOTS OR 14000 YARDS (7·9 MILES) AT 29·9 KNOTS. THE DEPTH KEEPING GEAR WAS DESIGNED TO GIVE A RECOVERY RANGE OF NOT MORE THAN 400 YARDS. PROVISION WAS MADE TO ADJUST THE OPERATING DEPTH BETWEEN 6 TO 44 FT. HORIZONTAL RUDDER CONTROLLING GEAR WAS FITTED. THE WARHEAD CONTAINED 750 LBS OF T.N.T. THE WEIGHT OF THE TORPEDO 3731 LBS. 109 WERE FIRED DURING WORLD WAR TWO.

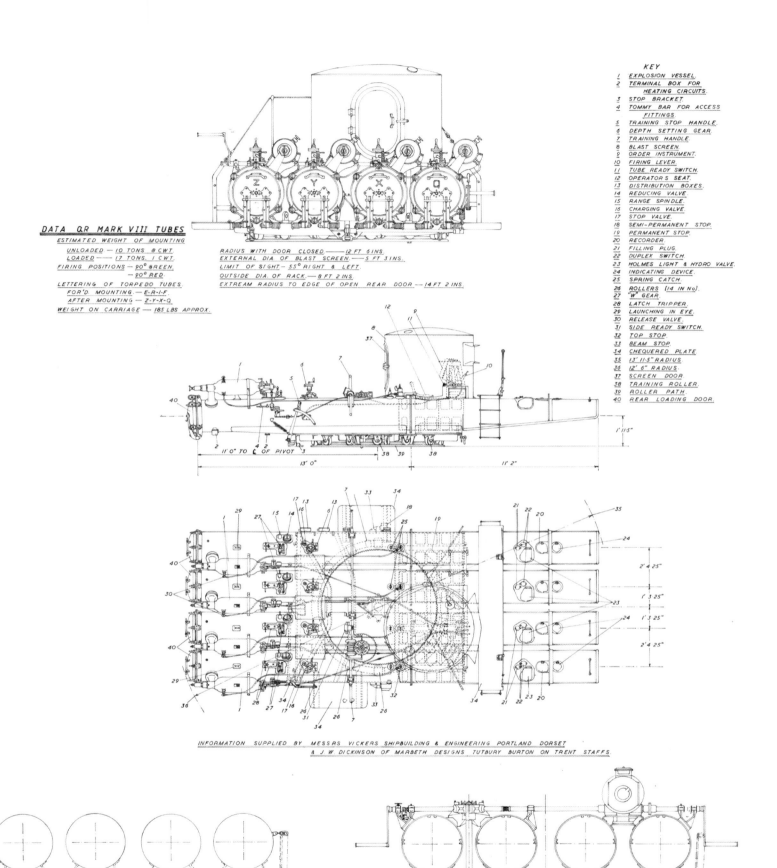

DATA QR MARK VIII TUBES

ESTIMATED WEIGHT OF MOUNTING
UNLOADED — 10 TONS 8 CWT.
LOADED — 17 TONS, 1 CWT.
FIRING POSITIONS — 90° GREEN.
— 90° RED.
LETTERING OF TORPEDO TUBES.
FOR'D. MOUNTING.— E-R-I-F.
AFTER MOUNTING — Z-Y-X-Q.
WEIGHT ON CARRIAGE — 185 LBS APPROX.

RADIUS WITH DOOR CLOSED.— 12 FT 6 INS.
EXTERNAL DIA. OF BLAST SCREEN.— 5 FT 3 INS.
LIMIT OF SIGHT — 55° RIGHT & LEFT.
OUTSIDE DIA. OF RACK.— 8 FT 2 INS.
EXTREAM RADIUS TO EDGE OF OPEN REAR DOOR.— 14 FT 2 INS.

KEY

1. EXPLOSION VESSEL.
2. TERMINAL BOX FOR HEATING CIRCUITS.
3. STOP BRACKET.
4. TOMMY BAR FOR ACCESS FITTINGS.
5. TRAINING STOP HANDLE.
6. DEPTH SETTING GEAR.
7. TRAINING HANDLE.
8. BLAST SCREEN.
9. ORDER INSTRUMENT.
10. FIRING LEVER.
11. TUBE READY SWITCH.
12. OPERATOR'S SEAT.
13. DISTRIBUTION BOXES.
14. REDUCING VALVE.
15. RANGE SPINDLE.
16. CHARGING VALVE.
17. STOP VALVE.
18. SEMI-PERMANENT STOP.
19. PERMANENT STOP.
20. RECORDER.
21. FILLING PLUG.
22. DUPLEX SWITCH.
23. HOLMES LIGHT & HYDRO VALVE.
24. INDICATING DEVICE.
25. SPRING CATCH.
26. ROLLERS [14 IN No].
27. "W" GEAR.
28. LATCH TRIPPER.
29. LAUNCHING IN EYE.
30. RELEASE VALVE.
31. SIDE READY SWITCH.
32. TOP STOP.
33. BEAM STOP.
34. CHEQUERED PLATE.
35. 13' 11.5" RADIUS.
36. 12' 6" RADIUS.
37. SCREEN DOOR.
38. TRAINING ROLLER.
39. ROLLER PATH.
40. REAR LOADING DOOR.

INFORMATION SUPPLIED BY MESSRS VICKERS SHIPBUILDING & ENGINEERING PORTLAND DORSET
& J.W. DICKINSON OF MARBETH DESIGNS TUTBURY BURTON ON TRENT STAFFS.

FRAME DETAIL.

PART SECTION LOOKING TOWARDS REAR DOORS.
N.B. A LIGHT METAL GUARD IS FITTED OVER WORM.

© JOHN LAMBERT 26/2/86   L/0/33

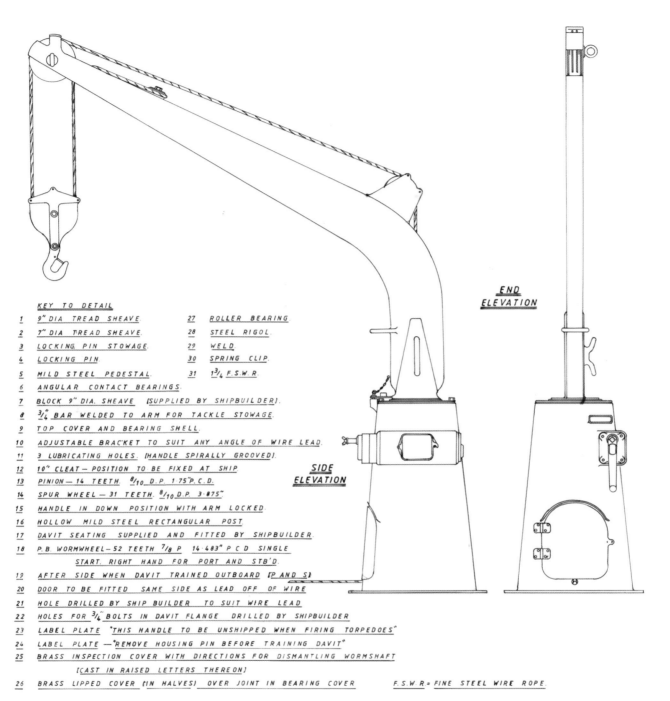

KEY TO DETAIL

1	9" DIA TREAD SHEAVE.	27	ROLLER BEARING.
2	7" DIA TREAD SHEAVE.	28	STEEL RIGOL.
3	LOCKING PIN STOWAGE.	29	WELD.
4	LOCKING PIN.	30	SPRING CLIP.
5	MILD STEEL PEDESTAL.	31	$1\frac{3}{4}$" F.S.W.R.
6	ANGULAR CONTACT BEARINGS.		
7	BLOCK 9" DIA. SHEAVE [SUPPLIED BY SHIPBUILDER].		
8	$\frac{3}{4}$" BAR WELDED TO ARM FOR TACKLE STOWAGE.		
9	TOP COVER AND BEARING SHELL.		
10	ADJUSTABLE BRACKET TO SUIT ANY ANGLE OF WIRE LEAD.		
11	3 LUBRICATING HOLES. [HANDLE SPIRALLY GROOVED].		
12	10" CLEAT — POSITION TO BE FIXED AT SHIP		
13	PINION — 14 TEETH. $\frac{8}{10}$ D.P. 1·75"P.C.D.		
14	SPUR WHEEL — 31 TEETH. $\frac{8}{10}$ D.P. 3·875"		
15	HANDLE IN DOWN POSITION WITH ARM LOCKED.		
16	HOLLOW MILD STEEL RECTANGULAR POST.		
17	DAVIT SEATING SUPPLIED AND FITTED BY SHIPBUILDER.		
18	P.B. WORMWHEEL — 52 TEETH $\frac{7}{8}$ P 14·483" P C D SINGLE START. RIGHT HAND FOR PORT AND STB'D.		
19	AFTER SIDE WHEN DAVIT TRAINED OUTBOARD [P AND S]		
20	DOOR TO BE FITTED SAME SIDE AS LEAD OFF OF WIRE		
21	HOLE DRILLED BY SHIP BUILDER TO SUIT WIRE LEAD		
22	HOLES FOR $\frac{3}{4}$" BOLTS IN DAVIT FLANGE DRILLED BY SHIPBUILDER		
23	LABEL PLATE "THIS HANDLE TO BE UNSHIPPED WHEN FIRING TORPEDOES"		
24	LABEL PLATE — "REMOVE HOUSING PIN BEFORE TRAINING DAVIT"		
25	BRASS INSPECTION COVER WITH DIRECTIONS FOR DISMANTLING WORMSHAFT [CAST IN RAISED LETTERS THEREON]		
26	BRASS LIPPED COVER [IN HALVES] OVER JOINT IN BEARING COVER		

F.S.W.R = FINE STEEL WIRE ROPE.

END ELEVATION

SIDE ELEVATION

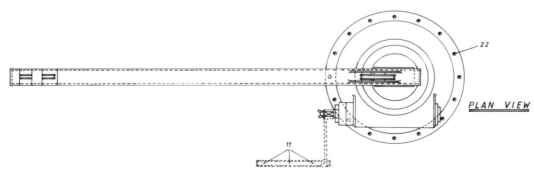

PLAN VIEW

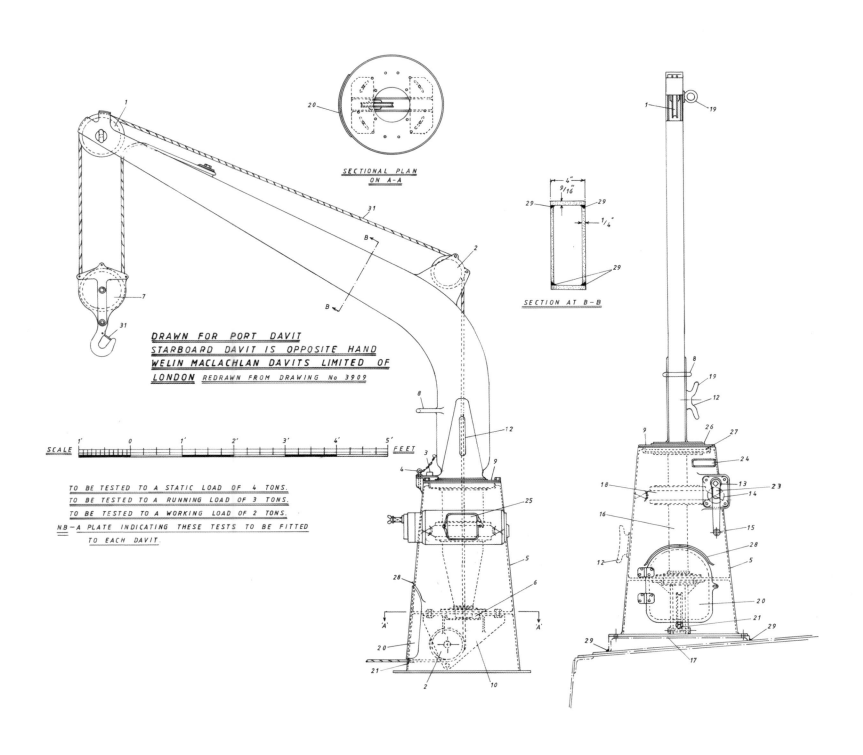

SECTIONAL PLAN
ON A-A

SECTION AT B-B

DRAWN FOR PORT DAVIT
STARBOARD DAVIT IS OPPOSITE HAND
WELIN MACLACHLAN DAVITS LIMITED OF
LONDON REDRAWN FROM DRAWING No 3909

SCALE   FEET

TO BE TESTED TO A STATIC LOAD OF 4 TONS.
TO BE TESTED TO A RUNNING LOAD OF 3 TONS.
TO BE TESTED TO A WORKING LOAD OF 2 TONS.
NB—A PLATE INDICATING THESE TESTS TO BE FITTED
    TO EACH DAVIT.

L/O/115

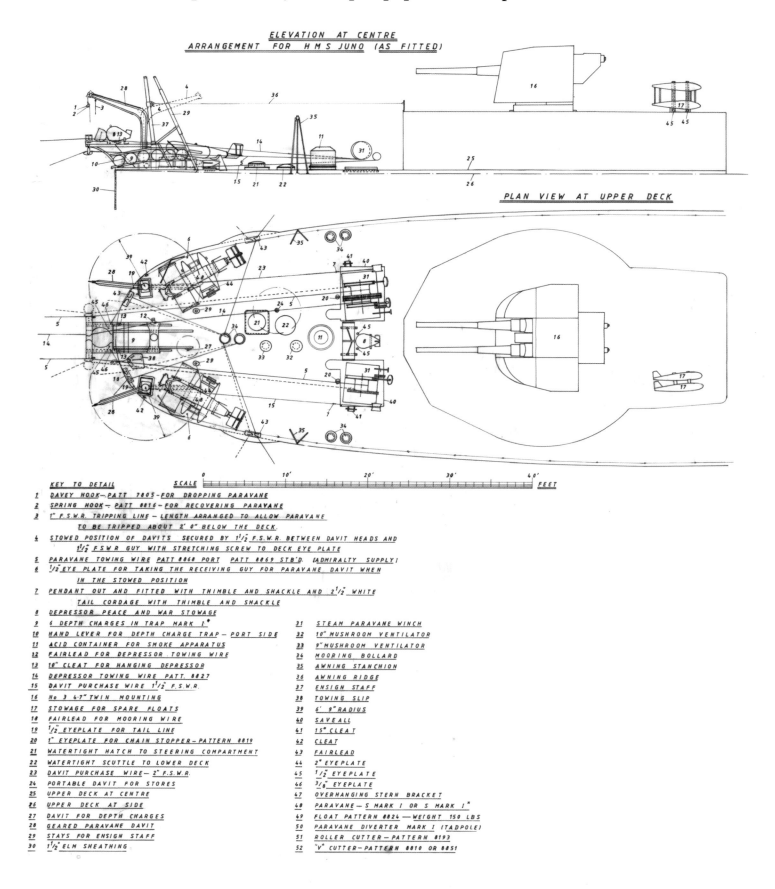

ELEVATION AT CENTRE
ARRANGEMENT FOR H M S JUNO (AS FITTED)

PLAN VIEW AT UPPER DECK

KEY TO DETAIL   SCALE   0   10'   20'   30'   40'   FEET

1 DAVEY HOOK—PATT 7805—FOR DROPPING PARAVANE
2 SPRING HOOK – PATT 8816–FOR RECOVERING PARAVANE
3 1" F.S.W.R. TRIPPING LINE – LENGTH ARRANGED TO ALLOW PARAVANE
      TO BE TRIPPED ABOUT 2' 0" BELOW THE DECK.
4 STOWED POSITION OF DAVITS SECURED BY 1½" F.S.W.R. BETWEEN DAVIT HEADS AND
      1½" F.S.W.R GUY WITH STRETCHING SCREW TO DECK EYE PLATE
5 PARAVANE TOWING WIRE PATT 8868 PORT PATT 8869 STB'D. (ADMIRALTY SUPPLY)
6 ½" EYE PLATE FOR TAKING THE RECEIVING GUY FOR PARAVANE DAVIT WHEN
      IN THE STOWED POSITION
7 PENDANT OUT AND FITTED WITH THIMBLE AND SHACKLE AND 2½" WHITE
      TAIL CORDAGE WITH THIMBLE AND SHACKLE
8 DEPRESSOR PEACE AND WAR STOWAGE
9 6 DEPTH CHARGES IN TRAP MARK I*
10 HAND LEVER FOR DEPTH CHARGE TRAP – PORT SIDE
11 ACID CONTAINER FOR SMOKE APPARATUS
12 FAIRLEAD FOR DEPRESSOR TOWING WIRE
13 10" CLEAT FOR HANGING DEPRESSOR
14 DEPRESSOR TOWING WIRE PATT. 8827
15 DAVIT PURCHASE WIRE 1½" F.S.W.R.
16 No 3 4.7" TWIN MOUNTING
17 STOWAGE FOR SPARE FLOATS
18 FAIRLEAD FOR MOORING WIRE
19 ½" EYEPLATE FOR TAIL LINE
20 1" EYEPLATE FOR CHAIN STOPPER–PATTERN 8819
21 WATERTIGHT HATCH TO STEERING COMPARTMENT
22 WATERTIGHT SCUTTLE TO LOWER DECK
23 DAVIT PURCHASE WIRE– 2" F.S.W.R.
24 PORTABLE DAVIT FOR STORES
25 UPPER DECK AT CENTRE
26 UPPER DECK AT SIDE
27 DAVIT FOR DEPTH CHARGES
28 GEARED PARAVANE DAVIT
29 STAYS FOR ENSIGN STAFF
30 1½" ELM SHEATHING

31 STEAM PARAVANE WINCH
32 10" MUSHROOM VENTILATOR
33 9" MUSHROOM VENTILATOR
34 MOORING BOLLARD
35 AWNING STANCHION
36 AWNING RIDGE
37 ENSIGN STAFF
38 TOWING SLIP
39 6' 9" RADIUS
40 SAVEALL
41 15" CLEAT
42 CLEAT
43 FAIRLEAD
44 2" EYEPLATE
45 1½" EYEPLATE
46 3/8" EYEPLATE
47 OVERHANGING STERN BRACKET
48 PARAVANE—S MARK I OR S MARK I*
49 FLOAT PATTERN 8824 —WEIGHT 150 LBS
50 PARAVANE DIVERTER MARK I (TADPOLE)
51 ROLLER CUTTER—PATTERN 8193
52 "V" CUTTER—PATTERN 8810 OR 8851

THE PRINCIPLES OF T.S.D.S.

HISTORY

THE HIGH SPEED MINE SWEEP (H.S.M.S.) HAD EVOLVED DURING WWI. DESTROYERS STEAMED AHEAD OF THE FLEET EACH TOWING A PAIR OF PARAVANES FROM AFT. TO MAKE THE SWEEP MORE EFFECTIVE THE TOWS WERE LED THROUGH SNATCH BLOCKS SECURED BY A WIRE SPAN TO A THIRD (DEPRESSOR) PARAVANE, KNOWN AS A TADPOLE. THIS SYSTEM HAD THE DISADVANTAGE OF A LIMITED SPREAD OF SWEEP AS AT HIGH SPEEDS THE SWEEP WIRES WOULD NOT STAND THE STRAIN OF THE FORCES IMPOSED BY THE GREATER SPREAD.
EXTENSIVE TRIALS WERE CARRIED OUT BETWEEN THE WARS TO DEVELOP A PARAVANE WHICH WOULD INCREASE ITS SPREAD BY ALTERING THE ANGLE OF ITS PLANE AS THE FORWARD SPEED DECREASED AND IN 1930 THE TWO SPEED DESTROYER SWEEP (T.S.D.S.) WAS INTRODUCED USING AN 'S' MARK I PARAVANE (O.U.5511/39)

REFERENCES – (SHEET A AND B)
PORT AND STARBOARD STEAM PARAVANE
WINCHES – CLARKE CHAPMAN AND COMPANY LIMITED
THE PARAVANE 'S' MARK I* – TECHNICAL HISTORY OF
BRITISH MINESWEEPING 1939–1945.
CAPABILITIES AND DETAILS OF GEAR – CB 1920
DRILL BOOK – O U 5430
GENERAL MINESWEEPING INSTRUCTIONS – CB 1842
T.S.D.S. SUPPLEMENT TO MINESWEEPING TACTICS
AND OPERATIONS — CB 1937A

DIAGRAM SHOWING THE TYPE OF GEAR USED FOR T.S.D.S.

NOTE ALTERNATIVE PATTERNS OF TYPE OF GEAR MAY BE SUPPLIED IN SOME CASES. FOR THE ESTABLISHMENT OF STORES SEE - B.R. 366.

VIEW FROM ASTERN

GENERAL ARRANGEMENT

PLAN VIEW

53   SLEEVE PATT 8800
54   FLOAT ROPE – 50 FATHOMS 3/4 PATT 8828
55   4' 3" GROMMET STROP 2 1/8" P.V. ROPE
56   CHAIN TAIL 16' 0" LENGTH 1/4" STUD LINK CABLE
57   EXTENSION LENGTH - 1 FATHOM 2 1/8" – 3 STRANDED
58   SLEEVE – STB'D PATT 8835 OR 8835A – PORT PATT 8836 OR 8836A
59   DEPRESSOR ROPE – 100 FATHOMS – 2 1/8" 3 STRANDED PATT 8827
60   SWEEP ROPE (WIRE) 125 FATHOMS PLAIN 175 FATHOMS SERRATED.
     STB'D. PATT. 8869 R.H. LAY.   PORT PATT. 8868 L.H. LAY.
61   THIMBLE PATT 1915B (5081) – SHACKLE PATT 2152 (5442) – SPLICE TAPERED AND SERVED WITH
     ROPING TWINE.
62   TRIP ROPE 1" F.S.W.R. – 2 THIMBLES PATT 1915 (5081) – 2 SHACKLES PATT 2051 (5441)
63   TAIL LINE FOR PARAVANE – 3 FATHOMS – 1 1/2" SISAL
64   DEPRESSOR SLIPPING LANYARD – 5 FATHOMS – 2 1/2" SISAL
65   LASHING FOR PARAVANE 1 1/2" S.W.R.
66   10 FATHOMS – 2 1/2" SISAL
67   10 FATHOMS – 1 1/2" F.S.W.R.
68   SHACKLE PATT.- 2156 OR 5445

69   SNATCH BLOCK PATT. 8821
70   SNATCH BLOCK PATT. 7873
71   1 1/2" E.S.W.R.

KEY TO DETAIL		F	390 YARDS
A	DEPTH AS ORDERED	G	340 YARDS
B	HIGH SPEED SETTING	H	150 YARDS
C	LOW SPEED SETTING		
D	200 FATHOMS (1200 FT)		
E	310 YARDS USING SWEEP MARK I. 320 YARDS USING SWEEP		
	MARK I*		

SHEET ONE OF THREE SHEETS

L/0/127/A

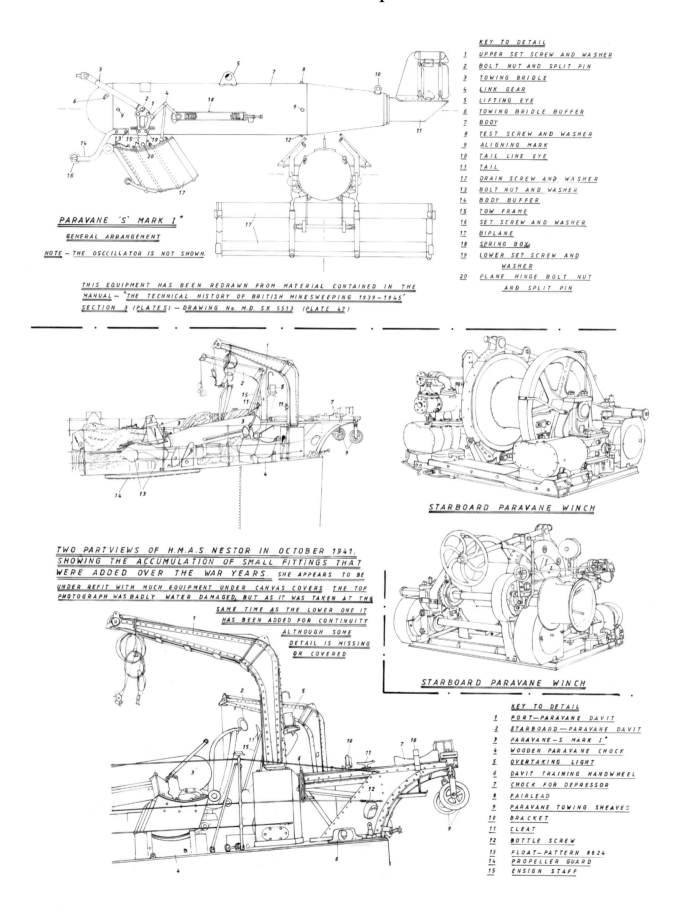

PARAVANE 'S' MARK I*

GENERAL ARRANGEMENT

NOTE – THE OSCILLATOR IS NOT SHOWN.

THIS EQUIPMENT HAS BEEN REDRAWN FROM MATERIAL CONTAINED IN THE
MANUAL – "THE TECHNICAL HISTORY OF BRITISH MINESWEEPING 1939–1945"
SECTION 3 (PLATES) – DRAWING No. M.D. SK 5513. (PLATE 47)

STARBOARD PARAVANE WINCH

TWO PARTVIEWS OF H.M.A.S. NESTOR IN OCTOBER 1941,
SHOWING THE ACCUMULATION OF SMALL FITTINGS THAT
WERE ADDED OVER THE WAR YEARS. SHE APPEARS TO BE
UNDER REFIT WITH MUCH EQUIPMENT UNDER CANVAS COVERS THE TOP
PHOTOGRAPH WAS BADLY WATER DAMAGED, BUT AS IT WAS TAKEN AT THE
SAME TIME AS THE LOWER ONE IT
HAS BEEN ADDED FOR CONTINUITY
ALTHOUGH SOME
DETAIL IS MISSING
OR COVERED.

STARBOARD PARAVANE WINCH

DATA ON T.S.D.S. – DESTROYER FIGHTING INSTRUCTIONS. – ADM 239/132

A = SPEEDS THROUGH THE WATER.

DROPPING PARAVANES – NEVER EXCEED 8 KNOTS

VEERING SWEEP WIRES, STANDARD METHOD 16 KNOTS, ALSO THE
   QUICKEST 8 KNOTS NECESSITATES A REDUCED RATE OF VEERING.

SWEEP CHANGES

S MARK I* P AND UP AT 11 KNOTS. DOWN AT 9 KNOTS

S TYPE C UP AT ABOUT 13½ KNOTS. DOWN AT 11 KNOTS

MINIMUM SPEED 8 KNOTS — FOR REASONABLE MINE CUTTING
   EFFICIENCY SPEED OVER GROUND MUST NEVER BE REDUCED
   BELOW 6 KNOTS.

MAXIMUM SPEED 25 KNOTS.

UNSTABLE SPEEDS (USING S MARK I* PARAVANES)
   SWEEP SHOULD NOT BE USED BETWEEN 11 AND 13½ KNOTS (OR
   10 AND 14½ KNOTS TO ALLOW FOR STATION KEEPING).
   LOSS OF SPEED IS TO BE EXPECTED DUE TO THE SWEEP LOW
   SETTING, – 1·4 KNOTS. HIGH SPEED SETTING AT 15 KNOTS – 1·0 KNOTS.
   HIGH SPEED SETTING AT 18 KNOTS – 1·2 KNOTS. HIGH SPEED
   SETTING AT 20 KNOTS – 1·5 KNOTS.

B = SPREADS

1 – SINGLE SHIP HIGH SPEED SETTING 150 YARDS, LOW SPEED SETTING 315 YARDS.

2 – DIVISION OF FOUR SHIPS, PROTECTING SWEEP, LOW SETTING 700 YARDS. PROTECTING SWEEP
   HIGH SPEED SETTING, 345 YARDS (NOTE SPREAD OF SWEEP IS NOT REDUCED WHEN ALTERING
   COURSE)

3 – FLOTILLA SEARCHING IN SCREENING DIAGRAM 51, SEARCHING SWEEP COVERS ABOUT A TWO
   MILE FRONTAGE. PERCENTAGE OF WATER SEARCHED AT HIGH SPEAD = 32% PERCENTAGE OF
   WATER SEARCHED AT LOW SPEED = 65%.

C = DEPTH OF SWEEP.

PARAVANES COULD BE ADJUSTED TO RUN AT ANY DEPTH BETWEEN
   20 AND 60 FEET.

THE SWEEP WIRE WAS FLAT AT 12 KNOTS AND ABOVE 20 KNOTS.

THE SWEEP WIRE HAS A MAXIMUM SAG OF 5 FATHOMS AT 8 KNOTS.

THE SWEEP WIRE HAS A SAG OF TWO FATHOMS AT 15 KNOTS.

DEPTH OF DEPRESSOR AND POINT OF TOW VARIES WITH THE
   AMOUNT OF DEPRESSOR WIRE VEERED.

THE DEPRESSOR RUNS DEEPER IN HIGH SPEED THAN LOW SPEED
   SETTING.

D = DEPTH OF WATER REQUIRED

NORMAL DEPTH OF SWEEP IS 45 FEET.

E = WEATHER CONDITIONS

THE SWEEP CAN BE GOT OUT OR RUN IN WEATHER UP TO
   ALMOST ANYTHING A DESTROYER CAN STAND. (DOUBTFUL
   WITH 'D' MARK II DEPRESSOR). THE SWEEP CANNOT BE GOT
   IN WITHOUT DAMAGE IN WEATHER ABOVE ABOUT SEA 4,
   SWELL 4, WIND 6.

VEER = TO PAY OUT CABLE ETC UNDER CONTROL. (BY REVERSING
   WINCH RATHER THAN SURGING)

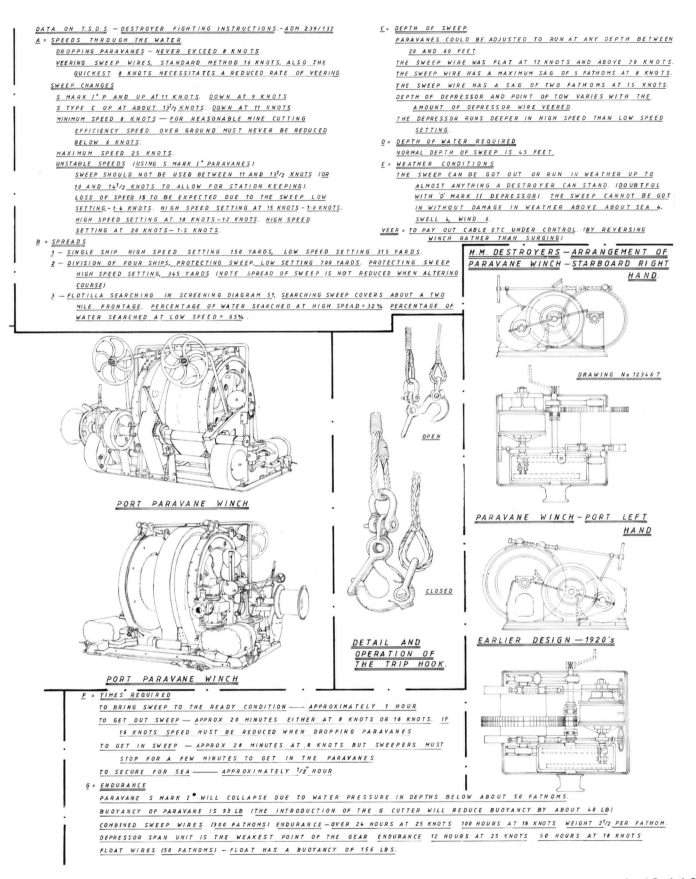

H.M. DESTROYERS – ARRANGEMENT OF
PARAVANE WINCH – STARBOARD RIGHT
HAND.

DRAWING No 12346 T

PORT PARAVANE WINCH

PORT PARAVANE WINCH

OPEN

CLOSED

DETAIL AND
OPERATION OF
THE TRIP HOOK.

PARAVANE WINCH – PORT LEFT
HAND

EARLIER DESIGN – 1920's

F = TIMES REQUIRED

TO BRING SWEEP TO THE READY CONDITION — APPROXIMATELY 1 HOUR

TO GET OUT SWEEP — APPROX 20 MINUTES EITHER AT 8 KNOTS OR 16 KNOTS. IF
   16 KNOTS SPEED MUST BE REDUCED WHEN DROPPING PARAVANES

TO GET IN SWEEP — APPROX 20 MINUTES AT 8 KNOTS BUT SWEEPERS MUST
   STOP FOR A FEW MINUTES TO GET IN THE PARAVANES

TO SECURE FOR SEA ——— APPROXIMATELY ½" HOUR

G = ENDURANCE

PARAVANE S MARK I* WILL COLLAPSE DUE TO WATER PRESSURE IN DEPTHS BELOW ABOUT 50 FATHOMS.

BUOYANCY OF PARAVANE IS 93 LB (THE INTRODUCTION OF THE G CUTTER WILL REDUCE BUOYANCY BY ABOUT 40 LB)

COMBINED SWEEP WIRES (300 FATHOMS) ENDURANCE – OVER 24 HOURS AT 25 KNOTS 100 HOURS AT 18 KNOTS WEIGHT 2½ PER FATHOM.

DEPRESSOR SPAN UNIT IS THE WEAKEST POINT OF THE GEAR ENDURANCE 12 HOURS AT 25 KNOTS 50 HOURS AT 18 KNOTS

FLOAT WIRES (50 FATHOMS) – FLOAT HAS A BUOYANCY OF 156 LBS.

SHEET TWO OF THREE SHEETS

© JOHN LAMBERT COMMENCED 2/4/2001 COMPLETED 22/5/2001 CH'D 25/5/2001

L /0 / 127 / B

M 1 General arrangement of Clarke Chapman & Co Ltd port & starboard steam paravane winches for the TSDS – for 'J', 'K' and following destroyers, 1938 onwards

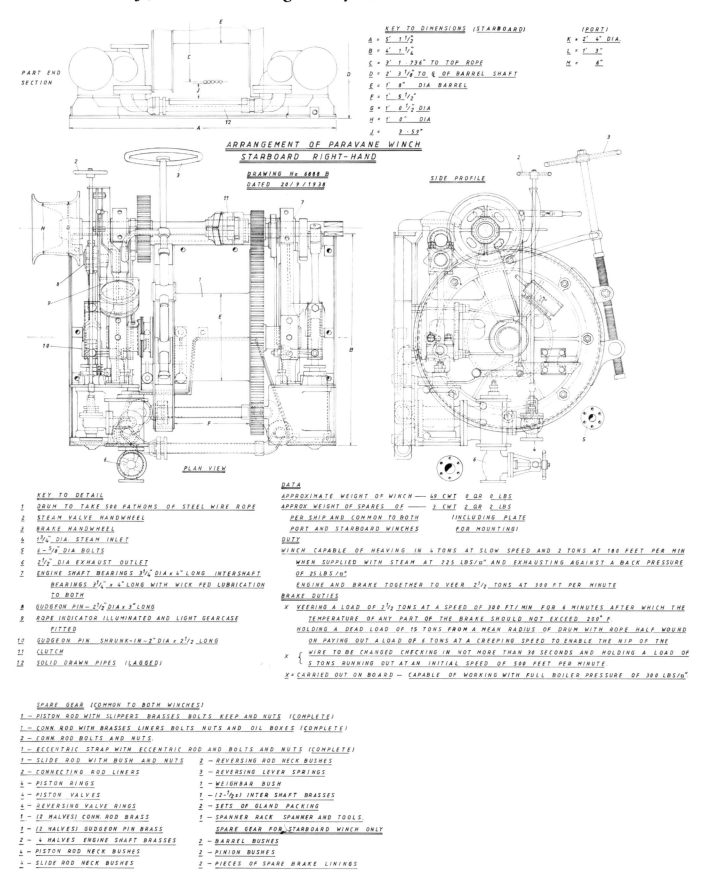

KEY TO DIMENSIONS (STARBOARD) (PORT)

A = 5' 1½"
B = 4' 1¼"
C = 3' 1·736" TO TOP ROPE
D = 2' 3⅛" TO ℄ OF BARREL SHAFT
E = 1' 8" DIA BARREL
F = 1' 5½"
G = 1' 0½" DIA
H = 1' 0" DIA
J = 3·59"

K = 2' 4" DIA.
L = 1' 3"
M = 6"

ARRANGEMENT OF PARAVANE WINCH
STARBOARD RIGHT-HAND

DRAWING No 6888 B
DATED 20/9/1938

PART END SECTION

SIDE PROFILE

PLAN VIEW

KEY TO DETAIL
1 DRUM TO TAKE 500 FATHOMS OF STEEL WIRE ROPE
2 STEAM VALVE HANDWHEEL
3 BRAKE HANDWHEEL
4 1¾" DIA. STEAM INLET
5 6 - ⅝" DIA BOLTS
6 2½" DIA EXHAUST OUTLET
7 ENGINE SHAFT BEARINGS 3¼" DIA x 4" LONG INTERSHAFT
   BEARINGS 3¼" x 4" LONG WITH WICK FED LUBRICATION
   TO BOTH
8 GUDGEON PIN - 2½" DIA x 3" LONG
9 ROPE INDICATOR ILLUMINATED AND LIGHT GEARCASE
   FITTED
10 GUDGEON PIN SHRUNK-IN - 2" DIA x 2½ LONG
11 CLUTCH
12 SOLID DRAWN PIPES (LAGGED)

DATA
APPROXIMATE WEIGHT OF WINCH ——— 49 CWT 0 QR 0 LBS
APPROX WEIGHT OF SPARES OF ——— 3 CWT 2 QR 2 LBS
PER SHIP AND COMMON TO BOTH   (INCLUDING PLATE
PORT AND STARBOARD WINCHES   FOR MOUNTING)

DUTY
WINCH CAPABLE OF HEAVING IN 4 TONS AT SLOW SPEED AND 2 TONS AT 180 FEET PER MIN
WHEN SUPPLIED WITH STEAM AT 225 LBS/□" AND EXHAUSTING AGAINST A BACK PRESSURE
OF 25 LBS/□"
ENGINE AND BRAKE TOGETHER TO VEER 2½ TONS AT 300 FT PER MINUTE

BRAKE DUTIES
X VEERING A LOAD OF 2½ TONS AT A SPEED OF 300 FT/MIN FOR 6 MINUTES AFTER WHICH THE
   TEMPERATURE OF ANY PART OF THE BRAKE SHOULD NOT EXCEED 200° F.
   HOLDING A DEAD LOAD OF 15 TONS FROM A MEAN RADIUS OF DRUM WITH ROPE HALF WOUND
   ON PAYING OUT A LOAD OF 6 TONS AT A CREEPING SPEED TO ENABLE THE NIP OF THE
X { WIRE TO BE CHANGED CHECKING IN NOT MORE THAN 30 SECONDS AND HOLDING A LOAD OF
   5 TONS RUNNING OUT AT AN INITIAL SPEED OF 500 FEET PER MINUTE.
X = CARRIED OUT ON BOARD – CAPABLE OF WORKING WITH FULL BOILER PRESSURE OF 300 LBS/□"

SPARE GEAR (COMMON TO BOTH WINCHES)
1 - PISTON ROD WITH SLIPPERS BRASSES BOLTS KEEP AND NUTS (COMPLETE)
1 - CONN. ROD WITH BRASSES LINERS BOLTS NUTS AND OIL BOXES (COMPLETE)
2 - CONN. ROD BOLTS AND NUTS.
1 - ECCENTRIC STRAP WITH ECCENTRIC ROD AND BOLTS AND NUTS (COMPLETE)
1 - SLIDE ROD WITH BUSH AND NUTS   2 - REVERSING ROD NECK BUSHES
2 - CONNECTING ROD LINERS   3 - REVERSING LEVER SPRINGS
4 - PISTON RINGS   1 - WEIGHBAR BUSH
4 - PISTON VALVES   1 - (2-½s) INTER SHAFT BRASSES
4 - REVERSING VALVE RINGS   2 - SETS OF GLAND PACKING
1 - (2 HALVES) CONN. ROD BRASS   1 - SPANNER RACK SPANNER AND TOOLS.
1 - (2 HALVES) GUDGEON PIN BRASS   SPARE GEAR FOR STARBOARD WINCH ONLY
2 - 4 HALVES ENGINE SHAFT BRASSES   2 - BARREL BUSHES
4 - PISTON ROD NECK BUSHES   2 - PINION BUSHES
4 - SLIDE ROD NECK BUSHES   2 - PIECES OF SPARE BRAKE LININGS

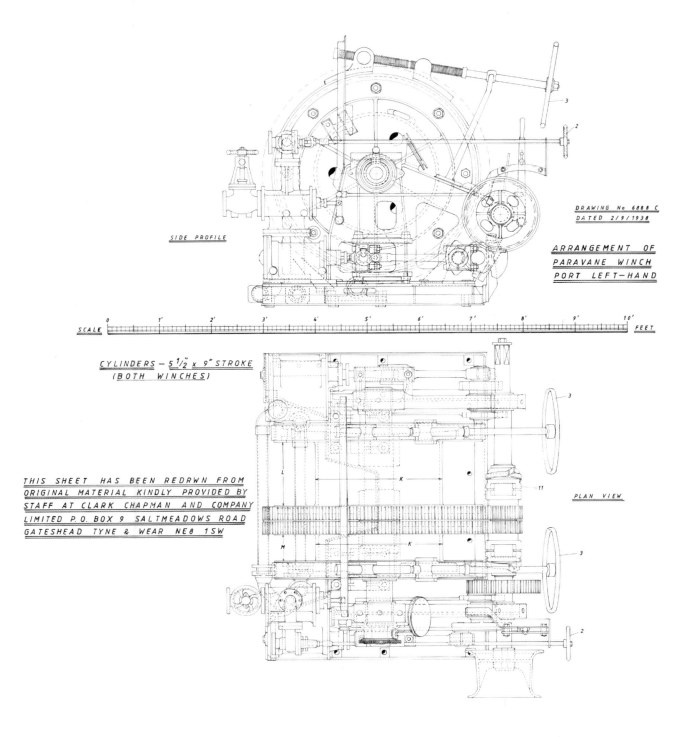

SIDE PROFILE

DRAWING No 6888 C
DATED 2/9/1938

ARRANGEMENT OF
PARAVANE WINCH
PORT LEFT—HAND

SCALE |0   1'   2'   3'   4'   5'   6'   7'   8'   9'   10'| FEET

CYLINDERS — 5 1/2" x 9" STROKE
(BOTH WINCHES)

THIS SHEET HAS BEEN REDRWN FROM
ORIGINAL MATERIAL KINDLY PROVIDED BY
STAFF AT CLARK CHAPMAN AND COMPANY
LIMITED P.O. BOX 9 SALTMEADOWS ROAD
GATESHEAD TYNE & WEAR NE8 1SW

PLAN VIEW

DATA (CONTINUED FROM SHEET B)

H = MANOEUVRING

GETTING OUT SWEEP ANY SPEED BETWEEN 8 AND 25 KNOTS AND ANY WHEEL MAY BE USED WHEN
THE PARAVANES ARE AT SHORT STAY. (UNLESS WIRES ARE BEING STREAMED FOR THE FIRST TIME)
SWEEPING IN LOW SPEED SETTING — AT SPEEDS BELOW 10 KNOTS, NO ALTERATIONS OF COURSE
EXCEPT FOR STATION KEEPING
AT SPEEDS OF 11 KNOTS ALTERATIONS UP TO 40° USING NOT MORE THAN 15° OF RUDDER.
SWEEPING IN A HIGH SPEED SETTING — 20° OF RUDDER CAN BE USED UP TO A MAXIMUM OF 25 KNOTS
BUT AT A SPEED OF LESS THAN 17 KNOTS THROUGH THE WATER THE INNER PARAVANE MAY
CHANGE SETTING IF THE TURN IS LARGE.

I = EFFECTIVENESS — DETAILED SUMMARY

LOW SPEED SETTING — SWEEP IS NOT SAFE AGAINST ANTI SWEEPING DEVICES.
HIGH SPEED SETTING — MOST SATISFACTORY AT SPEEDS ABOVE 18 KNOTS, WHEN IT WILL HAVE A LARGE MEASURE OF SUCCESS
AGAINST ANTI-SWEEPING DEVICES.

J = DEPTH CHARGE ATTACK

DESTROYERS TOWING TSDS MAY COUNTER ATTACK A SUBMARINE BY DROPPING
DEPTH CHARGES SUBJECT TO THE FOLLOWING RESTRICTIONS :-

i)   DEPTH CHARGES FROM THE TRAP MUST BE SET TO 150 FEET
ii) DEPTH CHARGES FROM THROWERS MAY BE SET TO ANY DEPTH
iii) THE SHIP MUST BE STEAMING AT 16 KNOTS OR MORE THROUGH THE
     WATER (MAY NOT APPLY TO D MARK II DEPRESSOR)

NOTE

ASDIC DOMES MUST BE IN THE HOUSED POSITION WHEN THE SPEED OF
THE SHIP IS OVER 24 KNOTS.

SHEET THREE OF THREE SHEETS

L/O/127/C

© JOHN LAMBERT COMMENCED 2/5/2001   COMPLETED 14/5/2001   CH'D 17/5/2001

M 2 HMS Napier, 'N' class fleet destroyer, depth charge arrangements

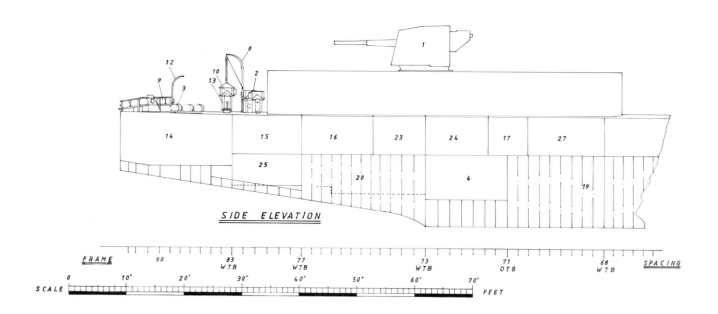

SIDE ELEVATION

FRAME SPACING

SCALE FEET

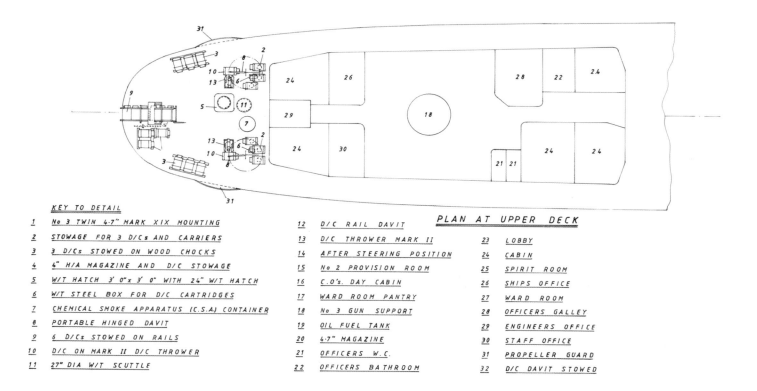

PLAN AT UPPER DECK

KEY TO DETAIL

1	No 3 TWIN 4·7" MARK XIX MOUNTING
2	STOWAGE FOR 3 D/Cs AND CARRIERS
3	3 D/Cs STOWED ON WOOD CHOCKS
4	4" H/A MAGAZINE AND D/C STOWAGE
5	W/T HATCH 3' 0" x 3' 0" WITH 24" W/T HATCH
6	W/T STEEL BOX FOR D/C CARTRIDGES
7	CHEMICAL SMOKE APPARATUS (C.S.A) CONTAINER
8	PORTABLE HINGED DAVIT
9	6 D/Cs STOWED ON RAILS
10	D/C ON MARK II D/C THROWER
11	27" DIA W/T SCUTTLE
12	D/C RAIL DAVIT
13	D/C THROWER MARK II
14	AFTER STEERING POSITION
15	No 2 PROVISION ROOM
16	C.O's. DAY CABIN
17	WARD ROOM PANTRY
18	No 3 GUN SUPPORT
19	OIL FUEL TANK
20	4·7" MAGAZINE
21	OFFICERS W.C.
22	OFFICERS BATHROOM
23	LOBBY
24	CABIN
25	SPIRIT ROOM
26	SHIPS OFFICE
27	WARD ROOM
28	OFFICERS GALLEY
29	ENGINEERS OFFICE
30	STAFF OFFICE
31	PROPELLER GUARD
32	D/C DAVIT STOWED

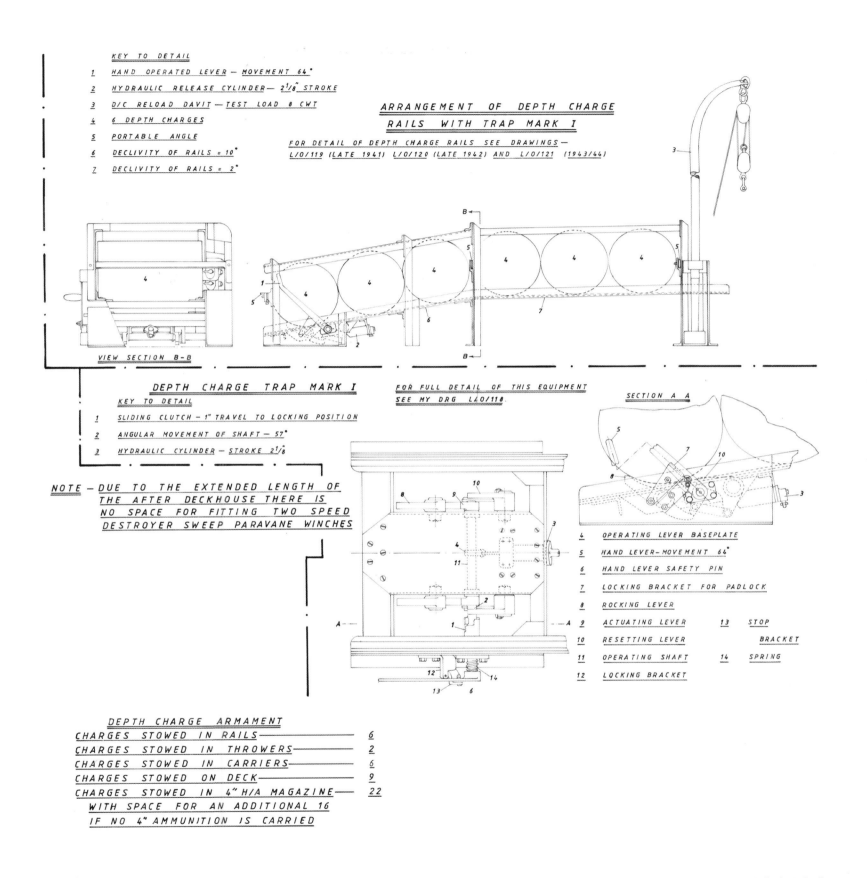

KEY TO DETAIL

1. HAND OPERATED LEVER — MOVEMENT 64°
2. HYDRAULIC RELEASE CYLINDER — 2⅛" STROKE
3. D/C RELOAD DAVIT — TEST LOAD 8 CWT
4. 6 DEPTH CHARGES
5. PORTABLE ANGLE
6. DECLIVITY OF RAILS = 10°
7. DECLIVITY OF RAILS = 2°

ARRANGEMENT OF DEPTH CHARGE
RAILS WITH TRAP MARK I

FOR DETAIL OF DEPTH CHARGE RAILS SEE DRAWINGS —
L/O/119 (LATE 1941) L/O/120 (LATE 1942) AND L/O/121 (1943/44)

VIEW SECTION B-B

DEPTH CHARGE TRAP MARK I
KEY TO DETAIL

1. SLIDING CLUTCH — 1" TRAVEL TO LOCKING POSITION
2. ANGULAR MOVEMENT OF SHAFT — 57°
3. HYDRAULIC CYLINDER — STROKE 2⅛"

FOR FULL DETAIL OF THIS EQUIPMENT
SEE MY DRG L4O/118.

SECTION A A

NOTE — DUE TO THE EXTENDED LENGTH OF
THE AFTER DECKHOUSE THERE IS
NO SPACE FOR FITTING TWO SPEED
DESTROYER SWEEP PARAVANE WINCHES

4   OPERATING LEVER BASEPLATE
5   HAND LEVER — MOVEMENT 64°
6   HAND LEVER SAFETY PIN
7   LOCKING BRACKET FOR PADLOCK
8   ROCKING LEVER
9   ACTUATING LEVER   13   STOP
10 RESETTING LEVER   BRACKET
11 OPERATING SHAFT   14   SPRING
12 LOCKING BRACKET

DEPTH CHARGE ARMAMENT

CHARGES STOWED IN RAILS	6
CHARGES STOWED IN THROWERS	2
CHARGES STOWED IN CARRIERS	6
CHARGES STOWED ON DECK	9
CHARGES STOWED IN 4" H/A MAGAZINE	22

WITH SPACE FOR AN ADDITIONAL 16
IF NO 4" AMMUNITION IS CARRIED

© JOHN LAMBERT   COMMENCED 21/1/2001   COMPLETED 26/3/2001   CH'D. 28/3/2001

L/O/129

M 3 'V' class destroyers *Veteran, Walrus, Waterhen* and *Witherington* – inboard smoke production apparatus as fitted at Malta, 1926

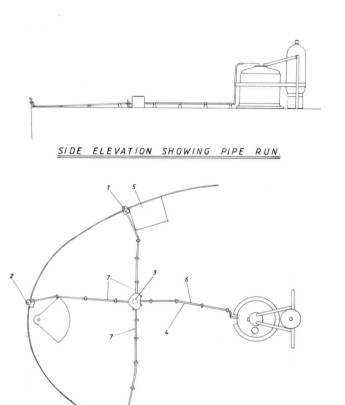

SIDE ELEVATION SHOWING PIPE RUN.

PLAN VIEW SHOWING PIPE ARRANGEMENT

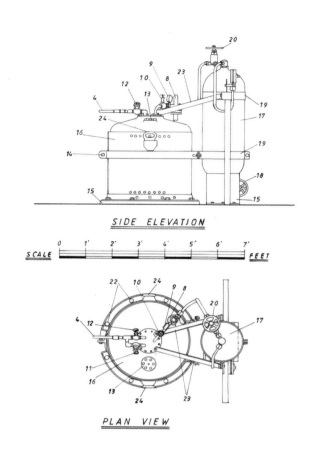

SIDE ELEVATION

SCALE   0   1'   2'   3'   4'   5'   6'   7'   FEET

PLAN VIEW

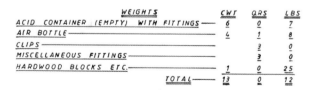

WEIGHTS	CWT	QRS	LBS
ACID CONTAINER (EMPTY) WITH FITTINGS	6	0	7
AIR BOTTLE	4	1	8
CLIPS		3	0
MISCELLANEOUS FITTINGS		3	0
HARDWOOD BLOCKS ETC.	1	0	25
TOTAL	13	0	12

NOTE
THE ARRANGEMENT OF PIPING SHOWN IS AS WAS FITTED ABOARD H.M.S. WATERHEN — LATER, H.M.A.S. WATERHEN. (FROM 1932). SIMILAR PIPE RUNS WERE FITTED TO OTHER SHIPS WITH SOME SLIGHT VARIATIONS TO AVOID EXISTING DECK FITTINGS.

REDRAWN FROM DRAWING   M.E.D. NO. 2664 DATED 10/9/1926
KINDLY PROVIDED BY THE NATIONAL MARITIME MUSEUM GREENWICH.